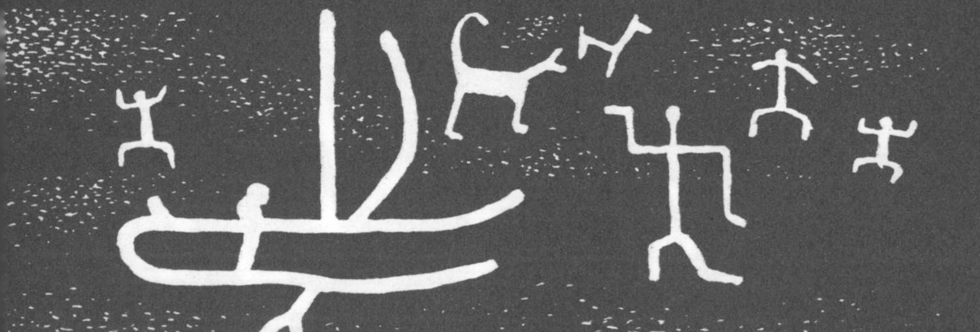

POLYNESIAN CULTURE HISTORY

PHOTO BY GEORGE TAHARA

KENNETH P. EMORY

POLYNESIAN CULTURE HISTORY

Essays in Honor of Kenneth P. Emory

EDITED BY
Genevieve A. Highland, Roland W. Force,
Alan Howard, Marion Kelly,
Yosihiko H. Sinoto

Bernice P. Bishop Museum Special Publication 56

BISHOP MUSEUM PRESS
HONOLULU, HAWAII

FOREWORD

K ENNETH PIKE EMORY began his career at Bishop Museum on August 1, 1920. The next day the First Pan-Pacific Scientific Conference, the genesis of the Pacific Science Association, was convened. This Conference was to outline the scientific problems of the Pacific Ocean region, suggest methods for their solution, make a critical inventory of existing knowledge, and devise plans for future studies. The most prominent resolution growing out of the Conference relative to anthropology noted the need for Polynesian research and recommended that the most prompt and efficient steps be taken to record the data necessary to the understanding of man's development in the Pacific area. The Conference adjourned on August 20, and the Section for Anthropological Research voted to request the National Research Council of the United States to formulate a comprehensive research program. The request was accepted and a report followed. The consensus was that the "Polynesian problem" was considered as the immediate primary undertaking in any approach to research in the Pacific.

Kenneth Emory served as a delegate to the First Pan-Pacific Scientific Conference and throughout almost a half-century thereafter he dedicated himself to Polynesian research. Over the years this dedication has taken him to the hinterlands of Hawaii, the Societies, the Samoas, the Tuamotus, the Cooks, Tonga, Fiji, a Polynesian Outlier, and to the museums of Europe. He has suffered administrative responsibilities as chairman of a department. He has taught university courses. He has diplomatically cultivated government administrators. His wartime survival courses comprised a form of applied anthropology. He has pioneered reconstruction techniques in archaeological sites and, when no other course was available, he has even presented public lectures. For nearly five decades Kenneth Emory has held appointment at one institution. He has seen it grow in stature and in scope of contribution and has, himself, been a vital participant in this growth. He possesses a distinction shared by few others in that he has served through the entire tenure of four of the five directors of this Museum.

From its inception Polynesia was a primary concern of Bishop Museum. Indeed, its mandate defines the Museum ". . . as a scientific institution for collecting, preserving, storing and exhibiting specimens of Polynesian and Kindred Antiquities, Ethnology and Natural History and books treating of, and pictures illustrating the same, and for the examination, investigation, and treatment for study of said specimens and the publication of pictures thereof and of the results of such investigation and study. . . ." Polynesia has been interpreted rather broadly through the years, and while the institution has always emphasized the investigation and study of the natural and cultural history of the great triangular segment of the Pacific we define as Polynesia, this emphasis has included a similar concern with all of insular Oceania and the littoral areas of the continental land masses and subcontinents, which, with the islands of the Pacific, comprise the Pacific Basin. Both the Resolution of the First Pan-Pacific Conference and the mandate of the Museum guided Kenneth Emory in his career as an anthropologist. His primary concern was and is Polynesian culture history.

There was a time in earlier days of the development of the discipline of anthropology when an anthropologist was something of a generalist, but as with other fields of study, specialization—even micro-specialization—has come to be the rule. Atomism must be considered inevitable in any field as broad as anthropology. There were even portents of this in the recommendations and reports of the special committee created by the Pan-Pacific Conference of 1920. Both ethnobotany and ethnozoology were remarked upon as areas of concern deserving of special concentration.

The more than one hundred publications by Kenneth Emory compel us to conclude that even with the growing tendency of anthropologists to specialize, he remains something of a generalist. Some would identify him as principally interested in archaeology; but this would ignore his considerable immersion in general ethnography, linguistics, and folklore. Over the years he has been concerned with decorative art, and early photographs depict him precariously suspended over a vertical surface covered with Hawaiian petroglyphs (see Danielsson). Some of his early field work involved the intricate recording of hundreds of genealogies. The coalescence of archaeology and linguistic research as a useful and productive approach to culture history owes a great deal to the pioneering efforts of Kenneth Emory (see Elbert; and Grace). He would make no claim to be identified as a physical anthropologist, yet his work and familiarity with Hawaiian skeletal collections and the anthropometric projects he has undertaken in other parts of the Pacific have required a certain competence. No "arm-chair" theorist, Emory has spent a good many years of his life in the field. Of "informal" expeditions in and around Hawaii, there are any number and we may count at least fourteen major ones to Polynesian locales plus visits of shorter duration to both Melanesia and Micronesia. Contrary to the pattern of many, who with increased years and responsibility tend to send their juniors to experience the rigors and discomforts of field work, Emory still manages to spend a portion of each year in the field.

Perhaps this remarkable commitment to field work is the most adequate explanation for the elapse of 27 years between his B.S. and Ph.D. degrees. He was immersed in the profession. To those who would criticize his timetable, I would quote the late President Kennedy who, upon receipt of an honorary degree from Yale, quipped that he had achieved the best of all possible states—he had a Yale degree and a Harvard education. Kenneth Emory earned a graduate degree from both Harvard (M.A.) and Yale (Ph.D.), as well as an undergraduate degree from Dartmouth. He even managed to spend a part of a graduate year at Berkeley between attendance at Dartmouth and Harvard.

This volume places its emphasis on Polynesia, for this is where Kenneth Emory has worked. It is also where culture history research in the Pacific has been most significant. Any listing of the salient features of the culture history of the Pacific world could be categorized as to the nature of the area under consideration, the nature of the population of the area, and the nature of the studies treating the area. Under the first of these headings it should be remarked that no other third of the earth comprises such vast ocean areas separating isolated land masses of relatively small size. A second point to note is that the distances between inhabited areas provided barriers to contact and often resulted in cultural differentiations and specializations conditioned by isolation (see Barrow). Conversely, the sea provided remarkably facile access between areas despite such limiting factors as distance, weather, and currents (see Green).

So far as population is concerned, it may be observed that for its size the proportion of human beings inhabiting the Pacific area over time is probably significantly smaller than that of any other comparable portion of the earth's surface. We may also say that settlement by man in the Pacific area, and particularly Polynesia, was more recent than in any other block of the earth's surface of similar size.

Compared with a number of other areas of the world, the Pacific has been studied by fewer anthropologists, and the studies which have been made are more recent. A number of Pacific studies are comparative. The region and its culture history not only allow a broad comparative approach, but demand it (see Biggs). Finally, and paradoxically, while isolation has in some cases tended to preserve the pristine quality of island cultures, the effects of rapid rates of cultural change and the impact of acculturation have often outstripped the capabilities of the anthropologists who have been concerned with Pacific studies to make essential observations before it was too late. The consequence has been detrimental.

Today we are much concerned with methodology; ethnoscience has become a specialty. Even with this concern, we have not yet achieved a real refinement of methodology in the field of culture history whose ultimate aim must be reconstruction; that is, the determination (through actual evidence or through inference) of the record of sequential events over a given span of time. In the Pacific the skein is greatly raveled and there will doubtless always be some considerable obscurity. At best, reconstruction is a matter of probabilities. Hypotheses and projections from the known permit generalizations to the suspected.

The contributions included in this book exemplify the kinds of problems to which students of Polynesia have addressed themselves. They constitute a compendium of the tools and techniques which have been applied to the study of culture history. These tools and techniques are familiar, not unique. They are included in the fields of investigation common to anthropological research; namely, archaeology with its stress upon stratigraphy; correlation of physical data; absolute and relative dating procedures; and keys to chronology, such as ceramic and fishhook traditions. The contribution of linguistics to the study of culture history is more as yet to be appreciated than to be pointed to significantly as a matter of past achievement. Contemporary linguistics, utilizing sophisticated computer techniques and guided by principles of lexicostatistics or glottochronology, has made significant strides in recent time, but the promise without question far outweighs the record to date.

So far as physical anthropology is concerned, newly developed notions of hybridization, genetic drift, gene frequencies, and mutation as factors affecting population (see Green) cause us to reconsider, if not to revise, more traditional conclusions about culture history based on broadly shared latter-day physical characteristics. The ethnographic approach to culture history (see Spoehr) has emphasized material culture (particularly decorative art and style), social structure, religion, and folklore. Over the years there has been an increased awareness of the value in reconstruction of documentary materials, such as personal, government, business or other institutional records. Similarly, there has been a growing emphasis on the cross-disciplinary approach in the study of culture history.

As the papers that follow attest, we have been, and continue to be, interested in refining our notions of Polynesian origins—both immediate and remote, migration routes, the nature of voyaging, settlement patterns, contact and isolation, and the development of cultural uniformity and differentiation as effects of the presence or absence of inter- and intracultural influences. In simpler terms, the questions to which we still seek answers are those which ask, "Where did the peoples of the Pacific come from? By what routes and means did they arrive? In what ways did they establish themselves in new island environments? How did they adapt to these environments? What was the nature of their contact or lack of contact with other peoples of the region?" And finally, "To what extent are the peoples of the Pacific alike and different culturally, and what factors may we conclude have effected the similarities and dissimilarities?"

Several things have militated against felicitous reconstruction of detailed culture history in the Pacific. There is a dearth of ethnographic studies of island cultures which detail their precontact nature. For example, as Kelly points out in her paper, there is no truly adequate account of Hawaiian culture as it was at the time of Cook's discovery of the Islands. Moreover, the impact and rate of cultural change in the Pacific were such that, coupled with other factors, we have no general ethnographic record comparable with that of the Americas or Africa. To illustrate, when Métraux worked on Easter Island in the early 1930's there were virtually no informants upon whom he could rely who could recall the ancient Easter Island way of life.

Coordinated field research which has contributed to our knowledge of Pacific culture history has been limited. The Thilenius Expedition probably stands as the most comprehensive and intensive approach to

Pacific island ethnography; and the Torres Straits Expedition, though more restricted in scope, must be cited, too, as a valid and early attempt to secure data through coordinated field investigation. They constitute the exception rather than the rule. We should not, of course, overlook the contributions of such pioneers as Dixon, Rivers, Malinowski, or later students of island cultures such as Beaglehole, Buck, Keesing, Gifford, Handy, Linton, Oliver, Mead, and others who worked, as did Emory, for the most part, on individual rather than coordinated collaborative projects. Their contributions have made it possible to generalize as much as we are able. Without them there would be a very small base upon which to draw any conclusion.

The years since World War II have seen more coordinated research in the Pacific than ever before: the U.S. Commercial Company (USCC) survey; three investigations initiated and sponsored by the Pacific Science Board of the National Academy of Sciences–National Research Council and known as the Coordinated Investigation of Micronesian Anthropology (CIMA), Scientific Investigations in Micronesia (SIM), and Scientific Investigations in the Ryukyu Islands (SIRI); and the Tri-Institutional Pacific Program (TRIPP) sponsored by Yale University, University of Hawaii, and Bishop Museum. In the years between the Bayard Dominick Expedition of the 1920's and these post-World War II approaches, the Yale-Bishop Museum Fellowship Program provided sponsorship for individual field workers, but of coordinated work there was little. Oliver developed a collaborative approach to Society Island studies in the late 1950's, and several of the papers in this volume are based in part on linguistic and archaeological research carried on by individuals from the United States, New Zealand, and Fiji under a 1965 National Science Foundation grant to Bishop Museum. Other coordinated programs worthy of mention are Watson's micro-evolution project in the New Guinea Highlands and Barnett's relocation study.

We know as little as we do of Pacific culture history for more reasons than that we lack valid early accounts and that there has been too little coordinated research. In answering the questions, "Why haven't we done more?" and "Why did we wait so long to do it?" I believe we must recognize that prior to the establishment of the major federal foundations in the United States following World War II, there were severe field research funding problems. No one would argue that there are adequate funds today, but conditions are vastly improved. Furthermore, transportation is not the problem today that it once was. Air travel enables people to get to and from the field with greater ease and in less time than ever before. A steamer voyage to the South Seas was an undertaking of months. Today the same journey can be accomplished in a matter of hours from anywhere in the world.

More important, however, than restrictions on productive results conditioned by inadequate funds or the slowness of transportation are such things as the geographical and topical strait jackets worn by Pacific anthropologists for far too long. We may conclude that broad regional perspectives have been slow to develop even if we recognize the excesses of yesteryear remarked upon by Elbert. Similarly we may admit to a parochial disciplinary approach to culture history. Cross-disciplinary research has never been fully exploited in the Pacific. Also, as noted by Danielsson and Davidson, archaeologists tended to operate until recently on erroneous assumptions regarding the retentive qualities of Pacific islands in respect to archaeological deposits, either because of hydraulic disturbance, recentness of events, or both.

Finally, it appears that we are not better able to offer generalizations about Pacific culture history because we have never provided sufficient manpower. In contrast, before this volume is issued, 150 Peace Corps volunteers will be posted to the Samoas, and Tonga will be provided with a contingent of 115. Within the past year approximately 600 young people were sent to Micronesia under the Peace Corps program. Leaving all arguments about the advisability of these assignments aside, the point I wish to make is that there has never been any comparable commitment from any nation to provide in a manner similar to that of the Peace Corps, a sizable number of zealous, intelligent, and reasonably well-educated individuals to work with professional scholars in the solution of problems of culture history.

Like the biologist whose frenetic race against the encroachments of "progress" that disturb the marine or terrestrial community in which he must pursue his investigations, the student of culture history, too, races against ever-increasing changes in the arena of his research. Anthropologists have to some extent become inured to the admonitions of those who counsel that there is too little time to do all that needs to be done while it may still be done. Such observations have been made many times over the years and they unquestionably predate Kenneth Emory's career. In this connection, however, it is of interest to note that one of the Resolutions of the First Pan-Pacific Conference contains the statement that a fuller knowledge of the history and culture of the Polynesian peoples was essential and further noted that the opportunities for obtaining information were rapidly disappearing. More recent spokesmen for this point of view have been Heine-Geldern and Lévi-Strauss, the latter of whom has proposed a most eloquent hypothetical parallel between anthropology and astronomy.

At first blush, it might appear that the archaeological record was the most secure of any of the subareas of interest to the culture historian. However, in the face of rapidly expanding world population and the physical disruption resulting from new highway systems, pipelines, harbors, power facilities, agricultural operations, mining, and so forth, as well as widespread urban expansion, there are no special guarantees which may be relied upon. Salvage archaeology is an accepted term. Though expressed usually in other terms—typically "urgent ethnological research"—we have also come to accept the need for "salvage" ethnology. Should we perhaps not also be increasingly concerned with what might best be defined as *salvage culture history?* This question is posed with an awareness of the appalling changes which have come about during the past 50 years and the conviction that those which we may anticipate in the next 50 will be inestimably greater (see Lavondès).

An estimate of the probable course of future research in culture history may be inferred from the papers in this collection. It would appear that out of our past experience should have grown by now an awareness that faulty assumptions greatly retard the pursuit of knowledge. Those involving culture history in the Pacific are worthy of constant review and analysis. Coupled with this should be a willingness to modify basic research philosophies, particularly those which would impose strictures of conceptualization in respect to artificial barriers, such as those between culture areas, disciplines, and subdisciplines. For instance, prehistory, ethnology, ethnohistory, and history tend to coalesce. The development of additional coordinated projects involving greater numbers of personnel than heretofore from a variety of fields of specialization is seen as beneficial. There is a need to recognize the changing nature of the object of our scrutiny. Tomorrow's Polynesia (or Oceania) is not yesterday's—or even today's (see Spoehr).

An extremely lucrative source of information on Pacific culture history is archival in nature. The use of documents in reconstruction generally needs to be encouraged. Oliver, in whose contribution we see an example of such use, is one of the stronger proponents of this view. There may well be a need for a marked change of philosophy on what constitutes an acceptable Ph.D. thesis project. Perhaps documentary research ought to be considered as legitimate as field projects.

It is probable that computers and other data-processing devices will be used to great advantage in the analysis of comparable data from multiple areas, the aim, of course, being the demonstration of how closely cultural configurations correspond to one another. Linguists have taken the initiative in this area and their example should be followed. Increasingly, key site or problem investigation approaches give promise of more significant results. To illustrate, migration routes and settlement patterns may well be most easily determined through investigations carried on in certain key locations, as for example among the Polynesian Outliers.

Finally, as Biggs comments, we would be well advised to develop a larger component of indigenous students of culture history. Perhaps there is even some degree of poetic justice in this proposal—for Polynesia at least, because Polynesians, with their enormous emphasis upon oral traditions and genealogies (a form of hypertrophy in Mead's terms), may be said to have been among the most enthusiastic and ardent proponents of the preservation (if not the reconstruction) of culture history.

Despite the title of this collection, I have been speaking of the culture history of the entire Pacific area—indeed I believe that we must so speak, especially as we look to the future. In sharp contrast to his catholic scholarly interests within the field of anthropology, Kenneth Emory has limited himself to Polynesian problems. However, he would be among the first to support the argument which stresses the need for breadth of purview. By virtue of their own field experience, those who salute him in this volume demonstrate that they, too, subscribe to the view. At least half of them have worked in parts of the Pacific outside of Polynesia. Each of the contributors to this volume, whether or not his experience is limited to Polynesia or goes beyond, counts Kenneth Emory both a colleague and a friend. A few, such as Barrère, Finney, Kelly, and Sinoto, might be identified as his students, but all have learned from him. Some would claim, as does Cox, a disciplinary affiliation outside anthropology. Most, however, concede a primacy of interest somewhere within the broad scope of the discipline. The roster of contributors is significantly international in character, and, in keeping with both the broad and growing concern with Pacific problems, it also offers testimony to the nature of the bonds formed by Kenneth Emory over the years which transcend political barriers. Represented are those whose national roots bind them to France, Sweden, Denmark, New Zealand, Japan, Great Britain, and Hawaii as well as the mainland

United States. There are many whose names do not appear in this book who might also have contributed had time and circumstance permitted.

Half a century is a considerable portion of anyone's lifetime. It is within but three brief years of that period of time that Kenneth P. Emory has been a member of the staff of Bishop Museum. In terms of years of continuous service, his tenure is the longest of any person now serving or who has previously served this institution. These considerations alone merit recognition. But volumes such as this in honor of any individual should be based on more than longevity of affiliation. The quality of a man's work is what should be acknowledged. Those whose comments follow are paying honor to one whose efforts are distinguished by both quality and longevity. More important, they honor one whose contributions are continuing.

ROLAND W. FORCE

Bernice Pauahi Bishop Museum
Honolulu, Hawaii
September, 1967

PREFACE

K IA ORA KENETI is the title of the biographical sketch of Kenneth
Pike Emory by Bengt Danielsson which opens this volume. It expresses, with true Polynesian elusiveness and rich variety of meaning, the
spirit which engendered and carried this project through. "Kia ora," we
are informed by linguist Bruce Biggs, expresses succinctly in the language
of the Maoris of New Zealand the idea, "may you enjoy long life and
the best of health." But it also parallels the more familiar Hawaiian concept of "aloha," which can mean anything from "love" to a casual
greeting. "Keneti" is the Tahitian form of "Kenneth," and he is undoubtedly known to as many or more persons as Keneti than he is as
Dr. Kenneth P. Emory.

The hard work of many persons has contributed to this volume's
completion. Although many have felt such a project greatly to be desired,
it began to take form on the suggestion of Dr. Alan Howard, and the
Editorial Committee was convened to consider its feasibility in the
winter of 1965. Dr. Howard, Mrs. Marion Kelly, and Dr. Yosihiko
Sinoto of the Museum's Department of Anthropology conferred with the
Museum Director, Dr. Roland W. Force, to select persons who might
contribute articles to such a volume.

Star-Bulletin Printing Company of Honolulu was asked to undertake
the printing, and its representative was queried as to just when we would
have to have the volume in type for it to appear on Kenneth Emory's
70th birthday, November 23, 1967. A tentative schedule was set up for
a book whose manuscript did not at that time exist.

Letters of invitation were sent to the far-flung contributors, who responded with gratifying speed, expressing their eagerness to participate.

All cooperated to keep the manifold phases of the work moving at all possible speed—the contributors, designer Joseph Feher, illustrator William Kikuchi, the printer, and Miss Sadie J. Doyle and Mrs. Dorothy Barrère of the Museum editorial staff.

The project had to be kept a secret from Kenneth Emory—not an easy thing to accomplish within the limited confines of Bishop Museum. An inquiring intelligence such as his, and one with so sincere an interest in the doings of those surrounding him, resulted in several perilous moments. But, so far as we of the Committee know, as of this writing "Code Project 70," although known to so many, has remained our secret.

All who have shared responsibility for this work feel, I am sure, as do I, an inherent satisfaction in the spirit that has propelled all of us forward to bring it to a successful conclusion. And we all join in a sincere "Kia Ora Keneti!"

GENEVIEVE A. HIGHLAND

Bernice Pauahi Bishop Museum
Honolulu, Hawaii
September, 1967

CONTENTS

KIA ORA KENETI

BENGT DANIELSSON

National Museum of Ethnography, Stockholm, Sweden

SOME ANTHROPOLOGISTS are constituted in such a way that they are utterly unable to write even the shortest scientific paper without injecting into it something of their personal experiences, feelings, and attitudes. As a rule, anthropologists of this breed also love to give public talks and regularly produce very readable and amusing accounts of their field trips and researches for the general reading public.

Other anthropologists abhor using material of a personal character, even if they have been through the most harrowing experiences and dangerous adventures. They are absolutely unable to write popular, salable books or articles and separate their private from their public lives by an insurmountable barrier. Kenneth Pike Emory definitely belongs to this latter category. There is even something evasive about his personality and the fact that the happiest years of his life have been spent on remote, isolated islands certainly entitles us to label him, without any malice whatsoever, an escapist, in the purest and most noble South Sea tradition.

It is exactly these self-effacing qualities—which make it impossible to learn anything about his personal life and struggles from a study of his many published works—that have persuaded us, his closest friends, of the necessity of opening this anniversary volume with a short biographical sketch. Another good reason for doing so is that a mere list of his publications, museum duties, field trips, lectures, excavations, and teaching positions would be very confusing and give the completely wrong impression; that his incredibly manifold and varied activities have been mostly unconnected and determined by fortuitous circumstances. As I hope that I shall be able to show clearly in the following pages, exactly the opposite is true: during all the 47 years that Kenneth has been on the staff of Bishop Museum, he has steadfastly kept the same goal in mind and pursued it with great obstinacy, sometimes against very heavy odds and handicaps, indeed.

The fact that Kenneth was born at Fitchburg, Massachusetts, a state that for more than a century supplied Hawaii with its most zealous and strict missionaries and dissolute beach-combers, of course greatly contributed to the shaping of his destiny. The decision to go West, in classic American tradition, was, however, not his own but his father's, for he was only three years old when the family sailed for the recently annexed new Territory of Hawaii in 1901. The senior Emory's main reasons for this bold move were the usual ones: the understandable appeal to a New Englander of the warm, tropical climate and the hope that the magnificent business opportunities there quickly would lead to a great fortune.

Honolulu at the beginning of the century was already a large modern city of 40,000 inhabitants, with numerous tall office buildings, an oil depot, a telephone system, a busy railway station, and modern street cars. But some tenuous links with the past still existed. There were, for instance, several clusters of settlers from the outer islands within the city boundaries, and Hawaiian was occasionally spoken in the streets of Honolulu. Kenneth's first attempts to learn the language were, however, made somewhat later, during his high school years at Punahou Academy. Many of his closest friends came from the other islands, and when visiting them during the school holidays, he was taken on long horseback trips to native villages, where Hawaiian was the mother tongue of the majority of the people and some of the old customs had survived. These repeated, direct contacts with genuine Polynesian communities of course made Kenneth curious about the still more primitive peoples in the southern part of the Pacific, and his enthusiasm knew no bounds when his father began to talk about setting out on a new voyage—to the Fly River in New Guinea in search of birds of paradise. Kenneth was ready to abandon his studies at a moment's notice. Fortunately, the preparations and the financing of this purely family expedition took such an unexpectedly long time that he managed to graduate from Punahou in the meantime. The year was 1916, and by then he was more interested in intellectual pursuits than in chasing dream birds in paradise. One way in which he clearly demonstrated this was the first appearance in print of an article signed by him. Its title was "Windward Molokai," which very aptly sums up the contents—except for the fact that it also describes a meeting with Jack London and his wife—

and it was published in the November issue for 1916 of *The Mid-Pacific Magazine*.

The highest institute of learning in the islands at this time was the forerunner of the present university, still called Hawaii College of Agriculture and Mechanical Arts. Since Kenneth was interested neither in tilling the soil nor in operating machines, the only solution left to him was the rather costly one of attending a good college on the mainland. Luckily he happened to have a benevolent uncle who lived only a few miles from Dartmouth. So there he went. The main subjects taught were the humanities, foreign languages, and natural sciences, and, in the absence of any definite plans for the future, Kenneth took courses in all three departments, acquiring what is euphemistically known as a "broad, general education." The only aberrant choice occurred during his junior year when he attended a course in Old World archaeology that he, however, quickly dropped.

These years in the climate of his ancestors, more austere from every point of view, strengthened Kenneth's determination to return and spend the rest of his life in the South Seas, preferably in some of the exotic, tropical islands south of the line, and in some profession that permitted him to lead a life in the open air. The only profession to offer an opportunity to do so seemed to be that of a missionary. As a preliminary step Kenneth joined one of the religious student clubs at Dartmouth. There is no doubt that Kenneth possessed—and still possesses—some of the more important character traits needed for missionary work, such as ascetic food habits and a complete disregard for physical comfort. But these are, after all, basically negative qualities, and to his great chagrin he soon discovered that he lacked the even more essential positive predispositions, such as a deep faith and a burning zeal to convert the poor heathens. Equally disqualifying was, of course, his broad-mindedness and tolerant attitude toward other people's quirks and foibles. So he pursued instead his rather vague aim of getting a "general education" with a somewhat unsuspected preference for botany.

Shortly before Kenneth graduated in 1920, Dr. Charles Montague Cooke, Jr., of Honolulu, who was a close friend of his father, suggested an alternative course of action. He advised Kenneth to make a trip to nearby Yale University and ask the new Director of Bishop Museum, Dr. Herbert Gregory, for permission to join some scientific expedition to the South Pacific. Dr. Gregory must have seen the determined glint in Kenneth's eyes and felt the contagious enthusiasm that has always endeared him to all his friends, for he promised to appoint him, immediately after graduation, as "Assistant Ethnologist" at Bishop Museum.

The salary he offered was magnificent, considering the circumstances: 85 dollars a month. Overwhelmed by joy, Kenneth accepted on the spot and then speedily went home and looked up the exact meaning of the strange new word "ethnologist."

On August 1, 1920, he took up his new post in Honolulu. The only ethnologist on the staff of the Museum at that time was John F. G. Stokes, who was curator of collections and therefore had little time to spare for initiating the neophyte in the mysteries of ethnological theory and the practical difficulties of ethnological field work. When six months later Kenneth's name was mentioned for the first time in the Annual Report of the Director, his qualifications were described in the following disarmingly frank manner: "Mr. Emory is familiar with surveying and field methods, and his residence in Hawaii has given him interest in Polynesian problems."

The early 1920's were a great period in the history of Bishop Museum, for this was the time when not less than three field expeditions were sent out simultaneously to Polynesian key areas south of the equator, thanks to the generous gift of 40,000 dollars by a New York businessman "deeply interested in primitive races," Mr. Bayard Dominick. Dr. Gregory summarized the state of Polynesian studies at this time in the following terse words, still worth quoting today as a useful memento to the overenthusiastic: "Data necessary to the understanding of the history of primitive man in the Pacific area are lacking, and the theories advanced rest on insecure foundations."

The anthropologists the Museum sent out on these salvage expeditions to record as much as possible of the aboriginal customs and traditions before they disappeared altogether, were either experienced field workers like Stokes and Aitken or young, well-trained men like Handy and Linton, whose splendid reports soon proved that they were the right men for the job. As to the inexperienced new assistant ethnologist, he was only asked to assist the expedition members with the packing. As a consolation he was, however, eventually dispatched to the Island of Maui to help Aitken to determine the truth of some recent reports that there were extensive stone ruins in the desertlike crater of Haleakala. The main reasons why Kenneth was chosen for this job were his long association with the von Tempsky family that had reported these new discoveries, his proficiency in the Hawaiian language, and his previous knowledge of the rugged, volcanic country, acquired during many school holidays spent on Maui. When Aitken shortly afterward had to sail forth on his long-planned expedition to the Austral Islands, Kenneth was left in charge of the crater survey. Launching into this new, exhilarating work with great vigor in spite of the dust and the heat, he repeatedly criss-crossed the crater, recorded the Hawaiian place names, mapped several dozens of stone terraces and shelters, and dug into the cinders, thereby making his first archaeological discoveries: a good number of skeletons and adzes.

It was nevertheless a poor substitute for a field trip to an island in the South Pacific with a living Polynesian culture. But Kenneth realized clearly that if he hadn't been entrusted with more important tasks it was solely because of his lack of proper academic training in anthro-

Chalking in petroglyphs on a boulder at Luahiwa, Kealiakapu, Lanai, Hawaii, in 1921.

pology. So as soon as his crater diggings were completed, he very sensibly sailed off to California and attended the graduate courses given at Berkeley during the spring semester of 1921 by Kroeber, Gifford, and Waterman.

On his return to Hawaii, he spent the next six months, from July 12 to January 28, 1922, on the most "backward" of all his home islands, Lanai. His investigations covered, in the thorough manner which later became his hallmark, not only all the ruins and petroglyphs, but also compiled extensive lists of place names, maps, and "a relationship tree including every native on Lanai." With this remarkable study Kenneth proved once and for all that he was a most gifted and accomplished ethnologist. Equally remarkable was the speed with which he completed the manuscript; it was ready in May, 1922.

Unfortunately, by then Bishop Museum had exhausted all the funds at its disposal for field work. So, in spite of all his progress and efforts, Kenneth was as far as ever from his goal: a prolonged stay in the islands in the South Pacific with a living, or at least a surviving Polynesian culture. While waiting for an opportunity to realize his dream he once more, very wisely chose to improve his knowledge and academic standing by continuing his studies on the mainland. This time he went to Harvard where America's great master of Oceanic studies, Roland Dixon, taught. Not less famous and learned were the other professors whose lectures he attended: E. A. Hooton and Alfred M. Tozzer. In addition to a thorough grounding in cultural and physical anthropology and archaeology, these three teachers gave their students some very sound practical advice. Tozzer, for instance, told them repeatedly: "If you want to take up archaeology as a profession, marry first a wealthy woman." While Tozzer soon acted in accordance with his own excellent principle, Kenneth, still a light-hearted bachelor, sailed back to Honolulu as soon as he had received his master's degree in July, 1923.

To nobody's surprise, no new benefactor with the same generous means and disposition as Mr. Bayard Dominick had appeared on the scene in the meantime. Doggedly Kenneth plunged into field work with Hawaiian informants. The farthest he got from the Museum was the uninhabited islands of Necker and Nihoa, where he and other members of the Tanager Expeditions found archaic stone sculptures and other stone remains that made the great Polynesian puzzle even more complicated and difficult to understand.

The Great Opportunity that Kenneth had been waiting for and preparing himself for so long eventually came toward the end of 1924 when a magnificent, 180-foot, four-masted yacht, very appropriately named *Kaimiloa,* "the long search," dropped anchor in Honolulu harbor, southward bound for Samoa, the most unspoiled of all the Polynesian groups. She was a former trading vessel that had just been refitted and equipped in a most thorough and lavish manner by her new owner, Mr. Medford Kellum, with the sole purpose of making a pleasure cruise. Not less than eight spacious staterooms and four bathrooms had been built below deck, along both sides of the central dining room which had a seating capacity of 24 persons. To ensure the passengers a varied and wholesome menu the ship was equipped with an enormous electric generator and enough cold storage space to carry fresh meat and vegetables for 30 persons for

90 days. The gigantic thirst that so rapidly develops in tropical countries could be quenched with the same ease, thanks to a separate refrigeration plant that produced 200 pounds of ice cubes every 24 hours. To look after the needs of the passengers and navigate the yacht there was a captain, a master's mate, a cook, a doctor, a nurse, and sixteen men.

Although Mr. Kellum had taken along his wife and four children, two friends, and two private tutors from the University of California, there was still plenty of room on board for additional passengers. With admirable impertinence Dr. Gregory sought out the owner of this floating hotel shortly after his arrival, and persuaded him to give free accommodation and transport to five members of the Bishop Museum staff, among them Kenneth. The only condition that Mr. Kellum made was that at least one of the scientists should be an experienced photographer, able to develop the movie films he planned to take of native scenes and customs. This task fell to Kenneth—mainly by default, since his companions knew even less about filming and laboratory work than he did. In keeping with the important mission with which he had been entrusted, Kenneth was, shortly before the *Kaimiloa* sailed from Honolulu on November 9, 1924, promoted to "Ethnologist," after having thus, for four years, been assistant and second to none in the Museum.

On the way to Samoa, Mr. Kellum kindly consented to make stops at several of the Line Islands to let Kenneth make surveys of the quite extensive *maraes,* temples and stone terraces, built there by the prehistoric Polynesian seafarers who had used the same route in their probably much more primitive and uncomfortable vessels. After having spent the day trudging across miles of sharp coral reefs and soft sand dunes in the dazzling heat, Kenneth then spent the greater part of his nights developing the footage shot by the delighted Kellum clan. Somehow the landscapes and persons filmed were often quite recognizable when the result was proudly shown on the screen.

As we all know, material comfort and lavish supplies do not automatically ensure success on a field trip. For this, a common goal and mutually shared interests are also necessary. In this case, no such common bond existed between the pleasure-seekers and the fact-seekers. So, while nobody in particular could be blamed, the tension between the two groups rapidly increased. Soon the point was reached where all messages were transmitted through the only person acceptable to both clans: the already overtaxed ethnologist *cum* photographer, Kenneth. Mr. Kellum who, as you may have gathered, was a man of action, solved the problem in a radical manner frequently resorted to by sea captains in the Pacific in the old whaling days. He simply decided to put the whole scientific

party on shore—no, not on the nearest island, as his predecessors used
to do, but on the nearest *inhabited* island with regular communications
with the civilized world. This happened to be Tahiti. Another quite remarkable departure from the traditional pattern was Mr. Kellum's quite
unexpected farewell gift, when they parted on January 1, 1925, of ample
funds for the scientists, to be used as they liked, either for continued
researches or for their speedy return to the United States.

Emory (left) and field team take shelter under a lean-to they constructed at
Popotaiaroa, in the interior of Papenoo Valley, Tahiti, 1925.

Tahiti in 1925 was an infinitely less rewarding field of study for an
anthropologist than Samoa, the original destination of the *Kaimiloa*.
True—unlike, for instance, Hawaii—the immense majority of the inhabitants in Tahiti were still more or less full-blooded Polynesians, who
spoke Tahitian and nothing else. But otherwise it was the same old, sad
story. Immoderate use of liquor, firearms, and preaching had completely
destroyed the pre-European cultural equilibrium. An alien, French administrative and legal system, incomprehensible to the natives, had been

imposed. The growing of cash crops and the introduction of a money economy had transformed their daily lives and prompted them to replace their food, tools, utensils, and dress with inferior imported factory products. The last keepers of the historical traditions and genealogies were dead, and the only tales the younger generations wanted to hear were those unfolded on the screens of the rickety movie theaters, where the programs consisted wholly of westerns, slap-stick farces, gangster, and war pictures. Of the traditional skills and crafts only fishing, leaf plaiting, and house building had survived, and they had all been ably studied and described by Dr. and Mrs. E. S. Craighill Handy two years previously.

When searching out the most skilled fishermen and craftsmen, the Handys had also, to their great astonishment, discovered that there existed not only in Tahiti but throughout the Society Islands a much greater number of well-preserved *maraes* and other stone structures than had hitherto been realized. They had, however, neither the time nor the necessary equipment to undertake any archaeological surveys. So here was at least one kind of study with which Kenneth had had previous experience and which might throw new light on the cultural relations of the Polynesian peoples and the much-disputed problem of their migration routes. He eagerly grasped this opportunity and started walking round the breathtakingly beautiful Island of Tahiti, penetrating deeply into every one of the sixty valleys. Everywhere he discovered hitherto unrecorded *maraes*.

At the same time he made two pleasant discoveries of a completely different sort. The first was that the Tahitians, in spite of all their sufferings and cultural losses, still were the same marvelously hospitable, cheerful, generous, humorous, and charming people as they had been at the time of European discovery, for which reason it was always stimulating and beneficial to be in their company. The second discovery was the gradual revelation of how delightful the social life of the few local, equally fun-loving French settlers was. Its most attractive feature, then as now, was the great freedom and tolerance that prevailed. For what had happened was simply that at the same time that the most stringent European norms had been abandoned, the permissive, and often libertine, philosophy of the Tahitians had been adopted to a very large extent. As a rule, it was not so easy for a recently arrived outsider to be accepted by this unique French colonial society, but Kenneth succeeded magnificently without really trying, just by being himself: an innocent, slightly bewildered young boy with tousled hair and an unwavering devotion to his work; that is, just the sort of person that everybody wants to help. Soon his constant companion was a famous local *belle,* Marguerite, whom he had

first met at a fancy dress ball, attired in the least self-revealing and appropriate costume he could have chosen, that of a pirate. Although—or
perhaps just because—they couldn't speak each other's languages, they
were in complete agreement, and before the year was up they were
married.

I don't think that Kenneth ever contemplated seriously remaining and
settling down for good in Tahiti, as so many others of us have done who
also by a lucky chance have been stranded there and succumbed to the
peculiar charm of this island. But then, the simple explanation is certainly that his work meant too much to him, and that it was at that time
absolutely impossible for a resident anthropologist or archaeologist to
make a living there. One thing is sure, however, and this is that he was
never again to be the same man, for he had now found a new compass
bearing to steer by during his future expeditions and travels in the Pacific.

The first fifteen-months-long visit and exploration of Tahiti and the
other Society Islands was immediately followed by a sort of scientific
honeymoon to Europe, where he and his young bride spent most of their
time studying and photographing the Polynesian collections in French,
Italian, and British museums. Not until December 14, 1926, after an
absence of more than two years, did he return with her to his home base,
Honolulu.

Although Kenneth was often temporarily distracted by his writing
labors, museum work, and family life (his first daughter was born in
1926), he spent much of his time during the next years propagandizing
for and planning a new expedition to the Etablissements Français de
l'Océanie which was then the rather incongruous and prosaic name for
the beautiful garland of green islands spread out on the ocean around
and including Tahiti. (The name has now been changed to the more
precise one of Polynésie Française). Of these islands he wanted particularly to visit and do field work on the Tuamotu atolls, east of Tahiti.

The Tuamotus were at this time by far the least known of all the
major Polynesian groups. The only published sources that contained
some useful information on the culture and language of this isolated
group were two or three short, biased accounts in mission journals and
scattered references in half a dozen travel books. The reason for this
almost complete lack of reliable information was, however, not that the
old culture was dead. On the contrary, on most of the atolls, the links
with the past were still numerous and strong. Kenneth's eyes had first
been opened to this fact by another New Englander gone astray. He was
J. Frank Stimson, who had settled down in Tahiti for good in 1912 and
gradually become absorbed by linguistic researches, even to the extent of

neglecting his original profession, which was that of an architect. After having been shown an impressive number of native manuscripts and made a quick exploratory voyage to two of the nearest Tuamotu Islands in 1925, Kenneth had drawn the correct conclusion that there existed in these islands the greatest reservoir of untapped traditional source material in all Polynesia.

The reason for this unusual cultural conservatism was simply that practically all foreign explorers, whalers, traders, and missionaries had deliberately avoided and by-passed these far-flung, barren coral islands, spread out over an ocean belt 900 miles long and 300 miles wide, full of treacherous currents and submerged reefs, because they lacked not only passes or good harbors, but also drinking water, fresh meat, vegetables, fruit and, most important of all, exploitable riches. Even at this late date in the long history of the European conquest of the Pacific there were no permanent settlers or resident administrators and only a handful of itinerant missionaries and Chinese traders in all of the 78 islands that make up the Tuamotu group. The most notable culture changes had of course been in the fields of religion and material culture. But basically the natives' mode of life had remained untouched, and in the eastern part of the archipelago, the islands most distant from Tahiti, there were still in the 1920's many elderly men and women who possessed a vast fund of knowledge, handed down in an unbroken line from the distant past, and who had been active participants in the ancient social and religious ceremonies. In addition, practically all family heads owned manuscript books, in which they or their parents had written down innumerable genealogies, chants, and tales in their native tongue, when and as soon as they had learned to write by attending occasional classes taught by the missionaries. Although the Tuamotuan culture thus was far from dead, it was slowly dying, and Kenneth had the immense merit of realizing immediately the importance of undertaking a vast salvage expedition before it became too late.

Wise from his previous cruise experience, he requested and obtained, toward the end of 1928, enough funds for chartering a schooner in Tahiti, and took the regular Matson liner to this island where he planned to establish his headquarters during the two years the Tuamotuan survey was to last. Of the other members of the field team, Harry Shapiro came out independently from New York, and Stimson, already living in Tahiti, waited eagerly there for his two companions. On their arrival, in March, 1929, they found that the most economical solution to their transport problem was to order a new boat from a local shipbuilder. This they did right away, and then quickly sailed off on a copra schooner for a first,

short cruise to Takaroa and Takapoto. Back in Tahiti, they spent the
rest of their waiting time working with Tuamotuans living there temporarily.

To everybody's surprise, the boat, which was designed by Charles
Nordhoff and baptized *Mahina-i-te-pua,* The Foam-of-the-Bow-Wave,
was ready by July. To build a whole ship in four months certainly seems
a most remarkable feat, especially on a small South Sea island. But one
is immediately much less impressed, if one knows that the *Mahina-i-te-
pua* was only 29 feet long—which is the exact length of two cars—and

With Dr. Peter Buck (Te Rangi Hiroa), right, at the coronation stone of
Marae Taputapuatea, Opoa, Raiatea, Leeward Society Islands, 1929.

that she had none of the conveniences and comforts that Kenneth had enjoyed on the *Kaimiloa*. Quite correctly, too, the *Mahina-i-te-pua* was never called "a ship" by the local knowledgeable inhabitants, but simply "the motor-launch."

The first duty the proud expedition vessel, the first ever owned by Bishop Museum, was called upon to perform was most fittingly to take the expedition members on a pilgrimage to the most sacred and famous of all Polynesian temples, Taputapuatea at Opoa, Raiatea. As agreed upon, they met there their own high priest, Te Rangi Hiroa Buck, who was then conducting field work in the nearby Cook Islands and who, like them, had never before visited Opoa. As usual, Kenneth didn't keep a

Emory, Dr. Harry L. Shapiro, and Mr. J. Frank Stimson, Hao, Tuamotu Islands, 1929.

diary and never found time to record his impressions. So it is most fortunate that we have the following account from Buck's pen of what they did and felt on this solemn occasion: "We took pictures of speechless stone and inanimate rock. I had made my pilgrimage to Taputapuatea, but the dead could not speak to me. It was sad to the verge of tears. I felt a profound regret, a regret for—I do not know what. Was it for the beating of the temple drums or the shouting of the populace as the king was raised on high? Was it for the human sacrifices of olden

times? It was for none of these individually but for something at the back
of them all, some living spirit and divine courage that existed in ancient
times and of which Taputapuatea was a mute symbol. It was something
that we Polynesians have lost and cannot find, something that we yearn
for and cannot recreate. The background in which that spirit was engendered has changed beyond recovery. The bleak wind of oblivion had
swept over Opoa. Foreign weeds grew over the untended courtyard, and
stones had fallen from the sacred altar of Taputapuatea. The gods had
long ago departed. To keep down the rising tide of feeling, I said bruskly
in the American vernacular, 'Let's go.' "

After having thoroughly repaired their vessel, which had proved a
little bit too leaky even by local standards, Kenneth and his two companions, with a Tahitian captain and two native sailors, set out early in
September on a long, adventurous cruise to the isolated atolls in the
northeastern corner of the Tuamotu group, to begin their field work in
earnest. They succeeded beyond their wildest expectations, as evidenced
by Kenneth's first, breathless interim report: "We have so many genealogies (we don't bother about them unless they are ten generations at
least) that we are laboriously copying down identical ones without knowing it. When you learn that one genealogy has 3,000 names, and another
1,700, and another 1,000, and that we have over 200 genealogies, you
will forgive us for not remembering all the names. We have 80 names of
the stars from Anaa, and about the same number from Fangatau. We
have the names of about 70 historical canoes, and the names of their
masters. It took me four days to make a rough index to Stimson's three
type-written, loose-leaf volumes of chants, genealogies, and traditions."

It would be tedious to describe here in detail all the cruises that Kenneth and Stimson made during the next year (Shapiro returned to the
United States in January, 1930). But that they went about their task
with extraordinary energy and go-ahead spirit is proven by the simple
fact that they sailed more than 4,000 sea miles in their little nutshell and
visited 27 atolls, for longer or shorter periods. Although they laid up the
ship during the hurricane seasons, they spent many frightful hours on
board when sudden storms blew them off course or suddenly a roar was
heard in the middle of the night from some unseen coral reef that happened to be much closer than the captain had foreseen. That these were
not the only dangers and hardships ship's travelers encountered in the
Tuamotus can easily be demonstrated by the following quotations from
an account written shortly afterward by one of Stimson and Kenneth's
companions on a later trip, Earl Schenck. Take this very common plague
for instance: "It seemed a hundred flies rode out with every sack of

copra. In addition, each visitor brought an escort of flies roosting on his hat and back. The mast and sides of the ship were covered with swarms of them like clotting blood. Eating became a nightmare." When they went ashore on some islands they were exposed to a slightly different but equally intensive attention. Tatakoto was such an island, says Schenck, for it was "a girl island, where women outnumbered the men four to one. We lost two of our crew. The captain sent out search parties, but at last

On the *ahu* of Marae Terangituatini at Farepue, northeast coast of Reao, Tuamotu Islands, 1930.

gave up." Not less trying and exhausting was the stiffling heat in the fancy plank houses, of European style, belonging to their wealthier native friends that they often were forced to live in. The most splendid belonged to the Chief of Vahitahi. Schenck calls the style "steam-boat gothic," and one is inclined to agree, for this is how he describes it: "The sun glared from a tin roof and four weather vanes. It bounced from rows of glass doorknobs, fastened all over the building, and struck into high relief a conglomeration of scrolled mill-work designs which ornamented the eaves, windows and doorways." The furniture consisted of armchairs, rocking chairs, clocks, brass beds with embroidered pillow slips and quilted counterpanes, night jars with pink roses, and several phonographs and sewing machines.

The intrepid explorers were, however, once more richly rewarded for their troubles and pains. On Tatakoto, for example, they met the daughter of "a warrior and cannibal who about 1865 was himself killed and eaten on a raiding expedition to the island of Vahitahi." On this latter island they were able to witness and film a three-day-long festival, anciently held in times of famine in order to hearten the people and enlist the help of the gods. On Reao they recorded fifty old *fangu* chants with the help of their queer-looking dictating machine that was of an equally impressive age. On Pukarua they found a fishing community of the pre-European type. And everywhere they were gladly given manuscript books to copy—by hand. Kenneth had a decidedly heavier work burden than Stimson, for on each of the islands they visited he also made measurements of the natives for Shapiro and surveyed all existing stone remains. Finally, in his spare time (?), he took thousands of photographs which are invaluable today, as the recent upheavals and transformations of the islanders' lives, brought about by the construction of French nuclear testing bases, have made the 1930's appear a period as remote and primitive as our own Stone Age.

As a result of the wealth of material that Kenneth and Stimson collected during their two-year-long field survey, it became for the first time possible to define and distinguish cultural subareas in the Tuamotu group and to determine more precisely its cultural relationships with the surrounding island groups. There were, of course, still at the end of it many gaps in the material, which also in many respects was uneven, mostly because unlucky circumstances and unfavorable weather and winds sometimes had prevented them from visiting certain islands or from staying long enough on certain other islands. Keenly aware of this, Kenneth concluded his report with the both hopeful and modest statement that their just-concluded field work should simply be considered as "preliminary" to a new Tuamotuan expedition lasting a year "or more."

Fortunately for Kenneth, the natural science staff of Bishop Museum, by now jealous of their colleagues in the anthropology department, soon began to clamor for a similar field trip to French Polynesia which, from the zoological and botanical point of view, was still very much a *terra australis incognita*. So all Kenneth needed to do was to fan their ambitions and generously offer his services.

Although 1932 and 1933 were the worst Depression years, in some miraculous way Bishop Museum managed to raise enough money to send out five scientists on such a cruise in 1934. Following the example of Kenneth and his companions in 1929, and in one respect even going a little bit farther, the leader of this new expedition, Dr. Charles Montague Cooke, hired a fishing sampan, engaged its competent skipper, Captain William Greig Anderson, and embarked with all his companions and

David Kaupiko's house at Kapua Bay, Kona, Hawaii, Museum field trip, 1932. Left to right: Lohiau, Jacob Hua, Sr., Jacob Hua, Jr., and Herbert K. Keppeler. Emory on second floor lanai.

equipment in Honolulu. *The Islander,* as the 87-foot, 75-ton sampan had been renamed, was small and the scientists' living quarters were extremely cramped. Furthermore, the smell from the powerful diesel engines penetrated every nook and corner. But the main purpose had been realized: the field party was completely independent and could go wherever they wished and stay on each island as long as necessary.

Kenneth wanted above all to make an intensive study on one of the culturally most conservative atolls in the Tuamotu group, Napuka, where he had only managed to spend a couple of hours during his previous Tuamotuan expedition. His companions, on the other hand, wanted to make extensive collections of plants, shells, and insects from as many different islands as possible in French Polynesia. Their ways were therefore bound to separate, but not until they had experienced many dangers and unforeseen difficulties during an adventurous cruise that took them first to the Line Islands and Tahiti. At long last, on May 15, 1934, the tiny atoll of Napuka, with its scattered clumps of wind-battered coconut trees and pandanus palms, rose up from the sea. There was no opening or pass in the reef ring. Some almost completely naked natives who came out in small paddle canoes through the tremendous surf, however, with big smiles, pointed out the spot where ships' boats used to shoot across the submerged reef. Undaunted, Captain Anderson started immediately disembarking Kenneth's voluminous equipment and provisions needed for a stay of several months.

Once more Kenneth had taken upon himself to perform the tasks of three men, those of anthropologist, archaeologist, and photographer. When, therefore, some time during the trip down from Honolulu, one of the crew members had volunteered to leave the ship and assist him in his work on Napuka, he had without hesitation gladly accepted this offer. Luckily, both for Kenneth and us, this courageous volunteer happened to have quite extraordinary qualifications for playing the role of Friday to Robinson Kenneth. He was actually the well-known, easy-going and practical-minded Honolulu journalist, Clifford Gessler, who had accepted the humble position of an ordinary sailor on *The Islander* in order to be able to see and write about the fabled islands in the heart of Polynesia. Whereas Kenneth, as usual, didn't find time for keeping a diary or writing articles, Clifford Gessler eagerly made copious notes for a charming and well-written book, *Road My Body Goes,* which gives us many excellent glimpses of Kenneth's life and work on Napuka.

As Kenneth had believed and hoped, the two hundred natives on this small, isolated atoll turned out to be true Polynesians in their behavior and thoughts to a much larger extent than those on any other atoll in the Tuamotu group on which he had previously lived. Which, among other things, meant that he and Gessler were right from the beginning received and treated like old, respected friends for whom all doors were always open. At the same time that they felt completely at home, they experienced, of course, also the wonderful peace of mind that only can be realized by leaving far behind all the noise, stress, hurry, and money problems so typical of our Western industrial societies. This is what Gessler has to say about what Napuka meant to both of them personally: "Peace flowed into the spirit. The surf curling over the ruddy reef; the wind in the tall fronds; the sunlight glowing over the rude land—these made our world. Concerns and conventions of that other world receded

With Te Mae, a resident of Napuka, Tuamotu Islands. Bishop Museum Mangareva Expedition, 1934.

and lost meaning. The country of the white men became but a confused
and troubled dream. Reality, for the moment, was this sun-washed ring
of coral, hard and clean in the vast sea."

The work was pure pleasure: "A detailed record of our days would
be a repetition of small incidents: this or that kind of food, a new dance
or chant; conversations with this or that old man who remembered pagan
times; the arising and adjustment of some dispute in the community, to
which we were interested witnesses. We arose at dawn, and walked by
the shore, marveling at its peace and beauty; then went together or
separately to continue our study of the people, returning at noon for a
swim in the lagoon and a meal at home or as guests of some native family.
In the afternoon we slept, as is customary, awakening to resume the same
business, or to take pictures, on Sundays, of people in their best clothes,
that we might photograph them later in a nearer approach to 'native'
costume. In the early evening we wrote our notes of the day's doings,
while the people were at 'evening school,' for after they returned, there
could be no work. The later evenings were gay with singing and dancing,
and the midnights solemn with old chants."

And let me add this last glimpse from Gessler's book in order to
give a well-rounded picture of the life and labors of our Napukan field
workers: "Most enthralling of all our foreign ways were the processess
of photography, which we practiced under extreme difficulties. Keneti
would get up at three or four o'clock in the morning, when the house
was dark and quiet, the water temperature down to seventy-eight degrees
or so, to develop film and hang them on cords across the house. In the
morning the people would flock around to examine them, exclaiming
'No good,' for they had no notion of a negative. To them a picture was
a picture."

Where to go next, when the last roll of film was taken, the last *marae*
surveyed, and the last chant recorded on Napuka, had been decided long
before *The Islander* left Honolulu. Peter Buck was this year to do field
work in Mangareva, the only major group in Polynesia unworked by
professional anthropologists. In order to finish quickly with this group,
once and for all, he had asked Kenneth to come over from Napuka and
map the *maraes* and other stone structures. The distance from Napuka
to Mangareva is not more than 500 nautical miles and can therefore
easily be covered in four or five days. That is, if one has a boat. *The
Islander* was, however, at this time somewhere in the Austral Islands and
unable to come to Kenneth's rescue, even if he could have sent a cable
to her from Napuka, which of course was not possible. The only thing
left for him and Gessler was to wait patiently for a copra schooner and

hope that she would head approximately in the direction of Mangareva. Such a schooner arrived at Napuka on July 29, and they embarked immediately. To their mutual, happy surprise, Kenneth and Gessler met Peter Buck and Frank Stimson only a month later on an island that was situated barely 300 nautical miles from Mangareva.

What happened next is typical of the hazards a traveler has to cope with in the Tuamotus and is told by Kenneth in his field report: "Buck and Stimson brought the news that *Tiare Tahiti* would not be along for at least three weeks and advised us to move on to a new field to await her, taking advantage of the schooner *Moana*. Though our work was not quite finished, we decided to push on to Reao, the quarantine which prevented an earlier visit having been removed, and, when the *Tiare Tahiti* arrived at Reao, to return to Tatakoto. En route to Reao, word came from Papeete that the *Tiare Tahiti* might be indefinitely delayed. Under these circumstances the *Moana* was chartered to take us from Reao to Mangareva and bring Stimson back to Tatakoto. The *Tiare Tahiti* was advised to go directly to Tatakoto, transfer Stimson to Vahitahi, and then report at Mangareva." Although some of his movements continued to be so complicated that we have to use a computer, if we wish to plot them in detail, Kenneth, against all expectations, eventually arrived safely in Mangareva on September 12 and immediately went to work. Apart from a nasty gale that blew the schooner widely off course half-way between Mangareva and Tahiti, nothing more remarkable happened during the long, homeward voyage.

As we all know, to collect data in the field is a relatively easy and pleasant task, compared to the long and tedious labors required to analyze and organize them so that they can be published. Yet, if we examine closely the impressive list of Kenneth's more than 60 publications—of which ten are full-length monographs—we cannot avoid being struck by the uncommonly long interval that elapsed between his return from the Tuamotus at the end of 1934 and the appearance of his first field report in print, in 1939.

One very understandable reason for this big gap in his otherwise uninterrupted chain of publications was that Bishop Museum at this time unfortunately lacked funds and therefore was badly understaffed. As a result of this sad state of affairs, the scientists on its staff were forced to fill simultaneously several posts, and even to perform a variety of tasks which normally are delegated to telephone operators, secretaries, exhibition guides, and janitors. The one with the heaviest burden was without any doubt Kenneth, simply because he was as usual too considerate to say no when asked to take on new duties. Since so much has been written about the exciting and adventurous life of Kenneth the field worker, I shall here try to correct the balance by offering some glimpses from the considerably more drab and inglorious existence of Kenneth the museum man, gleaned from the annual reports of Bishop Museum.

In 1935, the first year after his return to Honolulu, it is, for instance, recorded that he gave "considerable time to the classification of the

With Hawaiian *heiau* image at Bishop Museum, 1947.

ethnological collection" in the Museum. The following year, he assisted the new Director, Peter Buck, "in preparing a photograph catalog of Polynesian artifacts." This obliged him to postpone another chore, so "during his vacation, he took opportunity of working over Winslow M. Walker's manuscript on the archaeology of Maui by visiting various parts of the island." In 1937, he dashed off, right in the middle of a busy work schedule, to Mauna Kea on the Big Island of Hawaii "to study the adz workshop at the 12,500 foot contour of the western face." In the next report we read that for a change "Kenneth P. Emory devoted much time to rearrangement of exhibits in Polynesian and Hawaiian Halls, and to the arrangement of a special exhibition in Hawaiian Vestibule." In between, he supervised the work of graduate students from the University of Hawaii. Throughout 1939, "Mr. Emory served on the Labeling Committee of the Museum and devoted much attention to building up the photograph catalog file of the Museum"—which didn't prevent him from making a field trip to "the three famous burial caves in the district of Kohala, Hawaii." Whereupon, the following year, he sorted the Museum's large collection of dictaphone recordings. And all the time there was, of course, an endless stream of old ladies who wanted a Hawaiian name for their pet dog or cat, journalists who needed some hard facts for their fanciful articles, VIP's who expected personal guidance on their Museum tours, club presidents in quest of a colorful and witty dinner speaker, happy owners of ancient artifacts who wished to know how much they were worth, and loquacious amateur ethnologists who insisted on discussing for hours and hours their highly personal and original theories.

Under these circumstances, and considering that every new chore or unexpected visitor not only took so much time away from his Tuamotuan studies, but also distracted him and disorganized his whole work schedule, it is not surprising that the number of published papers and studies were fewer during these lean years.

But this is not the whole truth. There is another reason for the relative sterility of this period. Kenneth was most unfortunately forced into a bitter and time-consuming controversy with his fellow-worker during his two field trips to the Tuamotus, J. Frank Stimson. To reduce it to its simplest terms, the crucial question was whether there had existed in former times in the Tuamotu Islands a cult of a supreme god, called Kiho-Tumu or Kio-Tumu. Stimson affirmed that such a god had once secretly been worshiped by specially initiated natives, and published as early as in 1933 two Bishop Museum *Bulletins* containing a great number of chants and texts in support of this contention. Kenneth had from the outset serious doubts as to the authenticity of the material and became, as new texts and interpretations flowed from Stimson's pen, gradually more and more skeptical.

I am sure that many of my readers will be slightly dismayed that I touch upon this painful episode in a publication on a festive occasion like this one. But to pass it over in complete silence would certainly give the unfortunate impression that it is less flattering to Kenneth and doesn't stand up to scrutiny—which definitely is not the case. And is it, moreover, really satisfactory to ignore altogether, even in a short biographical sketch such as this, one of the most important problems in Kenneth's life, one that disturbed him continually for more than five years? I don't think so. Then, there is still a third reason why I want to include at least two short paragraphs about this episode; and this is the tendency some colleagues still have today to dismiss the whole controversy as essentially a clash of personalities. Those who have known both men well—and I think that I can count myself among this number, for I first met Kenneth fifteen years ago and was Stimson's neighbor in Tahiti during the last ten years of his life—can easily understand why such an erroneous interpretation has been put forward and believed. The most fitting way to describe how and why the two men differed, in my opinion, is to compare them to two common Polynesian character types. For whereas Stimson, with his bold speech, quick temper, enormous self-reliance, and marvelous, intuitive gift for generalizations closely resembled a Tuamotuan *kaito* warrior of old, Kenneth, on the other hand, with his mild manners, searching mind, and predilection for a contemplative life, has his perfect counterpart in a Tuamotuan *tahunga* sage. In fact, the only thing the two men actually had in common was their complete disregard for the normally and generally practiced methods of handling and driving a motor car—and that was of course not enough to avoid a break.

When the break finally did occur, it was exclusively for theoretical reasons, because the two men had reached diametrically opposed conclusions, using the same data. To begin with, Kenneth tried patiently to reason with Stimson and point out where he went wrong, mainly because he was deceived by his informants. When the result was only angry outbursts, Kenneth at long last and most reluctantly, in 1939 and 1940, published a series of articles in the *Journal of the Polynesian Society,* containing overwhelming evidence which proved that he was completely right and Stimson altogether wrong. It is as simple as that.

Having at long last definitely thrown off the heavy burden and anxieties that this unnecessarily prolonged controversy had created for him, Kenneth was now free to wind up the Tuamotuan studies he had been working on intermittently all these years. As a matter of fact, several manuscripts embodying all field data on the material culture, religion, and traditional history were by then practically completed, and a successful termination of the whole projected publication program within sight. But, during this long period of gestation, Kenneth had conceived an idea for still another study which he wanted to be a sort of all-embracing synthesis of them all: a comparative study of the cultural relations in Eastern Polynesia, paralleling Burrows' recent thesis on cultural differentiation in Western Polynesia. In addition to the great theoretical interest such a companion study presented, Kenneth had another and more personal motive for undertaking it. Like so many other colleagues before and after him, he had realized that purely formal, academic qualifications are a *sine qua non* requirement for a successful career (and higher income, ensuring a more decent living). He wanted, consequently, to present this study as a doctor of philosophy thesis at Yale. This desertion of his former university, Yale's arch-rival, Harvard, was not such a great treason as it may seem to many red-coats, but was simply dictated by the gradual evanescence of Harvard and the emergence during the 1930's of Yale as the principal center of Polynesian studies in the United States.

So, for the fourth time Kenneth sailed off to the mainland in August, 1940, for a year of academic courses and examinations. Although, for excellent reasons that soon will become apparent, Kenneth did not complete his thesis and obtain his degree until after the war, I should like to point out here two noteworthy features of it. The first one was that the final draft, both in its scope and emphasis, only very vaguely resembled the original project. For, instead of being based on inventories of the material culture of the principal island groups in Eastern Polynesia, it had become a penetrating study of the linguistic relationships of these groups, as evidenced by a comparison of the total vocabularies. The second and more remarkable feature of the dissertation is the often overlooked fact that it was a sort of glottochronological study, undertaken long before this new word and science had been invented.

Kenneth came back from Yale just in time to witness the bombing of Pearl Harbor. The immediate reaction at Bishop Museum was a truly Olympian *sang-froid,* for this is the only reference to this national and international disaster found in the annual report for 1941: "After the Pearl Harbor incident, the Exhibition Halls were closed for two weeks because the public had little time for recreation."

At the same time, however, the whole staff launched a febrile rescue operation as a precautionary measure against renewed air attacks. Unique and valuable specimens were removed to a fireproof building where they were locked up in steel cases. Other artifacts for which the Museum did not possess adequate records were photographed and manuscripts and other important documents were microfilmed. With the curator and several other staff members off on war service, and no hope of getting extra help, most of this gigantic and tedious work fell to the old handy man, Kenneth. It was also he who found an institution on the mainland willing to take all these records into safe-keeping. Do I have to add that it was Kenneth's old college at Dartmouth?

Lecturing before class in survival techniques for members of the armed forces during World War II at Bishop Museum, 1945. Photo by Jim Mooney.

Gradually, curious visitors of a new kind started arriving at the Bishop Museum. They were military intelligence officers in desperate need of reliable information on the Pacific islands, where a full-scale war was now raging. The Museum staff soon realized that it could make a modest but definite contribution to the war effort. As the fury and magnitude of the battles increased, more and more American pilots, soldiers, and sailors were set adrift on the ocean and stranded on remote, isolated islands, where they often perished quite needlessly because of their complete ignorance of how to locate and utilize the food resources. The toll was of course particularly heavy on the barren coral atolls. Most of the scientists at Bishop Museum had both theoretical and practical knowledge of the survival techniques evolved by and practiced for thousands of years by the natives and immediately decided to impart them to all potential castaways in the Armed Forces.

The first effort was a small guide book called *Castaway Baedeker to the South Seas,* a title evidently deemed a little bit too frivolous, since it was shortly afterward changed to *Native Lore for Castaways in the South Seas* and eventually to *South Sea Lore.* This excellent little guide was so frequently reprinted that it has become the greatest best-seller of Kenneth's books and as usual, of course, without making him richer.

The next step was the organization of an exhibit on the same theme, which opened at the Academy of Arts in downtown Honolulu but soon moved to, and became a permanent fixture at Bishop Museum. Finally, as the logical outcome of all this, Kenneth began to teach complete courses in island survival, both on the Museum grounds (for undergraduate students) and on the windward beaches and in remote mountain valleys of Oahu (for graduate students). The principal department in this Robinson Crusoe College, was, of course, that of Native Home Economics, with detailed demonstrations of how to catch fish, collect fruit, climb a coconut tree, open a nut, prepare an earth oven, make fire by friction, and so on. But there was also a School of Native Medicine, and an Engineering Department where the students were taught how to build a thatched hut. I doubt, however, that they found it quite as easy as it sounds to follow the instructions when, for instance, their professor casually remarked: "I demonstrated how a leaf thatch could be plaited in two minutes." Finally, there was even a Fashion Department, where the delighted students learned to make a complete island costume, starting with sandals of *hau* bast, progressing upward to loinclothes made from coconut stipules, and shoulder capes of *ti* leaves; and, to top it all, a graduation cap of plaited pandanus! The number of uniformed students who, with evident joy, attended these courses during the first year of the school's existence was 10,000.

In an article on this unusual combat training program, written at this time for *Natural History Magazine*—and which sounds very much like a propaganda piece but isn't—Kenneth summed up the impact the courses made in these words: "An unlooked for result of this preparation is the entire change of attitude of the men who face the prospect of fighting in the southern islands. Dread of the unknown and boredom of waiting are replaced by lively anticipation and the pleasure of learning to be self-reliant in a world new to them." What he omits is of course that the main reason for these changes in the men was his own enthusiasm and convincing demonstration of the often forgotten truth that we Westerners have much to learn from our so-called primitive or savage brothers. And I am sure that Kenneth, as I do myself, believed and still believes that they are able to teach us not only certain utilitarian skills and techniques but also the much more difficult art of how to be happy and lead a full life.

The courses were deemed so useful by the Armed Forces that from December, 1943, and for the duration of the war, Kenneth was relieved of all his duties at Bishop Museum and appointed Chief Instructor at the Armed Forces special Ranger and Combat School in Hawaii. When, finally, the eagerly awaited Victory Day came, the amazingly well-kept statistics showed that Kenneth had given a total of 913 lectures, and supervised the training of no less than 153,456 men.

Unwittingly, the military high command in the Pacific rewarded Kenneth in the way he appreciated most—by helping him to realize his life-long, up to then impossible dream to go and live on an unspoiled island with a Polynesian population that still clung to the ancient customs of their forefathers. The island where, miraculously enough, such a people still could be found was Kapingamarangi, which, against all reason and charity, had been part of the Japanese Micronesian empire, and had just been taken over by the United States as part of the Trust Territory.

Closed to all traders, explorers, and tourists, and not visited by any scientists since the German South Sea Expedition spent a week there in 1910, Kapingamarangi, as we now all know, had become the closest possible counterpart to the famous African lung-fish; that is, a living cultural fossil. From the scientific point of view, the most remarkable discovery that Kenneth made, at the end of his long voyage through space and time, was the amazing cultural and linguistic affinities that existed between the culture and language of Kapingamarangi and the geographically so-distant Tuamotu Islands. This is, however, not the place to go into the fascinating problem of how these affinities can best be explained, and I shall therefore limit myself to a few words about what the two field trips to Kapingamarangi, July to August, 1947, and June to November, 1950, meant to Kenneth personally.

What they entailed was, of course, a thorough, spiritual cleansing and rebirth of the kind that I think only a prolonged stay among a group of true Polynesians can give us. Kenneth lists in his monograph the following personality traits that he considers typical for the Kapingamarangians:

kindness, quietness, cooperativeness, hospitality, orderly conduct, neatness, cleanliness and industry.

Many other primitive peoples certainly possess some or most of these admirable traits, too. But I know of no people who have developed their hospitality to the same height and refinement as the Polynesians, and it seems to me that it is precisely this unique gift for making a stranger immediately feel at home, feel that he belongs, that always makes a stay on a Polynesian island such a moving experience. All those who have heard Kenneth talk about his field work on Kapingamarangi (particularly in connection with his splendid movie) can certify that he speaks the simple truth when, in his monograph, he calls it the highest point in his

With friends on Kapingamarangi, Polynesian Outlier in Micronesia, 1947.

life, and sadly adds: "The depth of our attachment, formed in our daily associations when we shared our thoughts and our property, and came to each other's aid in facing difficulties, was overpoweringly felt when time came to leave, and their farewell song faded as we paddled out to our waiting ship."

Kenneth had thus to wait for twenty-five years until he was able to realize his boyhood dream of sharing the life of a truly Polynesian people. But even so, he had been extremely lucky to see it fulfilled at all, considering the great cultural transformations that have occurred, and are still occurring at an increasingly rapid rate, in the Pacific, and which will soon completely engulf also Kapingamarangi. If I am allowed to make a very brief digression here, I should like to say that I fully share the grief that Kenneth feels in seeing how unnecessarily and thoughtlessly the old native customs and institutions often are destroyed, and, like him, I cannot cease asking myself, and all who care to listen, what will become of these Polynesian peoples in the future?

In the 1930's when the Great Depression suddenly cut off all outside sources of income for the islanders—thereby depriving them of all the imported tools, food, and clothing to which they had already become accustomed—they solved the crisis by returning to the simple subsistence economy of their ancestors. The same thing happened again on many islands isolated from the outside world by World War II. The next time a social, economic, or political disaster occurs in the so-called civilized world, this simple solution will, however, be out of the question in the islands, for by now all the old men and women who knew the ancient crafts and techniques are dead and the younger generations have refused to learn them. At any rate, even if no depressions and wars occur, many serious problems will arise in Polynesia for other reasons. A Western type of industrial civilization is impossible to achieve on these small islands because of the complete lack of exploitable raw material. Transportation costs are too high for the few exportable crops that can be grown. And most serious of all, the available, arable land area is everywhere extremely limited while all the time the population is increasing by leaps and bounds. So their only means of salvation evidently consists of strict birth control combined with an immediate abandonment of the obsolete, colonial type of monocrop production in favor of a return to the small plot, pre-European type of subsistence agriculture. Since so many of the ancient techniques and so much of the ancestral lore have been lost, we shall sooner or later reach the rather paradoxical situation in which we shall have to send out anthropologists to teach island survival programs also to the natives themselves. Which all means that Kenneth had been a much greater pioneer in the field of applied anthropology than he or anyone else has realized hitherto.

The Kapingamarangi expeditions marked the end of a whole era in the history of the scientific exploration of Polynesia. This era had begun about 1890 when the Polynesian Society, the Hawaiian Historical Society, and Bernice P. Bishop Museum were founded, and enthusiastic pioneers like Percy Smith, Elsdon Best, W. T. Brigham, and Karl von den Steinen went out into the field and began to collect data in a more systematic and accurate manner than had ever been done previously. The basic aim of these pioneers and their immediate followers was of course to reconstruct the whole prehistory of the Polynesian "race" and particularly to prove that their own migration theory was the only correct one. Later generations of ethnological salvage workers were more uncommitted *a priori* and concentrated on gathering new raw data and analyzing them carefully and critically.

As the 20th century passed its half-way mark, all major Polynesian groups, and the principal outliers as well, had been visited by competent field workers, who had overlooked very little vital information. There still existed, of course, many gaps in our knowledge of the pre-European culture of certain areas, but the reasons for these gaps were, as a rule, that many ancient customs had disappeared and that the last native informant had died before the arrival of the first anthropologist. On the whole we possessed, nevertheless, by 1950, thanks to the often heroic efforts of the pioneers, a fairly accurate idea of what the "pure" Polynesian cultures were like in all their essential aspects, at the time the islands were discovered by the first European and American sea captains.

As the impressive collection of dust-gathering studies in the recesses of our scientific libraries bears witness, many attempts were made by historically minded ethnologists during this period to penetrate still deeper into the past and reconstruct the movements of the proto-Polynesians, with the help of comparative studies, based on the distribution of cultural traits. Kenneth had never fallen for the false promises of such facile studies, which never managed to elucidate what they were supposed to do: the similarity or dissimilarity of the material culture of neighboring, contemporaneous peoples *in the remote past*. The courage Kenneth displayed when resisting the temptation to indulge in such *Kulturkreis* studies was considerable, if we keep in mind that his main lifelong interest has been the problem of the origin of the Hawaiians and their immediate Polynesian ancestors.

Elsewhere in the world, the problems concerning the cultural origins of the races and peoples had in the meantime frequently been solved by archaeologists, digging into the ground and analyzing their finds with rigorously scientific methods. Why then had nobody, during all these years, ever tried to unravel the past and reconstruct the Polynesian prehistory by making archaeological excavations? The question is particularly pertinent in Kenneth's case, considering that he had early in his career learned excavation techniques and considering how much mapping of archaeological surface structures he had done between 1920 and 1950.

The answer to this well-justified question is that no archaeological excavations were ever undertaken in Polynesia, prior to 1950, simply because everybody knew for certain that it was absolutely meaningless and useless to do so. With the feeling of superiority that so easily follows from hindsight, we find it today both incredible and ridiculous that such a dogmatic belief could have been established and maintained as the

At Kuliouou Shelter, Oahu, Hawaii, 1950. This is the site that produced the first radiocarbon date for the Pacific area.

ultimate truth, and this certainly forms a fascinating subject well worth study by someone interested in the history of scientific ideas. All I can do here, however, is to specify the premises on which this strange dogma was founded. These were the four more or less explicitly stated contentions that it was not worth while undertaking any archaeological excavations in Polynesia: (1) Because the arrival of man was so recent that no stratified earth layers could have had time to form; (2) Because the frequent hurricanes and tidal waves constantly overturned and scraped the soil bare, and would have destroyed anything left by early inhabitants; (3) Because no artifacts could have been preserved in the damp, corrosive climate except those of stone—of which there already existed rich collections in the museums; and (4) Because pottery, the key artifact that the archaeologists relied on elsewhere in the world for constructing their chronological sequences, was totally absent from all the islands.

The fact that some successful archaeological excavations had been undertaken in New Zealand didn't at all alter the universal belief in this dogma, for it was each time carefully pointed out that the reasons for these successful attempts were just precisely that the geological and climatic conditions were different in New Zealand.

It would certainly have made a much better story, if I could now have told how Kenneth with the sudden brilliant insight of a true genius, realized how hollow this time-honored dogma was and boldly challenged it. The somewhat less heroic but nevertheless highly meritorious truth is that when Kenneth eventually, in 1950, quite shockingly, decided to dig into the ground, his principal motive was that he had been asked by the University of Hawaii to teach a course in archaeological field methods and that without too much enthusiasm he had accepted to do so for the usual, prosaic financial reasons. Since his students were at the same time taking many other courses, the site where the demonstration in excavation techniques was to take place could not be located too far from the University. He chose a cave in the Kuliouou Valley, three miles east of the campus and half a mile from the beach, on the clever assumption that it might have been used by the first Polynesian immigrants as a first temporary shelter during the period immediately after their arrival, while they explored the new land.

To his and everybody else's great astonishment, his motley crowd of treasure diggers almost immediately encountered a series of fairly well-defined strata, each one containing artifacts, some of which were quite unlike the types found in ethnological collections. The most numerous category of artifacts was fishhooks, for they were found in profusion throughout all strata. It didn't take Kenneth long to realize he had here the key artifact he needed, in the absence of marked pottery sherds, for establishing a complete, relative chronology.

Only a couple of years previously, the first carbon-14 dating laboratory in the world had opened in Chicago. Kenneth of course immediately wished to take advantage of this new, revolutionary method of determining an absolute chronology. The result from the Kuliouou excavations, reported in February, 1951, and showing that the cave had been inhabited as early as A.D. 1004 ($\pm$ 180), was the first carbon date ever recorded for a Polynesian site.

Emory, William J. Bonk, Mary Stacey Judd, Tom Park, and Harry Uyehara, at Moomomi shelter site, Molokai, in 1952.

With more than usual enthusiasm and energy, but still operating financially on the proverbial shoestring, Kenneth went out with volunteer teams to sites all over the Hawaiian group. Each time the impressive results proved that every one of the basic premises of the old anti-archaeological dogma had been completely false. Soon again, and now with greater hope of being able to solve the intricate problem of the origin of the Hawaiians than during his first field trip twenty-five years earlier, Kenneth began to look south to his beloved Tahiti and to other islands in French Polynesia.

By now Kenneth's reputation and stature in the scientific world was such that he could with relative ease obtain a series of impressive grants for large-scale research projects, involving many assistants and colleagues. Thanks to the new impetus he gave Polynesian researches, one encounters today in the South Pacific, where the only foreign visitors used to be writers and movie makers, almost as often archaeologists, distinguished principally by their soiled clothes and happy countenances,

Dr. Yosihiko Sinoto and Emory recording postholes at the Sand Dune site (H1), Kau, Hawaii, in 1954.

owing of course to the splendid results of their excavations. One of the surest measures of their success is the alarming fact that during the last years an ever-increasing number of looters have started their own diggings, for purely commercial reasons.

Very fittingly, the most important scientific discovery so far has been made by Kenneth himself in 1962-1963, on the Island of Maupiti, where he found the long sought-after missing link—an archaic Society Island culture, identical to the early Moa Hunter culture in New Zealand.

*   *   *   *

However exciting and fascinating, the results obtained so far in the field of archaeology constitute but the beginning of a new era in the long history of the scientific exploration of Polynesia that undoubtedly also in the future for a long time to come will be marked by Kenneth's personality. I am therefore placed in the very unusual and embarrassing situation for a writer of a biographical sketch of a seventy-year-old, gray-haired professor emeritus to have to stop right in the middle of his life story. But there is no other solution when the subject of our admiration and homage is such an incredibly active, vital, and forward-looking young man as Kenneth.

Field team at Site K3, Nualolokai, Kauai, Hawaii, 1959. Left to right: James Corr, William Smith, Lloyd Soehren, Emory, Mike Manhart, and William J. Bonk. Photo by Robert Goodman.

BIBLIOGRAPHY OF
KENNETH PIKE EMORY

1916. "Windward Molokai: The Story of a Sampan Trip." *Mid-Pacific Mag.* **12**(5):443-447.

1921. "An Archaeological Survey of Haleakala." *B. P. Bishop Mus. Occ. Pap.* **7**(11):237-259.

1923. "Heiaus of Lanai." *Hawaiian Annual for 1923,* p. 138. Honolulu: Thrum.

1924. *The Island of Lanai: A Survey of Native Culture.* B. P. Bishop Mus. Bull. 12. Honolulu.

1926a. "Archaeology in the Society Islands." *Bull. Soc. Etudes Océaniennes,* No. 12, pp. 29-34.

1926b. "The Petroglyph Bowlder at Tipaerui, Tahiti." *Bull. Soc. Etudes Océaniennes,* No. 11, pp. 10-15.

1927a. "L'Art Tahitien." *Bull. Soc. Etudes Océaniennes,* No. 19, pp. 236-239.

1927b. "The Curved Club from a Rurutu Cave." *Bull. Soc. Etudes Océaniennes,* No. 21, pp. 304-306.

1928a. *Archaeology of Nihoa and Necker Islands.* Tanager Expedition Pub. 5. B. P. Bishop Mus. Bull. 53. Honolulu.

1928b. "Stone Implements of Pitcairn Islands." *J. Polynesian Soc.* **37**(2):125-135.

1929. "Ruins at Kee, Haena, Kauai (Famous Court of Lohiau)." *Hawaiian Annual for 1929,* pp. 88-94. Honolulu: Thrum.

1930. "Terminology for Ground Stone Cutting Implements in Polynesia." *J. Polynesian Soc.* **39**:174-180. (With P. H. Buck, H. D. Skinner and J. F. G. Stokes.)

1931a. "A Kaitaia Carving from South-east Polynesia?" *J. Polynesian Soc.* **40**: 253-254.

1931b. "The Marae at which Capt. Cook Witnessed a Rite of Human Sacrifice." *Bull. Soc. Etudes Océaniennes,* No. 41, 4(7):195-203.

1931c. "Recent Petroglyph Discoveries on Tahiti." *Bull. Soc. Etudes Océaniennes,* No. 39, 4(5):138-143.

1932a. "Cock's Comb Hooded Images." *J. Polynesian Soc.* **41**:66.

1932b. "The Curved Club from a Rurutu Cave: Additional Note." *Bull. Soc. Océaniennes,* No. 42, **5**(1):12-14.

1932c. "Découverte d'une Nouvelle Pierre Gravée." *Bull. Soc. Etudes Océaniennes,* No. 43, **5**(2):53-54.

1932d. "The Tuamotuan Survey." In H. E. Gregory *Report of the Director for 1931,* pp. 40-50. B. P. Bishop Mus. Bull. 94. Honolulu.

1933a. Review of A. C. Eugene Caillot *Histoire de l'Ile de Opara ou Rapa.*
       J. Polynesian Soc. **42**:116-117.
1933b. Review of A. C. Eugene Caillot *Histoire des Religions de l'Archipel Pau-
       motu. J. Polynesian Soc.* **42**:114-116.
1933c. Review of G. M. Desmedt "Les Funerailles et l'Exposition des Morts à
       Mangareva (Gambier)." *J. Polynesian Soc.* **42**:125-127.
1933d. *Stone Remains in the Society Islands.* B. P. Bishop Mus. Bull. 116. Hono-
       lulu.
1933e. "Wooden Utensils and Implements;" "Sports, Games, and Amusements;"
       "Warfare;" "Navigation." In Handy, Emory, Bryan, Buck, Wise and
       Others, *Ancient Hawaiian Civilization,* pp. 119-124; 141-153; 229-236; 237-
       245. Honolulu: Kamehameha Schools Press.
1934a. *Archaeology of the Pacific Equatorial Islands.* Whippoorwill Expedition
       Pub. 4. B. P. Bishop Mus. Bull. 123. Honolulu.
1934b. Bibliography of J. Frank Stimson *Legends of Maui and Tahaki.* B. P.
       Bishop Mus. Bull. 127, pp. 89-90. Honolulu.
1934c. *Tuamotuan Stone Structures.* B. P. Bishop Mus. Bull. 118. Honolulu.
1938a. "The Adz Makers of Mauna Kea." *Paradise of the Pacific* **50**(4):21-22.
1938b. "The Canoe Making Profession of Ancient Times." (Trans. by Mary
       Kawena Pukui, edited and annotated by K. P. Emory.) *Hawaiian His-
       torical Soc. Pap.* **20**:27-37. Reprinted in *B. P. Bishop Mus. Occ. Pap.*
       15(13):149-159.
1938c. "God Sticks, Hawaii."*Ethnologia Cranmorensis* **3**:9-10. Cranmore Ethno-
       logical Mus. Issued for private circulation.
1938d. "Hawaii: Notes on Wooden Images." *Ethnologia Cranmorensis* **2**:3-7.
       Cranmore Ethnological Mus. Issued for private circulation.
1938e. "The Tahitian Account of Creation by Mare." *J. Polynesian Soc.* **47**:45-63.
1938-1939. "Flying Spray." Newspapers *Honolulu Advertiser* and *Honolulu
       Star-Bulletin.* Weekly, Dec. 12, 1938 to Aug. 14, 1939. Under patronage
       of Castle and Cooke, Ltd.
1939a. "Additional Notes on the Archaeology of Fanning Island." *B. P. Bishop
       Mus. Occ. Pap.* **15**(17):179-189.
1939b. *Archaeology of Mangareva and Neighboring Atolls.* B. P. Bishop Mus.
       Bull. 163. Honolulu.
1939c. "Archaeology of the Phoenix Islands." (Abstract.) *Proc. Hawaiian Acad.
       Sci.* 14th Ann. Meeting. B. P. Bishop Mus. Spec. Pub. 34, pp. 7-8. Honolulu.
1939d. "Manihiki: Inlaid Wooden Bowls." *Ethnologia Cranmorensis* **4**:20-26.
       Cranmore Ethnological Mus. Issued for private circulation.
1939e. "The Tuamotuan Creation Charts by Paiore." *J. Polynesian Soc.* **48**:1-29.
1940a. "Tuamotuan Concepts of Creation." *J. Polynesian Soc.* **49**:69-136.
1940b. "A Newly Discovered Illustration of Tuamotuan Creation." *J. Polynesian
       Soc.* **49**:569-578.
1942a. "The Hawaiian God 'Io." *J. Polynesian Soc.* **51**:200-207.
1942b. "Oceanian Influence on American Indian Culture: Nordenskiold's View."
       J. Polynesian Soc. **51**:126-135.
1942c. "Polynesian Migrations and Culture: Spirited Defence of Dr. Buck's
       Book." *Pacific Islands Monthly* **13**(4):11.
1942d. *Castaway's Baedeker to the South Seas.* Honolulu: Army Printing Plant.

1943a. "Additional Illustrations of Tuamotuan Creation." *J. Polynesian Soc.* **52**: 19-21.

1943b. "Every Man his Own Robinson Crusoe." *Natural History* **52**(1):8-15.

1943c. "Meet Coconut Meat—Potential Life Saver." *Paradise of the Pacific* **55**(6):20-22.

1943d. "Native Crafts Have Gone to War." In P. H. Buck *Report of the Director for 1943*, pp. 26-30. B. P. Bishop Mus. Bull. 182. Honolulu.

1943e. Native Lore for Castaways in the South Seas. Honolulu Academy of Arts. Mimeo.

1943f. "Polynesian Stone Remains." In *Studies in the Anthropology of Oceania and Asia . . . in Memory of Roland Burrage Dixon*. Peabody Mus. American Archeology and Ethnology Paper 20, pp. 9-21. Cambridge.

1943g. *South Sea Lore.* B. P. Bishop Mus. Spec. Pub. 36. Honolulu.

1946a. Eastern Polynesia, its Cultural Relationships. Ph.D. dissertation, Yale Univ.

1946b. "Hawaiian Tattooing." *B. P. Bishop Mus. Occ. Pap.* **18**(17):235-270.

1947a. "Tuamotuan Bird Names." *J. Polynesian Soc.* **56**:188-196.

1947b. *Tuamotuan Religious Structures and Ceremonies.* B. P. Bishop Mus. Bull. 191. Honolulu.

1947c. "The Tuamotu Legend of Rongo, Son of Vaio." *J. Polynesian Soc.* **56**: 52-54.

1947d. "Tuamotuan Plant Names." *J. Polynesian Soc.* **56**:266-277.

1947e. South Seas Diary. Newspaper *Honolulu Advertiser Sunday Polynesian,* Aug. 31, Sept. 7, Oct. 19, Nov. 30.

1947f. "Kidnaped to London." Newspaper *Honolulu Advertiser Sunday Polynesian,* Mar. 30.

1949a. "Myths and Tales from Kapingamarangi, a Polynesian Inhabited Island in Micronesia." *J. American Folklore* **62**:230-239.

1949b. "The Tuamotuan Tale of the Female Spirit Who Assumed the Form of Tu's Wife." *J. American Folklore* **62**:312-316.

1951a. "The Native Peoples of the Pacific." In Otis W. Freeman *Geography of the Pacific,* pp. 44-60. New York: Wiley.

1951b. "The Original Background of the Micronesians." *Trust Territory of the Pacific Islands Basic Informaton* 1, pp. 61-69.

1951c. "A Program for Micronesian Archaeology." Recommendations of the Sub-Committee on Pacific Archaeology, National Research Council. *American Anthropologist* **53**:594-597. (With E. W. Gifford, G. MacGregor, D. Osborne, A. Spoehr.)

1952. "Advances in Hawaiian Archaeology." (Abstract.) *Proc. Hawaiian Acad. Sci.* 27th Ann. Meeting, pp. 8-9. Honolulu: Univ. Hawaii.

1953. "A Program for Polynesian Archaeology." Prepared at the request of the Sub-Committee on Pacific Archaeology, National Research Council. *American Anthropologist* **55**(5, pt. 1):752-755.

1954. "Archaeological Work in Hawaii, 1953." *News from the Pacific* **5**(1):5-6. Anthropological Soc. Hawaii.

1955a. "Oahu's Fascinating Petroglyphs." *Paradise of the Pacific* **67**(5):9-11, 26.

1955b. "Un Programme d'Archéologie Polynésienne." Trans. by B. Jaunez. *Bull. Soc. Etudes Océaniennes,* No. 110, **9**(9):382-387.

1956a. "Archaeology in Hawaii." *Paradise of the Pacific Holiday Annual,* pp. 38-40.

1956b. "Kilalowe Was Here." *Paradise of the Pacific* **68**(3):9-11.

1957.   The Natural and Cultural History of Honaunau, Kona, Hawaii. Vol. II: The Cultural History, pp. 1-37; 213-248. Prepared by B. P. Bishop Mus. for U.S. National Park Service. Typescript.

1958a. Editor. *COWA Bibliography. Current Publications in Old World Archaeology: Area 21—Pacific Islands.* Council for Old World Archaeology. Cambridge.

1958b. Editor. *COWA Survey. Current Work in Old World Archaeology: Area 21—Pacific Islands.* Council for Old World Archaeology. Cambridge.

1958c. Review of J. Frank Stimson *Songs and Tales of the Sea Kings. American Anthropologist* **60**(4):791-794.

1959a. "City of Refuge." *Paradise of the Pacific* **71**(7):66-70.

1959b. *Hawaiian Archaeology: Fishhooks.* B. P. Bishop Mus. Spec. Pub. 47. Honolulu. (With W. J. Bonk and Y. H. Sinoto.)

1959c. Natural and Cultural History Report on the Kalapana Extension of the Hawaii National Park. Vol. I: Culture. Prepared by B. P. Bishop Mus. for the U.S. National Park Service. Typescript. (With J. H. Cox, W. J. Bonk, Y. H. Sinoto, and D. B. Barrère.)

1959d. "Origin of the Hawaiians." *J. Polynesian Soc.* **68**(1):29-35.

1959e. "Origin of the Hawaiians." *Viltis* **18**(5-7).

1959f. "Rapport Publié par le Conseil d'Archéologie de l'Ancien Monde." Trans. by B. Jaunez. *Bull. Soc. Etudes Océaniennes,* Nos. 127-128, **11**(2-3):33-41.

1959g. *Radiocarbon Dates Significant for Pacific Anthropology.* Pacific Sci. Assn. Supplement to Information Bull. **11**(3). (With Y. H. Sinoto.)

1960.   Editor. *COWA Surveys and Bibliographies: Pacific Islands Area 21.* Council for Old World Archaeology. Cambridge.

1961a. Archaeological and Historical Survey of Honokohau Area, North Kona, Hawaii. Prepared by B. P. Bishop Mus. for the Dept. of Land and Natural Resources, State Parks Division, State of Hawaii. Typescript (With L. J. Soehren.)

1961b. *Hawaiian Archaeology: Oahu Excavations.* B. P. Bishop Mus. Spec. Pub. 49. Honolulu. (With Y. H. Sinoto.)

1961c. "Le Rocher des Petroglyphes de Tipaerui (Tahiti)." Trans. by P. Verin. *Bull. Soc. Etudes Océaniennes,* No. 135, **11**(10):281-287.

1962a. "Additional Radiocarbon Dates from Hawaii and the Society Islands." *J. Polynesian Soc.* **71**(1):105-106.

1962b. Changing Hidden Worlds of Polynesia. Paper presented before Social Sci. Assn. Dec. 3, 1962. Honolulu. In Bishop Mus.

1962c. "Découverte Archéologique aux Iles de la Société." *Bull. Soc. Etudes Océaniennes,* No. 140, **12**(3):125-127. (With Y. H. Sinoto.)

1962d. "Report on Bishop Museum Archaeological Expeditions to the Society Islands in 1960 and 1961." *J. Polynesian Soc.* **71**(1):117-120.

1962e. Review of Thor Heyerdahl *Archaeology of Easter Island, I. Science* **138** (3543):884-885.

1963a. "Archéologie de l'Ile de Pâques." *Bull. Soc. Etudes Océaniennes,* No. 145, **12**(8):347-354.

1963b. "East Polynesian Relationships: Settlement Pattern and Time Involved as Indicated by Vocabulary Agreements." *J. Polynesian Soc.* **72**(2):78-100.

1963c. "Prehistoric Burial Site, Society Islands." Parts I and II. *Conch Shell: Bishop Mus. News* **1**(3):31-33; **1**(4):46-47. Bishop Mus. Assn. Pub. (With Y. H. Sinoto.)

1963d. "Society Islands Archaeological Discovery." *Current Anthropology* **4**(4): 357-358.

1963, 1964, 1965. "Flying Spray." *Conch Shell: Bishop Mus. News* **1**(3):34-35; **1**(4):44-45; **2**(2):22-23; **2**(4):46-48; **3**(1):9-12. Bishop Mus. Assn. Pub.

1964a. "Les Conséquences des Récentes Découvertes Archéologiques en Polynésie Orientale." *Bull. Soc. Etudes Océaniennes,* No. 148, **12**(11):406-414. (With Y. H. Sinoto.)

1964b. "Eastern Polynesian Burials at Maupiti." *J. Polynesian Soc.* **73**(2):143-160. (With Y. H. Sinoto.)

1964c. "Maraes de Bora-Bora." *Bull. Soc. Etudes Océaniennes,* Nos. 146-147, **12**(9-10):370-377.

1964d. "Préhistoire de la Polynésie." Trans. by R. Bertrand. *J. Soc. Océanistes* **20**(20):39-41. (With Y. H. Sinoto.)

1964e. "Rapport Préliminaire de l'Expédition du Bishop Museum aux Iles de la Société: Découverte et Fouilles d'un Site Funéraire Préhistorique à Maupiti." *Bull. Soc. Etudes Océaniennes,* Nos. 146-147, **12**(9-10):378-383.

1965a. "Archaeological Investigations in Polynesia, 1962-1964." *Ka 'Elele* No. 21, pp. 2-3. Bishop Mus. Staff Newsletter. (With Y. H. Sinoto.)

1965b. Editor. *COWA Surveys and Bibliographies: Pacific Islands Area 21.* Council for Old World Archaeology. Cambridge.

1965c. *Kapingamarangi: Social and Religious Life of a Polynesian Atoll.* B. P. Bishop Mus. Bull. 228. Honolulu.

1965d. Preliminary Report on the Archaeological Investigations in Polynesia: Field Work in the Society and Tuamotu Islands, French Polynesia, and American Samoa, in 1962, 1963, 1964. B. P. Bishop Mus. Polynesian Archaeological Program. Prepared for National Science Foundation. Mimeo. (With Y. H. Sinoto.)

In press. "'Ana'a: Histoire Traditionnelle d'un Atoll Polynésien (Archipel des Tuamotu)." *J. Soc. Océanistes.* (With Paul Ottino.)

In press. Material Culture of the Tuamotu Archipelago. Honolulu: Bishop Mus. Press.

In press. Preface to D. B. Barrère, The Kumuhonua Legends. Honolulu: Bishop Mus. Press.

GENERAL POLYNESIA

POLYNESIAN ORIGINS AND MIGRATIONS
A REVIEW OF TWO CENTURIES OF SPECULATION AND THEORY

ALAN HOWARD[1]
Bernice P. Bishop Museum, Honolulu

> Who can give an account of the manner in which they were conveyed hither, what communications they have with other beings, and what becomes of them when they multiply on an isle. . . .
> —*Louis de Bougainville, 1772*

THE ISLANDS OF POLYNESIA have held an enduring fascination for Western man since the time of their discovery. It was perhaps inevitable that the tall, brown-skinned inhabitants would become romantic figures —they were physically attractive, generous, receptive, and from a European point of view, carefree and sexually uninhibited. Their style of life on the balmy tropical isles rendered them close to Rousseau's *l'homme naturale.* By no means the least romantic part of the Polynesian story is the question of their origins. Where was their homeland? When did they arrive on the scene, and by what routes? How did they negotiate the vast distances between the islands? Even the least imaginative of speculations must include a measure of adventure to answer these questions.

THE EARLY EXPLORERS

Conjectures concerning the origins and migration routes of the Polynesians began with the explorers. In Captain Cook's journals (Cook, 1784), for example, the outlines of a general theory are cast:[2]

---

[1] This paper was written with the assistance of Richard W. Bodman and Cedric C. I. Kam, both of whom spent considerable time searching and abstracting the literature. Mr. Bodman translated from the French and Mr. Kam from the German sources. Their judgment and skill has contributed enormously to the preparation of this essay. I am deeply indebted to both of them.

[2] Captain Cook's journals represent the observations and records of many of the men who sailed with him. It is therefore not entirely clear whose ideas the following quotes reflect.

From what continent they originally emigrated, and by what steps they have spread through so vast a space, those who are curious in disquisitions of this nature, may perhaps not find it very difficult to conjecture. It has been already observed, that they bear strong marks of affinity to some of the Indian tribes, that inhabit the Ladrones and Caroline Islands; and the same affinity may again be traced amongst the Battas and the Malays. When these events happened, is not so easy to ascertain; it was probably not very lately, as they are extremely populous, and have no tradition of their own origin, but what is perfectly fabulous; whilst, on the other hand, the unadulterated state of their general language, and the simplicity which still prevails in their customs and manners, seem to indicate, that it could not have been at any very distant period (Vol. 3, p. 125).

Also considered in the journals is the possibility of multiple sources for the vast Polynesian culture complex, but the conclusion is offered that a common origin was more likely. The discussion of this point foreshadows later anthropological arguments of diffusion versus independent invention to account for similar culture traits:

Possibly, however, the presumption, arising from this resemblance, that all these islands were peopled by the same nation, or tribe, may be resisted, under the plausible pretence, that customs very similar prevail amongst very distant people, without inferring any other common source, besides the general principles of human nature, the same in all ages, and every part of the globe. . . . Those customs which have their foundation in wants that are common to the whole human species, and which are confined to the contrivance of means to relieve those wants, may well be supposed to bear a strong resemblance, without warranting the conclusion, that they who use them have common source. . . . But this seems not to be the case, with regard to those customs to which no general principle of human nature has given birth, and which have their establishment solely from the endless varieties of local whim, and national fashion. Of this latter kind, those customs obviously are, that belong both to the North, and to the South Pacific Islands, from which, we would infer, that they were originally one nation. . . . But if this observation should not have removed the doubts of the sceptical refiner, probably he will hardly venture to persist in denying the identity of race, contended for in the present instance, when he shall observe, that, to the proof drawn from affinity of customs, we have it in our power to add that most unexceptionable one, drawn from affinity of language . . . (Vol. I, p. 373).

THE MISSIONARIES

In the wake of the explorers followed the missionaries. They were responsible for amassing the first large quantities of data upon which scholarly inquiries could be based. In order to preach the Gospel they had to learn native languages, and many of them produced usable dictionaries. Their interest in religious matters led them to record legends, myths, and cosmology. They also described customs, although often with an evaluative bias and perhaps with an overemphasis on the bizarre and exotic. Nevertheless, the content of their accounts strongly shaped the discussion of Polynesian culture history for the entire 19th century and the first decades of the 20th. The missionaries themselves led the way in the speculation. Some, such as Samuel Marsden (1932), were so committed to Biblical interpretations that they could not resist linking the Polynesians with groups from the Old Testament. Marsden suggested that the New Zealand Maoris, among whom he was working, "have sprung from some dispersed Jews, at some period or other ... and have by some means got into the island from Asia" (p. 219). He based his case on the similarity between selected religious customs;

> When they go to war the priest always accompanies them, and when they draw near to the enemy he addresses them in similar language to that which the Jewish High Priest addressed to the Jews of old, as recorded in the 20th Chapter of Deuteronomy, verses 2, 3 and 4 (p. 219).

and on a presumed similarity in character;

> They have like the Jews a great natural turn for traffic; they will buy and sell anything they have got (p. 219).

William Ellis (1830, Vol. 2), a missionary of somewhat sounder scholarly judgment, while not dismissing the possibility of Hebraic origin, considered the bulk of the evidence to favor "their derivation from the Malayan tribes inhabiting the Asiatic Islands" (p. 49). He acknowledged the similarity between some of the widely shared Polynesian myths, such as accounts of creation and a deluge, but offered the alternative explanation that they may have learned about these Mosaic events prior to leaving their Asian homeland. He also pointed out that certain Polynesian myths have "a striking resemblance to several conspicuous features of the more modern Hindoo, or Braminical mythology" (p. 42). Ellis was perceptive enough to doubt the validity of myths, however, and recognized the possibility that some may have been influenced by European storytellers. Basing his case primarily on linguistic data, he adhered to the view of a common origin not only for the Malayan, Madagasse, and Polynesian languages, but American Indian languages as well. This, in conjunction with his knowledge of the prevailing winds (from east to west) led him to conjecture that the migration routes took the ancestors of the Polynesians across the Bering Straits and down the west coast of the American continent before setting off into the Pacific. Heyerdahl's argument over one hundred years later, is markedly similar to that offered by Ellis:

Whether some of the tribes who originally passed from Asia, along the Kurile or Aleutian Islands, across Behring's straits, to America, left part of their number, who were the progenitors of the present race inhabiting those islands; and that they, at some subsequent period, either attempting to follow the tide of emigration to the east, or steering to the south, were by the northeast trade-winds driven to the Sandwich Islands, whence they proceeded to the southern groups; or whether those who had traversed the north-west coast of America, sailed either from California or Mexico across the Pacific under the favoring influence of the regular easterly winds, peopled Easter Island, and continued under the steady easterly or trade-winds advancing westward till they met the tide of emigration flowing from the larger groups or islands, in which the Malays form the majority of the population—it is not now easy to determine. But a variety of facts connected with the past and present circumstances of the inhabitants of these countries, authorize the conclusion, that, either part of the present inhabitants of the South Sea Islands came originally from America, or that tribes of the Polynesians have, at some remote period, found their way to the continent.

The origin of the inhabitants of the Pacific is involved in great mystery, and the evidences are certainly strongest in favour of their derivation from the Malayan tribes inhabiting the Asiatic Islands; but, allowing this to be their source, the means by which they have arrived at the remote and isolated stations they now occupy, are still inexplicable. If they were peopled from the Malayan Islands, they must have possessed better vessels, and more accurate knowledge of navigation, than they now exhibit, to have made their way against the constant trade-winds prevailing within the tropics, and blowing regularly, with but transient and uncertain interruptions, from east to west . . . (Vol. II, pp. 48-49).

On the other hand, it is easy to imagine how they could have proceeded from the east. The winds would favour their passage, and the incipient stages of civilisation in which they were found, would resemble the condition of the aborigines of America, far more than that of the Asiatics. There are many well-authenticated accounts of long voyages performed in native vessels by the inhabitants of both the North and South Pacific . . . (Vol. II, p. 50).

If we suppose the population of the South Sea Islands to have proceeded from east to west, these events illustrate the means by which it may have been accomplished; for it is a fact, that every such voyage related in the accounts of voyagers, or preserved in the traditions of the natives, has invariably been from east to west, directly opposite to that in which it must have been, had the population been altogether derived from the Malayan archipelago.

From whatever source, however, they have originated, the extent of geographical surface over which they have spread themselves, the variety, purity, and copiousness of their language, the ancient character of some of the best traditions, as of the deluge, &c., justify the supposition of their remote antiquity (Vol. II, pp. 51-52).

ORIGIN THEORIES

Alternative theories to either the Asiatic or American origin of the Polynesians also were presented early in the 19th century. Most prominent among them was that the Polynesian race originated in Oceania on an ancient continent that had since disappeared, leaving only the islands.

Although this argument was later demolished by geological evidence, it was not unsophisticated at the time it was first offered. Many questions had not been satisfactorily answered by the previous theories. Thus J. A. Moerenhout (1942; first ed., 1837) in criticizing the theory of Malayan origin, asked such questions as: how could the frail Malayan canoes have bucked the prevailing winds and currents to the eastern extremities of Polynesia, a third of the way around the globe; why are the physical characteristics of modern Malays found only in westernmost Polynesia; why is no such migration from west to east in evidence today? He asserts that the only strong link between Polynesians and Malays is the linguistic one, and that this can be explained by considering the Malays to be descendants of the Polynesians, blown westward by the prevailing winds. Moerenhout also attacked the theory of American origins. How, he asks, if the Polynesians are the descendants of American Indian tribes, can the existence of cotton and pigs among the islands be explained, when the two are foreign to America? And given the crudeness of American Indian navigation how could the islands have been settled from America? The similarity between American Indians and Polynesians had been based primarily on customs, he asserted, but similitude of customs alone does not indicate a common origin; the only true test is that of language, yet in considering cognates only exactly similar words can be accepted and none of the twisted and perverse forms admitted by some etymologists. The little linguistic resemblance between American Indian and Polynesian languages that has been offered is valueless, he cogently pointed out, for there are indeed chance resemblances between Polynesian and French, and who would be prepared to argue that they are related? In the light of this evidence, Moerenhout concluded that the Polynesians must be considered autochthonous to Oceania, and that their uniformity in customs, traits, and language can only be adequately accounted for by the existence of a great continent in Oceania. The Polynesian isles, he asserted, are the birthplace of the great Malay family, for in those isles alone does the race achieve a purity of form and the tongue a purity of idiom found nowhere among the Malayans, where the language, as well as customs and physical characteristics have become varied and corrupted.

Thus, well before the middle of the 19th century the three major possibilities to account for the origin of the Polynesians had been postulated. For the following hundred years arguments were put forth in support of one or the other of these views, in some cases with considerable elaboration or revision. The accumulation of evidence was slow and somewhat indecisive, with the exception of the geological evidence which reduced the plausibility of a lost continent. Many of the arguments got down to fine points of myth interpretation and spurious *ad hoc* philological comparisons, but there was also some brilliant scholarship. The work of Horatio Hale (1846), philologist with Wilkes' United States Exploring Expedition, is exemplary. Hale relied mainly on linguistic comparisons to build his theory, but he supplemented his philological findings with a critically sophisticated comparison of customs as well. He used genealogies for dating, but not without an awareness of their limitations. Genealogies were not treated as reign-periods, but as lists of generations. In the interest of accuracy, Hale cautioned, a fair number of first ancestors should be dismissed as mythological, as seems appropriate in each case. He took into account details of the winds and currents, and concluded that the islands were probably settled by accidental voyages and by outcasts defeated in war. Hale also anticipated glottochronology by using the degree of difference between languages to assign relative dates. On the basis of his research he concluded that the progress of emigration was from west to east, and that the Polynesians belong to the same race as that which peoples the East Indian Islands. In summarizing his argument for a west to east migration Hale states:

> This conclusion may be deduced from an examination of the comparative grammar and vocabulary of the various dialects. We see in those of the western groups many forms which are entirely wanting in the eastern tongues; others, which are complete in the former, are found in the latter defective, and perverted from what seems evidently their original meaning. . . . Other comparisons serve to confirm this general deduction. We find in the west a comparatively simple mythology and spiritual worship, which in the east is perverted to a debasing and cruel idolatry (pp. 117-118).

He also notes that the easterly trades are not constant throughout the year, and do not prohibit voyaging from west to east. At certain times of the year there is a northwest monsoon, and there are a fair number of accidental voyages from west to east. To support his conclusion that the Polynesians belong to the same race as the East Indians, Hale invokes the Samoan tradition of a homeland in Pulotu or Burutu, and notes that -*tu* is merely a suffix meaning sacred. "Now the easternmost island inhabited by the yellow Malaisian race, in the East Indian Archipelago, is that called on our maps Bouro or Booro . . . . if we derive the Polynesians from that one of the Malaisian islands which lies nearest to them, we should refer them to the above-mentioned Bouro" (pp. 194-195).

Hale's arguments concerning the settlement sequence within Polynesia are worthy of recapitulation, for they coincide in so many details with some of the most prominent contemporary views. He hypothesized Fiji as the original staging area:

The original scene is probably on the Feejce Group. A party of Melanesians, or Papuans, arrive first at this group, and settle principally on the extensive alluvial plain which stretches along the eastern coast of Viti-levu. Afterwards a second company of emigrants, of the Polynesian race, perhaps from some island in the East Indies, called Bulotu, make their appearance, and finding the western coast unoccupied, establish themselves upon it. The two thus divide the land between them, and are known to one another as eastern people and western people, or Viti and Tonga. After several generations, the blacks (or Viti), jealous of the increasing wealth and power of their less barbarous neighbors, rise upon, and partly by treachery, partly by superior numbers, succeed in over powering them. Those of the Tonga who are not made prisoners, launch their canoes, and betake themselves to sea, after the usual custom of vanquished tribes. In this way they reach the islands of the Friendly Group, which receive from them the name of Tonga . . . (pp. 178-179).

From Tonga and Samoa, which Hale also presumed to have been settled at an early period, the Polynesians moved on to the various groups: to the Society Islands:

. . . and we shall probably be thought justified in supposing that the first settlers of the Society Islands came originally from the Samoan Group, and landed or established themselves first at the place now called Opoa, on Raiatea, which they named Havaii, after the principal island of their native country (p. 124).

It seems certain, therefore, that between the time of settlement of Tahiti by Samoan emigrants, and the sending forth of the colonies which peopled the surrounding groups, sufficient time must have elapsed for the language to have undergone considerable alteration, and for their religious belief, tabu-system, and much of their social polity to have taken a new and peculiar form. If the Rarotongans have been established nine centuries in their present abode, and the Hawaiians fourteen, it seems impossible, on any calculation of probabilities, to allow less than three thousand years to the Tahitian people (p. 148).

To the Marquesas:

On the whole, it seems probable that the northern portion of the Marquesan Group was first settled by emigrants from Vavau (Tonga group), and the southern by others from Tahiti, and that their descendants have since gradually intermingled (p. 128).

Allowing, for the present, the ordinary estimate of thirty years to a generation, it will give us two thousand six hundred and forty years since the arrival of Oataia from Vavau. It seems probable, however, that the first part of the royal genealogical list of Nukuhiva will be found, like that of Hawaii, to be merely mythological; in which case, the foregoing computation will require a corresponding correction, and the time elapsed since the settlement of the island will be considerably diminished (p. 129).

To Hawaii:

The probability is that the Sandwich Islands were first peopled by emigrants from the Marquesas, of the mixed race (Both W. Polynesian and Tahitian elements) which is there found. . . . we have thirteen hundred and fifty years from the commencement of the Hawaiian records (and perhaps from the settlement of the country, though that is uncertain), to the accession of Tamehameha—or, reckoning to the present date, about fourteen centuries.

To Mangareva, or the Gambier Islands:

. . . if we suppose, as all the circumstances indicate, that they came from Rarotonga, they must have left that island about four generations, or one hundred twenty years, after it was settled (p. 140).

To the Australs:

These islands lie south of the Society Group, and west of Rarotonga, and are nearly equidistant from both. The probability is that they were settled from both directions, and at a very late day (p. 141).

On the whole, if we admit that Rarotonga was peopled not quite nine hundred years ago, and Tupuai only about a century before its discovery, we cannot suppose that more than two or three centuries have elapsed since the other Austral islands received their first inhabitants (p. 143).

To the Tuamotu archipelago: These islands seem to have been settled by two groups: by the Tahitians, some time before the peopling of the Australs, and by another unknown group, not terribly long ago.

From what source this foreign element which is here apparent was derived, cannot now be determined. A comparison of the peculiar words in the Paumotuan with the corresponding terms in various other languages of Oceanica has led to no satisfactory result. Perhaps, when the idioms of Melanesia are better known, the attempt may be renewed with more success (p. 144).

To New Zealand: New Zealand seems to have been peopled by Samoans, driven off-course on a voyage to Tonga.

. . . we might be induced to suppose that the emigrations by which New Zealand and Tahiti were peopled, took place at about the same time (p. 148).

Hale also hypothesizes that Rarotonga was settled partly from the Samoan group and partly from Tahiti, and that the Chathams were accidentally settled from the East Cape of New Zealand.

Hale's major conclusions were accepted by de Quatrefages in his book *Les Polynesiens et Leurs Migrations* (1866). De Quatrefages used the example of the Polynesians in an attempt to disprove the then current theory of polygenism—that each race has a separate origin in a definite motherland. The polygenists, he argued, had postulated the existence of a continent in Oceania to account for the uniformity in race, culture, and language of the present islanders; but if another continent, say South America or Europe, were to be submerged at the time he was writing about, the inhabitants of the projecting mountain peaks would be quite diverse in race, language, and culture. The polygenists had considered it impossible for peoples to sail from west to east into Oceania against the prevailing winds and currents, but they overlooked the equatorial counter-current and the period of the western monsoon. The polygenists had assumed that the Polynesians are original to Oceania, but they neglected the islanders' own traditions of coming from the west and of former homelands; traditions which are found throughout Oceania in essentially the same form. The polygenists had said that the Polynesians are not the descendants of the Malays, but it is a fact that the two are definitely related by language, physical characteristics, and culture. Moreover, the example of the Caroline Islanders shows that the Polynesians were exten-sive and able voyagers, and such voyages were recorded in their tradi-tions. Their geographical knowledge is another proof of the former extent of their voyaging; Tupaia's map[3] is our evidence. Nor were accidental voyages rare; they occur and have occurred both to east and west, for quite considerable distances. So argued de Quatrefages in his onslaught against the proponents of an autochthonous beginning for the Polynesian race. He concluded that none of the migrations could be traced back beyond historical times, and that some of the most important migrations took place a little before or after the Christian era. The others are con-siderably more recent, and there are some that are quite modern. Like Hale he made use of genealogies in arriving at his conclusions regarding the time of settlement, although he had similar reservations:

. . . these documents must be used with prudence, and require the control of a penetrating critic. Evidently they lend themselves to interpretations which permit one to fix with great certainty the relative dates of occurrences. But when it is a question of absolute dates, they give very different results, according to the value one gives to the phrases of the poem (p. 165).

Unlike Hale, however, de Quatrefages chose to treat genealogies as reign periods, and assigned a value of twenty-one and a fraction years per period, based on the average length of a European ruler's reign. He therefore arrived at settlement dates that are somewhat later than those postulated by Hale, who made his calculations on the basis of thirty years to a generation. De Quatrefages' dates are, incidentally, closer to current estimates.

The theory that the Polynesians were autochthonous to Oceania did not depend entirely upon the concept of a lost continent, however. Thus P. A. Lesson (1880-1884) argued that the Polynesians were descended

[3] Tupaia was a Tahitian chief who sailed with Cook. He apparently had a knowledge of many islands and successfully directed Cook to some of them.

from the Maoris, and that Maori was the mother tongue of all the Polynesian dialects. Their original homeland was the middle island of New
Zealand, or Kawai (=Hawahiki); from there they migrated to the North
Island, and thence followed the prevailing west and southwest winds into
Polynesia. The first islands they came across were in the Tonga region,
the next in Samoa; from there they spread through the rest of Polynesia,
all of which they found previously uninhabited, except for a few islands
on the Melanesian border. It is certain, Lesson argued, that the migrations had already been accomplished for a long while at the time that the
first Europeans arrived, but no more than that can be said. Polynesians
had mixed with Melanesians, although not as much as one might think,
and they were in contact with the inhabitants of Madagascar at a distant
time, and with the inhabitants of Africa and Egypt as well. They also
reached Siam, Cambodia, Laos, and India and had definite contact with
the Philippines and Japan. There were also some accidental and insignificant contacts with American Indian tribes, notably the Caribe Indians.

Lesson not only believed that the human race originated in many
different places, but also that each point of origin produced a pure and
perfect race, as well as a pure mother tongue. The Polynesians could
therefore not be descended from the Malays, he claimed, because there
are many Polynesian words in Malay, but very few Malay words in
Polynesian; this linguistic evidence suggested to him that the Malays are
descendants of the Polynesians. Moreover, the Polynesians are a pure
race and possess a pure tongue, while the Malays are of many mixed
races and have many different dialects. How then could they be ancestors
of the Polynesians?

Lesson also brought in botanical and zoological information to support his view. From the botanical point of view, he maintained, Polynesian vegetable life is distinct from that of Australia or Malaysia, and is
perhaps best represented in New Zealand. Polynesia is similarly distinct
zoologically; in contrast with Indonesia, which is rich in animal life,
Polynesia has very few species. Similarly, the pig was not found in pre-
European times in New Zealand, and those that the natives encountered in
the other islands are definitely of a species apart from the Malaysian pig.

A variation on previous theories was presented by Jules Garnier in
1870. He held that throughout the Tertiary period and the very early
Quaternary period of the earth's geological history a fairly large continent
existed in Oceania. This continent was inhabited by peoples whose like
are still found in Australasia. At the beginning of the present Quaternary
period the continent was destroyed by a series of calamities, and a few
volcanic and coral islands have taken its place. These new islands have

been populated by migrations from the surrounding continents. By far the majority of Oceania was populated by chance arrivals from America swept away by the prevailing winds and currents; these same winds and currents effected the population of Polynesia from east to west and brought the Polynesians as far west as China and Madagascar.

Besides relying on the winds and currents to support his argument, Garnier asserted that the Polynesian flora resembles that of the west coast of Panama and that the Polynesian physical type resembles that of the American Indians more than that of the Malayans. He also relies heavily on linguistic evidence, which he used selectively and somewhat indiscriminately to support his case while ignoring contrary evidence, managing to find linkages between Polynesian and the languages of Guiana and the Indians of New Mexico, and between Chilean and the languages of New Caledonia and the Philippines. By selectively gathering examples of customs from American Indian tribes, Garnier also finds a large number of shared culture traits between the American Indians and the Polynesians, including caste systems, property systems, feather ornaments, agriculture, megalithic architecture, writing, cannibalism, council meetings, the attribution of suffering to evil spirits, catching fish by poisoning, human sacrifice, and the existence of both common and ceremonial languages.

SCHOLARLY THEORIES

Despite these attempts to the contrary, however, the large majority of serious scholars from the mid-19th century on accepted the theory of west to east migration although each one generally offered a unique interpretation, or elaborated one or another aspect of previous views. John Lang (1877) for example, not only believed that the Polynesians were of Asiatic origin and of the Malayan race, but concluded that these same people continued eastward after populating insular Oceania and reached the coast of South America, where they landed near Copiapo, in Chile, a few hundred years after the deluge. From here their descendants spread out to both continents. He strongly rejected the theory that an emigration had ever taken place from Asia to America by Bering Straits, as others of his time asserted. For evidence Lang relied heavily on customs and architecture, and he concluded that the Polynesians and most of the Indo-Americans had degenerated from an original high civilization, remains of which could be found throughout Polynesia and in Central and northern South America.

In 1878 Abraham Fornander published the first volume of his classic work, *An Account of the Polynesian Race,* in which he presented the following complex theory of Polynesian origins and migrations:

> I think the facts collected . . . will warrant the conclusion that the various branches of the family . . . are descended from a people that was agnate to, but far older than, the Vedic family of the Arian race; that it entered India before these Vedic Arians; that there it underwent a mixture with the Dravidian race, which, as in the case of the Vedic Arians themselves, has permanently affected its complexion; that there also, in greater or less degree, it became moulded to the Cushite-Arabian civilization of that time; that, whether driven out of India by force, or voluntarily leaving for colonising purposes, it established itself in the Indian Archipelago at an early period, and spread itself from Sumatra to Timor and Luzon; that here the Cushite influence became paramount to such a degree as to completely engulf its own legends, myths, culte [*sic*], and partially [*sic*] institutions, upon the folklore and customs of the Polynesians; that it was followed into this archipelago by Brahmanised or Buddhist Ario-Dravidians from the eastern coasts of Deccan, with a probably strong Burmah-Tibetan admixture, who in their turn, but after protracted struggles, obtained the ascendancy, and drove the Polynesians to the mountain ranges and the interior of the larger islands, or compelled them to leave altogether; that no particular time can be assigned for leaving the Indian Archipelago and pushing into the Pacific—it may have occurred centuries before the present era, but it was certainly not later than about the first century of it; that the diversity of features and complexion in the Polynesian family—the frequently broad forehead, Roman nose, light olive complexion, wavy and sometimes ruddy hair—attest as much its Arian descent and Cushite connection, as its darker colour, its spreading nostrils, and its black eyes attest its mixture with the Dravidian race; and, finally, that if the present Hindu is a Vedic descendant, the Polynesian is *a fortiori* a Vedic ancestor (pp. 159-160).

He also worked out an approximate chronology of migrations:

> 1st. At the close of the first and during the second century of the present era the Polynesians left the Asiatic Archipelago and entered the Pacific, establishing themselves on the Fiji group, and thence spreading to the Samoan, Tonga, and other groups eastward and northward.
>
> 2d. During the fifth century A.D. Polynesians settled on the Hawaiian Islands, and remained there, comparatively unknown, until—
>
> 3d. The eleventh century A.D., when several parties of fresh emigrants from the Marquesas, Society, and Samoan groups arrived at the Hawaiian islands, and, for the space of five or six generations, revived and maintained an active intercourse with the first-named groups; and—
>
> 4th. From the close of the above migratory era, which may be roughly fixed at the time of *Laa-mai-kahiki* and his children, about twenty-one generations ago, Hawaiian history runs isolated from the other Polynesian groups, until their rediscovery by Captain Cook in 1778 (pp. 168-169).

For evidence Fornander relied mainly upon legendary information. Settlers in a new land invariably name places after those of their old home, he asserted, and Polynesian place names can be traced from Persia to Hawaii. For example:

> *Puna,* name of districts on the islands of Hawaii and Kauai, Hawaiian group; and *Puna-auia,* a district in Tahiti, Society group, and *Puna-he,* district on Hiwaoa, Marquesas group, refer themselves to / *Puna,* the name of a mountain tribe in the interior of Borneo, and to / *Puna,* a district in Deccan, India, south of Bombay, as well as to a river of that name in Northern India, supposed by Remusat to be the Jamuna or Jumna. It recalls, moreover, the old Egyptian name of *Pun* for Yemen, in South Arabia; a name older than the twelfth dynasty (p. 11).

He also asserted that the chaos idea of creation among the Polynesian tribes bears a striking resemblance to the old Babylonian and Hebrew accounts of the genesis of the world. The Tahitian *"Tino Taata* who floated on the surface" may be the original or the copy of the Hebrew legend. The Hawaiian legend of the lost homeland, the Hebrew legend of Lot and the Greek legend of Orpheus and Eurydice all seem to show a common origin in times before the departure of Abraham from "Ur of Chaldees," and among a people where superstition had already hardened into maxims and precepts. Fornander further maintained that Polynesian customs, usages, rites of worship, and modes of thought indicate an ethnic and social connection with the early peoples in the Mesopotamian basin; for example, circumcision and the use of tabu. Finally, if this is not sufficiently convincing, the numerical system of the Polynesians furnishes decisive testimony of relation to the Aryan stock. Counting did not go beyond four originally in both languages, and larger numbers were expressed in multiples of four. In Polynesia, a group of four was called *kauna;* in Sweden, a group of four small fish, especially herring, is called a *kast.*

Toward the close of the 19th century "wave" theories of migration began to appear in the literature. The underlying presumption was that Oceania was settled by a series of migrations by distinct racial groups, some of which could be found in their pure forms in certain geographical pockets. Other groups found occupying Oceanic islands are to be explained as mixtures of the "pure" types. The theory advanced by John Fraser (1895) provides an example:

> My explanation of the whole matter under discussion is briefly this: The main *officina gentium* for Oceania, long, long ago was India. The whole extent of that peninsula was at a very early period, probably more than twenty centuries before the Christian era, occupied by a pure black race, which I call Hamite; later on, there came into it a Cushite race, also black, but more mixed than the Hamites. Traces of two black races are to be found in all of these regions, and often of the two races apart, as in Australia and the New Hebrides; for the northern Ebudans are in many respects very different from the southern, and the Tasmanians differed

somewhat from the Australians. In Malacca there are dwarf blacks, as in the heart of Africa, and there are negroid blacks in the Philippines and even in Japan. In Eastern Polynesia, the aboriginal black population must have been very scanty, as these islands are so far removed from the Asian continent, and consequently the traces of their occupation have been swamped by the subsequent flow of Polynesian immigrants; but I ascribe the cyclopean structures on Ponape Island and Easter Island to these earliest settlers (for the black races everywhere—in India, Babylonia, Egypt—have shown a liking for hugeness of architecture); and in some of the islands of the eastern Pacific, as Mangaia, the inhabitants are at this hour decidedly blacker and coarser than other Polynesians, as if from a larger infusion of black blood mingling with the brown men. Fiji also has two black races, those of the interior and those of the coast, and these show important differences in customs; so also in New Guinea. In many of the Indonesian islands there are aboriginal black races in the mountains of the interior, and so also in various places in Further India. In fine, I think it could be established with the utmost probability that two black races, proceeding from India in succession, peopled the whole of the islands of Oceania.

Then, long after the Aryans had taken possession of the Indian plain, a Prakrit speaking fair race from the two Indias came to occupy the chief islands in Indonesia, driving the black aborigines into the mountains there, or further east towards New Guinea and Fiji; these are the ancestors of the present brown Polynesians. The in-comers may have intermingled to some extent with the blacks, but probably not much, for the brown Polynesians are mainly Caucasian in physique and character.

Then, in the more recent centuries of the Christian era, a race of Mongolian origin came into Indonesia from the Further Peninsula and drove the Polynesian ancestors from their possessions. Some of the expelled fled to the coasts of New Guinea; of these, the present Motuans are examples; others, and the greater quantity, seem to have passed northwards, then eastwards, past the north coast of New Guinea and onwards to Samoa, avoiding the Papuak and Fijian islands, which were occupied by the original blacks in force, and in such numbers and so fiercely as to prevent any settlement of invaders. From Samoa, as an original seat, the Polynesians have spread into all the other islands, absorbing or, in some cases, amalgamating with the native blacks. On my theory, the Mongolians who came to Indonesia adopted mostly the language of the conquered Caucasians (just as the Japanese are now adopting English), and when fresh bands of Mongolians arrived and enabled them to master all the islands, they all continued to speak that dialect which is now called the Malay, and is the lingua franca of the East.

On this theory, there must be a close connexion between the Polynesian and the Malayan languages, but not because the Polynesian is taken from the Malay. The process in my opinion was quite the reverse; they both came from the same stock, and the Malayan is Polynesian as to its origin. And, just as the Maldivean is evidently a mixture both of the Aryan Pali language of India and of the speech of the Dravida blacks of the Dekkan, so the languages of the Melanesian region and of Samoa and New Zealand show a resemblance in their vocabularies, being all, more or less, the product of a similar union, and sprung in the distant past from the same original sources in India (pp. 252-254).

Using primarily legends and genealogies, another prominent scholar of the late 19th and early 20th centuries, S. Percy Smith (1910), arrived at a comprehensive timetable from the time the Polynesians occupied their original homeland in India to the arrival of the "great fleet" in New Zealand. Smith was most familiar with Rarotongan legends and genealogies and used them as a basis for his theory, although he took pains to check with those of other Polynesian groups. The routes of migration were traced primarily by names of traditional homelands or by traditional (primarily Rarotongan) stories of migrations.

In 450 B.C., Smith maintained, the Polynesians inhabited their traditional homeland of Atia-te-varinga-nui, or India.

Great disturbances within the India of this time drove the Polynesians down the Ganges to the sea over the period of about a century. About B.C. 300, a large migration was led down the Javan archipelago, pushed onward by a following invasion of Hindus. By B.C. 65, the Polynesians were well established in the Ceram-Celebes-Java area. By that time, they had also come into contact with a white race from whom they obtained the fishing net and certain physical characteristics as well. During their stay in Indonesia, they acquired their highly-developed nautical skill, and mixed with and enslaved the already established Negrito population, who were to be called Menehune and Manahune. The first exploration of the Polynesian islands was undertaken at this time by Maui. In the next 400 years, up to A.D. 450, under the increasing pressure of Malays in Java, they traveled via Celebes, Ceram and Gilolo to New Guinea, whence they branched off past New Britain and the Solomons on their way to Fiji, leaving colonies all along their route. Tonga and Samoa were reached about this time, and the wars of that period caused much colonisation in that area; westward voyages were also undertaken, to the New Hebrides, Santa Cruz group, Tikopia, etc. From A.D. 650 to A.D. 1250 was the era of great voyages throughout Polynesia—from the Hawaiian Islands to New Zealand and antarctic waters and from the New Hebrides to Easter Island, as well as to Avaiki in Indonesia. During the big burst of voyaging ca. 650, the Hawaiian Islands were settled as well as the Tahitian group. New Zealand was first settled ca. 850, and Rarotonga in 875. A new wave of voyaging broke out in 950, but contact was not reestablished with the Hawaiian Islands until 1150 and then lasted only until 1325. In 1250, a new group of Maori-Rarotongans settled Rarotonga, and at this same time, contact between western and eastern Polynesia was broken off. The fleet settled New Zealand from Tahiti (for the second time) ca. 1350.

Underlying Smith's analysis were three basic assumptions that he explicitly defended. First, he considered it axiomatic "that all tradition is based on fact—whilst the details may be wrong, the main stem is generally right" (p. 19). He criticized European ethnologists for being too ready to discredit tradition. Second, he assumed that "the Polynesian genealogies are reliable within certain limits and go very far back" (p. 26). Smith treated the genealogies as representing generations rather than reign periods and made his calculations on the basis of 25 years per generation. His third assumption was that the Polynesians were excellent navigators, and that in the main their migrations were planned rather than accidental. All three of these assumptions were to be seriously challenged by subsequent scholars, and even his contemporaries, although they made use of similar information, voiced their doubts of the validity of native traditions. Thus Gudgeon (1902), while relying heavily on traditional sources to trace "The Whence of the Maori" back to Egypt, expressed the following concern for fabrication on the part of storytellers:

> Unfortunately, we can never know the real history of the Maori people. We can never do more than advance theories founded on traditions, which are but imperfectly known even to the most learned Maoris of the present day, and which, not unfrequently, appear to have been made up for the occasion. . . . But his (the Maori's) education has reached this point, that he is now capable of noting the extreme value we place on minute information, and is inclined to be ashamed that he does not know more of his history. The result of this dual feeling is, that when he really comprehends what you want to know he draws upon his imagination for your benefit (pp. 188-189).

And Edward Tregear (1904) prefaced his detailed philological analysis in support of the hypothesis that the original homeland of the Polynesians was "that locality wherein those branches of the Indo-European family now occupying North-Western Europe had their birth," with the admission that:

> After studying the question for years, I by no means approach any discussion of it with the light-hearted confidence of absolute ignorance. I know some of the immense difficulties, the absence of written records or of monumental inscriptions, the maze of baffling and imperfect traditions, the delusions of linquistics, the fallacies of customs-comparisons, the phantoms of genealogy (p. 105).

ANTHROPOLOGY AND ARCHAEOLOGY

Such comments signaled a concern for fresh evidence, or at least hitherto unsystematically explored evidence, that would shed new light on the problem of the Polynesian migrations. Two kinds of data that had not yet been fully exploited were physical anthropology and archaeology, which at the beginning of the century were gaining the attention of the academic world. J. Macmillan Brown (1907) was the first scholar to propose a comprehensive theory of Polynesian origins and migrations on the basis of such data. The three primary problems of Polynesia were, according to Brown: (1) Whence came the fair, European-like people; (2) what is the origin of the many megalithic monuments; and (3) what is the origin of the extraordinary resemblance between British Columbian

culture and Polynesian? The three problems taken together are, he believed, mutually solvent.

> Caucasians had reached the Pacific coast of Asia and British Columbia long
> before the Mongoloids were driven out of the central plateau and drawn across
> Behring Straits. . . . Megalithic monuments mark their path right from the Medi-
> terranean to the Pacific, and across that ocean by Micronesia and Polynesia into
> Central and South America. Only in New Zealand and British Columbia did the
> huge timbers of the forests substitute wood for stone. . . . They also left waymarks
> all the way in the long head and wavy hair and often fair complexion. . . . No
> Mongoloid immigration obscured the Caucasian in Polynesia, the only non-
> Caucasian features being negroid, brought in by the last immigrants and con-
> querors (p. xxx).

However, the problem of problems was, according to Brown, "the
origin of the strangely varied web of culture in the region, a singularly
advanced barbaric [that is, neolithic] woof crossing a palaeolithic warp"
(Brown, 1907, p. xxx). To explain this he postulated a distinction between the household culture of women and that of men:

> The solution lies in the distinction between the household culture and that
> of the men; it is the former that is palaeolithic—which means that the only women
> that came in with immigrant expeditions came in palaeolithic times. . . . This
> implies that with the elementary navigation of palaeolithic peoples there must
> have been some island-bridge not nearly so incontinuous as at present from the
> coast of Asia into Polynesia; this must have been the subsiding belt that runs
> from Japan south-east to Easter Island. . . . It could not have been continuous
> enough to allow of animals or plants migrating as well as man; and the whip
> that goaded man on to the sea was doubtless the glacial. . . . After that immigra-
> tion all communication with the continent must have been cut off for tens of
> thousands of years. . . . Once man began to venture into this isolated region again,
> he had entered the neolithic period, and learned the art of digging out huge
> single canoes; with his neolithic weapons, and unhampered by the necessity of
> protecting his household and women, he always came as conqueror, and settling
> down as aristocrat left the palaeolithic women of his new household to follow
> their own ways. . . . The process went on for thousands of years, till he had to
> seek realms to conquer farther afield away to the south. New Zealand and Easter
> Island would be the last to be populated. . . . In all the spheres of Polynesian life
> there are evidences of this long infiltration of men from Asia in the variant and
> often contradictory phases of the culture. . . . Much of this it would be difficult
> to disentangle and assign to the north and the south of Asia, especially in the
> language and mythology, though the legends of the spirit-world and the culture-
> heroes point to the north, whilst the cosmogony points to the south. . . . In the
> arts it is easier; for what belongs to the household and to women is ancient, and
> came from the north; what belongs exclusively to men is neolithic; but part of the
> latter is from the north, part from the south, of Asia; the huge single dugout
> canoe, the arts of carving and designing, the art of fortification, much of the
> house-building and the agriculture, and the aute or paper-mulberry tree came

from the north; edible bulb-culture, the edible domestic animals, and the final healing art came from the south. . . . So did negroid features and cannibalism come in with the South Asiatic conquerors, but the former only sporadically and the latter as an intermittent habit. The pig and the domestic fowl missed some of the groups. . . . All the immigrants from the north came in by the sixth century before our era; all those from the south came in by the beginning of our era. . . . Nor did any of them come from a Semitic race, or any race that had a script several thousand years ago (Brown, 1907, pp. xxx-xxxi).

Brown's theory bears the unmistakable stamp of social evolutionism, particularly as it was espoused by Lewis Henry Morgan in his classic book, *Ancient Society* (1878).

In a later publication, Brown (1919) raised the issue of the absence of pottery from Polynesia. There is no sign of pottery in any of the groups of Polynesia, he pointed out, but right up to its portals the art flourished —in the New Hebrides, the Solomon Islands, along the north and south-west coasts of New Guinea, and had developed into elaborate nests of well-glazed water vessels in Fiji. He interpreted the situation in the light of his general theory:

The only explanation I have been able to find . . . is that the households of the Polynesians left their continental homes before man had invented the art. In and around the Pacific Ocean at least the art is a household one; it is a woman's art. . . . The beginning of the Polished Stone Age may go back as far as fifteen to twenty thousand years ago. In other words, women with their families came into Polynesia as long ago as that. And after that the expeditions were purely masculine (pp. 135-136).

In the same publication he referred to the development of social stratification in Polynesian society. Polynesian social organization revealed, in his view, an imperialistic capacity and trend that must have come from the continent after the empires had begun to form. Every group in Polynesia developed toward kingship, but these imperial tendencies are only remnants of far past history. It is clear, he maintained, that Hawaiki, the original homeland of the Polynesians, was imperially organized. His explantation, which was also consistent with his overall position, reflected a strong belief in environmental determinism:

We may conclude then that a masculine migration accustomed to the art of great stone building came into Polynesia by way of Japan and Micronesia. By the same route came the empire builders that gave the imperial tendency to the Polynesians. And it must never be forgotten that no masterful people, no imperial race has ever come from the tropics. It is the hard breeding of the north temperate zone winters that has alone produced the will-power and practical organizing ability implied in empire building; for these make foresight and self-control on the individual and organization in the community imperative (p. 138).

The contention that Polynesian languages were not derivative from Malayan was supported by William Churchill (1911). Basing his case mainly on published vocabularies for the Polynesian and Melanesian areas, Churchill concluded that the most ancient Polynesians, the Proto-Samoans, swept into the Pacific some two thousand years ago. Two swarms left from Indonesia; one came around the north of New Guinea and entered the Pacific by way of Saint George's Channel and settled in Samoa; the other was driven by advancing Malays into the Arafura Sea and south of New Guinea through Torres Straits and thence onward to a new home in Fiji. There in "Nuclear Polynesia" they reunited and sent out further expeditions to Hawaii, New Zealand, and eastward. He assumed that the Polynesians were competent navigators and that this skill was already developed in their place of origin (Indonesia) and that they island-hopped through Melanesia without knowing where they were going, on the fastest course that the wind would take them.

The designation of Malayo-Polynesian as a basic speech family has no basis, Churchill contended. His researches revealed that there is neither ethnic nor linguistic unity between Indonesians and Polynesians— even that Polynesian outdates Indonesian. He rejected the Semitic, Aryan, and Indian theories of Polynesian origins, maintaining that the linguistic evidence takes them back no farther than Java. Churchill also opposed the contention of the German ethnologist, Thilenius, that the Polynesian Outliers (that is, those islands geographically within Melanesia occupied by a Polynesian people, such as Tikopia and Ontong Java) received their Polynesian elements from castaways washed westward from central Polynesia. Although the currents would favor Thilenius' argument, the linguistic evidence shows that Polynesian traces in Melanesia outdate any elsewhere in Polynesia.

Physical anthropology, linguistics, and a consideration of sailing capabilities figured heavily in the theory of Georg Friederici (1914). He suggested that there were three basic elements concerned with the peopling of the region stretching from Sumatra in the west to Easter Island in the east, and from Formosa and Hawaii in the north to New Zealand in the south, with Madagascar as a far-western outpost. First, a dark-skinned, coarse or wooly-haired, short race with a broad, flat nose spread through the Malay Peninsula, the Melanesian islands, and south to the Australian area—the Negrito. The second element was the Papuan, a dark, coarse-haired, tall to medium race with a projecting, slightly aquiline nose. This group remained mostly around New Guinea. A new element was added with the coming of the Malayo-

Polynesians, or Austronesians. Their original home lay in Indo-China near the sea, and they quite early developed into a sea-faring people. Their reason for leaving Indo-China was possibly geographic—a food shortage from overpopulation or a change of climate, or possibly political pressure from the Mongolian peoples to the north. They were a light-skinned people, but two varieties can be noticed—a tall "Indo-nesian" and a short "Proto-Malayan." Possibly the latter had some Negrito blood picked up in the Sunda Islands.

The Malayo-Polynesians left the Indonesian area before the time of its Hinduization. Their language has no Sanskrit elements in it, but Javan has 110 Sanskrit words per 1,000, and the Sunda language has 40 per 1,000. Some of them traveled southwest, through the islands west of New Guinea, where they were influenced by the Papuan element. Another group went from Borneo to the Philippines, and from there to Formosa. It has often been reported, Friederici pointed out, that the Polynesians found a dark people already living on the islands they discovered in the South Seas. Legend tells of them, and every so often an individual will show Melanesian features. It has been suggested that these are the survivors of a now sunken continent; however, it is very probable that in their wanderings the Polynesians mixed with dark peoples, or possibly the dark element is from a slave group that came with them. Or a group of Melanesians could have been blown off course and landed in Polynesia. For example, there are foreign words in the Tuamotu dialect that could be Melanesian.

The peak period of Polynesian wanderings was from A.D. 700 to 1200, according to Friederici, when there was a knowledge among the larger Polynesian island groups of one another. In contrast to the Melanesians, the Polynesians settled, sailed, and colonized with planning and knowledge. Their history involves the development of sailing from small beginnings to complete high-sea voyaging, followed by a decline of the sailing art. The most primitive water craft of the Malayo-Polynesians was a raft of three beams laid side by side. In the course of development, the central beam became larger, and the side beams took on the functions of outriggers, resulting in the double outrigger canoe. From the double outrigger came the single outrigger canoe, and then the double canoe. The latter were true ships, 30 to 40 meters long with room for 200 to 300 people. A further development was the mast and sail. They made their long voyages on these great high-sea canoes under the leadership of trained captains. After the peak of Malayo-

Polynesian sailing, characterized by the double canoe, a decline set in. When Cook visited the Maori they had only a few double canoes and fewer outriggers. The Chatham Island Moriori had sunk even lower; they were building simple rafts from the tough flowering stalks of the *Phormium tenax*.

This whole developmental sequence is of great interest when we note that the Mangarevan type of wooden raft with twin masts and the Tuamotu type of sail spread between them was found on the coasts of the Incan empire. This particular type of sail is the only one found in pre-Columbian America, and pre-Columbian double canoes were known on the Pacific coast of Central America. Large numbers of cultural parallels between South America and the South Sea lands, and especially the words *kumara* (sweet potato) and *ubi* (yam?) which are used both in Polynesia and parts of South America show that the Polynesians reached the American coast.

An increased measure of sophistication in the use of physical anthropology was introduced into Polynesian ethnology by two American anthropologists during the 1920's, Louis R. Sullivan and Roland B. Dixon. In reviewing "The Status of Physical Anthropology in Polynesia" at the First Pan-Pacific Scientific Conference in 1920, Sullivan remarked that "the data is [sic] entirely inadequate for conclusions as to the racial or inter-insular affinities of the Polynesians" (1921, p. 63). Although physical anthropology cannot offer a solution to the problems of origin and migration routes, he cautioned, "It can accurately define and describe the Polynesian groups. It can prove beyond reasonable doubt the racial origin and affinities of the Polynesians. It can designate fairly accurately to what branch of a given race they belong" (p. 64).

In a later paper (1924), using craniometric and osteometric literature and field data obtained from living Polynesians by members of the Bayard Dominick expeditions sent out by Bishop Museum, Sullivan asserted that:

> . . . the "Polynesians" are in no sense to be considered a uniform racial type. The "Polynesian type" is an abstract concept into the composition of which have entered the characteristics of several physical types. It is roughly comparable to an "American type," defined by the average characteristics of the Anglo-Saxon, Slavic, Mediterranean, Indian, Negroid and Mongol elements which inhabit America.
>
> Anthropologists have disagreed on the racial affinities of the Polynesians. Some have classified them as Mongols, others have classified them as Caucasians, while still others have maintained that they are a separate race. This in itself is strong evidence that the Polynesians are a badly mixed people for whenever there

has been a general disagreement as to the racial affinities of any group it has been found almost invariably that the group was a non-homogeneous group (p. 22).

Sullivan concluded that the population of Polynesia was composed of at least four distinct elements. Two he considered to be Caucasoid, one Negroid or Melanesian, and the fourth, which was of doubtful affiliation, showed several Negroid as well as some Mongoloid characters. These types combined in various proportions to make up the populations of the different island groups, and even different islands in the same groups contain elements in different proportions. He terminated his paper with the question of whether or not the four local types had differentiated by isolation on the different islands, and answered it in the negative:

> This seemed at first plausible to me for it was something of a strain on my credulity to believe that some of these remote island groups had been reached by man not only once but in a few instances as many as four separate times. But when I found each and every one of these types outside of Polynesia I was forced to abandon the idea of local differentiation. No one of these four types is confined wholly to Polynesia. The distribution of these types both within and without Polynesia argues strongly against a local origin of these types in Polynesia (p. 26).

Roland Dixon analyzed all the available information on crania measurements for the peoples of Oceania and Southeast Asia and in 1920 wrote a short article which he entitled, "A New Theory of Polynesian Origins." Using three basic indices—cephalic, length-height, and nasal—and making the assumption that those groups whose indices were all extremes either at one end or the other of their several series constituted fundamental types, while those having one or more of their indices medial in value were blends or crosses, he concluded that four racial types were represented in Polynesia. These were: (1) a Brachycephalic, Hypsicephalic, Platyrrhine type which was practically identical with the Negrito. Geographically this fundamental type survives in any strength only in the Hawaiian Islands, especially Kauai. The influence of the type in its derivative forms may be traced in most of the marginal groups in the east and south of Polynesia, but on the basis of very scanty data from Tonga and Samoa seems to be absent in the west. (2) A Dolichocephalic, Hypsicephalic, Platyrrhine type, whose proximate affiliations lie with the Negroid populations of Melanesia and Australia. It is marginal in occurrence, and appears most strongly in Easter Island. It makes its influence felt in the northern islands of the Hawaiian group, in the Marquesas and Central Polynesia, and plays a notable part in New Zealand. Here, there is interesting evidence to show that one of its most common derivatives, very numerous throughout Melanesia, has played a double role, entering into the composition of the Maori people not only at an early date, but reappearing again much later as a relatively recent factor in the make-up of that people.

[3] The third and historically clearly the latest type which has contributed to the making of the Polynesian people, and the one whose influence has for long been preponderant over a large part of the area, is one which is Brachycephalic, Hypsicephalic and Leptorrhine. This type is one which forms a very important factor in the rather complex Malayan and Eastern Asiatic populations. . . . In Polynesia, this type seems strongest in Samoa and Tonga in the west, and of great importance in the southern islands of the Hawaiian group, while it plays a considerable part in Central Polynesia and New Zealand. Curiously, little trace of it occurs in Easter Island to the east (p. 265).

(4) There are indications of a small minority of a fourth fundamental type—a Dolichocephalic, Hypsicephalic, Leptorrhine type, whose affiliations may be said to be distinctly Caucasic. It survives only in small proportions, but especially in Hawaii and New Zealand. From its marginal distribution, it seems to be early in historical sequence, and in company with the Austro-Melanesian stratum.

After having arrived at this typology Dixon suggested that the racial history of Polynesia is even more complex than had previously been supposed:

The underlying stratum here, as well as further westward, appears to be indistinguishable from the Negrito, although the problem of how it reached this remote region is not yet wholly clear. This stratum was followed by a wave of negroid peoples whose most numerous modern representatives in this portion of the world form the bulk of the population of Melanesia and Australia. As a result of this influx, the earlier Negrito type was largely absorbed, and survives today as such, only in remote marginal areas into which it was driven by the negroid immigrants. Following the negroid came the Malayoid or Mongoloid wave, which, spreading over the area, absorbed and apparently quite submerged the preceding types and blends in western Polynesia, and flooded in force into the central, southern and northern portions, so that the Austro-Melanesians or negroid type and its predecessor were left in any degree intact, only in the marginal areas. These successive waves must not, however, be thought of as rapid conquests, but rather, for the most part, as slow drifts requiring generations or centuries for their completion, with periods of halting, and as following moreover somewhat different paths (pp. 266-267).

In a later paper (1929) Dixon modified his earlier position. The Pacific was peopled, he suggested in this later view, in a series of five waves. Probably the earliest racial type to reach the Pacific region somewhere about the end of glacial times, was that commonly known as the Negrito. Coming from southeastern Asia, probably at a time when many of the larger islands of Indonesia still formed part of the Asiatic continent, and when much of Melanesia was similarly joined to Australia, the Negrito spread northward to the Philippines and eastward, crossing one or more narrow strips of sea, to New Guinea and some of the adjacent island groups of Melanesia. There he was free to expand southward along the eastern edge of Australia to Tasmania, which then may still have been connected with continental Australia (p. 196).

A second racial type is that characteristic of the Australian aborigines. They represent a very early wave of immigration, which spread from southeast Asia eastward through Indonesia and Melanesia to Australia, displacing, destroying, and to some extent absorbing the older Negrito stratum in the latter area, but were themselves largely destroyed or assimilated by later comers throughout most of the area over which they had spread (p. 196).

Probably next in sequence came the Oceanic Negroids. They seem to have spread out eastward from southeastern Asia and to have reached many, if not all, of the islands of Indonesia, and then streamed into Melanesia where they replaced the older Australoids, driving the Negritos into the mountainous interiors of the larger islands and penetrating ultimately some distance into northern Australia, where they blended with the older population. Whether or not the Oceanic Negroids penetrated farther eastward into Polynesia is still a moot question. They had some knowledge of the sea and of navigation, and might have perhaps reached the nearer islands of Western Polynesia, although as yet there is no clear evidence for it. The strong infusion of their blood which we find in Central and particularly Eastern Polynesia is to be attributed to later immigrations of the so-called Melanesian peoples who represent in large measure a fusion of the Papuan with the later Indonesian and Mongoloid types (p. 196).

Seemingly next in order of sequence was the type which may be called the Indonesian. Undoubtedly mixed in origin, the type includes an unmistakable Caucasic element—one known to have reached the east Asiatic coast region as early as neolithic times. It is uncertain whether they entered Indonesia mainly from Indo-China, or from the central and southern Chinese coast region. At any rate, they were able to spread easily by sea, not only throughout the Indonesian and Melanesian areas where by then, as a result of slow subsidence of the land, the islands had become more widely separated, but also into the remoter islands of Micronesia and parts, at least, of Polynesia (p. 197).

The last of the great racial waves to enter the Pacific was the Mongoloid. Spreading peripherally toward the eastern and southeastern coasts of Asia, they doubtless mixed in varying degree with the older Indonesian-like peoples of the coast and then, following their lead, poured into Indonesia. From Indonesia the Malays, as they have also been called, began spreading eastward. Like the Indonesians they came into Micronesia and dominated at least the western portion. They swept along the New Guinea coasts, and both left large strains of their blood there as well as took with them some admixture of darker peoples as they passed on farther into Polynesia, into whose remotest groups they were able to penetrate owing to their skill as navigators. In Western Polynesia, which bore the brunt of their movement, they almost entirely swamped and destroyed the older, mixed Indonesian and Papuan population. From various evidences we may place the movement from Indonesia to the eastward as taking place in the very early centuries of the Christian era.

In three other works Dixon dealt with nonracial matters that were at issue in the problem of Polynesian migrations. His classic book, *The Building of Cultures* (1928), included a section discussing the possibility of extensive cultural diffusion across the Pacific, a possibility which he rejected. The book was largely an attack against the British Egyptianist diffusion school of G. Elliot Smith and William J. Perry, who proposed that high civilization had originated only once on earth —in the Nile Valley—from where the "Children of the Sun" spread Egyptian culture, first in the Old World, then into the Pacific Islands, and on to the Americas, where their influence was manifest in pyramids, mummification, and many religious and art motifs. Given the distances and the hardships involved, Dixon reasoned, the number of persons reaching the New World on any one voyage could hardly have been great, and upon reaching South America their fate would be doubtful at best. Most damaging for the diffusionist theory, however, was the necessity to presume that most of the "civilized" traits found in the New World had either been lost in Polynesia or had come from Melanesia, adding several thousand more miles to an already almost impossibly long voyage. The question of Polynesian contact with South America was the subject of two other papers. One dealt with "The Problem of the Sweet Potato in Polynesia" (1932) and the other with "The Long Voyages of the Polynesians" (1934). In the article on the sweet potato Dixon reviews Friederici's argument that the tuber was introduced by the Spaniards, and concludes that the evidence contradicts such a possibility. Therefore, he asserts:

> . . . we are brought face to face with the problem of pre-Columbian contacts between South America and Polynesia, and must explain the presence of the sweet potato in the Pacific as due either to Polynesian voyagers who, reaching American shores, brought back the plant with them on their return to their homeland, or to Peruvian or other American Indians who sailed westward and carried the sweet potato with them to Polynesia . . . (p. 59).

In the article on Polynesian voyaging Dixon postulates that although historical evidence indicates that journeys were rarely more than moderate in length (five or six hundred miles), previous voyages had been made between Tahiti and Hawaii, and therefore the Polynesians were capable of reaching the New World. Having established this point he then argued: If, then, voyages to the New World were made, we are led to relegate them in time to the considerably earlier period when the hitherto empty lands received their first human settlers. The sweet potato seems to make this a certainty. Originating in America, it could only have reached Polynesia with human aid. Since we have no evidence that at any time the Indians of the Pacific coast of South America where the sweet potato was grown had either craft or skill for making long sea journeys, we are forced to conclude that the transference was made by Polynesians (pp. 173-174).

The position that significant diffusion had taken place from Polynesia to the American continent was not limited to the Egyptianists. P. Minnaert (1931), for one, speculated that it was probable that isolated expeditions of Polynesians arrived on the coasts of Peru or Ecuador. It seems legitimate to suppose, he continued, that under favorable conditions certain of these expeditions took root and formed prosperous colonies, or at least brought new traditions, customs, and techniques to the original population. The fact that throughout the Polynesian islands there exist traces of megalithic architecture, far beyond the capacity and know-how of the Polynesians to create, proves that the islands were formerly inhabited by a race superior in construction, art, and social organization. The fact that these constructions have certain narrow affinities with those which exist on the western coast of South America, makes one suppose that migratory elements belonging to this race, established themselves on this coast and left the imprint of their civilization with the Polynesians as well. The pre-Inca civilizations of Peru and the Polynesians then adapted these cultural elements to their own environment and way of life. It is difficult to say whether the Incas were also a branch from the

Polynesian source, but it is probable that the Polynesian or pre-Polynesian civilization was at least one of the formative elements of Inca civilization.

For supporting evidence Minnaert relied upon: (1) *Tradition*—there are South American legends of invasions of giants on rafts, with loose sexual morals. They could be equated with Polynesians. (2) *Religion*— both areas had sun worship, human sacrifice, seclusion of virgins. One of the Peruvian gods was *Con-Ticci-Viracocha*—Kon-Tiki; some Polynesian gods are called tikis. A certain area near the island of Puna, Peru, is called Tangorara, perhaps after the Polynesian god Tangaroa. Both areas had a similar concept of mana; the Peruvian term was *huaca*. (3) *Social Organization*—both areas were very hierarchical. The basic unit was the family or clan, usually localized in one valley. Among the royalty of both areas, brother-sister marriages were the custom. (4) *Customs*—genealogies were kept on knotted cords in both Peru and Polynesia; cannibalism was practiced in both areas; there was pottery in Fiji and Peru. (5) *Architecture*—both were high stone cultures; both had megalithic architecture of the same nature.

Using Tahiti as a model from which to reconstruct Polynesian culture history, E. S. Craighill Handy (1930) evolved a theory which attributed variations within Polynesia to two separate migrations, the first of which was associated with the more "primitive" elements while the second brought the more "civilized" traits. The first wave was represented in Tahiti by the commoner classes, particularly the *manahune* whom Handy categorizes as tenants or serfs, while the second wave is represented by the *arii,* or chiefly caste. The more primitive cultural elements in Polynesia are found by Handy to correlate with the vestiges of a neolithic phase of culture that was spread in Indonesia at a time prior to the entry of the Malay peoples and of Indian (Hindu) culture into Malaysia. The race of the area seems to have a substratum of Caucasoid with an intermixture of secondary and sometimes dominant Mongoloid, with Negroid in Melanesia—the same mixture that is found in the "old Polynesian" substratum. The language is Austric (that is, Malayo-Polynesian), to which Polynesian belongs. The phase of culture in Indo-China and Malaysia that succeeded this prehistoric period was one of Brahmanical civilization carried by conquest, trade, and missionaries from India—mainly from South or Dravidian India—into Malaysia or Indo-China. Many of the old Polynesian culture traits, such as rites for the firstborn, phallic symbolism, and priestly traditions were probably derived from this phase.

With the *arii* the problem is more complicated, for their culture appears to include traits of Brahmanical, Buddhist, Indian, and Chinese origin.

> The interesting thing is, however, that just this complication of matters is what would be expected if the *arii* originated in the region under discussion during the period following the spread of Buddhism out of India into Malaysia, Indo-China, and China, for during this period and since that time there has been perpetuated an amalgamated cult and culture that combines Brahmanical and Buddhistic traits, while there have been at the same time continuous commercial and political contacts, with consequent cultural influence, with India on the one hand and South China on the other (p. 15).
>
> . . . the *arii* . . . trace their descent from Tan-ga-loa. [They] were related to the river population of Kwantung, in South China, who are known as the Tan-ka-lo. . . . The Tan-ka-lo, although they have thoroughly assimilated Chinese culture, were not originally Chinese. . . . Their maritime life, physical type . . . and their relationship to the Cantonese . . . would indicate that they are an intrusive river folk from Indo-China or maritime people from Indonesia. If this is true it is quite within reason that as refugees from some disrupted civilization, those reaching Polynesia may have succeeded in establishing themselves as rulers, while others, taking refuge in the rivers of Southwest China may have fallen into the outcaste position in which we find the Tan-ka-lo (pp. 18-19).

During this period there was great maritime commerce in the region between Arabia and China, Handy asserted, and the ships that might have been swept into the Pacific were large commercial vessels, not primitive craft. He rejected the notion of discrete migrations in "fleets of canoes:"

> I submit that henceforth the habit of talking of Polynesian migrations in canoes should be abandoned. . . . Almost certainly the later Asiatics or Malaysians who came into Oceania started their voyages, which were probably accidental, in ships. . . . Furthermore, the word "canoe" is not a correct designation for the large seagoing vessels which Polynesians were building in historic times, such as the Tahitian *pahi* with two pontoon hulls 110 feet long, which Captain Cook measured on his second visit to Tahiti. As to the word "migration," I find myself more and more incapable of thinking in terms of movements of fleets at stated periods, such as this implies. . . . I believe we shall conceive the picture of the peopling of Polynesia more truly if we think in terms of a process of repeated, occasional, and generally accidental drifting and sailing of boats and their crews eastward, northward, and southward, and also westward, through a period extending over several millenia (pp. 22-23).

During the 1930's anthropologists began to pay more attention to internal distinctions within Polynesia, and to relationships between the island groups. How much of the diversity within the area could be accounted for on the basis of diffusion and how much on the basis of local evolution? The development of systematic archaeology by professional

anthropologists, along with a careful recording of material culture, facili-
tated the discussion. One of the foremost pioneers in this work, along
with Peter Buck (Te Rangi Hiroa) and Kenneth Emory, was H. D. Skinner. In a summary of "Archaeology in Polynesia" given at the Fifth
Pacific Science Congress, Skinner (1934) divided Polynesia into two
areas, a western one which included the Samoan and Tongan groups, and
an eastern and southern area, including the Society Islands, the Marquesas, the Hawaiian Islands, the Tuamotus, Easter Island, the Australs, the
Cook Islands, and the New Zealand-Chatham area. To the first area he
gave the designation "Western Polynesia," to the second, "Marginal
Polynesia."

Skinner reviewed, as of that time (1933), the status of archaeological
work in terms of three kinds: stratigraphical work, surveys of sites and
structures, and typological studies. He considered the first of these to
be most important, but up to that time the only stratified sites investigated were in the South Island of New Zealand. From the surveys of sites
and structures by Emory, Buck, and others, he concluded that the structures of Western Polynesia appear, on the whole, to be simpler than those
of Marginal Polynesia. The Western Polynesian structures include features absent from Marginal Polynesia, but whether this was because of
a process of simplification from a common Polynesian ancestor is not
clear. Regarding typological studies, Skinner reported that studies in this
field had just begun. Relying heavily on evidence provided by Emory
and Buck, he found fairly conspicuous differences between the adzes of
Western Polynesia and those of Marginal Polynesia, with the former
being simpler and less diverse in type. However according to Skinner, the
whole field of Polynesian material culture was awaiting typological
investigation.

A systematic attempt to document the differences between "Western"
and "Marginal," or "Central," Polynesia using all available evidence was
attempted by Edwin Burrows. In an article entitled "Western Polynesia:
A Study in Cultural Differentiation" (1938), Burrows demonstrated the
distinctiveness of Western Polynesia by plotting the distribution of a
number of traits and culture complexes. The traits which distinguish
Western from Central-Marginal Polynesian cultures he traces to eastern
Melanesia and Micronesia, and he attributes the differentiation within
Polynesia to a combination of several historical processes, including diffusion, local development, and abandonment or rejection. Previous writers
had failed, in Burrows' opinion, to give proper consideration to these
processes. Some, like Churchill, Handy, and Smith, had taken as a point
of departure traditions from one region within Polynesia. They then

allotted cultural differences among hypothetical immigrant peoples, fitting available data from all Polynesia into a scheme based on traditions from one region. They were so preoccupied with early voyages that they failed to reckon with at least two alternative possibilities: (1) that earlier and later elements in the population of one part of Polynesia may not correspond to those of another part, and (2) that cultural differences within Polynesia may result from the processes of diffusion, local development, and abandonment or rejection. Another line of procedure, followed by Dixon and others, began not with local traditions but with regional similarities and differences in culture. Their conclusions still take the form of simple subdivisions of Polynesian culture into two or three hypothetical strata of immigration. These writers, Burrows claimed, like those who followed the other course, had stressed early voyages to the neglect of processes less spectacular and nearer at hand.

His study, in Burrows' opinion, although based on fuller data than were available to earlier writers, shed little light on original immigration into the Pacific. One hint, however, was that certain traits shared by Central-Marginal Polynesia, Micronesia, and some intermediate islands were absent or rare in Western Polynesia. These include simple fishhooks, *Ruvettus* fishhooks, stone or wooden food pounders, tanged adzes, drums, carved human images, nights of the moon, and lack of kinship terms for some of the relationships emphasized in Western Polynesia. This situation suggested to Burrows that one immigration had taken place into Central-Marginal Polynesia by way of Micronesia, while another had gone into Western Polynesia by a different route, probably through Fiji. In summary, however, insofar as his inquiry bore upon the remote period of first settlement, it suggested to him a fundamental unity of Polynesian culture corresponding to the unity of language.

Burrows' belief in the unity of Polynesian culture was lent support by Harry Shapiro (1943), a physical anthropologist who collected and analyzed anthropomorphic data from twenty-six living Polynesian populations. On the basis of his research Shapiro concluded:

The Polynesian population possesses a fundamental unity in physical type which necessarily implies that the successive immigrants were derived from a common people. It is extremely doubtful that the various waves of invaders were profoundly different racially. This homogeneity does not, however, mean that the Polynesians are a pure-line stock. The present thesis that the Polynesians adhere basically to a uniform physical type differentiable by cephalic dimension and proportion need not be taken to run counter to the hitherto prevailing picture of a composite stock. The present data throw no light on the components of the Polynesian people and consequently are not in conflict with the idea that they are ultimately of mixed origin. Like most other populations, they undoubtedly are. But I believe that the essential composition of these diverse elements occurred before the invasion of Polynesia began. Somewhere outside this area the Polynesians had become welded into a recognizable and distinct population which served as a source from which migrants streamed into the limits of Polynesia. This hypothesis does conflict with the widely held opinion that Polynesia was settled by a number of distinct migrations each characterized by distinct physical type. Such a conception rests heavily on the discernible differences between the island groups but neglects the broad and consistent [sic] similarities which could never have arisen by admixture within Polynesia.

The differences, however, which do occur within Polynesia should not be minimized . . . some of them may be explained as local variants likely to arise among small inbred groups. Others, more significant in this context, are distributed according to a geographic pattern that conforms admirably with the direction of migration. These are the variations in head length, head width, cephalic index, and, to a lesser extent, minimum [sic] frontal diameter. Indeed, the only reasonable explanation of this arrangement is on the basis that the successive migrants were differentiated primarily in these particular cephalic dimensions.

If it be borne in mind that a considerable gap in time occurred between the first and the latest comers, it is possible to conceive of a gradual and progressive modification of the fundamental type in those particulars by which the successive waves are now distinguishable.

It may be significant that in southeastern Asia and Indonesia an important area of brachycephaly now exists. In Indonesia there is some reason to believe that the earlier populations were more dolichocephalic and were supplanted by rounder headed groups. This expansion of brachycephaly into Indonesia may very probably have been associated with a vast population movement which not only forced out the ancestors of the Polynesians but eventually stamped the last wave with brachycephaly. Whatever this brachycephalic stock may have been like, it was not vastly different from the proto-Polynesian, since the later immigrants to Polynesia were essentially similar to the earlier ones (pp. 7-8).

An argument in favor of a Micronesian migration route was presented by Peter Buck (1938), the first scholar of Polynesian background to develop a comprehensive theory of his ancestral origins. Using racial, linguistic, archaeological, genealogical, and mythological data to buttress his thesis, Buck proposed that the Polynesians' original homeland was in India. Although he was in agreement on this point with some previous theorists, such as Percy Smith, he was critical of their use of isolated word comparisons and loosely interpreted legends, basing his own argument on racial data. From India the ancestors of the Polynesians moved into Indonesia and were forced from there by the pressure of the Mongoloids. They then took a northern route through the atolls of Micronesia. From the end of the Micronesian chain, possibly from the Gilberts, a first wave of settlers set out. This migration was probably a forced one because of the inferior social status of those expelled; these early settlers were poorly equipped with food plants and domestic animals. The Hawaiian Islands, the Society Islands, and Samoa all have traditions of early settlers. In Hawaii, they were called the Menehune; Hawaii-Loa, the mythical first settler of the islands, is said to have arrived ca. A.D. 450. In the Society Islands, these first inhabitants were called Manahune, and in Samoa were called "sons of worms." From Samoa, this early group settled Tonga.

This first group was followed by another composed of people of the same stock but of higher social grade. They sailed southeast from Micronesia to the Society Islands, where they first settled at Havai'i (modern Raiatea). Dissensions then caused a rebellious group to settle Tahiti. Increasing population and domestic political struggles were the cause of the large number of colonizing expeditions that left Central Polynesia after the first theology had been established by the priests at Opoa; these migrations took place from the 12th to 14th centuries. Junior members of chiefly families, with little prospect of advancement at home, organized these expeditions into the unknown. Settlement was by individual canoes, not by large migrations.

The Marquesas were settled early and were used as jumping-off places for the colonizing of Mangareva and Easter Island. They may also have been used as way-stations for voyagers to Hawaii. The Cook Islands were settled by followers of Tane who left Tahiti after the imposition of the god 'Oro from Havai'i (Raiatea). The people that settled Hawaii passed through the Equatorial Islands and left coral monuments and coconut palms as indications of their presence. When they reached Hawaii in the early 12th century, the Menehune were pushed from their center on Kauai northward to Nihoa, Necker, and beyond. New Zealand was discovered by Polynesians in the 10th century, but it was only sparsely settled by off-course voyagers until the 14th century, when the Maoris, forced from Hawaiki (Raiatea) by internal conflicts, made it their home.

In refuting the hypothesis that Polynesia was settled primarily through Melanesia, Buck emphasized several distinctions between the two areas, including the following: (1) Polynesians are physically very different from Melanesians; (2) the bow, though used in Polynesia, is not employed for warfare as it is in Melanesia while on the other hand warrior helmets of the same type are found both in the Gilberts and Central Polynesia; (3) social customs such as brother-sister avoidance and certain burial practices that are found throughout Melanesia occur in Polynesia only on its Melanesian borders; (4) Western Polynesian mythology, such as that reported by Gifford for Tonga, has many more Micronesian elements than Melanesian. He accounted for the linguistic similarities between Polynesia and eastern Melanesia by postulating, along with

Thilenius, Ray, and others, a colonization by Polynesians of the Melanesian islands showing Polynesian affinities. Besides, Buck argued, despite the overlay of Mongoloid elements, Polynesian words are found in Micronesia.

A position consistent with this view was taken by Alexander Spoehr (1952), one of Buck's successors as Director of Bishop Museum. Spoehr stated that, although the racial, linguistic, and cultural differences between Micronesia and Polynesia are evident, in technology, social organization, mythology, and art there are basic similarities as well as differences. He also suggests that Micronesia and Polynesia taken as wholes are much more closely similar to each other in the physical type of their inhabitants, in language, and in culture than either is to Melanesia. Therefore our perspective would be clearer, Spoehr maintained, if we avoided a rigid separation of the two regions and for the purposes of historical analysis combined Micronesia and Polynesia into a single major area. He suggested the term *Micro-Polynesia* for the combined region, and stated: "Grouping Micronesia and Polynesia together in a larger area . . . assumes . . . that the main migration route of the Polynesians was through Micronesia. This I believe to have been the case" (p. 460).

Using the first four carbon 14 dates available from archaeological excavations in the region, Spoehr formulated a "working hypothesis." These dates were:

1. A.D. 1005 ± 180 from Oahu, Hawaii (collected by Kenneth Emory).

2. A.D. 1002 ± 300 from Viti Levu, Fiji (collected by E. Gifford).[4]

3. 1527 B.C. ± 200 from Saipan, Marianas (collected by A. Spoehr).

4. A.D. 845 ± 145 from Tinian, Marianas (collected by A. Spoehr).

Spoehr's working hypothesis was that by 2000-1500 B.C. a form of sea-going transport had been developed in the Malaysian-Southeast Asian region sufficient to carry men into western Micronesia. Quite possibly it was the single outrigger canoe. The eastward migrations into and through Micro-Polynesia took place over at least a two and a half thousand year period. The terminal points of this are set by the Saipan and Oahu dates, and to this lengthy period must be added the increment of

---

[4] This sample did not come from the lower levels of excavated cultural material, which are considerably earlier, indicating an occupation date by at least the beginning of the Christian era.

time between A.D. 1000 and the point of first European contact. Spoehr speculated that the cultural differences within the area would eventually be accounted for on the basis of local evolution rather than of distinct migrations. It seems most likely, he held, that the first voyagers brought with them the principal adaptations that were at the core of the historic cultures. Because of the island environment, diffusion could not have taken place except locally, and even major island groups must have experienced considerable periods of isolation.

While concurring with the probability of a Micronesian migration route on the basis of linguistic evidence, H. D. Skinner (1951) took issue with Buck's belief that Raiatea was settled prior to the islands in Western Polynesia.

> Consultation of the map will show that geographical considerations are so much against this view as to outweigh decisively Buck's single argument in support of it. It seems much more probable that the Samoan islands were the first group in Polynesia to be settled by the Proto-Polynesians and that the Tahitian group was settled after, though probably at no long interval (pp. 43-44).

Skinner also argued against Buck's contention that the Proto-Polynesians had lost virtually all aspects of Indonesian culture by the time they reached Tahiti. In his opinion many elements in Polynesian material culture "go back beyond Tahiti to Indonesia and Eastern Asia, and, in some cases, further still" (p. 44). His thesis, based largely upon material culture and art forms, was that the Polynesians' ancestors had moved out of Indonesia and the Philippines about the 7th or 8th centuries A.D. They were part of a seafaring community, and their culture was allied to elements from all parts of Indonesia, including areas strongly influenced by India. In the central Carolines sultanates were probably set up, and movements were made southward to the New Guinea coast and the northern islands of Melanesia. Many went southeast to Samoa and Tahiti at the same time, as well equipped colonists, taking with them all the domesticated animals and plants their vessels could carry. The culture that developed in the Tahitian group differed from that left behind. Metal and pottery were lost because there were neither metal ores nor clay, and distance forbade trade. The first culture established was characterized by elaborate arts and crafts. When groups of Tahitians left between A.D. 1000 and 1300 for the marginal areas, they took with them a well-developed decorative art as well as purely utilitarian arts. In the new settlements, representational and decorative art either declined, as in Hawaii, the Tuamotus, and Mangareva, or continued to flourish, as in the Marquesas and New Zealand. In

Tahiti itself, representational and decorative art dwindled to almost nothing, perhaps because the energy formerly expressed in them was deflected into the immense elaboration of socio-religious ritual seen by European discoverers and explorers—ritual directly linked with the development of the *marae* in the Tahitian Islands. The Maori developed a characteristic local art style. So also the Polynesians of the Cook and Austral area, and the Marquesans. But the more closely the art of these areas is studied, the more numerous are found to be the motives they have in common (pp. 45-46).

In 1947 Thor Heyerdahl and five companions dramatically drew world attention to the problem of Polynesian origins by drifting in a balsa-wood raft from the shores of Peru to Raroia in French Polynesia. Heyerdahl organized the *Kon-Tiki* expedition in order to prove that Peruvian Indians in pre-Inca times could have drifted in balsa-wood rafts and settled Polynesia. His adventure book (1950) describing the journey was a best seller. Heyerdahl's theory, elaborated in a later book (1952), was that a band of Kwakiutl Indians from the American northwest coast was forced to vacate their homeland by an invading group of Salish Bella Coola Indians. Fleeing for their lives, they loaded their wives and children into canoes and let the wind and current carry them south into the unexplored ocean. Ultimately they reached the Hawaiian Islands (pp. 177-178).

About the same time, a Caucasian-like people with light skins and red hair left the Peruvian coast on rafts and sailed west into the Pacific Ocean, landing first at Easter Island. These people had been the culture bringers of Central and South America—the intelligent, bearded wanderers who brought learning, civilization, and leaders to the dark, short, beardless, and less intelligent Indians. The Incas were their descendants who remained in the Americas (pp. 219-345).

The Peruvians and the Northwest Indians found a short, dark race with Negroid features already living on many of the Pacific islands. These were known as the *Menehune,* and were possibly a Melanesian group (pp. 182-187).

The spreading and mixture of the three groups—the Northwest Indians south from Hawaii, the Peruvians west from Easter Island, and the "aboriginal" *Menehune*—resulted in the Polynesian race as it is known today. The culture became homogenous, but the race remained a bit heterogenous. Even today there can be found fair and red-haired Polynesians (*uru-kehu*) and short, dark, and flat-nosed Polynesians in addition to the "standard" Polynesian type (pp. 187-188).

Heyerdahl backed up his theory with a wide array of evidence gleaned from archaeology, mythology, linguistics, physical anthropology, and ethnobotany, but the mainstay of his argument has been the winds and currents. Those theorists who have committed themselves to Malayan or Indonesian origins had in his opinion been overly impressed with absolute distances. The only realistic measure is the time required to make a voyage, and this would bring the Polynesian islands much closer to the Americas than they appear on a world map.

As a test of his theory Heyerdahl led an archaeological expedition to Easter Island, the results of which he initially reported in a popular book entitled *Aku-Aku* (1958). Easter Island was settled, he speculated, by two successive populations, the "long-ears" and the "short-ears." The long-ears were inhabitants of pre-Inca Peru; they were a fair, white race with abundant skill in stone architecture and an ability to navigate in reed boats. Before the Incas came to Peru, the majority of this population sailed west into the Pacific, following the current. Some of them landed on Easter Island, and were responsible for the paved roads, the stone quarries, and the giant images now found there. The date of their settlement was ca. A.D. 400. From Easter Island or perhaps from Peru itself, other settlers sailed into Oceania, reaching Rapa-Iti, Pitcairn, and the Marquesas.

The short-ears were originally from Indonesia; from there, they followed the current to the Pacific Northwest and mingled with the populations there. These Indians of the Pacific Northwest then set out in their large canoes and followed the current down to Hawaii, and spread out thence into the rest of Polynesia; these were the majority of the Polynesians. The short-ear population reached Easter Island very late, perhaps only 100 years before the arrival of the Europeans. Having arrived on Easter Island, the descendants of the long-ears, attempted to enslave them; a civil war ensued, and all but one long-ear was massacred.

Heyerdahl's position has been met with a storm of criticism by the majority of Oceanic specialists. Heine-Geldern, for example, in two review articles (1950, 1952) takes the Norwegian adventurer to task for apparently being ignorant of the archaeology and ethnology of eastern Asia, Indonesia, and Melanesia. "He does not know that in material culture, in art styles, in myths, and in social customs, these regions have infinitely more in common with Northwest America than have the Polynesians" (1952, p. 356). There is every reason to assume, claims Heine-Geldern, that the majority of cultural parallels between

Polynesia and Northwest America are due to derivation from a common Asiatic source rather than to direct contact. Most damaging to Heyerdahl is his failure to account for the strong affinity between the Polynesian and Southeast Asian languages and the shared floral and faunal syndrome between the two areas. His view that Northwest American and Oceanic languages exhibit a basic unity is rejected by almost all serious comparative linguists, thereby rendering highly improbable his contention that some language elements may have spread with migrants from Southeast Asia to Northwest America, and so into the Pacific (Heyerdahl, 1951). Concerning Heyerdahl's problem with accounting for the flora and fauna Heine-Geldern observed:

> In making the bold assertion that "there is nothing in Polynesian race or culture that is not also shared by the American Indian," Heyerdahl cautiously adds, "or else available through intimate neighbourly trade with the nearest marginal islands to the west, in Melanesia." He obviously wanted to keep a door open in order to explain just such embarrassing facts as the possession of those Old World plants and animals by the Polynesians. I am afraid that it will not prove of much help to him. It might be different if the plants and animals in question were restricted to the westernmost islands, but they were found also in eastern Polynesia. Even the Easter Islanders had fowls, bananas, yams, and the sugar-cane. Thus we are faced here with the same inescapable conclusion as in the case of the outrigger canoe. After having crossed the Pacific from America to the margin of Melanesia and there obtained from their new neighbors the fowl, the pig, and the various Old World crop plants, some of those Peruvian and North-West American Polynesians would have had to recross most of the Pacific from west to east, "against all prevailing winds," a feat which, according to Heyerdahl, they ought to have been incapable of accomplishing. Thus Heyerdahl's argument, as far as it is based on conditions of winds and currents, completely collapses (p. 323).

Another severe critic of Heyerdahl's thesis has been Robert Suggs. In a volume presenting his own theory of Polynesian migrations (1960a), Suggs devotes an entire chapter to a critique of the Kon-Tiki theory. He points out temporal inconsistencies in Heyerdahl's attempt to account for culture traits on Easter Island by presuming a migration from Peru:

> Heyerdahl's Peruvians must have availed themselves of that classical device of science fiction, the time machine, for they showed up off Easter Island in A. D. 380, led by a post-A.D. 750 Incan god-hero, with an A.D. 750 Tiahuanaco material culture featuring A.D. 1500 Incan walls, and not one thing characteristic of the Tiahuanaco period in Peru and Bolivia. This is equivalent to saying that America was discovered in the last days of the Roman Empire by King Henry the Eighth, who brought the Ford Falcon to the benighted aborigines (p. 224).

And concludes by dismissing the scientific merit of Heyerdahl's position:

> In conclusion, the *Kon-Tiki* theory is seen as a *revenant* from the past, clothed in a more attractive shroud. Its basis is mainly the success of a modern raft voyage that could not even hope to prove anything concerning ancient Peruvian navigation. The meager scientific evidence for the theory is weak, even in the few instances where it is completely acceptable. Otherwise, the similarities which are purported to show Polynesian-Peruvian relationships are completely equivocal. The *Kon-Tiki* theory is about as plausible as the tales of Atlantis, Mu, and "Children of the Sun." Like most such theories it makes exciting light reading, but as an example of scientific method it fares quite poorly (p. 224).

Nevertheless Heyerdahl has not been without equally passionate supporters. They include a small minority of scholars (for instance, H. Lavachery, 1965) and at least one religious group that has a stake in the *Kon-Tiki* theory, the Mormons. According to the *Book of Mormon,* which is based on the revelations of Joseph Smith, the American Indians are descendants of a colony of Hebrews who came from Jerusalem ca. 600 B.C. These Semites settled in Central America and northern South America where they built a civilization, the ruins of which are still extant. During the year 58 B.C., two shiploads of people, led by Hagoth (that is, the legendary Polynesian character *Hawaii-Loa*) left the northwest coast of South America and did not return. These ships settled in Hawaii, from which they settled all the other islands of Polynesia.

Other commentators have been more balanced in their response to Heyerdahl, allowing the possibility if not probability of American influences without going to the extreme of trying to explain virtually all Polynesian culture on the basis of such contact. Thus Paul Adam (1955) suggested that the nature of contacts between Polynesia and Peru was sufficient to account for the presence of the sweet potato, syphilis, and blond hair without being as extensive as envisioned by Heyerdahl. The first contact was probably made by Polynesians, who took a southerly route from the vicinity of Easter Island to Peru. Having thus heard of lands to the west, the Peruvians may have sent out a flotilla of rafts which, following the path of the *Kon-Tiki,* would have ended up in the Tuamotus or perhaps Easter Island. The small fleet of Peruvians, however, would find themselves unable to conquer the already established Polynesians, and unable to traverse the seas back to Peru in their clumsy rafts. Thus, they would inevitably have been absorbed into the Polynesian population. The statues of Easter Island are given two possible explanations: either they were monuments set up by Polynesians to ensure the safe return of their travelers farther east, or they were the product of Peruvians cut off from their homeland.

And Edwin Burrows (1956) after criticizing Heyerdahl for presenting his data in the manner of an advocate rather than a dispassionate scientist, and for ignoring the possibility of local development and convergence, remarks that "Despite many dubious details, the cumulative evidence of early contact between Polynesia and South America is convincing; and it may well have been more important than most Oceanists have been willing to admit" (p. 18).

Heine-Geldern and Suggs have both offered theories of their own to account for Polynesian origins. A summary of Heine-Geldern's position, which is based largely upon adz types (1932), was translated from the German by Skinner (1957) and presented in the *Journal of the Polynesian Society*. He postulates eight successive cultural developments, and makes use of three technical terms to describe adz types: *Walzenbeil,* an adz with rounded surface and oval cross section; *Schulterbeil,* an adz with marked shoulders; and *Vierkanterbeil,* an adz with flat surfaces and rectangular cross section. Here is Skinner's translation:

1. Penetration of a branch of the Walzenbeil Culture, either from Japan via Formosa, Philippines, Celebes, Moluccas, etc. to New Guinea and Melanesia, where the Walzenbeil culture influenced deeply the culture of Papuans and Melanesians; they may even have taken it over completely. This culture is, in part, the same as the "two-class culture" of Graebner; probably the partial Neolithisation of Australia is the result of it. The form of the boat was a plank-built boat without outrigger (Botel Tobago, "orembai" of East Indonesia, "mon" of Melanesia); the technique of the potters was based on building up pots from rings of clay. The people who brought the Walzenbeil culture from East Asia to East Indonesia and Melanesia were also the bearers of at least a part of the so-called Papuan languages (which fundamentally have nothing to do with the Papuans) especially the North Halmahera languages.

2. Diffusion of groups speaking an Austroasiatic language and probably having Mongoloid bodily characteristics, with Neolithic Schulterbeil Culture, from a region not yet known via South-east Asia to the south Chinese coast, Formosa, Philippines, North Celebes, Japan, N. E. Korea, perhaps also to a part of India.

3. In the first half or middle of the second millenium B.C., the penetration of people with Neolithic Vierkanterbeil culture (the Uraustronesians) from China to S.E. Asia. Their culture is most nearly related to the late Neolithic Yang-shao culture of China, and therefore shows like the Yang-shao culture elements, definite relations with the "cstbandkcramic" culture. Among their culture elements may be listed the following: rectangular sectioned adzes of different forms (long adzes, chisels (?)), stone-sawing technique, kronbohrer, net-and-band ceramic, manufacture of vessels in Treibtechnique; spear-points from schist (?), implements and arrow points of bone and stone, and clam-shell armlets as ornaments and perhaps also as money, decoration by Steinperlschmuck, especially Roehrenperl, pile houses, rice, horse, pig, cattle, megalithic monuments, head-hunting, the most primitive form of river outrigger canoe, possibly (but not certainly) the making of the tapa cloth.

4. Mixture between Austronesians and Austroasiatics, Vierkantbeil and Schul-terbeil culture. Penetration of the bearers of this mixed culture into Further India.

5. Even before the beginning of important mixture of cultures, penetration of a part of the Uraustronesians into the southern part of the Malay Peninsula which, until then, was populated only by Palaeolithic or a little neolithicised primitive tribes. Development of the primitive river outrigger boat to the real outrigger (canoe).

6. Further wanderings of a branch of the Uraustronesians able now through the developed outrigger canoe to pass by sea from the Malay Peninsula (to the common Urheimat of these, part of the Uraustronesians from which the present Austronesian tribes are descended) (a) via Sumatra, Java, and the chain of the little Sunda Islands, southwest and southeast into the extreme east of the archi-pelago, where they mixed with the Walzenbeil population (the bearers of the so-called Papuan languages) and with the still present remnants of the real Papuans. (b) A second branch via Borneo, the Philippines, and Formosa to Japan.

7. Formation of the Polynesian culture, or at least of one of its most impor-tant components in the Formosan-Philippine-North Celebes area out of a mixture of Austronesian Vierkanterbeil and Austroasiatic Schulterbeil cultures.

8. Formation of the Melanesian languages and Melanesian cultures (Mela-nesian bow-culture) out of a mixture of Austronesian language and culture with pre-Austronesian languages (Papua languages) and with the Walzenbeil culture. (pp. 206-207).

Robert Suggs, an archaeologist, did extensive excavations on Nuku Hiva in the Marquesas during 1957, and his theory of Polynesian migrations has been heavily influenced by the data he collected there. He traces the ancestors of the Polynesians back to a group of tribes living in South China along the coast and in the river valleys about 2200 B.C. (1960a, 1962). These tribes depended upon livestock (pigs), fishing, shell fishing, and garden agriculture for a livelihood. They were well adapted to their environment as sailors and spoke dialects of a common language, Malayo-Polynesian. Physically these people were a stabilized admixture of an old Asian Caucasoid stock with elements of Mongoloid and Oceanic Negro. The development of the Chinese state (Hsia and Shang dynasties) put pressure on them, causing them to take to the sea to find a home on the offshore islands or to move down the coast a few miles at a time. Gradually, in this fashion, the Malayo-Polynesians passed from the mainland of Asia into the Pacific. The archaeological records of the islands of the western Pacific indicate that the main route followed by the Malayo-Polynesians was through the Philippine Islands and then south into Melanesia and Papua. Distinctive Polynesian types of artifacts, such as tanged and stepped adzes, tapa-cloth beaters, and fighting clubs permit us to trace this route in general terms, although in the current state of archaeological knowledge precision is impossible.

By A.D. 1000 at a minimum, the Melanesian islands of Fiji and New Caledonia, on the fringe of the Polynesian triangle, were occupied by Malayo-Polynesians. Possibly by 750 B.C., the inhabitants of Fiji had explored the sea to the east and discovered the islands known today as the Tongan and Samoan groups. These islands were subsequently occupied, and it is at this point that the ancestors of the modern Polynesians branched from their parent stock, which was of course already considerably ramified as a result of the continual movements through the islands of the western Pacific.

The settlers of Western Polynesia did not remain long in their new-found homes, however, as restless splinter groups soon began to search in the sunrise for lands farther to the east, discovering some of the islands of Eastern Polynesia. The Marquesas were settled by the second century B.C. and Tahiti was undoubtedly settled by approximately the same date, if not somewhat earlier. From these two major "seedings" within the eastern half of the Polynesian triangle, the occupation of the other islands in that area was accomplished. The population of the Marquesas grew rapidly, and soon the canoes were heading off again into the unknown, carrying Marquesan explorers to settle Easter Island, Mangareva, and the eastern islands of the Tuamotu Archipelago.

Colonization parties crossed the 2,200-mile stretch of open sea between Tahiti and Hawaii by A.D. 100. Others reached New Zealand, far to the southwest, at the end of the first millennium after Christ, while still others discovered the Austral Islands and settled the western Tuamotu Archipelago. This process of island jumping along the major archipelagoes of Eastern Polynesia was probably still going on when the Europeans sailed into the Pacific from the west coast of South America in the sixteenth century.

In this fashion, the Polynesians managed to occupy all the habitable islands of the Polynesian triangle and visit those that could not support human life. Perhaps the most remarkable thing about the entire migration is the relative speed with which it took place, despite the fact that the Polynesians were obviously not particularly interested in making a quick crossing. Between approximately 1800 and 200 B.C. the greatest part of the Pacific had been spanned by the swift-sailing double canoes, while the contemporary cultures of the Mediterranean and Near East were still regarding as major undertakings their relatively short voyages along the coasts of the Mediterranean and the Indian Ocean (Suggs, 1960a, pp. 226-227).

Thor Heyerdahl is not the only contemporary scholar who has raised an issue from the past for re-examination. Almost all the premises that have underlain previous theories have recently been discussed anew, often with equally inconclusive results. Andrew Sharp, for example, resurrected the question of Polynesian navigational abilities in a book expounding his belief that the islands were settled almost entirely by accidental voyages (1957). He accepted the probability that short, deliberate voyages were eventually made within local island groups, but only after courses had been discovered by accidental voyages. Polynesian navigators would have been helpless to counteract the unknown set and drift caused by ocean currents, Sharp maintained, and would have been unable to reorient themselves after a storm. At best the stars would have been of assistance in gauging latitude, but they would have been of no help in determining longitude. If the Polynesians had made deliberate voyages, he insisted, there would not be such uneven distributions of food plants, pigs or rats, nor would the difference between Western and Eastern (that is, marginal central) Polynesian languages and culture be so clear. Sharp's views have been debated pro and con, in some quarters as zealously as the *Kon-Tiki* theory.

Captain Brett Hilder, an experienced European navigator who had spent many years in the Pacific, placed himself in 99 percent agreement with Sharp. "In considering the question of what forms of navigation were possibly used by the Polynesians," he wrote, "it is quite unrealistic to assume that their small and scattered communities could, without mathematics and written records, without sundials, clocks, charts, magnetic needles, astrolabes or sextants of any kind, achieve a better system of navigation than the combined civilisations of Christiandom and Islam in the year 1500" (1962).

A. P. Vayda (1959) attempted to test some of the implications of Sharp's thesis by re-examining cultural distributions in Western and Eastern Polynesia. Why, he asks, was the distinctiveness between the two areas not obliterated by accidental voyaging between the two areas? Sharp's answer had been that "no one lot of new arrivals would have sufficient impact to dominate the existing culture or language, but would be absorbed" (p. 71). This is probably quite true on the large volcanic islands, Vayda admitted, but what about the small atolls? The population on them is not very large to begin with, and hurricanes, drought, or other natural disasters can decimate it. One would therefore expect that on the central atolls the distribution of east-west traits would be about equal, while on the high islands the traits would be predominantly east or west. He tested this hypothesis using the traits listed by Burrows in his trait distribution study (1938), and found that with the single exception of Niue, the expectations were realized. In the coral atolls of the Tokelaus, the Ellice Islands, and the Northern Cook group, there is a more nearly equal representation of western and eastern traits than in the high islands of Tonga, Samoa, the Lower Cooks, and the Society group. This finding could be interpreted as consistent with Sharp's viewpoint.

Among Sharp's major critics have been G. M. Dening, Captain G. H. Heyen, G. S. Parsonon and Robert Suggs. Dening (1962), in discussing the geographical knowledge of the Polynesians, concludes that there were a number of "contact areas" in Polynesia within which return voyages of over 1,000 miles were made, although the longest open stretches were less than 350 miles, and averaged between 150 and 230 miles. "The possibility that they were occasionally undertaken when the proper incentive was offered seems just as strong" (p. 125). Captain Heyen (1962) also believes that the possibility of deliberate voyages cannot be ruled out:

> . . . the ancient Polynesians were expert seamen and competent coastal and inter-island navigators. For long-distance voyaging they would have been dependent upon wind and swell direction and bearings of sun and stars for directional purposes. They undoubtedly had some method of keeping a reasonably accurate dead-reckoning, and possibly some crude method of calculating or observing relative latitude and differences of latitude. Since determination of longitude depends upon time observation, it is extremely doubtful whether they had any means of computing longitude or observing differences of longitude except by visual contact with known islands (p. 71).

North-south voyaging would have been natural, and it is significant that all long-distance trips attributed to the Polynesians, either legendary or true, have been made in this fashion. The old canoes had a sea-keeping endurance of about three weeks, which would have allowed perhaps a 2,000 mile round trip. Some voyages were undoubtedly made by outcasts who would not have returned; accidental voyages were indubitably made as well; but it is possible that some canoe captains did discover new lands and returned to tell of their wanderings. Why else would tales of such voyages have been recorded?

Parsonon (1962) is more direct in his support of the opposite hypothesis, that deliberate voyaging played a considerable role in the migrations. After criticizing Sharp on his method of argument, use of evidence, inconsistencies, and unreliabilities, he offers his own theory:

> The legends suggest, more reasonably, that the Pacific was occupied at a comparatively late date and within a quite short period following a far-reaching agricultural revolution which stimulated not merely a sudden growth of population and a fierce rivalry for cultivable land but the emergence of new and more complicated social and political institutions. In this case, the movement cannot but have been very considerable, involving the migration of whole clans . . . (p. 61).
>
> The early inhabitants of Oceania were essentially nomadic . . . discovering islands not by chance . . . but where birds and fish led them. The scattered archipelagoes of the Pacific were settled . . . initially by small groups of oceanic rovers, and then, much later, by numerous deliberate colonists who, so far as a very different environment and the inescapable tendency towards cultural divergence in

virtual isolation would allow, succeeded in establishing in remote lands societies similar in most respects to those they had left behind.

The original pressure in Hawaiki having been relieved, the great migrations of the 10-13th centuries naturally soon dried up. . . . The expansion of the Polynesians westwards, whether from eastern or western Polynesia, was in the final analysis checked at Buston's line (border of the malaria area of Melanesia). . . .

A new burst of maritime activity in the 18th century . . . was cut short by wasting civil wars and more especially by the appalling ravages of newly introduced diseases. The abrupt and irreversible eclipse of the canoe-maker's art and the rapid growth of foreign shipping . . . brought to a close even the lesser voyaging of later times. The wide expanses of the Pacific were thus left at last to those whose misfortunes in tiny boats and outriggers have led theorists in Cook's day and this to underestimate the achievements of the Polynesians and the Micronesians in mastering the world's greatest sea (p. 63).

Suggs (1960a) takes Sharp to task for ignoring contradictory evidence and maintains along with Luomala (1958) that Sharp's "entire presentation of the thesis has more of the aspect of a pet notion than that of a scientifically developed theory" (Suggs, 1960a, p. 83). Suggs reviews the present state of knowledge of Polynesian navigation in the following manner:

1. The Polynesians had a well-developed technology, producing extremely seaworthy vessels of a wide size range.
2. Empirical navigation techniques were numerous, and their value, even today, cannot be arbitrarily dismissed. A dearth of scientifically recorded information, however, does not allow us to state their value objectively.
3. Definite archaeological evidence exists proving that well-provisioned expeditions occupied both Hawaii and the Marquesas. This accords with legendary evidence from all over Polynesia that not all settlements were made by chance, although some may have been.
4. Although there is evidence of a curtailment of voyaging in historic times, this has no bearing whatsoever on the state of navigation 2,000 years previous.
5. The "accidental voyage" thesis explains nothing, being applicable to any situation in the world owing to its lack of specificity. Although such voyages undoubtedly often occurred, they seldom would have resulted in permanent settlement (pp. 84-85).

A somewhat less virulent but nonetheless significant debate can also be found in the recent literature concerning the validity and usefulness of Polynesian legends and genealogies in reconstructing the region's culture history. Ralph Piddington, a student of Malinowski's and an avowed functionalist, expressed the same doubts concerning the validity of Polynesian legends that his pioneering professor had expressed for all orally transmitted historical legends. Historical traditions should be compared not with historical documents, Piddington maintained, but with Arthurian legends (1956). That genealogies are subject to gross distortion was clearly illustrated by Dorothy Barrère (1961). She shows that during the latter part of the 19th century several writers rearranged ancient genealogies and interpolated names to bolster Biblicized traditions of the Hawaiian people. Robertson (1956, 1962) has argued that although distortions may creep into legendary material they can be compensated for by proper analytical techniques, and that such data cannot be dismissed as unworthy of serious consideration as history. He distinguishes between what he calls "factual" and "conceptual" traditions:

> Factual tradition would consist of such traditions as genealogies and detailed narrative, which purport to be true records of fact, whether valid or not, and which are capable of being analysed and compared with a view to assessment for *prima facie* validity. How satisfactory the assessment can be will depend on the quantity and the quality of the material available for analysis. Validity does not necessarily follow from consistency, but experience shows that there is a very high degree of consistency to be found over a wide range of tribal tradition, and especially as between the traditions of different groups, which cannot be fortuitous. If the consistency is not fortuitous it must be the result either of accurate recording or else of the most painstaking invention. The existence of very important and widely accepted versions which can be shown by analysis to be utterly impossible in terms of the main body of consistent tradition would rule out the latter. This consistency is most easily demonstrated in genealogies, but the close limitations of a chronology dictated by detailed analysis of the genealogies provide a stringent check on the narrative. Survey of a wide field of tradition sometimes brings to light clear historical sequences which are not always recognised in traditional concept, and this constitutes a further pointer to a general validity. Absolute validity cannot be claimed for traditional evidence any more than for other evidences of prehistory, which all depend on consistency of a pattern of some kind. In the case of very early traditions it must inevitably happen that frequently there is little material for analysis and comparison. In such a case continuity with subsequent tradition which can be shown to have *prima facie* validity must be a strong point in favour of its acceptance, and on the other hand, isolation in context calls for extreme caution. Authentic tradition has by long custom been defined as that which has been transmitted by the trained experts. . . . As a general rule experience teaches that such tradition will stand the test of severe analysis, but it is not safe to assume validity without detailed analysis in every case.
> Traditional concept is more difficult to define. It tends to be expressed in gen-

eral terms which are not amenable to direct analysis. To a large extent it would
be in the nature of interpretation of factual tradition. It could be expected to
tend towards enhancement of prestige. It could easily be the cause of transfer of
factual tradition into a wrong context, and it could as easily be the origin of
false factual tradition. There is little doubt that some Pakeha [European or
Caucasion] theories have come to be accepted as traditional concepts by both
Pakeha and Maori. All these strictures notwithstanding, traditional concepts are
not necessarily erroneous (pp. 293-294).

Robertson concludes his evaluation on the following note:

> There is no doubt that factual tradition has been so overlaid with concepts
> and theories that it is possible only by careful study and comparative analysis to
> ascertain what is authentic factual tradition and what is theory. It would be well
> if the theories evolved by the pioneers in the study of tribal tradition, based gen-
> erally on a much narrower field of recorded material than is now available, could
> be forgotten while a fresh approach is made. In the past the approach has been
> made from the remote past to the present. Much more profit is to be expected from
> an approach in the reverse direction, namely from what is known of the recent
> past back towards the more nebulous remote past (p. 308).

Robert Suggs (1960b), in a critical review of the use of historical
traditions, asserts that "More often than not traditional evidence has
been seized upon quite uncritically to support shaky hypotheses" (p.
771). For appropriate usage consideration must be given to the manner
in which the material was collected. Sound comparative studies of form
and content, including legends not only from Polynesia, but Micronesia,
Melanesia, and Papua, are also called for. "Traditions are apparently
most valuable when they are thought of as providing a body of general
data which can be used in a positive fashion," Suggs suggests, "as a
kind of palaeo-ethnology for the culture in question, to aid in the interpretation of the cold facts and sequences of archaeology and to facilitate
the ultimate reconstruction of the subject culture's prehistory. There is
good reason to believe that Polynesian historical traditions concerning
the origin of island settling parties may often be reliable" (pp. 771-772).
Concerning genealogies Suggs points out that, when compared with
radiocarbon dates, genealogical dating has generally been found to be
unreliable, with errors of as much as one thousand to two thousand
years. He concludes his discussion with the statement that "Polynesian
historical traditions can no longer form the sole basis for prehistoric
reconstructions as they did in the past, but they still constitute a valid
source of evidence which, when properly used, will contribute substantially to prehistoric studies" (p. 772).

NEW TECHNIQUES

In recent years new techniques in linguistics, physical anthropology, ethnobotany, and archaeology have kindled the flame of interest in Polynesian culture history to a peak intensity. In linguistics, two main approaches have been developed that promise to yield results of a more compelling nature than were obtained by earlier *ad hoc* philological comparisons. The first is based upon the analysis of phonological, lexical, and grammatical innovations shared exclusively by a few languages; the second is based upon calculations of sameness and differentness, particularly of vocabularies, between pairs of languages within the same family. The goal, as it has been put by Bruce Biggs, "is to postulate a sequence of linguistic splits that will account for the similarities and differences found among the contemporary daughter languages of now extinct proto-languages, themselves descendants of proto-Austronesian. The solution to such a problem may be displayed in the form of a family tree" (1965, p. 8). The main proponent of the first approach to this goal has been George Grace. In a monograph aimed at determining the position of the Polynesian languages within the Austronesian language family (1959), Grace concludes that Polynesian is most closely associated with Rotuman and Fijian, and "that Rotuman, Fijian, and the Polynesian languages have passed through a period of common history apart from all the remaining languages of the Austronesian family" (p. 65). These languages are part of a grouping he terms "Eastern Austronesian," which represents a unity "as opposed to all other Austronesian languages for which sufficiently extensive comparative studies exist" (p. 65). Included in this grouping are nineteen subgroups encompassing most of the languages in Micronesia, Polynesia, Melanesia, and New Guinea (1955). Isidore Dyen (1965) has taken the second approach to the problem of subgroupings within the Austronesian language group. He compared basic vocabulary lists of 371 languages and dialects (requiring some 7,000,000 decisions as to cognacy or otherwise of word pairs), and with computer assistance over 68,000 cognate percentages between pairs of languages were calculated. The resulting groupings overlapped only partly with those postulated by Grace. On the basis of his findings Dyen rejects Grace's category of Eastern Austronesian, stating that this grouping "contains many languages and groups of languages that are independent and cannot be united by lexico-statistical argument" (p. 80). Based on the discovery that Melanesia represents the area of greatest linguistic diversity, Dyen suggests that the Malayo-Polynesians may not have spread out from western Indonesia, but rather from the Melanesian-New Guinea area. The New Hebrides, in Dyen's opinion, are the most likely origin point of the subgroup that contains Polynesian (along with Rotuman, Fijian, and several languages of the southeast Solomons and the central New Hebrides). A Melanesian point of origin for Polynesian languages is also proposed by Biggs (1965). After reviewing the literature he concludes with this statement:

> One thing is clear. Polynesia's close relatives are all to be found in eastern Melanesia. There is no linguistic evidence for a direct migration from anywhere further west. As far as language goes Polynesia is a branch of Melanesia (p. 11).

Within Polynesia itself there have been several recent attempts to define subgroupings and to plot genetic relations between languages. Samuel Elbert (1953), using glottochronology, a lexicostatistical technique which presumes a relatively constant rate of change between languages which have separated from a parent language, concluded that pre-Tongan was the first language to branch off from a parent proto-Polynesian language. Pre-Samoan split off next, followed by Kapinga-marangi and the languages of Eastern Polynesia (including New Zealand). From an older form of Tongan came the languages of Futuna, Uvea, Niue, and modern Tonga. Early Samoan produced the languages of Tikopia, Ellice, and modern Samoa. Elbert's analysis confirmed the existence of a schism between Western and Eastern (that is, Central-Marginal) Polynesian. Other contributions have been made by Pawley, Emory, and Green. Pawley (1966), using comparative morphology, makes the claim that all the well-described Polynesian languages spoken within the Polynesian triangle apart from Tongan, Niuean, and possibly Uvean, belong to a single subgroup which he terms "Nuclear Polynesian." Tongan and Niue are regarded as comprising a second major subgroup, co-ordinate with Nuclear Polynesian, and called "Tongic" by Pawley. Nuclear Polynesian can be subdivided into "Eastern Polynesian" and "Samoic." There is therefore considerable agreement between the results achieved by Pawley on morphological grounds and those obtained by Elbert using lexicostatistics. Emory (1963), using total vocabularies and modified lexicostatistical procedures, suggested that Easter Island was colonized from the Marquesas, that Hawaiian derives both from Tahiti and the Marquesas, and that New Zealand Maori stems from the Eastern Polynesian homeland either in Tahiti or the

Marquesas with a stopover in the Cook Islands. Green (1966) uses a combination of linguistic techniques, including an analysis of shared innovations and lexicostatistics. An archaeologist, he also is concerned with the relationship between the linguistic data and those obtained by archaeology. He concludes that the major cultural differences between Eastern and Western Polynesia are not fundamental to an understanding of the sequence of settlement so much as they are "a reflection of the extensive nature of contact that obtained both with Melanesia and within the West Polynesia area versus the more restricted nature of such contact in East Polynesia" (p. 33).

The position of the Polynesian Outliers (Tikopia, Kapingamarangi, Nukuoro, Rennell) is still a matter of controversy. Thus Capell (1962) maintains that the Outliers represent colonies left behind during the eastward movements of the Polynesians and are therefore actually older than either Western or Eastern Polynesian. His views are shared by Marshall (1956), although most recent theorists have interpreted the evidence to indicate that the Outliers represent a westward "backwash" from Polynesia proper.

In physical anthropology the use of blood groups as a means of classifying genetic connections has been applied to the Polynesian problem. Initially the results lent what appeared to be strong support to Heyerdahl's thesis. Thus Graydon (1952), upon examining the known distribution of ABO, MN, and Rh blood types to mid-1951, concluded that Polynesians are clearly closer to American Indians than either the Melanesians or Micronesians; and Mourant (1954) wrote:

> Observations on the *ABO, MNS and Rh* blood group systems are . . . all consistent with the theory of Heyerdahl. The results of tests for the other blood group systems in America are not sufficiently uniform to allow detailed comparison with the Polynesians . . . The Maori and North American Indians agree in showing very high frequencies of tasters of phenylthiocarbamide, but while the Maori have a rather high frequency of non-secretors of *ABH,* the American Indians have a high frequency of secretors. Thus it may be said that a large part of the genetic constitution of the Polynesians can be accounted for on a basis of an American, and especially a north-west American origin, but there must have been a considerable amount of mixing with other peoples, presumably the islanders to the west, to account for the *MNS* and secretion frequencies. Even if the hypothesis of migrations from America to Polynesia should prove untenable there would still be a strong suggestion that Polynesians and North American Indians had in the not very distant past received many genes from a common pool (pp. 146-147).

But more recently Simmons (1962), summarizing his own work and that of his associates, has painted a more complex picture:

. . . blood grouping data show that all unmixed Polynesians to-day are basically of the same stock. Contributions to this stock have undoubtedly come from the west (Tonga and Samoa), the north-west (Indonesia) and the east (South America) to form a common gene pool and a different physical type. The original numbers were few and came (as others have said) in canoes, often at the mercy of wind and current. Just as we have shown that in isolated areas, for example New Guinea . . . human types evolve with slightly different characteristics such as skin colour and an occasional gene mutation, so a blood pattern in one area differs slightly from those in isolation over the next mountain range, or in the adjacent inaccessible valley, or deep in the rain-forest. The variations in blood group frequencies we have shown in Polynesia from island population to island population, reflects again the results of small numbers breeding in isolation as in New Guinea, and in other parts of the world. It could be that the original limited numbers, or basic stock of men and women from the west or north-west lacked by chance the glood group B, and this nucleus with additions from the east (South America) also lacking B, but rich in the Rh genes R^2 (cDE) and M, increased in numbers and covered most of Polynesia. Group B was then only introduced in marginal areas, when numbers became sufficiently great many centuries later for the interchange of visits, mostly with Melanesians and Micronesians. It seems likely that the original men and women who entered Polynesia lived and bred in isolation for at least 1,000 years, dispersing to adjacent areas by design, but to distant areas by accidental voyages. Population additions from the coast of America would have represented a voyage of no-return, and these individuals made their contributions to the Polynesian way of life.

In conclusion, points of broad serological similarity may be drawn with Polynesians as follows:

American Indians:	No B, high M, high R_2, moderate Fy^a.
Australian aborigines:	No B, high A.
Melanesians:	Nil.
Micronesians:	Nil.
Indonesians:	High M.
Ainu:	Nil.

If one makes and accepts such comparisons with Polynesians, then there are four points of similarity with American Indians, two with Australian aborigines, one with Indonesians, and none with Melanesians, Micronesians, and Ainu.

If the comparisons are valid, then American Indians and Polynesians shared in a common gene pool, more so than Polynesians and other races to the west and north-west.

After 25 years of progress, we serologists have mapped most of the known blood group genes for racial groups throughout the world, and while clear-cut gene markers are known in respect to some human races, it seems clearly evident that blood group genetical studies do not tell us the racial components of the Pacific peoples or their paths of migration. I believe that the blood grouping percentage variations demonstrate the impossibility of equating a component of one racial group, with the possible component of another some thousands of miles away. If the gene frequencies as calculated do hold the clues, then posterity alone will provide the proof and the answers.

It seems evident that there were no planned migrations into Polynesia, and that the Polynesian people spread mainly by accidental voyages to all the distant Polynesian islands. Blood group serology does not prove to us who they were or from whence they came. There is then no Polynesian problem, other than that created by ourselves, for it would seem that a handful of men and women from the east and the west, and not racial groups as we know them to-day, produced the Polynesian people as a distinctive entity amongst the races of Man (pp. 208-209).

Recent research in ethnobotany demonstrates that this comparatively new field may help solve some of the puzzles of human migrations in the Pacific. For example, St. John (1962) summarized his analysis of the distribution of crop plants in the following manner:

The Polynesians had a highly developed agriculture based upon the growing of 27 species of crop plants. One, *Piper methysticum,* was a beverage plant, the others were food plants. By the known source and by phylogeny, the home land of these crops can be determined. One, *Ipomoea batatas,* is demonstrably of American origin, but in aboriginal times was carried by native people as far west as New Guinea. One was domesticated in Polynesia; three in Polynesia and adjacent Melanesia, two in Melanesia, and one in Micronesia. These central Pacific ones make 25 per cent. The great majority of them came from farther west, 7 from Malaysia, 6 from Malaysia and southeast Asia, 3 from the shores of the southwest Pacific and the Indian Oceans, and 3 from India or Ceylon. These Oriental ones total 70.4 per cent. Hence, the geographic origin of their crops implies that the people brought them from Southeast Asia.

Evidence of origin can also be found in the vernacular names used by the many tribes of aborigines. It was pointed out by S. H. Ray . . . that the coconut, *Cocos nucifera,* was known by the name "niu," in that same or in a cognate form of the word, all the way from Madagascar to Hawaii. The same wide usage is true of the name "taro" for *Colocasia esculenta.* Others of the 27 crops have names with a wide use, but over area of less size than the whole tropical Indo-Pacific.

Since all but one of these crops are of Asiatic or Pacific origin, it would be of interest to find the route over which they were imported, that is, either through Micronesia direct to Polynesia, or through Indonesia and Melanesia to Polynesia. The aboriginal occurrence and use of the crop plants gives the best evidence. In aboriginal times, in all Micronesia 4 of the crops were missing, while in the Marshall, Gilbert, and Ellice Islands, all of which are atolls or coral islands, 11 were missing. On the other hand, all 27 were in use by the natives in all or in several parts of the East Indies. This supports the theory that Polynesians, emigrating from Southeast Asia, followed the chain of islands of the East Indies or skirted and touched them while migrating through Malaysia and Melanesia to Polynesia (p. 308).

Perhaps the main single enigma remains the sweet potato. Until a few years ago it was generally accepted that it was of American origin, therefore posing a problem for those theorists advocating a west to east migration across the Pacific. However, several scholars have recently suggested the possibility that Oceania or Africa may prove to be the place of origin. In a symposium on "Plants and the Migration of Pacific Peoples" held at the Tenth Pacific Science Congress in 1961, three papers were offered presenting data on the sweet potato. Yen (1963), after a careful analysis of variation throughout the regions of its cultivation, concludes that the sweet potato is a single species and that an American origin seems to be strongly reaffirmed. Nishiyama's research (1963) confirms Yen's conclusions and Conklin (1963) addressing himself explicitly to a consideration of the hypotheses that the sweet potato may have been of African or Oceanic origin, rejects the possibility on the grounds of ethnoecological, historical, and lexical evidence. The problem of how it got into the Pacific and the manner and course of its distribution therefore remains unsolved.

Without doubt the most dramatic advances in accumulating evidence with a bearing on Polynesian culture history has come from archaeology. Prior to World War II there was hardly any systematic digging beneath the surface; it was assumed by many that island deposits would be too shallow for meaningful stratigraphy. This has proved to be a false presumption and the past decade has seen a tremendous proliferation of well-planned excavations throughout Polynesia, with substantial beginnings in Melanesia and Micronesia as well. The findings have been extremely encouraging. Even the atolls appear to have sufficient depth to promise significant results, as Janet Davidson's (1967) excavation of Nukuoro has demonstrated. The introduction of techniques such as radiocarbon dating is providing a sounder method of anchoring time, and methods of artifact comparison suitable to the area are being developed. The fishhook classification scheme worked out by Emory, Bonk, and Sinoto (1959) is an example. It is therefore to archaeology that most serious scholars look for dramatic new evidence. However, it is clear that an adequate theory of Polynesian origins and migrations must take into account evidence from many disciplines. Unraveling the mysteries of prehistory is indeed a team game.

It should be evident from this review that the problem of Polynesian culture history has lost none of its fascination as the result of two centuries of inquiry and speculation. What is most remarkable about this is that the game of theory has had to be played in an arena of limited possibilities, and almost all of them were clearly spelled out well over a hundred years ago. Each new bit of evidence, each new approach, has therefore had the effect of shifting the balance toward one or the other of possible solutions rather than suggesting radically new or innovative ones. Why then the fascination, the excitement, the heat of debate? Why do some men find it worthwhile to spend their lives trying to discover how a people in the distant past found their way to the remotest corners of the globe? Would it not be more gratifying to concern ourselves with fields in which theoretical revolutions can occur? But is there any story that better illustrates the height of human endeavor and the resilience of the human spirit than the settlement of the Polynesian islands? Are not our modern astronauts the same breed of men, with different faces and speaking different tongues? I would say that they are, and that the Polynesian story takes on fresh significance with each new exploration undertaken by man. It is therefore fitting that no final resolution is likely to be forthcoming, so that each generation can continue to be intrigued by a people who overcame all obstacles to create such remarkable societies at the ends of the earth.

LITERATURE CITED

ADAM, PAUL
  1955. "Etude sur les Migrations Polynésiennes." *La Revue Maritime* **105**: 9-31. Paris.
BARRÈRL, DOROTHY B.
  1961. "Cosmogonic Genealogies of Hawaii." *J. Polynesian Soc.* **70**:419-428.
BIGGS, BRUCE
  1965. "Comparative Linguistic Research in the Pacific." *Council for Old World Archaeology.* Surveys and Bibliographies, Area 21, No. III.
BROWN, J. MACMILLAN
  1907. *Maori and Polynesian: Their Origin, History and Culture.* London: Hutchinson.
  1919. "The Peopling of the Pacific." *Mid-Pacific Mag.* **17**(2):133-138.
BUCK, PETER H.
  1938. *Vikings of the Sunrise.* New York: Stokes.
BURROWS, EDWIN GRANT
  1938. "Western Polynesia: A Story in Cultural Differentiation." *Etonologiska Studier* **7**:1-192.
  1956. "Champion Explorers of the Vast Pacific." *UNESCO Courier* **7-8**:18-21.
CAPELL, ARTHUR
  1962. "Oceanic Linguistics Today." *Current Anthropology* **3**:371-431.
CHURCHILL, WILLIAM
  1911. *The Polynesian Wanderings.* Carnegie Inst. Washington Pub. 134. Washington, D.C.

CONKLIN, HAROLD C.
    1963. "The Oceanian-African Hypotheses and the Sweet Potato." In J.
        BARRAU (editor), *Plants and the Migrations of Pacific Peoples,* pp. 129-
        136. Honolulu: Bishop Museum Press.
COOK, JAMES
    1784. *A Voyage to the Pacific Ocean . . . in the years 1776, 1777, 1778, 1779,
        and 1780. . . .* 3 vols. (Vols. 1 and 2 by Cook, Vol. 3 by King.)
        London: Strahan.
DAVIDSON, JANET
    1967. "Archaeology on Coral Atolls." In *Polynesian Culture History: Essays
        in Honor of Kenneth P. Emory.* B. P. Bishop Mus. Spec. Pub. 56.
        Honolulu.
DENING, G. M.
    1962. "The Geographical Knowledge of the Polynesians and the Nature cf
        Inter-Island Contact." In J. GOLSON (editor), *Polynesian Navigation.*
        Polynesian Soc. Mem. 34, pp. 102-131. Wellington.
DIXON, ROLAND BURRAGE
    1920. "A New Theory of Polynesian Origins." *Proc. American Philosophical
        Soc.* **59**:261-267.
    1928. *The Building of Cultures.* New York: Scribner.
    1929. "The Peopling of the Pacific." *Philippine Mag.* **26**(4):195-197, 244-
        245.
    1932. "The Problem of the Sweet Potato in Polynesia." *American Anthro-
        pologist* **34**(1):40-66.
    1934. "The Long Voyages of the Polynesians." *Proc. American Philosophical
        Soc.* **74**(3):167-175.
DYEN, ISIDORE
    1965. *A Lexicostatistical Classification of the Austronesian Languages.* Inter-
        nat. J. American Linguistics Mem. 19. Indiana Univ. Pub. Anthropol-
        ogy and Linguistics.
ELBERT, SAMUEL
    1953. "Internal Relationships of the Polynesian Languages and Dialects."
        Southwestern J. Anthropology **9**:147-173.
ELLIS, WILLIAM
    1830. *Polynesian Researches.* 2 vols. London: Fisher, Son, and Jackson.
EMORY, KENNETH P.
    1963. "East Polynesian Relationships: Settlement Pattern and Time Involved
        as Indicated by Vocabulary Agreements." *J. Polynesian Soc.* **72**(2):
        78-100.
EMORY, KENNETH P., WILLIAM J. BONK, and YOSIHIKO SINOTO
    1959. *Hawaiian Archaeology: Fishhooks.* B. P. Bishop Mus. Spec. Pub. 47.
        Honolulu.
FORNANDER, ABRAHAM
    1878. *An Account of the Polynesian Race.* Vol. 1. London: Trubner.
FRASER, JOHN
    1895. "The Malayo-Polynesian Theory." *J. Polynesian Soc.* **4**:241-255.
FRIEDERICI, GEORG
    1914. "Malaio-Polynesische Wanderungen." Paper read at 19th meeting of
        German Geographers in Strassburg (June, 1914). Leipzig: von Simmel.

GARNIER, JULES
    1870. "Les Migrations Polynésiennes." *Bull. Soc. Géographie* (Cinq. Ser.)
          19:5-50.
GRACE, GEORGE W.
    1955. "Subgrouping of Malayo-Polynesian: A Report of Tentative Findings."
          American Anthropologist **57**:337-339.
    1959. *The Position of the Polynesian Languages within the Austronesian
          (Malayo-Polynesian) Language Family.* Internat. J. American Lin-
          guistics Mem. 16. Indiana Univ. Pub. Anthropology and Linguistics.
          B. P. Bishop Mus. Spec. Pub. 46.
GRAYDON, J. J.
    1952. "Blood Groups and the Polynesians." *Mankind* **4**:329-339.
GREEN, ROGER
    1966. "Linguistic Subgroupings within Polynesia: The Implications for Pre-
          historic Settlement." *J. Polynesian Soc.* **75**:6-38.
GUDGEON, C. M. G.
    1902. "The Whence of the Maori." *J. Polynesian Soc.* **11**:179-189.
HALE, HORATIO
    1846. "Ethnography and Philology." *United States Exploring Expedition,* Vol.
          VI. Philadelphia: Sherman.
HANDY, E. S. CRAIGHILL
    1930. "The Problem of Polynesian Origins." *B. P. Bishop Mus. Occ. Pap.*
          9(8):1-27.
HEINE-GELDERN, ROBERT
    1932. "Urheimat und früheste Wanderungen der Austronesier." *Anthropos*
          27:543-619.
    1950. "Heyerdahl's Hypothesis of Polynesian Origins: A Criticism." *Geo-
          graphical J.* **116**(4-6):183-192.
    1952. "Some Problems of Migration in the Pacific." *Kultur und Sprache,
          Wiener Beiträge zur Kulturgeschichte und Linguistik* **9**:313-362.
HEYEN, G. H.
    1962. "Primitive Navigation in the Pacific—I." In J. GOLSON (editor), *Poly-
          nesian Navigation.* Polynesian Soc. Mem. 34, pp. 64-79, Wellington.
HEYERDAHL, THOR
    1950. *The Kon-Tiki Expedition by Raft across the South Seas.* F. H. Lyon,
          translator. London: Allen and Unwin.
    1951. "Voyaging Distance and Voyaging Time in Pacific Migration." *Geo-
          graphical J.* **117**(1):69-77.
    1952. *American Indians in the Pacific: The Theory Behind the Kon-Tiki Ex-
          pedition.* London: Allen and Unwin.
    1958. *Aku-Aku, The Secret of Easter Island.* American edition. Chicago:
          Rand McNally.
HILDER, BRETT
    1962. "Primitive Navigation in the Pacific—II." In J. GOLSON (editor), *Poly-
          nesian Navigation.* Polynesian Soc. Mem. 34, pp. 81-97. Wellington.
LANG, JOHN DUNMORE
    1877. *Origin and Migrations of the Polynesian Nation.* London: Sampson
          Low, Marston, Low, and Searle.

LAVACHERY, HENRI
    1965. "Thor Heyerdahl et le Pacifique." *J. Soc. Océanistes* **21**:151-159.
LESSON, P. A.
    1880, 1881, 1882, 1884. *Les Polynesiens: Leur Origine, leurs Migrations, leur
        Langage.* 4 vols. Paris: Leroux.
LUOMALA, KATHARINE
    1958. "Review of *Ancient Voyagers in the South Pacific* by Andrew Sharp."
        American Anthropologist **60**(4):776-778.
MARSDEN, SAMUEL
    1932. *The Letters and Journals of Samuel Marsden.* J. R. ELDER (editor).
        Dunedin: Coulls Somerville Wilkie. (Journals written between 1814
        and 1838; excerpted passage dates from 1819.)
MARSHALL, DONALD S.
    1956. "The Settlement of Polynesia." *Scientific American* **195**(2):59-72.
MINNAERT, P.
    1931. "Polynésiens et Andéens." *Bull. Soc. Americanistes de Belgique.* March.
        pp. 3-28.
MOERENHOUT, J. A.
    1942. *Voyages aux Iles du Grand Ocean.* 2 vols. (Reproduction of the first
        edition of 1837. Paris: Maisonneuve.)
MORGAN, LEWIS HENRY
    1878. *Ancient Society.* New York: Holt.
MOURANT, A. E.
    1954. *The Distribution of the Human Blood Groups.* Springfield, Ill.: Thomas.
NISHIYAMA, ICHIZO
    1963. "The Origin of the Sweet Potato Plant." In J. BARRAU (editor), *Plants
        and the Migrations of Pacific Peoples,* pp. 119-128. Honolulu: Bishop
        Museum Press.
PARSONON, G. S.
    1962. "The Settlement of Oceania: An Examination of the Accidental Voy-
        age Theory." In J. GOLSON (editor), *Polynesian Navigation.* Polynesian
        Soc. Mem. 34, pp. 11-63. Wellington.
PAWLEY, ANDREW
    1966. "Polynesian Languages: A Subgrouping Based on Shared Innovations
        in Morphology." *J. Polynesian Soc.* **75**:39-64.
PIDDINGTON, RALPH
    1956. "A Note on the Validity and Significance of Polynesian Traditions."
        J. Polynesian Soc. **65**:200-203.
QUATREFAGES DE BRÉAU (J. L. ARMAND DE)
    1866. *Les Polynesiens et Leurs Migrations.* Paris: Bertrand.
ROBERTSON, J. B. W.
    1956. "Genealogies as a Basis for Maori Chronology." *J. Polynesian Soc.*
        65:45-54.
    1962. "The Evaluation of Maori Tribal Tradition as History." *J. Polynesian
        Soc.* **71**:293-309.
ST. JOHN, HAROLD
    1962. "Origin of the Sustenance Plants of Polynesia, and Linguistic Evidence
        for the Migration Route of the Polynesians into the Pacific." (Ab-
        stract.) *Proc. Ninth Pacific Sci. Cong.* (Bangkok) 1957.

SHAPIRO, HARRY L.
  1943. "Physical Differentiation in Polynesia." In *Studies in the Anthropology of Oceania and Asia* pp. 3-8. Peabody Mus. Pap. Vol. 20. Cambridge.
SHARP, ANDREW
  1957. *Ancient Voyagers in the Pacific.* Baltimore: Pelican Books.
SIMMONS, R. T.
  1962. "Blood Group Genes in Polynesians and Comparisons with other Pacific Peoples." *Oceania* **32**:198-210.
SKINNER, H. D.
  1934. "Archaeology in Polynesia." *Proc. Fifth Pacific Sci. Cong.* (Canada) Vol. IV, pp. 2847-2849. Toronto: Univ. Toronto Press.
  1951. "Some Aspects of the History of Polynesian Material Culture." *J. Polynesian Soc.* **60**:40-46.
  1957. "Migrations of Culture in South-east Asia and Indonesia." *J. Polynesian Soc.* **66**:206-207.
SMITH, S. PERCY
  1910. *Hawaiki: The Original Home of the Maori.* London: Whitcombe and Tombs.
SPOEHR, ALEXANDER
  1952. "Time Perspective in Micronesia and Polynesia." *Southwestern J. Anthropology* **8**(4):457-465.
SUGGS, ROBERT C.
  1960a. *The Island Civilizations of Polynesia.* New York: Mentor Books.
  1960b. "Historical Traditions and Archaeology in Polynesia." *American Anthropologist* **62**(5):764-773.
  1962. *The Hidden Worlds of Polynesia.* New York: Mentor Books.
SULLIVAN, LOUIS R.
  1921. "The Status of Physical Anthropology in Polynesia." *Proc. First Pan Pacific Scientific Conf.* (Honolulu) 1920. Part I, pp. 63-69.
  1924. "Race Types in Polynesia." *American Anthropologies* **26**(1):22-26.
TREGEAR, EDWARD
  1904. "Polynesian Origins." *J. Polynesian Soc.* **13**(50):105-121.
VAYDA, ANDREW PETER
  1959. "Polynesian Cultural Distribution in New Perspective." *American Anthropologist* **61**(5, Part 1):817-828.
YEN, D. E.
  1963. "Sweet-Potato Variation and its Relation to Human Migration in the Pacific." In J. BARRAU (editor), *Plants and the Migrations of Pacific Peoples,* pp. 93-117. Honolulu: Bishop Museum Press.

REVISIONS AND ADULTERATIONS IN POLYNESIAN CREATION MYTHS

DOROTHY B. BARRÈRE
Bernice P. Bishop Museum, Honolulu

THE ANCIENT POLYNESIAN concept of creation was of a universe originating in a "void," "source," or "night," and produced by the pairing of personifications of various phases of cosmic development. The pairings were arranged in genealogical sequences, and the evolutionary process described as "births." In the sequences, sky and land, gods, men, and plants and animals appear in a merging cosmos, with no clear-cut demarcations between divine and earthly beings. This concept of creation has been preserved in variants of chants and traditions in different island groups, and they are the standard by which to judge degrees of revision or adulteration of ancient native myths. Where the concept itself varies we look for localized revisions of older myths by the native priesthood, or for adulterations caused by an outside influence, namely Christianity, with its introduced concepts of creation.

As rituals of religious worship developed in the organized society of men, Tane, Tu, Tangaroa, and Rongo, present in most cosmogonies as children of the "Sky Father" (Atea) and the "Earth Mother" (Papa), assumed the functionary powers of major gods. In turn, one or another of these four might gain superiority in status over the others in some island groups, and in the Society Islands the ultimate in superiority was reached when Taaroa (Tangaroa) was not only elevated to be the supreme god, but a god of creation. This was accomplished by the priests of Opoa on Raiatea, and the revision in the cosmogony which they originated spread through the Society group, to some of the nearby islands of the Cook and the Tuamotu groups and perhaps to Mangareva. (Buck, 1938, pp. 84-85).

SOCIETY ISLANDS

By the 1820's, when the English missionaries Ellis, Barff, Williams, and Orsmond were recording native traditions in the Society Islands, cosmogonic chants featured Taaroa as the supreme god, creator of the universe and maker of man. By this time the Tahitians had been exposed to Europeans for some fifty years, and to active missionary work for twenty. Although the Raiatean-introduced concept of Taaroa as a supreme creator god was already established in Tahitian mythology, the chants of the creation of the universe and of man collected by Orsmond show occasional parallels in phraseology with the Bible (Henry, 1928, pp. 337, 344, 403), and raise the question as to whether these chants had received a further reworking after exposure to Christian thought.

In the two versions of creation chants recorded by Orsmond (Henry, 1928, pp. 336-340) Taaroa lived in the shell Rumia, where he made all things. These chants do not describe the creation of man, however. Both merely say that Taaroa first created *(tupuraa)* or conjured forth *(rahu)* gods, and that "it was much later," "when Tu was with Taaroa," that man was made *(hamani),* or conjured up *(rahua).* The creation-of-man incident is given in another chant (Henry, 1928, pp. 402-403). In it, Taaroa and Tu consult and decide that "We must now make man." Taaroa then conjures up Tii, "The very first man in this world," who mates with Hina-te-uuti-mahai-tua-mea, daughter of the god Te Fatu. Among their children is Hina-ereere-manua.

In the Mare chant published by Emory (1938, pp. 53-58), Taaroa, the supreme creator, mates with Te-Papa-raharaha, and born of their union were gods, among them Te Fatu, given as the father of the Hina who mated with Tii in the Orsmond chant. The Mare chant does not include an account either of the "birth" or of the "creation" of first man, Tii.

In the Orsmond chant describing the creation of man by Taaroa and Tu, Tii is given several epithets: Tii-ahu-one, Tii-maaraa-uta, Tii-maaraa-i-tai, Tii-haamomou-huna, and Tii-faaina-toi. Two of these epithets, Tii-maaraa-uta and Tii-maaraa-i-tai, are found in a prose tradition collected by Barff on Huahine and published by Ellis (1829, Vol. 2, pp. 40-42). This tradition is clearly Polynesian in thought throughout, and may reflect an earlier Tahitian tradition of man's beginning than the chant version. The story runs:

> Hina [a goddess-daughter of Taaroa] is reported to have said to Taaroa, "What shall be done, how shall man be obtained? Behold, classed or fixed are

gods of the Po, or state of night, and there are no men." Taaroa is said to have answered, "Go on the shore to the interior, to your brother." Hina answered, "I have been inland, and he is not." Taaroa then said, "Go to the sea, perhaps he is on the sea; or if on the land, he will be on the land." Hina said, "Who is at sea?" The god answered, "Tiimaaraatai." "Who is Tiimaaraatai? is he a man?" "He is a man, and your brother," answered the god; "Go to the sea, and seek him." When the goddess had departed, Taaroa ruminated within himself as to the means by which man should be formed, and went to the land, where he assumed the appearance and substance which should constitute man. Hina returning from her unsuccessful search for Tiimaaraatai at sea, met him, but not knowing him, said, "Who are you?" "I am Tiimaaraatai," he replied. "Where have you been?" said the goddess; "I have sought you here, and you were not; I went to the sea, to look for Tiimaaraatai, and he was not." "I have been here in my house, or abode," answered Tiimaaraatai, "and behold you have arrived, my sister, come to me." Hina said, "So it is, you are my brother; let us live together." They became man and wife; and the son that Hina afterwards bore, they called Tii. He was the first-born of mankind. Afterwards Hina had a daughter, who was called Hina-ereere-monoi [Hina-ereere-manua?]; she became the wife of Tii, and bore to him a son, who was called Taata, the general name . . . for man throughout the Pacific. Hina, the daughter and wife of Taaroa, the grandmother of Taata, being transformed into a beautiful young woman, became the wife of Taata or Man, bore him a son and a daughter, called Ouru and Tana, who were the progenitors of the human race.

An obvious addition to Tahitian mythology took place after European contact. There now appeared a prose tradition of the creation of first man and first woman that closely followed the Biblical tradition. Ellis says (1829, Vol. 2, p. 38):

A very generally received Tahitian tradition is, that the first human pair were made by Taaroa, the principal deity formerly acknowledged by the nation. On more than one occasion, I have listened to the details of the people respecting his work of creation. They say, that after Taaroa had formed the world, he created man out of *araea,* red earth, which was also the food of man until bread-fruit was made. In connexion with this, some related that Taaroa one day called for the man by name. When he came, he caused him to fall asleep, and that, while he slept, he took out one of his *ivi,* or bones, and with it made a woman, whom he gave to the man as his wife, and that they became the progenitors of mankind. This always appeared to me a mere recital of the Mosaic account of creation, which they had heard from some European, and I never placed any reliance on it, although they have repeatedly told me it was a tradition among them before any foreigner arrived. . . .

Emory (1938, p. 47) observes that "Ellis reveals that the missionaries were alert and on guard in their recordings, and that they wished to obtain only what was anciently taught." We therefore look for other than missionary influence for the source of the story.

Between the time of Tahiti's discovery by Wallis in 1767 and the arrival of the first missionaries from London in 1797, the Tahitians had had a good deal of contact with Europeans and several individuals had had opportunities to become acquainted with Christian mythology (Henry, 1928, pp. 10-31). However much the Europeans did or did not tell of their Biblical stories, the story of the creation of first man and first woman would probably have been the most common, and, of course, completely consistent in each telling. Twenty to thirty years before the first missionaries arrived in Tahiti, and forty years before Ellis and his associates were recording native traditions, a number of Tahitians had no doubt heard the Biblical account of man's creation. In Polynesian terms this represents two or three generations, and it is not surprising to find the natives insisting to Ellis that the story of the creation of first man out of red earth, and the first woman from his bone, were sincerely thought by them to be a pre-European tradition.

A fragment of purportedly ancient tradition recorded by de Bovis in 1855 (1909, p. 45) introduced another supreme god to Tahitian myth:

> In the beginning there was nothing but the god Jhoiho; there was next an expanse of water which covered the abyss, and the god Tino-ta'ata floated on the surface.

Emory (1938, p. 48) corrects the spelling of Jhoiho to Ihoiho, which "seems to be a reduplicate form of *iho* . . . having numerous connotations centering around the idea of core, self, essence, that which animates or gives life." He disputes the credibility of this fragment having come from ancient Tahitian tradition:

> It is noteworthy that in all which Ellis and Orsmond have put on record there is no mention of a god named Ihoiho. Should we assume from this that what De Bovis gives was a sacred teaching concealed from the early missionaries who were prying deeply into native learning? De Bovis himself does not imply that it was an esoteric teaching. He attaches importance to it because it seems to him to resemble very much the Hebrew teaching: "The Spirit of God moved upon the face of the waters." De Bovis does not take into account that his informant was in all probability quite familiar with the opening words of the Bible with which his statement runs parallel, and that he may well have been influenced by them. It is difficult to believe that the priests, who destroyed their own *maraes* and delivered their images to the flames, would have purposely withheld from the missionaries a teaching so in accord with the new teaching.

Tregear had accepted de Bovis' fragment as coming from an authentic independent cosmogony, and had equated Ihoiho with the Maori god Io (Tregear, 1904, p. 456). He thus introduced the idea that the concept of a supreme creator god was perhaps a widespread one in Polynesia, rather than what is now seen as late localized revisions by certain priesthoods in the Society Islands and in New Zealand. Thirty years later Emory (1938, p. 52) showed that the basis for Tregear's equation of Ihoiho and Io was an unsubstantiated one. Before this, however, Tregear's conclusion that Io and Ihoiho were equivalent had been accepted and "made to support sweeping statements as to the probable spread of the Io cult in Polynesia." It also colored the thinking of investigators for some time (Emory, 1940a, p. 117).

NEW ZEALAND

The commonly accepted cosmogony among the New Zealand tribes, according to Buck (1949, p. 433), "consisted of applying proper names to the phenomena of nature, arranging them in an ordered sequence, and reciting them in the same way as a genealogical table of human descent." In other words, it was the basic Polynesian concept of the evolution of the universe, with Te Kore (The Void) the originating point, and "Earth Mother" and "Sky Father" appearing as Papatuanuku and Tangi. In this cosmogony, the first human being was a female whose body was moulded out of earth by Tane, although there were alternate stories that the first human was a male, and in one, which Buck calls a variant, the first man was made out of red clay (Buck, 1949, pp. 449-452). This last version is suspect as being a late adulteration of the myth, since red earth or clay as the substance of first man's body probably was derived from missionary-taught knowledge that in Hebrew "Adam" means "Red," with the Biblical corollary that a first man made of earth would be made of some reddish soil. Reddish soil is also present in Tahiti (araea), and in Hawaii ('alaea), where other versions of man's creation out of "red earth" are found (Ellis, 1829, Vol. 2, p. 38; Fornander, 1878, p. 62).

Io, the supreme god of an esoteric Maori cult, has been the subject of considerable study since the disclosure of the teachings of the Matohoranga school of priests by Percy Smith and Elsdon Best in the years 1913-1924 (Smith, 1913-1915; Best, 1924). Unlike Taaroa in Tahiti, who was elevated from his original place as one of several gods of more or less equal status, Io seems to have been a new "character" (Buck, 1949, p. 531) selected by certain priests to head a cosmogony that showed him as creator of all things.

Perhaps the most discerning of the scholars who have discussed the origin and development of the Io myth was Sir Peter Buck (Te Rangi

Hiroa). He introduces his discussion with the words (Buck, 1949, p. 435):

> The select, or esoteric, version of the cosmogony has been written up . . . from the Maori text compiled from the teaching of the school of Te Matorohanga. In spite of its source, it is confused and contradictory, probably reflecting the state of mind of the experts who tried to build a more pretentious structure on the narrow foundations of an older and simpler school.

After a discussion of the component parts of the myth, in which he discriminates between the elements of the myth he believes were retained from the older cosmogony, those composed and added by the priests of Io, and those patterned after Genesis (Buck, 1949, pp. 435-438, 443-449, 450-451), Buck says in summary (1949, pp. 535-536):

> The Maori concept of Io was . . . a local development in New Zealand and apparently originated with the Ngati Kahungunu tribe, from which rumors of the cult spread to a few other tribes. I believe that the elaborations on the popular version [of cosmic evolution] over the period after the birth of the family of Rangi and Papa were composed in the Ngati Kahungunu houses of learning. . . . On the other hand, the cosmogony of separating light from darkness, the waters from the dry land, and the suspension of the firmament appear to have been post-European additions made after knowledge was acquired of the biblical story of the creation. The separation of the spirits at Hawaikinui so that the righteous went through the east door to ascend to supernal realms and the sinners through the south door to the Underworld, is contrary to the Maori and Polynesian concepts of the future world: It is too closely allied to the Christian teaching of heaven and hell to have originated in an ancient house of learning before European contact.

In a later study of the Io cult, Prytz Johansen (1958, pp. 36-63) lays stress on the rituals connected with the cult, and says (p. 56), "To my mind the myth of Io is actually based more on Maori ideas than on Genesis. The similarity to Genesis is unmistakable, and that an inspiration from there has taken place shall not be disputed. . . ."

The modern summation of the Io myth may perhaps be stated thus: In late pre-European times a god called Io was elevated to be a supreme god of an esoteric Maori cult, and a myth based on the older cosmogony was modified and expanded into a cult with rituals based on Maori cultural concepts; after European contact, the myth was adulterated with elements adapted from the Biblical story of Genesis.

HAWAII

Few Hawaiians had heard of Io until 1920, when a group of visiting Maoris formed warm relationships with a number of prominent Hawaiians, and discussions of their common Polynesian traditions took place among them (Emory, 1942, pp. 202-203). Apparently these discussions led to a conviction among some of the Hawaiians that they, too, had once had a supreme deity, whose name, they said, was 'Io. This view was presented by Ahuena Taylor in 1931 (Ahuena, 1931), who called 'Io "the Holy Spirit of the Ancient Maolis of Hawaii," and who said, "Io to us is Jehovah to other peoples."

A decade later, Handy (1941) and Emory (1942) discussed the evidence of 'Io in Hawaii, and showed that 'Io, far from being a "Jehovah," was linked as a god or as a cult to the Hawaiian hawk, 'io, which received its name from its cry, and not from a god. They differed only in their assessment of the role of 'Io in Hawaiian religion and ritual. Handy, after receiving two family chants from Taylor and discussing their interpretation with her, expressed the view that 'Io was an esoteric name for the god Uli, and was indeed a god superior to Kane, Ku, and Lono in a cult or priesthood which had been revealed by Taylor (Handy, 1941, pp. 136, 158). Emory felt such a god to have too much of the Maori Io. In his interpretation of the evidence, 'Io emerges as a hawk-god or as the hawk body form of the god of "justice," Uli. He says (Emory, 1942, p. 206):

> . . . in Hawaii all cults were esoteric, some more rigidly than others, but the breaking-down of the ancient religion which resulted in the revelation of all those about which we have learned was such that no cult of importance is likely to have survived until 1932 [1931], then to be revealed for the first time. The informant who revealed "the cult of 'Io" was obviously striving to show that the Hawaiians had a cult equivalent to the Maori cult of Io.

The attempted introduction of 'Io as a supreme god in ancient Hawaii was disclosed as a modern innovation before it became accepted as an authentic tradition to be considered in studies of Hawaiian mythology. Unfortunately the same cannot be said of an earlier introduction of a supreme god when that Christian concept was presented by two Hawaiian scholars, Kepelino and Kamakau, in the years 1865 to 1870. Kepelino, in his composition "Moolelo Hawaii" (Beckwith, 1932), and Kamakau, in newspaper articles of 1865 and 1869 (Kamakau, in press), reveal the beginnings of an effort on the part of some Hawaiians of that day to manipulate certain Hawaiian traditions to show parallels to Christian beliefs. In the process, the Hawaiian gods Kane, Ku, and Lono (Tane, Tu, and Rongo) became a "threefold god," and Kanaloa (Tangaroa) became a Satan.

In their writings, Kepelino and Kamakau, who had been educated in Catholic and in Protestant mission schools, presented stories of the creation of the universe and of man which they patterned on Genesis.

They later elaborated on these stories in conversations with Abraham Fornander (1919, Vol. 6, pp. 266-276), and expanded them to include tales similar to the Biblical stories of the fall of man, the Flood, and the Exodus. Fornander found in these stories "evidence" which strongly supported his theory of the Semitic origin of the Polynesians, and retold them, with some added interpretations of his own, in Volume One of his *Polynesian Race* (1878, pp. 59-100). As part of the series of tales, called the "Kumuhonua legends," Fornander's two informants fur- nished him with a "genealogy of Kumuhonua," their "Adam." It began with thirteen generations from true Hawaiian cosmogonic genealogies and ended at Papa and Wakea, with an interpolated sequence of twenty- two generations of their own invention. They also furnished "biograph- ical notes" on names in the genealogy, which show decided similarity with Old Testament characters, and which also introduced a "discoverer of Hawaii" in the person of Hawaii Loa, and ancestors of the Hawaiian people as descendants of Kalani Menehune, their "Isaac."

Fornander's uncritical acceptance of the invented "Kumuhonua legends" and the weight of authority given them by his publication have distorted the study of ancient Hawaiian traditions for some two genera- tions. It is only recently (Barrère, in press) that a detailed analysis of the origin and development of the Kumuhonua legends has been made. The study was based on the same sources that Fornander used, and two others not then available to him: Kepelino's own written story; and the Hawaiian cosmogonic chant, the Kumulipo (Beckwith, 1951, pp. 187- 240). The adaptations and borrowings from Biblical stories and from Hawaiian folklore and tradition are traced, and provide evidence that any and all stories or theories originating in the "Kumuhonua legends" are not a part of true Hawaiian tradition, but are traceable to adultera- tions made in Hawaiian mythology in the mid-19th century.

The Kumulipo, the so-called "Hawaiian creation chant," was ac- tually an honorific "name chant" composed for the birth of a particular Hawaii island high chief, a 17th century ancestor of King Kalakaua. It is not a ritual chant of the priesthood, but a private family chant, the legacy of the direct descendants of the chief for whom it was originally composed. The chant begins in Po, or "Night," and ends with the name of the newborn chief, Lono-i-ka-makahiki (Kalani-nui-'i-a-mamao, first- born of Keawe-i-kekahi-ali'i-o-ka-moku). Just when the Kumulipo was set down in written form is unknown; but a manuscript copy, perhaps the only one in existence at the time, was in the possession of King Kalakaua when Adolf Bastian, a German anthropologist visiting in

Hawaii, obtained a copy and published a portion of it in 1881. The chant was published in full in 1889, in 1897, and again in 1932 (Beckwith, 1951, pp. 1-2), with varying translations and interpretations of the text.

In its pairing of male and female personifications, the Kumulipo follows the pattern of ancient Polynesian creation chants, resulting in various forms of plant, animal and human life being "born." In it, and in other myth chants (Fornander, 1916, Vol. 4, Pt. 1, pp. 12-15; 1919, Vol. 6, Pt. 3, p. 360), Wakea (Atea) and Papa are not the parents of gods, as they are in most Polynesian cosmogonies, but together, and with other mates, give birth to the islands. However, Malo (1951, p. 4) states:

> . . . in the genealogy called [O] Lolo . . . the first native Hawaiian (*kanaka*) was a man named Kahiko. His ancestry and parentage are given, but without defining their character; it is only said he was a human being (*kanaka*).
>
> Kupulanakehau was the name of Kahiko's wife; they begot Lihauula and Wakea. Wakea had a wife named Haumea, who was the same as Papa. In the genealogy called Pali-ku it is said that the parents and ancestors of Haumea the wife of Wakea were *pali,* i.e., precipices. With her the race of men was definitely established.

Both the Ololo and the Paliku sequences of genealogy are incorporated in the Kumulipo (Beckwith, 1951, pp. 230-231, lines 1711-1734; pp. 231-232, lines 1735-1764) and lead down to Wakea and Haumea (Papa). In her incarnation as Papa, Haumea gives birth to the islands, and in "reincarnations" she mates with her own "human" descendants for seven succeeding generations (Beckwith, 1951, p. 232, lines 1765-1771; p. 236, lines 1948-1957). This aspect of Haumea's nature may be an elaboration of a dimly remembered Tahitian tradition of the Hina who mated with her son Tii, "the first-born of mankind," and who, upon "being transformed," mated with her grandson Taata and so became a progenitor of the human race (Ellis, 1829, Vol. 2, pp. 40-42; p. 104 this text). The statement that Malo makes of Papa, "With her the race of men was definitely established," is also reminiscent of this Tahitian Hina, but in Hawaii mankind descends through Haloa rather than through Tii, or Kii, as "first man." In the Kumulipo, the only extant genealogical source for this name, Kii, is "born" at the same time as Kane, *he akua* (a god), and Kanaloa, *"ka heʻe-haunawela"* (the "hot-striking" octopus (Beckwith, 1951, p. 203, lines 613-615; p. 98, line 615), in the eighth period of the genealogical sequence, while Papa does not appear until the thirteenth period.

THE TUAMOTUS

The ancient Tuamotuan creation myths followed the early Polynesian concept of an evolving cosmos and led to Atea and Faahotu as progenitors of their active gods, Tane, Tu, Rongo, and Tangaroa. It may be mentioned here that Faahotu, or Hakahotu, shares with Papa the functions of the primary female element in Polynesian mythology. As Buck (1938, p. 128) puts it, "Hakahotu [Faahotu] belongs to coral atolls, and Papa to volcanic islands." Despite the close relationship between Tahitian and Tuamotuan cultures, Tangaroa was not generally elevated to a supreme position and made a creator god. This retention of Tangaroa in his original position indicates that the rise of Taaroa in the Society Islands was perhaps of more recent development than had hitherto been supposed (Emory, 1938, p. 22; 1940a, pp. 106, 115-116, 125-126).

Inevitably, revisions took place in the native cosmogonies. Some of these revisions were influenced by Christian teaching, which had begun in the Tuamotus in 1817. One was the delineation of Tangaroa as a "Satan." Sometime about 1859, high chief Paiore, a Protestant convert of Anaa island, the scene of the earliest and most sustained Christian proselytizing (Emory, 1938, p. 20; 1940b, pp. 573-574), gave such an account to a French naval officer, Xavier Caillet. This account was given by Caillet to Teuira Henry in 1890, and it is published in *Ancient Tahiti* (Henry, 1928; pp. 347-349). The passage reads:

> Aito and Fenua [children of Atea and Fakahotu] begat Tangaroa-i-te-po, an evil genius of great power who afterwards ruled the netherlands. . . .
> The creation of the universe was scarcely terminated when Tangaroa, who delighted in doing evil, set fire to the highest heaven, seeking thus to destroy everything. But fortunately, the fire was seen spreading by Tama-rua, Oru, and Ruanuku, who quickly ascended from the earth and extinguished the flames.
> Although Tangaroa was the strongest, these three men combined, fearlessly surrounded him, seized hold of him, and bore him down to the lowest layer of earth, which was in utter darkness, and there banished him. He became the supreme ruler of that region and remained the powerful god of death. Te-Tumu was the god of life and rewarded spirits according to their deserts.
> After these events human beings became mortal; and the spirits of the wicked went down to dwell with Tangaroa, those of the good soared up to the higher regions.

Emory (1939, p. 13) says of Paiore's revision of the myth:

> It . . . reveals that Paiore had equated Tangaroa, because of his association with the *po,* or nether world, with Satan of the missionaries. . . .
> In ancient Tuamotuan teaching Tangaroa was called Tangaroa-i-te-po (Tan-

garoa-of-the-nether-world) . . . and he was associated with fire through the incident of setting fire to the skies during the struggle between Tane, the sky raiser, and Atea (Space). Also, Tangaroa was called "the supreme ruler of the nether world." . . . It is small wonder that he should have come to be regarded as the equivalent of Satan of the Bible.

Paiore had begun his account with (Henry, 1928, p. 347):

> The universe was like an egg, which contained Te-Tumu (The-Foundation) and Te-Papa (The-Stratum-rock). It at last burst and produced three layers superposed, one below propping two above. Upon the lowest layer remained Te-Tumu and Te-Papa, who created man, animals, and plants.

In the *Annuaire Etablissements Francais de l'Oceanie* for 1863 appeared another version of this story of the strata, also by Paiore (Emory, 1939, p. 4), which reveals a further reworking to conform to Christian ideas:

> According to the ancient tradition, the earth was composed of three layers superposed. Each of these layers has its own sky: the upper layer is designed for happy souls, the living inhabited the middle layer, and in the third layer wandered the souls in distress. . . .

It was this latter account which Fornander paraphrased in *The Polynesian Race,* and upon which he based his assertion, "The allusion to the three heavens connects it with the Hawaiian legend . . ." (Fornander, 1878, p. 65) The "Hawaiian legend" is the spurious "Kumuhonua legend" of creation, which incorporated the detail that the trinity of gods "created the heavens—three in number" (Fornander, 1878, p. 62).

Actually, the "three heavens" defined by Paiore were but three strata of ten in Tuamotuan cosmogony (Emory, 1939, p. 6; 1940b, p. 573). This cosmogony has been illustrated in several charts showing the stages of evolution of the world, and have been thoroughly studied and described by Emory (1939; 1940a; 1940b; 1943). He cautions against the charts being accepted as of truly native origin, saying (Emory, 1943, p. 19):

> While these illustrations serve to clarify the several accounts of creation and to add various details, the drawing of them is now beyond [doubt] the outcome of foreign example, and they must be accepted, therefore, with a certain amount of reserve.

In subsequent years, other revisions of the Tuamotuan cosmogonies took place, and, by the 1930's, myths showed Tane or Atea elevated to positions of supreme creator gods. Emory (1940a, p. 116) sums up the transition from the older concept of an evolving cosmos to one of a created cosmos:

. . . in pre-European times the Tuamotuans were more or less exposed to the Tahitian teaching that one of the gods, hitherto regarded as an offspring of Heaven and Earth, was the creator of them. In post-European times Biblical teaching has thoroughly accustomed the Tuamotuans to the idea of a supreme god and creator of Heaven and Earth. This has led to the identification of Atea or Tane as a supreme god and creator, or of Atea, Tane, and Tangaroa as a Trinity.

As in Hawaii, outright "plagiarism" of Genesis also took place. The "traditions" collected by A. C. Eugene Caillot in 1912, and found again by Stimson and Emory in the 1930's (Emory, 1939, pp. 19-20; 1940a, p. 87), are unmistakably Biblical in origin. Emory (1939, p. 19) summarizes them:

> In these biblicized accounts it is stated simply that Atea, Tane, and Tangaroa were the three gods of the Tuamotuans. Atea made heaven and earth and all that in them is. He formed Tiki, the first man, out of sand, and took a rib from his side to make Tiki's wife, Hina. Through the anger of Atea a flood overwhelmed the land. Rata (i.e., Noah) escaped in his ship (the Ark) with his wife, children, and all the animals and birds. His three children became the progenitors of the three races of mankind: the whites, the blacks, and the Polynesians. A tower (*kaua*) was built to reach Atea. He destroyed the tower and changed the language of the people into a number of languages, so that they could not understand each other.

In 1929, when Stimson and Emory began collecting material in the Tuamotus, another creator god made his appearance in the mythology. This was Kiho, or Kiho-tumu, the supreme god of an "esoteric" cult now "revealed" for the first time by an informant of Anaa. Over the course of the next few years "corroboration" received from several other informants convinced Stimson that the cult was indeed an ancient one. Emory, on the other hand, was skeptical of the genuineness of the evidence, and had cautioned against accepting it (Emory, 1947, p. 6). Stimson, however, prevailed, and the "cult of Kiho" entered the literature (Stimson, 1933a, 1933b). Believing that the cult had been made up in response to their quest for ancient lore, Emory continued investigations, and the documentary evidence he gathered has convincingly exposed the Kiho cult as a late attempted adulteration of Tuamotuan mythology (Emory, 1939, pp. 22-26; 1940a, pp. 116-126; 1947, pp. 5-6).

THE MARQUESAS

Marquesan myths appear not to have been widely collected until the 1920's, when Handy (1923, 1930) investigated the social culture of those islands. From his collection of traditional stories Buck reconstructed the ancient mythology, which he introduced by saying (Buck, 1938, p. 149):

Marquesan myths had evidently been partially forgotten when they were first recorded in writing long after European contact. The creation myths lack many details that the old priests must have known. However, some of the general themes have been transmitted in a confused form that may yet be translated by those who can interpret the displaced sequence of events.

His reconstruction reads in part (Buck, 1938, pp. 149-152):

Creation begins with Papa-'una (Upper-stratum) and Papa-'a'o (Lower-stratum) as primary parents. Their offspring were numerous, and among them were Atea, Tane, Tu, 'Ono-tapu (Rongo-tapu), Tonofiti, Tiki and Aumia [and Moepo (Handy, 1923, pp. 244, 328)]. . . .

The Marquesan myth departs from the pattern previously observed in that one Papa married another Papa and produced Atea. In other islands, Atea married Papa, but since Papa was already given in marriage, the Marquesan school created the new personage, Atanua, as wife for Atea. . . .

Atea retained importance by being made the direct ancestor of man. Atea also married various personified females and produced mountains, rocks, earth; various food plants . . . ; and the pig. . . .

One of the most striking features of Marquesan myth is the absence of Tana'oa (Tangaroa) among the progeny of Papa'una and Papa'a'o. He functions, however, as the god of the winds, the sea, and fishing. . . .

It is evident that the Marquesan school had the original myth in which Tiki is credited with being the direct ancestor of man. . . .

In the Bishop Museum manuscript collection are letters and papers of Thomas Clifton Lawson which show the extremes of adulteration in Marquesan mythology. Lawson had been the mate on an English whaler, which he left at the Marquesas in 1843; he lived the remainder of his life in these islands. Judging from his letters, Lawson did some vigorous proselytizing of his own among the natives, who had been exposed off and on to missionary proselytizing since 1797. Apparently he made friendships among the American missionaries from Hawaii who were active in the Marquesas in the 1850's, and upon their return to Honolulu kept up a correspondence with them. His letters, dated 1862-1865, were occasionally accompanied by manuscripts which he apparently hoped would be published in the mission-slanted periodical *The Friend,* of which the Reverend Samuel C. Damon was editor and publisher. It is evident that the missionaries themselves took no stock in Lawson's arbitrary equations of Marquesan mythological characters with Biblical characters or in his Bible-oriented interpretations of their chants, since none of his material of this type was published in *The Friend.* However, J. Linton Palmer, an English naval officer who made

Lawson's acquaintance in the Marquesas in 1852, published three of his chant translations in 1877 (Palmer, 1877), and Fornander used two of his chants (1878, pp. 214-219, 225-235) in furtherance of his argument for the Semitic origin of the Polynesians. Of the first of these, a "creation chant," Handy (1923, pp. 328-329) says bluntly:

> What is called *Te Vanana na Tana-oa,* which Fornander published . . . I feel to be certainly a fictitious fabrication of a European mind. . . . This so-called *vanana* is built around the idea of Atea as a "God of Light" and Tanaoa as a "Prince of Darkness" who was cast out. [An excerpt from] The chant is as follows:

> > Born is his (Atea's) first son, his princely son.
> > O the great prince, oh, the sacred superior,
> > O the princely son, first born of divine power!

> > O the son, equal with the father and with Ono ("Spirit")
> > Joined are they three in the same power,
> > The Father, Ono, and the Son.

> These English lines are a literal translation of the Marquesan lines which accompany them. It is obvious to one acquainted with the idiom of native chants and the native religious thought that the original translation of this so-called *vanana* was from the English into Marquesan and not the other way.

Of the second chant published by Fornander, called "The Deluge," Lawson himself reveals the extent of his adulteration. He had said in one letter (to Damon, December 20, 1862), "their ideas about the Deluge is all about a lot of pigs set afloat in a hogpen by a sea roller and about fighting by water and catching human sacrifices." The chant itself, however, as Lawson roughly translated it, and as Fornander (1878, pp. 90-91) explains it, contains such elements as "animals who were to be reserved from the Flood" . . . "a house to be built high above the waters" . . . "the animals fastened with ropes, tied up in couples" . . . "the waters retreating" . . . "the grounding of the house" . . . "A bird . . . is sent out over the sea" . . . "after a while it returns to the vessel" . . . "another bird is sent out" . . . "It lands on the dry land, and returns with young shoots or branches it had gathered." These two birds Fornander (1878, pp. 231, 232) translates as "the travellers" of Tanaoa and Moepo; Lawson had equated the gods Tanaoa and Moepo directly with the Raven and the Dove. In another letter (to Damon, April 29, 1863) Lawson recounts a conversation he had had with two priests in connection with this chant, which indicates that in its original form the chant was an old one. The priests say to him, "you have a very strange way with you in transforming an Atua into a ship . . . and a stinking sea into a generation of stinking men . . . and making us believe them, but one thing . . . don't use any more of your logic in trying to make us believe that the two great Atuas Tanaoa and Moepo are two birds."

In Lawson's collection is another chant declared to be partially the composition of two of his informants, and a comparison of it with the chants of "creation" and of "the Deluge" may disclose to a competent reader changes and additions they may have made within the framework of older chants. Between what were introduced elements in the chants themselves and the interpretations given them by their Western translators, these survivals of Marquesan chant-myths show too much parallelism with Christian teaching to be accepted as wholly genuine.

In one of Lawson's letters (to Damon, December 20, 1862) is a revealing incident as to the reaction of natives to their Christian proselytizers:

> I once asked a young chief to explain a certain passage of a vanana to me. He went on his knees and repeated the Lord's Prayer and then asked me what that was called among white men. I told him. He then replied that their vananas was to them what the Lord's Prayer was to us. He then asked if every white man understood everything in the Bible. I told him no, it had to be explained by ministers. Then, says he, neither do we understand our own vananas. All we know is the words and everybody puts their own meaning to them. And some hard old meanings they do put to some of them; they almost beat Baron Maunchausen [sic]. And they seem particularly fond in dealing in the wonderfull, marvelous and the impossible and where things have a double meaning they are sure to cling to the wrong one until they are bawled out and logically convinced that they are wrong.

A review of Polynesian creation myths shows that while isolated changes in concepts and widespread variations in details were made by native priesthoods, most of the revisions, and all of the adulterations, took place after European contact. The above quotation from Lawson may well illustrate how the later revisions came about: through the interpretation of existing myths in the light of "logic," that is to say, dogma, expounded by the proselytizers of the introduced religion, Christianity. Adulterations to the myths then followed, as influential natives accepted and adopted the new teachings as their own.

LITERATURE CITED

AHUENA [Mrs. Emma Davison Taylor]
    1931. "The Cult of Iolani." *Paradise of the Pacific* 44(12):78.

BARRÈRE, DOROTHY B.
    In press. The Kumuhonua Legends. Honolulu: Bishop Museum Press.

BECKWITH, MARTHA WARREN
    1932. *Kepelino's Traditions of Hawaii.* B.P. Bishop Mus. Bull. 95. Honolulu.
    1951. *The Kumulipo: A Hawaiian Creation Chant.* Chicago: Univ. Chicago Press.

BEST, ELSDON
    1924. *Maori Religion and Mythology.* Dominion Mus. Bull. 10. New Zealand.

BOVIS, DE, DE VAISSEAU
    1855. "Etat de la Société Taitienne à l'Arrivée des Européens." *Revue Colonial.* Reprinted by French Government, Papeete, 1909.

BUCK, PETER H. (TE RANGI HIROA)
    1938. *Vikings of the Sunrise.* New York: Frederick A. Stokes Co.
    1949. *The Coming of the Maori.* Wellington: Maori Purposes Fund Board.

ELLIS, WILLIAM
    1829. *Polynesian Researches.* . . . 2 vols. London: Fisher, Son, and Jackson.

EMORY, KENNETH P.
    1938. "The Tahitian Account of Creation by Mare." *J. Polynesian Soc.* 47(2):45-63.
    1939. "The Tuamotuan Creation Charts by Paiore." *J. Polynesian Soc.* 48(1):1-29.
    1940a. "Tuamotuan Concepts of Creation." *J. Polynesian Soc.* 49(1):69-136.
    1940b. "A Newly Discovered Illustration of Tuamotuan Creation." *J. Polynesian Soc.* 49(4):569-578.
    1942. "The Hawaiian God 'Io." *J. Polynesian Soc.* 51(3):200-207.
    1943. "Additional Illustrations of Tuamotuan Creation." *J. Polynesian Soc.* 52(1):19-21.
    1947. *Tuamotuan Religious Structures and Ceremonies.* B.P. Bishop Mus. Bull. 191. Honolulu.

FORNANDER, ABRAHAM
    1878. *The Polynesian Race.* Vol. 1. London: Trubner & Co.
    1916-1919. "Hawaiian Antiquities and Folk-Lore." *Mem. B.P. Bishop Mus.* Vols. 4, 5, 6. Honolulu.

HANDY, E. S. C.
    1923. *Native Culture in the Marquesas.* B.P. Bishop Mus. Bull. 9. Honolulu.
    1930. *Marquesan Legends.* B.P. Bishop Mus. Bull. 69. Honolulu.
    1941. "The Hawaiian Cult of Io." *J. Polynesian Soc.* 50(3):134-159.

HENRY, TEUIRA
    1928. *Ancient Tahiti.* B. P. Bishop Mus. Bull. 48. Honolulu.

JOHANSEN, J. PRYTZ
1958. *Studies in Maori Rites and Myths.* Historisk-filosofiske Meddelelser Det Kongelige Danske Videnskabernes Selskab. Bind 37, Nr. 4.

KAMAKAU, SAMUEL M.
In press. *Na Moʻolelo a ka Poʻe Kahiko.* (MARY KAWENA PUKUI, trans.; DOROTHY B. BARRÈRE, editor.) Honolulu: Bishop Museum Press.

MALO, DAVID
1951. *Hawaiian Antiquities.* B. P. Bishop Mus. Spec. Pub. 2 (2nd ed.). Honolulu.

PALMER, J. LINTON
1877. "Marquesan Tradition of the Deluge." In *Proc. Literary and Philosophical Soc., Liverpool.* No. 31, pp. 271-292. London: Longmans, Green, Reader & Dyer.

SMITH, S. PERCY
1913-1915. "The Lore of the Whare-wananga. . . ." Parts 1 and 2. *Polynesian Soc. Mem.* Vols. 3 and 4. Wellington.

STIMSON, J. F.
1933a. *Tuamotuan Religion.* B.P. Bishop Mus. Bull. 103. Honolulu.
1933b. *The Cult of Kiho Tumu.* B.P. Bishop Mus. Bull. 111. Honolulu.

TAYLOR. See Ahuena.

TREGEAR, EDWARD
1904. *The Maori Race.* Wanganui: A.D. Willis.

HOMOGENEITY AND HYPERTROPHY

A POLYNESIAN-BASED HYPOTHESIS*

MARGARET MEAD

The American Museum of Natural History, New York

E THNOLOGICAL AREAS, like historical periods, make a double contribution to human knowledge, in terms of their distinctive
characteristics and the work of the particular group of scholars who
have used them as a basis for generating hypotheses and conceptualiz-
ing human history. Polynesia, early explored and imaginatively appeal-
ing, has been the source of an impressive array of hypotheses and
theories. The peculiar circumstances of the great isolation and the
striking similarities among the peoples of these far-flung islands, and
the cultural features that have lent themselves to historical hypotheses,
have fostered speculations as diverse as those of Graebner (1911) and
Rivers (1914); G. Elliot Smith (1916) and Perry (1923); Handy
(1927), Heine-Geldern (1937), Heyerdahl (1958); as dependent upon
a finer analysis of island interrelationships as those of Linton (1923);
and as spirited as the current discussions of whether the early voyages
were accidental or planned (Suggs, 1961; Sharp, 1964; Golson, 1962).
Studies of migrations have been combined with the measurement of
physical traits, from the classic work of Shapiro on the descendants of

*This article is based upon Polynesian library research, for my dissertation,
completed in 1925, *An Inquiry into the Question of Cultural Stability in Polynesia,*
1928, and my field work in American Samoa in 1925-1926, as a Fellow in the
Biological Sciences of the National Research Council, combined with later field
work in Melanesia, New Guinea, and Bali (Mead, 1964, appendix B). It owes its
specific inspiration to the request to honor Kenneth Emory, to the preparation of
a new edition of *Social Organization of Manua* (Mead, 1930a), and to the field
work of T. Schwartz and myself under an NIH Grant (No. MH-07675-01/5) to
The American Museum of Natural History project, *A Study of Cultural Systematics in New Guinea.*

the mutineers of the *Bounty* (1936), to contemporary studies of blood types (Simmons, 1962). In the field of social organization and kinship, Morgan early included Hawaiian kinship terms in his *Systems of Consanguinity and Affinity of the Human Family* (1870), and Murdock used the Hawaiian system as type (1949). Studies of balanced structure and function have extended from Rivers' "The Father's Sister in Oceania" (1910), through the invocation of Tongan-Fijian behavior by Radcliffe-Brown in "The Mother's Brother in South Africa" (1924), or elaborations recently adumbrated in Schneider and Homans (1955). Sahlins (1958) and Goldman (1957) have recently used Polynesian materials to present alternative theories of the importance of class versus ecological determinants, and the work of Douglas Oliver and his associates (Oliver, n.d.; Finney, 1964a, 1964b, 1965, 1966; Green, 1961a, 1961b, 1966; Hooper, 1966, in press; Kay, 1963a, 1963b, 1963c, 1964; Levy, in press; Moench, 1963) has added a new dimension to the study of social structure. My early work on Manua provided the basis for an understanding of the dynamic relationships between the descendants of brother and sister in subsequent work in the Admiralty Islands (Mead, 1934a), and has been amplified in recent Admiralty Islands researches by Schwartz (1963). In the fields of religion and psychology, Polynesian materials contributed to Freud's work on tabu (1918); and later discussions of tabu (Mead, 1930b, 1934b, 1963; Steiner, 1956), and to discussions of mana (Marett, 1909; Firth, 1940b), and the role of the relationship between ancestor worship and high gods (Frazer, 1922). Keesing's study of change among the Maori was one of the very earliest studies of social change (1928), followed by his *Modern Samoa* (1934) and *The South Seas in the Modern World* (1941); by the Beagleholes' *Some Modern Maoris* (Beaglehole and Beaglehole, 1946), *Pangai* (1941a) and E. Beaglehole's studies of Rarotonga and Aitutaki (1957), which combined, as did the studies of Pukapuka ethnology, with modern psychological theories and psychological testing (Beaglehole and Beaglehole, 1938, 1941b). There have been specific contributions to psychological theory from my *Coming of Age in Samoa* (1928a), Cook's early Samoan Rorschachs (1942), the contribution of Linton's (1923) Marquesan materials to psychoanalytic theories of the role of culture in personality formation (Kardiner, 1939), Ausubel's studies of Maori youth (1961), Ritchie's intensive particularization of the Beagleholes' early work on the Maori (Beaglehole and Ritchie, 1958; James E. Ritchie, 1956a, 1956b; Jane Ritchie, 1957), and Levy's current work in Tahiti (in press). Polynesian art styles have been used to hypothesize far-flung lines of diffusion (Heine-Geldern, 1937); for intensive analyses of style (Robley, 1896; Hamilton, 1896; Linton and Wingert, 1946); for the delineation of ethos (Bateson, 1946); and for global types of surveys like those of Firth (1936b) and Guiart (1963).

Firth's massive monographs on Tikopia (1936a, 1940a) were followed by a restudy in the light of recent theories of cultural change (1959); Keesing followed his earlier work on the political scene with a study of *Elite Communication in Samoa* (Keesing and Keesing, 1956); Beaglehole his earlier work on culture and personality with a more specific use of tests combined with derivation based on ethnohistorical materials in his Aitutaki work (1957). We have had the benefit of ethnographies which ranged all the way from David Malo's *Hawaiian Antiquities* (1951) through Firth's functionalist study of a living Polynesian community (1936b, 1940a) to Emory's contemporary study of Kapingamarangi (1965), and Oliver and his colleagues' re-examination of traditional Tahiti as seen in the light of contemporary field work. Polynesian work has contributed to contemporary linguistic controversies (Grace, 1959) and Gloria Cooper's (n.d.) recent field work in Samoa brings Polynesian materials into the field of paralinguistics and kinesics. The involvement of Samoans in the wider world, as recruits in the American Navy and as migrants to Hawaii and New Zealand, has resulted in their use as subjects in contemporary psychological testing experiments (Grinder and McMichael, 1963), and Ausubel's studies of Maori youth (1961) are closely related to contemporary American interests in problems of cultural deprivation.

Work in Polynesia continues to depend upon theories of origin and contact among Polynesian groups, modified as they have been through time as students have moved from almost Biblical exegesis of oral tradition (Percy Smith, 1904; Williamson, 1937) through the comparison of surface finds and the beginnings of archaeology (Linton, 1925; Skinner, 1921), through the new and often contradictory formulations of modern archaeology (Suggs, 1961; Green, 1961a, 1961b), linguistics (Grace, 1959; Walsh and Biggs, 1966), ecology (Barrau, 1965), and serology (Simmons, 1962). The hypothesis that I propose to develop here can only be relatively independent of changes in our knowledge of Polynesian origins and migrations. It is concerned with the expression in Polynesian culture of special types of response to the colonization and isolation attendant on migration. To the extent that Polynesian culture may be analyzed into different layers, levels, or waves, during which its distinctive characteristics were evolving, the hypothesis which I will propose would have to be further elaborated, but should not be invalidated.

So in this paper, I propose to add to the Polynesian-generated set of hypotheses. I want to examine briefly one of the contrasts between Polynesia and Melanesia which has been a perennial interest to Oceanic scholars; the homogeneity of Polynesian culture and language in contrast to the extreme degree of diversity found in Melanesia. The diversity of Melanesia was responded to by ethnologists in an emphasis on the study of very small groups, so that, particularly in the 1920's and 1930's, each linguistic group was treated as a virtually separate isolated unit, or "culture" (Malinowski, 1922, 1929, 1935; Fortune, 1932; Powdermaker, 1933; Hogbin, 1936; Wedgwood, 1934; Bateson, 1937, 1946; Mead, 1930a, 1930c, 1938, 1940). This was of course partly because of the new interest in studying living cultures in great detail, but it was also, I think, a response to the attempts to treat Melanesia as a culture area, in such studies as those of Rivers (1914) and Seligman (1910), which accentuated the sense of unmanageable heterogeneity. But when Hogbin worked first on Ontong Java (1934), and then in Melanesia (1939), and I worked first on Samoa (1928a, 1930a), and then in Melanesia (1930c), the treatment we gave local cultures from the two areas reflected this difference in attributed homogeneity and heterogeneity. I doubt if I would have treated Manus kinship as an integral part of an areal pattern (Mead, 1934a) if I had not previously worked in Polynesia and been interested in the special characteristics of Nuclear or Central Polynesia (Mead, 1930c), with the stimulating comparisons between Samoa, Tonga (Gifford, 1929), and Fiji (Hocart, 1913a, 1913b, and 1915). This Polynesian-based areal emphasis can also be regarded as a precursor of my interest in 1931-1935 in the Sepik Aitape area, in treating New Guinea as an area with widely diffused common cultural elements depending upon different local styles of affective organization (Mead, 1938, 1949). This interest fed back again into a renewed interest in the Admiralties as an areal culture, where Schwartz is now expanding his earlier formulation on an archipelago-wide scale (Schwartz, 1963).

Wherever we have focused upon the problem of local differentiation, there has been abundant material to document the contrast between Polynesia and Melanesia, and we are beginning to understand at least some of the dynamics. The peoples we have studied emphasize and highlight every small difference of custom, dialect, accident. The uniqueness of the own group and other groups is simultaneously brought into focus by the identification of these small differences. "The people

of Mbuke are different," said the Manus in 1928, of one of the other
Manus-speaking villages, "because in Mbuke a widow must turn her back
to those who speak to her, when she is mourning." "The people of Liwo
say *arur* instead of *alul* and also some people in Alitoa speak like the
people of Liwo," said the Arapesh of Alitoa. "It is becoming the custom
of Ahalesimihi [a small hamlet] for a man to marry a mother and daughter both at once," said the people of Alitoa, when this had in fact happened only twice (Mead, 1947). Small differences in vocabulary, minor
differences in ritual, and new or slight differences in social organization
are thus taken up and remarked upon, by those who practice them and
by their neighbors, emphasized, amplified, and reified, and this increases
the sense of diversity.

I have proposed (1938), as one explanatory principle for this
ubiquitous diversity in language and custom that is found in island
Melanesia and fringing New Guinea (I believe that we may find that
we have to treat Highland New Guinea somewhat differently), the
particular style of diffusion which results in trading, not only tangible
concrete objects like pots or ornaments, but religious beliefs, art forms,
specific types of marriage. This readiness to engage in the diffusion of
intangibles such as marriage with the father's sister's daughter, or a
fourfold phratry system either as vendors or as purchasers or borrowers,
is of a piece with the way in which the people of the area see their
culture as an assemblage of identified and discrete customs. Integration
in any local group is accomplished by setting an ethological imprint on
clusters of customs each of which is very widespread. In this formulation
there is no contradiction, such as Vayda (1966) attempts to construct
in his recent paper, between the emphasis on the diversity in Melanesia
and the recognition that the repertoire of *traits* in Melanesia-New Guinea
is not itself enormously diversified. If the emphasis on local differentiation is seen as a concomitant of an excessively high and uncritical style
of diffusion, then the similarity when the shared traits are treated as a
list, and the diversity when attention is paid to local clusters, can be
seen as part of the same cultural style (Mead, 1949). Vayda, in his
discussion (Vayda, 1966), in addition to ignoring this possibility altogether, postulates a set of ecological conditions to account for the
attributed diversity in Melanesia's degree of contact between the groups,
degree of difference in the environment between the groups, difference
in the tasks at hand, and difference in the personnel at hand. Yet differences of this sort all occurred in Polynesian archipelagoes, and yet the
influence of these factors was not sufficient to produce as much linguistic

diversity among islands thousands of miles apart as we find in groups living a few miles apart in Melanesia-New Guinea.

Whether we consider language, myth, genealogies, rank, or art style, the great homogeneity of Polynesia contrasts with the persistent local diversification of language and custom in Melanesia-New Guinea.

I therefore wish to suggest that within Polynesia there has been an attempt to conserve a culture which was developed elsewhere and brought to each particular empty island by migrants, who were conscious that they were migrants who had brought a tradition with them which would have to be established and maintained in the new environment. Whatever the resolution of the current discussions about the accidental or purposeful nature of the voyages that led to the colonization of Polynesia, the fact remains that all Polynesian groups were migrants, and with a few revealing exceptions (like the extreme reactive ethnocentrism of the village of Fitiuta in Manuʻa) kept this circumstance in mind.[1]

We need not, therefore, be surprised to find the Polynesians displaying some of the conservatism that is associated with other colonizing groups that have been conscious of their isolation. In cases where we have completely documented rather than inferential histories of migration and colonization, such as the recent migrations of English-speaking peoples to many parts of the world, we find many examples of extreme conservatism in language, as among the mountaineers of the American Southeast, and in architecture and town planning (Garvan, 1951). Pitcairn and Norfolk islands, with their pitifully small fragment of Tahitian and English tradition, are a particularly conspicuous example of the conservatism that is associated with a cultural tradition which has been cut off from its source (Shapiro, 1936).

We may make the assumption that the emphasis upon origins and explicit tradition, upon genealogical ties between men and gods and between men and the cosmos, was a feature of early Polynesian culture, wherever and whenever that culture was originally developed. We may further assume that, given this preoccupation with tradition, in

---

[1] A further question with which I do not propose to deal here is the relationship between political centralization and homogeneity. The Melanesian styles of diversification and political centralization of any sort are demonstrably incompatible (Schwartz, n.d.), the Melanesian style of "big men" puts a premium on fission and short time depth for genealogical validation. Thus local diversification, scotomazation of the past, and articulate creation of a sense of contemporary diversity, and with a low level of political organization, go together. A Polynesian type of homogeneity could both generate and be maintained by a different political structure. Further data on where and when Polynesian culture took its historical far-flung form should throw more light on this question.

each island settlement the problem of conservation of tradition was experienced as a task and was responded to by certain forms of behavior,
such as an insistence on the unity of the language in spite of various
kinds of phonemic and lexicographic differentiation. It is striking that,
when a speaker of a Melanesian language encounters one of the small,
familiar shifts among stops, from a *t* to a *k* to a *j*, or from an *r* to an *l*,
he will use these shifts to insist that two languages are different, whereas
a Polynesian visiting another Polynesian island uses the same kind of
shifts to insist that Polynesian is the same language, and points to the
fact that everywhere the same word—*fale, hale, fare, fa'e, whare*—is
used for house, for example, and so the people who speak the same
language—Samoan, Hawaiian, Tahitian, Marquesan, Maori—are the
same people. So the shallowness of time depth in Melanesia, compared
with the great time depth in Polynesia, may be seen as a rejection of
common origins in the first case and a perpetuation of the sense of
common origins in the other.

This is even true in Samoa where the interest in a shared and immutable version of the past has been modified by the use of titles rather
than names and the preoccupation with the construction of local hierarchies by the manipulation of the relative rank of the titles (Krämer,
1902; Ella, 1893; Stair, 1897; Churchill [1955]; Mead, 1930a; Grattan,
1948; Freeman, 1964). But even this manipulation of titles, itself quite
self-conscious and explicit, is used in Polynesian style to insist that all
the contemporarily arranged hierarchies in villages, districts, and regions
of Samoa are part of an assumed system, the Great Fono (Assembly)
in which every title is allotted a place. So where the Melanesians
obliterate the past, and amplify the extent of differences in the present,
the Samoans, in spite of exercising a fair amount of local autonomy in
rearranging the system, end up with a reassertion of their unity, and an
insistence on a common past.[2]

This Samoan behavior is the more striking because it occurs in a
Polynesian culture where insistence on genealogical time depth is low—
for Polynesia.

The efforts of different Polynesian groups to preserve genealogies,
cosmologies, accounts of settlements, and the correct discharge of ritual
duties in such institutions as the *whare wanganga* (Best, 1924) of the

---

[2] In a paper presented to the American Association for the Advancement of
Science in Cleveland in 1950, Gordon Macgregor discussed the way this attributed
past political unity had been used in arguments about the inappropriateness of the
division of Samoa between New Zealand and American rule, a unity which we
have no reason to believe ever existed.

Maori and the hula of Hawaii are too well known to need elaboration here. Comparative students of education do, however, recognize that they are unexpectedly formal for cultures without a written language, and in comparison with the West African bush schools, the choice of subject matter—tradition rather than morality—was striking. The fact that in some cases the attempt to preserve the records of overseas origin failed, as in Fitiuta, only throws into relief the possibility that the most sophisticated, conscious attempts to preserve tradition could fail and a short time scale replace the carefully cultivated memories of the past.[3]

It is illuminating also to consider the way in which the island of Bali has handled the question of local diversification (Bateson and Mead, 1942; Belo, 1960; McPhee, 1966; Geertz, 1959). Balinese villages are largely endogamous and local laws and customs have proliferated through the continuous contribution of trance experience in which local situations are met by the enunciation of new rules and usages. Both the earlier Javanese migrants who established a loose hegemony over the local population, and the Dutch during the some fifty years of Dutch rule, respected the right of each village to insist on its own customary law. The differences were continually verbalized, as local specialists argued about some law of their own, in comparison with other villages, or a local offering specialist cooperated with a ritual specialist imported for some particular ceremony. In matters of ritual, only the most painstaking cross referencing of ritual details, each treated as discreet by the ritual specialists, revealed the symbolism of any particular item, as, for example, the offering of a live deer horn, a bit of deer skin, or a miniature of the enclosure in which a deer could be kept, found in different ritual versions. The common referent of these various items is not articulated. People travel from village to village, to large religious centers, or attend great cremation ceremonies in other parts of Bali; dance troupes go about performing in other villages; religious practitioners are summoned from a distance to perform special ceremonies, ceremonial practices are enacted within the theatrical settings of plays given by strolling players (Mead, 1939). Families move from one part of Bali to another and set up family temples which preserve parts of the ceremonial style

---

[3] Haiti presents a situation in which the origins of the present-day inhabitants are known and yet are outside the living tradition of the peasantry. Educated Haitians minimize their colonial history and emphasize, instead, the struggle of the Arawak Indians against the Spanish explorers which ended early in the 16th century. Haitian peasants have no knowledge of the origins of their society in slavery. In their vocabulary "African" carries the meaning of "savage" or "uncouth," and African place names occur only ceremonially as, for example, in a religious invocation of the abode of the ancestors and the dead (R. Métraux, personal communication).

of the place from which they came. The ways in which different ritual forms echo and complete each other is visible and palpable but not articulately recognized among a people whose verbalizations, characteristically have very little to do with the matter in hand. There are also considerable dialectical differences in Bali, especially in the use of alternate modes of word formation. The Balinese deal with such dialectical differences by a kind of studied half attention in which one's ear is, as it were, thrown out of focus so that similarities in stem rather than differences due to choices among affixes become salient. So ubiquitous is this attention that Balinese, speaking to Europeans whom they expected to reply in Pasar Malay, did not notice when the European replied in Balinese.

At the same time there is, in a system like the Balinese, with its great particularity of verbs, and its thousands of named ritual items, a great deal of dependence on rote memory, and the underlying similarities of form are not made explicit. And in spite of all of these minute differences, the underlying homogeneity of Balinese culture is overwhelming, maintained by a cross referencing calendarization within which there was no linear time perspective. In the Balinese calendar, there were many interlocking systems of weeks, 3-day, 4-day, 5-day weeks, and so forth, but a sequential yearly dating, although available, was seldom used. With a special version of reincarnation theory, the belief that individuals were reborn within the same family line, life consisted of a series of repetitive cycles within which individuals suffered variable fates. But the nature of life itself did not change (except in rare instances when individuals of high rank were raised to permanent godhead position). So the Balinese could say, "all of Bali is the same," and "each part of Bali is different," without either intensifying or denying the diversification of speech and usage. What the Polynesians accomplished by insistence on origins and history, the Balinese achieved by the denial of history or change.[4]

These other methods of dealing with history and with diversity and similarity have been cited here simply to throw into relief the Polynesian handling of their traditions. We may now turn to a consideration of

---

[4] In 1957 I found that, faced with the need to deal more explicitly with their Hindu religious heritage because of the modern Indonesian definition of what constituted a religion and a sect, the Balinese were attempting to deal with the sacredness of the Ganges, intrinsic to Hinduism and geographically inconvenient for Balinese theology. The intellectuals who were grappling with the problem had suggested that an under-ocean stream flowed from the Ganges to Bali and came up again in Balinese sacred springs so that in fact, when a Balinese bathed in one of his own springs, he was bathing in the Ganges!

another feature of Polynesian cultures, the recurrent tendency toward hypertrophy, or efflorescence.[5]

This tendency may be identified at many levels, in the overelaboration of tools until they become useless, as in the adzes and paddles of the Cook group (Buck, 1927); in the featherwork of Hawaii (Brigham, 1899, 1903, 1918); in the tattooing of the Marquesas, where the body was first painfully and laboriously tattooed into delicate and complex designs, only, in order to reach even higher status, to have these designs obliterated by total tattooing (von den Steinen, 1925); in the monotonous giantism of the Easter Island statues (Métraux, 1940). In social organization the same tendency can be found in the long repetitious chants that had to be memorized verbatim, in the excesses of the Areoi of Tahiti (Ellis, 1829), the elaboration of the position of the Tui Tonga Fafine (Gifford, 1929), and the cumulation of maternal and paternal rank in an unmarriageable lady of high rank among the Maori (Tregear, 1904). In all of these instances, we find features which are associated with the exhaustion of a style in other parts of the world, such as the late period of Gothic architecture or the end of the Bronze Age. In a continental culture or a culture in frequent friendly and/or hostile relations with other cultures or a wider cultural world, hypertrophy signals the end of a period and the imminent beginning of a new style. On isolated islands, this type of cross fertilization with other cultures is not possible, especially if there is a persistent attempt to deny local differences. It is as if the culture, limited by the emphasis on conservatism, was like a city built on a small island, such as Manhattan. Limited in available space, it had nowhere to go but up. Similarly, in Polynesia, with a limitation on expansion in the form of local differentiation, there was hypertrophy and overelaboration of existing forms.

Again Samoa, notable for the apparent lack of excess in social organization, religion, or art, is a useful test case. I have already discussed the handling of titles which could be rearranged within a theoretically immutable and timeless system. In the dance and in decorative art, very, very small differences were treated as giving originality to the style of an *individual* dancer or tapa maker. This attention to small details of innovation or difference at first glance recalls the Melanesian attention to such details. But the Samoans, by treating them as the elements characteristic of a single individual, where the Melanesians would have

---

[5] When I originally noted this in my first comparative work on Polynesia, Professor Boas was unhappy about the word efflorescence, although he was himself fascinated with such problems as the sudden end of the Bronze Age, and used to say speculatively: "Perhaps they just got bored."

attributed them to an imputed village or linguistic group difference, preserve the tradition of the homogeneity and conservatism of the style itself.

The Samoan handling of the acquisition of script and the concurrent shift from the *t–ng* form to a *k–n* form (*tangata* to *kanaka*) was another example of complex conservatism. At the time that script was introduced by Christian missionaries, the shift from *t* to *k* had already begun in Western Samoa. The first transcription of the Bible was done with a *t,* and this became standard written Samoan. In 1925, when I was learning Samoan in Eastern Samoa, the use of the *t* was the appropriate pronunciation in all formal speech, and in writing. But in everyday life, people spoke with a *k*. Children who had never yet used the *t* form, would nevertheless rebuke me if I, as a highly educated person, used the *k* form that characterized their own speech. Thus the ability to recognize and include within one system the two forms resulting from a characteristic Oceanic sound shift, had now been expressed in an elaboration of the Samoan fondness for differentiations of rank.

This Samoan handling of accommodation of the new within the system, also points up the extent to which these self-contained types of change can also produce, under culture contact, conditions of either efflorescence, as when steel tools gave a tremendous impetus among the Maori to the decoration of every sort of wooden object, or impoverishment. Samoan vocabulary has been stretched to accommodate one new idea after another, thus preserving the homogeneity of the language at the expense of precision of reference. This lack of precision may account for some of the unsatisfactory responses of Samoans to verbal intelligence tests.

I suggest that the sort of areal characteristics that I have discussed here, the contrast between Melanesia and Polynesia, should be included when we attempt to describe the cultural dynamics of an area, or areal clusters such as the Admiralties or the Samoan Islands, or whole culture areas such as Melanesia and Polynesia. To the lists of characteristics that can be conveniently handled in trait lists or form elements we should add such matters as the less tangible and definite but significant ways of dealing with the past, with change, with discernible differences and discrepancies between individual performance and local and more widespread custom. Matters such as these may become constant features of a culture and persist through many generations of migration, colonization, political division, and geographical separation. Where the Melanesians specialized by village or small linguistic group, and trade in the tangible and the intangible flourished, the Polynesians emphasized high levels of craftsmanship within the group itself. Where the Melanesians responded to differences in the languages spoken by their neighbors by learning to hear them as different languages and to culture contact by the enthusiastic use of a lingua franca, the Polynesians not only emphasized the abiding unity of diversifying dialects but also, in contact with an alien and conquering language, remained purists preserving their language from degeneration into intermediate forms.[6]

In time it may be possible to include such intangible aspects of the style of a culture area in predictions about the way in which constituent cultures will respond to different kinds of change, to assess their relative strength and vulnerability, brittleness or flexibility, and so plan to accelerate or decelerate various kinds of cultural change. As methods of recording are perfected, examples of vanishing art styles, particularly in dance and oral poetry and song, can be preserved as reservoirs, sources of future creativity for members of those cultures in which there is a strong preference for conservation and permanence.

We are moving toward a planetary society which may—within the setting of the solar system, and if no accessible intelligent life is found in the cosmos—place the whole of the human race in the same position as that of the inhabitants of a single Polynesian island—people who have no way to retrace their long voyage into the present, no notion of anywhere else to go, and who are in full and continuous communication with each other. In such a case, a foreknowledge of the dangers of hypertrophy as a part of dead-end conservatism, and the contrasting dangers of superficial variations which can result from imputing significance to small variations in local styles, may be valuable components of the process of directed cultural change as we take our evolutionary direction under conscious advisement.

---

[6] I. L. G. Sutherland once told me an amusing story of a visit to a Maori village where he had spoken in English to a Maori group and then ventured one final phrase in Maori. The interpreter, who had been rendering his English into Maori, meticulously rendered the single Maori phrase into English,

LITERATURE CITED

AUSUBEL, DAVID P.
 1961. *Maori Youth.* Wellington: Price, Milburn.

BARRAU, JACQUES
 1965. "L'Humide et le Sec." *J. Polynesian Soc.* **74**:329-346.

BATESON, GREGORY
 1937. "An Old Temple and a New Myth." *Djawa* **17**:291-307.
 1946. "Arts of the South Seas." *Art Bulletin* **28**:119-123.

BATESON, GREGORY, and MARGARET MEAD
 1942. *Balinese Character: A Photographic Analysis.* New York: New York
 Academy of Sciences. (Reprinted in 1962.)

BEAGLEHOLE, ERNEST
 1957. *Social Change in the South Pacific: Rarotonga and Aitutaki.* London:
 Allen and Unwin.

BEAGLEHOLE, ERNEST, and PEARL BEAGLEHOLE
 1938. *Ethnology of Pukapuka.* B. P. Bishop Mus. Bull. 150. Honolulu.
 1941a. *Pangai: Village in Tonga.* Mem. Polynesian Soc., Vol. 18. Wellington.
 1941b. "Personality Development in Pukapukan Children." In LESLIE SPIER
 and OTHERS (editors), *Language, Culture and Personality.* Menasha:
 Sapir Memorial Publication Fund.
 1946. *Some Modern Maoris.* New Zealand: Council for Educational Research.

BEAGLEHOLE, ERNEST, and JAMES E. RITCHIE
 1958. "The Rakau Maori Studies." *J. Polynesian Soc.* **67**:132-154.

BELO, JANE
 1960. *Trance in Bali.* New York: Columbia Univ. Press.

BEST, ELSDON
 1924. *The Maori.* 2 vols. Mem. Polynesian Soc., Vol. 5. Wellington.

BRIGHAM, W. T.
 1899. "Hawaiian Feather Work." *Mem. B. P. Bishop Mus.* **1**(1):1-81.
 1903. "Additional Notes on Hawaiian Feather Work." *Mem. B. P. Bishop
 Mus.* **1**(5):437-453.
 1918. "Additional Notes on Hawaiian Feather Work." *Mem. B. P. Bishop
 Mus.* **7**(1):1-69.

BUCK, P. H. (TE RANGI HIROA)
 1927. *The Material Culture of the Cook Islands (Aitutaki).* New Plymouth:
 Avery.

CHURCHILL, WILLIAM
 [1955.] Fa' Alupega i Manu'a. Manuscript in Bishop Museum. (On Samoa,
 pp. 1000-1097.)

Cook, P. H.
    1942. "The Application of the Rorschach Test to a Samoan Group."
        Rorschach Research Exchange **6**:51-60.

Cooper, Gloria S.
    [n.d.] An Analysis of the Paralinguistic Phenomena of the Samoan Lan-
        guage. Ph.D. dissertation. In preparation. Cornell Univ.

Ella, S.
    1893. "Samoa." In *Report of the Fourth Meeting of the Australasian
        Association for the Advancement of Science* **4**:620-645. Tasmania.

Ellis, William
    1829. *Polynesian Researches.* . . . 2 vols. London: Fisher, Son, and Jackson.

Emory, Kenneth P.
    1965. *Kapingamarangi: Social and Religious Life of a Polynesian Atoll.*
        B. P. Bishop Mus. Bull. 228. Honolulu.

Finney, Ben
    1964a. "Notes on Bond-Friendship in Tahiti." *J. Polynesian Soc.* **73**:431-435.
    1964b. "Notes sur les Relations Urbaines-rurales à Tahiti." *Bull. Soc. Etudes
        Océaniennes* No. 149, **12**(12):413-418.
    1965. *Polynesian Peasants and Proletarians.* Wellington: Polynesian Soc.
    1966. "Resource Distribution and Social Structure in Tahiti." *Ethnology*
        5:80-86.

Firth, Raymond
    1936a. *We, the Tikopia.* London: Allen and Unwin. (Reprinted 1963, Bos-
        ton: Beacon Press.)
    1936b. *Art and Life in New Guinea.* London: Studio.
    1940a. *The Work of the Gods in Tikopia.* 2 vols. London: Lund, Humphries.
    1940b. "The Analysis of Mana: An Empirical Approach." *J. Polynesian Soc.*
        49:483-510.
    1959. *Social Change in Tikopia: Re-study of a Polynesian Community after
        a Generation.* New York: Macmillan.

Fortune, Reo F.
    1932. *Sorcerers of Dobu.* London: Routledge. (Reprinted 1963. New York:
        Dutton.)

Frazer, James G.
    1922. *The Belief in Immortality and the Worship of the Dead. II. The Belief
        among the Polynesians.* London: Macmillan.

Freeman, Derek
    1964. "Some Observations on Kinship and Political Authority in Samoa."
        American Anthropologist **66**:553-568.

Freud, Sigmund
    1918. *Totem and Taboo.* New York: Moffat, Yard. (Reprinted 1960, New
        York: Random House.)

GARVAN, ANTHONY N. B.
   1951. *Architecture and Town Planning in Colonial Connecticut.* New Haven: Yale Univ. Press.

GEERTZ, CLIFFORD
   1959. "Form and Variation in Balinese Village Structure." *American Anthropologist* **61**:991-1012.

GIFFORD, E. W.
   1929. *Tongan Society.* B. P. Bishop Mus. Bull. 61. Honolulu.

GOLDMAN, IRVING
   1957. "Variations in Polynesian Social Organization." *J. Polynesian Soc.* **66**:374-390.

GOLSON, JACK (Editor)
   1962. *Polynesian Navigation: A Symposium on Andrew Sharp's Theory of Accidental Voyages.* Mem. Polynesian Soc. No. 34. Wellington.

GRACE, GEORGE W.
   1959. *The Position of the Polynesian Languages within the Austronesian (Malayo-Polynesian) Language Family.* Indiana Univ. Pub. in Anthropology and Linguistics Mem. 16. Bloomington.

GRAEBNER, F.
   1911. *Methode der Ethnologie.* Heidelberg: Winter.

GRATTAN, F. J. H.
   1948. *An Introduction to Samoan Custom.* Apia, Samoa: Samoa Printing and Pub. Co.

GREEN, ROGER C.
   1961a. "Pacific Commentary: The Tenth Pacific Science Congress. 1. Archaeology." *J. Polynesian Soc.* **70**:477-481.
   1961b. "Moorean Archaeology: A Preliminary Report." *Man* **59**(200):169-173.
   1966. "Linguistic Subgrouping within Polynesia." *J. Polynesian Soc.* **75**:6-38.

GRINDER, ROBERT E., and ROBERT E. MCMICHAEL
   1963. "Cultural Influence on Conscience Development." *J. Abnormal and Social Psychology* **66**:503-507.

GUIART, JEAN
   1963. *The Arts of the South Pacific.* London: Thames and Hudson; New York: Golden Press.

HAMILTON, AUGUSTUS
   1896. *The Art Workmanship of the Maori Race in New Zealand.* Dunedin: Fergusson and Mitchell.

HANDY, E. S. CRAIGHILL
   1927. *Polynesian Religion.* B. P. Bishop Mus. Bull. 34. Honolulu.

HEINE-GELDERN, ROBERT VON
   1937. "L'Art Prebouddhique de la Chine et de l'Asie de Sud-Est et son Influence en Océania." *Rev. Arts Asiatiques* **11**: 177-206.

HEYERDAHL, THOR
    1958. *Aku-Aku: The Secret of Easter Island*. London: Allen and Unwin.

HOCART, A. M.
    1913a. "The Fijian Custom of Tauvu." *J. Royal Anthropological Institute*
        43:101-108.
    1913b. "Heralds and Envoys in Fiji." *J. Royal Anthropological Institute*
        43:109-118.
    1915. "Chieftainship and the Sister's Son in the Pacific." *American Anthropologist* **17**:631-646.

HOGBIN, H. IAN
    1934. *Law and Order in Polynesia*. New York: Harcourt, Brace.
    1936. "Adoption in Wogeo, New Guinea." *J. Polynesian Soc.* **44**:208-215;
        45:17-38.
    1939. *Experiments in Civilization*. London: Routledge.

HOOPER, ANTONY
    1966. Marriage and Household Structure in Two Tahitian Communities.
        Ph.D. dissertation, Harvard Univ.
    In press. "Adoption in Tahiti." In VERN CARROLL (editor), *Oceanic Fosterage*.

KARDINER, ABRAM
    1939. *The Individual and His Society*. New York: Columbia Univ. Press.

KAY, PAUL
    1963a. "Urbanization in the Tahitian Household." In A. SPOEHR (editor),
        Pacific Port Towns and Cities: A Symposium, pp. 63-73. Honolulu:
        Bishop Mus. Press.
    1963b. "Tahitian Fosterage and the Form of Ethnographic Models." *American
        Anthropologist* **65**:1027-1044.
    1963c. "Aspects of Social Structure in a Tahitian Urban Neighborhood." *J.
        Polynesian Soc.* **72**:325-371.
    1964. "A Guttman Scale Model of Tahitian Consumer Behavior." *Southwestern J. Anthropology* **20**:160-167.

KEESING, FELIX M.
    1928. *The Changing Maori*. Mem. Board of Maori Ethnological Research,
        Vol. 4. New Plymouth.
    1934. *Modern Samoa, Its Government and Changing Life*. London: Allen
        and Unwin.
    1941. *The South Seas in the Modern World*. New York: Day.

KEESING, FELIX M., and MARIE M. KEESING
    1956. *Elite Communication in Samoa*. Stanford: Stanford Univ. Press. London: Oxford Univ. Press.

KRÄMER, AUGUSTIN
    1902, 1903. *Die Samoa-Inseln*. 2 vols. Stuttgart: Schweizerbartsche.

LEVY, ROBERT
    In press. "Child Management Structure and its Implications in a Tahitian
        Family." In E. VOGEL and N. BELL (editors), *A Modern Introduction
        to the Family*. (New ed.) New York: Free Press.

LEVY, ROBERT (Cont.)
  In press. "Maohi Drinking Patterns in the Society Islands." *J. Polynesian Soc.*
  In press. "Tahitian Fosterage as a Message." In VERN CARROLL (editor), *Oceanic Fosterage.*
  In press. "On Getting Angry in the Society Islands." In W. CAUDILL and TSUNG-YI LIN (editors), *Mental Health Research in Asia and the Pacific.* Honolulu: East-West Center Press.

LINTON, RALPH
  1923. "The Material Culture of the Marquesas Islands." *Mem. B. P. Bishop Mus.* **8**(5):263-471.
  1925. *Archaeology of the Marquesas Islands.* B. P. Bishop Mus. Bull. 23. Honolulu.

LINTON, RALPH, and PAUL S. WINGERT
  1946. *Arts of the South Seas.* New York: Simon and Schuster.

MACGREGOR, GORDON
  1950. Patterns and Policies of Administration of American Samoa. Paper presented at the meeting of the American Association for the Advancement of Science in Cleveland, December 29.

MCPHEE, COLIN
  1966. *Music in Bali.* New Haven and London: Yale Univ. Press.

MALINOWSKI, BRONISLAW
  1922. *Argonauts of the Western Pacific.* New York: Dutton.
  1929. *The Sexual Life of Savages in North-western Melanesia.* London: Routledge.
  1935. *Coral Gardens and Their Magic.* London: Allen and Unwin.

MALO, DAVID
  1951. *Hawaiian Antiquities.* B. P. Bishop Mus. Spec. Pub. 2 (2nd ed.). Honolulu.

MARETT, R. R.
  1909. *The Threshold of Religion.* London: Methuen.

MEAD, MARGARET
  1928a. *Coming of Age in Samoa.* New York: Morrow. (Reprinted 1949, Mentor. New York: New American Library).
  1928b. *An Inquiry into the Question of Cultural Stability in Polynesia.* Columbia Univ. Contributions to Anthropology, Vol. 9. New York: Columbia Univ. Press. (Reprint in press.)
  1930a. *Social Organization of Manua.* B. P. Bishop Mus. Bull. 76. Honolulu.
  1930b. "An Ethnologist's Footnote to *Totem and Taboo.*" *Psychoanalytic Review* **17**(3):297-304.
  1930c. *Growing Up in New Guinea.* New York: Morrow. (Reprinted 1962, New York: Morrow.)
  1934a. "Kinship in the Admiralty Islands." *Anthropological Pap.*, American Mus. Nat. Hist. **34**(2):181-358. New York.
  1934b. "Tabu." In EDWIN R. A. SELIGMAN and ALVIN JOHNSON (editors), *Encyclopedia of the Social Sciences,* pp. 502-505. New York: Macmillan.

MEAD, MARGARET (Cont.)

 1938. "The Mountain Arapesh. I. An Importing Culture." *Anthropological Pap.,* American Mus. Nat. Hist. **36**(3):139-349. New York.

 1939. "The Strolling Players in the Mountains of Bali." *Natural History* **43**:17-26, 64.

 1940. "The Arts in Bali." *Yale Review* **30**:335-347.

 1947. "The Mountain Arapesh. III. Socio-Economic Life. IV. Diary of Events in Alitoa." *Anthropological Pap.,* American Mus. Nat. Hist. **49**(3): 161-419. New York.

 1949. *Male and Female.* New York: Morrow. (Reprinted 1955, Mentor. New York: New American Library.)

 1963. *"Totem and Taboo* Reconsidered with Respect." *Menninger Clinic Bull.* **27**:185-199.

 1964. *Continuities in Cultural Evolution.* New Haven: Yale Univ. Press. (Reprinted 1966, New Haven: Yale Univ. Press.)

MEAD, MARGARET, and THEODORE SCHWARTZ

 [n.d.] A Study of Cultural Systematics in New Guinea. In preparation.

MÉTRAUX, ALFRED

 1940. *Ethnology of Easter Island.* B. P. Bishop Mus. Bull. 160. Honolulu.

MOENCH, RICHARD

 1963. "A Preliminary Report on Chinese Social and Economic Organization in the Society Islands." In A. SPOEHR (editor), *Pacific Port Towns and Cities: A Symposium,* pp. 75-89. Honolulu: Bishop Mus. Press.

MORGAN, LEWIS H.

 1870. "Systems of Consanguinity and Affinity of the Human Family." *Smithsonian Contributions to Knowledge* **17**(218). Washington: Smithsonian Institution.

MURDOCK, GEORGE P.

 1949. *Social Structure.* New York: Macmillan.

OLIVER, DOUGLAS

 [n.d.] Ancient Tahitian Society. In preparation.

OLIVER, DOUGLAS, and OTHERS

 In press. Social Change in Tahiti: 1767-1964.

PERRY, W. J.

 1923. *The Children of the Sun.* London: Methuen.

POWDERMAKER, HORTENSE

 1933. *Life in Lessu.* New York: Norton.

RADCLIFFE-BROWN, A. R.

 1924. "The Mother's Brother in South Africa." *South African J. Science* **21**:542-555.

RITCHIE, JAMES E.

 1956a. *Basic Personality in Rakau.* Victoria Univ. College Pub. in Psychology No. 8. Wellington.

 1956b. "Human Problems and Educational Change in a Maori Community." *J. Polynesian Soc.* **65**:13-34.

RITCHIE, JANE
    1957. *Childhood in Rakau: The First Five Years of Life.* Victoria Univ. College Pub. in Psychology No. 10. Wellington.

RIVERS, W. H. R.
    1910. "The Father's Sister in Oceania." *Folklore* **21**:42-59.
    1914. *The History of Melanesian Society.* 2 vols. Cambridge: Cambridge Univ. Press.

ROBLEY, HORATIO G.
    1896. *Moko: Or Maori Tattooing.* London: Chapman and Hall.

SAHLINS, MARSHALL D.
    1958. *Social Stratification in Polynesia.* Seattle: Univ. Washington Press.

SCHNEIDER, DAVID M., and GEORGE C. HOMANS
    1955. "Kinship Terminology and the American Kinship System." *American Anthropologist* **57**:1194-1208.

SCHWARTZ, THEODORE
    1963. "Systems of Areal Integration: Some Considerations Based on the Admiralty Islands of Northern Melanesia." *Anthropological Forum* **1**:56-97.
    [n.d.] New Bunai—An Amalgamated Village. Manuscript.

SELIGMAN, CHARLES G.
    1910. *The Melanesians of British New Guinea.* Cambridge: Cambridge Univ. Press.

SHAPIRO, HARRY L.
    1936. *The Heritage of the Bounty.* New York: Simon and Schuster. (Reprinted 1962, Natural History Library, Garden City: Doubleday.)

SHARP, ANDREW
    1964. *Ancient Voyagers in Polynesia.* Berkeley: Univ. California Press.

SIMMONS, R. T.
    1962. "Blood Group Genes in Polynesians and Comparisons with Other Pacific Peoples." *Oceania* **32**:198-210.

SKINNER, H. D.
    1921. "Culture Areas in New Zealand." *J. Polynesian Soc.* **30**:71-78.

SMITH, G. ELLIOT
    1916. "The Influence of Ancient Egyptian Culture in the East and in America." *Bull. John Rylands Library.*

SMITH, S. PERCY
    1904. *Hawaiki.* (2nd ed.) Christchurch and London: Whitcombe and Tombs.

STAIR, J. B.
    1897. *Old Samoa.* London: Religious Tract Soc.

STEINEN, KARL VON DEN
    1925. *Die Marquesaner und Ihre Kunst.* Vol. I. *Tatauierung.* Berlin: Reimer.

STEINER, FRANZ
    1956. *Taboo.* London: Cohen and West. New York: Philosophical Library.

SUGGS, ROBERT C.
  1961. "The Archaeology of Nuku Hiva, Marquesas Islands, French Poly-
      nesia." *Anthropological Pap.,* American Mus. Nat. Hist. **49**(1):1-205.

TREGEAR, EDWARD
  1904. *The Maori Race.* Wanganvi, New Zealand: Willis.

VAYDA, ANDREW P.
  1966. "Diversity and Uniformity in New Guinea." *Acta Ethnographica Sci-
      entiarum Hungaricae* **15**:293-300.

WALSH, D. S., and BRUCE BIGGS
  1966. *Proto-Polynesian Word List I.* Te Reo Monographs. Linguistic Soc.
      New Zealand. Auckland.

WEDGWOOD, CAMILLA H.
  1934. "Report on Research in Manam Island, Mandated Territory of New
      Guinea." *Oceania* **4**:373-403.

WILLIAMSON, ROBERT W.
  1937. *Religion and Social Organization in Central Polynesia.* Cambridge:
      Cambridge Univ. Press.

NEW PERSPECTIVES ON POLYNESIAN VOYAGING

BEN R. FINNEY

University of California, Santa Barbara
Bernice P. Bishop Museum, Honolulu

THE TRADITIONAL VIEW that planned exploration and colonization played a major role in the Polynesian expansion into the Eastern Pacific has been challenged recently by those who see drift and random one-way voyages as the primary means by which the islands of Polynesia were settled. This controversy over the issue of what type of voyaging was involved in the settlement of Polynesia has usually been phrased in terms of the "accidental" versus the "purposeful" theory of Polynesian voyaging. Although writers supporting one or the other theory have filled many a journal and monograph page during the last decade, minimal progress has been made in understanding the nature of Polynesian voyaging. In part this may be due to the polemical approach of opposing writers whose exchanges have often taken on an air of "Yes, they can!" "No, they can't!", to paraphrase the song from Irving Berlin's *Annie Get Your Gun*. But it also is traceable to a lack of reliable data on canoe performance, navigational capabilities, and other points crucial to the issue. Until recently the only sources available on such points have been the sketchy and often ambiguous reports by the first European visitors to Polynesia, reports which lend themselves to selective citation to support either side. This paper attempts to avoid polemics and to advance our knowledge of the voyaging phase of Polynesian culture history by applying new and experimentally derived data on Polynesian canoe performance and navigation to the issue.[1]

---
[1] This analysis originated from experimental research on Polynesian voyaging supported by the National Science Foundation (Grant No. GS-1244), the University of California, Santa Barbara, and Bernice P. Bishop Museum.

Experimental research is not new to anthropology (Ascher, 1961), or to research on primitive voyaging, but its meaning in these fields is often misunderstood. Much of the misunderstanding arises from the belief that all experiments are "crucial experiments" in the sense that they will definitely "prove" or "disprove" a disputed theory. However, neither the 1893 voyage of a reconstructed Viking ship to North America (Philips-Birt, 1966, pp. 56-57) nor the 1947 voyage of the *Kon-Tiki* (Heyerdahl, 1950) validates a particular theory of settlement.[2] Yet these and other experiments in voyaging are useful insofar as they provide new information, where before only crude estimates existed, to be used for refining or reformulating hypotheses concerning the nature of the voyaging in question. It is in this spirit that my experiments in Polynesian voyaging were attempted, and in the same spirit that preliminary interpretations based on the results of my work, and that of others who have applied the experimental method to the problem, are offered.

The utility of this attempt to apply experimentally derived data to the voyaging issue is, I believe, enhanced by applying the data to a particular voyaging situation, not just the issue in abstract. Hawaii, its settlement, and subsequent contact between it and other Polynesian islands, provides the voyaging situation. This restriction to one voyaging situation involves a narrow focus but one which should illuminate the issue considerably, for an examination of Hawaii can tell us much about Polynesian voyaging in general. This is so because of Hawaii's isolated geographical position thousands of miles to the north of other major Polynesian centers, and because recent archaeological and linguistic work provides us with a firm hypothesis concerning where Hawaii's first settlers came from (Marquesas Islands), and the source of subsequent contacts from the outside (Tahiti). By applying our data to the probable conditions faced by the voyagers crossing the seas between the Marquesas and Hawaii, and Tahiti[3] and Hawaii, we can examine two of the longest reputed examples of Polynesian voyaging.

THE ISSUE: ACCIDENTAL VERSUS PURPOSEFUL VOYAGING

The publication in 1956 of Andrew Sharp's *Ancient Voyagers in the Pacific* initiated the modern controversy on Polynesian voyaging. His

---

[2] Heyerdahl (1950, p. 297) recognizes this and cautions that "My migration theory, as such, was not necessarily proved by the successful outcome of the *Kon-Tiki* expedition. What we did prove was that the South American balsa raft possesses qualities not previously known to scientists of our time. . . ."

[3] Tahiti is used in this paper to denote the entire Society group.

views, which are still central to the controversy, are cited to provide background for the analysis presented later.

Sharp's thesis is simple, and—as he himself admits—by no means new. Except for voyaging between adjacent islands, the Polynesians did not have the means to sail out to distant and unknown islands, discover them, retrace their course to their home island, and then send out men and women on great colonizing expeditions loaded with food plants, domesticated animals, and other cargo necessary to start a new colony. The most distant purposeful voyaging Sharp accepts is that known from early European records: the several hundred miles separating Tahiti and the Society group from the Tuamotus, and the slightly greater distances separating Tonga, Fiji, and Samoa. Beyond that, all voyaging and settlement is "accidental" to Sharp. That is, islands with no near neighbors, such as New Zealand, Hawaii, the Marquesas, the Australs, or Easter Island, were discovered and settled by two means: either by the chance arrival of a canoe-load of people driven off some known course in one of the regular navigating areas (such as between Raiatea and Tahiti, or Tahiti and Ana'a); or by the arrival of a canoe-load of exiles—men and women who, because of war or famine, were driven from their native island, and who were searching blindly for some new and virgin island on which to settle.

The use of the word "accidental" to describe the latter form of settlement—that by a randomly searching group of exiles—was unfortunate, for it led to much needless controversy and obscured—at least to some of his critics—Sharp's actual argument. In the new edition of his book, Sharp (1964) clears the air immensely by substituting "one-way" for "accidental," thereby making clear that his thesis is not primarily concerned with accidents but with one-way voyages with little or no probability of return. The crux of Sharp's position then comes down to the idea that once Polynesians reached, by either drift or exile voyage, an island of more than 300 or so miles from their homeland, they did not have the necessary maritime equipment or skills to return to that homeland, much less to return, organize a colonizing expedition, and retrace their course to the new island in order to found a colony.

Sharp's argument in support of his proposition rests ultimately on his assessment of Polynesian marine technology and the environment facing the voyagers. From Sharp's portrayal of the Pacific one gains the impression that the islands of Polynesia are but tiny specks of land, that clouds often obscure the stars from navigators, and that shifting winds, often whipped to gale force, as well as shifting currents, make voyaging extremely hazardous. He points out that the Polynesian navigational system

did not allow any absolute reckoning of longitude, and could not predict-
ably guide the islander to a distant landfall because the shifting winds
and currents would render his rudimentary skills useless (Sharp, 1964,
pp. 34-53). The navigator was further at the mercy of the winds, according to Sharp (1964, pp. 54-61), because his craft was unequal to the
task; it could not be sailed well to windward, and if pointed to windward
the vegetable fibers holding the hulls together were vulnerable to the
stress imposed by pounding headseas. In addition, Sharp maintains that
the broad beam and high freeboard of ocean-going canoes would eliminate paddling as a significant aid in long-distance voyaging. Although
Sharp (1964, pp. 52-53) gives credit to the Polynesians for outstanding
short-range navigational feats, because of the deficiencies he posits for
their canoes and navigational system he can only come to negative conclusions about the long-range navigational capabilities of Polynesian
voyagers.

The above is, I believe, a fair rendering of Sharp's position. Arguments brought to bear against his position have been many—too many
to summarize here—although interested readers might consult Golson's
(1963) critical monograph on Sharp's thesis, and Sharp's latest monograph (1964) for discussion of these arguments and for citations of the
many critical papers.

THE POLYNESIAN DOUBLE CANOE

It is generally agreed that the double canoe, because of its greater
carrying capacity and greater stability, and not the outrigger canoe, was
the craft primarily used in long-distance voyaging.

From this starting point, after having identified the voyaging craft,
most writers discussing Polynesian voyaging immediately jump to estimates of that craft's sailing characteristics and seaworthiness without
specifying the design of the hulls, the type of sail used, or the other design
features crucial to sea handling. This disinclination even to sketch the
voyaging canoe design features is understandable in light of the paucity
of information. There is no written, pictorial, or detailed traditional account which can furnish direct evidence of the details characteristic of
voyaging canoes used during the era of settlement, the period from, say,
the time of Christ to A.D. 1400. The only clues we have are the designs
of the double canoes characteristic of each island group as recorded by
European observers in the 17th, 18th, and early 19th centuries. Using
these sometimes excellent representations, and inferences based on the
distribution of design features, along with accounts of design changes

early in the European era, it is possible to make a reasonable hypothesis as to the basic features of early voyaging canoes.

Fortunately, two works, *Canoes of Oceania* by A. C. Haddon and James Hornell (1936–1938), and *An Analysis of the Design of the Major Sea-Going Craft of Oceania* by H. P. Whitney (1955), have covered much of the ground for the analysis, which is summarized below.

The double canoes of Polynesia known from early European reports fall into two categories: (1) combination sailing and paddling craft with a relatively low freeboard, definite bow and stern structurally differentiated, and some form of the oceanic sprit sail (a triangular sail lashed apex down to a mast, with a single yard); (2) a primarily sailing craft with relatively high freeboard, double-ended hulls (either end could serve as the bow or stern), and some form of the oceanic lateen sail (a triangular sail with two yards coming together at the apex which is attached to the bow, the whole sail being slung from a mast located aft of the apex attachment). The double canoes of Tahiti, the Marquesas, and Hawaii are the best representatives of the former category, whereas the double canoes of Samoa and Tonga influenced by Fijian designs (and the Fijian canoes themselves, if Fiji may be included in this survey of Polynesian canoe types), and the Tuamotu double canoe fall into the latter category. Working on the principle that the most widely distributed form is likely to be the oldest in time, it would seem that the combination paddling and sailing craft best represents the design of the early voyaging canoes, and that the more sophisticated designs known in the Tuamotus and Western Polynesia represent modern innovations. For Western Polynesia there is good evidence from European reports that the double-ended feature of their canoes, and the true form of the oceanic lateen sail, came there from Fiji early in the European era, and there is inferential evidence that Micronesia is the ultimate home of these innovations.

The above inferences indicate that the settlement of Polynesia was accomplished by voyagers (whether drift, exile, or purposeful navigators) sailing, and perhaps paddling at times, in canoes of a relatively unsophisticated design. Compared to the lateen sail, the sprit sail is less efficient, particularly in going to windward. The double-ended feature, plus the lateen sail—which is moved to the opposite end of the canoe in tacking—provides a much more maneuverable combination than the fixed bow and stern, sprit sail combination. Probably because of the higher efficiency of their sail and hull design, the double-ended, lateen sail canoes could raise their freeboard high above the water, whereas the less efficient fixed bow and stern, sprit sail canoes probably retained a relatively low freeboard so that paddling could aid in maneuvering and moving the craft through the water.

Beyond the essentials—sprit sail, fixed bow and stern, and a low freeboard for paddling—it is difficult to refine our reconstruction of the double canoes known in Polynesia a thousand or so years ago. However, some idea of the nature of the basic design can be gained by considering the Hawaiian double canoe, which according to Haddon and Hornell (1936, Vol. I, p. 339) is the one known canoe type most conservative of the basic voyaging design.

There are well-documented reports of Hawaiian double canoes of 70 feet in length, and one less well-documented report of a canoe 108 feet in length.[4] Little detailed information on carrying capacity was recorded, although there are reports of loads of up to 80 men. Each hull had a definite bow, marked by a narrowing of the hull, an increase in the sheer line, and a high cutwater, and a definite stern. The hulls were not decked over, leaving maximum room for paddlers, although woven pandanus covers, with holes for paddlers, helped to prevent swamping in heavy seas. Also, probably for the benefit of paddling, the freeboard was relatively low, perhaps not much over 2 feet in the largest canoes. On the larger canoes, at least four main crosspieces and a bow and a stern crosspiece joined the hulls. Along the top of the crosspieces a narrow platform was lashed, but except for a portion near the stern of the craft where an extra platform was sometimes erected across the hulls, enough room was left between the inboard sides of the hulls and the central platform to permit paddlers to alternate their outboard strokes with inboard strokes for full paddling efficiency. One or two masts were set into U-shaped steps lashed to the central platform. Lashed to the mast or masts was a sail made of woven pandanus formed into a triangular shape (apex down) with a curved boom lashed along the outer edge. Steering was accomplished by large paddles held, but apparently not permanently lashed, against the hulls near the stern.

Concerning the performance of voyaging double canoes there are three main points in dispute: (1) the ability of canoes to sail to windward; (2) the ability of paddlers to aid or replace the sails in providing forward propulsion, particularly in headwinds and calms; and (3) the ability of the craft to stand up to stresses imposed by heavy seas. On each of these points information from the European record on modern double canoes is sketchy or seemingly contradictory. Recently,

---

[4] This summary is based on descriptions of Hawaiian canoes by Haddon and Hornell (1936, Vol. 1, pp. 6-23) and Buck (1957, pp. 253-284), and my own unpublished research.

however, some light has been shed on the first two of these points by experimental work in two sets of experiments: one by Charles Bechtol (1963), who worked with 30-inch models of sailing canoes; another by the author, who worked with a 40-foot replica of a Hawaiian double canoe.

Bechtol's work with sailing models was primarily directed toward finding out if Polynesian canoe designs were capable of being sailed to windward. Using double-canoe models with sharp V-shaped hulls, and models with rounded hulls and very large steering paddles, he found that these designs were capable of sailing within 45 degrees of the wind. Models with rounded hulls but comparatively small steering paddles (the size of the steering paddles, he reasons, may be limited by the ability of the steersman to brace it) could, however, only sail within 60 to 80 degrees of the wind. In concluding his discussion on the windward capabilities of Polynesian canoes, Bechtol cites the difficulties experienced by racing yachts and old-time sailing ships to argue against the possibility that Polynesians could have made lengthy crossings sailing very close to the wind. He thinks it likely that the Polynesians, to avoid punishment to both crew and canoe, did not force their canoes closer than 70 or 80 degrees to the wind on extended voyages.

My work was concerned with both the sailing characteristics of the double canoe and the ability of paddlers to aid in its propulsion. The experimental program is, unfortunately, only partially completed; more sailing tests must be performed, and the data taken from the physiological tests of paddling have not been fully analyzed. The findings stated here are, therefore, both incomplete and tentative, although it is felt that they are sufficiently valid and interesting to warrant disclosing at this opportune time.

Following detailed plans made by Paris (1841, Plate 127) and other data on Hawaiian canoes, a Hawaiian double canoe was reconstructed. The overall length is 40 feet. Each hull has a maximum depth of almost 3 feet and a maximum beam of almost 2 feet. The hulls are placed approximately 3½ feet apart and are joined by four major crosspieces and a bow and a stern crosspiece. A central platform is lashed along the top of these crosspieces. Because of the high costs and difficulty of reviving lost skills, modern materials were used throughout the construction. The hulls, for example, were formed of fiberglass in a mold taken from the hull of a large Hawaiian outrigger canoe, and the crosspieces were made of laminated oak. The whole assembly was built solidly, both for safety and to simulate the weight of a double canoe made from local hardwoods. The total weight (unloaded) is just over 3,000 pounds, which is a few hundred pounds in excess of the estimated weight of a canoe of equal dimensions made from Hawaiian materials. The use of modern materials eliminates the possibility of performing any experiments concerning the double canoe's ability to withstand stress, but because Hawaiian design is followed throughout, the canoe can be used to provide useful data on sailing and paddling performance.[5]

Testing began in Santa Barbara, California (where the canoe was built) during July and August, 1966, and continued in the Hawaiian Islands during September and October of 1966. To complete the experiments, tests will be resumed during the summer months of 1968.

Testing under sail was done off the shore of Oahu Island in light and moderate seas, and in trade winds varying from a few knots to about twenty. Most of the testing time was occupied with learning how to sail the Hawaiian rig, which is radically different from modern sailing rigs, and also different from anything in the experience of Hawaiian crewmen employed to handle the sails and to steer. Some idea, however, was gained of the performance characteristics of the Hawaiian design. For example, as could be expected, the craft sailed well downwind, with speeds of at least 8 knots reached in moderate trade winds. In heavier winds the speed would probably increase. The canoe was also efficient in sailing across the wind (90 degrees to the wind), making at least 6 knots. However, in sailing to windward the craft was much less efficient: in very light airs it was difficult to make much headway to windward, although in heavier winds the windward ability of the craft picked up markedly. Speeds of about 4 to 5 knots were reached in moderate trade winds, with the canoe making way 75 degrees to the wind. The canoe can actually point closer to the wind than 75 degrees, but because of its lack of keel or deep steering paddles, it makes considerable leeway, so that the resultant angle is not less than 75 degrees.

It should be emphasized that the Hawaiian design is not necessarily

---

[5] A sail of heavy canvas cut in the shape of a Hawaiian sprit sail was used in place of a sail made of pandanus matting. I doubt that the performance of this sail was superior to a pandanus sail because: (1) it was poorly cut and did not draw well; (2) a cloth sail is not necessarily better than a pandanus sail. Many Micronesians, for example, still prefer the performance of pandanus sails to those of canvas (Samuel Falanruw, personal communication, November 13, 1966). Also it should be mentioned that the test paddles were made of heavy hardwood to simulate the heavy *koa* paddles formerly used in Hawaii.

the same as that of earlier voyaging canoes. The Hawaiian design appears to embody modifications adaptive to the conditions prevailing in Hawaiian waters (the seas and wind in the channels separating the Hawaiian Islands are usually rougher and stronger than those found on the high seas between Hawaii and its southern neighbors). Adaptation is apparent in the crosspieces connecting the hulls, the manner of lashing the crosspieces to the hulls, the rigging and mast and sail, and in the hull form.[6] While these features may add to the ruggedness and ease of handling the canoe in rough water, they would not appear to enhance the canoe's overall sailing performance. If anything, the special hull form of the Hawaiian canoe—which is rounded and shaped in such a way (deep aft, but shallow toward the bow) to make it manageable in rough seas—probably detracts from the ability of the canoe to resist making leeway sailing to windward. The windward ability of the Hawaiian canoe as determined in our tests would therefore certainly represent no improvement over that of voyaging canoes, which perhaps had hulls better adapted to resisting leeward movement.

Bearing the above in mind, the finding that the Hawaiian double canoe can sail within 75 degrees to the wind may be accepted as a conservative estimate[7] of the double canoe's windward sailing ability. This figure agrees with Bechtol's results on tests on models with rounded hulls and small steering paddles. If either the hulls of our test canoe were made more V-shaped or deep steering paddles were used, windward performance might be increased. However, if Bechtol's strictures concerning extended windward sailing are to be accepted, the 75 degree figure probably represents a realistic estimate of the windward performance capability of a voyaging canoe.

Paddling tests involved physiological testing of experienced Hawaiian racing paddlers to gain information on speed and endurance in paddling a heavy double canoe, and the "cost" of paddling in terms of energy expenditures and food and water intake needed to maintain the required level of effort.[8] The major test was a round trip of about 52 miles, paddled in two days by a crew of twelve men (eight regular paddlers,

---

[6] These adaptations are the subject of a paper in preparation.

[7] Maximum performance of the ancient Polynesian double canoe would certainly not approach that of the modern catamaran. Although the latter is based on the Polynesian double-hull concept, modern materials, construction techniques, and design innovations give it a speed and windward ability in excess of most mono-hull racing yachts (Finney, 1959).

[8] Physiological measurements were taken and are being analyzed by the staff of the Institute of Environmental Stress, University of California, Santa Barbara, under the supervision of the director, Steven M. Horvath.

two relief paddlers, and two steersmen) in the test canoe loaded to a total weight of about 6,000 pounds. Physiological data from this and other tests are still being analyzed, but a preliminary estimate of the results may be hazarded.

The paddlers showed that they could move the test canoe through calm water at slightly over 3 knots when paddling at a relaxed rate for eight consecutive hours (maximum speed at a racing pace was over 6 knots), and felt that they could, if given sufficient rest, food, and water, keep this up for at least several consecutive days. The apparent food and water requirements would appear to be high. Although data on caloric expenditure are not yet available, preliminary figures on water loss indicate about 5 pounds per day per man. Paddling against wind and current, though possible, proved to be extremely difficult and slow (even though, as would be done on a voyage, mast and sail were lowered to reduce wind resistance). The speed of the canoe was slowed to about 1 knot when paddling against a slight current and a 20-knot headwind. The paddlers estimated that if there had also been a strong headsea (the paddling was done in the lee of Oahu), little or no forward progress would have been possible. Paddling would, therefore, appear to have been useful to voyagers in calms or light wind and sea conditions, but not in the face of contrary wind, current, and seas—at least for any long distances.

The above indicates that given sufficient food and water, paddlers could materially speed the progress of a double canoe through calm seas and winds at the rate of approximately 25 miles a day. This assumes that only one paddling crew is available and that it works only 8 hours out of 24. A canoe longer and larger than the experimental canoe would accommodate a bigger crew which could split paddling shifts and increase daily progress, although the increased bulk of the canoe might slow the paddling speed, and thus detract from the advantage of a bigger crew.

THE POLYNESIAN NAVIGATION SYSTEM

Most authors agree that the Polynesian navigators used a stellar navigation system, although many are hazy about the system's actual features. Fortunately, Frankel (1962), an engineer and former navigator, has realistically described the system, the main features of which are summarized as follows:

(1) *Sidereal Compass.*—Bearings taken off the rising and setting points of stars provide a sidereal compass. The navigator uses this compass for general orientation and to sail toward an island by steering toward the star on the horizon, and the other stars that subsequently appear on the horizon at approximately the same point, that indicate the desired course.

(2) *Zenith Star.*—The navigator tells when he has arrived at the latitude of his destination by observing when the zenith star or stars are directly overhead his canoe.

(3) *Latitude Sailing.*—The navigator has no means to determine longitude. Instead of trying to hit the destination directly, he attempts to sail to the windward side of his destination (using the sidereal compass for direction), and upon reaching the latitude of his destination (determined from the zenith stars), he sails downwind along that latitude to make his landfall. Observations of land birds, floating debris, cloud effects over the island, as well as distant sights of the island, aid in making the landfall.

Although the skeptic might accept the above features as adding up to a theoretically workable navigation system, he still would have room for questioning the accuracy of the system. Can, for example, a navigator follow a given course just by observing a succession of stars on the horizon? Or, can he find his latitude with any accuracy by the zenith star method? To answer these and other questions, David Lewis attempted, in 1965, to sail from Tahiti to New Zealand via Raiatea and Rarotonga by using the Polynesian navigation system exclusively (Lewis, 1966). The passage was made in a modern catamaran, with a European navigator—banished to the other hull—making constant checks on Lewis' accuracy. Except for one error in the Cook Islands, Lewis' Polynesian navigating was reasonably accurate for he was able to hit his ultimate objective and to keep fairly good track of his position as he progressed across the Pacific. His voyage did not, of course, prove that the Tahitians navigated to New Zealand, but it did indicate that the features of the navigation system and their combination were workable: Lewis was able to use the stars and other heavenly bodies as a compass and to direct his craft where he wanted it to go; he was able to use zenith stars to tell his latitude, usually well within one degree (60 miles); and he was able to hold his latitude fairly well to make his final landfall.

A paper published by Lewis (1964) prior to this voyage should serve to forestall critics who would note that finding the huge mass of New Zealand does not tell us anything applicable to the voyaging situation in tropical Polynesia where islands are tiny dots amid the huge expanse of the Pacific. The point Lewis makes is that most of the islands of Polynesia are not lone islands but islands within groups, and that when one realizes that each island within a group may be sighted many miles away at sea (particularly if it is a large volcanic island like Hawaii or Tahiti) it is apparent that most navigation within Polynesia can be done between "island blocks" of sizable dimensions. Lewis (1964, p. 369) calculates, for example, that the Tonga block extends 260 miles on its north-south axis, and 140 miles on its east-west axis. To find an island within such a huge island block, the navigator must aim for the block as a whole and, once having made a landfall in the block, work his way by short interisland journeys to his destination. Absolved of the necessity of searching only for tiny dots of islands, the Polynesian navigator's burden—and the requirements of accuracy placed on his system—is considerably lessened.

HAWAII AND POLYNESIAN VOYAGING

Kenneth Emory, on the basis of archaeological and linguistic work done by him and his associates (Emory, 1946, 1963; Emory and Sinoto, 1965; Green, 1966; Sinoto, 1962), posits a case for two distinct settlements of Hawaii. The first settlement appears to have come from the Marquesas Islands about A.D. 750. The second settlement appears to have come from Tahiti, the archaeological, linguistic, and traditional evidence indicating a prolonged relationship between these two areas occurring between the 12th and 14th centuries A.D. We have, then, firm evidence of settlement along two long voyage routes: the 1,890 miles that separate the Marquesas and Hawaii; and the 2,220 miles that separate Tahiti and Hawaii. Our problem is to estimate the nature of the voyaging—whether drift journeys, one-way exile voyages, or planned colonization involving two-way voyaging—that occurred along these routes. But before immediately offering hypotheses based on our experimental data, it is necessary to consider the natural conditions along the sea routes.

Hawaii, Tahiti, and the Marquesas lie within the trade-wind area of the Pacific, but since Hawaii is north of the equator and the other two are south of the equator, the angle and intensity of the trades vary. From Tahiti and the Marquesas north until about 5 degrees above the equator, the trades blow predominantly from the east-southeast, mostly in the range of from 5 to 15 knots. The next few hundred miles, usually up to about 9 degrees north, although the boundaries are always shifting, are known as the doldrums or equatorial calms. Here the trade winds often slacken and sometimes die, and humid rainy conditions marked by cumulus clouds and frequent squalls interrupt the relatively cool and clear trade-wind conditions. Above 9 degrees north and for several hundred miles north of Hawaii the trade winds return in strength, blowing this time predominantly from the east-northeast mostly in the range of from 10 to 20 knots. Except for the doldrum area, the trades of this region of the Pacific are remarkably constant, although they often fluctuate in their exact direction and intensity. Only in the summer months around Tahiti and the Marquesas do westerly winds occasionally intrude, as northwest storms sweep through the area. During the same time, which is Hawaii's winter, the trades there are sometimes interrupted by southerly winds and very occasionally by westerlies.

The trade-wind area, it should be emphasized, is an ideal "fair weather" sailing area since cloud cover and rainfall is slight and gales and hurricanes are rare.

Ocean currents in the trade-wind area generally follow the wind: in the trade-wind belts north and south of the equator the currents flow westward at an average of between 10 and 20 miles a day. In the doldrums, although the wind and current do not always coincide, the equatorial countercurrent flows in an easterly direction at between 20 and 25 miles a day.

We are now ready to match the performance of the double canoe with the winds and currents of the eastern Pacific to consider the probable nature of the voyaging along the routes in question. The Marquesas–Hawaii route will be considered first, followed by the Tahiti–Hawaii route.

Archaeological and linguistic data indicate that the first settlement of Hawaii came from the Marquesas. The relevant questions before us are: (1) How was the settlement voyage (or voyages) accomplished —by a drift, or by an actual sail in search of new land? (2) Could the settlers have returned to the Marquesas and initiated two-way communication between the groups?

To aid in considering the probabilities involved in these questions, a map (Fig. 1) of the area has been drawn on which prevailing winds and currents are indicated, with possible routes drawn in. The winds and currents are indicated as means which have been derived from data recorded since the last century during the months of June, July, and August, the period of fair weather and steady trade winds most

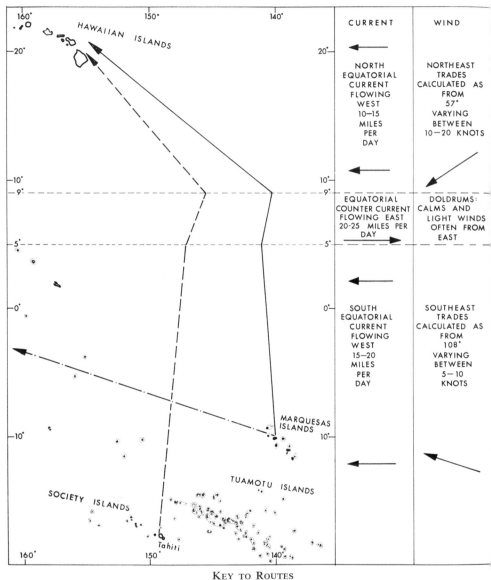

KEY TO ROUTES

1. ————————————————————————

2. — · — · — · — · — · — · —

3. — — — — — — — — — — —

FIGURE 1.—Discovery routes to Hawaii. 1, Discovery route from the Marquesas to Hawaii sailed at 105 degrees to the wind. 2, Westerly track of a canoe drifting from the Marquesas before wind and current. 3, Discovery route from Tahiti to Hawaii sailed at 95 degrees to the wind. Sailed courses assume that the canoes will average 144 miles a day in trade-wind areas and 48 miles a day in the doldrums. (Map drawn by William K. Kikuchi, Bishop Museum.)

favorable for voyaging.[9] Although it is unlikely that conditions in any one year, particularly some year ten or more centuries ago, would exactly follow these means,[10] the figures do provide an explicit starting point for the analysis. Once probabilities are established using these figures, estimates could be made, for example, of how much a shift in mean wind direction would affect voyaging possibilities on a given route.

From an examination of prevailing winds and currents it is apparent that unless there was a most aberrant and prolonged reversal of conditions, a canoe could never drift, in the sense of moving directly with the wind and current, from the Marquesas to Hawaii. The route would have to be sailed at approximately 105 degrees to the wind, a favorable angle for a double canoe since the wind would be slightly behind the canoe pushing it forward at about 5 to 6 knots with little tendency to make leeway to the west. Assuming that the canoe could average 6 knots in the southeast and northeast trades, and 2 knots in the doldrums (calculated on the basis of paddling 25 miles in one day of calms, and sailing 72 miles in alternate days of light easterly winds), such a voyage would take about 20 days if made directly.

Since the Marquesans would have no foreknowledge of Hawaii, we must assume that such a voyage might be one of many expeditions that set off to search for new lands to the northwest. It would only be pure chance that Hawaii would be discovered, although the huge bulk of the Hawaiian Island block would allow canoes pointing slightly north or slightly south of the islands to sight and reach the new land.

It would seem unlikely, however, that once the Marquesans reached Hawaii they could have returned to their homeland and initiated two-way communication. Hawaii lies approximately 850 miles west of the Marquesas, and the dominant easterly wind and current would prevent a canoe from making the necessary easting to make a direct landfall on the Marquesas. The improbability of such a voyage is compounded if we consider that in order to navigate safely to their home islands, Marquesan navigators would want to be sure to reach the latitude of the Marquesas well to the windward, or eastern, side of the group.

---

[9] Data on winds and ocean currents were abstracted from Navy Pilot Charts (United States Navy, 1960, 1965) and Marine Climatic Atlas (United States Navy, 1959).

[10] Since the direction of the earth's rotation has not changed in the last millenium, it is not likely that the pattern of winds and currents this rotation spawns would have greatly changed, although variation from year to year probably occurred.

To do this, the canoe would be required to sail at least within 65 degrees to the wind, 10 degrees more than our estimate of the maximum windward ability of the Polynesian double canoe. Sailing to windward at the estimated best possible angle of 75 degrees would bring a canoe to within about 270 miles of the Marquesas on the downwind, or western, side, with little prospect of being able to beat to windward to make a landfall. A canoe continuing on this tack would eventually reach the Tuamotu Islands, and from there—by waiting for westerly winds that occasionally occur during the summer months (November-March)— might be able to sail to the Marquesas. However, the difficulty of such a return passage makes it unlikely that any significant two-way voyaging between the Marquesas and Hawaii could have been initiated along such a circuitous route.

A glance at Figure 2 will suffice to show the improbability of a drift voyage across the wind and current from Tahiti to Hawaii. Just as it would have to be on the Marquesas-to-Hawaii route, a voyage from Tahiti to Hawaii would have to be made under sail. In this case a canoe sailed at 95 degrees to the wind—still a very favorable angle for a double canoe—could make a landfall on Hawaii, the main island of the Hawaiian group. Again, as in the Marquesan case, a course slightly closer to the wind or away from the wind would still bring a canoe to within the range of the island block formed by all the Hawaiian Islands.

Unlike the Marquesan case, however, there is some possibility that a canoe from Tahiti which reached Hawaii could be sailed back to Tahiti and that two-way communication might thereby be initiated. Hawaii and Tahiti are almost ideally aligned for long-distance two-way communication, for they lie almost in a north-south relationship with a dominant easterly wind blowing over the course almost at right angles. If these island groups did lie exactly on a north-south course, and if the winds were directly from 90 degrees, and there were no current, then canoes could sail back and forth on a broad reach (90 degrees to the wind) between groups. The actual situation departs somewhat from the ideal, necessitating some windward sailing on at least one of the legs. The Society Island block lies about 150 miles east of the Hawaiian Island block; the dominant current tends to push any craft westward as it sails between the groups; and the Polynesian navigation system requires that the canoe arrive at a comfortable distance to the windward side of the objective before the canoe can be turned downwind to its objective. All this makes it imperative that a canoe have some windward ability.

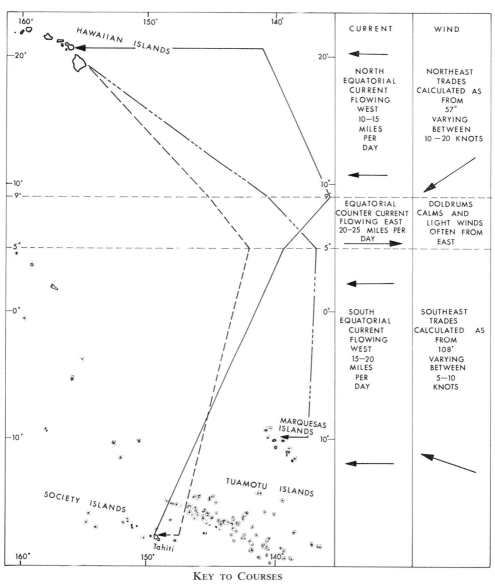

KEY TO COURSES

1. — — — — — — — — — — —
2. ——————————————
3. — — - - - — — — - - - — — —

FIGURE 2.—Two-way voyaging between Tahiti and Hawaii. **1,** Navigated course from Hawaii to Tahiti sailed at 75 degrees to the wind. **2,** Navigated course from Tahiti to Hawaii sailed at 75 degrees to the wind. **3,** Navigated course from Hawaii to the Marquesas requiring a canoe to sail at 65 degrees to the wind. Sailed courses assume that the canoes will average 96 miles a day in trade-wind areas and 48 miles a day in the doldrums. (Map drawn by William K. Kikuchi, Bishop Museum.)

But the windward ability required would appear to be within the capabilities of the Polynesian double canoe. Sailed at 75 degrees to the wind it could just make a safely navigated course to Tahiti, as Figure 2 indicates. Because of the northerly component in the northeast trades, a course held close to the wind from Hawaii to the doldrums would bring the canoe some miles to the east. Sailing at 4 knots, this portion of the route would require about 9 to 10 days. In the doldrums, calms and light winds would slow progress to perhaps a 2-knot average, requiring a passage of 6 days or more. Even though contrary winds might keep the canoe from sailing eastward, the strong equatorial countercurrent acting on the slow-moving canoe would probably allow some gain in mileage to the east. However, once out of the doldrums and into the southeast trades the canoe would be forced onto a course slightly west of south. If the 4-knot average were held, the canoe would arrive within 14 or 15 days at the latitude of Tahiti, slightly on the windward, or west side. A day or so of downwind sailing along Tahiti's latitude would suffice to make the landfall, ending a passage of 30 days or more.

Since Hawaii lies west of Tahiti, a navigated return to Hawaii would not require the canoe to be held so close to the wind, although the lack of any method to gauge longitude might require that the canoe be held at 75 degrees to the wind to insure that Hawaii would not be passed on its leeward (western) side.

The Hawaiian and Society groups present large targets for the Polynesian navigator. The Hawaiian Island block measures about 330 miles on the north-south axis (Hawaii to Kauai), and about 440 miles on its east-west axis (Hawaii to Kaula), while the Society Island block measures about 160 miles on its north-south axis (Borabora to Tahiti) and 290 miles on its east-west axis (Maupiti to Tahiti). Given the size of these targets, the generally favorable wind and weather conditions prevailing in the trade-wind area, and a skillful application of Polynesian navigation principles, a navigator should have more than an even chance of finding his objectives.

As an example of how a successful voyage would be navigated, take the Hawaii–Tahiti trip, the most difficult portion of the postulated two-way communication route. The navigator would have to be able to carry out three main tasks: (1) recognize the cardinal points from the stars and bear as far east of south as the wind would allow him; (2) recognize the latitude of Tahiti from its latitude stars; and (3) hold the canoe on Tahiti's latitude while sailing downwind to make the landfall.

Recognition of the cardinal points presents little problem—skilled Tahitian seamen still retain this ability, and even if it were difficult, the desired course could be set by tacking closely to the dominant easterly winds. A Tahitian navigator returning to his homeland would not be likely to have forgotten his latitude stars, and the north-south spread of the Society group would allow an error of 1 degree (60 miles) or more. If Lewis' experiments are any indication, an experienced navigator's margin of error would probably have been less. Since the course would carry the canoe through the Tuamotu Islands before reaching Tahiti's latitude, a nonhostile reception at any atoll encountered in this group would provide additional navigational information for the last leg into Tahiti. Once onto Tahiti's latitude, the downwind leg could be carefully sailed so that Tahiti or one of the leeward islands of the group could be sighted and reached.

So far in this analysis we have not dealt with two problems that faced the Polynesian seamen: durability and seaworthiness of their craft; and their own survival at sea. Concerning the first, we have no experimental data to offer. It must be accepted, however, that accidents might befall a double canoe and fatally terminate a voyage. If a heavy double canoe were overturned there would be little hope of righting it, and although it would form a raft for crew and passengers, its slow drift would make survival difficult unless land were close by. A major structural failure, such as the splitting of a hull or the breaking of the cross-pieces holding the hulls together, would lead to a quicker end since the chances of repairing such failures—especially in the heavy seas that would be likely to have caused them—would be slight. Although lesser structural failures, such as worn lashings or torn sails, might be mended along the way without affecting the success of a voyage, there is little doubt that major structural failures or mishaps, like those mentioned above, took their toll among Polynesian voyages.

The human element has also been neglected in this analysis. Long voyages require adequate food and water supplies, and these would surely become critical on voyages lasting 30 to 35 days, like those postulated between Tahiti and Hawaii. Large double canoes could take considerable quantities of food that keeps well—pandanus flour, yams, sweet potatoes, dried bananas, fermented breadfruit poi, and dried fish —as well as water stored in bamboo joints, gourds, and coconuts, but the balance between adequate and inadequate food and water supplies on crowded canoes undertaking long voyages must have been fine. Because of miscalculation, mishaps along the way, delaying winds, or a difficulty in making a landfall, many a canoe must have run perilously and often fatally low on food and water.

How much these supplies could be supplemented by fishing and collecting rain water is a question amenable to research. Fishing from a slow-moving canoe, particularly if considerable growth had accumulated on the hulls, might help supplement the supply of protein. The doldrums might provide a unique "watering spot" for canoes traversing them because they are often covered with clouds and experience frequent rainstorms and squalls.[11] Although rainfall in the trade-wind stretches from Hawaii to the doldrums and from the doldrums south to Tahiti is relatively slight, cumulus clouds rising from the humid calms of the doldrums release over 150 inches of rain a year (Sadler, 1959, p. 14). Using the auxiliary power the crew can provide, a canoe might be paddled to squalls or under cumulus clouds promising rain to replenish the water supply depleted during the long sailing periods in the relatively rainless trade-wind areas. To a thirsty crew the doldrums might therefore have been more of a blessing than the name suggests.

A possibility of disaster through capsizing, structural failure, or exhaustion of water and food supplies might not have greatly deterred voyaging by the Polynesians of the settlement period. Implicit in arguments citing these and other dangers as deterrents to planned exploration and colonization is a very modern premise about safety in travel. Few of us would commit ourselves to an ocean voyage, or any journey, if chances of survival were anything less than well over 99.9 percent. Yet our ancestors traveled willingly with much less security. Modern safety standards cannot be applied to Polynesian voyaging any more than they can be applied to the wagon journeys of the pioneers across the United States. If anything, given the apparently casual Polynesian approach to the dangers of voyaging that modern Polynesians still exhibit,[12] and the probable necessity of leaving famine-stricken or strife-ridden islands, as well as the prospects that the discovery and colonization of a new land offered, the ancient Polynesians may have planned and undertaken voyages where chances of survival were perhaps as low as 50 percent, or even less.

[11]Weather satellite photographs indicate the frequent occurrence of heavy cloud cover averaging about 150 miles wide between 5 and 9 degrees north latitude (James C. Sadler, personal communication, November 15, 1966).

[12] For example, on several occasions in recent years Easter Islanders have sailed for Tahiti in tiny craft ill adapted for long voyages, and without adequate food supplies or proper navigational equipment (Laguesse, 1954).

CONCLUSION

A summary of our argument may now be made. Because of the dominant easterly set of wind and current, it would seem highly improbable that a drift voyage from either the Marquesas or Tahiti could ever have reached Hawaii. These same winds and currents, however, would allow a Polynesian double canoe to sail—at favorable angles to the wind—to Hawaii. This conclusion indicates that if, as culture-historical data show, Hawaii was settled from both the Marquesas and Tahiti, the voyages involved were planned voyages of exploration or colonization. Data on Polynesian canoe performance indicate that once Marquesans reached Hawaii it would have been extremely difficult for them to have returned to their homeland against wind and current, and that it is therefore improbable that there was any significant two-way communication between these two archipelagoes. Matching this same canoe data with the route, winds, and currents in the Tahiti case does, however, indicate the feasibility of a return voyage from Hawaii to Tahiti and therefore the possibility of some two-way voyaging—perhaps with a high rate of disasters—between these two Polynesian centers.

The above estimates would have to be modified if (1) the data on canoe performance were significantly inaccurate, or (2) the mean wind and current patterns employed in the analysis did not reflect actual conditions at the time of voyaging. For example, if the Polynesian canoe could sail within 65 degrees of the wind, 10 degrees better than our estimate, the possibility of a return voyage from Hawaii to the Marquesas and the initiation of two-way voyaging between these groups would have to be considered. Or, if the double canoe could only sail within 85 degrees of the wind, the possibility of two-way communication between Hawaii and Tahiti could be questioned. Similarly, if the direction of the prevailing winds shifted to force a canoe either farther east or west, the possible patterns of voyaging would also be altered.[13]

However, lest this analysis end with a note of doubt, some arguments supporting the postulated patterns of voyaging should be briefly cited.

Archaeological evidence pointing to the Marquesan derivation of the

---

[13] If the Polynesians could recognize and utilize the eastward-flowing equatorial countercurrent, they might have been able to make extra miles of easting to approach Tahiti well on the eastern side, or even to reach the Marquesas. Modern yachtsmen, using thermometers to recognize the temperature differential marking the current, sometimes motor eastward in the current to make their easting on trips from Hawaii south. If the Polynesians could have recognized the current, perhaps by observing their drift in calms in relation to stationary cumulus clouds, they might have paddled eastward to take advantage of both the current and light wind conditions to gain miles to the east.

first Hawaiians also indicates that this settlement may well have been the result of a planned expedition, for bones of the dog and pig—the main Polynesian domesticates—are found in the early sites.[14] These animals are more likely to have arrived with colonizing parties, in canoes loaded with the domesticated plants and animals needed to survive in a virgin land, than in an accidentally drifting canoe. That the Marquesas was the source of such expeditions is known from the journal of Captain David Porter, U.S.N., who occupied part of the Marquesas during the War of 1812. Porter (1823, p. 93) reported that: "The grandfather of Gatta-newa [Porter's informant] sailed with four large canoes in search of land, taking with him a large stock of provisions and water, together with a quantity of hogs, poultry and young plants. He was accompanied by several families, and has never been heard of since he sailed." A European who had been living in the islands for some years prior to Porter's arrival also told Porter of such voyages, calculating that during his sojourn more than 800 Marquesans had fled in search of new lands.

Necessity rather than adventure appears to have been the main motive for these expeditions. The Marquesas are subject to alternate periods of drought and ample rainfall, and therefore, to alternate periods of poverty and plenty in food resources (Freeman, 1951, p. 374). During drought periods when food supplies diminished, some islanders, fearing starvation, might have left voluntarily to search for new and more fertile lands, or under pressure from powerful neighbors coveting their meager resources, might have been forced to flee for their lives. Following a course to the northwest (Fig. 1), a course that would indicate no desire to return home since it would take the voyagers too far downwind to allow them to tack home, a group or groups of such exiles may have made a fortunate landfall, thus becoming the first Hawaiians. Lacking the motive to leave a fertile land for a drought-stricken and perhaps war-stricken one, and faced with contrary winds and currents, it is doubtful that these first Hawaiians would have tried to return to their homeland. The postulated Marquesan settlement of Hawaii would therefore appear to be a classical case of one-way exile voyaging.

The unstable rainfall and food production pattern, and the periodic pressures on a population grown large in times of plenty, may have made the Marquesas a spawning ground for exile voyages seeking new lands for survival. This view would seem to help explain the evidence of Marquesan settlement in Hawaii and the other islands of Eastern Polynesia,

---

[14] Bird bones also found in early sites cannot be identified as definitely coming from domesticated chickens (Kenneth P. Emory, personal communication, January 13, 1967).

but the same hypothesis applied to Tahiti—whose influence is also wide-spread in Eastern Polynesia—does not fit the facts. Although population pressures were evidently experienced on Tahiti, and perhaps partially dealt with through infanticide, Tahiti's rainfall and food harvest were probably fairly stable (Freeman, 1951, p. 369), so that the Tahitians would probably not have felt the extreme and sudden population pressures characteristic of the Marquesas. Some different type of explanation would seem to be required to explain Tahitian expansion.

Chiefly rivalry and an adventuresome spirit of political-religious aggrandizement may well have been central to the Tahitian expansion to islands like Hawaii. Taking our clues from the history of chiefly rivalry in Tahiti, Vayda's (1958) suggestion that rivalry over status was an important motive for voyaging and colonization, and Fornander's (1919-1920, pp. 239-257) analysis of Hawaiian traditions dealing with Tahitian contact, the following conjectures on the Tahitian expansion to Hawaii may be offered.

Hawaiian legends are silent about the first settlement of the islands,[15] but they do contain some references to the coming of Tahitian voyagers. These legends relate mainly to the exploits of high-status individuals who do not appear as refugees from an impoverished homeland, but as culture-bearers coming to a politically and ritually underdeveloped land. In the legend of Pa'ao, for example, this Raiatean priest discovers that the Hawaiian rulers are greatly lacking in power, and he returns to Tahiti to fetch a high chief to restore the prestige of rank among the Hawaiians. The chief's assumption to power in Hawaii involved not only a reform of the chieftainship, but also—according to the tradition—the introduction of important ritual elements like the red-feather girdle for the investiture of a high chief, the *heiau* type of temple, and human sacrifice (Buck, 1959, pp. 262-263). Although we need not accept these and other traditions following a similar theme of Tahitian aggrandizement as literally true, they do suggest that the Tahitian coming to Hawaii was not a movement of desperate exiles, but rather of opportunistic and adventuresome individuals who were perhaps frustrated in efforts to improve their status at home and were seeking new opportunities far away.

The course from Tahiti is, as we have seen, one that would allow a return to Tahiti. It may, in fact, represent the track of an exploring canoe sailing swiftly with the wind on its beam, but not pointing too far downwind so as to make it impossible—as in the Marquesas case—to return home (see Fig. 1). The Hawaiian legends telling of Tahitian voyages

---

[15] The tale of Hawaii-Loa's discovery of Hawaii appears to be a post-European fabrication, not an ancient tradition (Emory, 1965).

often feature—as in the above-cited legend of Pa'ao—two-way voyaging between the groups. Perhaps the most complete legend of this type is the story of Moikeha, which, in the space of two generations, features three round trips between Tahiti and Hawaii (Buck, 1959, pp. 260-262). Again, we need not accept the details of such legends as literal history, but neither can we ignore that two-way voyaging was a common feature in Hawaiian traditions of the Tahitian contact era. This traditional remembrance combined with our demonstration of the feasibility of navigated voyages to and from Hawaii and Tahiti, argues for the acceptance of the possibility that two-way voyaging in Polynesia was not limited to closely spaced islands, but may have taken place between archipelagoes separated by over 2,000 miles of blue water. The Tahiti-to-Hawaii route may well have witnessed the maximum achievements in Polynesian two-way voyaging.

LITERATURE CITED

ASCHER, ROBERT
    1961. "Experimental Archaeology." *American Anthropologist* **63**:793-816.

BECHTOL, CHARLES
    1963. "Sailing Characteristics of Oceanic Canoes." In J. GOLSON (editor), *Polynesian Navigation,* pp. 98-101. Polynesian Soc. Mem. 34, Wellington.

BUCK, PETER H.
    1957. *Arts and Crafts of Hawaii.* B. P. Bishop Mus. Spec. Pub. 45. Honolulu.
    1959. *Vikings of the Pacific.* Chicago: Univ. Chicago Press.

EMORY, KENNETH P.
    1946. Eastern Polynesia, its Cultural Relationships. Ph.D. Dissertation, Yale Univ.
    1963. "East Polynesian Relationships: Settlement Pattern and Time Involved as Indicated by Vocabulary Agreement." *J. Polynesian Soc.* **72**:78-100.
    1965. "Comments on Chapter 2: Polynesian Migrations." In E. S. C. HANDY *et al., Ancient Hawaiian Civilization,* pp. 319-320. Tokyo: Tuttle.

EMORY, KENNETH P., and YOSIHIKO H. SINOTO
    1965. *Preliminary Report on the Archaeological Investigations in Polynesia.* Mimeographed. B. P. Bishop Mus. Honolulu.

FINNEY, BEN R.
    1959. "The Modern Hawaiian Double Canoe." *J. Polynesian Soc.* **68**:36-39.

FORNANDER, ABRAHAM
1919, 1920. "Hawaiian Antiquities and Folk-Lore." *Mem. B. P. Bishop Mus.* Vol. 6. Honolulu.

FRANKEL, J. P.
1962. "Polynesian Navigation." *Navigation* 9:35-47.

FREEMAN, OTIS W.
1951. *Geography of the Pacific.* New York: Wiley.

GOLSON, J. (Editor)
1963. *Polynesian Navigation.* Polynesian Soc. Mem. 34. Wellington.

GREEN, ROGER
1966. "Linguistic Subgrouping within Polynesia: The Implications for Prehistoric Settlement." *J. Polynesian Soc.* 75:6-38.

HADDON, A. C., and JAMES HORNELL
1936, 1937, 1938. *Canoes of Oceania.* 3 vols. B. P. Bishop Mus. Spec. Pubs. 27, 28, 29. Honolulu.

HEYERDAHL, THOR
1950. *Kon-Tiki: Across the Pacific by Raft.* Chicago: Rand McNally.

LAGUESSE, JANINE
1954. "Migration Polynesienne Moderne." *Bull. Soc. Études Océaniennes* 9:354-357.

LEWIS, DAVID
1964. "Polynesian Navigational Methods." *J. Polynesian Soc.* 73:364-374.
1966. "Stars of the Sea Road." *J. Polynesian Soc.* 75:85-94.

PARIS, F. E.
1841. *Essai sur la Construction Navale des Peuples Extra-Européens.* Paris: Berthaud.

PHILIPS-BIRT, DOUGLAS
1966. *Ships and Boats, the Nature of their Design.* London: Studio Vista.

PORTER, DAVID
1823. *A Voyage in the South Seas, in the Years 1812, 1813, 1814. . . .* London: Phillips.

SADLER, JAMES C.
1959. "A Study of Some Recent Climatological Data of the Line Islands." pp. 12-16. *Proc. Ninth Pacific Sci. Cong.* (Bangkok). Vol. 13, Meteorology.

SINOTO, YOSIHIKO H.
1962. "Chronology of Hawaiian Fishhooks." *J. Polynesian Soc.* 71:162-166.

SHARP, ANDREW
1956. *Ancient Voyagers in the Pacific.* Polynesian Soc. Mem. 32. Wellington.
1964. *Ancient Voyagers in Polynesia.* Berkeley: Univ. California Press.

UNITED STATES NAVY
1959. *U. S. Navy Marine Climatic Atlas of the World, Vol. 5. South Pacific Ocean.* Washington: U. S. Govt. Printing Office.

UNITED STATES NAVY (Cont.)

    1960. *Pilot Chart of the South Pacific Ocean.* June, July and August, No. 2601. Hydrographic Office Pub. 107. Washington.

    1965. *Pilot Chart of the North Pacific Ocean.* June, July and August, No. 1401. Hydrographic Office Pub. 143. Washington.

WHITNEY, HARRY P.

    1955. An Analysis of the Design of the Major Sea-Going Craft of Oceania. M. A. Thesis, Univ. Pennsylvania.

VAYDA, A. P.

    1958. "A Voyage by Polynesian Exiles." *J. Polynesian Soc.* **67**:324-329.

CYLINDRICAL HEADDRESS IN THE PACIFIC REGION

H. D. SKINNER*

Otago Museum, Dunedin, New Zealand

THE CYLINDRICAL HEADDRESS, which is ancient and widespread in Europe, doubtless rendered imposing the chief or priest who wore it. Conspicuous among present or recent European examples are the top hats of stockbrokers, bankers, archdeacons, bishops, patrons of Ascot, and schoolboys of Eton, and also the derivative bourgeois stovepipe hat or bell-topper. More typical of the ancient form from which they are descended is the cylindrical headdress of clerics of the Greek Orthodox Church. In ancient times this form of headdress appears to have been widely spread in Asia. The present study deals with the cylindrical headdress in two ethnographic areas of coastal and insular Pacific—that of the Haida people, Northwest Coast of North America (see Figs. 1-2), and that of the islanders of northern Melanesia and of Polynesia (see Figs. 3-20).

The culture of the North American Northwest Coast has received many elements from the circumpolar Arctic region and from Asia. The immediate source from which its cylindrical headdress was derived is not at present known.

The Protestant missionaries, who began work in Oceania at the close of the 18th century and increased their activities in the earlier decades of the 19th century, very frequently on important ceremonial occasions wore the bell-topper. It is to be supposed that their converts were considerably impressed by the new rendering of the cylindrical headdress long familiar to them from ancient ritual. This has been clearly demon-

---

* I have had the good fortune to know Kenneth Emory over a period of forty years and, for a brief time, to have served in Tahiti under his direction. It is an honor to be asked to contribute to this book.

strated in carvings from the Solomons. Even more convincing data are provided by Smith (1910, p. 248). Quoting Captain Gilbert Mair, he says:

The late Rev. Mr. Spencer told me when he settled at Tera-wera, in 1848, Te Mapu-Takanawa came to him and extorted a promise which he never allowed Mr. Spencer to forget to the effect that all his discarded "bell-toppers" should be given to Te Mapu, one of which was always carefully placed on the stone marking the spot where Te Amotu fell. [Smith adds:] I saw the stone with the hat myself in 1874. I feel pleased through Captain Mair's help to place on record the noble action of Te Amotu in sacrificing himself to save his fellow tribesmen.

A similar reaction was reported by Williams (1838, p. 59) at Aitu-taki:

Finding that we did not repose entire confidence in their assertions, some held up their hats. The European shaped hat was worn only by the Christian party, the idolaters retaining their heathen head-dresses.

It was, I think, commonly held that the cylindrical artifacts of red tufa originally placed on the heads of human figures set up on the Easter Island *ahu,* shown and described in Figures 19 and 20, were headdresses of this kind. However, in 1917 Henry Balfour presented a new view:

I wish to urge as a tentative and heterodox suggestion, that the reason was that these red cylinders were not intended to represent hats at all, but hair. A red tufa was selected in order to conform with the practice, common enough in Melanesia, of bleaching the hair to a reddish colour with lime, or of coating it with red ochre.

Métraux (1940, p. 301) was inclined to agree with this view, saying that "The theory that these crowns were merely a crude attempt to ornament the statues with a structure similar to a topknot (*pukao*) is the most logical assumption." Heyerdahl (1952, p. 371) accepts this explanation and asks: "Is it not probable . . . that the Easter Island statues directly depict this early red-haired ideal? May they not represent ancestor-portraits of chiefs and heroes of this venerated appearance?" He discusses the seafaring, white-skinned redheads, and brings them to Easter Island from Peru.

The cylindrical headdress is an ancient feature in Eurasian culture, impinging at some undetermined date on western Oceania. Its presence has here been demonstrated in the Northwest Coast, in New Britain, the Solomons, Santa Cruz, New Caledonia, New Zealand, the Cooks, Tahiti, the Hawaiian Islands, the Marquesas, and at Easter Island. In Melanesia both red and black cylindrical headdresses are recorded. In Polynesia the only color was the ritual red. On reaching Easter Island the Polynesian pioneers entered an environment lacking some of the most attractive

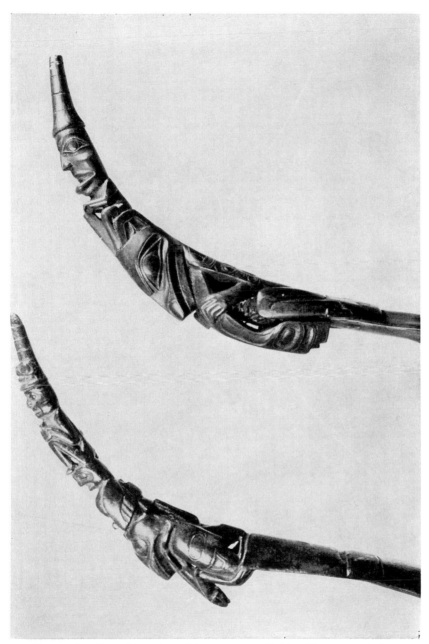

FIGURE 1.—Carved handles of horn spoons. Haida. Above, terminal human figure with lip plug. Base of headdress expands slightly to fit human head. Crown contracts slightly upward in four stages. Length from top to neck of human figure 2½ inches. (Otago Museum. D.21.349. Exchange.) Below, terminal human figure. Headdress in two parts, the lower carved to represent a birdlike face, the upper crown contracting slightly in four sections. Length from top to neck of human figure 1¾ inches. (Otago Museum. D.56.23. Fels Fund.)

FIGURE 2.—Upper part of slate totem pole. Haida. Topmost figure, a bear. Below it are a pair of flanking human figures, each crowned with a cylindrical headdress. Headdresses are parallel-sided and divided in three sections, with bases expanded to fit head. Length from crest of bear to neck of human figure 4½ inches. (Otago Museum. D.21.396. Exchange.)

FIGURE 3.—Bark cylindrical headdress painted scarlet. New Britain. Decorated by a pair of shell disks suggesting eyes, and by two vertical rows of perforated shells flanked by two rows of perforated dog teeth. Height 8 inches. (Otago Museum. D.20.1013. Fels Fund.)

FIGURE 4.—Wooden human figure from canoe prow. Roviana, Solomon Islands. Head crowned by cylindrical headdress painted red. Height 9½ inches. (Otago Museum. D.34.1973.)

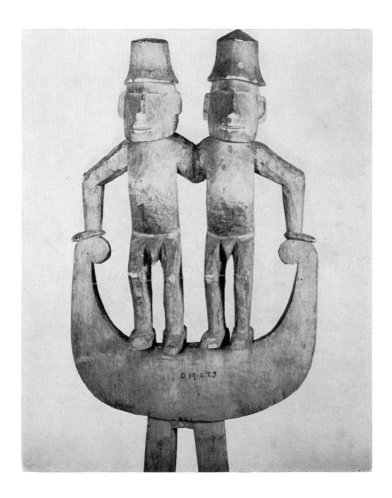

FIGURE 5.—Pair of human male figures from roof decoration of canoe shed. Solomon Islands. Heads crowned by cylindrical headdresses. Wood unpainted. Height of figures 10½ inches. (Otago Museum. D.19.423. Fels Fund.)

FIGURE 6.—Two human male figures, terminal of a lime spoon. Solomon Islands. Paired dance presumably based on European fashion. Headdresses clearly influenced by European fashion. Wood, unpainted. Height of figures 2½ inches. (Otago Museum. D.23.956. Fels Fund.)

FIGURE 7.—Wooden male figure. Solomon Islands. Cylindrical headdress profoundly influenced by missionary bell-topper. Ear lobes perforated and elongated until they reach the shoulders. Painted black. Height 13 inches. (Otago Museum. D.53.513. Fels Fund.)

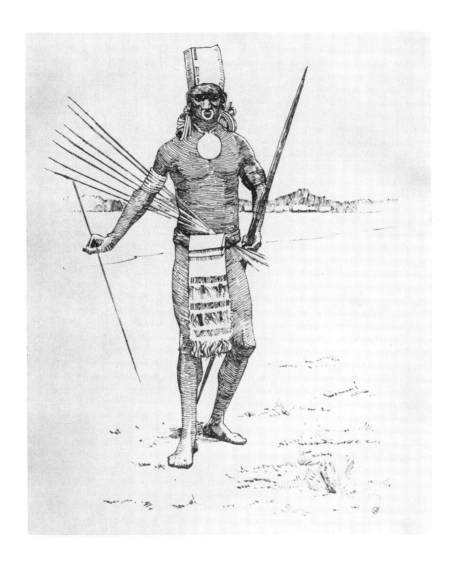

FIGURE 8.—"Man of Santa Cruz Fully Equipped for Ceremonial or War."
Drawing by James Edge-Partington. The headdress appears to be of bark, color
not specified.

FIGURE 9.—New Caledonian chief. Drawing by William Hodges, illustrator with Captain James Cook's second voyage (1772-1775). Headdress described as "a kind of . . . cylindrical, stiff black cap, which appeared to be a great ornament among them, and, we thought, was only worn by men of note, or warriors. A large sheet of strong paper, when they got one from us, was generally applied to this use" (Cook, 1777, p. 119).

FIGURE 10.—Cast of upper terminal of *tekoteko* (gable); Maori chief wearing cylindrical headdress. Arawa. Originally painted with red hematite, *moko* in black. Lower margin of headdress expanded slightly to fit head. Height 18 inches. Described by Hamilton (1905). (Dominion Museum.)

FIGURE 11.—Upper end of Maori chief's *tokotoko* (staff), cut down from *tao* (double-ended spear). Arawa (?). Lower edge of headdress is clearly cut and shows no expansion. Height of figure 3¾ inches. (Otago Museum. D.34.513.)

FIGURE 12.—Upper terminal of *tekoteko* (gable-end carving of *uhata*). From *pa* near Raglan. Rendering influenced by European headdresses. Original color scarlet. Height of figure 24 inches. (Otago Museum. D.24.891. Fels gift.)

FIGURE 13.—(Opposite) "Te Po, a chief of Rarotonga," Baxter print published by Williams (1838). Cylindrical headdress lavishly decorated with feathers and human hair. Above the brow is a rectangular panel of scarlet feathers.

FIGURE 15.—Three stone figures in *marai,* Taiohae, Nukuhiva, Marquesas. From von den Steinen, 1928, after Krusenstern, 1805. Draftsmanship indifferent, but all three appear to be carved from stone. Figure on right has cylindrical headdress, to upper margin of which some visitor, perhaps a festive mariner, has added in paint a decorative diadem.

FIGURE 14.—(Opposite) Three figures in house in *marai,* Atui, Hawaiian Islands. From an engraving in John Webber's folio illustrating Cook's third voyage (1776-1779). Two of the figures appear to be carved from wood, one from stone. All wear cylindrical headdresses. Color not specified.

FIGURE 16.—Bier of Chief Taiuao, and wooden figure with cylindrical headdress. *Marai*, Menaha Takaoa, Hakamoui, Uapu, Marquesas. From von den Steinen, 1928.

FIGURE 17.—Three wooden figures, each with cylindrical headdress. Marquesas. Height of central figure, 180 centimeters. From von den Steinen, 1928. (Leipzig Museum.)

FIGURE 18.—Tahitian priest wearing cylindrical headdress of type commonly worn in Cook's time. Drawing by Sydney Parkinson, artist with Cook's first voyage, 1768-1771. Front decorated with small feathers, presumably scarlet.

FIGURE 19.—Two Easter Island statues, the nearer one wearing a cylindrical headdress of red tufa. From an engraving after W. Hodges, illustrator, Cook's second voyage (1772-1775).

materials present in other Polynesian groups, the most conspicuous absentee being large timber. Thus the fleets of the Tahitian islands and the canoes and woodcarving of New Zealand were impossible at Easter. But the Polynesians found there limitless supplies of easily worked vesicular lava, and energy was therefore concentrated on such stone work as the *ahu* and on the sculpture of stone statues. In addition to vesicular lava the island supplied a deposit of red tufa, from which red cylindrical headdresses were easily quarried. Owing to the vigor and enthusiasm of Thor Heyerdahl, the present-day Easter Islanders have demonstrated the method by which statue and headdress were raised on the *ahu*. As to the explanation of the color, it is unnecessary to invoke red hair.

A further point arises and should be touched on briefly. In the discussion of stonework, a Polynesian viewpoint should be considered. In Polynesia generally, stonework is not a conspicuous feature, although it is widely distributed. Probably the most conspicuous single masonry unit in the whole area is the Haamonga a Maui in Tongatabu. The three pieces of quarried coral rock of which it is composed are of great size and weight, and for their handling must have required considerable disciplined manpower. Even a brief examination of the structure invites the conclusion that the basic constructive art of the builders was woodwork or carpentry. All the discussions of the method of building it that I have read agree on that. I am not among the fortunate who have visited Easter

FIGURE 20.—Easter Island statue, in vesicular basalt. Purchased in Papeete, 1931, from a member of the Brander family. Collected by Tati Salmon, Easter Island agent of the Brander firm. It had stood for many years in the family grounds. Assurance was given that the headdress, of red tufa, belonged to the figure as recovered at Easter Island. (Otago Museum. D.66.1685. Fels Fund.) An almost identical figure with cylindrical headdress, presumably from same *ahu*, is exhibited in the Ethnographic Museum, Hamburg.

Island, but I have read some part of the literature relating to it. As a student of Polynesian material culture, I ventured in 1958 to suggest that Easter Island masonry was based, like the Haamonga a Maui, on woodwork and that its cultural relationships were Polynesian, not Cuzcan. This suggestion I see no ground for abandoning.

LITERATURE CITED

BALFOUR, HENRY
   1917. "Some Ethnological Suggestions in Regard to Easter Island, or Rapanui." *Folklore* **28**:356-381.

COOK, JAMES
   1777. *A Voyage towards the South Pole and Round the World . . . in . . . the* Resolution *and* Adventure . . . Vol. 2. London: Strahan and Cadell.

EDGE-PARTINGTON, JAMES
   1898. *An Album of the Weapons, Tools, Ornaments, Articles of Dress, etc. of the Natives of the Pacific Islands.* Manchester: Issued for private circulation by James Edge-Partington and Charles Heape.

HAMILTON, AUGUSTUS
   1905. [No title.] Colonial Museum Bull. 1.

HEYERDAHL, THOR
   1952. *American Indians in the Pacific: The Theory behind the Kon-Tiki Expedition.* London: George Allen and Unwin.

MÉTRAUX, ALFRED
   1940. *Ethnology of Easter Island.* B. P. Bishop Mus. Bull. 160. Honolulu.

PARKINSON, STANFIELD (Editor)
   1773. *A Journal of a Voyage to the South Seas in the* Endeavour. *Faithfully transcribed from the Papers of the late Sydney Parkinson.* London: Printed for Stanfield Parkinson.

SKINNER, H. D.
   1955. "Easter Island Masonry." *J. Polynesian Soc.* **64**:292-294.

SMITH, S. PERCY
   1910. *Maori Wars of the Nineteenth Century.* (2nd ed.) Wellington: Whitcombe and Tombs.

STEINEN, KARL VON DEN
   1928. *Die Marquesaner und Ihre Kunst.* Berlin: Ernst Vohsen.

WILLIAMS, JOHN
   1838. *A Narrative of Missionary Enterprises in the South Sea Islands.* London: J. Snow.

MATERIAL EVIDENCE OF THE BIRD-MAN
CONCEPT IN POLYNESIA

T. BARROW*
Bernice P. Bishop Museum, Honolulu

THE PURPOSE of this paper is to establish the existence of bird-man images in several Polynesian areas and to postulate a general theory in relation to them. The style of each area is illustrated by selected museum specimens and by petroglyphs *in situ*. Although the mythological and religious ideas relating to birds and bird-men are beyond the scope of this descriptive paper, certain references to them have been included. With few exceptions the specimens described appear in the illustrations.

The bird-man idea is an abstract concept which cannot be handled as archaeological or factual ethnological data. Therefore the speculative nature of the interpretations suggested here is to be acknowledged at the outset. However, any evidence for distinctive bird-man images in Polynesia has direct bearing on the analysis of ordinary ancestral or god sculpture, according to the theory presented here, namely that avian elements are often superimposed on images which are basically anthropomorphic, that features such as claw hands, staring eyes, and beaked lips are superimposed on the image. This is clearly seen in the New Zealand material. When this "hybridization" reaches a certain point we arrive at forms that are conveniently called "bird-men." This process may be seen as simple and obvious, yet has long gone unrecognized or rejected as invalid. Here it is postulated that the combination of

* Thanks are extended to museum authorities for access to specimens or for photographs. Miss Paula Ortiz, student assistant in the Department of Anthropology of Bishop Museum, helped in the compilation of the material presented. The paper was written in honor of Kenneth P. Emory, who is forever unfailing in his friendly help to all.

human and bird elements is consistent in Oceanic art from the island world of Southeast Asia through Melanesia to Polynesia.

A bird-man is here defined as any carving that combines both human and avian features in the one image. The combination may take a number of variations; for example, a bird head may be placed on a human body, or a human head on a bird body. At one end of the scale we find almost wholly avian forms, while at the other we have predominantly anthropomorphic forms. Between the two extremes, that is, between the two component elements, there is an infinite range of hybrids or variants.

In most areas birds are closely associated with the supernatural, often serving as vehicles for gods or the spirits of the dead. The association of these ideas in the carvings of bird-men, or in ancestral or god images, seems natural to South Sea craftsmen.

The existence of material symbols of bird-men on an island does not necessarily indicate the former presence of a bird-man cult or consciousness of bird-man ideas. Some styles became firmly established, then persisted long after the original inspiring idea was forgotten or submerged in the unconscious.

There are themes and motifs in Polynesian carving that have their origins in the distant past. For example, Skinner (1964) demonstrated the survival of the crocodile form in New Zealand and other Polynesian carving, and related lizard forms to earlier crocodile ideas. Wittkower (1939) illustrated the widespread dispersal of the bird-grasping snake motif. This is well represented for Polynesia in Maori woodcarving where the *manaia* is seen grasping a snakelike creature that never existed in New Zealand fauna.

Polynesian styles and themes are studied better in relation to other Oceanic areas than when these are treated separately. An illustration of this is the relationship of bird and man in Polynesia which has a close parallel in the bird and man relationship in Melanesian carving. The better documentation of the Melanesian material makes it significant for comparative use.

The specimens illustrated here were collected historically, or are found *in situ* as petroglyphs or rock drawings (which lack known tribal or religious association). The scanty nature of bird-man material from Polynesia is not encouraging to systematic research, yet it is necessary to record it in an attempt to determine its character and to discern some pattern in its sporadic distribution.

The association of birds with the supernatural has been widespread among mankind throughout human history. The origin and distribution of beliefs relating to birds, and their persistent magico-religious associations, have been well documented (Armstrong, 1958). In the Oceanic world, birds appear to have held a mystical relationship with the gods and ancestral spirits to a degree that is unsurpassed elsewhere. The explanation is probably to be found in the isolated environment of the South Seas where land mammals and other conspicuous creatures were generally lacking and where birds were usually present on both land and sea. Also sea birds have always had a strong influence on the imaginations of seafaring peoples. In Polynesia, birds served as omengivers, guides, family totems, a source of food, and vehicles for the spirits of the dead or of the gods. Certain birds were especially important in certain areas; for example the frigate bird was revered in the Solomon Islands, the sooty tern in Easter Island, and the owl in New Zealand and Hawaii. The invention of the bird-man idea and the manufacture of material symbols to represent this idea is simply explained.

Handy (1927) makes a number of references to the supernatural association of birds in his study of Polynesian religion. He notes that birds were widely held as representatives of celestial deities and that priests used birds as omens or as vehicles of their power. Whether a bird was the spirit or the messenger of a spirit was always difficult to determine: "Thus in Samoa the plover (*turi*) is spoken of in the mythology of creation as the *ata* (reflection), of Tangaloa-savali (Tangaloa-the Messenger)," which was explained by a translator to signify that the plover was the "shadow" or second self of Tangaloa (Handy, 1927, p. 20). Throughout Polynesia red feathers were identified with the *mana* of the gods. J. G. Frazer (1924) in his classic study of Oceanic religions entitled *The Belief in Immortality and the Worship of the Dead,* provides abundant documentation from original sources on the magical associations of birds. Among the Micronesians he notes the use of an owl as a vehicle of a goddess of Ponape (Vol. 3, p. 154); that the Marshall islanders believed the spirits of the dead take up their abode in birds and fish: "Such ghostly fish and fowl" he says, "live on or near the atolls, and their presence places a certain degree of restraint on the activities of living men, whether it be by the prohibition to set foot on an island that is haunted by a spirit, or by the rule that certain words may not be spoken" (Vol. 3, p. 148), and the Mortlock islanders held that at death when the soul quits the body it assumes the shape of a sea bird (Vol. 3, p. 118). The subject is one that easily ramifies. From these general observations on the importance of the bird in South Sea life (and observations on bird-man images) we may move to specific areas considered in relation to the material images of bird-man ideas,

EASTER ISLAND

Easter Island is the only place in Polynesia where there is a recorded bird cult with associated bird-man images of several distinct types. This cult provided a diversion for the inhabitants who lived in an environment that did not offer the luxuries of the lush Society or Marquesas Islands. In spite of the depredations of slavers and the ravages of introduced diseases, the bird-man cult survived into the second half of the

FIGURE 1.—Petroglyphs at Orongo, *in situ,* Easter Island. Photographed by Alfred Métraux, 1934.

19th century and was recollected long enough to provide later visitors with substantial outlines (Routledge, 1917; Métraux, 1940). Archaeological remains of the cult were more recently recorded by Heyerdahl and Ferdon (1961). The accumulated materials for Easter Island bird-men are considerable, yet they call for reclassification and coordination of the many sources that now exist.

The bird-man cult of Easter Island centered around the arrival, between August and October, of the sooty tern (*manu tara*) which nested on small islets below the village of Orongo where the cult headquarters were established. This site is marked by the splendid engraved rocks (Fig. 1) which have been illustrated in a dozen or more books on the nonexistent mysteries of Easter Island. The appearance of the sooty tern caused great excitement and inaugurated events which led to the annual competition to secure the first egg of the season from Motu Nui islet. The man whose retainer secured the first egg for him became the elected bird-man (*tangata-manu*) of the year. The triumphant bird-man appears to have held his divine office under the sanction of the god Make-make for the year that followed his success. Irksome *tapu* surrounded the honor of being nominated bird-man of the year, but economic privilege for the man and his family made the position one to

FIGURE 2.—Bird-man on boulder, Easter Island. British Museum, London.

be sought after and suffered gracefully. A special bird-man name awarded to the successful candidate also became the name of the year.

Thus a system of chronology as well as social and religious life focused on the activities of the cult. A cycle of feasts was held at the village of Orongo, which is also notable for the striking petroglyphs depicting bird-men grasping the all-important egg (Fig. 1). A large engraved rock (Fig. 2) in the collection of the British Museum depicts the same theme, which is easily understood as the relation of the egg to the bird-man. In addition there are illustrated three kinds of wooden images of the bird-man type which almost certainly belong to the cult of Make-make. The first (Fig. 3, *a*) has been described by Cranstone

FIGURE 3.—Clockwise: a, Bird-man, Easter Island, British Museum, London. Height 26.5 cm. b, Bird-man, Easter Island, American Museum of Natural History, New York. Height 43 cm. c, Bird-man, Easter Island, British Museum, London. Length 33.5 cm.

(1955). It is a male figure, substantially a human image, with arms converted to wings, and a masklike bird's head on a basically human head. Tapa masks are recorded from Easter Island so it is possible that this figure is shown wearing a mask. The second image (Fig. 3, *b*) is more birdlike in its general characteristics, although the body remains anthropomorphic while the beak has a nose mounted to it. A third image (Fig. 3, *c*) is unlike the first two in that it has a naturalistic human head on a bird body.

It is appropriate to introduce at this point comparative material from the Solomon Islands by drawing attention to the valuable studies of H. Balfour. Balfour (1893) became a pioneer in the analysis of bird-men motifs by demonstrating the amalgamation of avian and human elements in Solomon Island canoe-prow images. He later expanded this thesis (Balfour, 1905) with added material, then extended it (Balfour, 1917) to a paper covering the same general theme with added suggestions concerning ethnological parallels between Easter Island and the Solomon Islands. His argument is based on forms of sculpture and similarities in art motifs. Although art material does not yield to exact scientific analysis, Balfour's results appear valid apart from his speculation on origins. According to Balfour (1917) the relationship is readily explained by migrations from Melanesia to Easter Island, a point of view that is not now tenable. The value of these papers is in the demonstration of hybridization of bird and human elements. His practical analysis has wide implications.

Balfour also noticed a strong similarity between the Easter Island tablet ideographs and certain Solomon Island symbols, particularly those based on the frigate bird, namely that the bird figures on the Easter Island "talking boards" are frigate birds and not the sacred sooty tern of the Easter Island bird cult. Regardless of the weakness of Balfour's assumptions on Melanesian migrations to Easter Island, his observations of bird-man hybrids of the Solomon Islands and the consequent influence on human images are valid and original. It seems probable that related influences were at work in Easter Island and that the style of the great stone statues with their prognathous and elongated faces can in fact be explained by the same process. The sculptural style of Easter Island appears to relate closely to that of the Solomon Islands.

Three of the specimens that Balfour used as line drawings to illustrate part of his thesis are here reproduced as photographs (Fig. 4). They are net floats from New Georgia collected by Lieutenant B. T. Somerville of the British Royal Navy in 1895. The specimens illustrate the human head on bird body theme (Fig. 4, *a*), a type known from

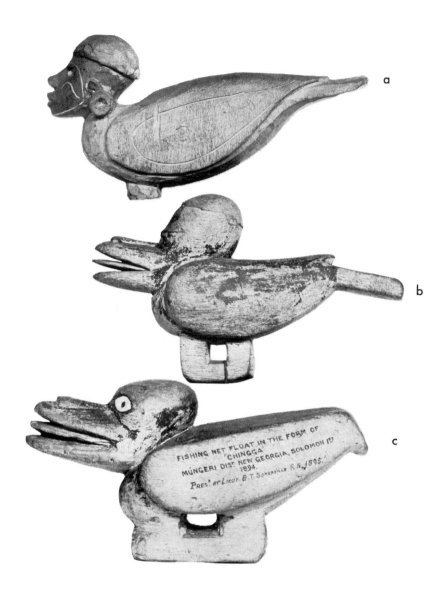

FIGURE 4.—Net-floats in bird-man form, New Georgia, Solomon Islands. Presented to the Pitt Rivers Museum, Oxford by Lieut. B. T. Somerville RN, 1895. Specimens range in length from 15 cm. to 21 cm.

Easter Island. Figure 3, c, is a bird with strongly humanized head. Figure 4, b, is a birdlike image with head form and nostril retained as typical human features. The bird part of these floats is of course the frigate bird which was held as sacred, particularly by canoe men and fishermen. According to Codrington (1891) the frigate bird was believed to be the vehicle of a potent ghost of a deceased person of importance and was called *tindalo* (these *tindalo* were placated before canoe voyages or fishing expeditions because they were regarded as guardians). The association of the frigate bird with dead humans readily explains the bird-man form of many Solomon Islands carvings.

FIGURE 5.—Bird-form box with human head, Marquesas. Collected on Hivaoa by Ralph Linton in 1921. Bernice P. Bishop Museum. Length 65 cm.

MARQUESAS

The combination of bird and human elements is found in the Marquesas in the bird-form bowls with human heads, two of which are illustrated (Figs. 5 and 6) from the collection of Bishop Museum. Some of the oldest canoe models, such as two in the Peabody Museum (Salem) figured by Handy (1923, Pl. XLIV, A and B) are of obvious bird form, with prows terminating in human masks. These specimens show that the Marquesas (an area ancestral to much of Hawaiian, New Zealand, and Easter Island culture) has material evidence of the bird-man idea in its carving art.

HAWAII

Birds held an important place in Hawaiian beliefs concerning the supernatural. They served as vehicles for personal spirits (*'aumakua*). There are many stories of the owl as an *'aumakua*. The plover (*kolea*) and the chicken (*moa*) were also important. There is no evidence suggesting a true bird cult, but the mythology of ancient Hawaii portrays a good number of flying humans and gods (Fornander, 1916). In view of these distinctive beliefs it is unfortunate that there are not more obvious bird-men in collections of Hawaiian images. However it

FIGURE 6.—Bird-form box with human head, Marquesas. Bernice P. Bishop Museum. Length 40 cm.

is reasonable to assume that the cockscomb surmounting a number of carved figures (Buck, 1957, Figs. 302-304) implies a connection between birds and the person or god represented; therefore such images qualify for inclusion here. The widespread destruction by the burning of the images at the abolishment of Hawaiian religion and the breakdown of the *kapu* system in the first quarter of the 19th century removed for all time the mass of evidence relating to Hawaiian iconography. What remains is a fragment of what once existed. We can only speculate on what has been.

The quality of early material is seen in the image (Fig. 7) collected by Andrew Bloxam at the *heiau* Hale-o-Keawe, Honaunau, in 1825. This image possesses a human body, a cockscomb, and a face

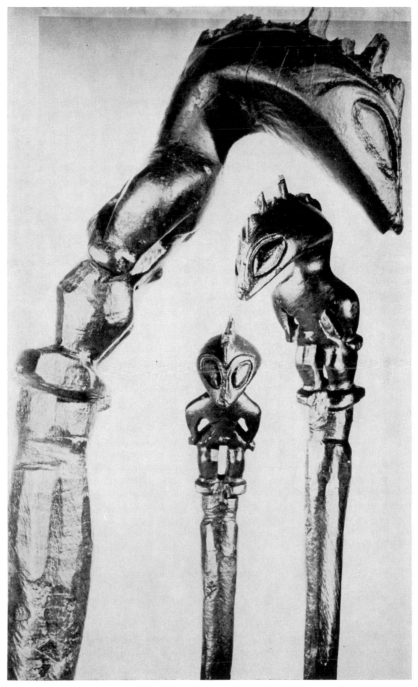

FIGURE 7.—Crested god stick, Hawaiian Islands. Collected on Hawaii at Honaunau (Hale-o-Keawe) by Andrew Bloxam in 1825. Bernice P. Bishop Museum. Height 37 cm.

that has been described as that of a lizard. There may be reptilian influences present (in fact Polynesians tended to link birds and lizards as vehicles of potent power: a similar overlay of reptilian features is seen in the New Zealand bird-man shown in Figure 11; otherwise it is a distinctive bird-man).

Petroglyphs provide the best example of pure bird-men for Hawaii, the finest being those on Lanai which were described and illustrated by Emory (1924, p. 120). These impressive flying or leaping figures located on the west bank of Kaunolu are here reproduced (Fig. 8).

A second example of bird-man petroglyphs is found in Moanalua Valley, Oahu (Fig. 9). They were described by McAllister (1933, Pl. 10, C) who does not identify them as bird-men. In view of the characteristics of the Lanai group, and the other Polynesian evidence, there can be little doubt that they represented bird-men. Their antecedents, personality, maker, and meaning, have been lost, however.

NEW ZEALAND

Material evidence for bird-man concepts in New Zealand falls into two categories. First, there are a few obvious bird-men drawn on limestone walls (Fig. 10) along with others in ornamental form (Skinner and Phillipps, 1953, p. 188, Fig. 24, A). These appear to be associated with the early or archaic period of Maori culture. Second, there is a wide range of woodcarvings of the classic period which incorporates a creature called the *manaia* (Fig. 12). The *manaia* has been hotly discussed for half a century, some claiming that it is a bird-man or a lizard (or the reptilian fabulous monster *taniwha*) and others that it is merely a human form rendered in a profile.

Supporters of the bird-man theory have their chief exponent in Skinner (1933), followed by Phillipps (1958), and Barrow (1956). The opposite school of thought which states the *manaia* is merely a human form has an expounder in Archey (1933, 1936). McEwen (1966), who is himself a skilled carver and an authority on Maori art, supports the human identity of *manaia* when he says: "It is quite clear that most, at least, of the *manaia* in carving are grotesque human figures shown in profile." Whether these two authors have reviewed the *manaia* sufficiently in relation to Oceanic carving in general appears uncertain. The evidence of bird-man relationships of Melanesia and the Polynesian

FIGURE 8.—(Opposite) Bird-man petroglyphs, *in situ*, Kaunolu, Lanai, Hawaiian Islands. Photographed by Kenneth P. Emory, 1921.

bird-men such as are illustrated here must have direct bearing on such studies. The *manaia* illustrated (Fig. 12) is classified here as a representative of the bird-man tribe of Polynesia.

No one would deny that the dancing (or flying) figures (Fig. 10), located on a limestone wall at Frenchman's Gully, South Canterbury, are other than bird-men (in fact they bear close resemblance to the Hawaiian petroglyph bird-men (Fig. 8). They establish beyond a doubt the existence of the bird-man idea in New Zealand. The persistence of the idea is provided by a late 19th century rendering of a bird-man (Fig. 11) with *manaia* head on the door of the Rotorua meeting house Nuku-

Figure 9.—Bird-man petroglyphs, *in situ,* Moanalua, Oahu, Hawaiian Islands. Photographed by J. G. McAllister, 1930.

te-Apiapi. The fabulous personage depicted, who is connected with the ancestors of the house, is rendered with feathers and claws in accordance with the European ideas of realism that influenced late Maori carving. The head is that of the *manaia* type which has been in existence in this general form since prehistoric times, as indicated by Shawcross (1964) who excavated at Tauranga a number of wooden combs with *manaia* heads carved on them. Hundreds of *manaia* are found on carvings collected from the time of Captain James Cook, whose first visit to New Zealand was in 1769. Since the *manaia* is second only to the human figure in frequency of appearance in Maori carving, some basic understanding of it is essential to an appreciation of Maori art. Although it

FIGURE 10.—Three bird-men with fish and birds drawn on limestone, *in situ*, Frenchman's Gully, South Canterbury, New Zealand. A record by T. Fomison, 1961.

was very much the motif of carvers on the east coast of the North Island of New Zealand, there is evidence that the idea of *manaia* was formerly widespread. What is the relationship of *manaia* to the ancestral image? The way the symbol is used can be readily studied from specimens in museum collections or on meeting houses *in situ*. Its form is different and its "behavior" is aggressive for it apparently attacks or bites into parts of the image it accompanies (for example the shoulders of Fig. 13). *Manaia* is often fragmented to fit into a design but in its complete form it has (as in Fig. 12) upper and lower limbs, clawed hands, large round eye, and an elongated beak surmounted with a horn.

FIGURE 11.—Bird-man from the door of the meeting house Nuku-te-Apiapi built at Rotorua, New Zealand, late 19th century.

FIGURE 12.—Bird-headed *manaia*, New Zealand. Detail from the hull of an ornamented canoe. K. A. Webster Collection.

Many New Zealand meeting houses which can be dated to the year of construction provide remarkable assemblages of *manaia*, one of the best being the Te Hau-ki-Turanga house which was built in 1842 and recently described (Barrow, 1965).

The ancestral image illustrated as Figure 13 is from the Te Hau-ki-Turanga house, and like the numerous human images in the same house

FIGURE 13.—Ancestral panel. From the meeting house Te Hau-ki-Turanga, built at Manutuke, New Zealand, 1842. Dominion Museum, Wellington.

is best explained in terms of avian features overlying the basically human image. Maori craftsmen had clear ideas of their own. For example, they rendered the head large because of the sacred (*tapu*) nature of it; they spread the figure out to fill an oblong panel, and (according to this theory) they gave some images claw hands, elliptical staring eyes, and a beaked mouth to express ideas which have their origin in the old Oceanic practice of relating the soul of the deceased to birds.

Sea and land birds played an important part in Maori life, both in the economy and religion. They served as an important source of food, vehicles for spirits, couriers, and conveyors of omens; also as pets, decoys, and family guardians. Accounts also of their use and personification in New Zealand are provided by Best (1924). Bird-men are also frequent in the compilation of mythological stories by Reed (1963). The last illustration (Fig. 14) is a carved representative of the owl (*ruru*), probably in its personified form of Kououru. Reference to the Kououru form in carving is made by Best (1924, p. 559), who provides positive information that the Maori believed birdlike persons were depicted in carvings, thus providing us with bird-men of a very human type. He says:

> East coast myths attribute carving to one Rua-i-te-pukenga, who introduced the art into this world, having acquired it in the realm of Rangi-tamaku, the second of the twelve heavens, counting upward. Rongo also acquired his knowledge of carving and carved designs from the house of Warekura in that celestial realm. When he constructed his own house he used Kououru (personified form of owl) as a sacred offering, and buried his body under the rear wall of the house. The Maori tells us that this is the reason why carved figures have large glaring eyes: they are the eyes of Kououru.

What evidence could more clearly state the presence of avian elements in Maori carving?

CONCLUSIONS

The specimens described above are from records of bird-man images found after extensive searching of museum collections and relevant literature. They establish the existence of bird-men images in several Polynesian areas and thus the former existence of the bird-man concept in Polynesia. The survey has revealed that bird-men carvings have a marginal distribution in Polynesia (namely Hawaii, New Zealand, and Easter Island) and that they appear not to have survived in collections from Western or Eastern Polynesia. This marginal dispersal may be related to and explained by the pattern of distribution of primary artifacts such as

FIGURE 14.—Image on the ridge beam of a meeting house. New Zealand. Dominion Museum, Wellington.

types of adz blades and fishhooks which are also commonly shared by Hawaii, New Zealand, and Easter Island.

To explain the relationship of the three areas there is no need to postulate direct contact, because there is abundant evidence to indicate dispersal from a central area (namely from the Society and Marquesas groups) where the comparatively rapid rate of change has been maintained through regular intergroup contact and the arrival of new immigrants. The peripheral or marginal Polynesian areas have, through isolation and consequent conservatism, retained old forms. This seems a logical thesis which can be used to explain the marginal incidence of bird-man symbols. Although Marquesan material is presented with that from the Hawaiian, Maori, and Easter Islands, it may be considered as of older origin and ancestral in an area of survival of archaic features less influenced by the forces of change so evident in the Society Islands.

The subject of bird-men and the bird-man concept in Polynesia calls for monographic treatment, including an assemblage of all material available and the study of it in relation to archaeological evidence, mythology, religion, and pre-European Polynesian society in general. In such a study it would be essential to relate the bird-man ideas and bird beliefs of Polynesia to those of Melanesia, Micronesia, the island world of Southeast Asia, and the ancient cultures of China and India. Polynesian sculptures depicting ancestors and gods should also be reviewed in relation to the same areas and to beliefs concerning birds and bird-men. The theory that avian features tend to be superimposed on human images, thus giving rise to features that are difficult to explain in any other terms, should be worked out thoroughly in relation to the abundant material that exists (notably for New Zealand and the *manaia*). This paper has attempted to establish the importance of the bird-man in Polynesian art, the ideas that inspired it, and the significance of this material to Polynesian iconography in general.

LITERATURE CITED

ARCHEY, GILBERT
    1933. "Evolution of Certain Maori Carving Patterns." *J. Polynesian Soc.* **42**:171-190.
    1936. "Maori Carving Patterns." *J. Polynesian Soc.* **45**:49-62.

ARMSTRONG, EDWARD A.
    1958. *The Folklore of Birds.* London: Collins Clear-Type Press.

BALFOUR, HENRY
    1893. *The Evolution of Decorative Art.* London: Percival.
    1905. "Birds and Human Designs from the Solomon Islands, Illustrating the Influence of One Design over Another." *Man* **5**(5):81-83.
    1917. "Some Ethnological Suggestions in Regard to Easter Island, or Rapanui." *Folklore* **28**(4):356-381.

BARROW, T. T.
    1956. "Maori Decorative Carving—An Outline." *J. Polynesian Soc.* **65**(4): 305-331.
    1965. *A Guide to the Maori Meeting House Te Hau-Ki-Turanga.* Wellington: Dominion Mus.

BEST, ELSDON
    1924. *The Maori.* 2 vols. Polynesian Soc. Mem., Vol. 5. Wellington.

BUCK, PETER H. (TE RANGI HIROA)
    1957. *Arts and Crafts of Hawaii.* B. P. Bishop Mus. Spec. Pub. 45. Honolulu.

CODRINGTON, R. H.
    1891. *The Melanesians. Studies in the Anthropology and Folklore.* Oxford: Clarendon Press.

CRANSTONE, B. A. L.
    1955. "An Easter Island Bird Figure." *British Mus. Quarterly* **20**(1):22-23.

EMORY, KENNETH P.
    1924. *The Island of Lanai.* B. P. Bishop Mus. Bull. 12. Honolulu.

FORNANDER, ABRAHAM
    1916, 1917. "Hawaiian Antiquities and Folk-Lore." *Mem. B. P. Bishop Mus.,* Vol. 4. Honolulu.

FRAZER, JAMES GEORGE
    1913. *The Belief in Immortality and the Worship of the Dead. Vol. I: The Belief Among the Aborigines of Australia, The Torres Straits Islands, New Guinea and Melanesia.* London: Macmillan.
    1922. *The Belief in Immortality and the Worship of the Dead. Vol. II: The Belief Among the Polynesians.* London: Macmillan.
    1924. *The Belief in Immortality and the Worship of the Dead. Vol. III: The Belief Among Micronesians.* London: Macmillan.

HANDY, E. S. CRAIGHILL
1923. *The Native Culture in the Marquesas.* B. P. Bishop Mus. Bull. 9. Honolulu.
1927. *Polynesian Religion.* B. P. Bishop Mus. Bull. 34. Honolulu.

HEYERDAHL, THOR, AND E. N. FERDON, JR. (Editors)
1961. *Reports of the Norwegian Archaeological Expedition to Easter Island and the East Pacific. Vol. 1: Archaeology of Easter Island.* School American Research and Mus. New Mexico. Monog. 24, Pt. 1. London: Allen and Unwin.

LINTON, RALPH
1923. "The Material Culture of the Marquesas Islands." *Mem. B. P. Bishop Mus.,* Vol. 8, No. 5. Honolulu.

McALLISTER, J. GILBERT
1933. *Archaeology of Oahu.* B. P. Bishop Mus. Bull. 104. Honolulu.

McEWEN, J. M.
1966. *Maori Art: An Encyclopedia of New Zealand,* Vol. 2, pp. 408-429. Wellington: New Zealand Govt. Printer.

MÉTRAUX, ALFRED
1940. *Ethnology of Easter Island.* B. P. Bishop Mus. Bull. 160. Honolulu.

PHILLIPPS, W. J.
1958. *Maori Carving Illustrated.* Wellington: A. H. and A. W. Reed.

REED, A. W.
1963. *Treasury of Maori Folklore.* Wellington: A. H. and A. W. Reed.

ROUTLEDGE, MRS. SCORESBY
1917. "The Bird Cult of Easter Island." *Folklore* **28**(4):337-355.

SHAWCROSS, WILFRED
1964. "An Archaeological Assemblage of Maori Combs." *J. Polynesian Soc.* **73**(4):382-398.

SKINNER, H. D.
1933. "Maori Amulets in Stone, Bone, and Shell." *J. Polynesian Soc.* **42**(3): 191-203.
1964. "Crocodile and Lizard in New Zealand Myth and Material Culture." *Rec. Otago Mus. Anthropology,* No. 1, pp. 1-43. Dunedin.

SKINNER, H. D., and W. J. PHILLIPPS
1953. "Necklaces, Pendants and Amulets from the Chatham Islands and New Zealand." *J. Polynesian Soc.* **62**(2):169-195.

WITTKOWER, R.
1939. "Eagle and Serpent. A Study in the Migration of Symbols." *J. Warburg Inst.,* Vol. 2, No. 4.

THE IMMEDIATE ORIGINS OF THE POLYNESIANS

R. C. GREEN*

Bernice P. Bishop Museum, Honolulu

IN A RECENT ASSESSMENT of current thought on Polynesian origins, Ferdon (1963, p. 505) suggests that the culture had many possible sources and utilized many possible routes of travel, the variety of which in his view are infinite, and only a portion of which we can ever hope to document. Also it is certainly true, as he (Ferdon, 1963, p. 499), Heyerdahl (1952, p. 8), Suggs (1960, p. 48; 1963, p. 1252) and many others have emphasized, that the range of theories on Polynesian origins which began with the speculations of early European explorers of the 18th century is now "only slightly exceeded by the variety of evidence mustered to support particular concepts." Especially is this true if one simply lists the various views as they have developed historically (see for instance Heyerdahl, 1952, pp. 4-8). Others of us, however, are unconvinced that the origins of the Polynesians are quite so diverse or complicated as Ferdon's statements would seem to imply, or that the evidence once used in their support, or that which is now available, does not allow us to reject a great many of the older theories as being unsupported by critical examination of these facts. In this respect Emory (1959, p. 34) speaks for many when he writes:

---

* The origins of the Polynesians and their dispersal throughout their island world have long been a concern of Kenneth P. Emory, as anyone familiar with him or his writings is well aware. It therefore seems fitting that an essay which explores one aspect of this fascinating subject should be among those offered to him on this occasion, for in the past decade we have probed, often as a direct result of his leadership and stimulus, more deeply than ever before into this subject. As a result, a "Prehistory of Polynesia" is slowly being pieced together by students of historical linguistics, physical anthropology, and archaeology, which not only reopens avenues long considered closed, but serves to pioneer efforts in new directions.

I wish to acknowledge here the assistance of Miss Janet M. Davidson in reading this manuscript and to thank her for helpful comment and criticism.

Therefore, it seems reasonable to view the arrival of man in Polynesia as having taken place through the migrations of a few small groups of canoe-borne people from islands not far to the west of Polynesia. These several groups formed the nucleus of the population which was to arise out of their descendants, and these original groups need not have come from one single island or an identical ethnic group of people. . . .

It seems therefore erroneous to consider that there ever was a migration to Polynesia of a people physically identical with the Polynesians as we know them, and as already possessing the distinctive features of Polynesian language and culture. What now appears most likely is that people of somewhat diverse origins came together in a western archipelago in the Polynesian area about B.C. 1500, and, in comparative isolation, their descendants, their language, and their culture took on the features which Polynesians now share in common and which give them their distinctive characteristics.

Because my own views parallel to a degree those of Emory, in this essay I propose to examine only three of the many theories of Polynesian origins. In doing so, little or nothing will be said about ultimate origins, or even origins at any great remove from the immediate peopling of the Polynesian area proper. The reason is that I find the known evidence on the subject not yet sufficiently great to add anything to that which has recently appeared in the literature (Suggs, 1960; Chang, 1964; Solheim, 1964; Grace, 1964). On the other hand, evidence is rapidly accumulating on the basic form of ancestral cultural patterns in Polynesia, which, as they changed, were disseminated throughout Polynesia. The basic pattern, as Emory recognized, seems to have developed first in West Polynesia as a distinct entity, probably as a result of slow differentiation from the still earlier cultural forms found not far to the west in areas of Eastern Melanesia and as the result of marked cultural changes in Eastern Melanesia itself, only some influences of which reached Polynesia.

In Polynesia, little doubt can exist any longer that the basic pattern was further elaborated and diversified over time both by internal mechanisms of cultural change (Buck, 1944, pp. 501, 507; Goodenough, 1957, pp. 146-153), and through later contact at different times and places throughout Polynesia, in which a host of traits, probably from rather diverse sources, many of them outside the Polynesian area, have been grafted onto the basic pattern. This process has long been recognized in West Polynesia, where contacts in both directions between later Melanesian cultures and slowly differentiating cultures of the island groups of West Polynesia have often been noted (Burrows, 1938, p. 152; Buck, 1938, p. 311; 1944, p. 505; Watters, 1958, pp. 49-50). A similar process between Micronesia and Polynesia has recently been examined in some detail by Koch (1966), whose field work has been in a principal point of exchange, the Gilbert and the Ellice Islands. Finally, in more cautious statements than characterized his *American Indians in the Pacific,* Heyerdahl (Heyerdahl and Ferdon, 1961, pp. 493-526; Heyerdahl, in press) reviews the evidence for a similar process between South American prehistoric cultures and those of Easter Island. In fact, in view of the accumulating evidence for long-distance prehistoric voyaging in the Pacific, even though much of it be one way and without adequate navigational aids so that landfalls are open to many chance factors, Ferdon rightly stresses, I believe, a point made many times by others, that the Pacific is composed of a great number of highways that offer opportunities for a wide and rather diverse range of cultural contacts, and we should anticipate these rather than seek to deny or dismiss them. As a result, distributions of traits, or of certain lexical items, or of particular physical characteristics, are simply not all going to fit the classic patterns imposed by an earlier generation of scholars devoted to the culture area concept, with its cultural centers, subcultural areas, and marginal survivals.

All this does not preclude, however, setting out the increasing evidence that the proto-languages, cultures, and populations ancestral to the basic Polynesian pattern are most likely to have their immediate sources in Eastern Melanesia. This evidence is made more impressive, in fact, if brief consideration is given first to the Micronesian area, which until fairly recently was the more highly favored route, and to Easter Island and the Hawaiian chain which Heyerdahl (1952, pp. 706-707) singled out as the two island groups of Polynesia that were settled from two maritime centers on the west coast of the American continent; the first by raftsmen of the Andean high cultures and the second by canoe-builders of the northwest coast. The essay therefore falls into three parts, the last of which attempts to sum up the evidence for an immediate origin of the Polynesians in Eastern Melanesia.

MICRONESIA

During the late 1930's and early 1940's, a route from Indonesia via Micronesia was favored by many Pacific scholars for the movement of the Polynesians into their far-flung island world. Indeed in the widely disseminated writings of Buck (1938, 1944) and Weckler (1943), these views were given particular prominence. Up to 1952 some, like Spoehr (1952, p. 460), continued to reiterate this view. Spoehr even proposed the concept Micro-Polynesia (1952, p. 468), although he subsequently admitted his indiscretion (1957, p. 177). Since the late 1940's, and in particular since the Seventh Pacific Science Congress in 1949 (see Heyerdahl, 1952, pp. 54-56, 67-68 for a summary), this view has steadily lost favor.

A Micronesian route has also long been one part of the theories of certain German and Swiss scholars, and has been reiterated recently by Schmitz (1962, p. 418). This theory postulated a two-pronged settlement of Polynesia, in which an earlier Austro-Melanid culture reached West Polynesia first and was subsequently transformed into its Polynesian type by a northern wave of Austronesians, who, not touching Melanesia, but traveling by way of Micronesia to West Polynesia, were able to give to later Polynesian culture its dominant Austronesian nature.

Viewed in this context, Buck's concept of a Micronesian path for Polynesian origins was the exact opposite of the Swiss-German school, for his Polynesians arrived in West Polynesia having lost in Micronesia the food plants, domestic animals, stone tools, and much of the material culture that had previously been developed in the volcanic islands of their ancient homeland in Indonesia. In his view they recovered these items and the art of their manufacture in the volcanic islands of West Polynesia, as the required materials again became available, or they borrowed them, as with the food plants, paper mulberry, gourd, and domestic animals, from the neighboring Fijians and other people of Eastern Melanesia (Buck, 1944, pp. 477, 520).

The case against a Polynesian movement through Micronesia has become even more sharply drawn today than it was a decade ago. As Koch (1966) puts it, if the cultural boundary between the traditional concepts of Polynesia and Micronesia (made possible only by stressing the fundamental unity of the Polynesian cultures, and the hybrid character of the Micronesian cultures) is examined today in the light of much recent ethnographic evidence, the boundary is found to be sharper than would be expected if the two cultures were immediately related to a common ancestor. Thus he finds it impossible on ethnographic evidence to "recognize clear traces of an Austronesian ('Polynesian') immigration via Micronesia and the Gilbert and Ellice Islands," where his knowledge of cultures is firsthand. Instead, the likelihood of diverse origins for various of the cultures, languages, and even human populations of different parts of the Micronesian area is clearly perceived.

In the field of linguistics, for instance, Palau and Chamorro are separate members of Dyen's Malayo-Polynesian Linkage, while Yapese is a separate member of the Austronesian Linkage, groupings which imply they have diverged from other subgroups in the Austronesian language family a very long time ago (Dyen, 1965, pp. 33-34, 39-40). The Carolinian subfamily, including Ponapean and its dialects, Trukese, Marshallese, and Kusaiean, forms another subgroup, also belonging to the Austronesian Linkage. The internal evidence from this subgroup implies, moreover, according to Dyen (1965, p. 55) that the Carolinian languages from Truk to the west stem from the Ponape area, while overall an east-to-west movement is clearly discernible, starting from the Kusaie–Ponape–Marshalls–Gilberts area. Grace (1964, p. 365), too, finds that Palauan and Chamorro belong outside a single postulated subgroup that includes all other Austronesian languages of Melanesia, Polynesia, and Micronesia. Within Micronesia itself the evidence suggests, he believes, that all the languages except Palauan and Chamorro "belong to a single group which has its closest relations with the languages of the New Hebrides, although not with those languages which are most closely related to Rotuman, Fijian, and Polynesian" (Grace, 1964, p. 367). Yap and Nauru are included in this group but regarded as quite aberrant. This implies, he suggests: (a) a movement from the New Hebrides to Micronesia, and (b) a greater internal diversity in Eastern Micronesian than in Polynesian, and consequently an earlier differentiation of the languages of Micronesia, probably considerably before the time of Christ. Recent linguistic evidence, then, points to some diversity for the origin of the Micronesian languages (Izui, 1965, p. 350), an east-to-west movement in those of Eastern and Central Micronesia, and a possible origin for them in the Melanesian area of the New Hebrides at a time before the Polynesian languages had become differentiated. This is hardly encouraging evidence for the movement of the Polynesians through Micronesia, in view of the fact that the Polynesian languages that are in Micronesia (Kapingamarangi, Nukuoro) seem definitely to derive from subgroups centered in West Polynesia (Bayard, 1966; Pawley, 1966, and personal communication).

No summary which coordinates data on the physical anthropology of Micronesia is available beyond that by Hunt (1950), and the coverage in recent studies remains patchy. Still a number of articles based on results of blood-group identifications for samples from various Micronesian populations have appeared (Simmons et al., 1965; Sussman et al., 1959; Myrianthopoulos and Pieper, 1959; Giblett, 1961). Results, when compared with those from Polynesian populations, are difficult to interpret, but Simmons (1965, p. 343) is unable to find any broad points of serological similarity between the two groups. Sussman *et al.* (1959, pp. 644-645) found the Marshallese population to be fairly homogeneous with extremes in gene frequencies which related them more closely to the populations of Indonesia and Southeast Asia than to Polynesia. Myrianthopoulos and Pieper (1959, pp. 105-108) found in data on the ABO group that the Chamorro are similar to the Palauans, but different from the Eastern Micronesian Trukese and Gilbertese, on the one hand, and the Polynesians from Kapingamarangi on the other. Simmons *et al.* (1965, p. 165) also studied the ABO, MNS, and Rh systems in samples from Yap, Palau, and Truk and compared their results with all previous surveys. They found a Polynesian relationship favored by three of the three gene frequencies for Gilbertese and Kapingamarangi, an Indonesian relationship in two of the three frequencies by Marshallese and Palauans, while either a Polynesian or an Indonesian relationship may be favored in two of three gene frequencies among Trukese, Ellice Islanders and Yapese. These studies show general agreement with Hunt's proposed division of geographical Micronesia into a Chamorro group with Mongoloid metrical affinities, a "trans-Micronesian" group from Sonsorol and Tobi to the Marshalls and Gilberts, and the Polynesian speakers of the islands of the Ellice group, Nukuoro, and Kapingamarangi. A study of precontact male crania from Guam has also suggested that they were metrically related to an "essentially Mongoloid type" found today in the populations of the Western Carolines, but bear little resemblance metrically to contemporary groups from Northeast or Southwest Micronesia, or a generalized type in Central Micronesia (Pettay, 1959, p. 58). Marshall and Snow (1956, pp. 416-418), in their study of Polynesian crania, also compared them with small samples from Guam and Fiji and found those of Guam to be less like the Polynesian ones than the Fijian. Thus these results do not encourage the view of any clear-cut uniformity in Micronesian populations, nor do they encourage the view of close physical relationships with the various Polynesian populations in the Micronesian area or in Polynesia.

The archaeological evidence for Central and particularly Eastern Micronesia is fragmentary and sketchy, most of it resulting from surface surveys and collections (Davidson, in press, a). That from the pottery area of Western Micronesia (see Spoehr, 1957, Fig. 1) is much fuller and based on the intensive survey of Palau by Osborne (1966), the excavations by Gifford and Gifford (1959) in Yap and those on Saipan, Tinian, and Rota in the Marianas by Spoehr (1957). The data from sites in this pottery area are still not well integrated but do demonstrate the likelihood of some basic relationships as well as later contact and influence among the three island groups. They also serve to suggest that the origins of some of these cultures, perhaps going back as far as the 1500 B.C. level indicated by Spoehr's (1957, p. 169) earliest date, are either in the Philippine and Malaysian area (Spoehr, 1957, pp. 174-175; Osborne, 1966, pp. 462-463, 472) or, with respect to some of the earlier Marianas pottery and fishhooks, perhaps to the north in the Jomon of Japan (Solheim, 1964, pp. 401-402). The earlier archaeological assemblages from Western Micronesia which are presently known, however, do not furnish much evidence for an ancestral culture from which the Polynesian pattern could derive. In fact, on the Polynesian outlier of Nukuoro where a Polynesian pattern was to be expected, the prehistoric assemblage of fishhooks, shell adzes, and a variety of other items is more easily compared to surface collections and ethnographic specimens from the adjacent islands of Micronesia, or to shell artifacts in the New Hebrides and other parts of Melanesia, than with those in Polynesia (Davidson, in press, b). Thus such archaeological evidence as is available from Micronesia is not in support of close Micronesian-Polynesian connections either, although some items in each cultural area may have been borrowed from the other through contact.

In summary, Buck's statement that: "Strong support in favor of the Micronesian route lies in the positive evidence against the route through Melanesia" (1938, p. 45) could now easily be inverted. The positive evidence from linguistics, physical anthropology, ethnology, and archaeology, while still very fragmentary, is against such a movement in Micronesia, but tends, as will be demonstrated below, to favor an immediate origin in Eastern Melanesia.

POSSIBLE AMERICAN SOURCES

Heyerdahl (1952, pp. 207-208) based his argument for the two initial settlements of Polynesia from the east on a rejection of the Melanesian and Micronesian areas as possible sources, and on the calculation that the first organized settlements in Samoa and Tonga were established as recently as A.D. 900-1000. In his view, this meant that Western Polynesia was not permanently settled until many centuries later than A.D. 400 to 500, the date when, along with other Polynesian scholars of that era, he believed the traditional accounts to indicate that man first entered Polynesia. In contrast to many others, however, he

assigned the first settling of Easter Island to this initial period and postulated for it an origin among the maritime cultures of the South American
coast. As he says "genealogical computations were the only available
means for an attempt of approximate dating" and "it should be stressed
that this profound difference in timing arose directly from the fact that
both attempts at dating were based on purely preconceived opinions as
to the voyaging directions of the first immigrants, combined with the
mutual acceptance of the current theory that the 5th century A.D. represented the initiation of human migration into the Polynesian island
world" (Heyerdahl, in Heyerdahl and Ferdon, 1961, p. 494). With the
advent of modern archaeology and the technique of radiocarbon dating,
the general use of genealogical dating has become suspect, while his
basic assumption, the primacy of East Polynesia, in particular Easter
Island and Hawaii, as the original points of entry from America of the
first peoples in Polynesia would seem to be in error.

Securely dated materials from Tonga and Samoa belonging to the 1st
to 3rd centuries A.D. are now known (Green and Davidson, 1965; Poulsen, 1966, p. 195). In Tonga an earlier date of 2,380 ± 51 years before
1950 for a fire pit beneath a pottery-bearing stratum has also been
reported. Moreover, the early Tongan adzes, shell ornaments, and many
of the stylistic elements of the pottery are directly related to similar
materials from Fiji and New Caledonia, also dated to between 400 and
800 B.C. (Poulsen, in press; Green, in press). They form part of an
early horizon associated with a distinct pottery tradition, one of the
main elements of which is decoration in the Lapita style, that stretches
from Tonga and Fiji in the east to New Caledonia, Efate in the New
Hebrides, and west to the island of Watom off the northeast coast of
New Britain. In further support of considerable time depth in West
Polynesia, stratigraphically earlier materials than those dated to the 1st
century A.D. have recently been recovered in Western Samoa, although
they are not related to the Lapita pottery tradition. Through such finds
it is becoming increasingly obvious that the time depth for initial occupation of West Polynesia is something of the order of 2,500 or more
years.

On the other hand, the time depth established by archaeology in
East Polynesia is probably not more than 2,000 years, and in many
island groups will be considerably less. Securely dated sequences presently go back to the 11th century A.D. in New Zealand, and to A.D. 700
to 900 in the Marquesas and Society Islands (Sinoto, in press, a; Emory
and Sinoto, 1965, pp. 95-96; Groube, in press). Two earlier dates for

the Marquesas in the first centuries B.C. have been recorded (Suggs, 1961, p. 20), but for some of us it remains an open question whether or not they can be used to date the earliest materials excavated by Suggs (Sinoto and Kellum, 1965, pp. 37-41; Sinoto, in press, b).

A similar position has to be adopted for the two early dates from Easter Island. One of A.D. 380 ± 100 is for the Poike ditch, and another, rejected by the excavator because it is in conflict with one of A.D. 1629 ± 150 for bone from the same grave, is A.D. 318 ± 250 for *totora* reed (Smith, in Heyerdahl and Ferdon, 1961, p. 394). Yet carbon-dating of bone consistently yields too recent results in Polynesia, while modern samples of *totora* reed were tested and shown to be reliable, so that the earlier sample of the same material is not suspect on that basis. In fact, as Golson (1965, pp. 75-77) points out, in terms of what we do and do not know about its archaeological associations and the history of Tepeu 1 site where it was found, the date need not be totally unacceptable, for the grave could equally well be of the Early Period as of the Middle one to which it has been assigned on the basis of the later radiocarbon date. Actually the difficulties do not lie in accepting these ages as an estimate for the settlement of Easter Island, but in the insistence that the one from the Poike ditch may be used to date the various features of Easter Island culture thought not to be of Polynesian origin and to derive instead from South America. Meggers (1963, pp. 330-331) in a review of this work put the issues for evidence of this contact very well:

If we accept this hypothesis, however, it seems somewhat peculiar that the closest resemblances should be with the Tiahuanaco cultures centered on Lake Titicaca in the highlands of Peru–Bolivia, rather than with one of the coastal complexes. Furthermore, Classic Tiahuanaco begins around A.D. 800 and its influence on the coast lags by some 200 years. If these dates are accurate then the beginning of the Early Period on Easter Island, which the authors believe to predate A.D. 400, is anterior to the appearance of the Tiahuanacoid on the mainland, to the detriment of their argument of derivation from that direction.

There would appear to be two ways out of this dilemma. The first is that the early date does not reflect human occupation of Easter Island. The authors suggest in several places that the charcoal may be of natural origin. Furthermore, its temporal isolation seems suspicious, the next earliest date being 857, nearly 500 years later. If 857 were selected as dating the beginning of the Early Period, it would fit much better with what is known of the chronological position of the relevant traits in the mainland sequence and strengthens the argument for connections. The second possible explanation is that dismissal of some of the elements as rare in Oceania reflects lack of knowledge about the archaeology of this area rather than actual absence.

Emory (1963, p. 566) in a review of the same work, tends to reinforce Meggers' point by following another line of argument. He is willing to accept the early date for the Poike ditch as a possible one for estimating the age of settlement in Easter Island but he advances evidence that the ditch was used for horticulture instead. He then quite legitimately points out that the famous dressed stone *ahu* religious structures have nowhere been securely established as existing at the early end of this poorly defined Early Period. Rather the evidence suggests they occurred at a point some 500 years later in a structurally defined portion of the Early Period, or at about the time that they could more easily have been derived from South America.

Golson's (1965, pp. 73-77) analysis raises further questions about the early dating of the Poike ditch. Noting the 1,300-year disparity between the date of ditch construction implied by the A.D. 380 ± 100 date for secondary charcoal under the mound of spoil derived from the ditch, and that for a primary deposit of charcoal in the ditch of A.D. 1670 ± 100, he observes that, in the interpretation of the charcoal from the ditch, the accepted tradition is that it was built about A.D. 1680 to meet a particular military need which it immediately fulfilled. This contemporaneity is supported, he notes, by the occurrence of two identical sling stones, one in the layer dated to A.D. 1670 and the other in the spoil of the mound itself. Similarly, Evans (in Heyerdahl and Ferdon, 1965, pp. 472-473) found that one piece of obsidian from the base of the ditch on the sterile soil and another from the base of the mound on the natural surface yielded almost identical hydration rims which suggested ages between 360 and 400 years ago making them quite compatible with the later radiocarbon date. As he noted, these results indicate the construction of the ditch to be a single event at the end of the Middle Period, rather than a feature re-used over a period of 1,000 years. Thus, in the lack of any clear stratigraphic evidence for two periods in the formation of the mound with a long interval between, the construction of the ditch which gave rise to the mound is best interpreted as having occurred at the end of the Middle Period. The question is then, how does one account for the secondary charcoal derived from the burning of wood found in the underlying soil as well as on its surface, if one does not accept the excavator's assertion that he "is certain that the carbon was deposited immediately prior to its having been covered by earth from the ditch (Smith, in Heyerdahl and Ferdon, 1961, p. 391).

Golson (1965) also makes a full and careful review of the sequence of religious structures postulated for Easter Island, including an evaluation of the A.D. 857 ± 200 date associated with the initial building of the plaza wall at Vinapu 2. He shows that, if we accept it as a date for the initial building of the *ahu* structure as well, then it is likely that it marks a much earlier point in the sequence of construction of religious structures of the Early Period than is allowed by the excavator's interpretation (1965, p. 82). He also develops an argument on the basis of the excavator's own evidence to show it is equally likely that Vinapu 2 with this early date bears the closest resemblances in form and execution to other Polynesian religious structures and is earlier than Vinapu 1, the masterpiece of Easter Island construction in stone. This reversal in the sequence therefore not only places the parallels used for connections with South America later in time, but also allows some time for the initial development of these religious structures in Easter Island itself.

In summary, a date for the settlement of Easter Island by A.D. 400 is still open to question, although in the view of some Polynesian archaeologists a date of this order for settlement by Polynesians is not at all unreasonable. Dated materials with which valid comparisons may be made are all much later, however.

These facts tend to answer some of the questions which concern us here. On the first point—did the initial settlement of the Polynesian area begin in West or East Polynesia—the evidence would seem to be fairly clear that West Polynesia with its older materials and longer sequences was settled before East Polynesia, including Easter Island. However, on a related point—had Polynesians settled in other islands of East Polynesia before Easter Island—the evidence is still not secure. All that can be said is that a well-supported sequence of Polynesian materials, which goes back in time as far as any reasonably dated materials from Easter Island, is known from the Marquesas, a postulated source for Easter Island's Polynesian culture. Also sequences with Polynesian materials almost as early as materials from Easter Island are known from New Zealand, Hawaii, and the Society Islands, with a scatter of additional radiocarbon datings quite as valid as that of A.D. 380 for Easter Island, suggesting that in each of these groups we have not yet reached the earliest levels, and that in some of them we may expect to go back as much as 2,000 years.

In turning to Heyerdahl's other notion of the settlement of Polynesia by people coming into the area through Hawaii via the American northwest coast, we find that it has received no support whatsoever, and now seems largely to have been abandoned or forgotten. All the linguistic and archaeological data assembled to date, in fact, point to the initial settlement of Hawaii from the Marquesas after A.D. 800, with later contacts from Tahiti about the 13th century A.D. influencing the course of cultural change in that group (Green, 1966, pp. 29-30). We are left then chiefly with the possibility of a later entry into an already settled Polynesian area of a non-Polynesian population on the still uninhabited Easter Island, which was subsequently replaced by one that was predominantly Polynesian.

I will not go into this vexed question of cultural continuity, versus evidence for replacement of one culture by another on Easter Island. Suffice it to say that Golson (1965) develops a strong case for continuity and change without replacement throughout the known portion of the Easter Island sequence, including that of the religious structures. It is also true that to most Pacific archaeologists the portable material culture of the Middle and Later Periods of the Easter Island sequence is overwhelmingly Polynesian, tending to substantiate Meggers' other possible explanation that "dismissal of some of the elements as rare in Oceania reflects a lack of knowledge about the archaeology of this area rather than actual absence." These deficiencies are now being corrected, and will, I believe, remove traits such as bone needles, stone and bone fishhooks, tanged obsidian knives, the pentagonal or rectangular fire pit of dressed slabs, and even the metatelike shallow grinding slabs from the list given by Heyerdahl (in press) as possibly indicative of contacts with South America, simply because they are without sufficient Polynesian parallels.

In fact, the items which Ferdon (Heyerdahl and Ferdon, 1961, pp. 533-535) or Heyerdahl (in press) select as rare or absent in the rest of Polynesia and for which they can cite apparent parallels in America, although not necessarily in any one single archaeological complex, belong to two clusters. In one group may be placed two useful fresh-water plants, *Polygonum acuminatum* and *Scripus totara,* the use of well-fitted masonry construction in religious structures, the emphasis on solar observation and orientation in them, and three statuary types; for all of these they believe they have reasonable evidence of an Early Period date. The remaining traits form a slightly larger second group and are known only after the beginning of the Middle Period, starting about A.D. 1100, although some may eventually be found to have been present earlier. To either group may be added the sweet potato, present in South America for perhaps 1,000 years before the first settlement of Polynesia, and therefore available to be brought at any period. On the evidence supplied by Heyerdahl and his collaborators, as pointed out by their reviewers, especially Golson, the assignment of these first traits to the Early Period is not always sound and certainly none is as yet securely dated to any point much before A.D. 800, while some may be several hundred years later. In the light of the difficulties caused by seeking too early relationships with South America, it seems to me therefore more economical to view all these traits as a single group dating somewhere between A.D. 800 and 1300, and to cite them as probable evidence for one period of contact with South America rather than two, as suggested by Ferdon (Heyerdahl and Ferdon, 1961, p. 535).

Nor is the pollen evidence necessarily in conflict with this view, for the clearing of the extinct palm on the crater of Rano Raraku that gave access to the extensive stone quarries seems to be the event which also gave rise to the soot particles with which the first appearance of the two fresh-water plants is associated (Heyerdahl, in press). Some quarrying may have been done earlier around the crater, to which the two unique Early Period statues near there could be witness, but in the main, mass-production quarrying for statues to place on *ahu* is clearly a Middle Period event (Skjölsvold, in Heyerdahl and Ferdon, 1961, pp. 343, 374), so it seems rather unwarranted to assign the initial appearance of the soot to the first settlers, as Heyerdahl (in press) has done.

Finally, and most important for our purposes, the very fact that these "non-Polynesian" traits are often rare, or even absent in the rest of Polynesia is evidence that South America was not a main source for the immediate origins of a majority of the Polynesian populations.

Heyerdahl (in press) also continues to stress the former presence of a non-Polynesian language in Easter Island, as well as the fact that Tahitian over the last century has had a marked effect on the language spoken today. However, many of these Tahitian borrowings in the language of Easter Island can easily be identified by the application of the comparative method, while the same technique reveals that the Easter Island language, despite all this influence, preserves certain items that could not have been borrowed at any recent date, because they have been lost some time ago in all the other languages of the Eastern Polynesian group. Instead these features reflect some of the earliest forms in a proto-language from which all the languages of East Polynesia derive, and as such serve to demonstrate that the language of Easter Island was the first to become differentiated in that group. This fact, in itself, suggests that it was one of the earliest island groups in the Eastern area to be settled by Polynesian-speaking peoples (Green, 1966, pp. 17-18, 25-26).

MELANESIA

Having examined some of the evidence bearing on two of the sources favored in the past few decades for the immediate origins of the Polynesians, Micronesia and America, we return to a third source, long favored by many, namely Melanesia, and in particular Eastern Melanesia, consisting principally of the Solomon, Santa Cruz, New Hebrides, New Caledonia, Loyalty, and Fijian Island groups. And here I believe one must concur with Emory that it is "erroneous to consider that there ever was a migration to Polynesia of a people already physically identical with the Polynesians as we know them and as already possessing the distinctive features of Polynesian language and culture." Many early theorists who have used the Melanesian route have made precisely the mistake to which Emory refers, while in the view developed here we will be searching for proto-languages, earlier cultural assemblages, and ancestral populations which were not Polynesian, but from which the Polynesian languages, the basic form of their culture, and even their general physical type could derive and subsequently develop within Polynesia itself.

In my view the ethnographically known populations, cultures, and languages of Eastern Melanesia are the result of a long, complex, and diverse cultural history which we are only now beginning to unravel. But the degree to which migrations need be involved is only that which is required to move people continually from one island group to the next, although not always in a systematic fashion or direction. The object, then, is not to trace the route of the Polynesians through Eastern Melanesia, but to show there are no insurmountable obstacles to deriving them from the ancestors of some populations still in that area, to demonstrate that related languages among those now spoken in Eastern Melanesia allow the postulation of proto-languages from which both they and Polynesian could have come, and to find among the earlier cultural assemblages that are now being recovered archaeologically, those which constitute adequate sources for many items in the early cultural assemblages of West Polynesia, and which contrast with many of the later cultural assemblages in Eastern Melanesia that do not. In this respect I have often noted a certain tendency to regard the recent Melanesian cultures as accurately reflecting basic patterns that have prevailed in the area from the distant past, just as racially a similar assumption is so often made as to the deep antiquity of populations of the so-called Melanesian race now in the area. It is almost as if cultural, linguistic, and physical change were not an aspect of Melanesian prehistory, whereas in my view such change is probably far greater than that found in either Polynesia or Micronesia.

It is notable in most of the previous theories discussed (Buck, 1944, pp. 477, 520; Schmitz, 1962, pp. 418-419; Heyerdahl, 1952, pp. 61-65) that the Southeast Asian and Pacific food complex that includes most of the domestic plants and animals present in Polynesia is either borrowed or brought in from Melanesia, whatever the postulated origins of the population or their culture. Barrau (1965, pp. 73-74) provides a recent summary of the botanical evidence which shows that the immediate sources of most of the Polynesian food plants are likely to be in the adjacent areas of Melanesia, while an earlier study by St. John (1957) demonstrates that only a few of these plants could have been derived from Micronesia. Barrau (1963, pp. 5-6), using linguistic evidence, shows that at least two of them may have been.

What has always made an immediate origin in Melanesia difficult to accept, however, was a matter of race, for it has long been thought that these dark-skinned peoples of Melanesia were among the first populations to be established throughout the area, and therefore that the Polynesians must have arrived by some other route or they surely would have picked up some of the racial characteristics of these resident Melanesian groups as well as a number of the cultural items which they possess, but which the Polynesians lack. This theme is elaborated fairly fully by Heyerdahl (1952, pp. 15, 50-52) in rejecting a Melanesian route, but is more cogently put by Schmitz (1962, p. 418).

> There is one undeniable fact with which we could start our discussion. Melanesian and Polynesian dialects, both belonging to the Austronesian family, are spoken by human groups of different race types. The negroid (melanid) Melanesians cannot be connected genetically with the polynesid Polynesians. I do not have to cite all the authorities. . . .

It seems therefore that one major stumbling block is a somewhat false assessment of the physical nature of the populations in Melanesia, for the linguistic and archaeological evidences for immediate origins in this direction are fairly straightforward. Thus when I reviewed the evidence for Fiji as the immediate source of the Polynesians, racially, culturally, and linguistically (Green, 1963, pp. 245-250), I proceeded simply to set out the rather substantial evidence available in each of these fields. But the recent physical evidence from Fiji was not as satisfactory then as it is now, and it will be discussed in more detail below, along with other recent evidence on the physical nature of the Melanesian populations.

In making the case for a Fijian origin, however, I was guilty of at least one major indiscretion in labeling this culture proto-Polynesian, a linguistic term for the original language spoken by Polynesians *after* they left their presumed homeland in Fiji, and their language and that in Fiji began to differentiate. Clearly it is a proto-language ancestral to both Fijian and Polynesian, which, if any, is to be associated with an earlier cultural assemblage from which the Polynesian culture derives and then develops. Also it is a fact to be demonstrated, and not something simply to be assumed, that a particular proto-language may be associated with a particular ancestral culture. Such an assumption tends to occur if both are called by the same term. I would therefore withdraw the proto-Polynesian identification of the Sigatoka Phase materials as being unsound both in theory and practice and warn others from repeating it. Still this does not lessen the case I made there initially and have subsequently developed further (Green, in press) that ancestral forms which may be postulated as sources for the language, culture, and even physical make-up of the earliest Polynesians are to be found in Fiji and other immediately adjacent island groups of Eastern Melanesia, although it would be wrong to refer to them on that basis as Polynesian. It remains then only to present additional material which has appeared more recently, most of which further serves to support that case. At this point it is also relevant to note the close parallels between my position and that of Emory's cited at the beginning of this paper.

One recent study of some populations in Melanesia (Swindler, 1962) finds that they are sufficiently homogeneous to be regarded as a major breeding unit or Geographical Race. This refers to the fact that they occupy a geographically delineated area in which the various populations have been exchanging genetic materials for a sufficient length of time to be more like each other than they are like groups outside this geographical area. It does not help in establishing the origins of the basic racial elements which have gone to make up the present race, for this is usually the result of a long and complex history of genetic changes which may be owing to a large number of factors. Thus the fact that the Melanesians are now somewhat like does not mean that the populations which now compose that race were always so like. Moreover the general likeness of these populations can be overstressed, with a resultant failure to see their great diversity or to appreciate fully some of the basic evolutionary factors which are responsible for it. Thus Swindler (1962, p. 39) is able to support an earlier finding of Howells (1943, p. 42), that there is a great deal of physical or morphological diversity within the geographical boundaries of Melanesia, especially as one moves into Southeastern Melanesia. It has been fashionable to explain much of this diversity as the result of intrusions of Polynesian populations from the east, and clearly this has happened, but such hybridization is unlikely to explain completely all such variation in these small populations, and certainly is not a main factor where it has been well studied, as is the case in Fiji. Thus, while Howells suggested it for other parts of Eastern Melanesia, he did not then support it when he made his study of the Fijian populations, as I have pointed out in the previous review of this subject. A more thorough recent genetic survey of blood-grouping systems for numerous subpopulations throughout the entire Fijian group by Ward (1967, pp. 120-121) arrives at this conclusion:

> One final point may be made about the importance of random genetic drift in the Fiji islands and this concerns the relationships between Fiji and other island groups of the South Pacific. The amount of variation between subpopulations is, for some genetic systems as great as the variation occurring between island groups to the west. With such a degree of genetic heterogeneity the Fijians should be regarded as a biologically significant population in their own right. This means abandonment of the idea that the Fijians are a smoothly blended mixture of Polynesians and Melanesians, and also the idea that the heterogeneous Fijian population is composed of refugee Melanesians in the interior, and the more recent Polynesian arrivals on the coast. . . . The genetical conclusion is that the Fijian population has been evolving as a distinct entity for some time, mainly under the influence of genetic drift (migration, and selection will have also played some part).

In line with the morphological evidence cited by Howells (1933, 1943, p. 42, fn. 25) that the Fijians completely resemble Samoans and Tongans, except for slightly shorter faces and greater platyrrhiny, is his statement that before the 11th century A.D. they may have been entirely Polynesian of the Tonga-Samoa type (1933, p. 335). Thus there are morphological as well as genetical reasons to expect that among those populations ancestral to the present-day Fijians, who have been evolving as a distinct population in their own right for several thousand years, there were some groups which could have given rise to the Polynesians.

In a recent blood-group genetic survey of populations from New Guinea, Bougainville, the British Solomon Islands, New Hebrides, New Caledonia, Fiji, Tonga, and New Zealand by Simmons and Gajdusek, (1966, pp. 168-172, and Tables 5, 6) the restricted published materials which were used for the Fijians showed that they stood in an intermediate position between the Polynesian populations on the one hand, and those populations to the west cited above on the other. In actual fact Ward's thorough survey results mentioned above suggest that the various subpopulations of Fiji almost completely encompass in some systems the entire range of variations exhibited by the above groups. Thus it seems likely that populations once existed in more than one area of Eastern Melanesia from which one could derive both the Polynesians and the wide variety of populations which occur within Melanesia. In contrast to Ward, Simmons and Gajdusek, (1966, p. 172) feel that hybridization, together with the unusual historical events caused by man and nature, would have been most important in varying the gene frequencies found in this area, while random genetic drift would come next among the various continuously operating forces of selection, mutational pressure, and hybridization, all of which have affected these populations. The distinct line between Melanesian and Polynesian populations, however, need no longer be drawn simply because the present-day populations exhibit certain differences in skin color, hair or head form, or shape of the nose.

Evidence continues to accumulate which demonstrates that a series of proto-languages once spoken by populations living somewhere in Eastern Melanesia are the likely linguistic communities from which Polynesian and its closest relatives may be derived. The concept of the Melanesian languages as forming a single group coordinate with Polynesian and Micronesian on the one hand and Indonesian on the other has had to be abandoned and the true extent of linguistic diversity among the Austronesian speakers of Melanesia recognized by the identification of numerous subgroups in that area. Dyen (1965, pp. 38-39), for instance, places the Polynesian subfamily of languages in a group he calls the Heonesian Linkage along with the languages of Efate (New Hebrides), Fiji, Rotuma, Kerebuto (Central Solomons), Mota (Banks Islands), Motu (Port Moresby, Papua, New Guinea) and the Lauic Subfamily (S.E. Solomons). Interpreting this evidence, he finds that "a migration from the New Hebrides is probably the source of the languages of the Heonesian Linkage," in which Fiji may have been the first stop, although not necessarily (Dyen, 1965, p. 55).

Grace (1959, 1961) postulated and attempted to support by shared innovations and lexicostatistical results a subgrouping of Fijian, Rotuman, and Polynesian. He (1964, p. 366) has suggested 1000 B.C. as an approximate date for the dissolution of the proto-language ancestral to the languages in this group. He is also "convinced that Fijian, Rotuman, and Polynesian are members of a slightly larger grouping, the other members of which are found in the Central New Hebrides" (1964, p. 366), including Efate, Epi, Malekula, and Espiritu Santo. To a certain extent he is agreeing with Dyen in thinking it likely that the proto-language of this larger grouping was spoken in the central New Hebrides. Dyen (1960, pp. 180-184; 1965, p. 52), however, considers both Grace's Rotuman, Polynesian, and Fijian subgroup and his larger grouping as unproven, or not well supported by Dyen's own classification, while Goodenough (1961) would include West Nakani of New Britain in Grace's putative Fijian–Rotuman–Polynesian group. Finally Biggs (1965, p. 383) postulates a subgroup which includes all languages in Dyen's Heonesian Linkage except Motu, and adds a few others in the Solomon chain; Arosi, Ulawa, Sa'a, Kwara'ae, Nggela, and Vaturanga. He calls the proto-language of the subgroup Eastern Oceanic.

Thus while the precise relationship of the Polynesian language to those in Eastern Melanesia is still not agreed upon, there is a large measure of general agreement on the languages to which it is most closely related. There is agreement also that the probable location of the proto-languages from which they all derive is somewhere in Eastern Melanesia, with at least one of the basic proto-languages centered in the New Hebrides. Grace's placing of Fijian in the Fijian–Rotuman–Polynesian group as the closest cluster of dialects and languages to Polynesian is, in general, acknowledged, but the position of Rotuman is regarded with more suspicion because of the large amount of borrowing from Polynesian languages which Biggs (1965, pp. 412-413) has demonstrated. Recent work by Pawley (personal communication; see also Pawley, 1966) suggests, however, that if the Fijian cluster of dialects and languages, in which there is greater diversity than many have been suspected (Schütz, 1963, p. 71; see also Grace, 1964, p. 367), is compared with the Polynesian cluster, and with representatives from the clusters of related languages in the New Hebrides and in the Solomons, Fijian and Polynesian appear to share a number of innovations beyond those noted by Grace which are not found in the other two clusters. As such, a proto-language ancestral to Fijian-Polynesian located in Fiji remains a distinct possibility.

Like the linguistic evidence, archaeological data bearing on cultural continuities between early assemblages in Fiji and New Caledonia on the one hand, and Tonga and Samoa on the other, have continued to accumulate and to support the already substantial information available in 1962 (Green, 1963, pp. 249-250). Because this information has recently been reviewed both by myself (Green, in press) and by others (Palmer, in press; Poulsen, in press), it would appear unwarranted to repeat that evidence in detail here. Rather it seems more appropriate to comment on some of the major points which I believe that data reveal.

The first point is evidence for significant cultural change in New Caledonia and Fiji. At least three major pottery traditions followed one another in New Caledonia and Fiji, each with an associated assemblage of other artifacts suggesting change not only in the pottery but in other aspects of the culture as well. Similar evidence of cultural change is also known for the New Hebrides. Thus the fact that the more recent Melanesian cultures adjacent to Polynesia now differ from the Polynesian pattern reflects nothing more than the fact that such change has occurred along with internal changes in Polynesian culture itself. What seems evident is that certain more recent pottery and adz-making traditions, along with other items of culture, have been diffused from west to east in Melanesia, replacing or being added to earlier patterns, but that these have in general not moved into Polynesia except as individual elements, and in many cases not at all. If some of these later complexes are associated with significant movements of people from farther west in Melanesia including New Guinea, as seems not unlikely, then the possibility of the introduction of new genetic materials into resident populations by hybridization must also be considered.

The second and related point is that while some traits from later cultures also reached Polynesia, entire complexes which did so are restricted to the early assemblages and the horizon associated with the Lapita style of pottery found in Tonga, Fiji, New Caledonia, and points farther west in Melanesia. Here I believe it important to note that the Tongan materials of the 1st to the 3rd century A.D. are only to a small degree differentiated from those found earlier in the Sigatoka Phase of Fiji or other related sites in that group. Thus the real difference between materials of this age in Tonga and those in Fiji lies in the fact that in Fiji this earlier cultural assemblage has now been replaced by a new one of the Navatu Phase. Similar replacement of this Lapita cultural horizon by other assemblages seems to have occurred as early or even earlier in other island groups of Melanesia. The point all this makes, I believe is one made by Emory; that it was in the comparative isolation of Polynesia that the Polynesians, their language, and their culture took on the distinctive features which they now share in common. Certainly this is so in their language, where 1,000 years has been estimated for this process (Grace, 1964, p. 366), and it is equally to be expected that parallel processes effected similar changes in their physical make-up and their basic cultural pattern.

In fact, the archaeological evidence from Samoa suggests that by the 1st century A.D. cultural differentiation in assemblages from West Polynesia had already proceeded to a fair degree (Green, in press). This is supported by more recent excavations which have revealed the existence of a new pottery assemblage stratigraphically under one that may be compared to that at Vailele dated to the 1st century A.D. This earlier pottery consists of a thinner and better-made paddle-and-anvil ware, with a finer temper, a greater range in pot forms and rims, and even pieces of rim with intermittent decoration. Both pottery wares are associated with a wide range of adz types and a number of other artifacts in stone. However, the pottery and some, although not all, of the adz forms differ from those found in Tonga or Fiji at this general period or those found earlier in Fiji. Thus while there are important continuities in the Samoan pottery and adzes with assemblages in Eastern Melanesia, these Samoan complexes cannot be directly compared with any single assemblage known in the island groups to the west.

This raises several issues and presents certain possible choices. Either these Samoan materials, which would serve quite adequately in some ways as the basis for a common Polynesian pattern, are a result of the perhaps 1,000 years or more of differentiation away from an earlier cultural pattern from which they derive, and thus are truly Polynesian, or they are the result of intrusion into Polynesia from an as yet unidentified but early cultural tradition in Eastern Melanesia. Either or both possibilities may prove to have occurred. If so, the case for cultural continuity in Tonga made by Poulsen (in press) may have to be reexamined, for it may be that in either the earliest Tongan or Samoan materials, we are dealing not with Polynesian culture at all, but with a descendant of a more distantly related culture that was changed into one predominantly Polynesian by either contact and internal change, or secondary settlement, or a combination of both. This, however, does not prevent us from drawing the conclusion that the immediate origins of the cultural pattern from which the Polynesian forms developed all lie in Eastern Melanesia, a theory for which there is increasing archaeological evidence.

CONCLUSION

This essay offers no new theories on the immediate origins of the Polynesians. Rather it examines three of those current in the more recent literature, and suggests that the bulk of the positive evidence favors a theory in a form initially postulated by Emory. This is that of an origin in the Eastern Melanesia islands immediately west of Polynesia itself, with subsequent development of the distinctive Polynesian pattern within

West Polynesia. The essay thus is offered as an attempt to substantiate and elaborate this theory by drawing on the recent evidence assembled by many in the fields of linguistics, archaeology, and physical anthropology. Moreover it is important to stress that the theory differs from many earlier ones which attempted to bring Polynesians through already settled areas of Melanesia according to some particular route, by dismissing the theory of a distinctive Polynesian migration or route within Melanesia. This is replaced with the concept of development within Polynesia itself of the Polynesian racial, linguistic, and cultural patterns which were based on ancestral forms found in Eastern Melanesia and in particular in Fiji.

LITERATURE CITED

BARRAU, JACQUES (Editor)

    1963. Introduction to *Plants and the Migrations of Pacific Peoples: A Symposium*, pp. 1-6. Honolulu: Bishop Mus. Press.

    1965. "Histoire et Préhistoire Horticoles de l'Océanie Tropicale." *J. Soc. Océanistes* **21**:55-78.

BAYARD, D. T.

    1966. The Cultural Relationships of the Polynesian Outliers. Master's thesis, Univ. Hawaii.

BIGGS, B. G.

    1965. "Direct and Indirect Inheritance in Rotuman." *Lingua* **14**:383-445.

BUCK, P. H.

    1938. *Vikings of the Sunrise*. New York: Lippincott.

    1944. *Arts and Crafts of the Cook Islands*. B. P. Bishop Mus. Bull. 179. Honolulu.

BURROWS, E. G.

    1938. "Western Polynesia: A Study in Cultural Differentiation." *Etnologiska Studier* **7**:1-192.

CHANG, KWANG-CHIH

    1964. "Movement of the Malayo-Polynesians: 1500 B.C. to A.D. 500; Prehistoric and Early Historic Culture Horizons and Traditions in South China." *Current Anthropology* **5**:359, 368-375.

DAVIDSON, J. M.

    In press, a. "Preliminary Archaeological Investigations on Ponape and Other Eastern Caroline Islands." *Micronesica* **3**.

    In press, b. "Nukuoro—Archaeology on a Polynesian Outlier in Micronesia." In I. YAWATA and Y. H. SINOTO (editors), *Prehistoric Culture in Oceania: Symposium Presented at the Eleventh Pacific Science Congress*. Honolulu: Bishop Mus. Press. (Paper read at the Congress, Tokyo, September, 1966.)

DYEN, ISIDORE
1960. Review of G. W. GRACE, *The Position of the Polynesian Languages within the Austronesian (Malayo-Polynesian) Language Family. J. Polynesian Soc.* **69**:180-184.
1965. *A Lexicostatistical Classification of the Austronesian Languages.* Internat. J. American Linguistics Mem. 19. Baltimore.

EMORY, K. P.
1959. "Origin of the Hawaiians." *J. Polynesian Soc.* **68**:29-35.
1963. Review of T. Heyerdahl and E. N. Ferdon, Jr., editors, *Archaeology of Easter Island. American Antiquity* **28**:565-567.

EMORY, K. P., and Y. H. SINOTO
1965. Preliminary Report on the Archaeological Investigations in Polynesia. Prepared for National Science Foundation. Mimeo.

FERDON, E. N., JR.
1963. "Polynesian Origins." *Science* **141**:499-505.

GIBLETT, E. R.
1961. "Haptoglobins and Transferrins in Pacific Populations." *Abstracts of Symposium Pap., Tenth Pacific Sci. Cong.* (Honolulu), p. 437. See also summary in A. H. SMITH, 1962, "Micronesia," *Asian Perspectives* **5**:81.

GIFFORD, E. W., and D. S. GIFFORD
1959. *Archaeological Excavations in Yap.* Univ. California Anthropological Rec. 81, No. 2. Berkeley.

GOLSON, JACK
1965. "Thor Heyerdahl and the Prehistory of Easter Island." *Oceania* **36**:38-83.

GOODENOUGH, W. H.
1957. "Oceania and the Problem of Controls in the Study of Cultural and Human Evolution." *J. Polynesian Soc.* **66**:146-155.
1961. "Migrations Implied by Relationships of New Britain Dialects to Central Pacific Languages." *J. Polynesian Soc.* **70**:112-126.

GRACE, G. W.
1959. *The Position of the Polynesian Languages within the Austronesian (Malayo-Polynesian) Language Family.* Internat. J. Linguistics Mem. 16. Baltimore. B. P. Bishop Mus. Spec. Pub. 46. Honolulu.
1961. *Lexicostatistical Comparison of Six Austronesian Languages.* Archives of Languages of the World 3, 9. Bloomington: Univ. Indiana.
1964. "Movement of the Malayo-Polynesians: 1500 B.C. to A.D. 500; The Linguistic Evidence." *Current Anthropology* **5**:361-368.

GREEN, R. C.
1963. "A Suggested Revision of the Fijian Sequence." *J. Polynesian Soc.* **72**:235-253.
1966. "Linguistic Subgrouping within Polynesia: The Implications for Prehistoric Settlement." *J. Polynesian Soc.* **75**:6-38.
In press. "West Polynesian Prehistory." In I. YAWATA and Y. H. SINOTO (editors), *Prehistoric Culture in Oceania: Symposium Presented at the Eleventh Pacific Science Congress.* Honolulu: Bishop Mus. Press. (Paper read at the Congress, Tokyo, September 1966.)

GREEN, R. C., and J. M. DAVIDSON
  1965. "Radiocarbon Dates for Western Samoa." *J. Polynesian Soc.* **74**:63-69.
GROUBE, L. M.
  In press. "Research in New Zealand Prehistory since 1956." In I. YAWATA and
    Y. H. SINOTO (editors), *Prehistoric Culture in Oceania: Symposium
    Presented at the Eleventh Pacific Science Congress.* Honolulu: Bishop
    Mus. Press. (Paper read at the Congress, Tokyo, September, 1966.)
HEYERDAHL, THOR
  1952. *American Indians in the Pacific.* London: Allen and Unwin.
  In press. "Prehistoric Culture of Easter Island." In I. YAWATA and Y. H.
    SINOTO (editors), *Prehistoric Culture in Oceania: Symposium Presented
    at the Eleventh Pacific Science Congress.* Honolulu: Bishop Mus.
    Press. (Paper read at the Congress, Tokyo, September, 1966.)
HEYERDAHL, THOR, and E. N. FERDON, JR. (Editors)
  1961. *Reports of the Norwegian Archaeological Expedition to Easter Island
    and the East Pacific. Vol. 1: Archaeology of Easter Island.* School
    American Research and Mus. New Mexico. Monog. 24, Pt. 1. London:
    Allen and Unwin.
  1965. *Reports of the Norwegian Archaeological Expedition to Easter Island
    and the East Pacific. Vol. 2: Miscellaneous Papers.* School American
    Research and Kon-Tiki Mus. Monog. 24, Pt. 2. Stockholm: Esselte
    Aktiebolag.
HOWELLS, W. W.
  1933. "Anthropometry and Blood Types in Fiji and the Solomon Islands."
    Anthropological Pap. American Mus. Nat. Hist. **33**(4):279-339.
  1943. "The Racial Elements of Melanesia." In C. S. COON and J. M. AN-
    DREWS, IV (editors), *Studies in the Anthropology of Oceania and Asia
    . . . in Memory of Roland Burrage Dixon.* Peabody Mus. Pap. 20,
    pp. 38-49. Cambridge.
HUNT, E. E.
  1950. "A View of Somatology and Serology in Micronesia." *American J.
    Physical Anthropology* **8**:157-184.
IZUI, HISANOSUKE
  1965. "The Languages of Micronesia: Their Unity and Diversity." *Lingua*
    14:349-359.
KOCH, GERD
  1966. "The Polynesian-Micronesian 'Culture Boundary.'" *Abstracts of Papers
    related with Social Sciences and Anthropology, Eleventh Pacific Sci.
    Cong.* (Tokyo). Vol. 9 (Ethnology), p. 3.
MARSHALL, D. H., and C. E. SNOW
  1956. "An Evaluation of Polynesian Craniology." *American J. Physical
    Anthropology* **14**:405-427.
MEGGERS, B. J.
  1963. Review of T. Heyerdahl, *Archaeology of Easter Island. American J.
    Archaeology* **67**:330-331.

MYRIANTHOPOULOS, N. C., and S. J. L. PIEPER, JR.
1959. "The ABO and Rh Blood Groups among the Chamorros of Guam."
American J. Physical Anthropology **17**:105-108.

OSBORNE, DOUGLAS
1966. *The Archaeology of the Palau Islands: An Intensive Survey.* B. P.
Bishop Mus. Bull. 230. Honolulu.

PALMER, B.
In press. "Archaeological Investigations in the Sigatoka Valley, Viti Levu,
Fiji." In I. YAWATA and Y. H. SINOTO (editors), *Prehistoric Culture in
Oceania: Symposium Presented at the Eleventh Pacific Science Con-
gress.* Honolulu: Bishop Mus. Press. (Paper read at the Congress,
Tokyo, September, 1966.)

PAWLEY, ANDREW
1966. "Polynesian Languages: A Subgrouping based on Shared Innovations
in Morphology." *J. Polynesian Soc.* **75**:39-64.

PETTAY, LOUANNA
1959. "Racial Affinity of Prehistoric Guam." (Abstract.) *Proc. Indiana
Acad. Science* **68**:58.

POULSEN, JENS
1966. "Preliminary Report on Pottery Finds in Tonga." *Asian Perspectives*
8:184-195.
In press. "Contribution to the Prehistory of Tonga." In I. YAWATA and Y. H.
SINOTO (editors), *Prehistoric Culture in Oceania: Symposium Presented
at the Eleventh Pacific Science Congress.* Honolulu: Bishop Mus. Press.
(Paper read at the Congress, Tokyo, September, 1966.)

ST. JOHN, HAROLD
1957. "Origin of the Sustenance Plants of Polynesia, and Linguistic Evidence
for the Migration Route of Polynesians into the Pacific." *Abstracts of
Pap., Ninth Pacific Sci. Cong.* (Bangkok), p. 19.

SCHMITZ, C. A.
1962. Comment on Capell's "Oceanic Linguistics Today." *Current Anthropology* **3**:417-420.

SCHÜTZ, A. J.
1963. "Phonemic Typology of Fijian Dialects." *Oceanic Linguistics* **2**:62-79.

SIMMONS, R. T.
1956. "A Report on Blood Group Genetical Surveys in Eastern Asia, Indonesia, Melanesia, Micronesia, Polynesia and Australia in the Study of
Man." *Anthropos* **51**:500-512.
1965. "The Blood Group Genetics of Easter Islanders (Pascuense), and Other
Polynesians." In T. HEYERDAHL and E. N. FERDON, JR. (editors), *Reports of the Norwegian Archaeological Expedition to Easter Island
and the East Pacific. Vol. 2: Miscellaneous Papers,* pp. 333-343. School
American Research and Kon-Tiki Mus. Monog. 24, Pt. 2. Stockholm:
Esselte Aktiebolag.

SIMMONS, R. T., and D. C. GAJDUSEK
1966. "A Blood Group Genetic Survey of Children of Bellona and Rennell
Islands (B.S.I.P.) and Certain Northern New Hebridean Islands."
Archaeology and Physical Anthropology in Oceania **1**:155-174.

SIMMONS, R. T., J. J. GRAYDON, D. C. GAJDUSEK, and PAUL BROWN
    1965. "Blood Group Genetic Variations in Natives of the Caroline Islands
        and in Other Parts of Micronesia." *Oceania* **36**(2):132-154.

SINOTO, Y. H.
    In press, a. "A Tentative Prehistoric Cultural Sequence in the Northern Mar-
        quesas Islands, French Polynesia." *J. Polynesian Soc.* **75**(3).
    In press, b. "Position of the Marquesas Islands in East Polynesian Pre-
        history." In I. YAWATA and Y. H. SINOTO (editors), *Prehistoric Cul-
        ture in Oceania: Symposium Presented at the Eleventh Pacific Science
        Congress.* Honolulu: Bishop Mus. Press. (Paper read at the Congress,
        Tokyo, September, 1966.)

SINOTO, Y. H., and M. J. KELLUM
    1965. Preliminary Report on Excavations in the Marquesas Islands, French
        Polynesia. Prepared for the National Science Foundation. Mimeo.

SOLHEIM, W. G., II
    1964. "Movement of the Malayo-Polynesians: 1500 B.C. to A.D. 500; Pot-
        tery and the Malayo-Polynesians." *Current Anthropology* **5**:360, 376-
        384, 400-403.

SPOEHR, ALEXANDER
    1952. "Time Perspective in Micronesia and Polynesia." *Southwestern J. An-
        thropology* **8**:457-465.
    1957. *Marianas Prehistory, Archaeological Survey and Excavation on Saipan,
        Tinian and Rota.* Fieldiana: Anthropology 48. Chicago.

SUGGS, R. C.
    1960. *The Island Civilizations of Polynesia.* New York: Mentor.
    1961. "The Archaeology of Nuku Hiva, Marquesas Islands, French Poly-
        nesia." *Anthropological Pap. American Mus. Nat. Hist.* **49**(1):1-205.
    1963. "Polynesian Origins." *Science* **142**:1252-1253.

SUSSMAN, L. N., L. H. MEYER, and R. A. CONRAD
    1959. "Blood Groupings in Marshallese." *Science* **129**:644-645.

SWINDLER, D. R.
    1962. "A Racial Study of the West Nakanai." In W. H. GOODENOUGH
        (editor), *New Britain Studies.* Univ. Pennsylvania Mus. Monog. Phila-
        delphia.

WARD, R. H.
    1967. Genetic Studies on Fijians. Master's thesis, Univ. Auckland.

WATTERS, R. F.
    1958. "Culture and Environment in Old Samoa." In *Western Pacific: Studies
        of Man and Environment in the Western Pacific,* pp. 41-70. Dept.
        Geography, Victoria Univ. Wellington.

WECKLER, J. E.
    1943. *Polynesians: Explorers of the Pacific.* Smithsonian Institution War
        Background Studies No. 6. Washington, D. C.

A COMMENTARY ON THE STUDY OF CONTEMPORARY POLYNESIA

ALEXANDER SPOEHR

The University of Pittsburgh

RECENT YEARS have seen a growing interest in the culture history of Polynesia and noteworthy advances in knowledge of the Polynesian past. This is true for both the pre-European and postcontact periods. Increased concern with the latter is signified by the auspicious founding of the *Journal of Pacific History* in Australia last year.

Much anthropological research in Polynesia has actually been concerned not with particular historical problems per se, but rather with clarifying the social structure of Polynesian societies and the basic organizing concepts of Polynesian culture. The objective of such studies has been to contribute to comparative knowledge of the nature of kinship and descent groups, economic organization, religion, the social function of myth and oral tradition, or other aspects of human society and culture wherever they are found. Yet this effort, falling in the realm of what is often termed social anthropology, has made its own distinctive contribution to Polynesian culture history. In other words, regardless of the theoretical objectives of the researcher, the ethnographic product which he writes today becomes a part of culture history tomorrow.

The purpose of this paper is to offer a brief commentary on current forces underlying the changing patterns of life in Polynesia, to indicate certain shifting emphases in social anthropology, and to relate these two kinds of change by indicating a few promising areas for those investigations in Polynesia whose objectives are generalizing, comparative, and based on ethnographic observation. If the outlook of this paper is toward the future, its base is in events which are part of the framework of history.

PATTERNS OF CHANGE IN POLYNESIA

In common with the rest of the Pacific islands area, Polynesia is probably undergoing changes of greater magnitude than at any comparable period in the past. In somewhat impressionistic fashion there are enumerated below certain present trends which will generate important sociocultural changes in the years ahead.

POPULATION INCREASE AND MIGRATION PATTERNS

If one includes Fiji, there are in Polynesia today more than 800,000 people. Average annual rates of population increase are high, ranging between 3 and 3.6 percent (McArthur, 1961). Further improvement in public health and medical services will lead to increased chances of survival of individuals to reproductive age, so that this elevated rate of population increase can be expected to continue. It seems doubtful that family planning measures or a trend toward rising ages at marriage will have a substantial effect on the areawide birth rate for a number of years. McArthur (1961) has projected a total population of slightly over 1,000,000 for Polynesia by 1971, with Fiji accounting for about half the total (New Zealand and Hawaii are excluded). Allowing for the past depopulation of the islands, this dramatic increase means that Polynesia will not lack for plenty of people, granted their uneven distribution.

As demographers stress, the kind of population picture presented by Polynesia has a most important consequence. This is that the number of individuals entering the work force each year tends to increase at a higher rate than the population. It is the rapid growth of this economically active adult segment of the population that is particularly significant in considering future sociocultural change.

A second important point is that Polynesia remains primarily agriculturally based. Even with technological improvements and greater productivity, I share the view of those who believe that agriculture in Polynesia cannot support the increase in the work force. Alternative occupations are necessary if the total labor force is to be supported in anything but dire poverty. McArthur (1961) notes that more than two-thirds of the work force in Fiji soon may be seeking employment in nonagricultural industries. Polynesia is not alone in this regard. The same problem on a much larger scale is a critical one in the Philippines.

The high rate of increase of the economically adult population seems to be one of the principal forces underlying the migration patterns that are crystallizing in Polynesia. It is of course true that people migrate for reasons other than the search for economic opportunity alone, but making a living is still one of life's necessities. In any case, demographic factors are fundamental to the three major migration patterns to be observed today.

The first pattern is migration from the Cook Islands and Western Samoa to New Zealand, and from American Samoa to Hawaii and the continental United States. This is a movement into a metropolitan milieu. The second pattern has developed within the Pacific island area itself, not confined to Polynesia but excluding New Zealand and Hawaii. This pattern includes the movement of Tahitians to New Caledonia, of islanders from the Wallis and Futuna group to the New Hebrides and New Caledonia, of Gilbertese and Rotumans to Fiji, and of Fijians and Tikopians to Guadalcanal in the Solomons. It is interesting that the general direction of this movement is westward. It is also conditioned by political factors and the nature of the second language—that is, it takes place within either French or British administered territories. The third pattern is an internal one within each territorial social system and consists of movement from the hinterland to the port town, with some return flow, although an individual does not necessarily return to the hinterland area of his origin. Comparable to this third pattern is the increasing urbanization of Maoris in New Zealand and of Hawaiians in Hawaii.

URBANIZATION

The port towns of Polynesia, at least on the high islands, will continue to attract population from the hinterland, and will continue their path toward increasing urbanization. The majority of the migrants will be young adults seeking employment and the attractions of town life. Although Belshaw (1963) has argued convincingly that Pacific island towns can be conducive to combining idle hands, new ideas, and capital toward the goal of economic development, considerable urban unemployment may be inevitable. Whether the practical aspects of town planning will keep pace with town growth remains to be seen.

A characteristic of many Pacific island towns is their great ethnic diversity. In Polynesia, Papeete and Suva exhibit this characteristic, Apia, Nukualofa, and Pago Pago to a much less degree. Where ethnic diversity exists in the island urban milieu, new alignments of political and economic power and new patterns of social stratification will no doubt emerge, although the nature of this process is not yet clear. It is clear that the most sensitive foci of change are the towns, and that their rapid growth poses numerous governmental problems for an area where urbanization is a recent phenomenon (Rennie, 1962).

ECONOMIC DEVELOPMENT

In Firth's words, the islanders today are committed to the material civilization that is the hallmark of the West. They aspire to higher standards of living, including an expanding range of public services. On the other hand, the restricted resource base of Polynesia, the scattered population, and the frequent dependence on metropolitan countries for development services and capital investment are obvious. Although Fiji may contain an agricultural potential yet to be fully utilized, and although it is only common sense that increased agricultural productivity should be given full support and encouragement in all parts of the region, demographic trends alone force the seeking of solutions to economic development in nonagricultural sectors.

It has long been debated whether Pacific islanders can play a major role in an expanded commercial fishing industry. So far this has not come to pass. The large-scale exploitation of fish resources and the subsequent processing and marketing on an international scale are highly technical operations, involving large amounts of capital, which to date have been pursued successfully in Polynesia only by metropolitan countries. However, the commercial fishing operations based in American Samoa and Fiji have benefited the economies of those territories, and islanders still are important suppliers of local markets.

In terms of economic development, the most marked change in the last decade has been the growth of tourism. Tahiti and Fiji, both on the main air route, have been the first to participate, and are being followed by American Samoa. Tourism will undoubtedly flow out of these areas into those nearby which are most readily accessible, and bids fair to be Polynesia's most important industry. In the words of Henri Nettre, Senior French Commissioner on the South Pacific Commission, ". . . one of the characteristics of this area is its insularity . . . and although this is probably an obstacle to economic and social development, it may also contribute to make the Pacific the last abode of peace and happiness. How many people, in different continents, who are tired of the bustle, the noise, the smoke, the smells and congestion of big cities, dream of escaping to a far away, fragrant, and colorful island."

Tourism in Polynesia is linked to port towns and requires an array of supporting services in such towns. Although it will affect the hinterland in varying degrees, it will also encourage urbanization. Stemming from tourism, however, one can logically expect a stimulus to related industries. These will start as small enterprises, but some can be expected to expand. The clothing industry is often mentioned as a promising possibility.

EDUCATION

Included in the aspirations of the people of Polynesia is the whole matter of education. In this there has been a contrast between the British and French policy on one hand and the American on the other. The former have tended to opt for a broad base at the lower level of schooling and a rigorous selection of those who become the well-educated and relatively small elite. The Americans have attempted to project in their one small territory the concept of education for all, borrowed from the homeland. Neither approach has worked to the full satisfaction of the educators, their critics, or those involved as students in the process.

Without attempting to assess a field in which my competence is limited, I can point to certain developments which seem of interest. The first is the problem of bilingualism, whether the second language is French or English. The reason is that in Polynesia the second language at an early age becomes the language of instruction and the young student's comprehension of the second language thereafter determines the success of his mastery of all subjects in the curriculum. In a technological era this is inevitable, and it makes bilingualism a pervading and all-important matter as ever-increasing numbers of children enter the educational system. Yet quite apart from the shortage of competent teachers of the second language, there is the question of how the second language is to be taught. George A. Pittman, the outstanding specialist on bilingualism in the Pacific islands, has repeatedly stated that a fuller understanding of the marked morphological and hence conceptual differences between the Polynesian languages on one hand and French and English on the other is the key to the effective teaching of the second language. The bold experiment now going on in American Samoa in the use of television as a major tool in the teaching of English, initiated by Governor Rex Lee, will in the end depend for its success on this very point.

A second development is at the apex of the educational system. The creation of an elite in Polynesia large enough in numbers and possessing a broad range of talents and skills sufficient to provide the kind of leadership the islands require demands the support of a system of higher education. Although some students from the islands will study in New Zealand, Australian, French, English, and American colleges and universities as before, the time is ripe for a new university within the island area. Most of us whose Pacific experience stretches back for more than two decades are probably both somewhat astonished and gratified at the impending establishment of a university in Fiji to serve the islands, following upon that already in operation in New Guinea.

A third development is at a different level. It has taken place slowly, with many halts and starts, and its progress is difficult to evaluate. This is the concept of community education, whose ultimate locale is the neighborhood or village, and whose rationale is that those who are taught will teach others to help themselves. It more often involves adults than youngsters, takes place in terms of limited span training projects, and covers a wide field of special skills and attitudes. It is an approach with which the South Pacific Commission has been particularly involved.

POLITICAL DEVELOPMENT

The Polynesian territories have been politically in a state of flux, pulled on the one hand toward a greater measure of incorporation into metropolitan countries, and on the other toward a kind of political independence conditioned by economic limitations. This fluid situation will no doubt continue, although one can anticipate increased interest and action on the part of both administration and people in the further development of local self-government in the territories, regardless of where national sovereignty may reside.

Two aspects of social change seem particularly relevant to political development. The first is that there have already appeared the forerunners of new island-born elites, based on participation in formal education and in specific needs to be met, whether in education, public health and medicine, various technical fields, entrepreneurship, or politics. How will these new elite groups develop and how will they exercise their aspirations in leadership roles as these affect the political scene? This question seems especially important in areas where chieftainship, and precontact institutions of kinship and descent, retain significance. The second question pertains to non-Polynesian segments of the population. Excluding the Indians of Fiji, non-Polynesians are minority groups, consisting mostly of Europeans, Chinese, and mixed-bloods. As local self-government expands, as Polynesian elites come to the fore, what will be the future political role of these minority groups and what kinds of accommodations will be reached? The question is an interesting one to contemplate.

BROADER HORIZONS

Since World War II one can discern out of the complex of social forces at work in the Pacific islands a certain degree of consciousness among island peoples of common problems and of a larger unity. So far this is shared mostly by the few and is easy to overemphasize. Yet the situation has changed radically from the days when each territory's main line of communication was with its metropolitan country, with pronounced and artificial communication barriers separating territories from one another according to their nationality.

Although the South Pacific Commission has received its share of criticism, it is in this area that its main force has been felt. The work program of the Commission could have been bolder, at times it has responded very slowly to expressed needs, and it has been timid in evaluating its own work; but these limitations have been imposed on the Commission by the metropolitan countries who support it. Founded in 1947 as an international development agency, the Commission, often in cooperation with UNESCO, WHO, and FAO, has provided technical and advisory services to territories, has brought islanders together to review common problems through the medium of its periodic South Pacific Conferences, and, through its publication and technical conference program, has made possible an islandwide sharing of technical, research, administrative, and operational experience. Perhaps the most popular innovation originally sponsored by the Commission is the South Pacific Games, which were last held in Noumea in 1966. Despite the restrictions and limited support under which it has labored, the South Pacific Commission has been a constructive force in the Pacific islands, and merits full encouragement in its future work.

These brief remarks on the trends of change in Polynesia are incomplete and could be extended at length. They are derived from the common experience of scholars and observers familiar with the area, and in large measure were anticipated by Felix M. Keesing (1953) in his survey of social anthropology in Polynesia. The trends described do indicate certain of the dimensions of change in the patterns of life in Polynesia today and in the future.[1]

---

[1] After this paper was written, the author received the work by Doumenge (1966), which represents the most scholarly, comprehensive, recent review of the peoples of the South Pacific and the contemporary forces affecting their lives, written from the point of view of a geographer.

CHANGES IN ANTHROPOLOGICAL METHOD

Just as the Pacific scene is changing, so are the research interests of anthropology. Without presuming to characterize a fluid if not chaotic situation, I have selected three aspects of contemporary work in ethnology and social anthropology which will no doubt affect the nature of Polynesian studies.

SPECIALIZATION

Anthropologists have always had a catholic interest in their subject matter and have not felt any particular hesitation in moving from the study of kinship and descent groups to political organization, to economics, to religion, or to whatever problem area impelled their interest. The concepts of culture and of social structure are inclusive ones, and anthropology's view of man, society, and culture is holistic. The traditional units of field research have been relatively small in size and appropriate for investigations conducted by a single researcher, who could select as he wished and explore in depth various facets of his people's culture and social life.

Although there seems no immediate tendency to fragmentation, specialized interests are clearly developing in the study of contemporary, non-Western societies. Recent work in economic anthropology, political anthropology, medical anthropology, social stratification and urbanization, and a renewed interest in religion reflect an emerging specialization. In the economic anthropology of the Pacific islands, where Raymond Firth once perforce had to carry the torch almost alone, he has now been joined by other talented colleagues, such as Cyril Belshaw, Salisbury, and Paul Ottino.

If this specialization does not involve fragmentation, it does involve closer relations with those parts of the other social sciences with which anthropology is most immediately involved in the study of contemporary problems. This is particularly true where the field of observation encompasses new nations, developing countries, and other rapidly changing regions of the world. A higher degree of social science sophistication is being demanded of the anthropologist. The full impact of this trend is yet to be felt in the training of our students, who, I fear, are not entirely satisfied with the fare which they are offered.

THE SCALE OF THE SOCIAL SYSTEMS UNDER STUDY

Anthropology has built up a corpus of more than a half century's experience in the techniques of field research on village, band, or tribe.

There is no lack of opportunity in Polynesia and elsewhere for the continued exercise of this expertise. On the other hand, the local units of traditional anthropological inquiry are today articulated in new and changing ways with larger entities—towns, cities, regions, states. The nature of this articulation among the component entities of systems larger than the local group, the consequent effect on the cultures of the local groups themselves, and the examination of at least aspects of cities, regions, or states are all accepted as proper subjects for anthropological investigation today. The anthropologist has not thereby abandoned his hard-won gains in method and technique, but they are being applied in the context of larger scale social and cultural systems. He is already fully involved in the study of complex societies. His principal difficulty is not that of involvement per se, but is rather methodological—how to devise new theoretical models appropriate to the scale of the systems under study, particularly when they are not static but are undergoing change.

METHODOLOGY

Social anthropology today is in a state of considerable ferment in regard to its methodology. This ferment does not lie with abstract notions about society and culture, incorporating little demonstrable connection with the empirically gathered data of ethnography. The situation is precisely the opposite. There is a real concern which embraces the direct observation of behavior and the gathering of data (what is a "good" or "adequate" ethnography?), and the most productive uses of such data according to the kind of theoretical models applicable to description, most useful for comparison, and most conducive to generating future problems whose solution will lead to higher levels of generalization.

A partial explanation of this ferment is the sheer growth in the number of anthropologists. It is a bit as though the discipline had attained the state of a critical mass. Out of this condition has come the period of methodological experimentation into which we have entered.

A partial explanation is also the fact that in science generally the formulation of equilibrium models seems to precede the development of processual models. Much effort in anthropology has gone into the construction of equilibrium models, and a greatly improved understanding of social structure, for example, has resulted. At the same time, there is an evident dissatisfaction with the adequacy of the equilibrium models so far achieved, and a striving to develop models which will be more useful in understanding phenomena of process and change. This is not the place to review the already voluminous literature on the subject. It is sufficient to note that mechanical models, ideal models, statistical models, cognitive models, decision models, and formal analysis compose an interlocking methodological development toward the improved understanding of structure, process, and change. This is a stimulating time, because the innovators are both theoretically inclined and close to social reality as best they can perceive it. Their success will be measured by the degree to which theoretical problems can be resolved by empirically reached data (see, for instance, Roger M. Keesing, 1967). Turning the statement around, one can say that it is not the ethnographic data as such, but the kind of data and what is done with them that counts.

FUTURE RESEARCH POSSIBILITIES

In the first part of this paper I attempted to sketch a few trends which are shaping the pattern of life in Polynesia, and transforming its social morphology. In the second part I noted three aspects of change in social anthropology as a form of inquiry. My thesis is that it is in the conjunction of these two kinds of change—one in the field of observation itself, and the other in how we observe, describe, and interpret that field—that the most promising possibilities for future social anthropological research in Polynesia lie.

In proposing this point of view, I do not wish to imply that traditional Polynesian culture and social structure are no longer of major comparative interest. Obviously they are. They underlie contemporary change in Polynesia and in the last few years have become a focal point in anthropological theory. If one had to select a single major problem in the investigation of social structure, I would choose the nature of cognatic descent groups and of bilateral kinship organization. Polynesian societies are of special interest in the study of cognatic or nonunilineal descent, because it was a kind of Polynesian specialty and because the Polynesians developed a number of variations on the theme. Lambert (1966) has recently published a fine analysis of ambilineal descent groups in the northern Gilberts. His paper raises the question as to how much new and comparable material can still be obtained from Polynesian societies.

I would entirely agree with Howard (1963) that the significance of current interest in cognatic descent lies in the calling into question of the conceptual apparatus of structural analysis. Concepts of descent, filiation, succession, residence, and others, about which we felt a relatively comfortable degree of consensus have had to be re-examined. More important, the analysis of cognatic descent has stimulated the construction of decision models, in many ways fathered by Firth, and recently given trial formulation and application in the Pacific islands by Howard (1963) and Roger M. Keesing (1967). There is a further significance to these efforts in that decision models give promise of a theoretically applicable approach to the study of sociocultural change, where we have been groping to transcend the synchronic-diachronic polarization. As Keesing (1967) has noted, decision models are not a replacement for statistical analysis, but their further elaboration, refinement, and application does give hope of methodological advance in ordering the recalcitrant phenomena of sociocultural change, including that taking place in Polynesia today.

I offer two brief additional illustrations of my thesis. The first refers to the specialization of research interests in social anthropology and specifically to that concerned with social stratification under conditions of change. This interest has not been extensively cultivated in Polynesia (excluding Hawaii) and offers numerous possibilities. An intriguing one lies in the ethnic diversity of urbanizing port towns. The question here is what kind of social stratification emerges from ethnic diversity and what are the consequences? In this situation the study of the European component of the population is just as important as the Polynesian. It is my impression, for instance, that in the rather rigid plural society of Fiji social class is beginning to transcend ethnic and racial difference. If this is so, what fruitful comparisons can be made with Tahiti or Western Samoa? There is here an unexploited comparative framework for future investigation.

This question leads to the next illustrative example, which concerns the scale of the systems under examination. How can better analytical models be devised to accommodate a regional rather than a local group approach? I am not thinking here so much of spacial scale but of the sociocultural complexity which it encompasses. Hinterland–port town relations are certainly important, toward whose elucidation Howard (1961) and Finney (1965) have made substantive contributions. What is happening in town centers is important, whether it be the physical transformation of towns (Jullien, 1963), the growth of voluntary associations (Nayacakalou, 1963), the form of family life (Kay, 1963), or the internal organization of a minority group (Moench, 1963). Yet the analytical framework for the larger whole has yet to be clearly formulated.

Perhaps the necessary preliminary step is to isolate more precisely a limited number of interrelated and observable trends of sociocultural change which appear common to two or more subregional or territorial systems in Polynesia. This might then provide a base of comparison on a subregional or macro level. Thereafter these trends would have to be explored in the kinds of social groupings and in fields of activity in which they are most clearly manifest within the subregion itself. The objective, however, is to handle subregional or territorial systems as units of comparison, and to do this analytically. I look forward to the time when this will be possible.

In a previous paper (Spoehr, 1966), I offered the opinion that we have reached the stage in anthropology where more time should be devoted to examining the research potential of those areas into which we have divided the world for the purposes of special study. The remarks offered here form a tentative effort in reviewing a few of the prospects for social anthropological research in Polynesia. Polynesia today is of course difficult of definition as a culture area. Polynesians are not staying put, and others have moved in to enjoy their ancient homeland. It is an area of movement and change, spilling its influence into other parts of the Pacific. It remains an area which will always intrigue and reward the student of both its ancient and modern life.

LITERATURE CITED

BELSHAW, CYRIL
    1963. "Pacific Island Towns and the Theory of Growth." In A. SPOEHR
        (editor), Pacific Port Towns and Cities, pp. 17-24. Honolulu: Bishop
        Museum Press.

DOUMENGE, FRANÇOIS
    1966. L'Homme dans le Pacifique Sud. Publications de la Société des Océan-
        istes, No. 19. Paris: Musée de l'Homme.

FINNEY, BEN R.
    1965. Polynesian Peasants and Proletarians. The Polynesian Society, Reprints
        Ser. 9. Wellington.

HOWARD, ALAN
    1961. "Rotuma as a Hinterland Community." J. Polynesian Soc. 70:272-299.
    1963. "Land, Activity Systems, and Decision-Making Models in Rotuma."
        Ethnology 2:407-440.

JULLIEN, MICHEL
    1963. "Aspects de la Configuration Ethnique et Socio-Economique de Papeete." In A. SPOEHR (editor), *Pacific Port Towns and Cities,* pp. 47-62. Honolulu: Bishop Museum Press.

KAY, PAUL
    1963. "Urbanization in the Tahitian Household." In A. SPOEHR (editor), *Pacific Port Towns and Cities,* pp. 63-73. Honolulu: Bishop Museum Press.

KEESING, FELIX M.
    1953. *Social Anthropology in Polynesia.* New York: Oxford Univ. Press.

KEESING, ROGER M.
    1967. "Statistical Models and Decision Models of Social Structure: A Kwaio Case." *Ethnology* **6**:1-16.

LAMBERT, BERND
    1966. "Ambilineal Descent Groups in the Northern Gilbert Islands." *American Anthropologist* **68**:641-664.

MCARTHUR, NORMA
    1961. "Population and Social Change: The Prospects for Polynesia." *J. Polynesian Soc.* **70**:393-400.

MOENCH, RICHARD
    1963. "A Preliminary Report on Chinese Social and Economic Organization in the Society Islands." In A. SPOEHR (editor), *Pacific Port Towns and Cities,* pp. 75-89. Honolulu: Bishop Museum Press.

NAYACAKALOU, R. R.
    1963. "The Urban Fijians of Suva." In A. SPOEHR (editor), *Pacific Port Towns and Cities,* pp. 33-41. Honolulu: Bishop Museum Press.

RENNIE, J. S.
    1962. "Problems of Town Growth: An Inquiry into the Relationship between the Research Worker and the Administration in the Pacific." *J. Local Administration Overseas* **1**:183-192.

SPOEHR, ALEXANDER
    1966. "The Part and the Whole: Reflections on the Study of a Region." *American Anthropologist* **68**:629-640.

LINGUISTICS

A LINGUISTIC ASSESSMENT OF THE HISTORICAL VALIDITY OF SOME OF THE RENNELLESE AND BELLONESE ORAL TRADITIONS[1]

SAMUEL H. ELBERT

University of Hawaii

1. Language, archaeology, and tradition
2. The oral traditions of Rennell and Bellona
3. Origin of the language of Rennell and Bellona
    3.1. Hypotheses
    3.2. Phonology
    3.3. Morphology
    3.4. Glottochronology
4. Summary and conclusions

1. LANGUAGE, ARCHAEOLOGY, AND TRADITION

IN THE ROMANTIC PERIOD of the study of Polynesian prehistory, important facets of Polynesian culture were believed to have been transplanted bodily, perhaps by large numbers of people in fleets or "swarms," from various parts of Asia. The Easter Island *rongorongo* tablets were

[1] My work on the language of Rennell and Bellona began in 1957 with a grant from the Tri-Institutional Pacific Program, whose support I wish to acknowledge. Three trips in all have been made to the Solomons, plus work with a Bellonese informant, Taupongi, in Honolulu and in Copenhagen, where a Fulbright research grant permitted me to spend nearly full time working on the language of the two islands. This paper was reviewed by Donn Thomas Bayard, Bruce Biggs, George W. Grace, Saul H. Riesenberg, Laurence C. Thompson, and Albert J. Schütz, whose many helpful suggestions are much appreciated. I want to thank especially Torben Monberg, who has been my co-worker and fellow enthusiast since 1958 in attempts to study the language and culture of Rennell and Bellona. Another valued critic, to whom this book is dedicated, was not bothered this time for reasons of secrecy. He started me out with help and encouragement on my first article nearly three decades ago, and ever since in a multitude of ways has shared his insight and knowledge. Once before I wrote that anyone working on the language and culture of Hawaii has a debt to him. Now I would like to say instead, Hawaii and the Pacific.

believed by some to have come from Mohendjodaro in India. The Samoan *kava* ceremony was connected somehow with the Japanese tea
ceremony. The elevated philosophy had come from India. Even Alfred
Kroeber stated (1948) that Polynesian oral and religious traditions are
a "remnant" of a greater culture, perhaps of India or Indonesia.

The sober period of the study of Polynesian prehistory began with
Emory's 1946 thesis, in which he attempted to trace subgroups of East
Polynesian languages on the basis of a study of shared vocabulary, with
consideration of the total lexicon. This marked the end of the cultural
transplanting notion, and the end of romantic hopes of finding a Polynesian-speaking tribe in central India, Indonesia, or South China. Gradually the view was accepted that the racial, cultural, and linguistic
homogeneity of the Polynesians could only have developed after many
centuries in a single place, and that the place was probably in Polynesia
itself. This view seems more compelling now in the light of Grace's
theory (1959) that the neighboring languages spoken in Fiji and Rotuma
formed with Polynesia a single subgroup. In 1953 Tongan was mentioned
as the most "archaic" (Elbert, 1953, p. 163) of the Polynesian languages,
and the possible "homeland."

In 1966 (p. 13) Roger Green concluded after consideration of both
language and archaeology, that linguistic evidence alone was not con-
clusive, but that on the basis of geography and of recent archaeological
evidence, he believed that Tonga was settled first, and Samoa later.

The favored methods of historical reconstruction since 1946 have
been language and archaeology. Emory, although the leader in Polynesian
subsurface archaeology, has always stressed language, which he called
(1963, p. 78) "the most stable part of Polynesian culture." Each type
of research, he says in the conclusion to the same article (p. 100) "can
act as a corrective in interpreting the results of the other." Green (1966,
p. 35) warns that new findings in one field may fundamentally affect the
interpretation of results in another.

What of a third field of research, native oral traditions? In the romantic period the traditions were taken at face value as literal truth, and even
the long genealogies were considered infallible, although Buck (1938,
p. 25) wrote that, with all his love for his mother's stock, his father's
unbelieving blood kept him from thinking that genealogies would be remembered accurately for 2,000 years of history, a remark prompted by
Rarotongan genealogies going back 92 generations.

But certainly all Polynesian traditions are not as fanciful as this, and
some of them seem to stand the light of investigation, as the Maori
immigration canoes from Central Polynesia, and Gifford (1929, p. 232)

suggested that the Tongans did not evolve genealogical fictions, as did the Hawaiians and other eastern Polynesians. Many scholars considered that the traditions provide hints and hypotheses to be tested by language, archaeology, and ethnology.

The present study purports to assess linguistically and eclectically the validity of certain of the oral traditions of Rennell and Bellona, two Polynesian Outliers with a single language and culture in the British Solomon Islands. The techniques are phonology, morphology, and glottochronology. The investigation can be considered only an introduction, since some of the linguistic data for most of the compared languages (East Uvea, or Wallis Island, East Futuna, Ellice, Niuafo'ou, Takuu, Tikopia, and especially West Uvea in the Loyalty Islands) are fragmentary and questionable.

The oral traditions of Rennell and Bellona (hereafter written R/B) are preserved with great detail and clarity, and with a remarkable unanimity by informants from the east end of Rennell (RE) and Bellona (BE), and thus provide a convenient laboratory for an investigation of the validity of oral tradition.

2. THE ORAL TRADITIONS OF RENNELL AND BELLONA

The R/B traditions have been presented in the informants' words in great detail in Elbert and Monberg (1965, hereafter referred to as *Canoes*). Those concerning the discovery of the two islands, mostly in Chapters 8 and 9, are considered in this paper. Two versions of this tradition exist and will be only briefly summarized here.

(Unusual R/B letters are *gh,* a voiced velar fricative, and *g,* a prenasalized voiced velar stop. *b* is a voiced bilabial fricative, and ' a glottal stop. In BE, the RE *g* is replaced by *ng,* a velar nasal. See *Canoes,* pp. 19-22.)

RE version (*Canoes,* Text 67): Kaitu'u, living on 'Ubea, dreams of two gods who wish to possess a place called Mugaba. With three others, his mother, and his mother's brother, Kaitu'u sets out in a double canoe to find Mugaba. He takes along two stone gods. The canoe lands at various unnamed islands, where the three companions are killed (*Canoes,* Text 67, Verses 9-18). On one island, Kaitu'u escapes from a giant named Tongagegeba. Finally the survivors come to Ahanga at the northeast end of Mugaba. The two stone gods refuse to go ashore here or elsewhere on Mugaba, but consent to stay on nearby Mugiki. Kaitu'u returns to Mugaba, travels over that large island (*Canoes,* Text 67, Verses 28-

33), building temples and naming places 'Ubea or compounds with the name 'Ubea. (The RE map, Plate 1 of *Canoes,* contains eleven names with 'Ubea; five are on the BE map, Plate 2 of *Canoes.*)

BE version (*Canoes,* Text 66): Nine men come to 'Ubea Matangi ('East 'Ubea') from 'Ubea Ngango ('West 'Ubea'), bringing two stone gods, a sacred staff, and a temple. Kaitu'u joins them. They go to Ngua Hutuna ('Two Hutuna') and then to Henuatai ('Sealand'), where they obtain many gods. Most of the canoes swamp in the surf and a hundred persons drown. The two surviving canoes, captained by Taupongi and Kaitu'u, land at Ahanga on northeast Mungaba and then go to Mungiki (*Canoes,* pp.173-176).

Kaitu'u and Taupongi establish clans that survive today. Members of the Kaitu'u clan on both islands trace their ancestry back 23 generations to Kaitu'u (*Canoes,* Plate 8). Members of the small Taupongi clan live only on RE, and trace back 23 generations to Taupongi (*Canoes,* p. 59).

3. ORIGIN OF THE LANGUAGE OF RENNELL AND BELLONA

3.1. HYPOTHESES

The places mentioned in the traditions are assumed to be the following islands:

RE version: 'Ubea: East Uvea or Wallis Island.
             Mugaba: RE, the usual native name.
             Mugiki: BE, the usual native name.
BE version: 'Ubea Ngango: West Uvea, in the Loyalty Islands.
             'Ubea Matangi: East Uvea or Wallis Island.
             Ngua Hutuna: East Futuna and its close neighbor Alofi, collectively
                 also known as Hoorn Islands. (This hypothesis is strengthened
                 by two names with cognates of Futuna on RE, and one name
                 with cognate of Alofi on RE and one on BE. See *Canoes,* Plates
                 1 and 2.)
             Henuatai: unidentified, but perhaps an atoll such as Pileni in the
                 Reef Islands.
             Mungaba, Mungiki: BE for RE Mugaba, Mugiki.

The meanings of Mugaba and Mugiki may possibly be 'Big Mu' and 'Little Mu.' Related names might be Murua or Woodlark Island near New Guinea (see *Canoes,* Text 227A) or Ulawa, near San Cristobal (*lawa* is cognate with *gaba,* "big," in RE). Informants in present-day R/B have no use for such explanations, but their own translations seem fanciful: Mugaba = *mu'a baa* 'first sea'; Mugiki = *mugi ki* /Nukumaangongo/ 'later to /Unknown-island/'; these names are said to refer to the relative order in which Kaitu'u reached the two islands.

The purpose of this study is to attempt to discover the early linguistic affinities of R/B. (Space precludes consideration of later Melanesian affinities.) Could the ancestors of the present people have actually come from West Uvea or East Uvea and stopped en route at East Futuna? If they came from one or several of these places, where do the latter stand within the Polynesian family tree? Is there such a place as Henuatai?

The discussion concerns phonology (Section 3.2), morphology (3.3), and glottochronology (3.4).

We begin with portions of a Polynesian family tree recently published by Roger Green (1966, p. 34). R/B and West Uvean are not listed on the tree; data were not available.

Proto Eastern Oceanic
Proto Fijiic
Proto Polynesian (PPN)
    Proto Tongic
        Tongan and Uvean
        Niuean
    Proto Nuclear Polynesian (PNP)
    Proto Eastern Polynesian (PEP), all eastern languages
        Outliers?
        Proto Samoic
            Outliers
            Futunan
            Samoan
            Ellicean
            Tikopian

In an article published as a companion piece to that by Green, Andrew Pawley (1966, Footnote 8, p. 41) states that evidence is too conflicting for positive assignment of East Uvean to either the Proto Tongic or the PNP groups. Accordingly, considerable attention will be paid to this language.

3.2. PHONOLOGY

Only certain of the PPN phonemes are relevant to the placing of R/B and the possible source languages on a family tree. These are PPN /?, h, r/. PPN /1, s/ are also listed below, as they have clarifying value.

Abbreviations are as follows:

EFU	East Futunan		R/B	Rennell and Bellona
EL	Ellice		SAM	Samoan
EUV	East Uvean		SIK	Sikaianan
HAW	Hawaiian		TAK	Takuu (Mortlocks)
KAP	Kapingamarangi		TIK	Tikopian
M/F	Mele-Fila		TO	Tongan
NO	Nukuoro		WUV	West Uvean
PIL	Pileni			

PPN	* ?	*h	*r	*1	*s
TO	?	h	Ø	l	h
EUV	? Ø	h, Ø	1, Ø	l	h
PNP	* ?	Ø	*1	*1	*s
HAW	Ø	Ø	1	1	h
EFU	Ø, ?	Ø	1	1	s
SAM	Ø	Ø	1	1	s
WUV	Ø	Ø	1	1	s
TIK	Ø	Ø	1, r	1, r	s
EL	Ø	Ø	1	1	s
TAK	Ø	Ø	1, r	1, r	s
PIL	Ø	Ø	1	1	Ø
SIK	Ø	Ø	1	1	s
KAP	Ø	Ø	r, rh	r, rh	h
M/F	Ø	Ø	r	r	s
NO	Ø	Ø	1	1	s, h
R/B	?	Ø	g, ng	g, ng	s

In EUV and EFU double reflexes occur for some of the PPN phonemes. One purpose of the following discussion of PPN / ? h r / is to attempt to discover if one of the doublets in each case may be assumed original, and the other borrowed.

PPN /?/

The problems here are EUV and EFU /?/ and Ø as reflexes of PPN /?/.

Random counts were made of /?-/ in the TO and EUV dictionaries by Churchward (1959) and Bataillon (1932). Of about 800 TO entries with initial glottal stops (exclusive of loans from English or other European languages), some 250 have cognates in EUV, and of these, about 80 percent maintain the glottal stop. Some of the lacking glottal stops, especially in rare words, may be attributed to loans, extra-systematic losses, faulty recording, or misprints.

Initial glottal stops seemed entered so erratically in Grézel's EFU dictionary (Grézel, 1878) that a similar count was not made for EFU.

A second type of check was made by consulting a recent and very useful list of PPN reconstructions by Walsh and Biggs, Burrows' 1937 EUV ethnology, and an EUV vocabulary compiled during World War II by Alexander Coburn Soper. A few of Walsh-Biggs' words were modified, mostly on the basis of entries in Burrows (1937, p. 17, *mala'e* for Bataillon's *malae,* and p. 161, *fo'ou* for Bataillon's *foou*) and Soper (*ma'uga* and *ma'uri* for Bataillon's forms without glottals). *Fetu'u* by analogy was interpreted as having a glottal; PPN *alo* was omitted in the count as it seemed to be the same as PPN *aro;* EUV *'uo* was considered a reflex of PPN *'ura; 'api'api* and *'u'u* were counted only once.

The totals then came out:

	/?/	Ø
EUV	77	13 (86% have / ?/)
EFU	36	41 (47% have / ?/)

The EFU figures appear unreliable (the dictionary date is 1878), but a 50 percent estimate will be reckoned. But for EUV, 85 percent retention of PPN /?/ seems conservatively realistic.

It must not be assumed that the figures above represent all PPN words in the two languages with glottal stops, but are rather a small sampling.

PPN /h/

EUV and PPN /h/ cannot be analyzed without consideration of what seem best explained as PPN doublets with */h/ and */s/. This problem has been discussed indirectly by Milke (1961) and Milner (1963), both of whom give numerous examples, but apparently has not been confronted squarely in the few extant discussions of PPN reconstructions. The list in Table 1 shows a number of examples, but makes no claim to exhaustive inquiry. Inspection will show that forms in some languages reflect a PPN form with */h/, and others a PPN /s/, and that many languages have reflexes of both forms, this being the justification for doublets. Very little patterning is apparent in the distributions, except that reflexes of *siwa* 'nine' seem confined to the Outliers (see Section 3.4), and that a few forms are found ordinarily only in EPN (*hamu, *liha, *'oho), and others only in EPN and Kapingamarangi (*aha, *kehe).

The dictionaries used were Bataillon (EUV), Grézel (EFU), Milner and Pratt (SAM), Pukui-Elbert (HAW), and my own notes for R/B.

TABLE 1

PPN	EUV	EFU	R/B	SAM	HAW
*aha 'what?'	aa	aa	aa	aa	–
*asa	–	–	–	–	aha
*'aho 'cloud'	'ao	'ao	'ao	ao	ao
*'aso 'day'	'aho	'asu	'aso	aso	–
*'ahu 'smoke'	'ahu	–	'au/ahi	–	u/ahi
*asu	'ahu	'afu	–	asu	–
*-ha'a 'bad'	-a'a	-aa	-a'a	-aa	-aa
*-sa'a	-ha'a	–	-sa'a	-saa	–
*hai 'who?'	ai	ai	ai	ai	ai
*sai	hei	–	–	sai	ai
*ha'i 'copulate'	ha'i	f/ei/si	h/e'i/ti	f/ei/ti	
*sa'i 'tie'	ha'i	sa'i	sa'i/sa'i	sai	
*hake 'up'	ake	ake	ake	a'e	a'e
*sake	hake	sake	sake	sa'e	
*haku 'swordfish'	aku	–	aku	a'u	a'u
*saku	haku	–	–	sa'u	
*hama 'outrigger float'	ama	ama	ama	ama	ama
*sama	hama	–	sama	–	
*hamu 'eat scraps'	hamu	samu/ko	–	samu/samu	amu
*samu	hamu	–	samu	–	hamu
*hapai 'carry'	apai	–	–	–	hapai
*sapai	hapai	–	sapai	–	–
*ha'u 'come'	ha'u	a'u	a'u	sau	
*sa'u	ha'u	–	–	–	–
*hifo 'down'	ifo	ifo	iho	ifo	iho
*sifo	hifo	–	–	(si)sifo	–
*hiku 'end'	iku	iku	–	i'u	i'u
*siku 'tail'	hiku	siku	siku	siku	hi'u

*hiwa 'nine'	hiva	iva	iba	iva	iwa
*siwa		–	–	–	–
*hoka 'pierce'	hoka	'oka	–	o'a	o'a
*soka		soka	soka	so'a	–
*hola 'live, escape'	ola	–	oga	ola	ola
*sola	hola	sola	–	sola	–
*holo 'rub'	holo	olo	ogo	olo	olo
*solo		–	sogo	solo	–
*huhu 'breast'	huhu	uu	uu	–	uu
*susu		–	–	susu	–
*huli 'sucker'	huli	uli	ugi	uli	huli
*suli		–	–	suli	ulu
*huru 'enter'	huu	ulu	ugu	ulu	–
*suru		sulu	–	sulu	–
*kehe 'different'	kehe	kese	kese	kese	'ee
*kese		lia	gie	lia	lia
*liha 'nit'	liha	–	–	–	liha
*lisa		–	–	–	oo
*'oho 'rations'	'oho	oso	'oso	oso	–
*oso		–	baa	vaa	waa
*waha 'space'	vaa	vasa	basa	basa	–
*wasa 'open sea'	vaha	vae	bae	vae	wae
*wahe 'divide'	vae	vasi (?)	–	vase	–
*wase	vahe				

NOTES

aho: HAW *ao* 'daylight'

*'ahu: HAW *u/ahi* < *au/ahi*

*-ha'a: EUV *logoa'a*, EFU *logoa'a*, R/B *gongoa'a* 'noisy'; HAW *'aiaa* 'wicked'; SAM *saugaa* 'smell bad'

*-sa'a: EUV *logoa'a*, EFU *logoa'a*, R/B *pongisa'a* 'very dark'

*ha'i: R/B has also an unexplained *ei*

*sake: R/B *sake* 'stretch arms taut, strut'; SAM *sa'e* 'heel over, overturn'

*samu: R/B *samu* 'bite seeds and spit out pulp'

*Sifo: SAM *(si) sifo* 'west'

*hoka: R/B *'oka* should perhaps be *oka*

*wasa: EFU *vasa* 'space'

*wase: SAM *vase* 'draw lines'

The EUV reflexes are of three types:

(1) Those with a doubtful source. They have /h/, but EUV /h/ reflects PPN /h s/. Since in other languages reflexes of both PPN /h/ and /s/ occur, the EUV source is doubtful. The 13 doubtful words in this category are bracketed.

(2) Those with double reflexes, /h/ and Ø, numbering 12.

(3) Only one form has an unequivocal Ø as a reflex of PPN /h/: *aa* 'what.'

Summary:

(1) EUV /h/ < PPN /h s/:   13
(2) EUV /h/ < PPN /h s/:   12
(4) EUV Ø < PPN /h/:   12+1=13

(5) In addition, 17 words reflect PPN /h/: EUV fuhi, hafu, hakau, hanga, hangafulu, hapo, hingoa, honge, huu, kaiha'a, kakaha, kanahe, mohuku, pihi, tehina, 'uhila, 'uhinga.

(6) In addition, 7 words with EUV Ø < PPN /h/: ala, fia, foe, lou, moe, tai, 'ua.

Adjusted totals:

(1+2) EUV /h/ < PPN /h s/:   13+12=25.
(5)   EUV /h/ < PPN /h/:   17.
(4+6) EUV Ø < PPN /h/:   13+7 =20.

The (1 + 2) figures can be interpreted either way and are not considered. The ratio of /h/ to Ø reflexes of PPN /h/ is 17 to 20, or about 46 percent. EUV phonology needs a modern study. Burrows (1937, p. 16) remarks that "h, though sometimes strongly aspirated, appears to be used and dropped at will in some words," citing the article *he,* sometimes pronounced *e.* One wonders how prevalent such variation is.

PPN /r/

PPN /r/ is reflected in EUV by /1/ and Ø. Most of the following examples are from Walsh-Biggs:

PPN	EUV	
	l	Ø
*'ara 'wake'	'a'ala	
*'ariki 'chief'	'aliki	
*'aro 'front'	'alo	
*fara 'pandanus'		faa
*firi 'plait'		fii
*huru 'enter'		huu

*ma'uri 'alive'	ma'uli	
*mori 'offer'	moli	
*muri 'after'	muli	
*ngaarue 'work'	galue	gaaue
*raa 'branch'		va[1]
*rama 'torch'	lama	
*rano 'lake'		ano
*rara 'heat'	lala	
*refu 'ashes'	lefu	
*renga 'turmeric'	lenga	
*rofa 'fathom'	lofa	
*rongo 'hear'	logo	
*rua 'two'	lua	uo/fulu 'twenty'
*rufi, fish sp.	lufi	
*seru 'scrap'		seu 'put aside (scrappings)'
*tiro 'look at'		sio
*turi 'knee'	tuli	
*'ura, a crustacean		'uo
*waru 'scrape'	valu	

[1] See note under *drink*, Section 3.4.

Of the 25 EUV examples, 17 have /1/ and 10 have Ø for PPN /r/. Two PPN forms (*-ngaarue and *rua) exhibit both correspondences in EUV. This is a nearly 63 percent /1/ correspondence for PPN /r/. The 37 percent might be considered loans, a high percentage when compared with the loans reflecting PPN /? h/.

We may conclude that in respect to PPN /r/, EUV is closer to SAM than to TO, but not as close to SAM as the proximity to TO exhibited by EUV reflexes of PPN /?/.

CONCLUSIONS

Portions of the table of sound correspondences given at the beginning of this section may be redrafted as follows, with the split correspondences followed by estimated percentages.

PPN	TO	EUV	EFU	SAM	WUV	TIK	R/B
*?	?	?(85%)	?(50%)	Ø	Ø	Ø	?
*h	h	h(46%)	Ø	Ø	Ø	Ø	Ø
*r	Ø	1(63%)	1	1	1	1, r	g, ng

Portions of Green's family tree (Section 3.1) may be rewritten with certain phoneme correspondences listed, and with the addition of Niuafo'ou (NF). Little has been published about this language or dialect except that given in a short article by Collocott (1922) and two short texts collected by him (1928, pp. 34-38) that reveal a phonemic system similar to that of EUV and R/B, as well as numerous grammatical similarities that make it seem very unlike TO. Collocott states that intercourse between NF and EUV has been "considerable."

In the evaluation of any family tree, Bloomfield's caution (1933, p. 314) must be remembered: family trees are "unrealistic;" cleavages are frequently much less sharp; the diagrams are statements of methods.

PPN	*?	h	*r	*l	s
Proto Tongic	*?	*h	*r	*l	s
TO	?	h	Ø	l	h
EUV (?)	?	hᵃ	lᵇ	l	h
NF (?)	?	hᵃ	lᵇ	l	s
PNP	*?	Ø	*l	*l	*s
Proto Futunic	*?	Ø	*l	*l	*s
EFU	?ᵃ	Ø	l	l	s
R/B	?	Ø	g, ng	g, ng	s
PEPN	*?	Ø	*l	*l	*s
Proto Samoic	Ø	Ø	*l	*l	*s
SAM	Ø	Ø	l	l	s
WUV	Ø	Ø	l	l	s
TIK	Ø	Ø	l, r	l, r	s

ᵃ and Ø, probably in loans.
ᵇ and Ø, the many /l/ reflexes may be loans.

The positions on the family tree of EUV and NF are not certain. They have been placed doubtfully with Tongic, with the understanding that both of them have been greatly influenced by SAM borrowings— not surprising in view of their geographic position between Samoa and Tonga, and in view of traditions of centuries of raids by these larger and more powerful sea-going neighbors.

R/B is clearly an offshoot of PNP and more intimately of EFU, and has the same or cognate reflexes of the crucial phonemes, except that the PNP glottal stop is faithfully maintained. This connection of R/B with PNP rather than with Proto Tongic would be less certain were it not for the preservation of PNP /?/ in Easter Island, which guarantees this phoneme a place in PNP, and serves to separate the Samoic languages from all other protolanguages listed above.

What of the RE traditions, with their constant reiteration of 'Ubea as the homeland? Perhaps the traditions are wrong, or more likely, as Professor Grace has suggested orally, EFU or NF people were the first settlers of EUV, and the two RE heroes, Kaituʻu and Taupongi, left there before or because of the inundation of that island by the Tongans.

After advancing this hypothesis, based on study of phonology coupled with the R/B oral traditions, I reread Burrows' account (1937, p. 171) of the settlement of EUV. It is so germane as to be worth quoting in full:

> Kauulufonua may well have been the first Tongan invader. He found a numerous population in Uvea and was able to pick out the Tongan murderers of his father in the crowd because they alone wore their hair short. A few place names tend to confirm the suggestions in tradition that there was a pre-Tongan population. Nineteen of the Uvean place names correspond to names in Futuna, but not in Tonga. The hypothetical pre-Tongan population may have had an early western culture related to that of Futuna. All western Polynesian cultures are so much alike that the consistent similarity between those of Uvea and Tonga does not refute this suggestion.
>
> Uvean culture, then, is western Polynesia. It is mainly Tongan, but shows traces of a pre-Tongan population, and of minor influences from other Polynesian islands.

In his earlier book on Futuna (1936, p. 54) Burrows tells of four visits of Tongans to Futuna; none resulted in conquest. "Futuna was never subject to Tonga. . . . Futuna culture has been influenced hardly at all by that of Tonga."

In conclusion, the EUV and EFU traditional evidence, as presented by Burrows, lends considerable credence to the linguistic evidence, and to the oral traditions of RE and BE.

The suggestion of the three is that R/B were settled from 'Uvea, but that the early settlers of that island were East Futunans. Later EUV was overrun by Tongans (and it may be that Kaitu'u left EUV because of TO pressure), which accounts for the phonological similarity of TO and EUV.

The phonemic systems of SAM and WUV are identical, save for SAM /?/ = WUV /k/, and for the considerable Melanesian influences on WUV. This is at complete variance with the WUV traditions. These are discussed by Burrows in his book on Uvea (1937, p. 16). Comparing the traditions of the two Uveas, he concludes that EUV settled WUV in about 1800. The phonology does not support this claim. Only one reflex of PPN /h/ was noted in the limited data available: tehina 'younger sibling.' This vexing problem is treated in Section 3.3.

3.3. MORPHOLOGY

An attempt is made in this section to compare certain morphological features in TO, EUV, EFU, SAM, and R/B. None of the features is present everywhere, and most of them are shared between at least two languages. Some were taken directly from Pawley's pioneering article

(1966) on that subject, but here no effort is made to classify features as PPN or PNP.

	R/B	TO	EUV	EFU	SAM
PRONOUNS					
1. Intrusive -u- in pl. (TO kimautolu, kimoutolu)	−	+	−	−	−
2. -tolu, 3rd pl.	−	+	−	−	−
3. *kita, 1st sg., emotional diminutive	−	+	+	+	+
4. -n-, 3rd pl. (TO kinaua, kinautolu)	−	+	+	−	−
DEMONSTRATIVES					
5. *nei, 'here, now'	+	−	−	+	+
6. *laa 'there'	+	−	−	+	+
POSSESSIVES					
7. t-set (not l-)	+	−	+	−	−
8. Zero-set for pl. (SAM o'u)	+	−	+	+	+
9. Indefinite set (SAM so'u)	−	+	+	−	+
10. Reduplicated set (RE ta'aku)	+	+	+	−	−
11. Emotional set (TO si'eku)	−	+	+	−	+
12. -e-, var. of a-poss.	+	+	−	−	−
ARTICLES					
13. Sg. def. (contrasts with pl.)	+	−	+	+	+
14. Sg. indef. (contrasts with pl.)	+	−	+	+	+
15. l-formative of def. art., poss., demon., negatives	−	−	−	+	+
16. Pl. defined by Ø	−	−	+	+	+
17. Diminutive-emotional *si'i	−	+	+	−	+
QUALIFIERS					
18. *loa 'then, immediately'	−	−	−	+	+
19. *fua 'just, without purpose'	−	−	−	+	+
20. *lava, intensive, particular	−	+	−	−	+
21. *kese 'away,' post-verbal	−	−	+	−	+
PREFIXES					
22. *toka-, human number (not toko-)	+	−	−	+	+
23. *soko- 'each, any'	+	−	+	+	+
24. *ngaa-, pre. to locative bases (RE ngaatai)	+	−	+	+	+

In the following table, the number of shared pluses and minuses is given for each pair, and below that the percentage of shared features out of the 24 listed features.

	EUV	SAM	EFU	R/B
TO	12	6	3	9
	50	25	13	38
EUV		14	11	13
		58	46	54
SAM			19	11
			79	46
EFU				16
				66

In the morphological comparison, R/B is most closely allied with EFU. EFU, however, is closer to SAM than to R/B, and EUV is a little closer to SAM than to TO, making that language still more isolated from the standpoint of morphology. Strangely, R/B is closer to EUV than to SAM.

The family tree, based on morphology alone, would be redrawn:

PPN

TO

PNP

PEUV

PSamoic-EFU

SAM

EFU

R/B

These anomalies raise the question as to the reliability of statistical use of morphological features in determining linguistic subbranching— a feat no one has yet done satisfactorily. For one thing, contrary to the usual theories, some kinds of morphology may be more easily borrowed than phonemes, as here the use of *t-* in possessives, demonstratives, and articles (Items 7 and 15, EFU and SAM), or the *-n-* instead of *-l-* in the third person pronouns and possessives (TO and EUV). Another objection to morphostatistics is the rather arbitrary selection of items, versus the rigorous selection of phonemes for comparison.

We can be sure that the area between TO, EFU, and SAM was one with considerable intracommunication. The Tongans were noted as seafaring marauders and colonists, and small, fairly low islands such as EUV and NF provided scant opposition to their onslaughts. Even SAM was occupied at one time by Tongans (Collocott, 1924, p. 168, sets the date at about A.D. 1250, based on SAM genealogies), but as we have seen, Burrows thinks EFU was never conquered; this immunity may be perhaps attributed partially to the comparative isolation of the island, and to its precipitous jungle-covered mountains and absence of lagoons.

3.4. GLOTTOCHRONOLOGY

Much has been written, some of it rather intemperate, about glotto-chronology since Morris Swadesh first published his Salish findings in 1950. In general, anthropologists have been more sanguine about the value of glottochronology than have linguists. Only a few of the latter, however, call such studies completely worthless. Most linguists seem to think something may be revealed about subgrouping, but are skeptical about absolute dating. Glottochronological studies in PN have been made by Elbert (1953), Grace (1961), Emory (1963), Dyen (1965), and Bayard (1966).

Most workers have found the basic word list ill-suited to Oceania, especially such words as *few, freeze, ice,* and *snow,* and the many doub-lets or triads, as *and/with, animal/bird, bark/skin, black/dirty, breathe/belly, burn/warm, egg/fruit, fight/hit/kill, foot/leg, hand/five, husband/man/person, husband/old, husband/wife, lie/sleep, stick/tree, wife/woman.* Pairs hard to distinguish are *float* and *flow* and *push* and *pull.*

The languages studied follow:
In western PN proper: EFU, EUV, SAM, TO.
Outliers: KAP, M/F, NO, PIL, SIK, TAK, TIK, R/B, WUV.
In eastern PN: HAW.
Since this study is concerned with the linguistic position of R/B, not all the Outliers were compared exhaustively, and some of them were not considered at all.

The sources consulted in this paper included my own field notes, and Bataillon (1932) for EUV, Elbert (1950) for Kapingamarangi, Grézel (1878) for EFU, Milner (1966) for SAM, Leverd (1922) for WUV, and Durrad (1913) and Firth (1936) for TIK. Bayard's lists (1966) were also consulted. Forms with many undifferentiated glosses in a dictionary and no informant for consultation were omitted.

The R/B basic list is given in full, with methodological notations de-signed to help future workers in PN glottochronology attain consistency.

1. Parentheses enclose portions of items ignored in the determination

of cognancy. Some are members of compounds, as R/B *gau('ugu)* 'hair,' literally '(head) leaf.' Many are bound morphemes, as follows:

(a) Thematic consonant (as -s-, -t-, -'-, -Ø-) plus vowel(s):
   bite: SAM uu, EFU (u)'u(ti), WFU u(tia)
   hit: R/B taa, TO taa('i)
   know: SAM ilo(a), TO 'ilo('i), EUV ilo(i)
   meat: EL (ka)kano, R/B kano(hi)
   spit: SAM (fe)anu, TO ('a)'anu, WUV anu(si)

(b) Affixes, as *m(a)*-, stative, *fe*-, plural, and -a, transitive
   blow: R/B angi, TIK (mangi)angi(a)
   cut: R/B ta(a)
   fight: R/B (heta)ta('i), WUV (fefe)ta(i)

(c) Reduplications, partial or complete:
   smooth: EUV (mo)mole, R/B (moge)moge, SAM (laamole)-mole

(d) Assimilations (see below *hand, tail*), dissimilations (*grass*), and metathesis (*wing*) are considered cognate.

2. Vague terms are defined specifically; see *man, we.*

3. Forms not considered cognate are in some instances mentioned specifically (*and, they*).

4. To assist in later evaluation of the findings, retention rates for each item are given, based on the comparison of the retention of each item in five languages for which there seems to be the least evidence of distortion (TO, EUV, EFU, EL, and R/B). Thus, after *all* is RR: .4, to be read, retention rate, 40 percent: a cognate form was found in two of the five languages, whether R/B was one of the two or not. Animal has a 100 percent retention rate (RR: 1.).

Loan words and probable loan words are starred, whether from English or from Melanesian languages.

Vowel length is ignored as it is not always indicated in dictionaries, or by some collectors.

all (a. the people): ba'i. RR: .4.
and: ma (not *mo*): RR: .8.
animal: manu. RR: 1.
ashes: gehu. RR: 1.
at: i. RR: 1.

back (human): tu'a. RR: 1.
bad *songo (BE: maase'i): RR: .2.

bark: kigi. RR: .8.
because: i te me'a gaa. RR: .2.
belly: tina'e. RR: .4.
big (b. house): hu'ai-. RR: .8.
bird: manu. RR: 1.
bite: u'u. RR: 1.
black: 'ugi. RR: 1.
blood: toto. RR: 1.

blow (of wind): angi. RR: .8.
bone: ibi. RR: .6.
breathe: manaba. RR: 1.
burn (intransitive): kaa. RR: .4.

child: tama ('iti'iti). RR: 1.
cloud: 'ao. RR: .8.
cold (of weather): gogohi. RR: .6.
come (singular): a'u (see *drink*). RR: 1.
count: (haka)gau. RR: .6.
cut (as a banana tree): tu(a). RR: .4.

day: 'aso. RR: 1.
die (as a person): mate. RR: 1.
dig: kegi. RR: .8.
dirty: 'ugi. RR: .8.
dog: *tokitoki (Eng.). RR: .8.
drink: binu. (This is considered cognate with *inu*, just as R/B *boo* 'come' = SAM *oo*. TO also has *v* cognate with Ø elsewhere, as *vaku* 'scratch' and *va'akau* 'stick' < PPN *aku*, *ra'akau*. EL *vau* 'come' = R/B *a'u*). RR: 1.
dry (as dead leaves, not *masa* 'drained': *maamala. RR: .4.
dull (not sharp): *palugha. RR: .4.
dust: pebu. RR: .6.

ear: taginga. RR: 1.
earth (dirt): kege. RR: 1.
eat: kai. RR: 1.
egg: hua. RR: .8.
eye: mata. RR: 1.

fall (as from a height, not *hina* 'topple'): too. RR: .8.
far: mama'o. RR: 1.
fat (grease): ngako. RR: .8.
father: tamana. RR: .6.
fear: mataku. RR: .6.
feather: hugu. RR: 1.
few (a f. people, not 'the people are f.'): nisi. RR: .2.
fight (general term, including warfare, not boxing): (heta)ta('i) (= taa). RR: .2.
fire: ahi. RR: 1.

fish: *kaui. RR: .8.
five: gima. RR: 1.
float (not sink; as a canoe): tahe(a). RR: .2.
flow (as current, a river): migi. RR: .6.
flower: *laka. RR: .2.
fly (v.): gege. RR: 1.
fog: sau. RR: .4.
foot: ba'e. RR: 1.
four: haa. RR: 1.
freeze — RR: 0.
fruit: hua. RR: 1.

give (to me): 'au mai. RR: .4.
good: gaoi. RR: .6.
grass (a kind, not a general term for vegetation): mutie (*mutia*, ok). RR: .8.
green: usiusi. RR: .4.
guts: *ghoghughoghu. RR: .6.

hair (head): gau ('ugu). RR: .6.
hand: gima (*nima*, ok). RR: 1.
he: ia. RR: 1.
head: 'ugu. RR: 1.
hear: gongo. RR: 1.
heart: hatu (manaba). RR: .6.
heavy: (ma)maha. RR: 1.
here (the house is h.): (tee)nei. RR: .8.
hit: taa. RR: .6.
hold (grasp): tau. RR: .4.
how: (pe)hea. RR: 1.
hunt (chase, not *shoot*): 'agu'agu. RR: .4.
husband (spouse if no special term): matu'a. RR: .4.

I: au. RR: .8.
ice — RR: .2.
if: namaa. RR: .4.
in (inside): goto. RR: 1.

kill: taa (ta[mate] is cognate). RR: .8.
know (facts): *na'a. RR: .8.

lake: gano. RR: .6.
laugh: kata. RR: 1.
leaf: gau. RR: 1.
left (hand): sema. RR: .8.
leg: ba'e. RR: 1.

lie (1. down): moe. RR: .6.
live (alive): ma'ugi. RR: .8.
liver: 'ate. RR: 1.
long (not *short*): goa. RR: 1.
louse: kutu. RR: 1.

man (male): tangata. RR: 1.
many: 'eha. RR: .6.
meat (flesh): kano(hi). RR: 1.
mother: tinana. RR: .4.
mountain: ogo. RR: .8.
mouth: ngutu. RR: 1.

name: ingoa. RR: 1.
narrow: gau ('iti). RR: .8.
near: hetaiake. RR: .6.
neck: u'a. RR: 1.
new: ho'ou. RR: 1.
night: poo. RR: 1.
nose: isu. RR: 1.
not (n. good): he'e. RR: .6.

old (as a person): matu'a. RR: 1.
one: tahi. RR: 1.
other (the o. man): teegaa. RR: .4.

person: *pegea. RR: .4.
play (as a game): bage. RR: .2.
pull (jerk, not drag): huti. RR: .8.
push: toso. RR: .4.

rain: 'ua. RR: 1.
red: uga. RR: .8.
right (side): maui. RR: .4.
right (correct): tonu. RR: .4.
river: bai (mimigo). RR: .2.
road: aga. RR: 1.
root: aka. RR: 1.
rope (general name for all kinds): uka.
    RR: .6.
rotten (log): popo. RR: .8.
rub (as hands): sogo. RR: .4.

salt: *salt (Eng.). RR: .4.
sand: 'one. RR: 1.
say (speak): *hegeu. RR: .4.
scratch (as with fingernails to relieve
    itch): akuaku. See *drink*. RR: .8.
sea: tai. RR: 1.

see: ina. RR: .6.
seed: hatu. RR: .6.
sew: *lapui. RR: .8.
sharp: (ka)ka(i). RR: .6.
short: *pulu. RR: .4.
sing: taugua. RR: .4.
sit: noho. RR: 1.
skin: kigi. RR: .8.
sky: gangi. RR: 1.
sleep: moe. RR: 1.
small: mi'i-. RR: .4.
smell (t r.): songi. RR: .6.
smoke (n.): 'au(ahi) (This is cognate
    with reflexes of PPN *ahu*, but not of
    reflexes of PPN *asu*.) RR: .6.
smooth: (moge)moge. RR: .8.
snake: ngata. RR: 1.
snow — RR: .2.
some (s. people are good, plural): ko-
    gaa. RR: .4.
spit: nga'esu. RR: .6.
split: ha(ha'a). RR: .2.
squeeze: (natu)natu. RR: .4.
stab (pierce): tuki. RR: .2.
stand: tu'u. RR: 1.
star: hetu'u. RR: 1.
stick: ga'akau. See *drink*. RR: 1.
stone: hatu. RR: .6.
straight: tino gaoi. RR: .6.
suck: miti. RR: 1.
sun: ga'aa. RR: 1.
swell: (hu)huga. RR: .6.
swim: (ka)kau. RR: 1.

tail: siku (*suku*, ok). RR: .6.
that (t. person, far): teegaa. RR: .4.
there (over yonder): koo. RR: .4.
they (pl.): kigatou (not cognate with
    latou). RR: .4.
thick: matogu. RR: 1.
thin (as a board): manihi. RR: 1.
think: tegeu'a. RR: .4.
this (t. person, singular): (tee)nei. RR:
    1.
thou: koe. RR: 1.
three: togu. RR: 1.
throw (as a ball): tupe. RR: .2.
tie (as a large rope): nono'a. RR: .6.
tongue: 'agego. RR: 1.

tooth: niho. RR: 1.
tree: ga'akau. RR: 1.
turn: (taka)hugi. RR: .6.
two: gua. RR: 1.

vomit: gua. RR: .8.

walk: sehu. RR: .6.
warm (hot): (be)bega. RR: 1.
wash: (hu)hu'i. RR: .6.
water: bai. RR: 1.
we (pl. inclusive): kitatou (not cognate with *tatou*). RR: .6.
wet: suu. RR: .4.
what?: aa; TO haa is considered a
  metathesis of *aha* and hence cognate; cognate with reflexes of PPN,
  aha, but not of *asa*. RR: 1.

when (interrogative future): makaahea.
  RR: 1.
where: hea. RR: 1.
white: (su)sugu. RR: .2.
who?: ai. RR: 1.
wide: gau ('eha). RR: .4.
wife (spouse if no special term): ugu-
  ugu. RR: .4.
wind: oko. RR: .8.
wing: kapakau (*pakakau*, ok). RR: 1.
wipe: sogo. RR: 1.
with: ma. RR: .8.
woman: (ha)hine. RR: 1.
woods: mouku. RR: .8.
worm: ane. RR: .2.

ye: koutou. RR: .8.
year: *ghapu. RR: .8.
yellow: (hego)hego. RR: .4.

The percentages of shared basic vocabulary follow:

	EFU	WUV	TAK	EL	EUV	SAM	TO	R/B	
TIK	68.9	69.7	71.1	62.0	63.3	56.3	57.1	62.6	TIK
EFU		65.8		60.8	75.0	57.4	64.9	61.9	EFU
WUV				65.1	64.1	58.7	60.5	64.6	WUV
TAK				61.5				60.4	TAK
SIK								58.4	SIK
EL					56.8	54.4	52.9	55.9	EL
EUV						54.2	75.5	53.9	EUV
PIL								52.7	PIL
SAM							52.4	49.2	SAM
								49.2	TO
								47.2	KAP
								46.6	NO
								44.5	M/F
								42.6	HAW

Examination of the R/B relationships reveals surprises. Two are discussed here: the high figure for WUV, and the low figure for SAM.
From what we know of the phonology, WUV seems too high, and SAM
too low: one would expect SAM to be closer to R/B than TO. The
validity of the WUV and SAM lists will now be reviewed.

Of the various lists used in lexicostatistics and glottochronology
(Hymes, 1960, p. 7), the short 100-word list has the highest retention
rate: this is apparent in Grace (1961, Table 2); the percentage shared
by TO:Maori varies from 41 in the 200-word list to 56 in the 100-word

list. In the present study, the 100-word list was used in the field with a WUV informant, and additions were made much later from texts and Leverd (1922). The impression was that words easily elicited and found in vocabularies were included in the list, whereas "difficult" words were excluded, and that the former had higher persistence. Could this impression be tested objectively?

As mentioned previously, the retention rates in the long list have been entered in the R/B list just preceding. The average percentage of resistance of the 200 words was 72.8, that is, cognate forms were found on an average in 72.8 percent of the five test languages. The average retention of the 154 WUV items included in the count was 78.0 percent. We therefore assume a 5 percent inflation for the WUV percentages.

As for the two lists, the longer one is preferred because it halves the diagnostic load of individual items, thus halving perturbations resulting from poor or chance selection of fillers, and cognancy evaluation.

In 1964 (p. 362) Grace reviewed Elbert's 1953 study, and commented that the TIK percentages showed a higher cognate percentage with every language in the sample than the Samoan ones. Could this SAM deflation be objectively measured? An attempt to do so was made by studying the retention rates in closely related languages of the aberrant SAM items. Sixteen of these scored 100 percent retention in the other languages (*die, in, long, rain, sea, tongue*) or 80 percent retention (*bark, big, dirty, dog, kill, left, red, sea, skin, vomit*).

Many of these terms with high retentions elsewhere exist as rare variants in SAM today, as

> *maile* 'dog' and rare *'ulii*
> *muumuu* 'red' and rare *'ula*
> *sami* 'sea' and rare *tai*
> *timu* 'rain' and rare *ua*

Probably all languages have synonyms. It just seems that in SAM more, proportionately, of words common among the closely related languages have been driven out of everyday circulation. There may, possibly, be a connection with the elaborate language of respect developed in SAM after the daughter languages had left, a language consisting largely of euphemisms. Could there have been a peculiarly SAM focus on name changing? A similar suggestion was made by Fischer (1964) about accelerated vocabulary innovation and replacement in Ponapean and Kusaiean due to a "respect language."

To bring the SAM percentages more into conformity with those of the other languages, it has been assumed that half of the 16 aberrancies highly common elsewhere were actually regular. (This is to ignore the many other aberrancies of items with less high semantic retention rates.) Such manipulation would raise the R/B:SAM shared cognancies to 105 out of 197, or 53.3 percent, an increase of about 3.6 percent above the 49.2 percent previously computed. It therefore seems realistic to *increase* all the SAM percentages by 4 percent.

It seems unsafe to adjust other percentages. The inflation of the TIK list previously mentioned can hardly be measured objectively. Milke (1965, p. 450) attributes this inflation to the possibility that Durrad's TIK vocabulary had been assembled "with inter-Polynesian comparability in mind."

Loans affect lists in two ways. Those from related languages raise the cognancy rates, and this has certainly inflated the EUV/EFU percentages. (Burrows, 1936, p. 56, remarks that voyages to EFU from EUV "were too easy and too frequent to be memorable.") And loans from nonrelated languages usually lower cognancy rates. This is true of WUV, with presumably Melanesian loans for *bad, egg, kill, snake, tail, think,* but the perturbation is far less than the inflation due to the small list.

The R/B figures show evidences of deflation. The dozen or so loans from Melanesian languages and from English deflate the cognancy percentages. Another deflating factor may be that a compiler's greater fluency in one language may produce aberrant forms in the list for that language. Certainly a compiler fluent in a language will not be tempted to think that the form common in the language family is necessarily the proper choice; R/B, for example, has cognates for the common PN forms 'say, speak,' as *gea, hai, muna,* and *taga,* but it is my impression that they are heard less often than the Melanesian loan *hegeu.* (Monberg prefers *gea*—an example of the subjectivity in some decisions.) Hymes (1960, p. 15) has commented on how a list changes if a compiler is fluent in a language. This is in line with Milke's conjecture, just cited, about TIK inflation.

Some indications exist, furthermore, that the R/B change has been more rapid than is "normal." Emory (1963, p. 94) has suggested that cognate percentages for Kapingamarangi and Easter Island are abnormally low because of the isolation and unproductiveness of these islands. The R/B populace may have been reduced to almost nothing at various times during their long wanderings; food was difficult (especially at the lake on RE); and fighting and killing seem to have been constant.

TABLE 2

	R/B to			TIK to				WUV to		EL to			
	Dyen 1965	Bayard 1966	Elbert 1967	Elbert 1953	Dyen 1965	Bayard 1966	Elbert 1967	Bayard 1966	Elbert 1967	Elbert 1953	Dyen 1965	Bayard 1966	Elbert 1967
TIK	63	56	63					58	66	81	67	70	62
EFU		60	62	83		71	69	62	63	79		71	61
WUV		51	61			58	66					55	62
TAK			60			66	71	53				69	62
SIK			58			61		52				63	
EL	63	55	56	81	67	70	62	55	66				
EUV		52	54	78		60	63	48	61	74		55	57
PIL			53		61	56		45			61	52	
SAM	63		51	76	63	50	59	44	58	78	63	50	57
TO			49	70	64	53	57	45	57	64	64	56	53
KAP			47					45				48	
NO		41	47					42				45	
M/F		45	45					47				50	
HAW			43	67				40				49	43
R/B					63	56	63	51	61	68	63	55	56

Comparison of the present results with those obtained by previous studies is difficult because of different systems used, or because few scores have been published. In the summaries (Table 2), WUV cognancy percentages have been lowered 5 percent, and SAM raised 4 percent, on the theory that these shifts represent perturbations and after application give more realistic presentation of relationships. The Bayard figures are based on a minimal list of 94 items available out of a possible 200 for all languages compared.

EVALUATION

How close do these statements based on glottochronology of relative proximity of R/B to the other language agree with results obtained by consideration of phonology and morphology, and with the traditions?

Comparison of phonology and morphology reveals agreement in placing R/B closest to EFU. This is attested in the glottochronology, except that TIK is a shade closer. In phonology and morphology, as well as in the corrected (but not the uncorrected) glottochronology, R/B is closer to SAM than to TO. EUV's closest relative in the glottochronological studies by a wide margin is TO, with EFU second.

A surprise is the closeness of TIK to EFU in all the studies, and its closeness to EUV. Firth (1961, pp. 86, 160), mentions genealogical evidence of immigration to TIK from SAM and EUV in about A.D. 1700, and also from Rotuma, Samoa, Taumako (Duffs), Ongtong Java, and Anuta. Firth concludes (p. 160) "the general inference that the Tikopia are the result of an agglomeration of drift or exploratory voyagers, mainly from other Polynesian groups to the eastwards, is supported by the geographical position of the island." Firth devotes Chapter 6 in this book to the "Tongan" raiders on TIK, but admits that there can be no proof they were Tongans, and that they might have come from Samoa!

The figures in the various studies largely agree in *relative* relationships. Elbert's 1953 results are consistently higher because of the use of multiple cognates, and because of the inclusion of "cultural" words (as *canoe, coconut, house*); these are very stable in PN—although in other parts of the world they are claimed to be evanescent. Bayard's figures for WUV are uniformly lower than Elbert's, perhaps owing to nonacceptance of derivatives as cognates.

Probably the most baffling finding in the comparison of basic lexicon, and one not reflected in phonology, is the close proximity of R/B to WUV, TIK and TAK, even with the corrected and lower WUV percentages. The unmistakable inference is of considerable contact of R/B with these western Outliers. R/B traditions tell of castaways from Gotuma (Rotuma?), Taumako (perhaps in the Duff Islands), and TIK. The Outlier traditions need careful study. None of them seem to mention Mulava or Muliki. The EFU people claim they settled SIK (Burrows, 1936, p. 44). TAK traditions tell of migrations from Ttuila (Tutuila?), with stops at Savaiki, Lotuma, Niua, Avai, Taputapu, and Luaniua (Elbert field notes).

Certain words attest intra-Outlier contact. In the list following, the R/B forms precede the colons. Meanings are the same in other languages as in R/B unless otherwise indicated.

> *bilaabei* 'meet': EFU *felavei*, EUV *felaveʻi*, TIK *feravei*. Note R/B *gabe, ngabe* 'caught, entangled' and TO *felaaveaki* 'come upon or across, detect, as a thief.' This word entered R/B twice, as is discussed later.
> *ʻeha* 'many': EL, PIL, WUV *efa.*
> *gabe:* see *bilaabei.*
> *gaboi* 'good': PIL *lavoi.*
> *gaoi* 'good': SIK *laoi*, TIK *laui.*
> *hage* 'house, kind, variety': WUV *fale.*
> *manaha* 'village, plantation, patrilineal descent group': EFU *manafa* 'tomb'; TIK *manafa* (rare) 'patrilineal descent group,' TO *manafa* 'piece of open ground,' WUV *manaha* 'land, plantation.'
> *ngongole,* a kind of dance and song: TIK *ngore* (Monberg has recorded on TIK and BE almost identical *ngore/ngongole* songs, believed taught on R/B by recent visitors from TIK.
> *tahaata* 'morning': TAK *taataa*, WUV *atahata* 'tomorrow.'
> *hetaiaki* 'near': TO *fetaiaki* 'live together harmoniously,' WUV *taiaki* 'near.'

Widespread Outlier terms not found in R/B include:

> KAP *hiva;* Nukumanu, Ongtong Java, SIK, TAK *sivo;* TIK *siva*—all from PPN **siva;* elsewhere, except possibly in TO, PPN *hiva* is reflected, with Ø for PPN /h/. PIL has *iba,* but replaces PPN /s/ and /h/ alike by Ø. See discussion of */h/ in Section 3.2.
> *kai* 'story' is reflected in KAP, TAK, and TIK.

Most revelatory in the above data are the dual correspondences of R/B /1/ in Outlier (and also in Melanesian) languages, as exhibited here by R/B /g, ng/ < /1, r/ in an early stage (*gabe, gaboi, gaoi, hage*) and R/B /1/ < /1, r/ in a later stage (*bilaabei, ngongole*). Between the two stages is the R/B shift of */1/ to /g, ng/, a shift perhaps resulting from the influence of Melanesian languages. In the early stage many Melanesian words entered R/B (not presented here for lack of space), as Saʻa/Ulawa *apalolo* 'banyan species' = R/B *apagogo,* and Nggela *lami* 'crab eggs' = RE *gami*. In a later stage a smaller number of MN words also entered R/B, as Talise (Guadalcanal) *lughulughu* 'carry' = R/B *lughulughu*. The many place names with /1/ on R/B suggest that the R/B shift */1/ > /g, ng/ occurred *before* the immigrants reached the two islands, and that they must have tarried somewhere.

An attractive theory is that they tarried at Henuatai, mentioned in the traditions (Section 2). This unidentified name might be a low island, as one of the PN Reef (PIL, Nukapu, Matemaa, Nupani), or it may have been closer to San Cristobal in the eastern Solomons or even SIK, Nggela, or Guadalcanal. The R/B traditions of contacts with Melanesians are not discussed in this paper. They are very sparse, except for the many stories about the first inhabitants of the two islands, the *hiti,* whom they finally exterminated. (See Elbert, 1962, for the theory that the non-Polynesian phonemes in R/B, /1, gh/, and a large part of the lexicon, came from these people.)

Recent R/B: TIK contacts are described by Firth (1931), who reports an interview with two Tikopians who had been cast up on RE a few years before 1929. Text 226 in *Canoes* gives a RE version. One of the castaways was interviewed by Monberg on Tikopia in 1966: his story was almost identical to that recorded by Firth. The people of R/B all know of TIK, but almost no one has heard of Pileni or WUV, other than the brief mention in the immigration story quoted in Section 2.

In the conclusion to the study of the phonology, the Western Outliers (not including R/B) were placed in the Samoic rather than in the Futunic subbranch of PNP, principally because they, like SAM, have lost the glottal stop. According to lexicostatistics, however, EFU, is far closer than SAM to the Western Outliers, a term that might be used for these closely related Outliers. Possible explanations are that SAM has not been corrected sufficiently (5 percent) and is still deflated, or that the Western Outliers have lost the glottal stop at the mythical Henuatai.

These studies are in essential agreement with Bayard's conclusions (1966, p. 84):

> The position of Fu [EFU] in this study has in the end come to assume an importance much greater than its size and population would at first indicate. If the indices used here are at all a valid indication of historical relationship, Fu must be viewed as the source of primary settlement not only for the southern Outliers and perhaps for Ti [TIK], but also as the major contributor to the settlement of El . . . the answer awaits detailed linguistic, ethnographic, and particularly archaeological work there.

By "Southern Outliers" Bayard refers to those in the New Hebrides and WUV; the former (except M/F) have not been studied here. We would substitute "Western Outliers," and include WUV with this group.

TIME DEPTHS

The 23 generations' time (nearly 600 years at 25 years to a generation) revealed in the R/B traditions compares with 38 generations or 950 years (now 980) recorded by Burrows (1937, p. 18) for EUV, and 38 also for TO by Collocott (1924, p. 166).

The 62 percent shared by R/B with TIK and EFU is a little more than 1,500 years, or A.D. 450, with a margin of error of between 10 and 20 percent. Grace (1964, p. 363) dates the breakup of PPN at about 90 B.C., but Green (1966, p. 34) places it at about 500 B.C., and the separation of Proto Samoic and PEPN at about the time of Christ. These figures indicate the disparity in our reckoning, and that of the traditions.

Although the number of generations in the history of R/B is 23, there is some evidence that the genealogies are incomplete; the Rennellese and Bellonese did not, to use Gifford's phrase about the Tongans (1929, p. 232), evolve "genealogical fictions." Analysis of the semi-historical stories in *Canoes* shows considerable documentation of the seventh generation after Kaitu'u (Chapter 10), but little before that time, and almost nothing at all is remembered for the first few generations after the people had settled on both islands. There are vague accounts, however, of the return of the three ancestors immediately following Kaitu'u to 'Ubea for turmeric, so necessary for proper worship (*Canoes,* Text 124). This early period may well have been considerably longer than indicated in the genealogies.

The time depth indicated for the separation of even corrected WUV is far greater than the mere 170 or so years of the traditions. This was pointed out by Bayard (1966, p. 56), who lists numerous writers who look with approval upon the traditions of recent settlement from EUV. The journey from EUV in about 1800 seems well authenticated, but most likely the immigrants found a long-established PN community there that must have been started many centuries earlier. This also has been suggested by Bayard (1966, p. 81).

4. SUMMARY AND CONCLUSIONS

Prior to Bayard's 1966 thesis, most thinking about the origin of the PN Outliers had been speculative, and precise data had been lacking. The present study concerns the origin of one of them, that of RE and

BE. Some of the other Outliers are closely related and their basic vocabularies have been compared. The languages studied from the standpoints of phonology and morphology include TO, SAM, EUV, and EFU, and lexicostatistically EL, HAW, KAP, NO, PIL, SIK, TAK, TIK, and WUV. An unusual procedure was to *lower* the WUV figures and to *raise* the SAM figures by 5 and 4 percent, respectively, manipulations based on the low retention rates of the items missing in the WUV lists, and on the high retention rates elsewhere of the many SAM aberrancies. The findings are considered in relation to the oral traditions of RE and BE that their islands were settled 23 generations ago by persons from two Uveas who stopped en route at two Hutunas and at Henuatai.

The linguistic findings do not support EUV as the R/B homeland, but point to EFU or TIK. The EFU language, according to comparison of phonology and basic vocabulary, is an offshoot of Proto Futunic. EUV, with its history of invasions, is a language with mixed phonology and morphology, but in lexicostatistics, definitely of TO rather than of SAM origin.

The R/B traditions of an EUV origin are credible if one accepts the EUV traditions of an early people on their island before it was settled from TO. These people may have been East Futunans, who later from their own island may have settled WUV, EL, and TIK, and thence perhaps by stages to the other Western Outliers. In such an interpretation, these languages would have lost the Proto Futunic */?/ after leaving EFU.

The relationships shown by phonology, grammar, and the traditions fail to reflect a close connection of R/B with other Outlier languages, as is so apparent in the lexical comparisons. The history of these small places is extremely complex. To unravel the complexities, we need to know more about their grammatical structures, and more about loans to and from neighboring Melanesian languages; this latter is especially necessary for M/F, West Futuna, and Mae in the New Hebrides, WUV in the Loyalties, and R/B in the Solomons. Linguistics and traditions united with deep archaeology may be able to answer such questions as these: Do the Outliers fall in five groups: R/B, Western (most of those in this study), Eastern (in the New Hebrides), Northern 1 (Kapingamarangi), and Northern 2 (Nukuoro) and are all these groups in the Futunic subbranch? And are some of the many languages close enough to be considered dialects of a single language; perhaps Ongtong Java, Nukumanu, Takuu, and Nukuria?

Although our knowledge is incomplete, a slightly altered family tree may be attempted:

PPN
    Proto Tongic
        TO
        EUV
        NF (?)
   PNP
       Proto Futunic
          EFU
             R/B
             EL(?)
             Western Outliers (PIL, SIK, TAK, TIK, WUV and
                 others?)
       Proto Samoic
       PEPN (HAW and many others)
       Proto Samoic
         SAM

What of glottochronology as a means of ascertaining linguistic phylogeny? And what of the 600 years of the genealogies versus something approaching 1,500 years in glottochronology?

In this study, comparison of basic vocabulary has highlighted what has been merely suggested by comparison of phonology and morphology: that R/B is closer to EFU than to EUV, and that the latter belongs in the Tongic group. And it has emphasized strongly what is somewhat contrary to the phonology, that the Western Outliers are in the Futunic group, and that R/B is somehow related. Could this Henuatai of the traditions, this Sealand, have been a cover term for a homeland where the Polynesians survived for centuries in a Melanesian sea?

As for the long centuries, far longer than the genealogies indicate, we may recall Gifford, previously quoted, who said that the Tongans elaborated no genealogical fictions—which suggests Monberg's recent experience on BE. Baiabe, home after a night's fishing, said his helpers were bringing in a small fish. Then three men came staggering in with an enormous sailfish.

LITERATURE CITED

BATAILLON, PIERRE
    1932. *Langue d'Uvea (Wallis): Grammaire, Dictionnaire Uvea-Français, Dictionnaire Français-Uvea-Anglais*. Paris: Geuthner.

BAYARD, DONN THOMAS
    1966. The Cultural Relationships of the Polynesian Outliers. M. A. thesis, Univ. Hawaii.

BLOOMFIELD, LEONARD
 1933. *Language*. New York: Holt.

BUCK, PETER H.
 1938. *Vikings of the Sunrise*. New York: Stokes.

BURROWS, EDWIN G.
 1936. *Ethnology of Futuna*. B. P. Bishop Mus. Bull. 138. Honolulu.
 1937. *Ethnology of Uvea (Wallis Island)*. B. P. Bishop Mus. Bull. 145. Honolulu.

CHURCHWARD, C. MAXWELL
 1959. *Tongan Dictionary (Tongan-English and English-Tongan)*. London: Oxford Univ.

COLLOCOTT, E. E. V.
 1922. "The Speech of Niua Fo'ou." *J. Polynesian Soc.* **31**:185-189.
 1924. "An Experiment in Tongan History." *J. Polynesian Soc.* **33**:166-184.
 1928. *Tales and Poems of Tonga*. B. P. Bishop Mus. Bull. 46. Honolulu.

DURRAD, W. J.
 1913. "A Tikopia Vocabulary." *J. Polynesian Soc.* **22**:86-95, 141-148.

DYEN, ISIDORE
 1965. *A Lexicostatistical Classification of the Austronesian Languages*. Internat. J. American Linguistics Mem. 19. Indiana Univ. Pub. Anthropology and Linguistics.

ELBERT, SAMUEL H.
 1950. *Grammar and Comparative Study of the Language of Kapingamarangi, Text and Word Lists*. Co-ordinated Investigation of Micronesian Anthropology, Rep. 3. Washington. Duplicated.
 1953. "Internal Relationships of Polynesian Languages and Dialects." *Southwestern J. Anthropology* **9**:147-173.
 1962. "Phonetic Expansion in Rennellese." *J. Polynesian Soc.* **71**(1):25-31.

ELBERT, SAMUEL H., and TORBEN MONBERG
 1965. *From the Two Canoes: Oral Traditions of Rennell and Bellona Islands*. Honolulu and Copenhagen: Univ. Hawaii Press and Danish Nat. Mus.

EMORY, KENNETH P.
 1946. Eastern Polynesia, its Cultural Relationships. (Manuscript, Bishop Museum.)
 1963. "East Polynesian Relationships: Settlement Pattern and Time Involved as Indicated by Vocabulary Agreements." *J. Polynesian Soc.* **72**:78-100.

FIRTH, RAYMOND
 1931. "A Native Voyage to Rennell." *Oceania* **2**:179-190.
 1936. *We, the Tikopia*. London: Allen and Unwin Ltd.
 1961. *History and Traditions of Tikopia*. Wellington: Polynesian Soc.

FISCHER, J. L.
 1964. "Comment on the Linguistic Evidence," by George W. Grace." *Current Anthropology* **5**:388-389.

GIFFORD, EDWARD WINSLOW
1929. *Tongan Society.* B. P. Bishop Mus. Bull. 61. Honolulu.

GRACE, GEORGE W.
1959. *The Position of the Polynesian Languages within the Austronesian (Malayo-Polynesian) Language Family.* Internat. J. American Linguistics Mem. 16. Indiana Univ. Pub. Anthropology and Linguistics. B. P. Bishop Mus. Spec. Pub. 46.
1961. "Lexicostatistical Comparison of Six Eastern Austronesian Languages." *Anthropological Linguistics* **3**(9):1-22.
1964. "Movement of the Malayo-Polynesians: 1500 B.C. to A.D. 500: The Linguistic Evidence." *Current Anthropology* **5**:361-368.

GREEN, ROGER
1966. "Linguistic Subgrouping within Polynesia: The Implications for Prehistoric Settlement." *J. Polynesian Soc.* **75**:6-38.

GRÉZEL, LE PÈRE
1878. *Dictionnaire Futunien-Française avec Notes Grammaticales.* Paris: Maisonneuve.

HYMES, D. H.
1960. "Lexicostatistics So Far." *Current Anthropology* **1**:2-44.

KROEBER, A. L.
1948. *Anthropology.* New York: Harcourt, Brace.

LEVERD, A.
1922. "Polynesian Linguistics. I. Polynesian Language of Uvea, Loyalty Islands." *J. Polynesian Soc.* **31**:94-103.

MILKE, WILHELM
1961. "Beiträge zur Ozeanischen Linguistik." *Z. Ethnologie* **86**:162-182.
1965. "Experiments in Matrix Reduction: Applied to Austronesian Data," *Lingua* **14**:443-455.

MILNER, G. B.
1963. "Notes on the Comparison of Two Languages (With and Without a Genetic Hypothesis)." In H. L. SHORTO (editor), *Linguistic Comparison in South East Asia and the Pacific,* pp. 416-430. Univ. London: School of Oriental and African Studies.
1966. *Samoan Dictionary: Samoan-English, English-Samoan.* London: Oxford Univ. Press.

PAWLEY, ANDREW
1966. "Polynesian Languages: A Subgrouping Based on Shared Innovations in Morphology." *J. Polynesian Soc.* **75**:39-64.

PRATT, GEORGE
1960. *Pratt's Grammar and Dictionary of the Samoan Language.* (First ed., 1862). Samoa.

PUKUI, MARY KAWENA, and SAMUEL H. ELBERT
1957. *Hawaiian-English Dictionary.* Honolulu: Univ. Hawaii Press.

SOPER, ALEXANDER COBURN
    1943. Faka-Uvea, an Abridged Vocabulary and Grammar of the Wallisian
    Language. (Mimeographed.)

SWADESH, MORRIS
    1950. "Salish Internal Relationships." *Internat. J. American Linguistics* **16**:
    157-167.

WALSH, D. S., and BRUCE BIGGS
    1966. *Proto-Polynesian Word List I.* Te Reo Monographs. Auckland: Lin-
    guistic Soc. New Zealand.

EFFECT OF HETEROGENEITY IN THE LEXICOSTATISTICAL TEST LIST

THE CASE OF ROTUMAN*

GEORGE W. GRACE

University of Hawaii

K ENNETH EMORY may justly be accorded the role of pioneer in two aspects of the modern tradition of culture historical studies in Polynesia. First, he was an early exponent of the value of integrating the results of linguistic and archaeological investigations, and the degree to which linguistic and archaeological efforts are being coordinated in current Polynesian research may be viewed with some pride. Second, his pioneering work in lexical comparisons has had a series of followers, particularly within the framework of lexicostatistics.

However, lexicostatistics cannot be regarded as a perfected technique. The underlying processes are imperfectly understood, and the results obtained are sometimes suspect. A lexicostatistical study of six Oceanic languages which I carried out a few years ago (Grace, 1961) showed several features which I found somewhat puzzling. This paper represents an attempt to explain one of those features.

The six languages used were two Polynesian languages (Tongan and New Zealand Maaori), the two languages which I believe to be most closely related to Polynesian (Fijian and Rotuman), and two languages which I believe to be somewhat more remotely related (Mota of the Banks Islands, New Hebrides Condominium, and Sa'a of Malaita, British Solomon Islands). Thus, the hypothesis—which was generally supported by the results, although as some have pointed out, not by

---

* An earlier version of this paper was read at the Eleventh Pacific Science Congress, Tokyo, 1966.

very substantial margins—recognizes a grouping consisting of the Polynesian languages, Fijian, and Rotuman. It will be convenient to have a label for that set of languages. I will refer to it as "Central Pacific."

In the study to which I refer I made four separate computations of cognate percentages for each pair of languages. Two employed the 200-item test list and two the 100-item list. For each list one computation included items which had been scored as doubtfully cognate or doubtfully noncognate, while the other computation excluded all such items in calculating the percentages. D. S. Walsh (1963) has published a revision of my study using different lists, obtained entirely from informants. It is likely that his results are more reliable. Unfortunately, however, I do not have access to his lists or his decisions and could not use them in the present study. The particular problem with which this paper is concerned also arises in his results, in a slightly less conspicuous degree.

This problem is that Rotuman consistently showed fewer cognates and lower cognate percentages with Mota and Sa'a than did the other Central Pacific languages. The cognate percentages are given in Table 1.

TABLE 1

COMPUTATION	Mot To	Mot Ma	Mot Fi	Mot Rot	Sa To	Sa Ma	Sa Fi	Sa Rot
1	16	16	18	13	18	15	15	11
2	24	20	23	18	21	18	21	16
3	21	21	21	17	23	20	20	14
4	31	28	28	24	28	24	26	19

Computations 1 and 2 employ the 200-item test list; Computations 3 and 4, the 100-item list. Computations 1 and 3 do not count items scored as "doubtful cognates" or "doubtful noncognates"; Computations 2 and 4 do count them.

In all computations the averaged percentages for comparisons between Rotuman and non-Central Pacific languages was about one-fifth lower than the averaged percentages for comparisons between Central Pacific languages in general and non-Central Pacific languages.

Perhaps a word is required as to why I felt it necessary to attempt to explain a modest statistical discrepancy. Essentially it is because of my own conviction that the phenomena underlying lexicostatistics and glottochronology are too poorly understood and that they are considerably more complicated than they appeared at the outset. I believe that lexicostatistics as practiced now is an instrument of very uneven accuracy, but that its potential has been only very poorly explored and exploited. Whatever the ultimate potential of lexicostatistical techniques, an understanding of the underlying phenomena is a matter of interest in itself.

In the case of the unexpectedly low percentages for the comparisons of Rotuman with Mota and Saʻa, two possibilities which must immediately be considered are (1) that Rotuman has been misclassified—that it is actually more remotely related than the other Central Pacific languages to Mota and Saʻa, and (2) the percentages for comparisons involving Rotuman may consistently be deflated, presumably indicating that Rotuman has had a rate of retention somewhat lower than the average.

Although it is impossible conclusively to rule out either of these possible explanations, they are not supported by the remaining comparisons.[1] For example, in Computation 1 the percentages for all pairs of Central Pacific languages (excluding the much higher Tongan-Maaori percentage) range from 19 to 26, with an average of 21.6. Those for Rotuman and each other Central Pacific language range likewise from 19 to 26, with an average of 21.67. Thus, in this series of comparisons Rotuman does not appear divergent in the least.

The explanation which I will propose developed from an investigation of test-list heterogeneity. The test list would be homogeneous in the appropriate sense if the probability that any given item on the list would be replaced were identical with the probability that each other item would be replaced. The original model for glottochronology assumed that the list was homogeneous in this sense. By "heterogeneity" I mean simply any deviation from this ideal. That the test list is not homogeneous has been recognized for some time. Recently, there has been considerable interest in the problems raised by that nonhomogeneity (compare Dyen, 1964; Van der Merwe, 1966).

Heterogeneity in the test list is suggested when a number of languages have retained the same item. For example, in Computation 1 (from this point on, I will confine myself to the results of Computation 1 in order to hold the discussion within a reasonable scope) of my study seven items were counted as having been retained by all of the languages. In each of these cases, each of the 15 language pairs recorded a plus. To get some idea of the nature of the heterogeneity I counted the total number of pluses recorded in the study (that is, all pluses for all language pairs). The total was 448. I then proceeded to determine the smallest set possible of test-list items which would yield

---

[1] However, the explanation which I will ultimately propose does hold that Rotuman percentages are subject to a general deflation.

at least half of the total pluses recorded in the study. I found that 20 items were sufficient.[2] This set of 20 items yielded 234.25 of the total of 448 pluses.[3] Thus, a subset representing only about 10 percent of the list yielded approximately 52 percent of the pluses recorded.

The number of pluses yielded by these 20 items for individual language pairs ranged from 12.5 to 18.5 with an average of 15.62. (The individual figures for this and various other subsets of the list are presented in Table 2.) It is interesting to note that in the case of the particularly close Tongan-Maaori relationship there were 17 pluses, but that these represented only 27 percent of the pluses recorded for that pair of languages in the entire study. The other pairs of Central Pacific languages obtain an average of 15.8 pluses or 47 percent of their total pluses (range: 36–58 percent) from these 20 items. Those pairs such that one language is Central Pacific and the other is not (that is, is Mota or Sa'a) obtain an average of 15.4 pluses or 65 percent of their total pluses (range: 59–75 percent; note that this range does not overlap that for Central Pacific internal comparisons) from the top 20 items.

It is assumed that there are three degrees of relationship to be distinguished in the study: (1) the internal Polynesian relationship represented by the pair, Tongan-Maaori; (2) the internal Central Pacific relationship, represented by the remaining pairs of Central Pacific languages; and (3) the relationship between Central Pacific and non-Central Pacific languages. It seems fair to say that none of these distinctions is suggested by the scores on the first 20 items. On the other hand the distinctions come out particularly clearly when we consider only the complementary subset (that is, the remainder of the list). The average number of pluses representing each of these relationships in the latter subset are: (1) Polynesian, 46; (2) Central Pacific, 17.8 (range: 12.5–25.5); (3) Central Pacific with non-Central Pacific, 8.34 (range: 4.5–11.5). These results suggest that the less stable items on the list as a set provide a fairly accurate measure of the relative closeness of linguistic relationship, but that the more stable items tend rather to blur than to clarify the actual relations.

---

[2] The items are:

bird	fish	I	thou
die	five	road	three
ear	four	sky	two
eat	fruit	stand	vomit
eye	he	stone	who

[3] Fractions were recorded when my list for one language showed more than one equivalent, not all of which were cognate with the equivalent in the other language, for a given test-list item.

TABLE 2

	PN	Central Pacific					Central Pacific with Non-Central Pacific									Totals
	To MA	To Rot	To Fi	MA Rot	MA Fi	Rot Fi	To Mot	To Sa	MA Mot	MA Sa	Rot Mot	Rot Sa	Fi Mot	Fi Sa	Mot Sa	
0	63	40	39	29	30	30	25	28	24	23	20	18	27	25	27	448
1a	17	14.5	18.5	13.5	17.5	15	16	16.5	15.25	15.5	12.5	13.5	17	17	15	234.25
1b	46	25.5	20.5	15.5	12.5	15	9	11.5	8.75	7.5	7.5	4.5	10	8	12	213.75
2a	15	8.25	13.5	8.75	13.5	9	10.5	10.25	10.5	9.75	7	6.5	12	11.25	11	156.75
2b	48	31.75	25.5	20.25	16.5	21	14.5	17.75	13.5	13.25	13	11.5	15	13.75	16	291.25
3a	40.33	24.75	31.5	22.25	29.5	24.5	22.5	22.83	21.83	20.5	16.58	14	20.75	21.83	20.42	354.07
3b	22.67	15.25	7.5	6.75	0.5	5.5	2.5	5.17	2.17	2.5	3.42	4	6.25	3.17	6.58	93.93

Key.—0, Numbers of cognates for language pairs in the 200-item list in Grace (1961). (Computation 1.) 1a, Numbers of cognates for language pairs in the 20 items most frequently retained in Grace (1961). 1b, Numbers of cognates in the remainder of the list. 2a, Numbers of cognates in the first 20 items of Dyen's Malayopolynesian Cognate-Pair Frequency Ranking. 2b, Numbers of cognates in the remainder of the list. 3a, Numbers of cognates in the first 66 items of the Malayopolynesian Cognate-Pair Frequency Ranking. 3b, Numbers of cognates in the remainder of the list.

The preceding sentence represents a hypothesis about the behavior
of the test list. The hypothesis appears to be of some significance, but
it is extremely loosely formulated. I would like to attempt to confirm
it in further tests, but to do so requires that it be formulated in more
precise form. The expedient I will choose is to state the hypothesis in
the strongest form possible. This has several advantages. First, it provides a much simpler hypothesis for testing than any hypothesis which
tried to accommodate all of the known facts could possibly be. Second,
the known facts are far from adequate to specify anything which could
be regarded as an accurate hypothesis in any event. Third, if this very
strong form of the hypothesis receives any significant confirmation from
the tests, this confirmation transfers automatically to any proper weaker
version of the same hypothesis.

The hypothesis may now be specified as follows:

1. The test list can be partitioned into two subsets, one consisting
of the most stable items and the other of the remaining items.

2. In the subset consisting of the least stable items, the number of
retentions in any language over a given span of time is a simple mathe-
matical function of the length of the span of time.

3. In the subset consisting of the most stable items the number of
retentions in any given language is entirely independent of elapsed time
—that is, is determined *entirely* by factors (whatever they are) un-
related to time.

4. Dyen (1964) presents an ordering of the entire test list (except
for four items which were excluded on practical grounds) by the frequency of cognate pairs in those meanings in 89 Austronesian lists. His
ordering, called the Malayopolynesian Cognate-Pair Frequency Ranking (CFRMP), will provide the basis for determining the relative
stability of test-list items. Thus, in the hypothesis as now formulated,
the stable (or "high-yield") subset is defined as consisting of a consecutive series of items from the top of the CFRMP and the unstable
(or "low-yield") subset as consisting of the complementary consecutive
series from the bottom of the CFRMP. I will generally proceed on the
assumption that the stable subset consists of just 20 items (that is, the
20 most stable items[4] with the unstable subset consisting of the remainder of the list. However, at times, I will depart from this assumption

---

[4] The top 20 items of the CFRMP are:

die	four	name	thou
eat	fruit	new	three
eye	hear	nose	two
father	louse	one	we
five	mother	stone	ye

to the extent of assuming that the size of the stable subset is undetermined, and that the 20 most stable items represent only a sample of the subset.

TESTS OF THE HYPOTHESIS

Test 1.—I have pointed out that three different degrees of relationship are assumed to exist in my study. I pointed out further that the numbers of cognates recorded for the set of the 20 most frequently retained items in that study do not discriminate any of these degrees of relationship, while the cognates recorded for the set consisting of the remainder of the list discriminate them all. On the basis of the hypothesis now being tested, it would be predicted that the stable subset (now defined as the first 20 items of the CFRMP) would also not discriminate the degrees of relationship.

It will be recalled that the 20 items most frequently retained in my study yielded a total of 234.25 pluses—about 52 percent of the total pluses. The stable subset as now defined contains 10 of the same items, and yields a total of 156.75 pluses in my study—about 35 percent of the total pluses. The hypothesis that the high-yield subset does not discriminate degrees of relationship is still approximately confirmed, although not quite so clearly as with the other partition of the list. The average number of pluses from the high-yield subset representing each of the degrees of relationship is: (1) Polynesian, 15—however, two of these represent Polynesian innovations, and since this fact is known, can be subtracted, leaving a sum of 13; (2) Central Pacific, 10.60; (3) Central Pacific with non-Central Pacific, 9.72. Although these averages suggest that there is some tendency to discriminate, the figures for individual pairs of languages extensively overlap. Those for the internal Central Pacific relationship range from 8.25 to 13.5, while those for the relationship of Central Pacific with non-Central Pacific range from 6.5 to 12.

Test 2.—A related prediction is that the complementary (low-yield) subset will be found to make all of the discriminations. This prediction is satisfactorily confirmed. The average numbers of pluses are: (1) Polynesian, 48; (2) Central Pacific, 23; (3) Central Pacific with non-Central Pacific, 14. The ranges of the last two (16.50 to 31.75 and 11.50 to 17.75, respectively) overlap only to the extent that the lowest figure of the first is lower than the highest figure of the second.

Test 3.—According to the assumptions outlined, the high-yield subset should not discriminate even more distant relationships. Two languages which are generally assumed to be more distant relatives of the languages in my study, and for which I had lists, are Malay and Tagalog. I compared the Malay and Tagalog equivalents for the 20 items of the high-yield subset with those of each of the languages in my study. Malay showed an average of 11.08 (range: 8–13.5), and Tagalog an average of 10.75 (range: 9–13), cognates with the languages of my study. The average number of cognates found in the same subset for pairs of languages in my study was 10.45 (range: 6.5–13.5—or 15 if shared Polynesian innovations in Tongan and Maaori are counted). Thus, the presumably more distant relationship of Malay and Tagalog is not discriminated from the closer relationships existing among the languages in my study.

Test 4.—What the tests so far described have indicated is that the differences in numbers of shared cognates for the high-yield subset are (approximately) independent of divergence time. It is possible to determine with what appears to be a high degree of accuracy which Proto-Austronesian items in this subset have been retained by each of the languages. The number of such retentions in the several languages ranges from 10.5 (Rotuman) to 16 (Fijian). The number of pluses obtained by a language in the various comparisons seems to be an approximately exact function of the number of its retentions. This is to be expected according to the assumption that the high-yield subset is a homogeneous list. However, with a heterogeneous list (such as the 200-item test list) this would not hold true if some languages retained larger numbers of highly stable items than did others. Thus, it would be predicted that those languages in my study which had retained more items of the high-yield subset would tend to show higher percentages by the 200-item list with any other Austronesian languages than would those which had retained fewer items of that subset.

In Isidore Dyen's (1965) Austronesian lexicostatistical classification, Fijian, Rotuman, Mota, and the Polynesian Subfamily are all members of an open group—the Heonesian Linkage. In his procedure, an open group is linked with another language or group to form a larger group on the basis of the highest percentage of one of the members of the open group with the other language or group. This suggests the prediction that those Heonesian languages in my study which had retained more items of the high-yield subset would more frequently serve as links between Heonesian (or the Malayopolynesian Linkage, of which Heonesian is a member) and other languages and groups than would those which had retained fewer items of that subset.

The numbers of items retained were found to be as follows: Tongan, 14.75; Maaori, 14.75; Rotuman, 10.5; Fijian, 16; Mota, 13; and Sa'a, 12.25. Accordingly, it would be predicted that Fijian would serve as a link most frequently, Polynesian (if it can be assumed that Tongan and Maaori are representative) second, Mota third, and Rotuman fourth. This turns out to accord perfectly with the actual facts. Fijian serves as a link in 6 cases, Polynesian in 4, Mota in 3, and Rotuman in 1.

Test 5.—However, there is one member of the Heonesian Linkage which was not included in my study, but which serves as a link for Heonesian in 7 cases—one more than Fijian. The language in question is Kerebuto of Guadalcanal. This suggested that Kerebuto should show as many retentions in the high-yield subset as Fijian, or possibly more. I checked the Kerebuto list and found 17 retentions—one more than in Fijian. Thus, by these tests the assumptions receive a surprisingly high degree of confirmation.

Test 6.—I employed one further test, which, however, involved an additional hypothesis. In Dyen's Austronesian lexicostatistical classification there were 39 languages or small groups (single languages in 24 of the 39 instances) whose critical percentages (that is, the highest percentage shown with any other language or group in the study) were surprisingly low. Furthermore, these critical percentages showed a wide range—from 7.3 to 19.6. Most of these languages show their critical percentage with a representative of the Malayopolynesian Linkage. Accordingly, I hypothesized that Malayopolynesian was a valid subgroup and that each of the 39 aberrant languages and groups was, in fact, equally closely related to Malayopolynesian. This hypothesis in turn leads to the prediction that the differences in the critical percentages obtained are due to differential retention of the most stable portions of the test list.

It will be apparent that I have again formulated a stronger claim than is warranted by the known facts. Furthermore, another difficulty arises. The difference between the maximum and minimum critical percentages involved is (19.6—7.3=) 12.3 percent, which, in a list of 200 items, represents a difference of some 24 pluses. Obviously, no pair of languages could show 24 more pluses than another pair in a list (the high-yield subset) of 20 items. Therefore, it becomes necessary to assume that the 20 items represent only a sample of the stable subset, which is assumed to contain a larger, but unspecified, number of items.

There were further difficulties in testing the hypothesis. I examined the lists (which I had in my possession) for 18 of the aberrant languages. However, practically nothing is known of the phonological history of any of them. In only 8 of the 18 cases did I feel that I could make sufficiently accurate identifications of retentions to justify using the language in the test. The results obtained for those 8 are given in Table 3. The hypothesis is confirmed to the extent that in no case where a language shows more retentions than another does it show a lower critical percentage than the latter.

TABLE 3

LANGUAGE	No. RETENTIONS	CRITICAL PERCENTAGE
Paama (central New Hebrides)	15	19.6
Nale (Malekula, New Hebrides)	12	19.4
Nalik (New Ireland)	12	18.4
Dang (New Hanover)	12	17.4
Banoni (Bougainville)	11	13.6
Iai (Uvea, Loyalty Islands)	11	13.4
Tomoip (New Britain)	9	11.5
Zabana (Ysabel, Solomon Islands)	6	9.6

Of the ten cases which were excluded because the identification of retentions was too uncertain, there were only three in which it appeared probable that the above pattern would not be maintained. I believe these three cases can be explained, but the explanation would involve a more complicated set of assumptions about the subgrouping of these languages. That is, it would involve abandoning the assumption that Dyen's Malayopolynesian Linkage is a valid subgroup as defined, and that the other 39 languages and subgroups are all equally closely related to Malayopolynesian.

Although this test is unquestionably extremely crude in a variety of ways, it does seem to suggest that there probably is in these cases a significant relation between the numbers of retentions from the high-yield subset and the critical percentages.

APPLICATION TO THE ROTUMAN CASE

Let us return now to the original question: Why does Rotuman consistently show lower cognate percentages with Mota and Sa'a than do the other Central Pacific languages? The principal point has been foreshadowed—that Rotuman has retained relatively few items of the high-yield subset. The numbers of retentions in the 17 languages which have been considered were determined to be (in order of magnitude):

Kerebuto, 17; Fijian, 16; Paama and Malay, 15; Tongan and Maaori, 14.75; Mota and Tagalog, 13; Sa'a, 12.25; Nale, Nalik, and Dang, 12; Banoni and Iai, 11; Rotuman, 10.5; Tomoip, 9; and Zabana, 6. Thus, Rotuman is 15th in a series of 17.

Above, I proposed as working assumptions that the rate of retention of certain test-list items was a function of elapsed time, whereas the rate of retention of others was a function of lexicostatistically accidental factors; and that the first 20 items of Dyen's Malayopolynesian Cognate-Pair Frequency Ranking were items of the second type, and the remaining 176 items were items of the first type.

Let us begin by considering the conjunction of our two hypotheses —that is, (1) the assumptions just noted, and (2) the hypothesis that the relatively low percentages of Rotuman with Mota and Sa'a are due to low retention of high-yield items in Rotuman. On this basis we would expect that Rotuman would show as many cognates as the other Central Pacific languages with Mota and Sa'a in the *low-yield* subset (all items except the most stable 20).

Over the entire 200-item list the average number of cognates found in comparisons of a Central Pacific language with a non-Central Pacific language is 23.75. The average for comparisons of Rotuman alone with a non-Central Pacific language is 19. Thus Rotuman shows a deficit of 4.75 cognates which, according to our present assumptions, should result from differences in the cognate yield of the high-yield subset. Most of the deficit does turn out, in fact, to be explained in this way. In the low-yield subset Central Pacific languages share an average of 14 cognates with non-Central Pacific languages, whereas Rotuman alone shows an average of 12.25 cognates with the same languages. Thus, the deficit is reduced to 1.75.

One might argue that the remaining deficit is too slight to be of concern. However, I was interested in discovering whether or not it could be eliminated entirely with modified assumptions. I found that it could by a redefinition of the subsets so that the high-yield subset consists of the first 66 items (that is, the first third) of Dyen's Malayopolynesian Cognate-Pair Frequency Ranking, and the low-yield subset consists of the remaining two-thirds of the list. We find that, in the low-yield subset so defined, the Central Pacific languages show an average of 3.65 cognates with Mota and Sa'a, and that Rotuman alone shows an average of 3.71 cognates with them.

It will be recalled that my original study employed four different computations of cognate percentages, and that the figures considered so far are those based on Computation 1. However, the comparisons of

Rotuman with non-Central Pacific languages showed comparable
cognate deficits in all of the four computations. In the case of Computation 1 we have seen that it was possible to define a low-yield subset
in which the deficit disappeared. In that case the low-yield subset consisted of the most unstable two-thirds of the list. I have considered the
same question with regard to the other three computations and find
that in each case it is possible to define a subset consisting of a consecutive series of items beginning at the lower end of the CFRMP in
which the deficit does not appear. However, the maximum size which
a subset meeting this requirement can attain varies from one computation to another. This, of course, is only to be expected if we disregard
for the moment our highly idealized hypothesis and consider the probable
properties of the test list more realistically. That is, if we divide the
factors affecting the likelihood of replacement of a particular test-list
item into the two classes we have used—(1) elapsed time and (2) all
other factors, whatever they are—we do not really believe that the list
divides neatly into one set of items which are affected only by one and
another set affected only by the other. In reality all items must be somewhat subject to the effects of both kinds of factors, but in differing
degrees. And it is entirely possible that the relative effects of the two
kinds of factors differ somewhat for each different item on the list (so
far from the list partitioning naturally into two subsets).

However, one problem remains. If the cognate percentages of Rotuman are generally deflated because of the relatively small number of
retentions of highly stable items in Rotuman, why is this not also
apparent in the comparisons of Rotuman with other Central Pacific
languages? The average number of cognates found for pairs of Central
Pacific languages (excluding the pair Tongan-Maaori) is 33.6. The
average number of cognates shared by Rotuman and another Central
Pacific language is 33. There thus appears to be no significant deficit.

An explanation is suggested if we consider once more the subset
consisting of the most unstable two-thirds of the test list. In this subset
we find the following numbers of cognates: Tongan-Maaori, 22.67;
Tongan-Rotuman, 15.25; Tongan-Fijian, 7.5; Maaori-Rotuman, 6.75;
Maaori-Fijian, 0.5; and Rotuman-Fijian, 5.5. It is striking that the
Tongan-Rotuman figure is aberrantly high—as near the internal Polynesian range as the Central Pacific range. Moreover, 38 percent of the
total number of Tongan-Rotuman cognates are found in the low-yield
subset. This exceeds even the figure for Tongan-Maaori, which is 36
percent (24 percent of the Mota-Sa'a cognates are found in this subset;
for the other language pairs the percentage is smaller still).

This suggests that the Tongan-Rotuman comparison is somehow disturbed. If we eliminate it (along with Tongan-Maaori) from the comparisons we find that the average number of cognates for pairs of Central Pacific languages becomes 32 for the test list as a whole, and that the average for comparisons involving Rotuman is 29.5. Rotuman thus shows a deficit of 2.5.

The following explanation for the disturbance in the Tongan-Rotuman comparison is suggested. It is known that Rotuman has borrowed heavily from Tongan or a language closely related to Tongan (see Biggs, 1965). Some borrowings and some retentions can be identified with certainty from their sound correspondences, but in the case of some forms no decision is possible. It is quite reasonable to suppose that the Rotuman list contains some Tongan borrowings. This assumption accords with the relatively high concentration of Tongan-Rotuman cognates in the less stable portion of the list. It also accords with the fact that the Tongan-Rotuman cognate percentage is slightly higher than any other internal Central Pacific cognate percentage (excluding, of course, Tongan-Maaori). When we add the consideration that Polynesian borrowings in Rotuman could also have inflated other of its percentages, especially with Maaori, it seems very possible that Rotuman would indeed show the expected deficit in cognates with the other Central Pacific languages if the effects of borrowing could be identified and discounted.

CONCLUSIONS

The matters discussed suggest the following conclusions. (1) The stability of test-list items varies widely, a fact which has already been well established. (2) The number of retentions among the more stable items does not correspond closely with elapsed time. (3) The cognate yield for retained items which are highly stable is high, thus retentions among such items have a disproportionate effect on the overall cognate percentage. This disturbing effect becomes increasingly important as the overall cognate percentage decreases (that is, generally in the case of more distant relationships). (4) In the case of Rotuman, the low cognate percentages with Mota and Sa'a appear to be due to the low retention of stable items in Rotuman. However, the generally deflated percentages of Rotuman have been reinflated in its comparisons with other Central Pacific languages (in large part, at least) by borrowings from Tongan or a language closely related to Tongan. (5) Both the deflation and the reinflation of the Rotuman percentages were apparent from an examination of the *kinds* of items involved in these percentages. Thus, it seems possible that considerably more might be inferred from lexicostatistical results if the performance in each of various subsets of the list were considered separately.

LITERATURE CITED

BIGGS, BRUCE
  1965. "Direct and Indirect Inheritance in Rotuman." *Lingua* 14:383-415.

DYEN, ISIDORE
  1964. "On the Validity of Comparative Lexicostatistics." In HORACE G. LUNT
      (editor), *Proc. Ninth International Congress of Linguists,* pp. 238-247.
      The Hague: Mouton.
  1965. *A Lexicostatistical Classification of the Austronesian Languages.* Inter-
      nat. J. American Linguistics Mem. 19. Indiana Univ. Pub. Anthropol-
      ogy and Linguistics.

GRACE, GEORGE W.
  1961. "Lexicostatistical Comparison of Six Eastern Austronesian Languages."
      Anthropological Linguistics 3(9):1-22.

MERWE, NICHOLAAS J. VAN DER
  1966. "New Mathematics for Glottochronology." *Current Anthropology* 7:
      485-500.

WALSH, D. S.
  1963. "Dictionaries versus Informants: An Aspect of Glottochronology." *Te
      Reo* 6:30-38.

THE PAST TWENTY YEARS IN POLYNESIAN LINGUISTICS

BRUCE BIGGS
University of Hawaii

THANKS to the industry and devotion to their task of missionary scholars, who, in a number of instances produced exceedingly good grammars and dictionaries, the Polynesian languages have long been the best known languages of Oceania. Most of the missionary linguistic work was done during the latter half of the 19th century and in the early part of the 20th. Lean years followed, with a few lone scholars such as A. Capell (Outlier Polynesia), J. Frank Stimson (French Polynesia), H. W. Williams (Maori, Moriori), J. Prytz Johansen (Maori), C. M. Churchward (Tonga), and Spencer Churchward (Samoa) continuing to produce descriptive work.

In 1946 Kenneth Emory completed a comparative study of Polynesian lexicons which was never published. This was followed by a resurgence of interest in Polynesian as new descriptive techniques diffused belatedly to Australia and New Zealand, and as linguists and anthropologists from America and Europe rediscovered the south seas.

Earlier descriptions of Polynesian languages have been termed "anecdotal," because they described features of the grammar that happened to attract their authors' attention, and neglected others. It was usual to find fairly adequate descriptions of the preposed tense-aspect particles, but unheard of to find a reasonable description of the paradigmatic set of "manner" particles which are also ubiquitous in these languages. While active and passive verbs were almost always described, the equally fundamental distinction between those verbs which are capable of the active-passive transformation and those which are not was rarely discussed.

The new grammars aimed at being exhaustive and generative up to the level of the newly discovered phrase unit which was found to be fundamental in the structure of any Polynesian language. The term morphology-syntax has been used of the grammatical level which describes the composition of the phrase, and the term phrase-structure, or structure of the phrase (or piece, contour-word, and so on) is common in the titles of recent work.

The structure of the phrase has been described for Maori (Biggs, 1961a), Tongan (Morton, 1962), Tahitian (White, 1958), Rarotongan (Buse, 1960, 1963a, 1963b, 1965), Samoan (Pawley, 1961, 1962, 1966a, 1966b), and Nukuoro (Carroll, 1965). This last, though brief, is important as perhaps the first reasonably complete description of the morphology-syntax of an Outlier language. It is doubly fortunate that Nukuoro is one of the two Outliers (Kapingamarangi is the other) which are placed on lexicostatistical grounds as most different from the languages of Triangle Polynesia.

Earlier work on Outlier languages, by Capell on Sikaiana (1935-1936, 1936-1937), on Aniwa-Futuna (1931), on Fila (1942), and on Mae (1962), and by Elbert on Kapingamarangi (1948), lacked certain requirements of descriptive adequacy. It is nevertheless unfortunate that Elbert's Kapingamarangi materials, in particular, have never been published in an accessible form. The original mimeographed CIMA report is extremely rare.

In press is a grammatical description by Elbert of another Outlier language spoken on Rennell and Bellona.

At present descriptive work is proceeding on the languages spoken on Sikaiana (Sharples) Ongtong-Java (Luangiua) (Thorpe), Niue (Hohepa), the Nanumea dialect of the Ellice Islands (Ranby), Pukapuka (Moeka‘a) and Penrhyn (Yasuda). Both of the latter are islands in the Northern Cooks, but early indications are that Pukapuka may not be a dialect of the Cooks at all, but a separate language.

Lexicographical work has also proceeded apace during the last decade or so. New dictionaries have appeared for Hawaiian (Pukui and Elbert, 1957), Tongan (Churchward, 1959), Easter Island (Fuentes, 1960), Tuamotuan (Stimson and Marshall, 1964), and Samoan (Milner, 1966). With the publishing, in 1962, of Stephen Savage's early manuscript dictionary, linguists now have available for the first time a comprehensive, although admittedly imperfect lexicon for a Cook Islands language. Extensive dictionaries for Niue (McEwen) and Rennell-Bellona (Elbert) are in press, while work is proceeding on a dictionary of Nukuoro (Carroll).

The revision of Williams' Maori dictionary, still the best dictionary of any Polynesian language, has been completed prior to publishing a seventh edition. (The first edition was published in 1844.) For some reason, perhaps because it was published by a government printer rather than by a commercial publishing house, it is less well known than it should be among Malayo-Polynesianists. Dempwolff, for example, did not use it, although the fifth, and best edition had appeared in 1919.

On the level of syntax the first major attempt to proceed beyond the phrase level is Hohepa's Profile-Generative Grammar of Maori (1966). An earlier exploratory attempt to enumerate simple sentences in Maori with an item and arrangement model (Biggs, 1961b) has not been followed up.

When the present paper, in an earlier draft, was read at Tokyo in 1966, it was possible to say: "There are still important gaps in our knowledge. Those areas for which information is particularly deficient are (a) Ellice Islands, (b) Niue, (c) Tokelau Islands, (d) Pukapuka and Penrhyn in the Northern Cook Islands, (e) most of the Outliers, and (f) the Austral Islands." It was noted then that work was proceeding, or about to begin, that would fill most of these gaps, and it is gratifying to report, just a few months later, that further progress is indeed being made in several of the areas where it is most needed.

There are certain areas in which further descriptive work is necessary for special reasons, such as suspected multiple origins of the language spoken there, or suspected dialect differences amounting to language boundaries. East Futuna, East Uvea, the Marquesas, and the Tuamotu archipelago are all cases in point.

In spite of the present gaps in our knowledge it seems likely that basic grammatical descriptions and extensive vocabularies, if not full lexicons, will be available for all of the Polynesian languages within the next few years.

COMPARATIVE AND TYPOLOGICAL STUDY

The quality and quantity of the descriptive data (with the promise of more to come) suggests a rosy future for comparative and typological study of Polynesian. The close interrelationship of the languages, such that they fall readily into the same descriptive mold, should allow comparative study to proceed beyond the reconstruction of proto-vocabulary to a plausible picture of the proto-grammar. Such reconstruction could include the major parts of speech, with reconstructions of the shapes and order classes of the grammatical morphemes, and description of the grammatical categories which were marked in the language ancestral to those spoken throughout Polynesia today.

Traditionally and popularly Polynesian has been regarded as a separate branch of the Malayo-Polynesian language family, coordinate with other branches called Indonesian and Melanesian; Micronesian was sometimes listed separately, sometimes regarded as a branch of Melanesian. This has remained the popular view despite Dempwolff's demonstration of phonological innovations common to the Melanesian and Polynesian languages that he studied, which strongly suggests that Polynesian and Melanesian are subgroups of the same higher order branch of the family. In any case it is now clear that whether or not the Melanesian languages form a single branch of Malayo-Polynesian, Polynesian is certainly a low-order subgroup whose immediate external relations are to be found in Melanesia, especially in Fiji, in the southeast Solomons, the Central New Hebrides, and in Rotuma, although the true genetic position of the last may be confused by the amount of borrowing it has done. Linguistically Polynesia is part of Melanesia, which is not to say that its status as a well-delimited subgroup is in question. On the contrary, it is one of the few unquestioned closed subgroups in the Oceanic area.

It is the internal rather than the external relationships of Polynesian which are to be discussed here. Traditionally Polynesia has been regarded as consisting of three divisions, Eastern Polynesia, Western Polynesia, and the Polynesian Outliers. Eastern and Western Polynesian languages are all found within the Polynesian triangle subtended by joining Hawaii, New Zealand, and Easter Island. The division between east and west lay between Samoa and the Cook Islands, with New Zealand included in the eastern division. The linguistic position of the Outliers was always in dispute, some holding that they were (individually or collectively) a group or groups coordinate with the eastern and western divisions, others insisting that they marked later migrations, or drift voyages out of Triangle Polynesia, in which case they would be a subgroup or subgroups of Eastern or Western Polynesian, or both.

This was the position until an important paper by S. H. Elbert entitled "The Internal Relationships of Polynesian Languages . . ." (1953) was published. Its findings were based on the recently developed technique of defining linguistic relationships in terms of sameness and difference in basic vocabulary, plus some comparison of phonologies (involving reconstruction of a proto-sound system), and the listing of certain grammatical features which appeared to be diagnostic for subgroup membership. Earlier work by Emory (1946) comparing total, rather than basic vocabularies, had remained unpublished, but Elbert's paper seemed to spark off an interest in the subgrouping of Polynesian which still continues.

Elbert's paper contains a tree diagram which, unexpectedly, shows the first major split between Tonga and Niue on the one hand and all other Polynesian languages (except Kapingamarangi but including Samoa, Ellice and Tikopia) on the other. Although the article is not completely explicit on this point it seems that the grouping was made on phonological rather than lexicostatistical grounds. In any case, it suggested for the first time that Samoan belonged with the languages of the east, rather than with Tongan. Within his major groups Elbert suggested, on lexicostatistical grounds, further subgrouping (see Fig. 1). Of several Outliers for which basic vocabularies were available, Elbert grouped Tikopia with Samoa, but Kapingamarangi was itself coordinate with the whole Eastern group.

The phonological evidence which Elbert used for grouping Samoan with the Eastern languages is in fact meager, consisting only of the retention of the distinction between proto *s and *h, and innovations consisting of the reflection of *h as zero and the falling together of *l and *r.

It was left for Andrew Pawley to point out (1966b) that Elbert's table of cognate percentages also supported the grouping of Samoan (and Tikopia and Ellice) with the Eastern Polynesian languages rather than with Tongan. For instance Tongan shares 45 to 58 percent, and Niue 47 to 56 percent of cognates with the eight Eastern languages in the sample; but Samoan (with 52 to 67 percent), Ellice (61 to 67 percent) and Tikopia (62 to 71 percent) consistently share more cognates with these same Eastern languages than either Tongan or Niuean does. In several cases the difference is as much as 18 percent.

Pawley postulates a first split of Polynesian into Tongic and Nuclear Polynesian, with Samoan and all the Eastern languages deriving from the latter group (see Fig. 2). He lists six formal innovations in the grammatical markers which are shared uniquely by the languages of the Nuclear Polynesian subgroup, and seven other uniquely shared features which may be innovations.

Tongic became Tongan, Niuean, and (possibly) Uvean. Nuclear Polynesian split into Samoic and Eastern Polynesian, the former being ancestral to Samoan, Ellice, Tokelauan, East Futunan, and Tikopian; the latter resulting in all of the remaining languages east of Samoa, together with New Zealand Maori. The Outliers, other than Tikopia, are not included in the classification.

Roger Green accepts Pawley's classification but proposes a further subdivision of Eastern Polynesian into a Central subgroup and Easter

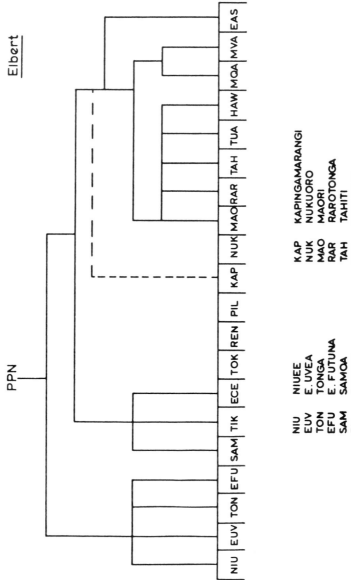

FIGURE 1

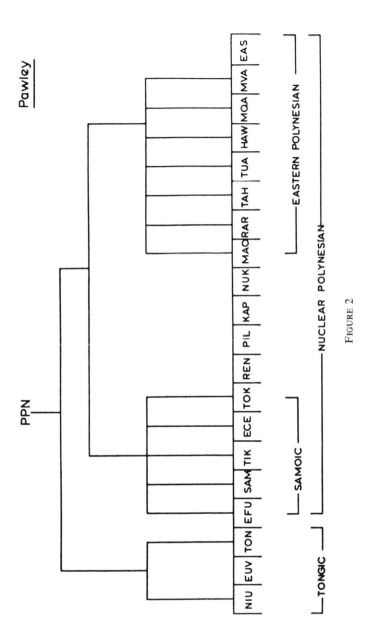

FIGURE 2

Island, the Central subgroup further differentiating into Tahitic and Marquesic, the former resulting in Maori, Tahitian, and Tuamotuan, the latter containing Marquesan, Mangarevan, and Hawaiian. Green argues further that Marquesan is two languages, with Hawaiian closer to southeastern than to northwestern Marquesan (see Fig. 3). Green's Central subgroup is established on the basis of one phonological and two lexical innovations; his Marquesic on the basis of six lexical innovations; his Tahitic on the basis of three lexical innovations.

Dyen (1963, 1965), using lexicostatistical calculations, finds that the subgroups of Polynesian, none of which is a closed group, are as shown in Figure 4. His subgrouping is traditional, that is, pre-Elbert, Pawley, and Green, in grouping Samoan with Tongan (and Niuean and Uvean) in a West Polynesian Cluster. The placing of Maori as coordinate with the other major subgroups is probably owing to the fact that Dyen's basic word list for Maori was unreliable; he notes that Maori "has marked Eastern Polynesian characteristics."

COMPARATIVE PROBLEMS

A special problem affecting the reconstruction of Polynesian and other Oceanic languages is presented by the number of doublets whose differences of form correspond to what has been termed the oral and nasal "grades" of certain proto-phonemes, or clusters of phonemes.

Milner's suggestion (1963) that in the Western Polynesian area they might result from borrowing among Fijian, Tongan, and Samoan would not account for the fact that doublets are frequent in all of the Polynesian languages. In a later paper (1965) he discusses the relationship of such doublets to possible proto-forms containing nasal and oral alternating phonemes.

As they have become better known the phonologies of certain Outlier languages have revealed features unusual in Polynesian. Elbert has shown for Rennellese how such features may be borrowed from nearby Melanesian languages (1965). In Mele-Fila and West Futuna nongeminate consonant clusters are also owing to the influence of neighboring non-Polynesian languages.

It is a puzzling feature of a number of widely separated Outliers that they have in common geminate consonant clusters which have resulted from the loss of a vowel, often the vowel in an initial syllable of a partially reduplicated base. Among the languages of Triangle Polynesia only Ellice has geminate consonant clusters, and these have arisen similarly. (In Maori the loss of a vowel sometimes results in a gemi-

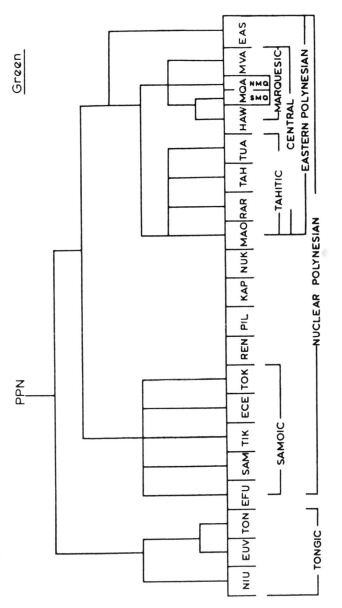

FIGURE 3

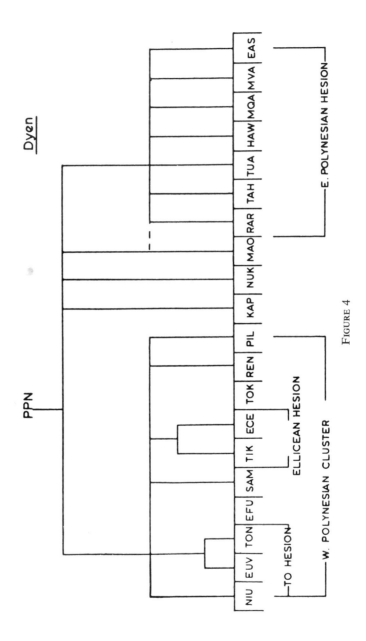

FIGURE 4

nate /t/ in fast speech.) Did the geminate consonants evolve independently in the various islands, or do several Outliers derive from the Ellice group?

In spite of evidence to the contrary in Capell (1958), it was often maintained that no Polynesian language had a contrast between L and R. Raymond Firth (1963) demonstrated clearly that both /l/ and /r/ do exist in Tikopia, but it seems evident that the contrast is a recent one. The two phonemes do not occur together in the same words, /l/ occurs in few basic words, /r/ in many, and both phonemes reflect either PPN *l or *r with no apparent phonological conditioning. For those Tikopian words containing /l/ borrowing from another Polynesian language is indicated. As described to me by Irwin Howard (personal communication) the /l/ and /r/ phonemes in Takuu (Mortlock Islands) also appear to be a secondary development. It is correct to say that no contemporary Polynesian language has directly inherited different non-zero reflexes of PPN *l and *r. (Tongan reflects *l as /l/ and *r as zero.)

Davenport (1962) and Elbert (1965) have described an interesting phonological situation on Pileni where, in some words, [h] alternates with [s], and in other words with [f]. Elbert is interested in stating the phonemic problem, but information provided by Davenport also elucidates the history of the phenomenon, a classic case of dialect mixing. As Davenport puts it in a personal communication to Elbert, "Aua people use /h/ and /s/ where the Taumakoans use /f/and /h/." It is apparent from examples given by himself and by Elbert that the Aua dialect reflects PPN *f as [h], and *s and *t before /i/ are reflected as [s]; Taumako on the other hand reflects *f as [f], and *s and *t before /i/ are reflected as [h]. With the recent mixing of the two populations "variable usage is . . . permitted everywhere." But from the examples given, alternation between [f] and [h] occurs only in reflexes of words containing PPN *f, while the alternation between [s] and [h] occurs in reflexes of words which contained PPN *s and *t.

This summary of comparative research since 1946 should not conclude without mention of a glottochronological study by D. S. Marshall (1956) which differed from the usual lexicostatistical study in comparing each language, not with each other language, but with a reconstructed proto-language; also a comparative study of certain features of the Easter Island language by Bergmann (1963) should be mentioned. Typological studies of Polynesian include C. F. and F. M. Voegelin's survey of Polynesian typology (1964) and two studies by Viktor Krupa (1966, and in press).

RESEARCH IN PROGRESS

Research in progress at the Universities of Auckland and Hawaii involves the comparison of the total lexicons of Polynesian languages. Chrétien once asked, "by what scholarly principle we neglect the great bulk of available lexical material in comparative work," and the extensive dictionaries available for many of the Polynesian languages suggested that the present project would be worth while.

It is perhaps not generally realized how many speech communities there are in Polynesia whose geographical isolation necessitates the initial assumption that they may be separate languages. We are distinguishing at present thirty-four such communalects, but this is almost certainly too few, since the Ellice, Tuamotu, and Marquesas groups are each being treated as units, which may not be valid, and there is at least one inhabited island, Anuta, which has not been included in the tally.

The aim of the research is the discovery of sets of cognates which will allow the reconstruction of a maximum number of Proto-Polynesian and sub-Proto-Polynesian words. Reconstruction is done according to the usual comparative techniques. Initially twelve languages for which good dictionaries are available have been used in the research. They are Easter Island, East Futunan, East Uvean, Hawaiian, Maori, Marquesan, Rarotongan, Samoan, Tikopian, Tongan, Tuamotuan, and Fijian.

A reconstructed form is labeled PPN if it occurs in either (a) Tongan or East Uvean and any other PN language, except Samoan; or (b) in Fijian and Maori or any language east of Samoa. Samoan is omitted from both (a) and (b) because the older subgrouping hypothesis and that now offered by Elbert and Pawley treat it differently. In the one case it is regarded as grouping with Tongan in a West Polynesian subgroup, in the other it is regarded as grouping with Maori and all languages to the east in a Nuclear Polynesian subgroup, which is further divided into Samoic and Eastern Polynesian. Both hypotheses agree that Tongan and the languages east of Samoa (including Maori) are in different subgroups of the highest order. We are therefore justified in setting up as Proto-Polynesian any reconstructed form which has reflexes in both areas. According to the older hypothesis, however, we would be unjustified in regarding as Proto-Polynesian a form with reflexes only in Samoan and Tongan. There is, moreover, the strong probability that there has been borrowing, which cannot now be identified as such, between Tonga and Samoa, areas which are admitted to have been in continuous contact, even on the most critical assessment of Polynesian voyaging capabilities.

Fijian is the best known non-Polynesian language of Eastern Oceania. It is also almost certainly the closest external relation of Polynesian. For these reasons it was included in this comparative study with the hope of establishing as Proto-Polynesian forms which do not have reflexes in all of the postulated major subgroups of Polynesian itself.

In a number of cases the inclusion of Fijian has enabled reconstructions of Proto-Polynesian forms to be made when the lack of a cognate in a particular language might otherwise have made this impossible. For example, the absence of a cognate in Tongan may leave uncertain whether a proto-form should be reconstructed with *r or *l; the occurrence of a cognate in Fijian solves the difficulty.

Since Fijian and the Polynesian languages are known to be in different subgroups of Austronesian we are justified in setting up as Proto-Polynesian a form which has reflexes in Fijian and in any Polynesian language. In fact, however, we do not reconstruct a Proto-Polynesian form if Tongan has the only Polynesian reflex, because Tonga is known to have been in contact with Fiji in pre-European times, and there is some evidence of linguistic borrowing between the two areas.

A set of cognates discovered by dictionary searching is entered on an edge-punched card, together with a reconstructed form, and a gloss. Where the meaning of a reflex in a daughter language differs from the gloss assigned to the reconstruction it is entered beside the reflex.

In the first stage of the research 1,000 cards have been processed, giving a total of 1,000 reconstructions, 644 of which are labeled PPN. This number will be at least doubled as more languages are brought into the comparison. Viktor Krupa of Bratislava, working on the basis of the number of actually occurring forms versus the number theoretically possible, in Fijian and various Polynesian languages, concluded that Proto-Polynesian contained 1,400 bi-vocalic forms. Our total of 620 reconstructed bi-vocalic PPN forms represents 44 percent of this theoretical total. Of course our reconstructions are not confined to bi-vocalic items.

This research would be justified simply in terms of the assemblage of available information, the addition of new information, and the storage of both in a readily retrievable form, together with hypothetical reconstructions of a large number of proto-forms. But as the work proceeds it will be possible to make use of the stored information in testing hypothesized subgrouping of Polynesian, thus throwing light on the prehistory of the area. For example, the total number of lexical items shared might be regarded as an index of relationship. More conventionally, the total number of items shared exclusively by certain languages might be regarded as evidence for subgrouping.

A question that invites testing concerns the existence of the proposed Nuclear subgroup of Polynesian, suggested by Elbert on phonological evidence, and by Pawley on the basis of shared innovations, and other shared features of the grammatical markers.

On the basis of the total number of items shared among Tongan, Samoan, and Maori (the latter being taken as representative of the widely accepted Eastern Polynesian subgroup), there is no confirmation of a Nuclear Polynesian subgroup. The figures obtained are: Samoa and Tonga shared 551 items; Samoa and Maori 546 items; and Tonga and Maori 553.

If Samoan does group with Eastern Polynesian, and Tongan does not, we might have expected Samoan to show a higher total number of words shared with Eastern Polynesian languages than does Tongan, and, with the exception of the comparison with Maori, such is the case. But in no case is the difference greater than 7 percent, and in several cases it is as low as 1 percent. We cannot say, therefore, that total comparison confirms the existence of the Nuclear Polynesian subgroup.

When we come to the case of exclusively shared items, however, it is found that Samoan shares with Eastern Polynesian languages eighteen items which are not found in Tongan, Niuean, or Uvean, while only twelve items shared by Tongan and Eastern Polynesian, to the exclusion of the Samoic languages, have been found.

We do not know how many of these exclusively shared items are retentions and how many are innovations, but the fact that there are 50 percent more lexical items shared exclusively by Samoan and Eastern Polynesian than by Tongan and Eastern Polynesian does suggest that the former relationship may be closer, as is also suggested by the phonology and by the morphology.

Eastern Polynesian is generally recognized as a subgroup of Polynesian and this is confirmed by the fact that no less than 176 out of 1,000 cards contain items that are widespread in the east but nowhere else. Because Niuean has not yet been brought fully into the comparison it is not possible to give comparable figures for Tongic, another generally recognized subgroup.

The first 1,000 reconstructed forms have been published (Walsh and Biggs, 1966), together with all the data on which they are based, in the hope that others interested in this field will provide addenda and corrigenda to expand and improve the list. The hope has already been realized. S. H. Elbert and J. M. McEwen have worked through the list adding Rennellese and Niuean forms respectively, and the former has provided information which will result in alterations to the reconstructed shapes of several forms. This help is gratefully acknowledged.

It may be of interest to conclude this paper with some mention of the use of native speakers of Oceanic languages, not only as informants, but as researchers. Our comparative work, in particular, has been helped by the employment of research assistants who are both trained in linguistics and speakers of a Polynesian language, or of Fijian. In searching two dictionaries for cognate forms, complete control of one of the languages was found to be a great advantage. Some of the deficiencies of existing dictionaries can also be overcome in this way. The first task of a research assistant from the Cook Islands was to correct the marking of glottal stop and vowel length in Savage's dictionary of Rarotongan.

In descriptive work, too, our native-speaking research assistants have been very valuable. At all times we have had on hand sophisticated informants for Maori, Tongan, Fijian, and Rarotongan who were themselves studying anthropological linguistics as undergraduates, or graduates of the University of Auckland. Two of these students have begun graduate thesis work on a Polynesian language other than their own.

Auckland is the largest metropolitan center of Polynesia. Among its thousands of non-Maori Polynesians can be found speakers of every language, with the possible exception of a few languages of French Polynesia, and some of the remoter Outliers. At the northern apex of the Polynesian triangle Hawaii has also become a mecca for Polynesians, with the East-West Center in Honolulu, and the Polynesian Cultural Center at Laie attracting numbers of potential linguistic informants from their remote island homes. It must be regarded as fortunate that both the University of Auckland and the University of Hawaii have seen fit to develop Polynesian linguistic studies.

The advantages of commencing the study of an unknown language with fully bilingual informants, and at a university specializing in the linguistics of the area are considerable. At Auckland all research students spend several years studying Maori before attempting the analysis of another Polynesian language. In each case fieldwork begins in Auckland, drawing informants from the local Polynesian community. Brief field trips to the home island can then be made, usually in the summer, and with excellent results. The fieldworker arrives in the island community with considerable insight into the language, and some speaking ability. Exposed to the linguistic community, rather than to a few informants only, he is now able to check his earlier work, observe dialectal and idiolectal variation, extend his lexical coverage, and get a better grasp of semantic features by observing the language in its cultural setting.

BIBLIOGRAPHY OF POLYNESIAN LINGUISTICS 1946-1966
(Including items prior to 1946 mentioned in text)

BAYARD, D. T.
> 1966. The Cultural Interrelationship of the Polynesian Outliers. M.A. thesis, University of Hawaii.

BERGMANN, HANS-GEORG
> 1963. Vergleichende Untersuchungen Uber die Sprache der Osterinsel. Ph.D. dissertation, University of Hamburg.

BIGGS, B. G.
> [n.d.] The Pronunciation of Maori: A Guide for Radio Announcers. Mimeo. New Zealand Broadcasting Service.

> 1958. "The Sound System of Maori." Paper read at Rotorua at the Refresher Course for Teachers of the Maori Language.

> 1960. "Morphology-syntax in a Polynesian Language." *J. Polynesian Soc.* **69**:376-379.

> 1961a. *The Structure of New Zealand Maori.* Archives of Languages of the World. Bloomington: Univ. of Indiana.

> 1961b. "Towards a Syntax of Maori." Paper read at the Tenth Pacific Science Congress (Honolulu).

> 1966. *English-Maori Dictionary.* Wellington: Reed.

BLIXEN, OLAF
> 1966a. "El Lenguaje Honorifico en Uvea (Wallis) y sus Conexiónes en Polinesia Occidental." *Moana: Estudios de Antropología Oceánica* **1**(1).

> 1966b. "Lenguaje Honorifico y Comportamiento Reverente en Samoa y Tonga." *Comunicaciónes Antropologicas del Museo de Historia Natural de Montevideo* **1**(6).

BUSE, J. W.
> 1960. "Rarotongan Personal Pronouns: Form and Distribution." *Bull. School of Oriental and African Studies* **23**:123-137.

> 1963a. "Structure of the Rarotongan Verbal Piece." *Bull. School of Oriental and African Studies* **26**(2):152-169.

> 1963b. "Structure of Rarotongan Nominal, Negative and Conjunctival Pieces." *Bull. School of Oriental and African Studies* **25**(3):393-419.

> 1965. "Problems of Morphology and Classification Illustrated from Rarotongan." *Lingua* **15**:32-47.

CAPELL, A.
1931. "Some Curiosities of Polynesian Possessives." *J. Polynesian Soc.* **40**: 141-150.
1935-1936. "The Sikayana Language." *J. Polynesian Soc.* **44**(175):163-172; continued in **45**(177):9-16; **45**(178):67-73.
1936-1937. "A Sikayana Vocabulary." *J. Polynesian Soc.* **45**(180):142-153; continued in **46**(181):24-31.
1942. "Notes on the Fila Language." *J. Polynesian Soc.* **51**:153-180.
1958. *The Culture and Language of Futuna and Aniwa, New Hebrides.* Oceania Linguistic Monograph No. 5. Sydney: Univ. of Sydney.
1962. *The Polynesian Language of Mae (Emwae), New Hebrides.* Auckland: Linguistic Soc. of New Zealand.

CARROLL, VERN
1965. "An Outline of the Structure of the Language of Nukuoro." *J. Polynesian Soc.* **74**:192-226.

CHURCHWARD, C. M.
1953. *Tongan Grammar.* Oxford: Oxford Univ. Press.
1959. *Tongan Dictionary (Tongan-English and English-Tongan).* London: Oxford Univ. Press.

DAVENPORT, WILLIAM
1962. "Comment on A. Capell's Article 'Oceanic Linguistics Today.'" *Current Anthropology* **3**:401.

DYEN, ISIDORE
1963. The Lexicostatistical Classification of the Austronesian Languages. New Haven. Mimeo.
1965. *A Lexicostatistical Classification of the Austronesian Languages.* Internat. J. American Linguistics Mem. 19. Indiana Univ. Pub. Anthropology and Linguistics.

ELBERT, SAMUEL, H.
1948. "Grammar and Comparative Study of the Language of Kapingamarangi, Texts, and Word Lists." CIMA Rep. 3. Pacific Sci. Board, National Research Council. (Mimeo.)
1953. "Internal Relationships of Polynesian Languages and Dialects." *Southwestern J. Anthropology* **9**:147-173.
1957. "Possessives in Polynesia." *Bible Translator* **8**(1):23-27.
1965. "Phonological Expansions in Outlier Polynesia." In G. B. MILNER and E. J. A. HENDERSON (editors), *Indo-Pacific Linguistic Studies*, Part I, pp. 431-442. Amsterdam.

EMORY, K. P.
1946. Eastern Polynesia, its Cultural Relationships. Ph.D. dissertation, Yale University.
1963. "East Polynesian Relationships: Settlement Pattern and Time Involved as Indicated by Vocabulary Agreements." *J. Polynesian Soc.* **72**(2):78-100.

FIRTH, R.
1963. "L and R in Tikopia Language." *Oceanic Linguistics* **2**:49-61.

FUENTES, JORDI
1960. *Dictionary and Grammar of the Easter Island Language.* Santiago: Editorial Universitaria, S. A.

GRACE, GEORGE
1959. *The Position of the Polynesian Languages within the Austronesian (Malayo-Polynesian) Language Family.* Supplement to International J. American Linguistics. Vol. 25, No. 2. Baltimore.

HOHEPA, P. W.
1966. A Profile-Generative Grammar of Maori. Ph.D. dissertation, Indiana Univ.

HOLLYMAN, K. J.
1959. "Polynesian Influence in New Caledonia: The Linguistic Aspect." *J. Polynesian Soc.* **68**(4):357-389.

KRUPA, VIKTOR
1966. *Morpheme and Word in Maori.* The Hague: Mouton.
In press. "The Phonemic Structure of Morphemic Forms in Four Oceanic Languages." *J. Polynesian Soc.*

MARSHALL, D. S.
1956. Polynesian Glottochronology. Ph.D. dissertation, Harvard Univ.

MILNER, G. B.
1961. "The Samoan Vocabulary of Respect." *J. Royal Anthropological Institute* **91**:297-317.
1962. "Active, Passive or Perfective in Samoan: A Fresh Appraisal of the Problem." *J. Polynesian Soc.* **71**:151-161.
1963. "Notes on the Comparison of Two Languages (With and Without a Genetic Hypothesis)." In H. L. SHORTO (editor), *Linguistic Comparison in South East Asia and the Pacific,* pp. 416-430. Univ. London: School of Oriental and African Studies.
1965. "Initial Nasal Clusters in Eastern and Western Austronesian." In G. B. MILNER and E. J. A. HENDERSON (editors), *Indo-Pacific Linguistic Studies,* pp. 416-430. Amsterdam.
1966. *Samoan Dictionary (Samoan-English, English-Samoan).* London: Oxford Univ. Press.

MOEKA'A, RANGI
1966. The Structure of the Pukapukan Verbal Piece. Typescript. Copy in Anthropology Dept., Univ. Auckland.

MORTON, E. J.
1962. A Descriptive Grammar of Tongan (Polynesian). Ph.D. dissertation, Indiana Univ.

PAWLEY, A. K.
1961. "A Scheme for Describing Samoan Grammar." *Te Reo* 4:38-43.
1962. "The Person-Markers in Samoa." *Te Reo* 5:52-56.
1966a. "Samoan Phrase Structure." *Anthropological Linguistics.* Vol. 8.
1966b. "Polynesian Languages: A Subgrouping Based on Shared Innovations in Morphology." *J. Polynesian Soc.* **75**:39-64.
[n.d.] The Phrase Structure of Polynesian Languages. Mimeo. Dept. Anthropology, Univ. Auckland.

PUKUI, M. K., and S. H. ELBERT
    1957. *Hawaiian-English Dictionary*. Honolulu: Univ. Hawaii Press.
    1964. *English-Hawaiian Dictionary*. Honolulu: Univ. Hawaii Press.

RANBY, R.
    1966. Notes on the Language of Nanumea I., in the Ellice Group. Mimeo. Dept. Anthropology, Univ. Auckland.

SAVAGE, S.
    1962. *A Dictionary of the Maori Language of Rarotonga*. Wellington: Dept. Island Terr.

SHARPLES, P.
    [n.d.] The Verbal Phrase of Sikaiana. Mimeo. Dept. Anthropology, Univ. Auckland.

STIMSON, J. F., AND D. S. MARSHALL
    1964. *A Dictionary of Some Tuamotuan Dialects of the Polynesian Language*. The Hague: Martinus Nijhoff.

THORPE, A.
    [n.d.] Notes of the Phrase Structure of Ongtong Java. Mimeo. Dept. Anthropology, Univ. Auckland.

VOEGELIN, C. F., and F. M.
    1964. "Languages of the World. Indo-Pacific Fascicles I and II." *Anthropological Linguistics*. Vol. 6, Nos. 4 and 7.

WALSH, D. S., and BRUCE BIGGS
    1966. *Proto-Polynesian Word List I*. Te Reo Monograph. Auckland: Linguistic Soc. New Zealand.

WARD, J. H.
    1952. Mutual Intelligibility between Certain Polynesian Speech Communities. M.A. thesis, Univ. Hawaii.
    1961. "A Recently Noted Easter Island Phoneme." *Abstracts Symposium Pap., Tenth Pacific Sci. Cong.* (Honolulu), p. 98.

WHITE, R.
    1958. A Linguistic Check-Sketch of Tahitian. Heliograph.

WILLIAMS, H. W.
    1957. *A Dictionary of the Maori Language*. (6th ed.) Wellington: Govt. Printer.

ONOMASTICALLY INDUCED WORD REPLACEMENT IN TAHITIAN

RALPH GARDNER WHITE
Punaauia, Tahiti

IN FEBRUARY, 1926, there was published an article by Edouard Ahnne entitled "On the Custom of 'Pii' and the Modifications Which It Imparted to the Tahitian Vocabulary." Using John Muggridge Orsmond's notes as his source material, Ahnne reported a custom ostensibly called *pii* wherein the name of an *ari'i* or high-ranking personage was considered as taboo /tapu/[1] and the common people were not allowed to pronounce the syllables making up the name. In other words, the sequence of sounds in the name of the *ari'i* were supposedly eliminated from the speech of his subjects, the punishment for failure to comply with this injunction being rectal impalement. Because this injunction was effective during the lifetime of the *ari'i* concerned, and some of the *ari'i* changed their names rather frequently, and since Tahitian names are usually composed of words of everyday speech, such a custom conceivably could have profound effects on the vocabulary of a people. Ahnne cites numerous examples of words purported to have been affected by such injunction and of the new vocabulary substituted for them.

In August, 1927, Mme. Marau Taaroa Salmon (Marau i Tahiti, Queen Dowager of Pomare V), in beautiful French, made a very lengthy

---

[1] Insofar as possible I have tried to give phonemic or quasi-phonemic renderings of all the Polynesian material which occurs in the text. To distinguish orthographic forms from phonological forms I have used italics for the former and enclosed the latter in slant lines, or diagonals / /. Everything between slant lines or brackets [ ] in this paper is mine, and I accept full responsibility for it. Most of my phonemic renderings are from first-hand observation, a few are inferred. All quotations in French, except for names of institutions and journals, have been translated into English, and I take the responsibility for these renderings also. In the bibliography I use the language of the original.

and polemic reply to Ahnne, in which she took up, item by item, the points of language and history postulated by Ahnne and evaluated them, for the most part repudiating them. Both she and Ahnne equated *pii* with /pi'i/ "to call," and she gave very adequate definition of this particular word as she knew it, fairly conclusively demonstrating that it could not have been the name of the custom in question.

Marau proposed a number of ways of referring to this custom, but they seem to me to be obviously inappropriate and they also show that, although her knowledge of Tahitian was broad and her reflective understanding of it deep, the Tahitian with which she was familiar had to be dated much later than the time of Orsmond's observations. Her knowledge of history seemed to go back to about the time of Pomare I and II, and of course her knowledge of genealogy went back much further.

She rejected Ahnne's statement about the punishment for breaking this taboo, in the following words:

> This chastisement [impalement] was reserved especially for those vanquished in war. . . . The punishment inflicted for a *lapsus linguae* [slip of the tongue], as I understand the word, was the chastisement called the "hoi-pu" [? /ho'i-puu/], which consisted of obliging him [the taboo breaker] to recite exactly a certain number of times, without making a mistake, a hundred or more times, the consecrated names. If he made a mistake in reciting the "hoi-pu," the transgressor was punished by having one eye removed, or both. The eyes of the victim were offered to the *arii* /ari'i/ whose name had been harmed by the use of the forbidden syllables.
>
> It is from this chastisement that the name "Aimata" /'ai-mata/ comes, which means the right to eat the eye.

In May, 1931, Ahnne published a nonpolemic follow-up in which he made a brief comparison of Tahitian *Pii* with a similar custom in Madagascar.

In 1948 an article by Charles Vernier appeared, entitled "The Variations in Tahitian Vocabulary Before and After European Contacts," in which he briefly summarized Ahnne's first article, mostly by quotation; but he does not even mention Marau's very learned rebuttal. Most of Vernier's article concerns new vocabulary from Hebrew and European languages.

In 1953, in an important and well-known article entitled "Internal Relationships of Polynesian Languages and Dialects," using Vernier as a source, Samuel H. Elbert says:

> The rate of change in Tahiti may have been unusually fast, and this may be attributed to a peculiarly Tahitian system of tabooing words after the death of a chief of the same name. [*Sic!* during the lifetime.] As an example, the old name

for water in Tahitian was *vai,* but after the death [*sic*] of a chief named Vai [?], the name for water was changed to *pape.* (The name of the capital was likewise changed from Vai-'ete to Pape-'ete.) Similarly, the names for the common numerals two and five were changed, as well as all words containing the common morpheme or even the sounds *tu.*

I have quoted Elbert in full because his statement seems to represent the final formulation of a scholarly myth, and to be the source of many similar statements made later on.

The Reverend John Muggridge Orsmond reached Tahiti in 1817, twenty years after the arrival of the original group of missionaries from the London Missionary Society in 1797 on the *Duff.* He had had Tahitian fellow passengers on his long trip to Tahiti from London via Sydney and could speak some Tahitian upon arrival. Orsmond asked Henry Nott to help him perfect his knowledge of Tahitian, but was told not to ask for help from the missionaries but to go to the source, to the Tahitians. As was usual with him, Orsmond took this as a personal rebuff. (Actually, Nott was overworked and very weary, and did not feel up to helping a vigorous young newcomer who was quite capable of helping himself.) But he did take Nott's advice and set forth with writing materials to interview native specialists of every sort. Probably he was the most intellectual of the early missionaries, and the best formal scholar; but Nott came closer to the heart of the Tahitian people and language. Orsmond did try to do his best at scientific reporting of his observations, but his religious and ethnocentric bias was so strong (I should say to the point of extreme bigotry) that even in a straightforward translation of a native text he could not refrain from interpolating his own very sarcastic interpretive remarks.

As for the Orsmond notes on which Ahnne based his article, there is some mystery as to just what notes these were and as to what happened to them. If they date about 1837, as Ahnne states, they were probably expanded or developed (as Orsmond calls it) from earlier notes. The following are perhaps slightly fragmentary and are derived from an essay by Orsmond called "Reception of the Gospel . . . ." From internal evidence this must date between 1819 and 1821, and since some of the phraseology is almost exactly like Ahnne's, it is probably at least a part of the basic source for the later writing. I quote everything that seems relevant:[2]

---

[2] Quoted from a typescript carbon copy in the possession of Dr. Niel Gunson, Australian National University in Canberra, who probably obtained it from the Mitchell Library in Sydney. Parts of the text are in Tahitian, which I translated for Dr. Gunson.

Pii. Custom. There is hateful pride among Barbarians, & to have a distinguished name was a very predominant feeling among the Tahitians. The name must stand alone, the pii enabled a chief to alter his name at pleasure, & to alter any word that contained a syllable like that which composed his name.

From Teu the husband, & Opiripoa the wife was born a son called (Tu nuiae te atua) /tuu-nui-e-'a'a-i-te-atua/ who is Vairaatoa /vai-ra'a-toa/.

Soon Vairaatoa gave his government to Tunuie te atua who is the Pomare now reigning. Vairaatoa was ill of a severe cough in the night (Po /night mare/ cough) and according to Tahitian custom he dropped the name Vairaatoa & was called by the name of the disease under which he suffered (Po mare) /poo-mare/. He gave this his name to his son who always has been & now is the patron & avaritious hard drinking friend of the Missionaries. . . . Tunuiae te atua continues as the grand/name, but Pomare is a circumstantial name & is daily, generally, & familiarly used.

Of all the Missionaries who came in the Duff Mr. Nott is able to speak the most readily & the plainest way in the Tahitian dialect, Mr. Bicknell stood next & Mr. Elder (Arara) next, but at the present the other brethern do not from incapacity in the language attempt to speak. Mr. Hayward, Wilson, Henry I have never heard since my arrival attempted to address the people, tho' it is said that after 20 years residence they are soon to begin.

There is also a rather unclear terminal note which seems to say that there were two words, *Moa* /mo'a/ and *Raa* /ra'a/ both meaning "sacred, prohibited," one being substituted for the other because of *Pii* (apparently *mo'a* was substituted for *ra'a*), and that there was also another word, *Rahui* /raahui/, meaning "to forbid."

I have combed the native literature available to me and find not a single example of the use of *pii* (or something similar) in this sense, nor any mention of the custom. In Teuira Henry's *Ancient Tahiti,* published in 1928, a standard source also based on Orsmond's notes, I find no direct reference to the custom, although she does mention an instance of temporary vocabulary change caused by an *ari'i*'s name becoming taboo.[3] Unfortunately, her example is erroneous.

It is possible that in the transactions or in the archives of the London Missionary Society some mention of this custom occurs; I am unable to consult these for this paper. However, mention is made in the Society's *Tahitian and English Dictionary* of 1851, but as *Pi,* not *Pii.* Their entry reads:

Pi /pii/, s. the custom of prohibiting the use of a word, or syllable, which had become sacred by its having been adopted as the whole or part of the

---

[3] "In ancient times breadfruit was always called *'uru* (head) until long, long ago a king of Ra'iatea, named Mahoru, took that name, and it was then called *maiore;* but gradually the name *maiore* wore out and *'uru* again became the common name of the fruit." Note that the word for "head" was /'uru/, not homophonous with /'uru/ "breadfruit," although some rather pretty stories have been concocted on the basis of this graphic identification.

name of some chief, when another word was substituted in its place; as *rui* /ru'i/ for *po* /poo/, and *hota* /hota/ for *mare* /mare/, as these two words formed the name of the late king Pomare /poomare/.

Tepano Jaussen, in his *Grammar and Dictionary of the Tahitian Dialect of the Maori Language* of 1898, has the following entry, probably derivative from the preceding one:

Pi /pii/, s. prohibition of a word consecrated as the name of the king. This custom disfigured the Tahitian language, in that it was necessary to replace the prohibited words. *Po* /poo/, became *rui* /ru'i/; *mare* /mare/, *hota* /hota/; *vai* /vai/, *pape* /pape/; *hou* /hou/, *ápi* /'aapii/; *tu* /tuu/, *tiá* /ti'a/; *mate* /mate/, *pohe* /pohe/.

I do not intend to make this a comparative study; but, since there is so little information about the occurrence of this word in Tahitian, I have gone through the general Polynesian literature to try to find some way to give it a bit of body and bring it to life. The only items I have been able to find which seem at all relevant are the following:

Stephen Savage's *A Dictionary of the Maori Language of Rarotonga*, published in 1962, says:

pī /pii/ n. the removal of tapu (sacredness) from a new fishing net, which really means the performance or observance of a kind of christening ceremony prior to a new net being used for fishing. akapī /'akapii/ v.t. to perform the ceremony of removing the tapu from a new fishing net.

Raymond Firth, *Primitive Polynesian Economy* (1939, p. 203), in reference to Tikopia, says:

The second type of prohibition consists primarily of a material token, but has no ritual to bring it into the *tapu* sphere. If, for instance, a man wishes to reserve the fruit for his own use, he lashes some sago fronds to the trunk. This is a sign to all that they should leave such trees untouched. It applies particularly to near relatives and friends who in the ordinary way might be expected to cull the fruit wthout first asking the owner's permission. This sign is called a *pipi* [probably /piipii/], being a form of the word *pi* [almost surely /pii/], to block. It is really an indication that permission is withheld. It may be put up by any commoner or chief. The same aim is sometimes sought by laying branches across a path or by filling up the entrance in the hedge which surrounds an orchard.

For the sake of convenience, from now on I will use the orthographic label Pi /pii/ for the custom, whether it has historical validity or not.

The reader may wonder why I, and Marau too, reject out of hand Ahnne's identification of the name with the word /pi'i/ "to call" (French "appeler") and why, if we are right, Ahnne would make this false identification. The answer to the first question is simply that it seems semantically absurd from the Tahitian point of view. Both the English "to call" and the French "appeler" have a primary meaning of "to emit a (strong) vocal sound to attract attention" and a secondary meaning of "to give a name to." This is not true of the Tahitian /pi'i/ which has only the first meaning. The second meaning is rendered by /topa/ or /tapa/ (dialectal variants), and /ma'iri/ at one period, and still in literary text. /ma'iri/ was apparently a temporary taboo substitute for /topa/ /tapa/; all of these have the primary meaning of "to fall."

There is one sense in which /pi'i/ is used in connection with names and it is quite in keeping with one of Orsmond's statements quoted above: "Tunuiae te atua continues as the grand/name, but Pomare is a circumstantial name . . . ." The Tahitian rendering of "a circumstantial name" would be "e i'oa pi'i noa," "simply a name of address." This is something like "nickname." There are many other similar expressions using the word /pi'i/, such as: e pi'i hia 'oona, ('o) Poomare, e 'ere raa i toona i'oa mau, "he is called Pomare, but it is not his real name." However, if it is from phrases like these that Orsmond has abstracted "a custom called Pii," the whole matter becomes very trivial and we descend into the realms of the ridiculous. Of course, Orsmond had been in Tahiti only a couple of years when he made his observations, and many other observers who stayed much longer have made much more ridiculous mistakes, so the possibility cannot be eliminated offhand. But what I think is much more likely is that there were two words /pii/ and /pi'i/ and that Orsmond was still naive enough about the language to consider the two as a single word. Such amalgamations of graphic sames which are phonologically different have happened again and again in the history of Tahitian scholarship.

The explanation of how such false identification could have come about lies partly in the English and French semantics already discussed and partly in orthographic history. In standard Tahitian spelling, a word written *pii* could represent the following phonemic sequences: /pi'i/, /pii'i/, /pi'ii/, /pii'ii/. In point of fact, the only single word sequence in this series which occurs is the first one, /pi'i/. To Ahnne, or Vernier, or even Marau, the sequence of letters *p i i* has no other possible reference. /pi'i/, "to call," derives from /pingi/ and did have a homonym meaning "to climb," which derives from /piki/ and seems to have been in use during the period from 1767 to 1821 but to have escaped the notice of the missionaries. This is evidenced by the fact that cats, when first introduced, were called /'uurii pi'i-fare/, "house climbing dog," which was later abridged to /pi'ifare/ and is now usually replaced by /miimii/, from French appellatives, in spite of popular etymologies such as Vernier's, "pii-fare, the-one-who-calls-in-the-house." Further, there is some indication that the word was transmitted to the Australs by native Tahitian missionaries shortly before Pomare II's death in 1821, where it still occurs in what might be called hinterland Tahitian.

"To climb" does not seem to fit our case any better than "to call." However, it may be worthwhile to indicate how etymological rationalization can surmount all obstacles. At one time Tahitians had a pastime called *pi'i-mato,* "cliff-climbing," which I have had explained to me by a Tahitian, in great detail, as consisting of standing before a cliff and declaiming at it and echoing back off from it rhythmic verses (paata'uta'u) or versified prayers ('upu); he claimed that this was a very powerful (*mana*-ful) way of casting spells.

But perhaps /pi'i/ from /piki/ "to climb" does fit our case. Kenneth Emory says of a Kapingamarangi custom:

> A section of coconut leaf wrapped around a tree reserved it for its owner's exclusive use. Such a sign is called a *piki* (clinger), and the act of affixing it also is known by that term. Formerly, should anyone climb a restricted tree without permission, he risked punishment by the gods. Although this fear is practically removed, the sign is still used and is respected.
>
> I noted the puzzlement on Hetata's face when I asked him what the punishment was for violating a *piki* sign. This was a coconut leaflet tied to a stick at the border of a land from which coconuts were not to be taken. "But why break the tabu?" was his only answer.

Compare this statement with Firth's about *pipi.*

To repeat, one can seem to solve almost any verbal puzzle with a proper use of etymological rationalization.

To complete the picture and give the reader a chance to etymologize on his own, there are two words, /pii/, in Tahitian which are well known but not too well covered in the dictionaries, so I will set up my own entries:

/pii/ stative verb, adjective: young, undeveloped, immature, green (in the sense of not being filled out) usually used of plants or fruits, and figuratively of intelligence. For small animals and birds this is usually compounded to /pii-nia/. The compound /'aa-pii/ is now the general word for "young, new," apparently substituted for an earlier /hou/ though not in all occurrences. (Allegedly a Pi substitution, although I have my doubts.)

'aita e faufa'a teriira, e raa'au pii ia, "That's no good, it's sapling wood."

'aita e aura'a te fee'ii pii 'ia 'amu, "Unfilled out plantains are tasteless to eat."

e piinia moa, "It's a chick, a chicken fledgeling."

e moa piinia, "It's a chick, a fledgeling chicken."

e ta'ata 'aapii 'oona, "He is a young person."

e tano teriira 'ohipa naa te u'i 'aapii, "That work is right for the younger/new generation."

e tipi 'aapii taana i noa'a mai, "He has acquired a new knife."

e mea fa'ahiahia te parau 'aapii, "The news is wonderful."

/pii/ active verb, "splash, dash with, squirt."

/piipii/, "to sprinkle."

pii 'oona i toona mata i te pape 'ia 'ore te vaare'a ta'oto, "He dashed water into his eyes to get rid of his sleepiness."

'aa piipii i te 'ahu ['ahau] i te pape 'a 'auri atu ai, "Sprinkle the clothes and then afterwards iron them."

e piipii maatou i te tiare 'ia 'ore ri'i te ahu [ahau] o te mahaana, "We (will) sprinkle the flowers when the heat of the sun/day has diminished."

To get back to the discrepancy between *pii* and *pi,* the explanation for this probably lies in the fact that Tahitian orthography had not become fully standardized at the time that Orsmond made his observations. The missionaries first tried spelling Tahitian as though it were English. This simply would not work for the vowels, so they worked out a five-vowel system but used Ee for what is now written Ii, and Greek epsilon Eε for what is now Ee. During the second decade of the 1800's they came up with approximately what is used now. But as lack of ways of indicating vowel length and the glottal stop created (and still create) problems, they, most particularly Orsmond, continued to experiment. Tahitians sometimes tried to indicate long vowels by doubling them. For instance, the word for "receptacle" is /faari'i/. In some of the early writing this is written *farii,* elsewhere *faarii.* Later, local scholars have been known to say that the word for "receptacle" is really (= was anciently) /fa'ari'i/. In his later notes, Orsmond did try to indicate both vowel length (usually with macrons) and the glottal stop (with a sort of mirror copy of the Arabic letter, because, I suppose, Arabic is written from right to left). This was later misinterpreted as a circumflex, which created confusion since the French used the circumflex instead of the macron to indicate long vowels. But he made a great many mistakes. In any case, as far as Orsmond's notes are concerned, *pii* could have stood for either phonemic /pii/ or /pi'i/.

[/hoo'e/ 'one' → hoe → hoe → hoê ~ ho'e ~ hoe

/hoe/ 'paddle' → hoe ——————————→ hoe ~ (hoê)]

This is just about all the information that I can provide about the word Pii or Pi. As for the custom itself, none of my sources tell us much about what actually happened, and some of what little they do say is highly gratuitous, and probably ex post facto interpolation. A few points may, perhaps, be safely inferred.

An *ari'i's* name was automatically /tapu/ and no ceremony was necessary to establish this fact. I suppose that there may have been some point in history when this was not true, but if so, it probably was pre-Tahitian.

Although Ahnne compares Pi with the Hebrew prohibition against uttering the real name of Jehovah, it is really more like the present-day prohibition against the use of God, the Devil, and so on, except as personal names. That is, there was no prohibition against using the name, only on using the sound of the name in other contexts.

Any ceremonies involved in Pi probably concerned the adoption of a new name by the *ari'i*. Marau says:

> It must not be imagined that changing a [royal] name or modifying a word was undertaken lightly. These matters were brought up and discussed first in the council of the royal family, which looked into the suitability of the measure. This matter was then passed along to the Supreme Council composed of three members, to wit: the king (the *ari'i*), one of the Hiva (the royal guard) who was a prince, chief of the army, etc., the *tahu'a* or high priest who had the name of *Teao* (the light). This Council either rejected the proposed measure or ratified it. In the case of approval, the decision was consecrated on the "marae," and became as the result of this ceremony a law to which everyone was subject.

Both Orsmond and Ahnne had implied that Tahitians changed names for very fickle reasons, and gave a rather simplistic explanation of the reason for the adoption of the name Pomare.

The strength of this /tapu/ and the native reaction to it are well illustrated by the following from Ahnne:

> At the time when Orsmond wrote, that is to say around 1837, although the custom of *pii* was no longer strictly observed, the effects could still be felt. . . .
>
> The names of the kings were still universally respected and considered as sacred. Thus, upon the construction of a schooner by the missionaries in Moorea /mo'orea/ /mo'ore'a/, the rumour went around that it would bear the name of Pomare. The day when the boat was to be launched, the Natives gathered by the hundreds, armed with axes, for the purpose of smashing it up, and they had to change its name. . . .
>
> A Spanish vessel on its way to the Tuamotus to hunt for pearls laid over in Papeete. Hoping to better their standing with the Natives, the shipwrights baptised her "Pomare." This name was inscribed on the poup and also appeared all over the vessel and silver plate aboard.

It was only with great difficulty that the Tahitians were prevented from seizing and smashing up this boat which fled to the Tuamotus where, we may say, it received no better reception, the inhabitants of these islands having always been enthusiastic supporters of the king, Pomare.

This last statement also gives some idea of the Pomarean influence in the Tuamotus and the probability that onomastic tabooing, at least as far as the names of the Pomare family were concerned, was in force there too. Pomare I started his political ascendancy by imposing his rule in the Tuamotus, which he claimed as his ancestral land. This is important because there is an obvious correlation between the changes in basic vocabulary in Tahitian and Tuamotuan (both of which seem to break the laws laid down by lexicostatisticians); often the substitute word in Tahitian is cognate with the colloquial word for the same thing in Tuamotuan, and often, when this is not true, both the Tahitian and the Tuamotuan words for the same thing are divergent from General Polynesian. Now, the question still remains as to whether the Pomare tabooing extended to Tuamotuan or whether Tuamotuan was the source language from which the substitute words were chosen. This passage would seem to indicate that the first possibility is the true one. But if so, it is hard to see where the new words (or sound sequences) did come from. In some instances, a synonym or metaphorical equivalent, or perhaps a dialectal variant, may have been chosen, but the data available are inadequate to show much about synonymy and metaphor in Tahitian and Tuamotuan before 1803, when most of the lasting changes took place, except by rather dubious inferences from later data.

Without going into Tuamotuan in any detail here, I shall simply state the possibility of its being a source of new Tahitian vocabulary, and the possibility of the custom of Pi itself having been imported from the Tuamotus. It is not my opinion that these things are so, or not so; I do not know. However, I will list a few examples to illustrate:

General Polynesian *vai* "water" (usually, fresh) is represented in Tahitian by /pape/ and in Tuamotuan by /komo/.

General Polynesian *fetuu~hetuu* "star" is represented in Tahitian by /feti‘a/ and in Tuamotuan by /fetika/ and /hetika/, connected with the /tapu/ on the name /tuu/. /fetuu/ occurs in very old Tahitian and /fetuu/ or /hetuu/ in old Tuamotuan.

General Polynesian *rua,* "two" is represented in Tahitian by /piti/ and in Tuamotuan by /ite/.

General Polynesian *rua,* "hole" is represented in Tahitian by /aapo‘o and in Tuamotuan by /maite/ and /rua/.

General Polynesian (   )*fatu*, "stone" is /ˈoofaˈi/ in Tahitian and /koonau/ in Tuamotuan.

I do not know what scientific conclusions can be drawn from the fact, but perhaps it is worth noting that it was the basic Swadeshan type of vocabulary which was most affected.

Now we come to a very important historical point. There is evidence of very similar practices in other parts of Polynesia. Something very similar seems to have been observed even recently in Samoa[4], although it is given no name and is not formalized. But it seems to have had very little lasting effect on Samoan vocabulary. It may be wondered why Pi should have affected the vocabulary so permanently in Tahiti but not elsewhere. The basic reason is quite simple. Until the Pomares came into power, after the arrival of Europeans, the *ariˈi* were many and ruled over small areas, or at least held sway of some sort there. No one *ariˈi* had ever reigned over the whole Tahitian-speaking area or even a large fraction of it. Thus, the tabooing of the name of an *ariˈi* was restricted to a small portion of the Tahitian-speaking population under his sway and during his lifetime. After his death, the tabooed term would gradually be reintroduced again from outside.

Pomare I was a very clever political opportunist and quickly understood that the Europeans had individual heads of states and that they assumed that Tahiti must have, too. So he gave them to understand that he was the rightful ruler but was having trouble with would-be usurpers. He was never quite able to carry the operation to completion, but his successor, Pomare II, did at the battle of the Fei Pi /feeˈii pii/ in 1815. Of course, all the missionaries were not completely taken in by this subterfuge, but they found it expedient to act as though they were.

Pomare II was born shortly after the arrival of the first European explorers and grew up with the development of the Tahitian writing system. He mastered each of the new orthographies as they were tried out and wrote Tahitian much better than any of his mentors, and in a better calligraphy. The whole early missionary movement centered about his person, primarily because of his status, but also because of his intellectual and linguistic talents.

Unfortunately, but quite naturally, Orsmond could not reconcile Po-

---

[4] It is obvious from this brief indication that if one wanted to make a comparative study of this kind of custom, much work should be done with Samoan. The custom here described is almost exactly the same as Pi; there is another, perhaps relevant, feature of the Samoan language: the use of different vocabulary by chiefs and commoners. This (or something rather similar) is mentioned and illustrated for Tahitian by both Ahnne and Marau, but is a matter extraneous to my present purposes.

mare II's intellectual attainments with his moral depravity. In fact, even long after Pomare's death in 1821, Orsmond despised everything Tahitian except for the elocutionary language and perhaps to some extent the arts and crafts. However, it must be admitted that his opinion of his fellow missionaries and of the London Missionary Society was hardly any better.

Quite a few of the words which have been listed as changed through Pi were names of Pomare I. Ordinarily, after his death, the /tapu/ would gradually have lost its force, and to some extent did. But Pomare II had the very special opportunity of helping formulate a standard literary language for Tahitian and of providing it with a large and firm corpus of literature: parts of the Bible and legal codes in his time, which paved the way and set the standards for other religious and legal and literary works later on. Furthermore, quite a bit of epistolary correspondence in Tahitian was carried on at that time, especially with the missionaries, or in connection with missionary work; most of the writers were very careful, sometimes obsequiously so, to follow Pomare's language precepts. A few, notably one of Marau's ancestors, expressed their opposition to the Pomare takeover by verbal independence, even downright insolence.

There is one point which I have avoided covering because it is hard to do without extending my bibliography inordinately and without assuming facts not in evidence. This concerns how extensively the substitute vocabulary was accepted and how lasting acceptance was.

For our oft-cited example of /ruʻi/ for /poo/, "night," and /hota/ for /mare/, "cough," we have a fairly clear case. /hota/, "to cough," has been accepted generally from that day until this, and /mare/ is known to only a few specialists. There was simply no reason to object to the change: one word is as good as the other.

The /poo/ to /ruʻi/ shift had a very different fate. In the straightforward meaning of "night," /ruʻi/ was satisfactory enough and it is still very well known, although not used much colloquially, but only for church work or literary effect. It is spoken of as being "the real old word." /poo/ was a very loaded term, a basic term in the oral literature, which was learned by rote, as well as basic to Tahitian philosophical and religious thought: it was a cultural necessity and soon revived and has survived to the present time, perhaps a bit the worse for wear, but not much. It is the usual colloquial word for "night," now.

Another interesting example is /rua/ which was homonymous, meaning both "two" and "hole." I cannot document the reasons for its being tabooed, but that it was is obvious from textual occurrences. In the meaning of "two," /piti/ was substituted and in the meaning of "hole,"

/aapoʻo/. These are the regular colloquial words today, but /rua/ is well known, especially in the meaning of "two."

In this case, there was a rather unusual side effect: for a short period an attempt was made to eliminate the /rua/ from the second person dual pronoun /ʻoorua/; the substitute chosen was /ʻoopiti/ which would seem to show that the Tahitians were able to abstract the semantic duality here. That is, there was no coinage such as */ʻooaapoʻo/, which incidentally does occur in the meaning of "hole digging, hole digger." It is rather humorous to read letters written at the time in which the writers would very manfully start out using ʻoopiti, but soon slip and use ʻoorua, and then catch themselves and use ʻoopiti again. But ʻoorua seems to have been too basic to the grammar, and ʻoopiti is no longer even known.

The /vai/ to /pape/ shift is harder to follow and it is not at all clear to me just who King Vai was. If it was Vai-raʻa-toa (Pomare I) there is some enigma involved, because the /vai/ here does not mean "water," but "to exist, or be located," and /vai-raʻa/ means "location." This second /vai/ is still used and I find no evidence that it was ever changed. In the meaning of "water, body of water," /vai/ was of very frequent occurrence as part of place names, usually the first element. The shift to /pape/ seems to have been fairly complete, although perhaps not over the whole Tahitian-speaking area, and /vai/ is still well known. /vai/ is reputed to be Leeward Islander and /pape/ Windward Islander, but I think that there is a certain amount of myth involved in this.

It may seem that, for a linguist, I have been approaching my subject backwards, and that the normal procedure would be to furnish a list of words which were changed through Pi, and to show just which portions of the vocabulary were affected and in what way, and perhaps at what time. Instead of that, I seem to have set myself up as an ethnological and historical critic. It is quite true that I am not an antiquarian, and feel at home only with data which I can verify at first hand, *in vivo* and not *in vitro*, as it were. I have always left history to the historians and ethnology to the ethnologists. In the present instance, I had already prepared several studies of vocabulary variation and change in Tahitian and Tuamotuan and then became interested in the possibility of categorizing the kinds of changes and variations, such as: dialectal variants, stylistic variants, changes due to euphemistic tabooing, to slang substitution, or metaphor: and one of the major categories seemed to be onomastically induced substitutions. But although this type of change was postulated by various competent scholars, I could not find any first-hand accounts of concrete events, of what actually happened. I then searched what literature I could lay my hands on, the results of which I have presented.

I can but hope that the reader is less disappointed than I have been.

For word lists, I refer the reader to Ahnne, and to Marau's re-evaluation. Besides the Pi list, there is also a list of words which only royalty were allowed to use, along with the required substitutions for commoners.

In connection with the rather odd basic vocabulary in Tuamotuan, Bruce Biggs (1965, p. 377) says: "It has become something of a linguistic folktale that there is a mysterious non-Polynesian element in Tuamotuan." I feel that this term "linguistic folktale" is very apt, and very applicable to many of the stereotyped statements about Polynesian languages which pass as scholarship.

Myth is usually thought of as an aspect of primitive thinking which, while of anthropological and literary interest, was appropriate for our ancestors, but beneath our dignity. Actually the formulation of myth is a basic kind of human abstraction, as normal to human beings as singing, praying, dancing, talking, or hunting for lice. It is true that civilization and sophistication seem to dampen some of these activities, whether for better or worse, and with what results is not easy to say.

The line of investigation followed in this paper can, I feel, help point up some of the characteristics of different abstractional attitudes and "views of truth and adequate statement of fact."

For instance, Americans and Frenchmen (not to mention others) are, or have been, very "spelling bound." To spell a word correctly is to have accomplished something and to have stated a truth. For people of this ilk it was an act of scholarly value to inform the world that the word taboo (French, tabou) should be spelled with a "p" instead of a "b" because there is no "b" in Polynesian. And French scholars have never quite understood why Englishmen heard a "b" there in the first place. Now, from a phonemic point of view, the picture looks very different; there is no contrast between "b" and "p" in the type of Polynesian under consideration, so it makes little difference which symbol is used, provided it is not both of them. The English distinction between "b" and "p" was not and is not the same as for French "p" and "b," with the result that a Frenchman is much less likely to hear a Tahitian bilabial stop as "b" than an Englishman is; besides, by the time that the French became interested, Tahitian had had enough polyglot contact to become more or less aware of a "b"–"p" contrast, which may have had the effect of reducing the articulatory range of the bilabial stop in Tahitian.

The make-up of the preceding paragraph is rather mythical in itself, but I do not think that this necessarily makes it untrue, or without value. I have given two different pictures of truths or facts. The phonemic picture I find much more meaningful than the "literal" one, but they are both kinds of abstractions from a given reality, and other kinds of abstractions are possible. A strictly phonetic description would be quite different.

The scholar or the scientist in the field, the first-hand observer, is always beset by the same problem: Just what constitutes an adequate description? He has to use his own judgment. About the only thing of which he can be sure is that if he accepts any ad hoc model, set of rules, or theory of observation, it is very likely that ten years hence the learned world will find his description of little value.

On the other hand, if he relates everything about that aspect of the world which is his particular interest in terms of his own evaluation of importance, future scholars will very likely be able to interpret it to their heart's desire, and his work may have a lasting interest.

Nevertheless, it seems to me that a basic aim of human endeavor should be the solution of this problem, and that the only way to do so is to increase and objectify human awareness of human nature. My purpose here has been to provide a few small insights.

LITERATURE CITED

AHNNE, EDOUARD
　　1926. "De la Coutume du 'Pii' et des Modifications qu'elle Apporta au Vocabulaire Tahitien." *Bull. Soc. Études Océaniennes,* No. 11, pp. 6-10.
　　1931. "La Coutume du 'Pii' en Polynesie et le 'Fady' de Madagascar." *Bull. Soc. Études Océaniennes*, No. 40, 4(6):181-182.

BIGGS, BRUCE
　　1965. Review of *A Dictionary of Some Tuamotuan Dialects of the Language* by J. Frank Stimson with the collaboration of Donald S. Marshall. *J. Polynesian Soc.* **74**:375-378.
　　1966. Notes and News in *J. Polynesian Soc.* **75**:3-5.

[DAVIES, JOHN]
　　1851. *A Tahitian and English Dictionary, with Introductory Remarks on the Polynesian Language, and a Short Grammar of the Tahitian Dialect.* Tahiti: London Missionary Soc. Press.

ELBERT, SAMUEL H.
　　1953. "Internal Relationships of Polynesian Languages and Dialects." *Southwestern J. Anthropology* **9**:147-173.

EMORY, KENNETH P.
　　1965. *Kapingamarangi: Social and Religious Life of a Polynesian Atoll.* B. P. Bishop Mus. Bull. 228. Honolulu.

FIRTH, RAYMOND
  1939. *Primitive Polynesian Economy*. London: Routledge.
HENRY, TEUIRA
  1928. *Ancient Tahiti*. B. P. Bishop Mus. Bull. 48. Honolulu.
JAUSSEN, TEPANO
  1898. *Grammaire et Dictionnaire de la Langue Maorie: Dialecte Tahitien*. Paris. (No publisher.) Reprinted in 1949. Paris: Braine-le-Compte.
MARSACK, C. C.
  1962. *Teach Yourself Samoan*. London: English Univ. Press.
ORSMOND, JOHN MUGGRIDGE
  [n.d.] Reception of the Gospel. Typescript copy at the Australian National University in Canberra.
SALMON, MARAU TAAROA (MARAU I TAHITI)
  1927. "Notes et Commentaires sur le *Pii*. Attributs Royaux, etc., etc." *Bull. Soc. d'Études Océaniennes* **20**:260-271.
SAVAGE, STEPHEN
  1962. *A Dictionary of the Maori Language of Rarotonga*. Wellington: Dept. of Island Territories.
VERNIER, CHARLES
  1948. "Les Variations du Vocabulaire Tahitien avant et après les Contacts Europeens." *J. Soc. Oceanistes* **4**:57-85.

ARCHAEOLOGY

ARTIFACTS FROM EXCAVATED SITES IN THE HAWAIIAN, MARQUESAS, AND SOCIETY ISLANDS

A COMPARATIVE STUDY

YOSIHIKO H. SINOTO*

Bernice P. Bishop Museum, Honolulu

THIS PAPER will attempt to interpret some of the results of fourteen years of archaeological fieldwork in the Hawaiian, Society, and Marquesas Islands, utilizing fishhooks excavated from stratified sites in all three island groups.[1] In Eastern Polynesia we are fortunate to have sites containing the widest variety of fishhooks and fishing gear of the entire Pacific island area. The first attempt at stratigraphic analysis and cross-dating between sites was based on a fishhook typology developed after a detailed study of over 3,500 fishhooks, which had been recovered from excavated sites throughout the Hawaiian Islands (Emory, Bonk, and Sinoto, 1959, pp. 7-13). Since that time the typology has been modified to provide for the analysis of head types (Sinoto, 1962), and also for additional fishhook forms found in the Marquesas (Sinoto and Kellum, 1965b, pp. 16-20) and Society Islands (Emory and Sinoto, 1965).

For the purposes of the present analysis, I shall discuss fishhooks recovered from three sites on the Island of Hawaii (H1 Sand Dune, H2 and H8 Cave Shelter sites), one site on Uahuka, Marquesas Islands (MUH1 Hane Dune site excavation, 1964), and one site in the Society Islands (M5, Afareaitu village site).

---

* My coming into the field of Polynesian archaeology was purely accidental. My great debt to Dr. Emory, accumulated ever since, can never be repaid by all that I am able to accomplish in my lifetime.

[1] Until recently pottery was unknown in Polynesia (Golson, 1957; Suggs, 1961; Sinoto and Kellum, 1965b; Green, in press; Emory and Sinoto, 1965). In Eastern Polynesia pottery has still not been found in sufficient quantity to be utilized in any detailed stratigraphic analysis.

TABLE 1

NUMBERS OF FISHHOOKS EXCAVATED FROM SELECTED SITES

	ONE-PIECE HOOKS	TWO-PIECE HOOKS	TROLLING HOOKS SHANK	TROLLING HOOKS POINT
Hawaiian Islands				
Hawaii: H1 Sand Dune site	1,101	582	8	16
H8 Cave Shelter site	560	462	3	4
H2 Cave Shelter site	250	160	2	4
Marquesas Islands				
Uahuka: MUH1 Hane Sand Dune 1964	780	—	47	21
Society Islands				
Moorea: M5 Afareaitu village site	59	—	2	2
TOTALS	2,750	1,204	62	47

HAWAIIAN ISLANDS SITES

The three Hawaiian sites are located at the southernmost tip of the Hawaiian Island chain, on the Island of Hawaii. H1 Sand Dune site overlooks a productive offshore fishing ground where ocean currents meet at land's end. From the point, the long slope of Mauna Loa, the largest volcano on the island, stretches upward through verdant rolling foothills, mountain forests, and, finally, barren lava fields to the summit. Everywhere there is evidence of past and recent volcanic activity. The southernmost point of land is in reality only half a point; part of it has dropped away, leaving a great cliff on its leeward side, and a large, protected bay. Even where the low-lying shore line resumes, the cliff, some 500 to 700 feet high, continues inland, producing a natural boundary between the high, verdant, soil-rich land at the top of the cliff and the low, dry, barren, lava-covered land below the cliff. It is here, at the base of the cliff, where H8 Cave Shelter site is found. Here, too, is a natural, protected landing site for Hawaiian canoes, which were safely beached and left while the occupants continued their way on foot to the windward parts of the island. In this way they avoided the miseries of sailing or paddling against the wind. H2 Cave Shelter, a large open lava tube, is located three-quarters of a mile inland from H1 (Fig. 1).

Both H1 and H8 sites were occupied by fishermen and probably H1 was a workshop where fishing gear was prepared. H2, located farther inland, was less extensively used for fishhook making by fishermen.

FIGURE 1.—An aerial view of Kalae, the south point of Hawaii, with the great fault, Kulani Pali, at the left and Mauna Loa in the background. Three important sites are in this area: H8, at the foot of Kulani Pali between the lava flow and the sea; H1, a sand dune next to the sea and to the right of Kalae; and H2, a shelter about half a mile inland from H1. Photo by Robert Wenkam.

MARQUESAS ISLANDS SITES

Hane site (MUH1) is located on a large sand dune at the mouth of the Hane Valley on the southern coast of Uahuka Island. It contains three successive paved occupation floors. Its cultural contents indicate that the site was one of the earliest settlement period dwelling sites in the Marquesas (Fig. 2) (Sinoto and Kellum, 1965b, p. 14).

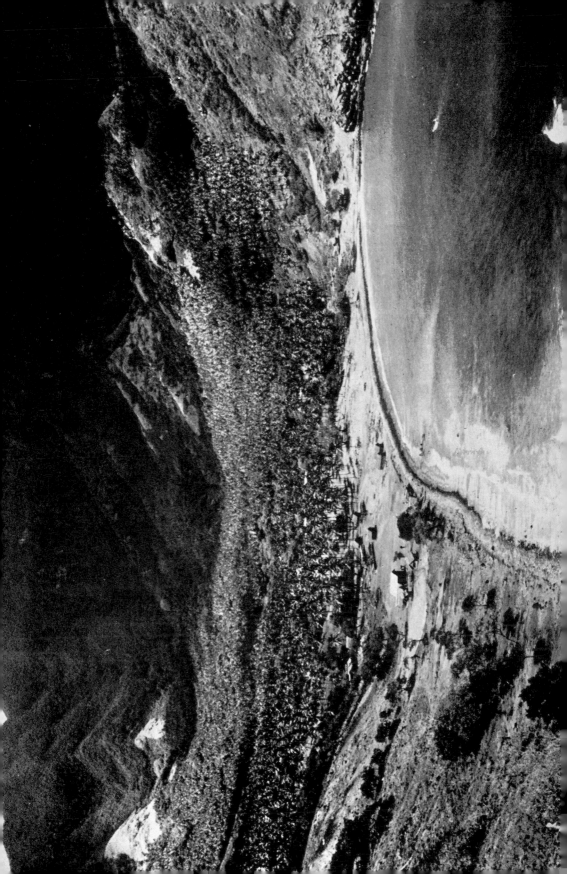

SOCIETY ISLANDS SITES

Afareaitu site (M5) is located on the west coast of Moorea and the area was known as a fishermen's village. The complex included a number of house sites and *maraes,* and excavation produced fishhooks as well as fishhook manufacturing tools. The site is one of two excavated coastal sites in the Society Islands (Fig. 3). The other is Papetoai, Moorea, excavated by Green in 1960 (in press). These two sites represent Tahitian culture immediately prior to Western contact. This has been determined by radiocarbon dates (Green and Davidson, 1962; Emory and Sinoto, 1965).

DISCUSSION

A cultural sequence based on fishhooks excavated from the stratified Hawaiian sites was established by Emory, Bonk, and Sinoto in 1959. It was discovered at that time that changes in fishhook forms and structural features, such as barbs and the lashing devices at the base of two-piece hooks, reflected chronological differences. Later, Green (1960) demonstrated the usefulness of this classification in analyzing his Mangarevan fishhooks. In that study he pointed out that the changing of line-lashing devices of the shank heads was the most useful and one of the most important elements in his fishhook chronology. This was confirmed by a restudy of Hawaiian fishhook head types (Sinoto, 1962) and its wide applicability for Polynesian and other Oceanic fishhooks was revealed. For Hawaiian fishhooks, the chronological characteristics are more distinct in the two-piece hooks. However, two-piece hooks have not yet been found from Central Polynesia, and any analysis must be based exclusively on one-piece hooks found in these areas. The restudy also demonstrated changes in the head-lashing devices of Hawaiian two-piece hooks. These changes parallel the changes in the one-piece hook head-lashing devices.

Changes in the typological and structural features of fishhooks are readily observable within an island group, but the ratio between point and shank heights, the materials used, the types of manufacturing tools, and the manufacturing methods are the distinctive elements observable between the island groups.

Only one-piece and trolling hooks are discussed in this paper,

---

Figure 2.—(Opposite) Hane Bay, Uahuka, Marquesas Islands, October 1963. The sand dune of site MUH1 is in the center of the photograph, where the trees begin, back from the water's edge.

because, among the three island groups considered, two-piece hooks were found only in Hawaii. One-piece hooks were made in a single piece, but two-piece hooks were made by lashing together a point and a shank at their bases. Trolling hooks, commonly called bonito-lure hooks, consist of a lure shank, a point, and chicken feathers or pig bristles lashed to the base. Two-piece hooks were developed in the fringe areas of East Polynesia; that is, Hawaii, Easter Island, and New Zealand. How the two-piece hooks developed in these areas is another subject and should be discussed separately. However, the significant point to be mentioned here is that the earliest Hawaiian two-piece hooks of the notched type (Emory, Bonk, and Sinoto, 1959, Fig. 4 and Pl. 2), found in H1 Sand Dune site and at the lowest level of H8 Cave Shelter site, were already well developed in form and they represented 40 percent of the fishhooks found in the two sites. These facts suggest two possibilities. One is that the two-piece hook form was introduced in this developed stage from another Polynesian area outside of Hawaii. Because no two-piece hooks have been reported from Central Polynesia, this first explanation has no evidence to support it. The other possibility is that it is a local innovation. If this proves to be the case, then there should be sites older than H1 and H8 elsewhere in the Hawaiian Islands and such sites should yield relatively fewer two-piece hooks, which should also be found in their incipient forms. This postulation of the existence of older sites is supported by the presence of barbs on one- and two-piece hooks in Hawaii because no barbed one- or two-piece hooks are found in Central Polynesia. The presence of a large number of Hawaiian fishhooks with head type HT1a, which gradually replaced HT1b, also suggests the existence of older sites in Hawaii (Sinoto, 1962, p. 163, Fig. 1). It is this head type, HT1a, which also is well represented in the early Marquesan fishhooks.

MATERIALS OF FISHHOOKS

Basically, Polynesians used pearl shell if it was available. The use of bone and other material is observed in the marginal areas of Polynesia; Hawaii, Easter Island, and New Zealand are good examples.

In Hawaii human bones were used most extensively. Dog and pig bones were used, but much less frequently. Pearl shells were used in-

---

FIGURE 3.—(Opposite) Excavation at site M5, Afareaitu, Moorea, Leeward Society Islands, 1962. [Neg. TR60-8]

frequently, except on Oahu and Kauai. This probably is related to the presence or absence of pearl shells in the waters around the islands.

In much smaller quantity, fish and bird bones, turtle shell, dog and whale teeth, cowrie shells, and wood were used. Presumably wooden shanks for the slender two-piece hooks were much in use, but, while some have been recovered archaeologically, most of them have disintegrated.

In the Marquesas bone hooks were found only in the lower levels of the Hane site. The rest are all pearl-shell hooks. The material of the Marquesas bone hooks is porpoise bone. After we discovered this, a re-examination of Hawaiian hooks revealed that some of the early ones are also made from porpoise bone. The material of Society Island hooks is mostly pearl shell, but excavations revealed that turbo shell was also used. Because of the small size of turbo shells, these hooks are small. At the Afareaitu site (M5) on Moorea Island, half of the hooks found were of turbo shell.

Some of the small trolling hook shanks are made from conus shell.

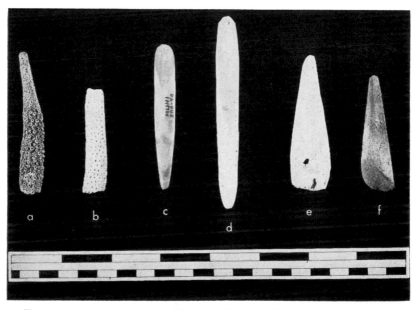

FIGURE 4.—*Acropora* coral files; *a,* Afareaitu M5 site, Society Islands, *b,* Huahine surface collection, Society Islands. Sea-urchin files; *c,* Hane MUH1 site, Marquesas, *d,* H1 site, Hawaiian Islands. *Porites* coral files; *e,* Hane MUH1 site, Marquesas, *f,* K3 site, Hawaiian Islands.

FISHHOOK MANUFACTURING TOOLS

Tools for making or reshaping fishhooks were recovered in great quantities from the Hawaiian sites. In the Marquesas they were found in much smaller quantities. There have been very few recovered from Society Island sites. Manufacturing implements are of three types, according to their function; cutting, filing, and drilling.

Tools were made of several types of material.

1. *Coral (Porites) saws,* oblong or oblong-triangular in shape. One edge is thinner than the other so that they are, to various degrees, triangular in cross section.

2. *Porous lava saws* with shapes similar to the coral saws.

3. *Stone flake saws.* Any stone flake with a sharp edge or edges was used as a saw.

4. *Coral files.* It is sometimes difficult to distinguish between saws and files, but generally files have sharper points with round or flat-triangular cross sections (Fig. 4, *e, f*).

5. *Spines of sea-urchin (Heterocentrotus mammillatus) files.* Predominantly the base end of the spines was used in filing, so that diago-

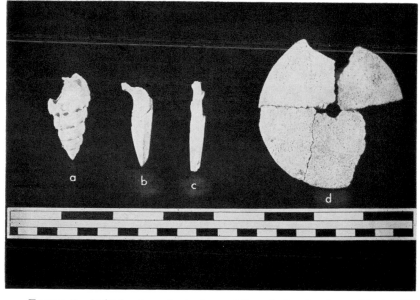

FIGURE 5.—Drill heads and whorls; *a, Mitra* shell point from H1 site, Hawaiian Islands, *b, Cymatiidae* shell point, H8 site, Hawaiian Islands, *c, Latirus* shell point, H8 site, Hawaiian Islands, *d,* coral pump-drill whorl, H1 site, Hawaiian Islands.

nally worn, thin facets result. The use to which a file is put determines the resulting shape of the file (Fig. 4, *c, d*). (See Emory, Bonk, and Sinoto, 1959, Pl. 6, Nos. 15–27.)

6. *Branch coral files*. Pieces of branches from *Acropora* coral were used to file fishhooks (Fig. 4, *a, b*).

7. *Chipping hammer*. In the preparation of chipped fishhook blanks, some as yet unknown object functioned as a hammer. From the Marquesas there are quite a number of chipped pearl-shell fishhook blanks, but no classifiable hammers known to have been used for this purpose. Probably some of the thin dyke stones were used in this manner. The only known examples of chipping hammers were made of *Cassis* shell and were found on Napuka Island in the Tuamotu archipelago (Sinoto and Kellum, 1965b).

8. *Pump drills*. These were used to drill holes, in the process of making the finished product from a fishhook blank. Drill points were made from the axis of the knobby spindle shell (Fig. 5, *b, c*), whole *Mitra* shell (Fig. 5, *a*), or obsidian.

Coral whorls used as weights on the pump drills were found from Hawaiian sites (Fig. 5, *d*). From ethnological collections it is known that wooden whorls were also used. The bows probably have disintegrated along with the other wooden parts of drills.

TABLE 2

	CORAL SAW	LAVA SAW	STONE FLAKE SAW	CORAL FILES	SPINE FILES	BRANCH CORAL FILES	DRILLS	PEARL SHELL HOOKS	BONE HOOKS
Hawaii	x	x	x	x	x		x	–	x
Society	–		x	–	–	x		x	
Marquesas	x		x	x	x			x	–

x = predominant
– = a few examples

Drilling tools have thus far been found archaeologically only in Hawaii. Pump drills were used in historical times in the Society Islands, but no archaeological specimens have been recovered. Probably some type of drill was also used in the Marquesas, because the drilling method of manufacturing hooks was extensively used in both the Marquesas and Society Islands. Sea-urchin spine files were predominantly used in Hawaii, but to a lesser extent and only in the early culture of the Marquesas. The choice of file material suggests a cultural relation similar to that exhibited in the fishhooks of the two areas.

Branch-coral files were found only in the Society Islands. There is a correlation between files of different materials and the materials used for making fishhooks. My own experiments showed branch-coral files to be more efficient than *Porites* files when used on pearl shell. In Mangareva only branch-coral files were used and only pearl-shell hooks were found (Green, 1960). In the Marquesas and Hawaii, pearl-shell hooks were made with the use of *Porites* files. There are two possible reasons for this: (a) in both areas the use of the traditional *Porites* coral files, which worked efficiently on bone material, was extended to hooks made of pearl shell; (b) in Marquesan and Hawaiian waters the relative scarcity of branch coral affected its use. It would seem that the former reason is more likely than the latter, because branch corals actually grow in the waters surrounding both groups, but much less extensively near the Marquesas and Hawaii than in the Society Islands.

The few spine files found in the Society Islands suggest that they were used on bone artifacts, such as human bone chisels, rather than on fishhooks.

MANUFACTURING METHODS

Preparation of hook tabs.—Manufacturing methods described here are the processes which take place after the preparation of the tabs. Tabs cut from bone or pearl shell are usually rectangular in form and are of various sizes. The cutting was done by sawing the raw material with coral, lava, or stone-flake saws (see Manufacturing Tools). In the next stage, both the inside and outside of the rectangular bone tab were ground flat. Among Hawaiian collections there are fishhooks that have retained the original curvature of the bone. Only the interior surface of the bone was ground to eliminate the spongy portions, and the exterior surface was left untouched.

The preparation of pearl-shell tabs involved a similar process. At first the exterior laminate of the entire shell was ground off with *Porites* coral files or rough grinding stones. Then tabs of various sizes were cut out with coral or stone-flake saws. Each side was cut halfway through and the weakened shell between the cuts was easily broken. This process of grinding the exterior of the pearl shells was employed in the Hawaiian, Society, Marquesas, and Tuamotu Islands. Shells were partially ground in Mangareva (Green, 1960).

It appears that the Marquesans ground the exterior very carefully and well, in comparison with other areas. The rectangular perforated shell tabs reported from Nukuhiva sites as probable ornaments, and those without perforation reported as shell plaques (Suggs, 1961, p. 134, Fig. 35, *b*, *c*), are most likely fishhook blanks.

In the case of turbo-shell tabs, the exterior laminate is taken off by repeated striking, until the iridescent inner shell shows through. Turbo-shell fishhooks always retain the curvature of the shell.

1. *Simple drilling method.*—The outside edge of a rectangular tab of bone or pearl shell was filed to form the rough outline of a hook (Fig. 6, *c*). A hole was then drilled in the center of the tab and a notch filed from the outside edge at the upper corner. This separated the point from the head of the shank (Fig. 6, *d*). This method was used in the manufacture of rotating hooks.

2. *Double drilling method.*—Two holes were drilled in the tab in the manufacture of inner and shank barbed hooks of either jabbing or rotating types (Fig. 6, *e*, *f*).

3. *Filing and notching method.*—A deep notch was cut straight or diagonally into the prepared tab from the top edge. Then the notch was enlarged to form the point and the shank. This method was used to make jabbing hooks (Fig. 6, *a*, *b*).

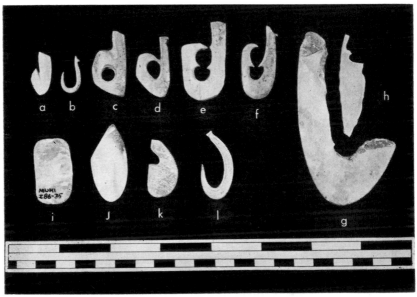

FIGURE 6.—Manufacturing methods. *a*, *b*, filing and notching (*a*, H14 site, Hawaiian Islands, *b*, H8 site, Hawaiian Islands); *c*, *d*, drilling (H51 site, Hawaiian Islands); *e*, *f*, double drilling (*e*, H101 site, *f*, H51 site, Hawaiian Islands); *g*, filing-out, hook, bend, and shank (Tuamotus); *h*, filing-out, inner reject (Tuamotus); *i-l*, filing and notching (Hane MUH1 site, Marquesas).

4. *Chipping and filing method.*—To make hook blanks, both direct and indirect chipping methods were applied. The center of the tab was chipped and worked with a coral or stone file (Sinoto and Kellum, 1965a, p. 147).

5. *Drilling-out method.*—This method was not only applied to drilling the core of the blanks, but also to cutting out the blank tab itself from the larger piece of bone. After the outline of a hook was made by filing the outer edge, the inside of the blank was drilled following the shape of the outer edge. A series of half-drilled holes on one side was matched by half-drilled holes from the other side. The center, inner piece was then broken out. The jagged inner edge was filed smooth to form the inner edge of the point and shank.

6. *Filing-out method.*—In this method the outer edge of a hook was filed or chipped. Filing from the outer edge into the blank to form the inner curvature of the hook was done with branch-coral files (Fig. 6, filed between *g* and *h*). Finally, the inner piece (Fig. 6, *h*) was filed away from the point and discarded (Sinoto and Kellum, 1965a, pp. 147-148).

TABLE 3

	FILING AND NOTCHING	SIMPLE DRILLING	DOUBLE DRILLING	CHIPPING AND NOTCHING	DRILLING-OUT	FILING-OUT
Hawaii	x	x	x			
Society	x	x				–
Marquesas		x		x	–	–

x = predominant
– = a few examples

As Table 3 indicates, the simple drilling method of fishhook manufacture was common in the island groups, but the filing and notching methods were used only in Hawaii and the Society Islands. The double drilling method was used only in Hawaii. Since this was the method used to make barbed hooks, it was not used in the areas where no barbed hooks were found. The drilling-out method was most commonly used in the Moa-Hunter period in New Zealand (Duff, 1956). The filing-out method was popular in the western Tuamotus. Neither of these methods was prevalent in the Marquesas and Society Islands. However, the evidence of the use of both methods in the two island groups indicates some historical relationship between the Marquesas and Tahiti, and Tahiti and New Zealand.

Size and ratio of point and shank heights of one-piece hooks.—The size of one-piece fishhooks is usually indicated by the length of the shank. When we compare the sizes of one-piece hooks from the three island groups, with the exception of those in the ethnological collections, they fall more or less within the same general range. Archaeological collections of Tuamotu and Mangarevan pearl-shell hooks and New Zealand whale-bone and moa-bone hooks are much larger. A significant point is the ratio between point height and shank height. If a hook has a shank height of 20 millimeters and a point height of 10 millimeters, its ratio is 2. (See Table 4.)

TABLE 4

	Jabbing Hook	Rotating Hook
Hawaii	1.65	1.46
Society	1.41	1.36
Marquesas	1.95	1.43

When the ratios of shank to point heights of the unbarbed hooks from the three island groups are compared, the rotating hooks have higher points than the jabbing hooks in all areas. In general, Central Polynesian hooks have a tendency toward longer points and the Mangarevan hook points are even higher than the shanks.

An analysis of the total collection of jabbing and rotating hooks from the three areas reveals a different shank-to-point ratio for each island group. If we divide the Hawaiian collection into stratified cultural levels, and for the purpose of analysis use the unbarbed jabbing hooks, the shank-to-point ratio displays a tendency to increase in the lower and upper levels, and decrease in the middle levels. (See Table 5.)

TABLE 5

Hawaii			Marquesas Hane Site	Society
H 2		1.80		
H 8	2-1	1.90	Upper Levels	Late Period
	I-2	1.62	2.13	1.41
	II	1.63		
			(Middle Levels)	(Middle Period)
H 1	I-u	1.60		
	I-1	1.45	1.92	Early Period
	II-u	1.76	Lower Levels	(Maupiti) 1.78
	II-1	1.80		

In Table 5, the reliability of the data is not very high, especially for the Society Islands, because the early level is represented only by a single hook. However, the general conclusion to be drawn from these data is that these ratios may be fairly close to the mean. Early Marquesan characteristics, and later characteristics from the Society Islands are revealed in Table 5. However, after a period of isolation each island group developed its own characteristic types of fishhook.

Barbed hooks.—Barbs on fishhooks are characteristic of the fringe areas of Polynesia. There have been, so far, no barbed hooks found in Central Polynesia.

Anell (1955, p. 118) pointed out that where the hooks are entirely or most frequently made of pearl shell, the barb is quite unknown. It would appear that it was very difficult to carve out barbs on shell hooks, presumably because this material was brittler than bone and turtle shell. Green (1960, p. 2) stated that this would account for the absence of barbs on Mangarevan pearl-shell fishhooks. However, in Hawaii the situation is quite different, although the use of pearl shell in Hawaii was not common. The proportion of the bone and pearl-shell hooks in H1 is 86 percent bone and 13 percent pearl shell. In the relatively later occupied site of H2, the proportion is 92 percent bone and

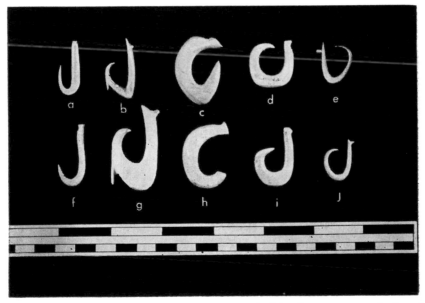

FIGURE 7.—One-piece hooks. All are pearl-shell hooks except *c, g, h, i,* and *j,* which are bone. *a, c, d, f,* Hane MUH1 site, Marquesas; *e,* Borabora surface collection, Society Islands; *b, g,* K3 site, Hawaiian Islands; *h, i, j,* from H8, H1, and H51 sites, respectively, Hawaiian Islands.

3 percent pearl shell. The proportion of bone and pearl-shell hooks thus has a chronological differentiation. There is also a geographic difference in the relative proportion of hooks made from these two materials. The use of bone decreases gradually in sites on the islands that are toward the northern end of the chain, while the use of pearl shell increases. At sites on the Island of Kauai, K1 and K3, the proportion shows 37 percent bone, 61 percent pearl shell, and 2 percent other materials. If the K3 site is considered alone, the difference in the proportion becomes greater; 30 percent are bone, and 68 percent pearl shell. The occurrence of barbs among the bone hooks in H1 site is 15 percent, and among the pearl-shell hooks is 7 percent.

In the K3 site, 22 percent of the bone (Fig. 7, g) and 7 percent of the pearl-shell hooks are barbed (Fig. 7, b). When we take into consideration all the Hawaiian hooks obtained by excavations, 21 percent are bone and 6 percent are pearl shell. These figures indicate that the occurrence of barbs on pearl-shell hooks is constant, regardless of the scarcity or availability of the material. The same is true for bone hooks. Based on this Hawaiian evidence, it would seem that the occurrence of barbs cannot be accounted for by the materials alone. There is also a cultural factor involved.

Head types.—The line-lashing devices at the head of the shanks are also significant in fishhook chronology and reveal observable characteristics for each island group. The original classification of the head types of Hawaiian fishhooks by Sinoto (1962) has been revised by the additional materials analyzed since then by Soehren and Sinoto (1966, Appendix B).

A tentative classification of head types of the Marquesas and the Society Islands fishhooks has been set up by Sinoto. They have greater variety than the Hawaiian hooks and are classified into eleven main types, with between two and seven types for each area. Some of the Marquesan fishhook head types are very distinctive and characteristic of fishhooks of a particular stratigraphic level. One good example is a one-piece jabbing hook of type IA(1)1 and IA(1)2 (Sinoto and Kellum, 1965b). This type is characterized by a thick, round, straight shank and a parallel thin, sharp, straight point, connected by a U-shaped bend. The line-lashing device of this hook consists of one or two horizontal grooves around and just below the top of the shank (Fig. 7, a). IA(1)2 hooks have a parallel point and shank of similar thickness connected by a U-shaped bend. The shank head is blunt, without the usual flare, and has a notch on the inner side of the shank just below the top for lashing the line to the hook (Fig. 7, f). IA(1)1 type has so far been found only in the lower levels of Hane site, but IA(1)2 type was found in the upper levels of Hane, in two other sites on Uahuka, in two sites on Nukuhiva, and in one site from Hivaoa. On the basis of radiocarbon dates (Sinoto and Kellum, 1965b), by the 14th century the IA(1)2 type of hooks had spread throughout both the northern and southern Marquesas groups. Hawaiian head types of the HT1a form were common in the bottom layer of H1 site. The early Marquesan bone fishhooks have the same type of heads (Fig. 7, c, d, h, i). However, early Marquesan pearl-shell hooks have the HT6 head type, which has not yet been found in Hawaii, but which is the type on the head of the only hook recovered in the surface collection at the site of the Maupiti burials (Emory and Sinoto, 1964, p. 151). It is this type of fishhook that was common in the Moa-Hunter period in New Zealand. The most common head type, HT4 of Hawaii, rapidly increased in the later period and the type was introduced among the later Tahitian hook head types (Fig. 7, e, j).

Trolling hooks.—The common uses of trolling hooks include catching bonitos, in Polynesia as well as in other parts of Oceania. Small shanks made of conus shell have been found in the Society Islands and at H1 site, Hawaii. However, what type of point was suitable for use with these shanks has not been established, especially for those of the Society Islands. Use of such small trolling hooks is seen among the Solomon Islanders, and thus their existence in Polynesia is not unlikely.

Pearl-shell lure shanks.—There are three types of lure shanks in the three island groups. (1) Shanks with sharp snood shoulders and flattened or blunt head ends (Fig. 8, a, and Emory and Sinoto, 1964, Fig. 5, a); (2) Shanks with slender shoulders and pointed head ends (Fig. 8, b); (3) Flat shanks with sharp shoulders without snood bulging. The line-lashing hole is ventrodorsal (Fig. 8, c), but the other two types have horizontal holes near the snoods.

The most common type of shank has slender shoulders. The flat shank is rare. Two examples were found in lower levels at the Hane site. Green found a similar shank made of pearl shell from the North Island of New Zealand (personal communication). Sharp-shouldered shanks were noticed for the first time in those from the Maupiti burials. More examples were later recovered from the Hane excavations and Maupiti finds. Based on the Hane stratification, the sharp-shouldered shanks and flat shanks are early types, and the slender-shouldered shanks are later in all three island groups.

As for point-lashing devices, the early types may be plain, or may have one pair of side notches, a groove across the back, or both. They may also have a V-shaped vertical groove on the back at the distal end.

The slender-shouldered, later type of shanks have multiple side grooves and vertical grooves on the back (Sinoto and Kellum, 1965b, p. 19).

Points.—Trolling-hook points are made of pearl or turtle shell, and bone. There are three major types: (1) Point with base proximal extension with two holes, the so-called Western Polynesian type (Fig. 8, *d-f*); (2) Point with distal extension with or without one or two holes (Fig. 8, *i, j*); (3) Point with no base extension (Fig. 8, *g, h*).

The points with base proximal extension have been found in the early sites in Hawaii (H1, for example), the Marquesas (Hane lower levels), the Maupiti burials, and the Wairau-Bar site in New Zealand (Duff, 1956, p. 204). There is slight variation in general form, except at the top end of the proximal base extension. Those with either knobbed or concave ends (Fig. 8, *f*) seem to be older forms than the blunt-ended ones. This type of point is always associated with a sharp-shouldered shank. This is most distinctive in points from the Hane and Maupiti sites. There are possibilities of survival of this type in later periods (from Papetoai site, excavated by Green, and from Haatuatua site, excavated by Suggs).

The points with distal extension vary among island groups in being with or without base knob or holes. Points with no base extension were found in Hawaii only. Two examples found in H1 site have inner barbs (Fig. 8, *g*).

TABLE 6

TROLLING HOOK POINTS	HAWAII	SOCIETY	MARQUESAS	
No base extension, without barb	x			
Base distal extension		x	x	Late
No base extension, with or without barb	x			
Base proximal extension	–	–	x	Early

x = predominant
– = a few examples

By the time points with distal extensions were made, the shanks had all been changed to the slender-shouldered type.

Although the point with base proximal extension has been called the Western Polynesian type (all the ethnological collections from both the areas are of this type), no archaeological finds have so far been reported. However, it should be noted here that the Tongan, Samoan, and Tikopian

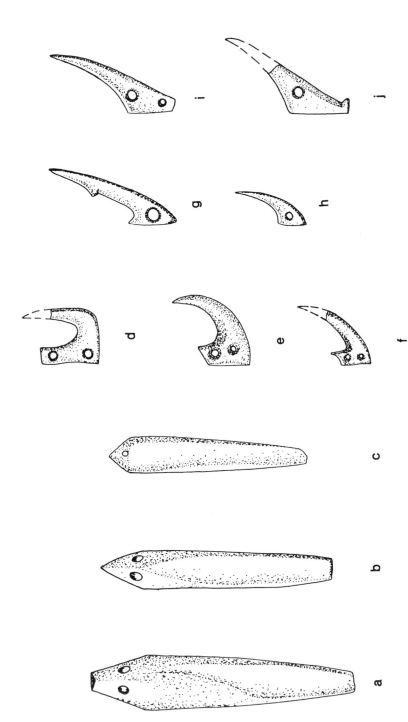

FIGURE 8.—Trolling hook shanks and points. Shanks, *a-c*, Hane MUH1 site, Marquesas. Points, *d-f*, Hane, MUH1 site, Marquesas; *g-h*, H1 site, Hawaiian Islands; *i*, Borabora, Society Islands; *j*, Hane, MUH1 site, Marquesas. (Drawing by William K. Kikuchi.)

ethnological trolling hook points have concave tops at the end of the base extensions.

SUMMARY

As described and demonstrated above, not only fishhook forms or structural features, but also the materials, tools, and methods of manufacture indicate the period and place of manufacture in the selected three island groups.

A postulated East Polynesian migration pattern is mainly based on fishhook studies, supplemented by other items of material culture (Emory and Sinoto, 1965; Sinoto, in press).

Establishing a relative chronology based on stratigraphically documented artifacts in Polynesia is far more important than reliance upon radiocarbon dating. Fishhooks and related artifacts are among the basic sources available in East Polynesia. The curious lack of such materials from West Polynesia makes comparative study difficult. A study of adzes, however, in both West and East Polynesia is another important source for establishing relative chronology. There are obvious gaps in the prehistory of each island group. Future investigations should fill these gaps.

LITERATURE CITED

ANELL, BENGT
    1955. *Contribution to the History of Fishing in the Southern Seas.* Studia Ethnographica Upsaliensia. IX. Uppsala.
DUFF, ROGER
    1956. *The Moa-Hunter Period of Maori Culture.* Canterbury Mus. Bull. 1 Wellington.
EMORY, KENNETH P.
    1962. "Additional Radiocarbon Dates from Hawaii and the Society Islands." *J. Polynesian Soc.* 71(1):105-106.
EMORY, K. P., and Y. H. SINOTO
    1964. "Eastern Polynesian Burials at Maupiti." *J. Polynesian Soc.* 73(2): 143-160.
    1965. Preliminary Report on the Archaeological Investigations in Polynesia: Field Work in the Society and Tuamotu Islands, French Polynesia, and American Samoa, in 1962, 1963, 1964. B. P. Bishop Mus. Polynesian Archaeological Program. Prepared for National Science Foundation. Honolulu. (Mimeographed.)
EMORY, K. P., W. J. BONK, and Y. H. SINOTO
    1959. *Hawaiian Archaeology: Fishhooks.* B. P. Bishop Mus. Spec. Pub. 47. Honolulu.

GOLSON, JACK
    1957. Report to Tri-Institutional Pacific Program on Archaeological Field-
    work in Tonga and Samoa, August to October, 1957. Univ. Auckland,
    New Zealand. (Mimeographed.)
GREEN, ROGER
    1960. Archaeological Excavations in Mangareva. Manuscript, American
    Mus. Natural History. (Typescript of chapter, "Mangarevan Fish-
    hooks," in Bishop Mus. Anthropology Dept.)
    1961. Moorea Archaeology: A Preliminary Report. Manuscript. (Copy in
    Bishop Mus. Anthropology Dept.)
    In press. "West Polynesian Prehistory." In I. YAWATA and Y. H. SINOTO
    (editors), *Prehistoric Culture in Oceania: Symposium Presented at the
    Eleventh Pacific Science Congress.* Honolulu: Bishop Mus. Press.
    (Paper read at the Congress, Tokyo, September, 1966.)
GREEN, ROGER, and J. M. DAVIDSON
    1962. A Preliminary Report of Investigations Carried Out on the Island of
    Moorea, French Polynesia, by the American Museum of Natural
    History from December 19, 1961, to March 1, 1962.
SINOTO, Y. H.
    1962. "Chronology of Hawaiian Fishhooks." *J. Polynesian Soc.* 71(2):162-
    166.
    In press. "Position of the Marquesas Islands in East Polynesian Prehistory."
    In I. YAWATA and Y. H. SINOTO (editors), *Prehistoric Culture in
    Oceania: Symposium Presented at the Eleventh Pacific Science Con-
    gress.* Honolulu: Bishop Mus. Press. (Paper read at the Congress,
    Tokyo, September, 1966.)
SINOTO, Y. H., and M. J. KELLUM
    1965a. "Hameçons Récoltés aux Tuamotu Occidentales." *J. Soc. Océanistes*
    21(21):145-149.
    1965b. Preliminary Report on Excavations in the Marquesas Islands, French
    Polynesia. B. P. Bishop Mus. Polynesian Archaeological Program.
    Prepared for National Science Foundation. Honolulu. (Mime-
    ographed.)
SOEHREN, LLOYD J., and Y. H. SINOTO
    1966. Hawaii Excavations, 1965. Preliminary Report Prepared for the Na-
    tional Science Foundation. B. P. Bishop Mus., Honolulu. (Mime-
    ographed.)
SUGGS, ROBERT C.
    1961. "The Archaeology of Nukuhiva, Marquesas Islands, French Polynesia."
    Anthropological Pap., American Mus. Natural History **49**(1):5-205.

ARCHAEOLOGY ON CORAL ATOLLS

JANET DAVIDSON

Auckland Institute and Museum, New Zealand

ARCHAEOLOGICAL EXCAVATIONS of all kinds are relatively new in the tropical Pacific, for it was once thought that the prehistory of the Pacific was too recent to have permitted deposits of any depth to accumulate. Since World War II, however, numerous excavations on high volcanic islands, and on large raised coral islands such as Tongatapu, have shown that excavations in coastal occupation sites, and even in and around structural remains in both coastal and inland situations, can be profitable and worth while. One type of Pacific island, however, has until very recent times been neglected because of these former beliefs. It is the atoll—so numerous in the Pacific and yet, in the eyes of the archaeologist, so unimportant and unprofitable.

There were two reasons for the presumed lack of archaeological deposits on atolls. First, and most important, it was thought that the low-lying atolls would be subjected to constant hurricanes and tidal waves that would sweep away any occupation remains which might otherwise have accumulated. Second, it was sometimes said that the inhabitants of small atolls with severely limited land areas would tend to deposit their rubbish in the sea, and therefore midden accumulations would not occur on the land. For these reasons archaeologists neglected atolls, despite the opportunities they offered to explore hypotheses concerning man's adaptation to specialized environments (Goodenough, 1957, p. 152).

As had formerly been the case on high islands, the only archaeological investigations on coral atolls for many years were surface surveys of structures, particularly *marae* enclosures. Examples of these include the work of Kenneth P. Emory on Tuamotuan religious structures and other atoll structures (Emory, 1933, pp. 119-121; 1934a; 1934b; 1947, pp.

42-56) and brief coverages of stone structures in ethnographic works
(Buck, 1932a, pp. 145-185; 1932b, pp. 138, 208-209, 217; Beaglehole
and Beaglehole, 1938, pp. 157-163). In only one case were sites other
than stone structures mentioned, but the existence of "kitchen heaps" on
Malden Island described by Dixon (1877) was not verified by Emory
(1934b, p. 26). In only one case was the possibility of excavation mentioned (Beaglehole and Beaglehole, 1938, pp. 157-163), although the
grave sites described were not investigated because of local superstition.

Recently, however, archaeologists have found it possible to undertake
limited excavations on atolls in French Polynesia, while in Micronesia,
more extensive excavations have been conducted on an atoll with considerable success.

The study of *marae* enclosures in Eastern Polynesia has been advanced beyond the stage of surface surveys by excavations in and near
such structures in the Society group (Green and Others, in press; Garanger, 1964, pp. 10-18; Emory and Sinoto, 1965, pp. 50-74). Similar
excavations on the western Tuamotuan atoll of Rangiroa have demonstrated that knowledge of structures on atolls also can be extended by
careful excavation (Garanger and Lavondès, 1966). These excavations,
and the accompanying survey, did not reveal occupation layers beneath
the *marae* structures, and it was concluded that Rangiroa was too often
disturbed by high seas for such deposits to accumulate. Subsequently,
however, workmen discovered traces of a fishhook-manufacturing site.
Although this was considered to be comparatively recent, the finds nevertheless demonstrated that systematic excavations could be conducted on
this site (Garanger, 1965). Surface collections of fishhooks from other
western Tuamotuan atolls (Sinoto and Kellum, 1965) suggest that shallow sites for excavation may exist on these atolls also, which would
enable at least the immediately pre-European period of occupation to be
documented by artifacts recovered from excavations.

Much more extensive were excavations carried out by the author in
1965 on the atoll of Nukuoro, a Polynesian outlier in the eastern Caroline
Islands. The entire area of the single village on Nukuoro is raised several
meters above high water mark by an accumulation of midden deposits.
Excavations at several localities within this area revealed cultural deposits
up to three meters in depth, yet these localities were not the highest
areas. Beneath the cultural deposits in each case there was a mere one-
half to one meter deposit of sterile sand before the high water mark was
reached. Brief visits to other atolls in the same area (Mokil, Pingelap,
Ngatik, and Pakin) revealed similar deposits showing that Nukuoro is
not unique among Micronesian atolls. Apparently Polynesian outliers

on atolls in Melanesia also have extensive deposits (de Loach, personal communication).

The existence on small coral atolls of occupation sites which can be excavated raises a number of interesting problems and possibilities. It is by no means true, however, that all atolls offer the same opportunities. Evidently there are some which have little or no evidence of human occupation in the past. There are a great many others, such as the Tuamotu group, on which middens have not accumulated to any great depth and on which structures have been damaged or destroyed by storms or tidal waves. On the first group of atolls, archaeology is out of the question. In the second group, however, excavation and reconstruction of damaged structures can be undertaken, while excavation of the shallow midden deposits may be expected to reveal evidence at least of the most recent period of prehistoric or protohistoric occupation.

By far the best prospects are offered by a third group: those on which there are abundant and deep stratified midden deposits covering a considerable area. Atolls of this kind exist in eastern Micronesia and probably elsewhere, in areas where hurricanes and tidal waves are less severe or more infrequent than in the Tuamotu group, for instance.

As Nukuoro is the only atoll so far investigated on which extensive and relatively deep archaeological deposits exist, it will be used as a basis for discussion. The nature of these deposits has been described elsewhere (Davidson, 1966); for purposes of the present discussion, however, they are again described here.

Nukuoro is a small atoll, with a land area of only .6 square mile distributed over forty-six islets, many of which are very small indeed. The village, the largest communal taro pit, and probably 90 percent of the existing archaeological evidence are situated on the largest islet, which is also named Nukuoro. There are very few structures. The bulk of the archaeological evidence is composed of raised areas of accumulated midden deposit. The deposits themselves consist of numerous thin layers and lenses of coral gravel, sand, and cooking debris, with abundant artifactual material. The majority of the coral gravel layers appear to be old house floors which have been replaced successively with fresh gravel as they became dirty and as new houses were built. The standard house platform in use today consists of a low rectangular platform formed from coral slabs set upright in the ground making a rectangular enclosure which is filled with coral gravel (cf. Beaglehole and Beaglehole, 1938, p. 116; Buck, 1932a, p. 147). Traces of a similar structure were encountered near the base of one of the excavated deposits.

Such a small atoll affords unique archaeological opportunities not encountered on larger islands. On a larger land mass any archaeological survey must of necessity be merely a sample, whereas on Nukuoro or a similar atoll it is possible for one person to carry out a total survey in a short time and quickly acquaint himself with those areas on which archaeological evidence, whether structural or in the form of midden deposits, has accumulated. By this means it is possible to learn which islets have been most heavily occupied in the time during which the deposits have formed.

On Nukuoro it appears that a majority of the population has always lived in the area of the single existing village. Gausema, the next largest islet, situated beside the single entrance to the lagoon, would appear to be the only other islet on which there has been prolonged occupation. Although there is much less area involved than on Nukuoro, there is a small area of substantially raised ground surface indicative of past occupation. Many of the other islets have some slight evidence of occupation, particularly on the lagoon shore and close to the intervening channels; but in general, the farther the islet from Nukuoro, the less the evidence of occupation. It should be emphasized, of course, that this relates only to the existing evidence and that traces of earlier occupation and settlement may have been destroyed by the sea. Indeed there is considerable evidence for disturbance of the smaller islets by storms. Many of them have in the past had retaining walls of coral blocks which now lie some distance from the present shore, stranded on the bare reef. Yet the archaeologist can work only with the evidence which survives, and this evidence points to a long tradition of nucleated settlement on the principal islet.

The occupation pattern of Nukuoro is repeated on Mokil and Pingelap, where again the heaviest past occupation seems to have been in the present village areas. On Ngatik, however, evidence of intensive occupation is scattered over the islet which is inhabited today in a pattern similar to that of the modern settlement. In each case the surface evidence of archaeological remains quickly provides a general picture of the nature of the settlement in the past. Only by excavation, however, can details of this settlement be learned; and because of the nature of the deposit and the means available to the archaeologist, these details are not easily obtained.

The archaeologist in Polynesia, it is to be hoped, not only aims to recover a chronological sequence of artifact types, but seeks to understand as much as possible of the way of life of the Polynesians in the past, and the changes in that way of life at various times and in adaptation to varying conditions. The archaeologist working on a high island must survey and explore a variety of ecological situations, and a variety of archaeological evidence and types of site. The archaeologist confronted with a small atoll, especially one isolated from frequent contact with a high island or islands, must consider how best to sample a small circumscribed area consisting perhaps of only a few acres of concentrated deposit, in order to learn as much as possible of the prehistory of its inhabitants. In some ways the situation is similar to that faced by an archaeologist working on a tell or on a large Indian mound. The inhabitants of these, however, had outside contacts and carried out a range of activities in areas beyond the bounds of their settlement, of which traces may remain, whereas the inhabitants of a small isolated atoll could go only to other minute fragments of land which are easily accessible to the archaeologist and his techniques, or onto the ocean, where no trace of their activity will survive which can be reached by normal archaeological methods.

Not all atolls are as small as Nukuoro. In general, however, atolls have a very much smaller land area than even the smaller volcanic islands. As the size of the atoll land area increases, so the difficulty of carrying out a detailed archaeological survey increases. In the case of an atoll with a lagoon area of many square miles, the practical problems of a thorough survey of all available land areas become considerable. Even so, on an atoll there will always be a uniformity of ecological setting and a lack of the diversity of land and resources available on a high island. These will greatly simplify the achaeological survey and raise special problems of excavation.

By far the greatest majority of archaeological evidence on a small atoll is likely to be concentrated within an area of a very few acres, which may coincide with the present settlement. The remainder will be close at hand on neighboring islets. Thus a small atoll provides an opportunity never otherwise encountered in the Pacific, where the total existing evidence for the prehistory of an island or group is usually scattered over a range of ecological settings and a diversity of types of archaeological site. It also provides an opportunity to explore the nature of man's adaptation to the unique and specialized atoll environment. Yet the concentration of centuries of prehistory in a small limited area means that the content of that area is complex in the extreme, and its excavation and unraveling is a challenge to the archaeologist.

It is possible to guess how the mass of material which is the existing evidence for the prehistory of an atoll such as Nukuoro accumulated. Certainly it did not rise evenly and uniformly over the several acres which it now covers. Today on Nukuoro, people dig downward into the ground to make wells, which are quite numerous around the village, or for taro excavations. They build upward for house sites, building up both the actual house platform and the area around the house by scattering fresh clean coral gravel from the beach on the surface. New houses are not always built on the same spots as the old; wells clog up and have to be cleaned out and renewed. Taro pits require constant care, or they likewise fall into disuse. With alterations in population size, taro pits would either have to be extended in area or some part of them allowed to fall into disuse. The material for building-up operations has to be obtained somewhere, likewise spoil from wells and taro excavations must be deposited somewhere. With these processes continuing for centuries on the same ground, it is inevitable that the stratigraphy is extremely complicated and that very limited excavations cannot hope to unravel the full story of the use of the area.

To reveal in detail the complicated processes by which such an accumulation built up, excavations on a scale seldom contemplated in the Pacific would be required. On Nukuoro, to reveal in detail the history of the village area, a trench the length of the village parallel to the lagoon shore, and several transverse trenches from lagoon shore to reef side through the village, together with extensive tests of other islets, would be the minimum required to examine fully the composition of the deposits. This would necessitate means, time, and manpower at present beyond the scope of Polynesian archaeology, and it would be debatable whether the end justifies the means, in view of our still limited knowledge in the field of Polynesian prehistory and the amount of valuable information which can be obtained from less ambitious projects.

The only practical method of investigating atolls at the present time is to adopt a sampling method designed to reveal as much as possible with the means available. But locations for excavation must be selected and interpretations undertaken, bearing in mind the complex nature of the total deposit.

On Nukuoro, there are no discrete sites whose boundaries are clearly marked. The entire area of the present village is one large amorphous archaeological site, whose different parts have traditionally been used for different purposes in the past. Of these differing activities, no visible traces or delimitations of discrete areas remain. Thus one may learn that in the still-remembered past, certain areas were set aside for god-houses, others for community houses, others for men's houses, although no visible remains of these structures exist and the boundaries of the localities where they stood are no longer known.

Eight localities on Nukuoro were selected for excavation, some because tradition assigned them particular functions in the past (men's house, cult house), others because their geographical position suggested that they should be tested to establish the functions of different areas in and around the village. Each locality was found to consist of numerous thin layers and lenses of clean coral gravel and sand, interspersed with layers of burned coral and charcoal. Most appear to have been occupied at various times by dwellings and by cooking areas. One locality, vaguely supposed by present inhabitants to have supported a cult house connected with a whale cult, yielded evidence of intensive and prolonged cooking activities. In only one instance was the traditional interpretation of a locality actually supported by the archaeological evidence. From a supposed men's house, extensive evidence of tool manufacture was recovered, separating this locality from those of dwelling and cooking activities. Thus it is likely that where structures are few or nonexistent, verification of traditional religious sites on the basis of excavation results will be extremely difficult. However, a general idea of the nature of the occupation and use of localities at various points in time can be obtained.

When the depth of deposit is as great as three meters, area excavation to determine the nature and extent of structures is likely to be difficult, particularly if a number of structures, of which few traces except postholes remain, may have succeeded one another on the same locality. Only those structures which appear on or near the surface can be fully excavated without considerable time. The existence of structures deep down in the deposits must be recorded, but their size and nature will remain undefined unless extensive excavations are carried out in a single locality.

The actual problems of excavation in a given locality are not likely to be unique to atolls. Indeed there is a close similarity between the Nukuoro deposits and the coastal midden deposits on high volcanic islands. Two main categories of middens on volcanic islands may be distinguished here: those in which natural stratigraphy is present and relatively undisturbed; and those in which for one reason or another natural stratigraphy is absent, and the archaeologist is confronted with an undifferentiated mass of material. Often the latter are shallow deposits which have been much disturbed by gardening activities. Such sites can be excavated by arbitrary levels, and a variety of techniques of midden analysis then becomes practicable. Most deep deposits on atolls, however, will probably contain natural stratigraphy similar to that which was encountered in a coastal midden deposit in Samoa (Davidson, 1964) as well as on Nukuoro.

A major problem in some coastal deposits has been disturbance by burrowing land crabs (Green and Others, in press). Although these crabs certainly exist in Nukuoro, as in Samoa, the amount of damage they have caused in inhabited areas appears to be negligible. They are numerous on other islets, where their burrows are large and ubiquitous, but they are seldom seen near the present village area; and, provided it has been constantly occupied (and there would appear to be no reason to assume otherwise), land crab damage may always have been slight. The smaller hermit crabs, which also burrow, are frequent even in the village area, but they do not seem to leave vertical burrows which could cause material in archaeological deposits to be displaced. In presently uninhabited areas, however, the effects on excavations of burrowing crabs would be significant, and exactly the same problem would arise as has already been realized and discussed in connection with excavations in coastal midden deposits on a high volcanic island (Green and Others, in press).

A source of error more common than crab burrows, both on atolls and in other coastal deposits, may be features occurring in the deposit which are not recognized. Experience has shown that postholes, ovens, and even pits are common in these sites, and that some of these, particularly postholes, are difficult to locate and excavate satisfactorily at the level at which they occur. Material from the fill of a posthole, if the posthole is not excavated at the level from which it was dug, may be seriously misplaced, yet it is extremely difficult to find postholes in deposits of loose coral gravel. Similar considerations apply to pits, and may even apply to firepits and ovens in deposits of concentrated cooking remains. The greatest care must be taken to find and excavate such features as they occur.

The occurrence of many features, and the irregularity, and in some cases thinness, of the natural layers, make excavation by arbitrary blocks alone unrealistic. A unit one meter square and ten or fifteen centimeters deep may include portions of several different layers and be perforated by the fill of a large posthole. All material in the block is not of the same or even approximately the same age, and such useful techniques of analysis as the concentration index devised by Willey and McGimsey (1954, pp. 43-45) become meaningless. Although excavation by arbitrary levels may be the only feasible method of dealing with disturbed deposits where cultural materials are mixed, or with deposits in which recognizable stratigraphy is absent, the archaeologist working with atoll

or coastal midden deposits having natural and irregular layers, must constantly strive to avoid mixing of materials by arbitrarily excavating several layers and features together. On the other hand, where the individual
layers are very shallow and there are no marked discontinuities representing time gaps, excavation at least partly by arbitrary levels may be
the only practical way of handling loose coral gravel deposits. Very
often it may be necessary to effect a compromise between following
natural layers, and excavation by arbitrary levels, excavating separately
individual layers which are clearly marked, and reverting to arbitrary
levels when deposits become loose and indistinguishable. It is important
to adopt a flexible approach to such deposits, which may be changed
according to the nature of the stratigraphy, and to be aware of the
probable existence of such features as postholes, and constantly on the
lookout for them.

Excavations of coastal midden deposits in the tropical Pacific are
so new that suitable techniques are still being sought. Archaeologists
working with such deposits need to think carefully about the methods
best suited to the excavation of the thin and irregular layers likely to be
encountered. Just as techniques of excavation must be tested and improved, so suitable methods of analyzing the total composition of the
excavated deposits must be sought. Certain special problems immediately
arise in connection with midden analysis in situations encountered on
atolls, and in certain other tropical midden deposits.

Because of the Polynesian habit of sprinkling coral gravel in and
around house floors, large quantities of coral will occur in archaeological
deposits and will be retained in screens if excavated material is screened.
Tedious labor must be expected to separate the artifactual and faunal
material, which is to be kept, from these coral fragments. The habit of
bringing coral gravel to the houses also raises problems in shell analysis.
Much of the shell which occurs in deposits of this kind (as distinct
from true shell middens, which do occur on some islands, for instance
Tongatapu) consists of waterworn fragments brought to the site together with gravel from the beach. Every effort must be made to distinguish remains of shell used for food or tool manufacture from shell
which is a by-product of the techniques used in constructing house
floors. Very often the only means of distinguishing house floors in the
deposits is by the heavy concentration of coral gravel. Means for
measuring this accurately have to be devised.

But the uniqueness of atoll archaeology does not lie in the excavation and analysis of individual localities. These present problems
exactly similar to those encountered in certain coastal midden deposits

of high volcanic islands, several of which have now been investigated. In particular, coastal deposits in Samoa and certain of the Society Islands closely resemble those of Nukuoro in content. Rather, the unique problems of atoll archaeology lie in the selection of localities for excavation, and in the ultimate interpretation of these localities in relation to the total composition of the site, and of their position in the prehistory of the atoll.

Only by good fortune can limited excavations encounter the earliest levels of occupation in an atoll such as Nukuoro. Some of the highest areas on Nukuoro are apparently rather recent in their entirety, where former depressions have been deliberately filled in and then built up to a commanding height to accommodate a religious structure. Total depth is unlikely to be in itself an indicator of antiquity. Nor can it be assumed that items from a similar depth below ground surface are in any way close to one another in time unless they are from the same stratigraphic context in a single locality, for the histories of two separate localities may be entirely different. Every effort should be made to establish correlations between localities and between individual layers of different localities, but depth below ground surface should not be regarded as a useful indicator in this process. Similarities and differences between artifact types can be useful markers, and also the presence or absence of certain faunal items. Radiocarbon dates where available are also useful, but experience on Nukuoro suggests that they cannot be used to provide more than a general indication of the age of the various deposits or to distinguish exactly between deposits which are not widely separated in time. If, however, as on Nukuoro, excavations provide abundant artifacts from stratified contexts, the interrelationships of the various excavated localities can be inferred from the presence or absence of a few diagnostic items.

From the individual histories of the excavated localities and their interrelationships where these can be determined, inferences must be drawn about the history of the total site. Concerning general interpretations, little can be said without detailed discussions of individual instances. Two particular aspects of interpretation of atoll prehistory may be mentioned. First, atolls have very limited resources, which are likely to be reflected in the technology if the atoll inhabitants are not in regular contact with the population of some neighboring high island. Excavations on an atoll are likely to provide material reflecting these limitations in the past and illustrating man's ingenuity in making the best use of what is available. Secondly, atolls generally have very small populations. It has been suggested that the small and fluctuating atoll populations offer the greatest possibilities for cultural replacement (Vayda, 1959, pp. 820-821). Archaeological research on coral atolls provides an opportunity to test this hypothesis.

Throughout this discussion isolated atolls have been considered. Yet atolls very often occur in groups. The archaeological prospects would, then, not be lessened, but could be increased in a group of atolls. A single atoll in a group would provide similar opportunities and problems to those of an isolated atoll such as Nukuoro, but excavations could only provide the basis for inferences about that single atoll. It would be unwise to make statements about the prehistory of the total group on the basis of finds from a single atoll, for there might be many small differences between members of the group. An innovation in one atoll might have spread at different times or not at all to other parts of the group. Not all members of the group might have felt the same effects of various natural disasters, such as tidal waves and cyclones, and the population of one might have been considerably more reduced at a given point in time than those of others. Likewise, some atolls might have preserved more archaeological evidence in the face of storms than others. A group of atolls, several of which were to be investigated in detail, would provide further opportunities to explore details of cultural adaptation and change in a given environment.

Only in the case of atolls that are satellites of high islands, such as Ant and Pakin which are within sight of Ponape, or Tetiaroa in the Society group, would the situation be different. In these instances the atolls are merely an extension of the varied resource zones of the neighboring high island or islands and offer similar problems and possibilities to the coastal flat areas of the high islands. Any material recovered would be studied in the light of the high island culture and not as part of an individual and separate culture. While the problems of selecting and excavating localities are the same as on an isolated atoll, interpretations will be influenced by different considerations.

There is no doubt that atolls which do contain abundant archaeological deposits provide an opportunity for important research. In particular, the small and isolated atolls offer opportunities which do not occur elsewhere. If our understanding of Polynesian, and indeed of Pacific prehistory, is to be a thorough one, we should not neglect this evidence of the history of man's adaptation to unique and specialized environments. Many of the problems likely to be encountered are those of technique and do not differ greatly from those encountered in dealing with any tropical midden deposit. The limited and concentrated nature of the archaeological evidence on an atoll, however, means that a greater understanding of the prehistory of the culture concerned can be gained in a relatively short time than would be the case in a large or diversified island or group.

LITERATURE CITED

BEAGLEHOLE, ERNEST, and PEARL BEAGLEHOLE
    1938. *Ethnology of Pukapuka.* B. P. Bishop Mus. Bull. 150. Honolulu.

BUCK, PETER H. (TE RANGI HIROA)
    1932a. *Ethnology of Tongareva.* B. P. Bishop Mus. Bull. 92. Honolulu.
    1932b. *Ethnology of Manihiki and Rakahanga.* B. P. Bishop Mus. Bull. 99.
        Honolulu.

DAVIDSON, JANET M.
    1964. "Preliminary Report on Investigations at Lotofaga Village, Upolu."
        In R. C. GREEN, *Preliminary Report on Archaeological Field-work in
        Western Samoa.* Auckland: Mimeographed.
    1966. "Nukuoro: Archaeology on a Polynesian Outlier in Micronesia." Paper
        presented to the Eleventh Pacific Science Congress (Tokyo).

DIXON, W. A.
    1877. "Notes on the Meteorology and Natural History of a Guano Island."
        J. Royal Soc. New South Wales 11:165-175.

EMORY, KENNETH P.
    1933. *Stone Remains in the Society Islands.* B. P. Bishop Mus. Bull. 116.
        Honolulu.
    1934a. *Tuamotuan Stone Structures.* B. P. Bishop Mus. Bull. 118. Honolulu.
    1934b. *Archaeology of the Pacific Equatorial Islands.* B. P. Bishop Mus.
        Bull. 123. Honolulu.
    1947. *Tuamotuan Religious Structures and Ceremonies.* B. P. Bishop Mus.
        Bull. 191. Honolulu.

EMORY, KENNETH P., and Y. H. SINOTO
    1965. Preliminary Report on the Archaeological Investigations in Polynesia:
        Field Work in the Society and Tuamotu Islands, French Polynesia,
        and American Samoa in 1962, 1963, 1964. B. P. Bishop Mus. Polyne-
        sian Archaeological Program. Prepared for National Science Founda-
        tion. Honolulu. (Mimeographed.)

GARANGER, J.
    1964. "Recherches Archéologiques dans le District de Tautira." *J. Soc.
        Océanistes* 20:5-21.
    1965. "Hameçons Découverts à Rangiroa, Tuamotu Occidentales." *J. Soc.
        Océanistes* 21:142-145.

GARANGER, J., and A. LAVONDÈS
  1966. "Recherches Archéologiques à Rangiroa Archipel des Tuamotu." *J. Soc. Océanistes* **22**:25-66.

GOODENOUGH, WARD H.
  1957. "Controls in the Study of Cultural and Human Evolution." *J. Polynesian Soc.* **66**:146-155.

GREEN, R. C., K. GREEN, R. A. RAPPAPORT, A. RAPPAPORT, and J. M. DAVIDSON
  In press. "Archaeology in the Island of Mo'orea, French Polynesia." *Anthropological Pap., American Mus. Natural History* **51**(2).

SINOTO, Y., and M. KELLUM
  1965. "Hameçons Récoltés aux Tuamotu Occidentales." *J. Soc. Océanistes* **21**:145-149.

VAYDA, A. P.
  1959. "Polynesian Cultural Distributions in New Perspective." *American Anthropologist* **61**:817-828.

WILLEY, G. R., and C. R. MCGIMSEY
  1954. *The Monagrillo Culture of Panama.* Peabody Mus. Archaeology and Ethnology Pap. **49**(2). Cambridge.

ARCHAEOLOGY AND THE SOCIETY ISLANDS

JOSÉ GARANGER*

Mission Archéologique ORSTOM-CNRS

THE SOCIETY ISLANDS, comprising the central archipelago of Eastern Polynesia, have long been considered to be the first dispersal center of East Polynesia, and the traditions are in agreement with this. Since World War II, archaeologists have focused their work on the study of Oceania's past, and it seemed particularly necessary in deciphering the prehistory of this archipelago to use modern methods of archaeological investigation. The hoped-for results should be of interest, not only in regard to the prehistory of these islands, but also of Eastern Polynesia and, in turn, of the entire South Pacific.

Research such as this, undertaken in 1960 by Bishop Museum and followed up to the present by the contributions of various universities, as well as by French research institutions (ORSTOM and CNRS), has not yielded all the expected results. However, these efforts were far from being in vain, because the difficulties encountered offer, in themselves, material for profitable reflection regarding the orientation of a new strategy for archaeological research in these islands. Certain results —in all respects positive—have shed new light on Oceanic prehistory; in short, Society Island archaeology, by bringing together investigators of different origins and backgrounds, has greatly profited from the confrontation of new ideas, men, and methods. After an initial few years of groping, of these efforts, successes, and failures, and in the light of each one's contributions, we can pause for a moment to consider the path taken and to survey the future. This is the purpose of the notes that follow.

---

* Translated from the French by Miss Marimari Kellum, University of Hawaii, Honolulu.

WORK BEFORE WORLD WAR II

Prior to World War II, knowledge of Polynesia's past was mostly based on linguistic studies and oral traditions. Material culture was not ignored, but its study was largely based on ethnographic and museum collections; the typological differentiations noted in spatial distribution did not suggest differentiation in time. Polynesian culture, which was considered to be homogeneous and a relatively recent phenomenon, intrigued the curious-minded as to its origin, but, it did not seem necessary to search beneath the surface for traces of cultural phases since these were not expected to differ from those observable on the surface.

We owe to E. S. Craighill Handy and to Kenneth P. Emory the first archaeological work carried out in the Society Islands. This was archaeological in the broad sense, in that it was concerned with the study of surface structures, *maraes* in particular, which provided durable evidence of a culture undergoing rapid acculturation. It was archaeological work also in the sense that investigations carried out by Emory, patiently and over a long period of time, led him to make a systematic classification of these religious structures (Emory, 1933). His classification was, first of all, functional, but it also had a secondary purpose closer to the usual preoccupation of archaeology—that of a differentiation of the structures in place and time. *Stone Remains in the Society Islands,* therefore, provided not only a vast amount of irreplaceable knowledge (240 sites were localized and often several structures were grouped within one site), but it also presented a classification into four types which remained the basis for all future studies. These types were: (1) Leeward Islands *maraes;* and three types of Windward Islands *maraes,* namely, (2) inland, (3) intermediate, and (4) coastal.

Through the use of other means, including the study of still existing ancient traditions, as well as linguistic investigations, Emory was able to lend life to these structures, to build a bridge between the oral information—often misleading, if not unintelligible, owing to its rich and multiple facets—and the silent traces represented by the ruins of these structures. *Stone Remains in the Society Islands* is still a Bible for new investigators in the field. The information it contains, including the naming and functional identification of the elements constituting the structures, as well as the traditional proper names of the sites, is all the more valuable today, when the traditions are disappearing at a rapid pace, and Polynesia is more and more being opened to foreign influences.

The book does not neglect to record and describe petroglyphs (pp. 171-179). The last chapter was the first record of an aspect of archaeology full of promise for an understanding of the cultures of the South Pacific.

WORK SINCE WORLD WAR II

Research in Polynesian archaeology gathered momentum after World War II, but was carried out in islands very distant from the Society Islands—New Zealand and Hawaii. The well-stratified sites revealed by excavations there, and the use of refined comparative typologies (in particular the work of Duff, 1959; Emory, Bonk, and Sinoto, 1959; Green, 1961a, 1961b; Sinoto, 1962), enabled investigators to differentiate definitely the exposed archaeological strata. This work, together with the radiocarbon method of dating, newly applied in Polynesia, will soon make an absolute chronological framework possible. Polynesian culture now appears to be much more complex than had previously been thought.

The Society Islands were the legendary place of origin of the New Zealanders and the Hawaiians. Thus they appeared to be one of the most important areas for an understanding of the processes of the peopling of the South Pacific (Emory, 1933), and were defined as such at the Tenth Pacific Science Congress (Emory, 1961). Since April, 1960, Emory and Sinoto have undertaken, under the auspices of Bishop Museum, and with the assistance of Pierre Verin of ORSTOM and of Marimari Kellum, a systematic exploration of the Windward and Leeward Islands. They were soon joined by Green (American Museum of Natural History and Harvard University), assisted by R. and A. Rappaport, and, in 1961-1962 by Janet Davidson (Auckland University). These latter investigations had, in a sense, a different but complementary aim from that of the Bishop Museum expedition. Archaeology in the Society Islands has thus benefited, from its beginnings, from the two methodological tendencies which divide archaeologists and archaeology itself; that is, the exhaustive study of horizontal layers and the search for sequences by deep stratigraphy.

THE SEARCH FOR SEQUENCES

The main preoccupation of the Bishop Museum expedition was to study the surface remains of the activities of the ancient Polynesians in the Society Islands and to construct as quickly as possible a framework for a relative and an absolute chronology. The evidence thus uncovered, when submitted to the critical techniques of rigorous excavation and comparative typology, should make it possible to state precisely the date of the first occupation of these islands by man, and of the successive changes in the culture that developed prior to the arrival of the Europeans. Comparison of the evidence thus gathered with that from other archipelagoes should clarify the ancient population movements across the South Pacific and, in particular, define the role played by the Polynesians of the Society Islands in the colonization of Eastern Polynesia.

In Oceania, more than elsewhere, cultural exchange does not necessarily signify migration. This area, as ethnologists have shown, is a web of relations—reciprocal or not, and more or less durable—between social groups at varying distances from one another. A technological custom may be introduced without the transportation of an ethnic group. A single drifting canoe from very far away can bring an object which is imitated, while its carriers may disappear, absorbed into the population that was accidentally met. Therefore, one can see the necessity of augmenting to a maximum the number of items to be interpreted and also of intensive prospecting and numerous excavations. This long and laborious task has been begun by Bishop Museum.

Finely stratified rock shelters and coastal sites in the Hawaiian Islands have provided much new evidence regarding the prehistoric activity of these islands. Fishing sites have yielded, in particular, an abundant collection of fishhooks. The study of these, a new focus of interest in the Pacific area since the work of Bishop Museum researchers Emory, Bonk, and Sinoto (1959), has greatly aided in the decipherment of Hawaiian Island prehistory (Emory and Sinoto, 1961; Sinoto, 1962). This fortunate experience guided the first steps of these archaeologists in the Society Islands. Emory released the results of their first two years of investigations (Emory, 1962), but they were not as satisfactory as the author and Sinoto had hoped. The abandonment of the interior of the islands after European colonization and the concentration of habitations along the coastal areas explain the rarity and extreme poverty of archaeological sites. Furthermore, both surface structures and stratigraphy have been ruined. The regions that are less disturbed by contemporary activity—and they are very few—have been disrupted by the vegetation and beach fauna, the *tupa* crabs in particular. Artifacts are practically nonexistent, having been removed a long time ago either accidentally or in agricultural or earth-moving work, and today are dispersed in public and private collections. In spite of intensive prospecting, Emory and Sinoto were able to collect from the surface in Tahiti over a period of four years only eighty-two artifacts; other expeditions had no better luck.

The excavation of coastal rock shelters has been no more profitable than coastal site prospecting. Contrary to the Hawaiian sites of this type, Tahitian caves and rock shelters—much rarer—are generally not favorable for human habitation. The cave ceilings are unstable because of disturbances of the rock. Only one rock shelter in Vairao, excavated in June, 1961, by Sinoto and Verin, revealed traces of successive temporary occupations. One hundred and four artifacts, consisting mostly of stone flakes and shells, and fragments of three hooks and four adzes, were stratigraphically recovered. Such an artifact assemblage, however, is of little comparative value, both in quantity and quality, compared with what was found in the Hawaiian rock shelters. The carbon samples from the lower levels dated back only about two centuries.

Rather disappointed with these first results, the Bishop Museum expedition switched its area of investigation to the other islands of the Society groups: Moorea and the Leeward Islands. Emory and Sinoto have completed a preliminary report on the work done between 1962 and 1964 (Emory and Sinoto, 1965). It would be beyond the purposes of this report to attempt to analyze here all the results before their final publication. However, we must point out the most important results included the discovery and excavation of the Maupiti site (Emory and Sinoto, 1964, 1965).

At this site an assemblage of burials was discovered by chance and studied in detail by Emory and Sinoto in 1962 and 1963. Sixteen skeletons were uncovered under a superficial sediment about 30 centimeters thick. Burial artifacts directly or indirectly associated numbered about seventy, including adzes, fishhooks, and ornaments, and yielded evidence of a material culture similar to that of the first occupants of New Zealand. The carbonate dates were not satisfactory because of definite contamination of the samples, but the collagen dates placed these burials between A.D. 860 (± 85) and 1190 (± 90). These are the oldest known dates for the prehistory of the Society Islands. Other dates obtained by Bishop Museum researchers, as well as by the Roger Green team and the ORSTOM-CNRS expedition, are later than the 13th century, with the single exception of Afareaitu, a site in Moorea (Emory and Sinoto, 1965, p. 51) which appears to have been occupied about A.D. 1000.

A relatively early time period for Society Island prehistory was finally determined. Its discovery was of equal importance for the prehistory of archipelagoes as distant from Tahiti as New Zealand and the Hawaiian Islands. It confirms, on the one hand, the legendary origin of the Moa Hunters of New Zealand, whose tools and burial ornaments are identical to those of Maupiti, and, on the other hand, it reveals the absence in Hawaiian sites of similar artifacts. This indicates a later Tahitian immigration to Hawaii, perhaps A.D. 1300 to 1500, which seems to have been an intrusion into a population probably Marquesan in origin. This last point contradicts the legendary information, according to which the first inhabitants of Hawaii were originally from Tahiti, but seems to confirm the archaeological results obtained both in Hawaii and the Marquesas (Emory and Sinoto, 1965), as well as the glottochronological studies now in progress (Green, 1966). The Tahitian materials, which also indicate a modification in burial customs, necessitate a modification in the evolutionary typology set up for Hawaiian fishhooks (Sinoto, 1962) and, very probably for the advent of the Tahitian type *marae* discovered by Emory on Necker Island (Emory, 1928). The absence of similar religious structures in New Zealand inclines one to deduce that the Tahitian *maraes,* such as we know them, are later than the period of the Maupiti burials.

SURFACE STRUCTURES

Although often of less interest to the general public than the discovery of rare or highly significant objects, or an unexpected sequence by the excavation of the deep stratigraphy, the detailed study of surface structures allows one to better apprehend "man" by the traces of civilization that he has created and then abandoned. This quest for "man," more than for events, is a major preoccupation for the archaeologists. They have borrowed techniques from the physical and natural sciences as precise, valuable tools, but humanism remains an end.

Such investigations, associated with the study of vertical stratigraphic sequences, have not been neglected by the various expeditions that have been working for the past few years in the islands. The Society Islands, rich in stone structures, offer abundant material for such work. In the coastal areas these structures are now detached from their ancient environment by contemporary human occupation. However, the study of their arrangement and of other associated remains offers not only a mass of evidence of an ethnological character, but also information regarding their chronological ordering. Modern activity renders their surface condition precarious, at least as far as the habitation structures are concerned (and one would like to be able to affirm the permanence of *maraes*!). Their current condition weakens the scruples of the investigator who can, after carefully recording the superficial documents, remove the successive layers and study each lower level with equal exhaustiveness.

Certain interior areas, such as in Moorea and on the Taiarapu peninsula of Tahiti, undisturbed by present-day activity, offer a much wider area of investigation. The ethnological landscape of the Polynesian settlement pattern can perhaps in part be reconstructed by the analysis of forms through study of the vestiges as organized in recently occupied space. The repartition of its inhabitants and of its socioreligious constructions can be traced by the study of remains left by artisans and agricultural activity. Such was the work done by the Roger Green team in Opunohu Valley, Moorea, and their publication will be a valuable contribution to the knowledge of ancient Polynesian civilizations. However slow and relatively unproductive the gathering of artifacts seems to be—their density was found to be thinnest in the Society Islands— such studies are of inestimable interest, and ample possibilities are open in the mountainous interior of the islands of the archipelago.

THE MARAES

These structures, because of their number, their originality, and their diversity, are one of the most characteristic phenomena of the cultures of Central Polynesia. The analysis of their structure is of interest to science, and complete restoration is desirable for the more important ones. Archaeology will thus save from destruction and oblivion a considerable part of the cultural heritage of Polynesia and, in rendering the structures more attractive, also contribute to the economic development of the Society Islands, for which tourism remains the most evident source of income. We will consider some of the problems posed by the religious structures, even though, as we have seen, the study of habitation sites has not been neglected by any of the three archaeological expeditions.

It was not among the intentions of the Bishop Museum expedition to concentrate in particular on the study of Society Island *maraes,* the preceding publications of Emory (1933, 1943) having rendered this area of archaeology less urgent. Nevertheless, Emory, Sinoto, Kellum, and Verin surveyed numerous *maraes* in the Windward Islands as well as in the Leeward Islands (Emory and Sinoto, 1965; Verin, 1962a, 1962b, 1962c). Some of these structures had previously been recorded (Emory, 1933); others were added to the earlier inventory. A few of these sites were excavated and useful data gathered, not only on their spatial organization, but also on their age and on the associated arti-

facts. The results of this work are presented in a preliminary report by Emory and Sinoto, and we will mention here only the most important.

MOOREA (AFAREAITU: SITE M5-3)

This coastal type of *marae* was constructed on the ruins of a more ancient *marae,* which, in turn, was constructed on the foundations of an ancient house site. Carbon dating places the construction of the coastal *marae* at a period slightly after the year A.D. 1470 ($\pm$ 240). The date is valuable in that it is in agreement with one obtained by Green for a coastal *marae* in the Opunohu Valley (1600 $\pm$ 350). The presence in the Afareaitu site of a skeleton of a small Polynesian dog is also to be noted.

RAIATEA (OPOA): TAPUTAPUATEA AND HITAI

The famous site of Taputapuatea *marae* and its surroundings were studied and an original survey was published by Emory in 1933. The survey was made more precise and augmented by several structures reassembled by Sinoto; notably, a rectangular platform and two archery platforms. The *ahu* of the large *marae* was consolidated, partially restored, and, for the first time, fully photographed. The attempts to date Taputapuatea seem to indicate that this *marae* was erected about the beginning of the 17th century, and this coincides with one of the traditions concerning its founding (Emory and Sinoto, 1965, p. 63). Undoubtedly this famous *marae,* one of the most important in the history of the Society Islands, merits exhaustive study and complete restoration, which would require more extensive means than are available to a single research expedition. Such restoration would also have to be accompanied by extensive excavation of sites without hindrances.

Emory's valuable work (1933) recorded the results of long and patient field reconnaissance of the surface structures. The author, alone with a compass and notebook in hand, could not map the sites in as detailed a manner as he wished, and as can be done by a team of

FIGURE 1.—(Opposite) *Marae* at Tautira, Tahiti, constructed in the mountains of Tairapu. This structure was preserved under a thick covering of sediments from the steep slope that dominates it. The photograph shows the site in process of being uncovered, and before the actual excavation. A, *ahu* and six stone uprights; B, a small structure annex to the *ahu* and common to *maraes* of Tahiti's inland type; C, cyst containing no bones; D, enclosing wall, separated from the *ahu* and of which the dressed stones, like those of the *ahu,* are typical of Tahitian coastal *maraes;* E, stone upright on a second *marae* situated to the right of the first and constructed earlier. Excavations disclosed a third *marae* beneath the two preceding ones. (ORSTOM-CNRS Mission.)

today's better-equipped archaeologists. This, however, was not the aim of this pioneer work; rather, it was concerned with the gathering of material and with opening the way for further research. Without complete clearing of the surface and the removal of the soil, satisfactory mapping of the stone structures (which are always partially destroyed by time) cannot be accomplished. Only excavation conducted with all the critical methods that we now possess can reveal (with the exception of artifacts, fireplaces, or burials which are easily notable) all the more subtle indices necessary for the understanding of the ancient functional arrangement of these religious structures. The work conducted in this direction by Emory and Sinoto, by Green and his team, and by the ORSTOM-CNRS missions was profitable. Such work is, by its very nature, very slow. Since lack of haste determines the value of the results, there must be much more such work done in order that it will bear the fruit necessary to carry on. Multiplicity alone will provide a sufficient amount of comparative information to interpret exactly the extreme diversity of these structures and the modality of their evolution. Such diversity was noted in the remarkable work of Green in Opunohu, where 200 sites, often grouping several structures within one, were analyzed (Green, 1961a, 1961b; Green and Davidson, 1962). It appeared that Emory's quadripartite classification, valuable though it was, had to be considerably refined within the previously established framework. The chronological problem of the evolution of these *marae* types is not yet perfectly elucidated; in particular, the relation between the coastal and the inland *maraes* needs verification and the placement in time of the inland preceding the coastal is not as certain as had been thought. The construction of a large inland *marae* in the Tautira Valley was dated to the beginning of the 18th century. Elsewhere, as in Opunohu, a coastal type of *marae* (Fig. 1) was constructed[1] not far from an inland type. Are these two exceptional cases? Is the coastal *marae* of the Tautira Valley evidence of the installation (not very likely in this district) of a family of higher social rank than that of the inhabitants of this high valley? It is not impossible, but only intensive prospecting of the interior regions, today difficult of access, will enable confirmation of this hypothesis. Perhaps the differences in the *maraes* reflect functional specialization rather than evolution through time. All the *maraes,* whether of inland, intermediate, or coastal type, that have been dated by the carbon-14 method have been shown to date from the last centuries of the pre-European Tahitian civilization.

---

[1] A.D. 1540 ± 100 (Universität Bern, Sample No. B. 768).

The nature and the age of the Leeward Islands inland *maraes,* the appearance of the classical *maraes* along the coastal areas, and their influence upon the coastal type of *maraes* of the Windward Islands are still problems that remain to be solved by proper archaeological methods. Their solution will throw light not only on the prehistory of the archipelago, but also on that of contact between distant archipelagoes. The relationship between the Tahitian inland *maraes* and the Hawaiian *maraes* of Necker Island offer but one example of the possible results of such a study. The study of these religious structures does not seem urgent if one considers their immutable character and the fact that they will always be available for science. However, their study becomes much more urgent when one considers the rapid economic and social evolution of the Society Islands. One has but to wander about the coastal plains of these islands with a copy of Emory's *Stone Remains in the Society Islands* in hand to measure the importance of the number of structures mentioned in the book which have been totally ruined, or which have entirely disappeared. It is equally a loss to the scientific record and to the cultural heritage of Polynesia.

THE CULTURAL SEQUENCES

Archaeology in the Society Islands has thus progressed remarkably since 1960. Knowledge of the stone structures has been enriched and refined, and a considerable number of artifacts have been collected, either *in situ* or on the surface, and measured and catalogued. Their study, as much as that of stone structures, offers a fairly clear picture of the last period of the prehistory of these islands. An older period was revealed by the discovery of the Maupiti site. It now seems that future research should adopt three principal orientations:

(a) Study of the most recent period, which extends from the end of the cultural period disclosed at Maupiti to the first European contacts—the "Period of the *Maraes,*" if it is necessary to give it a name. It is, indeed, the extreme proliferation of these structures and their architectural development which best characterize this period. Even if it is possible that, as elsewhere in Polynesia during the most ancient period, there existed well-planned places for religious and social purposes, we can surmise, relying on what we know about the first Polynesians of New Zealand, that the altars and meeting places were still distinct entities. The areas least disturbed by contemporary activities, including the high valleys of the interior and the coastal plains which are not easily accessible (such as, for instance, the east coast of Tai-

arapu) are the most promising for this study. They offer excellent
material for a better knowledge of stone structures, their variation, and
their evolution. In addition, the undisturbed groupings permit useful
work on the ancient Polynesian settlement pattern. The material culture
of this period, known mostly from specimens collected on the surface
and placed in private or public collections, would gain in value if supplemented by a more abundant *in situ* collection.

(b) The fortunate discovery of the Maupiti site disclosed the existence of an earlier cultural phase which can be distinguished from
the later one by the name "Maupiti Period." This is still known only
from the burials, and we know nothing of the house forms—whether
they were rectangular or oval—or of the nature of the religious sites.
It would be desirable to discover other sites of the same type in both
the Windward and Leeward Islands, so as to learn the geographical and
chronological extension of these burial practices. The prospecting of
many islets in the archipelago could aid in clarifying this question, if
it is confirmed that in this period burial places were situated on islets
isolated from the inhabited areas.

(c) The last problem—but not the least—is that of the existence
in the Society group of a period still more ancient than that of Maupiti,
which would begin with the settlement of the first Polynesians. Where
did these colonizers come from? How did their civilization evolve?
Did they have knowledge of pottery, as was suggested by Golson
(1959), and as did the first Marquesans (Suggs, 1961; Sinoto and
Kellum, 1965)? Was there such a period in reality? It would probably
be worth while to prospect and to dig test pits in the zones abandoned
by recent settlement, the small slightly alluvial plains situated at the
mouths of mountain streams and not yet disturbed by man or natural
agents.

THE SOCIETY ISLANDS AND SETTLEMENT OF EAST POLYNESIA

Following the discovery of the Maupiti site, and as an outcome of
results recently obtained from other Polynesian island groups, Emory
and Sinoto believe that we now ought to consider the Marquesas as the
first occupied area in the settlement of East Polynesia. In this view,
the Society Islands would have been settled from the Marquesas, thereby
occupying second place and losing the primary role that had formerly
been attributed to them. The successive stages of settlement would be
the following (Emory and Sinoto, 1965): (1) West Polynesia to the

Marquesas; (2) Marquesas to Society Islands; (3) Marquesas to Easter Island; (4) Society Islands to New Zealand (Maupiti Period); (5) Marquesas to New Zealand; (6) Marquesas to Hawaii; (7) Society Islands to Hawaii.

Based on the knowledge that we now have of Marquesan, Hawaiian, and New Zealand prehistory, this general scheme is beyond doubt for the third to seventh stage, but it does permit us to be more reserved concerning the first two stages. It seems, on the one hand, that Suggs' (1961) Marquesan chronology must be pushed forward in the light of recent results obtained by Sinoto in this same archipelago (Sinoto and Kellum, 1965); on the other hand, ignoring for the time being the possible existence of a pre-Maupiti Tahitian culture, we cannot definitely decide that it was the Marquesas and not the Society Islands which were colonized first from West Polynesia. The question of the existence of a pre-Maupiti, or proto-Tahitian culture is therefore important. It is of interest not only for the prehistory of this archipelago, but for that of the entire area of Eastern Polynesia.

A NEW STRATEGY

The prehistory of the Marquesas Islands, rich in archaeological sites and less disturbed by present-day activities than other areas, will soon be as clear to us as the prehistory of the Hawaiian Islands or of New Zealand. This is owing to the remarkable work undertaken in the Marquesas by Sinoto, complementing the first results of Suggs. The Society Islands, on the contrary, are a world which remains in part to be discovered, in spite of the efforts of three archaeological expeditions. Because Tahitian archaeology suffers from an illness common to many countries of the world, one must envision the methods to alleviate it, and this cannot be done without the aid of the present-day inhabitants of these islands.

The conditions under which the Maupiti site was discovered served as a very good lesson. Two years of intensive prospecting had not disclosed a single site of a satisfactorily early period, either in the Windward or Leeward Islands, until one day a pickax exposed a skull, two adzes, and two pendants. A very old site had finally been discovered and it was not the discovery of an archaeologist. A happy coincidence? Without doubt, but one which would not have borne fruit if the discoverer had not taken the trouble to notify Emory and Sinoto of his find, and if, during these two years, these two investigators had not made every effort to attract the attention of the inhabitants to their interest, and, for the benefit of science, to encourage them to report all accidental discoveries of early material. It is seldom like this, as there are a number of amateurs, more or less constant and obstinate, who destroy sites in order to extirpate some object to enrich their personal collections. This is done in ignorance, for they consider archaeology as a hobby and the artifact as a simple object for collection. Much less pardonable are those who, as has happened many times during the past five years, deliberately destroy *marae* and house sites to utilize the construction material or because the structures interfere with land utilization.

This interest in "curiosities"—and it is a very old one—explains in large part why artifacts in the Society Islands are now so rare on the surface, so rare that they do not lead to the detection of sites used for purposes other than construction. The Bishop Museum investigators have again given us the example of the aid that may be obtained from local collectors who, after their attention had been drawn to the scientific interest of these objects, gathered the greatest part of the 1,900 surface artifacts collected by this expedition. These same investigators have also been able to catalogue nearly 1,400 artifacts held in private collections, thanks to the understanding of their owners. But what amount of dispersed artifacts were illegally exported by the numerous voyagers drawn by the mirage of the "South Seas" and now irrevocably lost to science? During the general conference held in New Delhi in 1956, UNESCO, at a meeting of international experts, adopted a resolution. This recommendation underlined the urgency of measures to be applied to all countries to preserve their archaeological heritage. In particular, the following measures were suggested (Brichet, 1961):

A. The creation of an excavation service in charge of: Controlling accidental discoveries, repressing the destruction of sites and the degrading of monuments, and to ensure their conservation and upkeep; Operating archaeological excavations of which the financial backing would be assured by the State; Preventing illicit excavations and the illegal sale of artifacts of archaeological interest.

B. The preservation of the material recovered from excavations and from accidental discoveries in the territory of this State and their appropriation to a local museum with the understanding that a part of the material gathered may be kept by the excavator who would be in charge of placing it in a museum accessible to both.

C. The education of the public so as to develop its respect and attachment for the traces of the past.

French Polynesia long ago foreshadowed this recommendation by the creation of a commission of monuments and sites, and of a museum in 1917. For a number of years, the Société des Etudes Océaniennes has dedicated itself to the preservation of the museum collections and to the publication of all that concerns ancient Polynesian cultures. It is, therefore, neither legislative texts nor good intentions that are lacking; thus we find before us a paradoxical situation. The Society Islands are rich in enlightened minds who care about the full bloom of the culture of their country. The administration is armed with wise legislation, the offshoot of French legislation, which is one of the most precise and foresightful in the world in this matter. Yet they find themselves in an archipelago that is one of the regions of the South Pacific in which the prehistory is least well known and most difficult to uncover. Such a paradox is common in those countries that were among the earliest to be opened to intellectual curiosity, but it is particularly dangerous in a remote territory and one with accelerated economic and social development. The limited geographical extent of the Society Islands and its relatively elevated cultural level ought, nevertheless, to premit, more easily than elsewhere, the resolution of this paradox, provided that the methods of action be made simple and effective, and that efforts be aimed toward three interrelated spheres.

1. The Papeete Museum

Papeete Museum, lodged as it has been for many years in a small, uncomfortable, and very unattractive building, cannot efficiently carry out the proper functions of a museum. These functions include: (a) the conservation of artifacts; (b) the informing and educating of the public by the exhibition of representative collections attractively and meaningfully presented; (c) the taking of a scientific role in offering sufficient, well-equipped space for the study of the material collected by the various research expeditions working in French Polynesia, a point that is particularly important in a Pacific territory which is relatively strong from the economic and demographic point of view, but which cannot, without international collaboration, assure scientific guidance of all necessary excavations; and (d) the provision of a place for the activities of the learned societies, the Société des Etudes Océaniennes in the present case.

A solution happily seems to be in sight to the problem of creating such a museum, one long debated during the past few years (see Jacquier, in Lavondès, 1966; see also Lavondès, 1964).

2. The Protection of Archaeological Excavations

The monument and site commission, which is in charge of the protection of portable and nonportable artifacts and of artistic, historic, or picturesque sites, is competent in all that concerns decisions and procedures of classification. The problem of the protection of archaeological excavations is a different one. Such sites are supervised in metropolitan France by a special service, the Bureau des Fouilles et Antiquités, which directly depends upon the Ministère des Affaires Culturelles and is represented in the Conseil Supérieur de la Recherche Archéologique (Laws of 1/29/64 and 4/23/64). This bureau delegates, in each archaeological district, a regional director of antiquities, representing the Minister. The services of such an organization, with the responsibilities and competence provided by law, would undoubtedly be very profitable if French Polynesia were included as an archaeological region. Its mission would primarily be (see Meroc, 1966):

To supervise the application of legislation and the regulation of excavations and archaeological discoveries;

To grant authorization, for a period of one month, for test excavations;

To authorize urgent salvage archaeology;

To examine the petitions for authorization of excavations;

To control the authorized excavations;

To receive and to centralize reports of accidental discoveries;

To qualify certain persons to do systematic prospecting without making accompanying excavations or test pits;

To notify the competent authorities of secret excavations;

To keep the site records and excavations for each particular district up to date;

To give assistance in conservation and study of archaeological collections;

To orient and coordinate the activities of the local societies participating in archaeological research.

3. Volunteer Archaeologists and Local Learned Societies

In Polynesia, as in all relatively small and isolated territories, the professional archaeologist can only be present on a temporary mission. France has available only forty or so archaeologists for its own metropolitan excavations and, with the currently active French excavation sites scattered all over the world, collaboration with foreign investigators is thus indispensable in Polynesia. These missions are very costly because of the distances from the countries which finance them, so it does not seem wise for them to devote the greatest part of their time to the laborious collection of artifacts, the cataloguing of private collections, or the systematic prospecting of sites. Visiting specialists ought to be able to devote themselves entirely to the tasks assigned to them; to scientific study of genuine merit, and to the restoration of those structures which, despite the fact that they constitute one of the most evident cultural richnesses of the archipelago, are in great danger of disappearing. The amateur archaeologist, who has made important discoveries around the world, in Polynesia has a role to play in this scheme.

The learned societies as well as the universities could, thanks to larger administrative and financial facilities, intensify their action. They might multiply their contacts at local meetings, and cooperate in programming research regarding Polynesian prehistory. They might also inform the public and awaken intellectual curiosity about Polynesia's past by personal contacts, or by personal or radio-televised conferences.

Site prospecting, without test pits or excavation, could be organized on a local level. Two areas are to be considered: the areas currently inhabited and the interior areas of difficult accessibility. Concerning the first, the informative work carried out by Emory in the Leeward Islands should be amenable to systematic organization into the actual administrative framework, and on up to the level of districts.

The school seems to be the first and best center for such action, and surface finds and chance discovery of sites could there be centralized. Instructors could also organize prospecting walks. The history of the past, still to be discovered, would be for the children and young people a pleasant and valuable cultural pastime. The interior zones, previously very densely populated but at present difficult to penetrate and rarely visited, constitute a reserve of sites which would be desirable to catalogue and to preserve. Although still intact, it will not be long before these sites will disappear with the construction of new roads which will cut across and permit easy penetration and occupation of these areas. These regions could be prospected on a large scale by local societies, including mountain clubs, youth groups, and the Société des Etudes Océaniennes. The army could also contribute, as was recommended by the general UNESCO meeting.

Such programs, to be effective, should be coordinated and the results centralized by a responsible authority who could be the Museum Conservator or the Director of Antiquities of the administrative district.

Three indispensable conditions for the safeguarding of Polynesia's heritage and for the enrichment of her cultural and tourist potential are the following:

(1) The establishment in Papeete of a museum worthy of its name; (2) the assurance of efficiency in the area of the protection of excavations and archaeological sites; and (3) the increasing in numbers of volunteers who wish to devote themselves to the search for the past and the coordination of their work. This threefold action, coordinated with the work of professional archaeologists, would contribute to the progress of our knowledge of the prehistory of the Society Islands, as well as to that of the entire South Pacific.

LITERATURE CITED

BRICHET, ROBERT
1961. "Protection des Monuments Historiques, des Fouilles Archéologiques et des Sites." In *L'Histoire et ses Méthodes,* pp. 969-1023. Encyclopédie de la Pléiade. Paris.

DANIELSSON, BENGT
1966. *But et Organisation du Musée Polynésien.* Papeete: Service de l'Information du Gouvernment.

DUFF, ROGER
1959. "Neolithic Adzes of Eastern Polynesia." In J. D. FREEMAN and W. R. GEDDES (editors), *Anthropology in the South Seas* (pp. 121-147). New Plymouth, New Zealand: Avery.

EMORY, KENNETH P.
1928. *Archaeology of Nihoa and Necker Islands.* B. P. Bishop Mus. Bull. 53. Honolulu.
1933. *Stone Remains in the Society Islands.* B. P. Bishop Mus. Bull. 116. Honolulu.
1943. "Polynesian Stone Remains." In CARLETON S. COON and JAMES M. ANDREWS II, editors, *Studies in the Anthropology of Oceania and Asia.* Paper of the Peabody Mus. American Archaeology and Ethnology, Vol. 20, pp. 9-21. Cambridge: Harvard Univ.
1953. "A Program for Polynesian Archaeology." Prepared at the request of the Sub-committee on Pacific Archaeology, National Research Council. *American Anthropologist* **55**(5:1):752-755.
1961. "Report on Hawaii and Tahiti." *Abstracts Symposium Pap., Tenth Pacific Sci. Cong.* (Honolulu), p. 60.
1962. "Report on Bishop Museum Archaeological Expeditions to the Society Islands in 1960 and 1961." *J. Polynesian Soc.* **71**:117-120.

EMORY, KENNETH P. (Cont.)

1963. "East Polynesian Relationships: Settlement Pattern and Time Involved as Indicated by Vocabulary Agreements." *J. Polynesian Soc.* **72**:78-100.

EMORY, K. P., W. J. BONK, and Y. H. SINOTO

1959. *Hawaiian Archaeology: Fishhooks.* B. P. Bishop Mus. Spec. Pub. 47. Honolulu.

EMORY, K. P., and Y. H. SINOTO

1961. *Hawaiian Archaeology: Oahu Excavations.* B. P. Bishop Mus. Spec. Pub. 49. Honolulu.

1962. "Découverte Archéologique aux Iles de la Société." *Bull. Soc. Etudes Océaniennes* **140**:125-127.

1964. "Eastern Polynesian Burials at Maupiti." *J. Polynesian Soc.* **73**:143-160.

1965. Preliminary Report on the Archaeological Investigation in the Society and Tuamotu Islands, French Polynesia and American Samoa in 1962, 1963, 1964. Mimeo. In Bernice P. Bishop Mus.

GOLSON, JACK

1959. "L'Archéologie du Pacifique Sud. Résultats et Perspectives." *J. Soc. Océanistes* **15**:5-54.

GREEN, ROGER C.

1961a. "Moorean Archaeology: A Preliminary Report." *Man* **61**:169-173.

1961b. "La Plateforme d'Archer et le Marae d'Afareaitu, Opunohu, Moorea." *Bull. Soc. Etudes Océaniennes* **136-137**:310-315.

1962. "The Application of Matrix-Index Systems to Archaeological Material." *Asian Perspectives* **5**:257-264.

1966. "Linguistic Subgrouping within Polynesia: The Implications for Prehistoric Settlement." *J. Polynesian Soc.* **75**:6-38.

GREEN, R. C., and J. DAVIDSON

1962. A Preliminary Report of Investigations Carried Out on the Island of Moorea, French Polynesia, by the American Museum of Natural History. Submitted to the Governor of French Polynesia. Mimeo.

GREEN, R. C., and D. W. PURCELL

1962. "The Relationship of Length, Width, and Thickness in Central Polynesian Adzes." *J. Polynesian Soc.* **70**:451-465.

LAVONDÈS, ANNE

1964. Projet pour l'Etablissement d'un Nouveau Musée à Papeete. Mimeo.

1966. *Musée de Papeete: Catalogue des Collections Ethnographiques et Archéologiques.* Office de la Recherche Scientifique et Technique Outre-Mer (ORSTOM). Publication Provisoire. Papeete.

MEROC, LOUIS

1966. "La Législation Française des Fouilles et Découvertes Archéologiques." *Archeologia* **13**:49-51, 89.

SINOTO, Y. H.

1962. "Chronology of Hawaiian Fishhooks." *J. Polynesian Soc.* **71**:162-166.

SINOTO, Y. H., and M. J. KELLUM
   1965. Preliminary Report on Excavations in the Marquesas Islands, French
         Polynesia. Mimeo. In Bernice P. Bishop Mus.

SUGGS, ROBERT C.
   1961. "The Archaeology of Nuku Hiva, Marquesas Islands, French Poly-
         nesia." *Anthropological Pap., American Mus. Natural History* **49**(1):
         5-205.

VERIN, PIERRE
   1962a. "Documents sur l'Ile de Me'etia. (Extraits de 'Stone Remains in the
          Society Islands' par K. P. Emory.)" *Bull. Soc. Etudes Océaniennes*
          139:59-80.
   1962b. "Prospection Archéologique Préliminaire de Tetiaroa." *Bull. Soc.
          Etudes Océaniennes* **140**:103-124.
   1962c. "Relevé Archéologique de l'Ile de Mai'ao." *Bull. Soc. Etudes Océani-
          ennes* **138**:35-45.

HAWAII

SOME PROBLEMS WITH EARLY DESCRIPTIONS OF HAWAIIAN CULTURE

MARION KELLY

Bernice P. Bishop Museum, Honolulu

A CRITICAL ASSESSMENT of published materials about the Hawaiian people and their culture would be a distinctive contribution to anthropology as well as a contribution toward a more comprehensive understanding of ancient Hawaiian society. Between the writings of casual observers reporting hearsay gathered in a visit of a few days and those of Hawaiian scholars recording the remembered traditions of their ancestors, there is a vast quantity of unequal material. Otherwise relatively reliable texts contain extensive sections of pseudo-scientific theorizing on supposed origins of the Hawaiian people. An erroneous statement attributable to a single source may be repeated in several publications. Many authors had interests of a proselytizing nature, and each seems to have been endowed with his own particular bias, selective perception, and at times myopic self-concern.

A serious description of ancient Hawaiian culture based on the available data might pose more questions than it could answer. But the chances are that a large part of its contribution would be the evaluating of the degree of reliability of the sources and the correcting of some of the more obvious errors of fact.

Among the difficulties to be met in such an effort is the serious problem of clearly identifying indigenous and acculturated behavior recorded in these sources. The main concern of this paper will be the attempt to deal with this problem by (1) illustrating how some of the earliest publications on Hawaiian culture confuse indigenous and acculturated behavior, (2) identifying the elements of Hawaiian culture that seem to have been the earliest victims of the acculturative process, and (3) identifying some possible sources of these influences. Although this paper does not pretend to be a complete analysis, it does seek to open for discussion the problem of acculturated behavior that will be encountered by researchers who must eventually work with this material. Meanwhile, perhaps it may serve as a guide to those who must deal with the material in its present state. To illustrate the problem, two of the earliest data-rich sources will be used: the 1917 edition of William Ellis' *A Narrative of a Tour through Hawaii;* and the 1909 edition of Sheldon Dibble's *A History of the Sandwich Islands.* Material from George Vancouver's *A Voyage of Discovery to the North Pacific Ocean* (1798) will provide examples of the type of evidence supporting the conclusions set forth in this paper.

In 1822 the Reverend William Ellis, member of the London Missionary Society stationed in the Society Islands for five years, arrived in Hawaii with a deputation on a tour of the South Sea mission posts. The visit was unexpectedly extended to four months (Ellis, 1917, p. 39). Ellis' knowledge of the Tahitian language enabled him within a very short time after his arrival in Hawaii to address his Hawaiian congregation in their own language. His value was recognized and he was invited to join the American missionaries in Hawaii, which he did the following year.

The total length of Ellis' residence in the Hawaiian Islands was something under two years, but it resulted in the publication in 1826 of a remarkable collection of material with a wide range of topics pertaining to the Hawaiian people, their material culture, beliefs, customs, origins, and general island environment. Although each topic is treated only briefly, Ellis' material serves as the earliest—sometimes as the only— source of information on certain elements of Hawaiian culture. Without it our knowledge of the Hawaiian people would be much poorer.

As keen an observer as he was, Ellis occasionally suffered one of the most frequent afflictions of his calling: that of passing moral judgment on certain beliefs and customs of indigenous peoples. At times these communicated extremely negative impressions, against which he contrasted the enlightenment of the civilized world or the good works of his fellow missionaries. Some of these contradictions have been remarked upon by others (Anonymous, 1848). Still, because of his early publication and his wide range of subject matter, Ellis is probably the most widely quoted source, although not always being cited as such. His previous experiences in the Society Islands gave him the advantage of comparative data, which he utilized effectively.

There are other problems regarding his Hawaiian material for which Ellis cannot be held responsible, but about which anyone relying on his data should be aware. These deal primarily with results of early accul-turation.

By the time Ellis wrote, 45 years had elapsed since Cook's initial visit. Of these, the first seventeen years can be described as a period of increased chieftain rivalry intensified by the introduction of trade and firearms and the newly adopted techniques necessary for the effective use of the latter. The last twenty-eight years were characterized by a unique form of government adapted by Kamehameha to serve his special political needs and to accommodate the demands of the rapidly expanding eco-nomic activity of Western traders. Considerable inroads had already been made into the Hawaiian subsistence economy by the introduction of a market economy, especially during the years of intensive contact with the Northwest Coast fur and sandalwood traders. Because relationships between people and the land and between chief and commoner are es-pecially sensitive to the cultural elements of warfare, government admin-istration, and economy, it is important to approach any material in these particular areas with caution.

It should be remembered also that warfare and disease, which to-gether effected a rapid population decrease in those early years, carried off large numbers of older adults, thus preventing them from passing on their knowledge of ancient Hawaiian culture to their descendants. As Dibble (1909, p. 38) wrote, " . . . an extensive war . . . raged about the time of Vancouver's several visits; then the plague, which swept off the majority of the people; deaths were so sudden and frequent that the living could not bury the dead."

This brings us to the second source discussed, the Reverend Sheldon Dibble. About thirteen years after Ellis arrived in the Islands Dibble, who was headmaster of Lahainaluna Seminary, organized a group of ten Hawaiian scholars into a class of inquiry and instructed them to write down their knowledge and to collect information from elders who remem-bered the old ways. Dibble encouraged the Hawaiian students to study their own history because they were ignorant of it even while "they were becoming acquainted with other nations" (Dibble, 1909, p. iii). He developed a "list of questions, arranged chronologically" to serve as a guide. Each week one question was assigned to the students who were urged individually to seek out "the oldest and most knowing chiefs and people, gain all the information that they could on the question given out, commit each his information to writing and be ready to read it on a day and hour appointed." Dibble writes further (pp. iii-iv), " . . . dis-crepancies were reconciled and corrections made by each other and then all the compositions were handed to me, out of which I endeavored to make one connected and true account."

By the time this material was being written down, fifty-seven years had elapsed since Cook's visit, and the chance that the data were infused with acculturated material is, for all practical purposes, a certainty. The remembered experiences they recorded were for the most part those that had taken place during the reign of Kamehameha I. However, there was a tendency on the part of the Hawaiian scholars to qualify many statements, which probably reflects a greater depth of understanding and awareness of differences existing between precontact and postcontact behavior.

While Ellis was recording his observations of Hawaiians, he unconsciously searched for familiar signs by which he could identify a type of behavior or institution and communicate its identity to others in the terminology of his own language. The identification and grouping of like items is part of the scientific process, but if judged superficially, incorrect or misleading determinations can be made. Although aware that certain relationships in Hawaiian culture appeared similar to those found in Western culture, Ellis probably did not suspect that in some cases he was observing effects of early acculturation. He was satisfied to record what he observed, or what he was told, seldom distinguishing between indigenous and acculturative phenomena. In reality he described a society already considerably changed—one with a well-developed, operative, acculturative process.

My contentions are: that the resemblances to European feudalism remarked upon by Ellis (1917, p. 314) and Dibble (1909, p. 73) were familiar mainly because Western feudal forms had been used as the patterns after which Kamehameha I designed his particular form of government; that much of Kamehameha's government was structured according to descriptions provided him by agents of Western culture; and further, that Captain George Vancouver was perhaps the most resourceful and most important single figure among them.

Vancouver visited the Islands during the years of bloody rivalry between chiefs who were just beginning to use firearms obtained from traders. In writing of the disappointments of the first Christian mission in the Marquesas Islands, Dibble (1909, p. 252) said, "No government was the greatest evil." If this were true for missionaries in the Marquesas Islands, it would certainly be true for traders, whether in the Marquesas or the Hawaiian Islands. Perhaps the most essential requirement to continued successful trade is that of stable, responsible political control at the point where trade takes place. The need for this in Hawaii was clearly apparent to Vancouver, whose journal describes in detail the steps he took to lay the basis for a united kingdom of the Hawaiian Islands under Kamehameha's rule. The following examples will serve to illustrate this fact.

Vancouver was with the third Cook voyage when he met Kamehameha for the first time. He was sufficiently impressed to remember him some fifteen years later. By then, with the aid of his supporting chiefs, Kamehameha had elevated himself to the position of a ruling chief of the Island of Hawaii after eliminating his main opposition—his cousins, whose high rank qualified them as competitors for the position. But he still had opponents who ruled three of the island's six districts (Dibble, 1909, p. 36; Kamakau, 1961, p. 173). Also, following a particularly bloody battle on Maui, that island and Oahu had been promised to Kamehameha upon the death of High Chief Kahekili (Dibble, 1909, p. 45; Kamakau, 1961, p. 150).

On his visit to Hawaii in 1793, Vancouver met Kamehameha in Kona. Kamehameha was accompanied by John Young, his interpreter, and by Kaahumanu, his favorite wife. Acting perhaps on the inspiration of more than a single motive, Vancouver was liberal with gifts. He was greeted in equally generous fashion by Kamehameha, who arrived at Vancouver's ship accompanied by a large fleet of double canoes laden with gifts of feather helmets, nearly a hundred large hogs, and quantities of other food (Vancouver, 1798, Vol. 2, p. 127). Kamehameha entertained the British captain with a large sham battle between a hundred and fifty of his best warriors and took an active part in it himself. Vancouver finished the evening off with a grand fireworks display (p. 154). At this time Vancouver gave considerable advice to Kamehameha and his council members on how they should conduct themselves in their relations with the chiefs of Maui and Oahu (p. 156).

Vancouver's arrival in 1794, on the last of his three visits, was outside Hilo Bay during the *makahiki* festival. Kamehameha and a large group of chiefs came out with presents of fresh food and hogs. The weather being too uncertain for the ships to enter Hilo Bay, Vancouver desired to sail around the island to Kealakekua Bay to make repairs. With singular purpose he invited Kamehameha to make the trip with him. Kamehameha declined, explaining that preparations for the *makahiki* festival ceremonies were in progress and that his presence in Hilo was required for the period of the taboo. To leave, he would have to petition the priests for permission. Vancouver, unwilling to lose this opportunity to press for cession, suggested that instead of going ashore to present the petition himself Kamehameha send one of his chiefs to inform the priests of his decision to accompany the ship. When Kamehameha replied that this was impossible, Vancouver countered with a personal attack, calculated in advance to have the effect of forcing Kamehameha to oblige his desires. He accused Kamehameha of not being really sincere in his professed friendship for him, and of inventing excuses for not traveling with him. He insisted that a chief of Kamehameha's position could manage to leave if he really wanted to. As intended, this attack stung Kamehameha's pride, and he capitulated. Perhaps he did not want to admit that he did not have the kind of authoritarian control over his people that Vancouver seemed to have over the crew of his ship, or perhaps he feared losing the advantage of friendship with this powerful chief from Great Britain. In any case Kamehameha chose in that moment of stress to act independently of the priests. He sent his brother-in-law to inform them that he and the chiefs were making the trip to Kealakekua with Vancouver (Vancouver, 1798, Vol. 3, pp. 4-6).

The trip took several days and there was ample time for Vancouver to discuss the desirability of cession and numerous other subjects with Kamehameha and his chiefs (p. 7). They had long conversations in which Vancouver answered many questions about England, the European nations, and the British king. Kamehameha displayed an intense curiosity to learn how such a great nation as Britain managed its affairs.

Once at Kealakekua Bay, Vancouver insisted on obtaining the identical plot of land that Cook had used as an observatory camp. Kamehameha informed Vancouver that this could not be done without the consent of an elderly woman who happened to be the widow of the chief who was the first to stab Cook. Kamehameha went ashore to ask her permission, but she refused. He then appealed to Vancouver to pick another spot—any other. The British captain pressed his demands in such a way as to indicate that Kamehameha would lose Vancouver's esteem if he were unable to produce the desired permission. Kamehameha held a hasty council with a number of principal priests of the temple, and after solemn conference, approval was finally given. The seriousness of their action is evident in the fact that Kamehameha ordered very important chiefs, including his half-brother, and several priests to protect Vancouver's shore party (Vancouver, 1798, Vol. 3, p. 13).

Vancouver is an outstanding example of persistent and purposeful invasion by an agent of Western culture into the internal affairs of the Hawaiian chiefs. His immediate goal was cession of the Island of Hawaii to Great Britain; his long-range goal, a united kingdom under Kamehameha. Carefully laid plans assured his success. He overlooked nothing. A master at commanding compliance, Vancouver soon had the Hawaiian chiefs striving to keep in his good graces. A story that might be called "the case of the missing knives" illustrates his acumen. It concerns the party of chiefs who had accompanied Kamehameha on the trip from Hilo to Kealakekua Bay. By the time they were anchored in the bay the chiefs were very much at home on board the ship. Occasionally Vancouver handed out gifts which were much esteemed by the chiefs. To be a friend of the great chief from King George was recognized as desirable and profitable.

The story begins on Vancouver's ship with some handsome ivory-handled knives which the chiefs coveted. When five knives disappeared, Vancouver exploited the situation. He describes in his narrative how he first inquired pleasantly if the chiefs knew anything about the missing knives. Upon receiving a negative reply he then in a burst of rage ordered all the chiefs except Kamehameha off his ship, refusing them re-entry and shaming them by pointing out that this displayed their lack of gratitude for the gifts he had showered on them. He chided Kamehameha saying this was no way for chiefs to set an example for their subjects. By noon, three of the knives were returned. Vancouver continued to bear down on Kamehameha so that the chief retired from the ship in extreme dejection. The next day a fourth knife was returned. The fifth, Vancouver later discovered, had been presented to a very high personage over whom Kamehameha was unable to extend his control (Vancouver, 1798, Vol. 3, pp. 15-16). The incident was dropped; the point had been driven home that those who desired to remain in the good graces of England would have to conduct themselves by the rules laid down by her agent.

Perhaps the incident that serves to reveal the aplomb and perspicacity with which Vancouver performed his role was that of the forgiveness of the chief who had captured the ship *Fair American* and murdered its crew. This chief, Kameeiamoku, was the head of a large and important district and for some time had been jealous of the advantages other chiefs had received from Vancouver's friendship, while he, a proud man of equal rank, was banished from the Englishman's court. When voluntary cession of the island to Britain was to be discussed, Vancouver realized the necessity for including this chief in the agreement. He informed Kamehameha that England would forgive Kameeiamoku's misbehavior and receive him, providing he assured no recurrence of the incident. Word was immediately sent to Kameeiamoku. Possibly he believed this was his chance to get into Vancouver's good graces and secure a share of the rewards, or possibly he sincerely wished to confess and be forgiven, but he feared it might be some kind of trickery. He consulted the priests. They were not optimistic. Nevertheless, Kameeiamoku set out for Kealakekua Bay, escorted by a great many chiefs and a fleet of canoes, stopping along the way at each temple, making sacrifices, consulting the priests, sending messengers ahead to inquire if he were actually going to be received by Vancouver, and requesting that assurances be sent back to him. Vancouver did not return assurances each time they were requested, but frequently enough to keep the chief from turning back. The signs the priests saw as they approached their objective became more reassuring, and finally Kameeiamoku entered the bay in grand style.

The scene Vancouver describes is dramatic. As the fleet of canoes slowly approached the English ships, Vancouver sent word that they should retire to the opposite side of the bay and proceed on foot to Kealakekua village where Vancouver and Kamehameha would meet them. By the time Kameeiamoku and his chiefs had hiked around to the arranged meeting place, Vancouver managed to be absent from his encampment, tending to other business. When the British captain finally returned, the chief was seated at the entrance of the camp waiting for him. Completely in charge of the situation, Vancouver opened the discussion of the incident of the *Fair American,* putting in exact terms the requirements he demanded be fulfilled before forgiveness would be extended. Quickly the chief promised such a thing would never again occur, excusing his actions in that case by saying that he had been personally beaten by Metcalf, captain of the *Eleanor,* and that taking the *Fair American* was his revenge. His chiefs and the others concurred, informing Vancouver that this was the true situation, all promising never to let such a thing happen again. Vancouver then shook hands with Kameeiamoku and gave him gifts to seal the bargain. They feasted together with wine and spirits flowing freely and good humor among all (Vancouver, 1798, Vol. 3, pp. 35-36).

Vancouver left no stone unturned in preparing the groundwork for the success of his objectives. He even sought and finally obtained Kamehameha's permission to intervene in Kamehameha's domestic life to achieve a reconciliation with his wife, Kaahumanu, daughter of Keeaumoku, a chief of great consequence (p. 26). Vancouver feared that if Kaahumanu continued to be rejected, her father might add his ". . . strength and influence to the prejudice, if not totally to the destruction, of Tamaahmaah's regal power . . . " (p. 25). Vancouver kept reminding Kamehameha of this and wrote: " . . . whenever he was disposed to listen to such discourse, I did not cease to urge the importance and necessity of his adopting measures so highly essential to his happiness as a man, and to his power, interest, and authority as the supreme chief of the island" (p. 26).

The royal pair finally reunited on Vancouver's ship, and the way was now clear for securing the cession (p. 28). Chiefs had come from all parts of the island for the council (pp. 16-17, 29-32). The first proposal to Vancouver was that they should not acknowledge their subjection to a foreign power without being completely convinced that such power would protect them against "the ambitious vices of remote or neighboring enemies" (p. 29). When Vancouver failed to respond favorably, they then decided that they should at least be protected "against any future molestations of visiting ships" (p. 29). They cited the incidents of ships taking on refreshments and failing to pay the arranged-for price, or paying in defective goods or goods of no use to the inhabitants. This was the case with some arms and ammunition they had received in trade. The muskets and pistols obtained would burst on being discharged, burning and maiming the operator. Gunpowder was mixed with charcoal. Vancouver inspected some of the guns and gunpowder they brought to show him (pp. 29-30). His reply was that if they submitted themselves to "authority and protection of a superior power, they might reasonably expect they would in future be less liable to such abuses" (pp. 30-31).

Undoubtedly Vancouver was writing for his British audience. The actual extent to which he had to give out promises is not known. Some claim that he promised a force of five hundred men and a gunboat to protect the islands (Bradley, 1944, p. 45). It is fairly certain that Kamehameha expected something because in later years he sent letters asking King George not to forget him (Bradley, 1944, pp. 48-49). Kamehameha and the other principal chiefs of Hawaii officially ceded the island to Great Britain in a ceremony on Vancouver's ship, February 25, 1794, according to Vancouver (1798, Vol. 3, pp. 54-57). The Hawaiian view was that they were asking for aid and considered that they had placed their island under the protection of Great Britain, not that they had given it away (Westervelt, 1914, p. 21).

The foregoing examples give an unusually enlightening insight into Vancouver's role in support of Kamehameha's regency. It is rather clear that he was pressing Kamehameha to transform his chieftainship into a kingship. Vancouver's remarkably clear exposition illustrates culture contact in action and identifies the results of the process. This is not to claim that all ideas for the structure of Kamehameha's government were the direct result of discussions with Vancouver, but he undoubtedly can be identified as perhaps the strongest single factor in introducing change in this area.

Before his final departure from the islands, Vancouver had his ships' carpenter build the first foreign-type boat for Kamehameha (Vancouver, 1798, Vol. 3, pp. 17-18). He stopped at Maui and attempted to promote support for Kamehameha from the high chief of that island (Vancouver, 1798, Vol. 3, pp. 49-50; Kamakau, 1961, p. 165). A Hawaiian history states that Vancouver "taught Kamehameha's men how to drill as a body of soldiers" (Westervelt, 1914, p. 20). Vancouver encouraged Kamehameha to treat John Young and Isaac Davis, Young's companion, well and to utilize their knowledge of ships and guns. "Vancouver gave the king much wholesome advice about the protection of his own person, the management of his kingdom, and the course that would be wise for him to take in regard to foreigners" (Dibble, 1909, p. 35; Vancouver, 1798, Vol. 3, pp. 52-53). "His [Vancouver's] conduct toward them [Young and Davis] was such as to raise them in the estimation of the natives" (Kuykendall, 1947, p. 43). Undoubtedly these two men figured prominently in the development of the new government structure and controls, even to the extent that Young was for ten years governor of the Island of Hawaii under Kamehameha (Dibble, 1909, pp. 35-36; Kuykendall, 1947, p. 54).

In the material presented by Ellis, and to a lesser degree by Dibble and his Hawaiian scholars, we observe a tendency to telescope precontact and postcontact behavior and descriptions of cultural elements. If the "elder" chiefs whom the ten Lahainaluna scholars were sent to interview on ancient ways were two years of age at the time of Cook's arrival, they would have been sixty years old in 1836 when the scholars questioned them. They would have been only nineteen when Kamehameha organized his new government. In general they would perhaps have been more able to separate the indigenous from the acculturated when asked to describe ancient Hawaiian religion, than when asked about the relationship between chief and commoner, or administrative controls used by chiefs, or the relationship of the people to the land. In these latter areas of inquiry they would be likely to recall most vividly the period of the Kamehameha regime.

This failure to differentiate between behavior in precontact and postcontact times was perhaps particularly true in Ellis' material, since he did not make any special effort to question the Hawaiian elders. Although they would have been among the most likely to have knowledge about precontact times, Ellis was apparently more concerned with simply describing conditions as he perceived them at the time he wrote. In this connection it might be said that the problem of perception was real. Undoubtedly the Western, capitalistic concept that land had to be "owned" by someone figured strongly in questions put to informants and in the translation of their answers. Thus, Ellis writes, "The king is acknowledged in every island as the lord and proprietor of the soil by hereditary right, or the laws of conquest" (Ellis, 1917, p. 314). To the question, "Whose land is this?" the reply, "This is the chief's land" did not, and could not tell anything about the usufruct rights of the people in the land.

In the writings of the Hawaiian scholars, however, there is a notable tendency to qualify statements about the extent of authority that could be exercised by a chief in ancient times, a quality not as apparent in Ellis' remarks on the subject (Ellis, 1917, pp. 394*ff*; Dibble, 1909, p. 76).

Acculturated behavior seems more obvious in those areas where change is associated with introduced items of material culture, such as with guns and gunpowder. On the other hand, it is more difficult to assess the effects of the introduction of a market economy where local produce, formerly used for the subsistence of the community as a whole, is now sold and the proceeds appropriated by the chiefs. For other cultural elements the assignment of particular institutions or behavior to indigenous or acculturative factors may present even greater obstacles.

There are interesting insights into the problem given us by Vancouver. By the time of Vancouver's last visit to Hawaii, Kamehameha had achieved a leading position on that island. Presumably, according to later descriptions of the supposed powers of a high chief, he would have had complete, authoritarian control over all inhabitants. In Vancouver we find statements that indicate this was not so, or at least there were exceptions. There were ceremonial obligations a chief had to his office and there were people over whom he did not have complete control. Much the same situation is revealed at the time of the negotiations in 1779 for the return of guns used by the marines who were killed with Cook and for Cook's remains (Cook, 1784, Vol. 3, p. 81). There were people over whom the ruling chief of the island at that time did not have complete control. It is these exceptions that make the difference between the imagined complete authoritarian power of the chiefs postulated by Ellis (1917, pp. 319-320), and the delicately qualified description by Dibble (1909, p. 76). However, even Dibble hesitates to do more than nod in the direction of qualified power. He may have found it difficult to believe, considering the situation at the time he wrote; and also, to portray the Hawaiian chiefs in too benevolent a role would have lessened their contrast with the enlightened missionaries.

For the student interested in the acculturative process, Hawaii is a rich field, not only because there is so much material, but also because the records of the transitional phase are extensive and in some cases very detailed. However, most of the material, even that published in the early years, deals with behavior and institutions already in the process of transition. Not only were the early writers describing conditions already changed, but they were looking through Western eyes, making value judgments based on Western values, and making statements of fact from the viewpoint of their own Western concepts. In addition, those writers who actively represented special interest groups—religious, economic, or political—found it difficult, if not impossible to be objective, particularly in their own areas of concern.

LITERATURE CITED

ANONYMOUS [Mrs. E. Sanders]
    1848. *Remarks on the "Tour Around Hawaii," by the Missionaries, Messrs. Ellis, Thurston, Bishop and Goodrich, in 1823*. Salem: Printed for the author.
BRADLEY, HAROLD WHITMAN
    1944. *The American Frontier in Hawaii: The Pioneers, 1789-1843*. Palo Alto: Stanford Univ. Press.
COOK, JAMES
    1784. *A Voyage to the Pacific Ocean . . . in the years 1776, 1777, 1778, 1779, and 1780. . . .* 3 vols. (Vol. 1 and 2 by Cook; Vol. 3 by King.) London: W. and A. Strahan.
DIBBLE, SHELDON
    1909. *A History of the Sandwich Islands*. Honolulu: Thrum.
ELLIS, WILLIAM
    1917. *A Narrative of a Tour through Hawaii*. Honolulu: Hawaiian Gazette.
KAMAKAU, SAMUEL M.
    1961. *Ruling Chiefs of Hawaii*. Honolulu: Kamehameha Schools Press.
KUYKENDALL, RALPH S.
    1947. *The Hawaiian Kingdom, 1778-1854*. Honolulu: Univ. Hawaii Press.
VANCOUVER, GEORGE
    1798. *A Voyage of Discovery to the North Pacific Ocean and Round the World . . . in the* Discovery *. . . and . . .* Chatham. 3 vols. and atlas of charts. London: Robinson.
WESTERVELT, W. D.
    1914. "Kamehameha's Cession of the Island of Hawaii to Great Britain in 1794." *22nd Annual Report,* pp. 19-24. Honolulu: Hawaiian Historical Soc.

THE LEI NIHO PALAOA

J. HALLEY COX
University of Hawaii

IN THE WORLD of Polynesian artifacts there are a few objects which approach what can be called pure sculpture, objects in which the interest of the artists seems to have been directed toward a manipulation of formal elements and the achievement of technical perfection beyond the needs of function alone. Such forms are completely devoid of ornamentation and do not develop out of virtuosity, but from a craftsmanlike concern for the quality of the form itself. Examples can be found in a few of the more superbly finished and beautifully contoured of the "eared" food pounders from Tahiti, or in the abstract greenstone fishhook ornaments of New Zealand. The Hawaiian sculptors' efforts were channeled in this direction more noticeably than those of other Polynesian craftsmen, and the *lei niho palaoa,* the Hawaiian neck ornament of whale ivory, is a fine example of such sophisticated forms (Fig. 2 K). One of the major attributes contributing to the visual appeal of the *lei palaoa* is its apparent simplicity. On an elemental level of appreciation and understanding, this appearance of simplicity is because of the obvious bilateral symmetry and the two easily perceived basic shapes, the rectangular stem and the curving tip. These present a seemingly uncomplicated system of forms, which upon closer view extend into exceedingly rich variations in shape, subtleties of surface movements and contour, contraction and expansion of volumes and movements in space, providing a sculptural unity to the total form. There is also a suggestion of functionalism, as though the object were designed for some very specialized usage, a "tool in abstract." The sensing of this quality is accompanied by an aesthetic response to the technical perfection and to an imagined functional excellence.

The purpose here, however, is not to discuss these aesthetic values, although they will not be ignored, but to relate some of the possible sources of this unique form. This paper will be concerned only with the ivory pendant itself and not with the entire assembly made up of the bundle of braided hair and cords from which the ivory unit is suspended (Fig. 1). This assembly, and particularly the pendant, became quite strictly standardized as an emblem of chiefly rank in the period immediately before the first arrival of Europeans in 1778 and continued as such a symbol well into the historic period. A detailed history of the *lei palaoa* and a full account of the form probably can never be told, but some archaeological evidence is available, some reconstruction of a possible chronological sequence can be suggested, and certain areas of speculation concerning the source of the form seem worth while. It can be said that the final "classical" *palaoa* form has three generic sources: historical or traditional, technical, and symbolic. Obviously, these aspects of origin will interrelate and others might well be proposed; they are presented here, and in this order, mainly as a means of organizing this discussion.

HISTORICAL-TRADITIONAL SOURCE

The use of whale tooth[1] artificially shaped and drilled for suspension as ornaments was not an invention of the Hawaiians. Such items were in wide use in Polynesia and in some form were surely brought to Hawaii with the first Polynesian settlers. In addition to Hawaii, Buck (1957, p. 533) lists the Marquesas, Mangareva, Chatham Islands, and New Zealand as using single uncarved teeth of the sperm whale as pendants. The people of all of these areas are known to have also carved the tooth. Carved whale-tooth pendants have subsequently been found in archaeological excavations in New Zealand, the Society Islands (Emory and Sinoto, 1964, p. 148) and in the Marquesas Islands.

Most of the existing specimens, Hawaiian and otherwise, are late examples or from personal collections and surface finds, so that their age cannot be determined, but fortunately a few archaeological specimens provide some clues to the ancient form. As can be noted in the chart (Fig. 2) operations on the natural tooth generally took the form of the reshaping of the tip, with a tendency to emphasize its forward curve, and the preparation of the root end of the tooth for the drilling

---

[1] This is the tooth of the sperm whale or cachalot. The lower jaw contains 40 to 50 teeth ranging in size in the adult form from about 4 to 10 inches long, the middle size weighing on the average about 2 pounds.

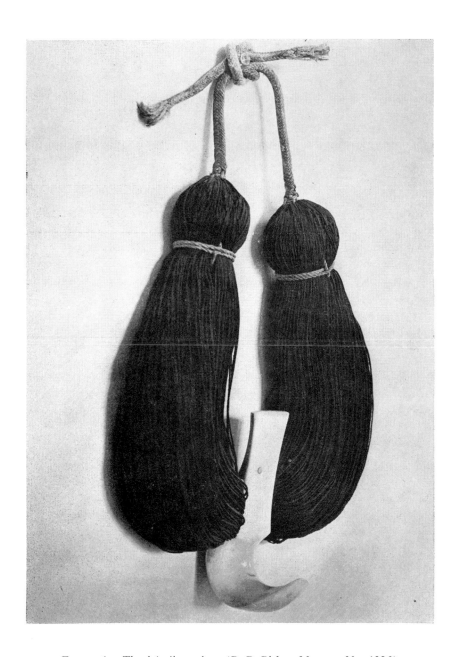

Figure 1.—The *lei niho palaoa* (B. P. Bishop Museum No. 1326).

of the suspension hole. In the earlier examples this reshaping was not very extensive, but was very likely carried out for the purpose of standardizing the size and shape, since the teeth were usually intended as single units of a continuous string. Their effectiveness as individual shapes was not as important as the pattern of the total array. This type of multiple unit necklace was probably prevalent in all of Polynesia in the early periods. Examples have been found in archaeological excavations in New Zealand and the Marquesas. In Fiji, Tonga, and Samoa the multiple tooth necklace was in use well into the historic period, but in the rest of Polynesia it seems to have been discontinued prior to the discovery period.

That the multiple unit type was used at an early period in Hawaii is suggested by the discovery of two pig tusks (Fig. 2 A). They were found in an archaeological site at South Point, Hawaii (Emory, Bonk, and Sinoto, 1959).[2] A number of these ornaments were probably strung together as a necklace. Estimating from the radiocarbon dates established for this site, this type of ornament could have been in use prior to A.D. 1000. Emory and Sinoto (1964, p. 150) suggest that the ornaments found in the burials at Maupiti in the Society Islands and similar ones found more recently in the Marquesas were strung as a necklace rather than being used singly. It was not until the later period in Hawaii and New Zealand, probably just prior to the discovery period, that the single tooth pendant became widely used. The change from the use of multiple tooth necklaces to single unit pendants probably accounts for the considerable elaboration in form in these later examples.

The Maupiti, Marquesan, and New Zealand Moa-Hunter[3] pendants (Fig. 2 L,M,N) are strikingly similar, tending toward a sharpening and some curving of the tip, and the forming of a lipped rim at the top. This rim may be a lashing notch for the tying of a series of teeth together to form a necklace in a manner similar to some of the Western Polynesian multiple tooth necklaces, which are lashed together rather than strung on a single cord. Although no definite chronology has yet been established for these archaeological finds at Maupiti and in the Mar-

------

[2] This archaeological report is limited to Hawaiian fishhooks but establishes dates and relative chronology for sites where pendants have been found. The Bishop Museum Anthropology Department has in preparation a similar report on ornaments from archaeological sites.

[3] See Emory and Sinoto (1964, p. 159) for a discussion of the similarity between the Maupiti and Moa-Hunter burials and artifacts.

quesas, Emory and Sinoto are of the opinion that the pendants are quite early, dating between A.D. 850 and 1300, which brings them very near to the period established by Duff (1956, p. xii) for the similar Moa-Hunter pendants.

To date, there is no example from Hawaii of this type, so it cannot be stated with certainty that it is the precursor of the conventionalized Hawaiian *lei palaoa*. In the Hawaiian examples, the nearest to

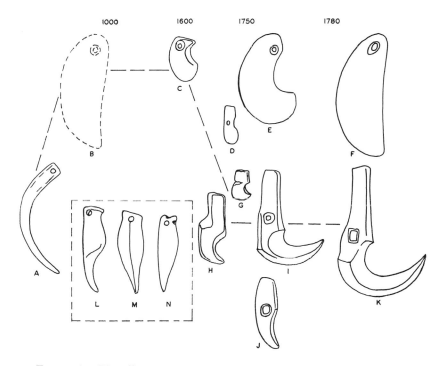

FIGURE 2.—Hawaiian pendant forms, arranged in a relative time sequence (with an insert of three early Eastern Polynesian types). **A.** Boar's tusk, archaeological (H8E5, 5-35), 3 in. **B.** Assumed early form. **C.** Whale-tooth bracelet unit, burial casket, 1 in. **D.** Dog-tooth bracelet unit, burial (C8939), ¾ in. **E.** Bone pendant, burial (C9702), 2½ in. **F.** Calcite pendant, *lei 'ōpu'u* (12013). **G.** Pig-molar pendant, unfinished, archaeological (H2-VII-3), 11/16 in. **H.** Coral pendant, unfinished, archaeological (H8E11-17), 1½ in. **I.** Shell pendant, burial, 1⅝ in. **J.** Whale-ivory pendant, burial (C8939), 1½ in. **K.** Whale-ivory pendant, final elaborated form (author's collection), 4¼ in. **L.** Whale-ivory necklace unit, Moa-Hunter, New Zealand (after Duff), 2 in. **M.** Whale-ivory necklace unit, Maupiti, Society Islands (after Emory), 3¼ in. **N.** Whale-ivory necklace unit, Uahuka, Marquesas, 1 in.

the lipped-rim Polynesian types is the *lei 'ōpu'u* (bud-shaped pendant) of almost natural tooth form (Fig. 2 B,F). Although no examples of this type have been found which can be accurately dated, one example is from a prehistoric burial. It is most likely a fairly ancient type.

It is surprising to note that of the thirteen pendants of the *lei palaoa* form from Hawaiian archaeological material, not one is made from whale tooth. They are of coral, shell, pig tooth, and animal and whale bone. Among the 176 nonarchaeological specimens in Bishop Museum, still other substitute materials are found: wood, stone, calcite, tortoise shell, walrus ivory, and elephant ivory. Of these 176 examples only 92 are whale ivory. The majority of the other 84 specimens are walrus ivory which was available only after the contact period. Since the emphasis in this report is on the form rather than the material or techniques of manufacture, I will not pursue this aspect further except to point out that quite a variety of materials was used. It is quite evident from this that to the Hawaiian the material from which the pendant was made was of secondary importance; his greatest concern was the form.

Examples of an intermediate form between the *lei 'ōpu'u* and the curved tongue style have been found with Hawaiian burials. Probably the oldest of these was found in the fiber casket containing the bones of a high chief of Ka'u and Puna on the Island of Hawaii who lived in about A.D. 1600.[4] The casket contained fifteen carved units, five of which were whale ivory, five of pig tooth, and five of tortoise shell. These were probably strung as a bracelet rather than as a necklace (Fig. 2 C). Each unit has a short, rounded, blunt tip turning sharply forward from the stem, the stem being pierced transversely near the top. A similar form was used as a single pendant, as in the specimen from burials found at Mokapu, Oahu (Fig. 2 E). This is made of bone and is considerably larger than the bracelet units. The Mokapu burials also produced another group of ornaments, seventeen small pieces of dog tooth 0.75 inch long (Fig. 2 D), and a larger rectangular piece of whale ivory 1.5 inches long, with its lower half curving slightly forward (Fig. 2 J). The small pieces are indented slightly in the center and are rounded at the lower tip. There is little doubt that these small bone pieces are a crude version of the blunt-tipped form such as that found in the fiber casket mentioned above. Buck points out that the indented

---

[4] This chief probably lived about five generations after Liloa, founder of the dynasty of supreme chiefs of Hawaii. The bracelet described here was removed after X-rays revealed some objects other than bones in the casket.

grooves on the outer surface of the bracelet pieces have affinity in structure with those in the turtle-shell bracelets and the larger boar-tusk bracelets. This is quite true, and the similarity to the blunt-tipped units from the fiber casket tends to put this bracelet at a mid-point in form between the turtle-shell bracelet and the *lei palaoa*. The small pieces and the ivory *palaoa* unit were found together and were as-sembled, for exhibition purposes, with the ivory piece as the center unit of a bracelet (Buck, 1957, p. 550, Fig. 338), but it is doubtful that this is an accurate reconstruction. The suspension hole is so much larger in the ivory piece than are the holes in the bone pieces that it must have been intended for a larger cord than would pass through the small units. Furthermore, the holes in the ivory piece and those of the small units do not line up properly for use as a bracelet. It is more likely that the larger unit was used separately as a single pendant. Another bracelet set of the same general type was found with a burial on the Island of Kahoolawe (McAllister, 1933, p. 44, Fig. 14, C). There are twelve units of animal bone carved in the same general shape as those found in the chief's fiber casket, but not as finely made nor as uniform in shape. The lower end protrudes in a rounded blunt tip; there is a lip at the upper front edge and a transverse hole about in the center. In two or three of the units the upper lip is wide and in one it is the same size as the tip, the groove between the two ends is in the center, again indicating an affinity with the turtle-shell bracelet pieces. There is little doubt, however, that the general form was intended to follow the *palaoa* shape.

The sharpening of the lower tip which leads to the extended curved tongue form occurs in two examples from archaeological sites near South Point, Hawaii.[5] One of these is of coral (Fig. 2 H), the other is of pig molar (Fig. 2 G). In neither of these pendants does the lower tip reach forward of the front of the stem, as it does in all cases in the "classical" *lei palaoa* form. It is doubtful if either is finished, but the tongue-tipped form is clearly established by these specimens. The coral specimen is from Site H2, found at a depth of only 6 inches, and consequently may not be of a date earlier than 1800. The pig molar is from the late period of Site H8 and hence is not likely to be dated earlier than about 1750. Although these two ornaments are the only datable specimens, they do establish that the pointed, nonprotruding tip was a prehistoric type.

---

[5] See Emory, Bonk, and Sinoto, 1959, for site description and chronology.

Two pendants from the Mokapu burials are of the fully developed protruding tongue type (Fig. 2 I), but in each the bottom curve of the tongue unit is comparatively slight, tending to extend horizontally rather than curving up, as in the "classical" type. This may be a local variation but, since these are very likely prediscovery specimens, they may mark an intermediate step in the development of the final form. With these examples from burials which seem to be from the prediscovery period, the two archaeological specimens from the South Point sites, and fragments and unfinished *palaoas* from other archaeological material, we can be fairly certain that the protruding tongue type of *palaoa* is a prehistoric form. However, this chronology does not establish much time depth for the "classical" type. It probably did not come into use until the 18th century.

Is the sequence in Hawaii then: (1) refined natural tooth (thin tusk and bud form), (2) lip-rimmed (Maupiti and Moa-Hunter), (3) blunt-tipped, (4) nonprotruding tongue-tipped, (5) horizontal protruding tongue-tipped, (6) curved protruding tongue-tipped ("classical" style)? Number 2 in this sequence, the lip-rimmed type, has not been found in Hawaii, and although it may seem to be a logical step in the series, it is not vital to the sequence and may never have been a part of the development of the Hawaiian pendants.

Since the legends and traditional history of Hawaii cannot be completely discounted as reflecting historic events, the references to the *lei niho palaoa* in ancient folklore are of some interest and importance. As a notable example, a whale-tooth pendant is featured in a story about Liloa (Elbert, 1959, pp. 114-166), the founder of the dynasty of supreme chiefs of the Island of Hawaii leading to the Kamehameha line. Reckoning by established genealogy, Liloa ruled the Hamakua district in about 1475.[6] The story is too involved to be told here, but a *lei niho palaoa* is the key object through which Liloa's son, 'Umi, is recognized as Liloa's rightful successor. In another instance, as a young man, 'Umi gets into serious trouble for contemptuously breaking a *lei palaoa* made of *wiliwili* wood belonging to the daughter of the chief of the district of Hilo. For this insult 'Umi is held prisoner and his own real ivory pendant (probably the one formerly belonging to Liloa) is forfeited as his ransom. 'Umi later waged a full-scale war against the chiefs of Hilo to regain the pendant, and incidentally to take over the district of Hilo.

---

[6] Liloa-ka-'ai, whose bracelet of whale tooth *palaoa* forms is described above, occurs in this genealogy as a grandson of Liloa generations prior to A.D. 1800.

Two factors, besides problems of authenticity and dating, must be considered in relation to the traditional accounts of the pendants. Nowhere in these stories is there a description of the form of the pendant, although, as above, the material is named. It would be of real significance if there was some indication of the form the *lei palaoa* took in 1475. The other point is that the legends were recorded in the mid-1800's when the meanings of terms as translated and written in English may have been considerably different from the ancient spoken language. Elbert (1959, p. 160) makes this comment in a footnote to the term *wiliwili* in the story of 'Umi:

> *Wiliwili, Erythrina monosperma,* a light white wood forming the ornament or tongue of the necklace. As this has been known generally of ivory, from sperm whale's teeth, with variations in shell and in bone, the name *palaoa* is confusedly applied to all alike as an ivory-tongued necklace. This account would imply that *palaoa* was the name of the peculiar curve-tongued ornament itself, not ivory, the material of which it was formed, though its general use and reference as *niho palaoa*—ivory tooth—is responsible therefor.

In spite of these problems such accounts of the *lei palaoa* do attest to a long traditional use of the object and to its special significance as an object of value.

TECHNICAL SOURCE

Hawaiians were not at all prolific in the area of pure decoration. It is only in tattooing, tapa making, gourd design, and feather work that any interest in two-dimensional surface decoration was exhibited and in these Hawaiian artists practiced a restraint, meticulous judgment, and control that reflect a considerable degree of reserve in decorative usage. The tapa and gourd designs (and possibly the tattooing patterns) are allied with the ancient Polynesian tradition of wood carving. In the gourd and tapa decoration the relationship to geometric wood carving patterns and techniques is direct. The outer layer of the gourd was incised, probably with a hafted shark tooth, the same type of knife used in wood carving, and the thin layer of epidermis was removed. The peeled and unpeeled surfaces took the coloring strain differently, creating the contrast in the pattern. The designs are universally angular geometric (Fig. 3 A). In the case of the tapa, two uses of surface wood carving with geometric pattern were employed. The bamboo stamps, used for transferring the dye to the finished tapa, were cut with sharp straight-sided angular patterns (Fig. 3 B). However, in the grooved and richly embossed hardwood tapa beaters (Fig. 3 C), which spread the fibers and gave remarkably soft flexibility to the Hawaiian tapa, the angularity of the pattern was softened by a tapering of the edges of the grooves. Similar patterns, when cut larger and deeper, as in the crests of the temple images (Fig. 3 D) show a greater slanting of the sides of the notches. This results from the sculptor finding the easiest and most efficient striking angle for the adz as it cuts across the grain of the wood. In the hair patterns of the Kona style[7] images (Fig. 3 E) this adjustment to technical needs

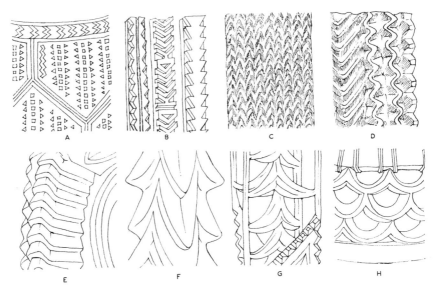

FIGURE 3.—Geometric carving, Hawaii. **A.** Gourd decoration. **B.** Bamboo tapa stamps. **C.** Tapa beater surface. **D.** Crest of a temple image. **E.** Hair pattern, temple image. **F.** Crest of a temple image. **G.** Crest of a stick image. **H.** Drum base.

tends to form longer down-slanting notches which in the deeper and individually worked units actually becomes a tooth-shaped curve (Fig. 3 F). It is basically a triangular block, but as it is freed from the base to become a volume in open space (Fig. 3 G), the best means of forming it is as a tapering curve rather than as an angular pyramid, since such a form would otherwise resist the cutting action of the adz or chisel and would surely split apart with the grain. Anyone who has carved or whittled wood will realize this. The similarity of the resulting form to the *lei palaoa* is clearly evident. The open screen pattern of

---

[7] This is the well-known temple image style with the large head, "figure eight" mouth and with the hair pattern curving back and down over the shoulders. Its production was apparently localized on the Kona coast of Hawaii at the time of Captain Cook's discovery of the islands.

the drum base (Fig. 3 H) is another example of the geometric patterns becoming curvilinear and triangular in cross section when developed in three dimensions. Certainly part of the reason for a convergence to this form lies in the techniques of wood carving, the materials, tools, and habits of the sculptor. This also suggests that this curving tongue-like form was developed in wood by the sculptors and thereby gained acceptance as a suitable motif. Its adaptation to a specific symbolic purpose was then fully acceptable as being within the prevailing style.

SYMBOLIC SOURCE

As a symbol the *lei palaoa* form is so highly abstract that a number of meanings might easily be applied to it. In fact, it is likely that it did have multiple signification. It is well known that it was a symbol of rank, its use limited to the noble class, the *ali'i*. This seems to be owing partly to the rarity of the material, whale tooth. Prior to the coming of the Europeans and their whaling activity, the Hawaiians' only source would have been from whales that floundered onto the reefs or were somehow washed ashore. These were declared *kapu* to all but the chief, giving him immediate control of the wealth which they contained. Could the teeth of the whale have been a material symbol of the chief's right to establish *kapus?* The story of 'Umi indicates the significance and value attached to the whale-tooth ornament, and a war was fought to regain possession of the heirloom. David Malo (1951, p. 77) names the *lei palaoa* as the object of second greatest value in ancient Hawaii, being second only to the *'ahu 'ula,* feather capes and cloaks. In third place is the *kahili,* the royal standard, also of feathers. It is of some interest to note that in this value structure, symbols take precedence over material wealth such as land, canoes, houses, food, and the like.

Since the form of the *lei palaoa* is the result of a sculptural develop-ment, it is helpful to turn to the wood sculpture for evidence of the symbolism that was intended. A great many of the images, particularly those of the *'aumakua* class,[8] have a strongly protruding chin, mouth, and tongue, which in extreme cases is precisely the *lei palaoa* form, even to such details as the medial ridge on the upper surface and the rounded lower side (Fig. 4). In all of these images the mouth is open and the tip of the tongue protrudes to terminate the forward-sweeping curve. The grimace that this represents must have had a special significance, pos-sibly as an indication of an attribute of the gods, a gesture of superiority,

---

[8] These are the images of ancestral deities or family gods as distinguished from the larger temple images.

defiance and contempt. In a few images all other facial features are subordinate to this jaw-mouth-tongue form and in some the shape is turned over and applied as a head crest or helmet. The similarity of these forms to the *lei palaoa* is unquestionable and certainly no coincidence. The tendency toward the chin-mouth-tongue complex in the image sculpture results in a wide range of treatments suggesting that the artists were free to—or were expected to—invent variations within a certain acceptable style range. The limits of this range seem to be anything from a comparatively naturalistic head form, always with the mouth open and tongue protruding, to something similar to the *palaoa* form, all understood as having similar meaning. Possibly the intensity of this meaning increased with the distortion toward the abstract and the ultimate symbol carries the pure essence of such meaning.

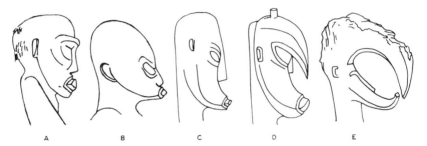

    A   B   C   D   E

FIGURE 4.—'*Aumakua* images, Hawaii, indicating the jaw-mouth-tongue elaboration. **A.** W. Munsterburger collection, New York. **B.** Bishop Museum (C9595). **C.** Bishop Museum (7654). **D.** Bishop Museum (1363). **E.** Bishop Museum (1341).

There is no such range of form in the whale-tooth ornament itself. It is surprisingly standardized and so far there is no evidence of its having much time depth. The form appears, full blown, probably as an adaptation of a form invented for the '*aumakua* images which were being produced in considerable numbers contemporaneously with the emerging *lei palaoa*.

The tongue is a significant element in other Polynesian images, notably the protruding tongue of the commemorative figures of New Zealand tribal ancestors where it is said to signify the fierce and violent fighting expression of the warrior chief. The protruding tongue also occurs in Cook Island god images and in Marquesan sculpture, but in a much more placid form. In none of these is the jaw line exaggerated as it is in Hawaii.

In spite of the sculptural emphasis on the conventionalized tongue form in the images, there are very few instances in the chants and legends of ancient Hawaii where the gods and tongue are mentioned together. This one, however, related by Kamakau (1964, p. 12) is revealing:

Hakau-a-Liloa, the high chief who ruled over Hawaii, was one of those laid on the altar as a burnt offering for the god by 'Umi. The story is well known, and thousands of persons were eyewitnesses that the god came down from heaven in a billow of floating clouds, with thunder and lightning and dark clouds, and the tongue of the god quivered above the *lele* [altar]. The god was not seen; his body was in the heavens, but his tongue quivered downward like lightning, and the burnt offering became a billow of smoke and rose up and was gone.

The name of the god of canoe makers was Kupa-'ai-ke'e, which translates as "Kupa [who] eats defects—referring to the belief that this god's tongue helped eat out the inside of the log to be made into a canoe" (Pukui and Elbert, 1957, p. 169). The word for tongue in Hawaiian is *lelo* (or *alelo*). *Lelo* is also the name of the front tip of the *lei palaoa* ornament. The term also has a second meaning relating it to the *palaoa:* "*lelo* . . . 2. Yellowish, especially the hue imparted to a whale-tooth pendant by smoking" (Pukui and Elbert, 1957, pp. 18, 187).

If the tip of the *palaoa* is the tongue, as its corresponding part of the images certainly is, the rest of the hooked curve is the chin and jaw which begins at the horizontal "brow-ridge" at the base of the upright stem. In this context, the *lei palaoa* can be taken to be a highly abstract symbol for the head of a god, reduced to the dynamic sweep of the "tongue" and the static upright "forehead." It carries with it associations of the vitality and spiritual force of the god, the ultimate source of all *mana*. Further speculation might lead one to suspect that the bundle of braided human hair used to support the ivory form symbolizes the hair of the image. Is it a counterpart of the human hair pegged into the head of the *'aumakua* image? Since a simple cord could serve as a support for the pendant, the hair bundle must have a more special significance. The shape of the hair bundle is strikingly similar to the hair pattern of the large Kona style temple images, thick and bulging at the forehead and gathered into two long tapering braids. The tendency to invent elaborated forms is always generated by some stimulus beyond the simple needs of function.

The tongue shape or anything similar to it was probably taken by the Hawaiians to mean the presence of abundant *mana*. Once it had become an accepted shape in the repertory of the sculptors, established both as a known symbol and as an aesthetically desirable form, the shape was used with one or both of these associations in a number of different objects. Its most significant function is as the chin-mouth-tongue complex of the *'aumakua* images, but it occurs also as hair and crest patterns in many of the stick and temple images. The form is reflected in the crests of the feather helmets. The crescent and half-crescent patterns worked in brilliant yellow, red, and black feathers on the capes and cloaks are probably the most strikingly beautiful use of this tongue-shaped *mana* symbol. Except for Buck's (1957, p. 227) suggestion that the curved motifs on the capes and cloaks resulted from the curving of the lower border which introduced a curved design into the feather decoration, there has been no explanation of these crescent designs. They are surely a two-dimensional version of the tongue of the *lei niho palaoa,* and in this as in other applications of the symbol, the objects carrying it were associated with the gods, *mana,* and the sacredness of the *ali'i.*

LITERATURE CITED

BUCK, PETER H. (TE RANGI HIROA)
  1957. *Arts and Crafts of Hawaii.* B. P. Bishop Mus. Spec. Pub. 45. Honolulu.

DUFF, ROGER S.
  1956. *The Moa-Hunter Period of Maori Culture.* (2nd ed.) Dept. of Internal Affairs. Wellington.

ELBERT, SAMUEL H. (Editor)
  1959. *Selections from Fornander's Hawaiian Antiquities and Folk-Lore.* Honolulu: Univ. Hawaii Press.

EMORY, KENNETH P., WILLIAM J. BONK, and YOSIHIKO H. SINOTO
  1959. *Fishhooks.* B. P. Bishop Mus. Spec. Pub. 47. Honolulu.

EMORY, KENNETH P., and YOSIHIKO H. SINOTO
  1964. "Eastern Polynesian Burials at Maupiti." *J. Polynesian Soc.* **73**:143-159.

KAMAKAU, SAMUEL M.
  1961. *Ruling Chiefs of Hawaii.* Honolulu: Kamehameha Schools Press.
  1964. *Ka Po'e Kahiko: The People of Old.* (MARY KAWENA PUKUI, trans., DOROTHY B. BARRÈRE, editor.) B. P. Bishop Mus. Spec. Pub. 51. Honolulu.

MALO, DAVID
  1951. *Hawaiian Antiquities.* B. P. Bishop Mus. Spec. Pub. 2. (2nd ed.) Honolulu.

MCALLISTER, J. GILBERT
  1933. *Archaeology of Kahoolawe.* B. P. Bishop Mus. Bull. 115. Honolulu.

PUKUI, MARY KAWENA, and SAMUEL H. ELBERT
  1957. *Hawaiian-English Dictionary.* Honolulu: Univ. Hawaii Press.

POI MAKING

MARY KAWENA PUKUI[1]
Bernice P. Bishop Museum, Honolulu

AMONG MY PEOPLE, a child learned to pound *poi* at the age of eight, and it was the custom that each beginner ate every bit of the first batch he or she pounded. Thus it was that I learned with a boy cousin from Puna, who had come to vacation with us at Kapuʻeuhi on the Island of Hawaii. We were told by our aunt, who was the instructor, to do our very best or eat lumpy *poi*. My hair was coiled up and pinned securely so that there was no danger of getting a strand of it in the *poi*. We both turned out a smooth batch, which my aunt blessed (*pule kahukahu*) before we ate. Heathen or Christian, my people were religious and believed in praying.

Poi making and *imu* cooking were usually the work of men and boys, but girls were taught in case of an emergency when masculine help might be unavailable. It was true in my situation, for at the age of sixteen I did our family *poi* pounding and enjoyed it. The women of our district were capable of replacing their men if need be, but I must confess that at *imu* making, I am no success. My mother could do almost anything a man did except deep-sea fishing.

Before I go on, let me tell about this place, Kapuʻeuhi. After the railroad station was completed there in 1903, the village was renamed Glenwood. Although the railroad station no longer exists, the new name is retained and the old one forgotten.

My people were particular about their utensils, never placing them where they would be stepped or sat upon. That was *kapu*. Therefore,

---

[1] In this account, which I originally recorded in June, 1958 (Bishop Museum Tape H-41 E), I use the terms of my own southern Hawaii people and describe their ways.

poi boards were leaned against the wall and the *poi* stones put on shelves. Boards were made of *ahakea,* or *'ohi'a* wood; those for one pounder were about 2½ to 3 feet long, and those for two persons were twice that length. We learned to name the parts of the stone pounder: the knob at the top was the *poheoheo;* the part gripped by the hands was the *ku'au;* the rim was the *ka'e;* and the base was the *mole.*

Prior to my arrival into this world, my ancestors baked taro in the *imu,* but in my childhood, they boiled it in five-gallon kerosene cans. After the cans were emptied of their original contents, they were cut open at the top, washed clean, and saved for many uses. Some had rounded sticks fastened across the top or handles made of heavy wire put on to make carrying easier. These cleaned kerosene cans were called *kini huinaha,* literally "square tins." Unless we expected company, three *kini huinaha* of boiled taro at a time were sufficient for our household, consisting of two women and two girls and an uncle who worked at the Experimental Station. My father and another uncle worked in Mountain View and came home only on weekends.

While the boiling was going on, the board and stone were washed and sunned, if the day was sunny. Then a mat was laid down, or a thick layer of banana, *ti,* or *hapu'u* leaves, depending on where the pounding was to be done. On this, the board was placed. Our boards were never laid on bare floor or earth when *poi* was pounded lest with every whack of the stone dust would rise into the *poi.* This my people did not like.

When the taro was cooked, most of the family pitched in with the work. Children often helped to pull off the outer skin or *'ili kalo.* Fingers were cooled by dipping into water. The removal of the outer skin was called *ho'opohole.* The skin was saved to be used later as fertilizer for plants. The taro was then passed to the peelers, usually adults, who scraped it clean of every vestige of peeling or flaws with a large *'opihi* shell. The scrapings, or *'ili kana,* were fed to the chickens or pigs. My people were very particular about cleanliness and food preparation and had a saying, *Hana kapulu ka lima, 'ai 'ino ka waha,* or "Careless work with the hands puts dirty food in the mouth."

Pounding was not so much a matter of strength, but of knowing how. The time taken in pounding depended on the kind of taro, whether hard or soft. Hard taro required pounding while hot, otherwise it would be like pounding a solid rubber ball. My folks were partial to the *la'aloa* because it could remain in the field longer without getting watery or *loliloli.* That meant that the pounding had to be done while the taro was hot. Everybody old enough in the family pitched in with the peeling and scraping, and one or two with the pounding. A little guminess or *'ulika* of the taro was not minded—we cut it off and ate it. We like it at that stage.

The first step in the pounding was the *pakīkī*. The taro was held on the board with the left hand while the stone was held in the right with knob tilted slightly toward the worker. With the rim of the stone the taro was gradually broken into small pieces. After several were thus broken up, moisture was added by dipping the fingers in water and slipping a hand under the mass to prevent its sticking to the board. A bowl of water was always near the pounder for this purpose. The mass was turned and brought back on itself from the outer edge to be pounded. If some of the taro had become slightly watery because of being overripe, the stone was worked back and forth with some pressure, *'anai,* to break any particles that had a tendency to form lumps. If the taro were in a perfect state of maturity, there was no need to work the stone back and forth. Overripe taro is somewhat gummy or watery, and underripe is flaky.

The moistening of the fingers and the turning of the edges to the middle continued until the mashed taro became a solid mass. This moistening and turning was called *pāku'iku'i,* and the forming into a solid mass was called *hui ka 'ai.* If this was to be carried or sent to a relative or friend who lived some distance away, the pounding stopped at this stage. *Ti* leaves were washed clean, then laid in rows overlapping each other. The mass of taro was placed on the leaves and a neat bundle, called a *pa'i 'ai,* was made. The person receiving the *poi* placed it on his board and went on with the pounding from there. The bundles were named according to size: very large was the *holo'ai;* smaller, the *pa'i 'ai;* and a still smaller one was the *pukele'ai.* Our folks referred to the *poi* sold in bags as a *pukele'ai.*

If the *poi* was for family use, the *poi* maker went on with the next step called *ho'opohā.* The left hand was dipped in water and the bottom of the stone moistened with a quick pat before it came down on the mass. The moistening and turning of the mass continued to the end of the work, and the only change was in the moistening of the bottom of the stone. The pat on the stone had a light sound and the pound a heavier one, and the rhythmic sound of this stage of *poi* pounding was always a delight to my ears. Little by little water was added, through the moistening of fingers, never by pouring, until the right consistency was reached and the mass perfectly smooth. This was the stage in which *poi* was sold commercially.

If the *poi* was for family use, the work did not stop there, for the next thing to do was to knead it on the board, as one would knead dough for bread. Here water was poured in, a small amount at a time, but the mass was not allowed to become too soft. This process, called *poho* or *kupele,* was to discourage any tendency to harden and dry. Should *poi* be allowed to harden, it became grainy, *oneone.*

After the pounding and kneading was done and the *poi* put away in the container, the sticky, watery residue on the board, called *kale'ai,* was saved. If a baby at the creeping or walking stage was around, his limbs and body were massaged with the *kale'ai* to strengthen them. As the *kale'ai* dried, it acted as an astringent. I cannot tell just exactly what it did, only what I saw done.

May I tell a tale of long ago that originated the saying *Hilea i kalo 'eka'eka,* or "Hilea of the dirty taro." Koha-i-ka-lani, chief of the district of Ka'ū in Hawaii, went to Punalu'u for a vacation, and it was the duty of the upland farmers of that section of the land to take turns bringing *poi* to him and his court. When it was Hilea's turn, the chief's *'ā'īpu'upu'u,* or steward, was shocked to find a speck of taro peeling in the *poi.* It was dirty! The *poi* makers were severely punished and Hilea became synonymous with uncleanliness. To say of a person that he was from Hilea, perhaps with some stress on the name of the village, was the equivalent of saying that he was dirty. The words *No Hilea paha* could cause a fight with a quick-tempered Ka'ū native in my childhood. Today, the insult can pass unnoticed.

Cleanliness in *poi* making was imperative, and until it became a commercial commodity, strainers were unknown.

With the coming of foreigners to Hawaii, the work of *poi* making gradually passed from the hands of the Hawaiians to those of the Orientals, especially the Chinese. Hawaiians took up employment on ranches, in *pulu* gathering, or on plantations, and by the 1870's there was hardly a sizable plantation village that did not have a Chinese *poi* shop. It was the Chinese who pounded the *poi* by hand and sold it in buckets of various sizes or in kegs. I did not see one that could be called particularly dirty, but they were not as meticulous in taro peeling as the Hawaiians were. The latter gouged out every flaw with the *'opihi* shell and scraped away every speck on the taro. I've seen the Chinese use spoons instead of the shell. This led to the use of scrim or cheese-cloth, *kānana poi,* to insure the Hawaiian that what he was eating was absolutely clean.

A *poi* shop was easily identified by a white flag, frequently just a washed flour sack, opened and tacked to a stick and set up near the doorway. Everybody recognized the *poi* flag. In the days when men tucked in their shirttails, one that hung out behind was dubbed the *"poi* flag."

First, *poi* was sold by the pail and later in cotton sacks, usually flour sacks reduced in size. Buyers would empty the bags, and wash and return them to the shops.

From infancy to womanhood, I've known *poi* made at home and also *poi* bought from the Chinese shops. I saw no machine-made *poi* until 1907 when I came to Honolulu, where it could be obtained at the Wilcox factory in Kalihi, on King Street near Mokauea.

Poi mixing was *ho'owali'ai.* Water was added in small quantities at a time so as to have it completely absorbed in the mixture. Too much water all at once made it *hakuhaku,* or lumpy. Working the *poi* so that it was forced between the fingers was called *'opā'opā;* the rotation of the hand in the mass while mixing was *'owai.* Now and then, the thumb side of the hand was worked upward against the side of the container to break up any lumps that might be in the *poi.* This motion was called *kō.* My mother reminded me when I first learned to mix *poi* to *hana a pau pono ka wai,* that is, keep working at it until the water was entirely absorbed.

Hawaiians preferred *poi* that had begun to ferment, forming air bubbles called *pohā.* Very fresh *poi* was called *'ai ko'eko'e* or *poi ko'eko'e,* and was usually fed to babies. The longer it remained, the more bubbly and sour it became, but my people never threw any away, no matter if it tasted like vinegar. They had a saying, *Ho'olei wale i ka 'ai a hiki mai no ka la e nānā mai ai ia 'oe,* or "Thow *poi* away and the day will come when it will just look at you," meaning, waste *poi* today and tomorrow you may want some and not get any. The sour *poi* was mixed with the very fresh to counteract its acidity.

There were no spoons in ancient times and *poi* was eaten with the fingers. To this day, we oldsters still enjoy eating Hawaiian food with our fingers. Dipping up the *poi* with the fingers was called a *miki.* A wad of *poi* adhering to the fingers was a *miki 'ai.* Dipping with one finger was *miki pāpākāhi,* with two fingers, *miki pāpālua.* My people never used three fingers, and whether they did in other localities or not, I don't know. I was taught as a small child never to separate the fingers in a *miki pāpālua,* and to insert them in the *poi* up to the first joint or perhaps just below them, rotate them about two times and bring the wad that adhered up to the mouth. The fingers should not be drawn through the *poi* toward one, that was *koe,* or *kīhelu,* scratch. I learned to wave my hand gracefully to and fro while talking and keep the *poi* balanced there until I was ready to eat it. There must be no jerky movement, *kā,* lest a dab fly off and smear somebody nearby. When two people shared the same bowl, one must wait until the other person had lifted his hand before inserting his.

After all had eaten, if there was any left in the container, the last to finish would run his finger around inside of the container to work the *poi* clinging to the sides down to the mass. All smudge must be removed and the sides clean. This was called *kahi.* Not to *kahi* the container called for a sharp rebuke from a parent or grandparent. Only at the end of eating did one *kahi* the *poi* bowl, for to do so while another was still eating was bad manners, like suggesting that he quit eating.

One should never serve very soft *poi* to a guest, that was not gracious. If it was a little thick, it could be thinned to suit one's taste, therefore it was not improper to serve such at a meal.

Watching a person eat was not good manners, nor was repeating to the others the amount of food consumed. My father's people, the *Haole,* might mention that someone ate six sandwiches and an apple, but my mother's people regarded this as abominable manners. One might say of a person, however, that he had a good appetite, *'ono ka 'ai.*

Business was never discussed over an open *poi* bowl, for Haloa, the god of taro, contradicted and denied the success of the project. Mealtime was the time for jovial conversation and cheerful recounting of anything except business. Children were never scolded at table and all unpleasant topics were avoided. Smacking the lips was polite, for only stingy people ate in silence or behind closed doors.

Any passer-by was hailed and invited to come in and eat when the people of the house ate, *Aloha mai e 'ai.* I remember being hailed and asked to share a meal many a time in the past. No traveler in old Hawaii need be hungry, for he could accept the invitation if he chose. The host was glad to share, even if his meal was a humble one of cooked taro greens, *kukui* nut relish, and *poi.* As long as a Hawaiian had his *poi,* and salt, he could get along with dried shrimps, *palula,* or sweet potato greens, or anything edible he could find.

Hands were always washed before and after eating and no household lacked a *po'i wai holoi,* or wash basin. In putting *poi* away, containers were always securely covered to prevent dust from entering and the surface from drying into a crust. This crust was called a *pāpa'a.* Anciently, all *poi* containers had rounded lids that resembled shallow basins and were sometimes used to hold meats when not employed as a lid. A carrying net, called *kōkō,* was placed on the outside of the container so that it could be hung up out of the way or suspended from the end of a *mamaka* or carrying stick when traveling.

In post-European days, prior to our present one, *poi* was sometimes kept in kegs or crocks beside the old wooden or gourd bowls. Crocks were probably introduced from Germany, for the Hawaiian name for such is *kelemania,* or German. When not in use, the openings of these containers were tied securely with clean dish towels before putting on the lids.

Empty *poi* containers were usually sunned after washing, to prevent a souring condition called *kūālani.* With porcelain bowls as we have today, this sunning is not necessary. My grandmother always declared that *poi* tasted much better when eaten from a gourd container than from a porcelain bowl.

There were three ways in which *poi* was fed to a small child. In the *kīhele, poi* was dipped up with the index finger and conveyed to the child's mouth. In the *pū'ā,* the feeder placed the *poi* and meat into her own mouth, masticated the food, then fed it from her mouth to that of the child, much in the way a mother pigeon feeds her young. In the *kau,* the child tilted back the head, opened the mouth wide, and the wad of *poi* was dropped into the open mouth from the fingers of the feeder held about six inches above. It was fun to be fed that way. I was fed that way by my grandmother.

Let me tell you about Haloa, since I had mentioned his name. There were two of them, brothers, who bore the same name. They were the sons of Wakea by Ho'ohokulani, chiefs and supernatural persons of remote antiquity. One was born a peculiar thing and so was tossed outside, against the wall of the house. From this sprouted the first taro, named Ha-loa, or Long-stalk. Its leaves were named Lau-kapalili and Lau-kapalala. The next to be born was a boy, who also bore the name Haloa, and from this brother, high chiefs were descended. They were the *mole o Haloa* or the root of Haloa. So one brother was a god whose form was the taro and the other was an ancestor of chiefs. We refer to our hereditary chiefs as *kalo kanu o ka 'aina* or "taro planted in the land," a source of life. One of King Kalakaua's genealogical chants refers to him as the offspring of Haloa. In designing his crown, the taro leaf was selected. Should you look at his crown, you'll see something resembling hearts with points turned upward. That is the symbol of Haloa.

There is a story often told of two taro plants that flew from Kona to Ka'ū. We know that taro doesn't fly. Writers of stories who do not know what it is all about, think that the flying taro is just a tale to amuse children. Not so! Big Taro was an important chief and Little Taro was his attendant. They were captives in war and had to dwell with Laka in Kona. Then one day Little Taro noticed activities denoting that someone was to be sacrificed, and he said to his master and companion: "When they look at my roots, they will find me of lesser importance than you. Yours is the bigger root." The other said: "Let us take flight to safety." Thus, they found their way to Punaluʻu in Kaʻū and there are two small places there that bear the names of Big Taro, Kalo-nui, and Little Taro, Kalo-iki.

Poi was made not only of taro but also of breadfruit and sweet potato. Breadfruit *poi* required pounding like taro *poi,* but sweet-potato *poi* was made with less work. The potatoes were mashed and water was added in small quantities until the right consistency was reached. Then it was set aside until it began to ferment. This was the principal food of people who lived in arid places, such as most of Kaʻū. In some places it was called *poi ʻuwala,* but my people called it *paʻi ʻuwala.*

In the last century a number of Hawaiians went to the west coast of North America to work as miners or salmon fishers. They got hungry for their native staff of life, *poi,* and someone found a way to make it out of flour. Letters were written home of their substitute *poi, poi palaoa.* Whether Hawaiians here learned from these descriptions or whether someone returned to show them how, I don't know, but some of my relatives made flour *poi* and liked it, mixed half and half with taro *poi.* Flour *poi* was not made by pounding but by stirring constantly while boiling water was poured into the flour. I have never made it, but I have watched my aunt who used a large coffee stick with bark removed to do the stirring. The bottom of the stick was flattened on both sides so that it could be worked against the side of the container to prevent the formation of lumps. Flour *poi* fermented just like taro *poi* did, and some people liked it. I have never acquired a taste for it and if I cannot get any taro *poi,* I am satisfied with the *paʻi ʻuwala* of my ancestors.

The word *ʻai* was much used by my people when referring to taro and the food prepared from it. To pound *poi* was *kuʻiʻai,* to mix it was to *hoʻowaliʻai,* to strain it was to *kānanaʻai.* Hard *poi* was *ʻaipaʻa.* My mother, in asking me to buy *poi* at the store, usually said, *E kuaʻi mai ʻoe i pukele ʻai na kakou.* "Buy us some *pukeleʻai.*" Sometimes she used the word *komou* in reference to *poi.* When asking whether we had any in the kitchen, she sometimes said, *He komou no ka kakou?* A thick-bottomed wooden bowl was a *kūmau* to my people, and the *poi* it contained was *komou* or *ʻai.*

Poi was the term used after the taro was prepared and ready for eating. Even then, a wooden or gourd bowl with *poi* was an *'umeke 'ai.* "Set the *poi* bowls down over there" would be *E ho'onoho aku i na 'umeke 'ai ma'ō.*

With porcelain bowls, *pola 'ai* and *pola poi* became interchangeable. "Bring the *poi* bowl" may be either *E lawe mai i ka pola 'ai,* or *E lawe mai i ka pola poi.*

To cook taro was *kahumu 'ai* or *kahu 'ai.* When anyone said, "Keola went to cook taro," it was frequently *Ua hele aku nei o Keola e kahumu 'ai.*

Cooked unpounded taro was either (*kalo*) *pa'a* or *kupu'u.* How often I was told where to get a cooked taro with this expression: *Aia no kahi kupu'u a kakou ma'ō.*

When Hawaiians grew taro for family use, the varieties were many: the kinds that matured quickly; those that could be left in the patches for a certain length of time without becoming soggy; those that could be made into attractive poi; and so forth. There were over two hundred varieties of this important plant.

The *paua* was the only taro that could grow in the arid sections of Ka'ū. Although ours were called dry-land taro, they were grown in the uplands near the forests where the rains kept the earth moist.

Poi ranged in color from white, yellow, pink, light gray to dark gray, depending on the variety of taro used. The *le'o* furnished yellow *poi* similar to that made of breadfruit, but for eating it was not good. Even the *poi* eaten on the day it was pounded caused an irritation of the throat. Only after it had fermented could *le'o poi* be eaten. It was tasty then. We grew it because we liked the color. The *lehua* and *'ula'ula* furnished pink *poi.*

Some taros were named for fish, like the *manini, 'ula'ula, kūmū, hīnālea, humuhumu,* and so on. When a *kūmū* fish was required as an offering to the gods and the sea was stormy, the taro was an acceptable substitute.

The *ipu-o-Lono, lauloa,* and *pi'iali'i* varieties were made into *poi* and served at religious ceremonies. The *haokea* was used when dedicating fish nets, and so the importance of the taro to the Hawaiian ranged from religious ceremonies to his daily diet.

A taro was named for Pele's smoke, *uahi-a-Pele,* another for her sister, Hi'i-aka. The latter taro was as attractive as any of our potted caladiums, having reddish-brown splotches. Another with pretty leaves splotched with white was named *'elepaio* for the bird loved by canoe makers. The *'ie'ie* taro was so named because its blossom was the same hue as that of the *'ie'ie* vine of the forest.

The young leaves, *lu'au*, stems, *hāhā*, and blossoms, *pua kalo,* were edible when cooked. The skin of the corm was excellent fertilizer, the scrapings were used as animal feed, and the cleaned taro was eaten, either pounded into *poi* or unpounded. The large mature leaf could be folded a certain way and water carried in it. The cooked taro greens were used on occasions as a substitute for a pig to be offered to the gods. It was then referred to as *pua'a hulu 'ole,* or "hairless pig." Where else in the world could a plant like this be found that was good as offerings, as medicine, as food for man and for animals, and for the soil? I almost forgot, taro is one of the ingredients of a pudding called *kulolo.* I have yet to see a Hawaiian who does not like it.

The Hawaiians had a riddle, *He 'ai ko lalo, he i'a ko luna,* that is, "The food is below, the meat is above." True, for many a day have we eaten the cooked taro greens with *poi.* We made a meal on *poi* and *lu'au,* or *hāhā,* or *pua kalo.*

As taro growing and *poi* making passed from the Hawaiians to the Chinese, some of our choice taros vanished. The *paua,* the only true dry-land taro, became extinct. The quick-maturing taro were grown more, and the slower but longer-lasting ones were found mostly in the patches of the Hawaiians. Although we grew some of the fast-maturing plants, we relied more and more on the *la'aloa* because it didn't spoil so fast.

Still we grew other varieties because we liked them, the *mana, lehua, 'ula'ula, 'ele'ele, hapu'u, le'o, kūmū, manini,* and others. The coloring of the stalks were so beautiful!

Constant picking of the *lu'au* was harmful, so we were taught only to break off the upper half and leave the lower half. When the leaves unfolded they looked like green butterflies sitting on the tips of stems.

When we first arrived at Kapu'euhi, we didn't have taro and had to buy plants, stalks and all, from other growers in various parts of Ola'a. Our source of supply between the first plantings and their maturing were the wild forest taro, *'aweu.* This taro grew in wet boggy places and had runners like the nut grass, which formed a sort of network in the mud. We looked for the main plant and, with a pull, drew all the taros to a spot where we could separate the corms from the stalk. One of the things our old folks taught us was that wild food plants did not belong to us but to the gods and we must replant. It was permissible to take a few stalks, but never all. The corms we took home to make into *poi*—and very tasty *poi* it was. This taro of the gods kept us well fed until our crops matured. We were also taught to observe where the *ti* grew the thickest. That indicated human habitation once upon a time, usually of bird catchers. Sometimes we found taro there, but not *'aweu.*

Once we found the *'ala,* a taro that gave out a fragrance when cooked. We replanted most of the stalks we found, but with a word of prayer, a please and a thank you, a few of the stalks went home with us to grow in our food patch. My people were strict in observing this law of the forest—always replant. *Ti,* taro, *'awa,* or banana—whatever we took, we replanted. We never asked: Why should we plant for some-body else to have some day? He was just as important to the gods as we were. Unfortunately, non-Hawaiians who were not taught that wild food plants belonged to the gods came to live there. They found the wild taros and took them, stalks and all, to boil for their pigs. Thus the supply we could go to, if need be, was depleted.

There is much more to be told of this wondrous plant that served my people as staff of life, vegetable, medicine, pudding, and offerings to the gods, but that will have to wait for another time.

So I'll say at the end of this story, *Pīpī holo ka'ao.* That was what my people always said at the conclusion of a narration: "It is sprinkled, the story has fled."

EAST POLYNESIA

FRIENDSHIP PACTS IN ANCIENT TAHITI

DOUGLAS OLIVER[1]

Harvard University

IN A SOCIETY so diffusely consanguineal and so pervasively hierarchical as that of ancient Tahiti, most of an individual's day-to-day interactions probably took place with persons explicitly identified as consanguines (or affines) or as having more (or less) authority or privilege of some kind or another. But interaction did take place between persons not thus categorized, or between persons whose ties of kinship, superiority, subordination, and the like were tenuous enough to ignore or override in favor of a more positive relationship of friendship.

The *Dictionary of the London Missionary Society* (Davies, 1851) lists three Tahitian words as having had the meaning of "friend": *hoa, taua* [tau'a] and *taio*. In the absence of adequate textual materials it is impossible to specify how these words overlapped or contrasted in meaning, but *taio* is certainly the one most frequently encountered in our sources,[2] and is the form used most often to refer to the more formalized kind of friendship relationship founded on a definite contract—that is, a friendship pact.[3]

---

[1] This descriptive article is a section from the writer's *Ancient Tahitian Society* (in preparation). Its appearance in print prior to the larger volume is occasioned partly by the interest evinced in this subject in recent publications by Gunson (1964) and Finney (1964), but mainly by the appropriateness of a discussion of friendship in a collection dedicated to Kenneth Emory. Grateful acknowledgment is made to officers of the London Missionary Society for their permission to make use of their unpublished documents on the Tahitian Mission, and to reproduce the excerpts quoted in this paper.

[2] *Hoa* may have had the most general, informal meaning as "companion," inasmuch as it is used in modern Tahitian not only for friend, companion, even acquaintance, but (in church parlance) for spouse as well. However, modern usage is no guarantee of pre-European meaning (Finney, 1964).

[3] But in a passage regarding women who save a slain warrior from being used as a sacrificial victim, Henry (1928, p. 311) wrote: ". . . the good woman who [thus] interposed became a *taua* (bosom friend) of all his family ever afterwards."

In any case, friendship pacts varied rather widely in reference and overlapped with the relationship we label "fosterage."[4] At one extreme such a pact seems to have been a formalized but rather casual way for two individuals to indicate peaceable intent toward one another, say a traveling chief with a dignitary met en route (Corney, 1913, p. 317). In many such cases the "contract" was probably short-lived and was concluded with nothing more than a temporary interchange of names and an exchange of presents.[5] At the other extreme was the kind of "friend-adoption" described by Morrison (1935, p. 189):

When a Man adopts a Friend for his Son the Ceremonie is the same [as a nuptial rite], only placing the Boy in the place of the Woman, the Ceremonie is ratified, and the boy & his friends exchange Names and are ever after looked as one of the Family, the New Friend becoming the adopted son of the Boys Father—this Freindship is most religiously kept, and never disolves till Death, tho they may seperate, and make temporary Friends while absent, but when they meet they always acknowledge each other. And should a Brother or one who is an adopted friend become poor or loose his land in War, he has nothing more to do but go to his Brother, or Friend, and live with him partaking of all he posesses as long as he lives & his wife and Family with him if he has any—or if any relation or Friend, tho not in immediate want, comes to the House of his Friend, he is always fed while he Stays and is Not only welcome to take away what he pleases but is loaded with presents.[6]

---

[4] In fact, there are grounds for asserting that, while the two basic axes of consanguinity—filiation and siblinghood—were derived mainly from descent (either biological or acknowledged) it was also possible to simulate them remarkably closely by contract. Indeed, some anthropologists might even claim that what we have to do with here is conceptually a single set of relationships, achievable by either descent or contract. Such possibly may have been the situation at some time in the Tahitian or more remote proto-Polynesian past (although there is no way of proving such a claim); but for the era under study we believe that not to have been the case. In the Tahitian society that we are attempting to describe, consanguinity was the prototype and fosterage-friendship the facsimile.

[5] Some such encounters may in fact have dispensed with name interchange, as witness the following report:

"We now took our leave of our friendly chief and proceeded along shore for about a mile when we were met by a throng of people at the head of whom appeared another chief. We had learned the ceremony we were to go through which was to receive the green bough which was always brought to us at every fresh meeting and to ratify the peace of which that was the emblem by laying our hands on our breast and saying Taio, which I imagine signifies friend. The bough was here offered and accepted and in return every one of us said Taio." (Beaglehole, 1962, Vol. I, pp. 254-255.)

The circumstance of the visitors having been European may have colored somewhat the Tahitians' view of the situation, but probably did not alter radically the ritual procedure.

[6] Gunson distinguishes dichotomously between *taio* pacts and what he labels "friendship nuptials," but I believe we have to do here with a more or less continuous series of contractual relationships rather than with two contrasting types.

Motivations for this kind of contract must have differed rather widely, both in terms of public avowal and private design. One such is described by Morrison (1935, p. 235):

If any Person wishes to have his son or Daughter instituted into the [Arioi] Society he procures an Areeuoy to be his Son or Daughters Friend and Adopts him for his Son and the Child is acknowledged an Areeuoy immediately the Ceremony is over, and May Continue to follow their Methods while He or she thinks Proper.

It goes without saying that friendship occurred among females as well as among males. If evidence were needed on this score there comes to mind a pretty little story about a young woman who gave her own life to save a female friend from the former's cannibal mother. The two friends are described as " . . . loving one another like sisters with the same father and mother" (Ropiteau, 1929, p. 289). On the other hand, we have found no specific references to friendship pacts between females.

Friendship, quite apart from kinship and casual sexual liaison, also occurred between females and males. When Europeans arrived on the scene, some women actively made *taio* pacts with their visitors—evidently for political advantage or for a more dependable source of European objects; but whether such pacts had been entered into previously, is not certain. In this connection, Wilson (1799, p. 346) wrote:

Lieutenant Corner [who had visited Tahiti in 1791 on the *Pandora* to capture the *Bounty* mutineers] also added that a tayoship formed between different sexes put a most solemn barrier against all personal liberties. Our brethren [the London Missionaries] who are returned, however, think this not to be the case; or that they have, since his visit degenerated.

This back-sliding, if such it was, must however have begun much earlier, for in his Journal of 1769, Molyneux wrote (Beaglehole, 1955, p. 553):

Individuals form Friendships with Individuals & every . . . [European] has his Tayo (or Friend) this might be productive of good consequences but the women begin to have a share in our Friendship which is by no means Platonick.

In this connection, another passage from Wilson (1799, p. 198) raises the possibility that women occasionally became *taio* of *mahu* (that is, male transvestites):

These mawhoos, being only six or eight in number [on Tahiti?], are kept by the principal chiefs. So depraved are these poor heathens, that even their women do not despise those fellows, but form friendships with them. This one was tayo to Iddeah [Iteia, wife of Pomare I].

Mahu, who spent much of their lives living and working as females, undoubtedly formed friendships with some women, but whether they entered into formal *taio* pacts with them is not altogether sure. It is quite possible that Wilson's use of the word *tayo* to describe Itea's relationship with this *mahu* may have been done on the basis of his own incomplete understanding of the *taio* institution, and not as the result of hearing the Maohi refer to the relationship as such.

Most of the friendship pacts reported in our sources were, however, between males, and between those of approximately the same age and social positions;[7] in these and other respects such relationships somewhat resembled brotherhood, but came even closer to approximating actual exchange of identity.[8]

Name interchange was a fundamental part of a friendship pact between Tahitians, but we are uncertain about the details of the arrangement (Parkinson, 1773, p. 68; Corney, 1918, p. 6). It may occasionally have involved titles, but perhaps more commonly soubriquets. Also, although some name interchanges may have become complete and permanent, others appear to have prevailed only when the principals were in each other's presence or proximity.

The extent of identity interchange involved in some friendship pacts is revealed in the following (Morrison, 1935, p. 168):

When a Chief is present in any Company the Men strip their Bodys to the Waist not suffering any Covering on their Head or Shoulders in His Presence—and all the weomen present uncover their Shoulders tucking their Cloth under armpits, to Cover their Breasts in token of obedience and respect, to his presence; the men are not always particular in this point except Upon the Chiefs Hereditary land *or that of His adopted friend,* where any neglect would be deemed an insult and punished accordingly. . . . (italics supplied)[9]

Our sources generally agree that a friendship pact had the effect of

---

[7] Finney (1964, p. 435*n*) makes the interesting but undocumentable suggestion that ". . . all chiefly youths ordinarily took a bond-friend in the course of growing up."

[8] In attempting to reconstruct the *taio* institution, we face the problem of deciding what was pre-European about it. Most recorded instances of it had to do with pacts between native and European; and while much of the native institution probably carried over into the new manifestations, it may be assumed that some changes were thereby introduced—in motivation as well as in degree of commitment and pattern of interaction. For example, the case of Ma'i excepted (see below, pp. 446–447), it is unlikely that cynical self-interest was as prominent in pacts between Tahitians as it was in some pacts initiated by Tahitians with their unsuspecting European visitors.

[9] Note the additional implications of this passage to the effect that "Chiefs" did not always conclude friendship pacts with other "Chiefs."

prohibiting sexual relations between a man and the sisters or daughters of his *taio*[10] (and presumably mothers); for example:

> . . . if a Man Makes a friend that Friend can never have any Connection with any female of the Family except his friends Wife, every other becoming His relations which they hold an abomination to have any Conexion with, nor can they be perswaded to alter that Custom on any Consideration, detesting as much as we do to have their own relations as wives (Morrison, 1935, p. 237).

I have discovered no evidence of the extension of this prohibition to other consanguines of each *taio*,[11] but an episode recorded by the missionary Crook (journal entry of April 10, 1826) provides an example of the consequences of friendship combined with fosterage (presumably, the friendship in question was of the pact variety):

> Some unpleasant things happened today which evinced the ignorance, pride and duplicity of our judges. A widow woman has been excommunicated for crim con. with a young man who is unbaptized. Her brother a chief of a district prevented their being married and therefore they ran into the mountains together. On Saturday last they were caught tied with ropes and used very cruelly by some of the inferior judges. Today the judges informed me that they were going to bring them to trial. I told them to do so and then allow them to be married to prevent further mischief. They seemed to consent but took every indirect method to counteract my design. They sentenced the man to be banished and the woman to work altho three months with child. As the man was forcibly led away the woman followed him, but was dragged from him with many struggles. I remonstrated against their proceedings.
>
> The chief judge a member of the church accused me with opposing the king and the laws and with opening a door for a commission of crime. After such an insult the people expected that we would leave them and were much alarmed. The chief of the district and a multitude of people thronged our house entreating that we would not leave them. The cause of the marriage being so much opposed is that the chief has adopted a boy who is a friend of the young man, and there-

---

[10] The case of Stewart, one of the *Bounty* mutineers, may have been an exception to this, but this matter is not altogether clear. Stewart was "married" to the daughter of a man described as being ". . . of great possession in landed property, near Matavy Bay" (Edwards and Hamilton, 1915, p. 106). At some point Stewart and this individual interchanged names, but whether before or after the "marriage" is not specified. It may be of course that this relationship was conceived less in terms of friendship than of fosterage, as was the case of Pomare II's fosterage of a prospective son-in-law.

[11] In fact, the question of how far a friendship pact involved relatives of the principals is unanswerable. Statements like the following imply a rather wide extension of the pact's undertakings—at least in terms of norms:

"Otu [Tu] show such a friendly attachment towards me [Rodriguez] that in a little while he adopted me as his brother, and as a son to his own parents and other kin people; and he exchanged his name for mine, an act which, among these people, is the bond of highest familiarity." (Corney, 1918, p. 6.)

But we are provided with little evidence concerning the actual implementation of such promises.

fore the young man is his friend or son as well as the boy according to their old customs and therefore must not marry his aunt.

In striking contrast with these proscriptions, a friendship pact appears to have licensed and encouraged sexual relations with a partner's wife, she having been considered " . . . a common property for the tayo" (Wilson, 1799, p. 346; see also Morrison, 1935, p. 237; Ellis, 1829, Vol. II, p. 369). According to Morrison (p. 184), however, the woman herself had a choice in the matter:

> . . . it is looked upon [as] a piece of Great friendship for a Man to Cohabit with the Wife of His adopted freind if she is agreeable: the Adopted friend being always allowed as a brother.

In one version of the *Legend of Honoura* warrior-heroes (*aito*), as an occupational category, are also described as licensed to "take liberties" with one another's wives. In the episode in question, while traveling to his home, a young *ari'i* and his bride met two other warriors, who said to him: "Give us charge of our little lady for a short while, since you and we are warriors all." The husband consented and the warriors had their pleasure with the woman. (As the translator added in an editorial note: "Women in those days were very passive.") However, these privileges evidently had their limits. Not content with such temporary entertainment the two warriors made off with the woman, but they were overtaken by the irate husband and killed (Henry, 1928).

Several legendary accounts indicate that hospitality sometimes included access to the host's wife (Adams, 1901; Salmon, 1904). Indeed, one may conclude from all such accounts that there prevailed a very general norm to the effect that whatever the intended degree of intimacy, the goods exchanged between males in the name of formal amicability quite often included access to one another's wife—but with varying degrees of access, ranging from tolerance of a one-time embrace to acquiescence in a continuing liaison such as the *taio* pact is alleged to have entailed.[12] Yet, in contrast to this norm, there is evidence that many husbands did not care for the arrangements when this involved their own wives; and this applies not only to absentee hosts but even to the case of

---

[12] Ellis (1829, Vol. 2, pp. 369-370) emphasizes the privileged nature of the friendship pact in the following:

"Their character in this respect [that is, sexual practices] presents a most unnatural mixture of brutal degradation, with infuriated and malignant jealousy; for while their conduct with respect to the taio, & c. exhibits an insensibility to every feeling essential to conjugal happiness, the least familiarity with the wife, unauthorized by the husband, even a word or look, from a stranger, if the husband was suspicious, or attributed it to improper motives, was followed by instant and deadly revenge."

close friends, as exemplified in the Legend of Turi and Mahu (Ahnne, 1931).

Hamilton, surgeon of the vessel *Pandora,* gave this account of the practice (Edwards and Hamilton, 1915, pp. 109-110):

In becoming the Tyo, or friend of a man, it is expected you pay him a compliment, by cherishing his wife; but, being ignorant of that ceremony, I very innocently gave high offence to Matuara, the king of York Island [Mo'orea], to whom I was introduced as his friend: a shyness took place on the side of his Majesty, from my neglect to his wife; but, through the medium of Brown the interpreter, he put me in mind of my duty, and on my promising my endeavours, matters were for that time made up. It was to me, however, a very serious inauguration: I was, in the first place, not a young man, and had been on shore a whole week; the lady was a woman of rank, being sister to Ottoo [Tu], the king of Otaheitee, and had in her youth been beautiful, and named Peggy Ottoo. She is the right hand dancing figure so elegantly delineated in Cook's Voyages. But Peggy had seen much service, and bore away many honourable scars in the fields of Venus. However, his Majesty's service must be done, and Matuara and I were again friends. He was a domesticated man, and passionatley fond of his wife and children, but now became pensive and melancholy, dreading the child should be Piebald; though the lady was six months advanced in her pregnancy before we came to the island."

The passage from Morrison quoted earlier (Morrison, 1935, p. 189) provides some notion of the range and amounts of objects and services involved in a friendship pact. This same writer added the following important detail (p. 194):

No Man ever Claims a right to any land but his own,[13] or His adopted Freinds, which he may Use during his Friends life, and should his Friend die without any Heir the Adopted friend is always considered as the right owner and no man disputes his right.

An example of this aspect of bond-friendship is provided in one traditional account of the establishment of the Pomare line on Tahiti (Adams, 1901, p. 85):

Tu of Faarava, having undertaken a visit to the distant land of Tahiti, came in by the Taunoa opening, which is the eastern channel into what is now the harbor of Papeete. Landing at Taunoa a stranger, he was invited to be the guest of Mauaihiti, who seems to have been a chief of Pare. Tu made himself so agreeable, or so useful to his host, that Mauaihiti adopted him as hoa, or brother, with the formal ceremonies attached to this custom, which consist in a grand feast, and union of all the families, and offering of all the rights and honors which belong to the host. Tu accepted them, and at the death of Mauaihiti he became heir and successor in the chief's line. He gave up all idea of returning to the Paumotus, and devoted his energy to extending his connections in Tahiti.

According to one account, an individual's title also could devolve

---

[13] Like many other assertions by Morrison this one is so very categorical that it can be taken, we suspect, as reflecting Tahitian *norms* rather than invariable practice.

upon his *taio,* but exactly what this title consists of is not altogether clear (Edwards and Hamilton, 1915, p. 110):

The force of friendship amongst those good creatures, will be more fully understood from the following circumstance: Churchill, the principal ringleader of the [*Bounty*] mutineers, on his landing, became the Tyo, or friend, of a great chief in the upper districts. Some time after the chief happening to die without issue, his title and estate, agreeable to their law from Tyoship, devolved on Churchill, who having some dispute with one Thomson of the *Bounty,* was shot by him. The natives immediately rose, and revenged the death of Churchill their chief, by killing Thomson, whose skull was afterwards shown to us, which bore evident marks of fracture.

Another statement by the missionary Crook (letter to Burder, December 4, 1824) indicates that six decades of European contact had altered only the sexual side of such practices among the Tahitians themselves:

. . . none of them know what it is to possess property in our sense of the word. If a native possess many articles of property, he must distribute and cannot withhold; all his friends have a kind of positive claim, and to refuse to give would be shocking. He would be a taata hamani ino, literally a man that works evil. It is to be observed that friendship, from whatever mercenary cause it was entered into is inviolate and is a kind of real relation in Tahiti. The friend was a representative of the person, and partner in everything, the wife not excepted. Our people have of course done away with the sinful part of it, but they are shackled by what remains, and will be many years before they can advance much in civilized life.

Undoubtedly underlying all such transactions was a tacit expectation of reciprocity—that is, the fundamental conception of the relationship was one of exchange, even though each contribution may have been phrased as an act of altruism, a nonreciprocable gift. Indeed, so apparently sincere were many such gifts that one observer took them to be such. (The observer was Bligh, and although the pacts in question involved Tahitians and Europeans, it is reasonable to assume that the transactions resembled those between Tahitian pact-friends, in this respect at least):

As it is the custom among these people whenever a Ship comes here, to have their separate Friend or Tyo as he is called so it has been the case among the people and Officers. Great friendship and disinterestedness from the Natives have been the result of this connection, for those who could not get a Canoe to come off in, swam to the Ship with bunches of Cocoanutts without any view of reward. (Bligh, 1937, Vol. II, p. 415.)

Against this attribution of "disinterestedness" is Cook's appraisal (Cook, 1784, pp. 8-9) of the reception accorded the Tahitian, Ma'i (Omai), when the latter returned to Tahiti after his visit to England:

When we first drew near the island, several canoes came off to the ship, each conducted by two or three men. But, as they were common fellows, Omai took no particular notice of them, nor they of him. They did not, even, seem to perceive, that he was one of their countrymen, although they conversed with him for some time. At length, a Chief, whom I had known before, named Ootee, and Omai's brother-in-law, who chanced to be now at this corner of the island, and three or four more persons, all of whom knew Omai, before he embarked with Captain Furneaux, came on board. Yet there was nothing either tender or striking in their meeting. On the contrary, there seemed to be perfect indifference on both sides, till Omai, having taken his brother down into the cabin, opened the drawer where he kept his red feathers, and gave him a few. This being presently known, amongst the rest of the natives upon deck, the face of affairs was entirely turned, and Ootee, who would hardly speak to Omai before, now begged, that they might be tayos, and exchange names. Omai accepted of the honour, and confirmed it with a present of red feathers; and Ootee, by way of return, sent ashore for a hog. But it was evident to every one of us, that it was not the man, but his property, they were in love with. Had he not shewn to them his treasure of red feathers, which is the commodity in greatest estimation at the island, I question much whether they would have bestowed even a cocoa-nut upon him. Such was Omai's first reception amongst his countrymen. I own, I never expected it would be otherwise; but, still, I was in hopes, that the valuable cargo of presents, with which the liberality of his friends in England had loaned him, would be the means of raising him into consequence, and of making him respected, even courted, by the first persons throughout the extent of the Society Islands. This could not have happened, had he conducted himself with any degree of prudence. But, instead of it, I am sorry to say, that he paid too little regard to the repeated advice of those who wished him well, and suffered himself to be duped by every designing knave.

A special kind of service exchanged between pact-friends is described by Morrison (1935, p. 174) in the following passage:

They take No Captives nor give any quarter, unless a man falls in with one who has formerly been His adopted friend, a breach of which they were never known to make. . . .[14]

---

[14] In this connection, we reproduce a somewhat puzzling statement by Bligh (1937, Vol. 2, p. 6) in which he distinguishes an individual's *taio* (his "friend") from his *ari'i* (his "champion, protector"):

"Every Person who comes among these people has or may have his Tyo or Friend, but the Commander or Erreerahigh (as he is called) has also his Erree [Ari'i] (in this sense signifies a Champion.) Now the Erreerahigh is beyond being an Erree to any one, and is only nominated a Tyo; it is therefore with me that Tynah is my Friend and Moannah my Erree, who is supposed to be determined to revenge any insult that may be given to me.

"When Captain Cook was here he was in the same situation. Tynah was his Friend and Poeeno his Erree, and it is from that circumstance that his Picture, which he gave to Otoo, now Tynah, is kept by Poeeno, which I have been long in discovering the Cause of. Poeeno is also my Tyo and in his own district by his people bears my Name and I his, but everywhere else I have the name of Tynah or Matte which are the two Names he has."

Gunson (1964, p. 66) writes:

To what extent the sexual element was present [in friendship contracts] is not clear, but there is reason to believe that it was. High ranking chiefs very often married much later than was usual amongst the people, the concept of continence was unknown, and pederasty (as in Hawaii) and other forms of sexual irregularity were regarded as chiefly prerogatives. Friendship rites with such implications are known in other cultures, and the suggestion is made to emphasize the commitment of the two parties to the contract.

I doubt very much that friendship pacts were deliberately entered into for homosexual purposes, although some contract-friends may very well have engaged in such practices—as indeed did many other pairs of males.[15]

Finally, I draw attention to that unusual and unelucidated manifestation of the friendship pact described by Morrison (1935, p. 175)[16] in which a warrior not only assumed the name of the individual killed by him in war, but ". . . adopts the nearest relation of the Deceased as his Friend, and by bearing his Name [presumably in addition to the name of the slain] becomes one of the Family and is ever after Treated as such and is as much beloved in the Family as if he had been born in it."

The account of friendship pacts just given leaves unanswered many important questions, such as: What proportion of the population entered into such pacts? Were they ever terminated by a specific ritual act?, and others. It would be of particular interest to know whether they were ever concluded between consanguines, or between same-genealogical-level affines (this latter situation would appear, however, to result in a status conflict vis-à-vis one another's sisters). Unfortunately, like so many other aspects of ancient Tahitian social structure, the available data run out of answers when the questions begin to become interesting!

---

[15] This qualification is also expressed by Dr. Gunson in a personal communication to the author.

[16] As with many such statements by Morrison, I recommend that this one be reviewed with some caution; but however exaggerated this one might be, it at least reflects, probably, what some Tahitians told Morrison.

LITERATURE CITED

ADAMS, HENRY
1901. *Tahiti. Memoirs of Arii Taimai e Marama of Eimeo, Teriirere of Tooarai, Terrinui of Tahiti, Tauraatua i Amo.* Paris.

AHNNE, E.
1931. "Turi et Mahu." *Bull. Soc. d'Études Océaniennes* 4:168-169.

BEAGLEHOLE, JOHN (Editor)
1955. *The Journals of Captain James Cook on His Voyages of Discovery.* Vol. 1. Cambridge: Hakluyt Soc. Extra Series 34.
1961. *The Journals of Captain James Cook on His Voyages of Discovery.* Vol. 2. Cambridge: Hakluyt Soc. Extra Series 35.
1962. *The Endeavour Journal of Joseph Banks.* 2 vols. Sydney: Angus and Robertson.

BLIGH, WILLIAM
1937. *The Log of the Bounty.* 2 vols. London: Golden Cockerel Press.

COOK, JAMES
1784. *A Voyage to the Pacific Ocean . . . in the years 1776, 1777, 1778, 1779, and 1780. . . .* 3 vols. (Vol. 1 and 2 by Cook, Vol. 3 by King.) London: W. and A. Strahan.

CORNEY, B. G. (Editor)
1913, 1914, 1918. *The Quest and Occupation of Tahiti by Emissaries of Spain during the Years 1772-1776.* 3 vols. London: Cambridge Univ. Press.

CROOK, WILLIAM
[n.d.] Journal and Letters. Manuscript in London Missionary Society Archives.

[DAVIES, JOHN]
1851. *A Tahitian and English Dictionary.* Tahiti: London Missionary Soc. Press.

EDWARDS, EDWARD, and GEORGE HAMILTON
1915. *Voyage of H.M.S. 'Pandora.'* London: Francis Edwards.

ELLIS, WILLIAM
1829. *Polynesian Researches.* 2 vols. London: Fisher, Son and Jackson.

FINNEY, BEN R.
1964. "Notes on Bond-Friendship in Tahiti." *J. Polynesian Soc.* 73:431-435.

GUNSON, NIEL
1964. "Great Women and Friendship Contract Rites in Pre-Christian Tahiti." *J. Polynesian Soc.* 73:53-69.

HENRY, TEUIRA
1895. "The Legend of Honoura." *J. Polynesian Soc.* 4:256-294.
1928. *Ancient Tahiti.* B. P. Bishop Mus. Bull. 48. Honolulu.

MORRISON, JAMES
1935. *The Journal of James Morrison.* London: Golden Cockerel Press.

PARKINSON, STANFIELD (Editor)

    1773. *A Journal of a Voyage to the South Seas in the Endeavour. Faithfully Transcribed from the Papers of the Late Sydney Parkinson*. London: Printed for Stanfield Parkinson.

ROPITEAU, A.

    1929. "Legende des deux amies." *Bull. Soc. d'Études Océaniennes* **3**:289-291.

SALMON, TATI

    1904. *The History of the Island of Borabora and Genealogy of our Family from Marae Vaiotaha*. Papeete: Privately printed.

WILSON, JAMES

    1799. *A Missionary Voyage to the Southern Pacific Ocean*. London: T. Gillet.

EARLY 'ĀTI OF THE WESTERN TUAMOTUS

PAUL OTTINO

Office de la Recherche Scientifique et Technique Outre-Mer

*Un chercheur aurait de grandes découvertes à faire dans les généalogies
classiques et légendaires de la Polynésie Française.*

R. P. Patrick O'Reilly

THE *'āti* to be discussed here may be briefly defined as a localized
descent group. The fieldwork for this study was done from 1962 to
1965 on the atoll of Rangiroa, located in the Western Tuamotus.[1] Some
material about early *'āti* on the atoll has been presented in a provisional
report (Ottino, 1965) and the present paper will be restricted to a discussion of the earliest *'āti* which can be traced.

The notion of *'āti,* while forgotten in the Society Islands,[2] and rather
hazy in the Marquesas[3] and Austral Islands,[4] is very much alive in the
western and central parts of the Tuamotuan archipelago, as well as in
the remote Gambier Islands.[5] However, in the present-day Tuamotuan
atolls, current *'āti* have little in common with the ancient ones, and the

---

[1] The research was sponsored by the Office de la Recherche Scientifique et
Technique Outre-Mer, Paris, France. Although the discussion is based upon
material from Rangiroa, the results are equally valid for the whole of the Western
and Central Tuamotus.

I wish to express my gratitude to Dr. Adrienne Kaeppler, for assistance with
the English version of this paper, and to William K. Kikuchi for drawing the
map and diagrams.

[2] In the Society Islands the word *'āti* is occasionally encountered in the topo-
nymy, for instance, the large plain of Āti/ma/ono in Tahiti, meaning literally
six *'āti.*

[3] Henri Lavondès (ORSTOM), personal communication.

[4] Pierre Vérin (ORSTOM–University of Madagascar), personal communication.

[5] According to Miss Sachiko Hatanaka (University of Tokyo), the word *'āti*
is not used at present in Pukarua atoll in the Eastern Tuamotus. The modern
grouping, called *'āti* elsewhere, is known there as *pupu* (personal communication).

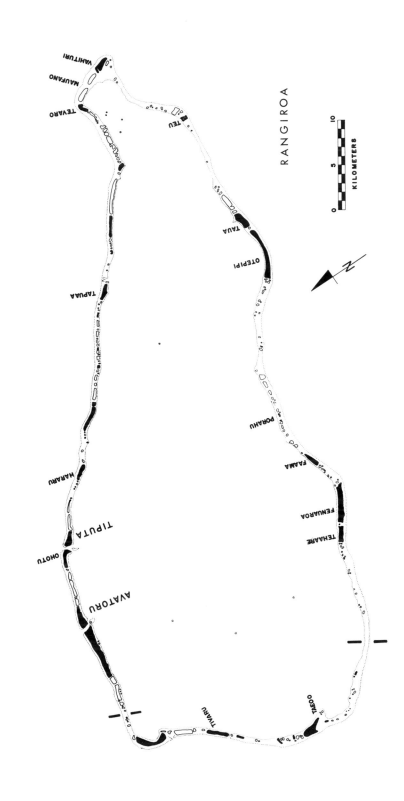

RANGIROA

VAHITURI
MAUFANO
TEVARO
TEU
TAUA
OTEPIPI
TAPUAA
HARARU
TIPUTA
OHOTU
AVATORU
PORAHU
FAAMA
FENUAROA
TEHAARE
TAEOO
TIVARU

N

KILOMETERS
0   5   10

use of the same term to describe such different entities cannot fail to be misleading, especially in matters of land tenure. This paper will not consider the historical evolution of the institution, but will be concerned only with the ancient 'āti as they were some three or four hundred years ago.

According to the evidence available from oral tradition, which has been partially validated by the first results of recent archaeological surveys and excavations (Lavondès and Garanger, 1966), the pre-European history of Rangiroa can be conveniently divided into two periods. The first one, encompassing some thirteen to fifteen generations, begins with the discovery of the Western Tuamotus by a group of Polynesians led by 'ŌIO,[6] the hero ancestor. This group of people had possibly sailed from the Leeward Islands, perhaps from Borabora, then known as Vavau. The first period ended with devastating tidal waves during the second half of the 16th century. The greatest part of the western end of the atoll, and particularly the extensive area known at that time as Tae'o'o, was swept away. The second period, beginning after the disaster, is considerably shorter, covering some eight or nine generations. Dominated by the fierce and ravaging wars carried on by attacking warriors (known as *parata* after the name of one of the most dangerous man-eating sharks) from the densely populated 'Ana'a atoll, this period came to an end with the flight of the Western Tuamotus' inhabitants to Tahiti.

The earlier period, following the landing of 'ŌIO, was one of isolation and the bonds with the high islands where the migration originated seem to have been completely severed. In contrast, the following period, which was characterized by strong demographic development, was marked by a complete change of former conditions after the establishment, probably through Makatea, of direct relations with Tahiti, and consequently strong Tahitian influence on the social, political, and religious evolution of the Western Tuamotus. It is for this very reason that I restrict myself to a discussion of the 'āti of 'ŌIO's period only, which is prior to any direct Tahitian influence.

PRESENT-DAY 'ĀTI

In Avatoru and Tiputa, the two villages of the atoll of Rangiroa, one often hears about 'āti, and it is not unusual to hear people stating that they belong to the same 'āti, or that certain lands pertain to such and such an 'āti. These problems of modern sociology are studied

[6] For the sake of simplicity, men's names both in text and diagrams are given in all capital letters.

elsewhere and, for the purposes of this paper, it is sufficient to recall three points about '*āti*. Present-day '*āti* are considered to be exogamous groups—which, in fact, is quite erroneous. Second, the notion of '*āti* is linked with the idea of a special land estate which, although nowadays split and shared, was in the past one of the important characteristics of the '*āti*. Another common present-day idea is that '*āti* affiliation is not exclusive and consequently that any person can be affiliated with different '*āti* through his different descent lines.

THE '*ĀTI* OF THE PAST

Reliable information concerning the ancient '*āti* is very limited, but still significant. In contrast with the situation today, '*āti* were widely scattered around the periphery of the atolls, forming diminutive communities which, according to my informants, did not exceed some thirty, forty, or, in rare cases, fifty people, including the children.

Informants are usually aware that all of the '*āti* were not contemporaneous. Some are recognized as old, or very old, while others are, known as more recent, or quite recent. One of the latter is the very important '*āti* Tetua of Tivaru and Avatoru. In the same way, every person who has some knowledge of the past is able to differentiate between important or very important '*āti*, such as '*āti* 'Ōio, Hoara, Fariua, and Marama, and the less important '*āti*. The relative importance of a particular '*āti* is evaluated on various grounds, including the number of its branches, '*ōpū*, the part played in the past history of the atoll (the facts of which are rarely remembered), the number of famous names appearing in its various genealogies, and last but not least, continuity through the course of time. Many of the earliest '*āti* have split into several branches, forming new '*āti*. Some of the branches are still in existence, whereas others have long since disappeared and would have been completely forgotten if their names had not been preserved in the genealogies.

The genealogies, transcribed for the first time some one hundred years ago when Tuamotuans were taught writing by the European missionaries, have been recorded, together with other traditions known as *parau,* or chants, *fa'atara, fa'ateniteni,* and, with quotations from the Scriptures, in the so-called ancestors' books, *puta tupuna.* All informants without exception considered genealogies to be identical with '*āti,* and a first problem is to ascertain to what extent this assumption is correct, and not misleading. To begin with, one may note that genealogies to be found in the *puta tupuna* are never labeled *tuatapapara'a* or *parau tuatapapa-*

ra'a, terms meaning genealogies, and expressing the correct recitation of a list of ancestors, starting always with the most remote, that is, "those who stand right at the bottom," *'i raro roa.* The *puta tupuna* genealogies are rather called *parau tupuna,* which literally means "ancestors' words," or traditions, or simply *parau,* that is, traditions.

Frequently lists of ancestors are presented under a much more complete heading, starting with the name of the *'āti,* the name of the land on which it lived, and even the limits, *'oti'a,* of the residential area, called *mata'eina'a,* a term which at that particular time conveyed only the idea of "residence" (Ottino, 1965). For example: *Parau tupuna no Taua/ te mata'eina'a no te 'āti Pau/ma'o/ e motu i Te/vai/Poa haere roa e Tahoro'ai/,* which means "Tradition of (the land of) Taua/ residence of the *'āti* Pau/ma'o/ (whose limits are from) islet Te/vai/Poa as far as (the land of) Tahoro'ai."

The list of ancestors' names can also be associated with certain parcels of land, as occurs in the "Tradition from Ahorehore," *Parau Tupuna no Ahorehore* (the ancient name of Taua). Or, on the contrary, the list may give the names of two or more *'āti* which are attached to the same land: *Parau tupuna no Teu* (Teu being the name of the land)/ *te mata'eina'a 'āti Pahorau, 'āti Ta'aroa/.* Even more confusion may arise when, as often occurs, different traditions from different lands refer to the same *'āti.* This may indicate either a shifting of residence, which shows that the genealogies do not cover the same historical period, or may represent a splitting process, in which case the genealogies may correspond to contemporaneous branches of a single *'āti* which have become localized in different places. When the *puta tupuna* do not give either the name of the *'āti* or of the land on which it resided, identification becomes still more difficult and often quite impossible. This happens when the list of names is written under a heading such as *"te hua'ai a* 'X' " which means no more than "X's descendants." This may refer to an actual genealogy, which was intended to provide a connection with a certain ancestor, often for the purpose of clearing land ownership, or, especially if the first name on the list is a woman's name, the line of ancestors may correspond to the offspring of a second union, possibly the origin of another branch of the *'āti.*

According to local theory, all the *'āti* had originated "from the interior" (*no roto mai*), that is, from a stem-*'āti,* which was the *'āti* 'Ōio, named after its founder, who was himself a member of a large social grouping or tribe known as the Marama. The *'āti* 'Ōio was located in the eastern part of the atoll on the land now called Vahituri. It was there that Ra'ipū, the oldest *marae,* was erected. In order to explain the process of formation of the several *'āti* from the stem-*'āti* 'Ōio, many informants have resorted to the image of an octopus whose head was supposed to symbolize the stem-*'āti,* or 'ŌIO himself, and whose tentacles stood for the separate *'āti* which "grew from within it."

Impressed by the octopus image, and having at my disposal the whole of the *puta tupuna* available in Rangiroa, I originally planned to reconstruct the splitting and branching process of all the Rangiroan *'āti,* starting with 'ŌIO and bridging the past down to the present living generations. This analysis, which I achieved partially for some of the most important *'āti* (Ottino, 1965), failed from the moment I attempted to grasp the totality of the *'āti.* This failure is relevant to the present discussion and can be accounted for by many reasons, of which the following are the most important. (1) The genealogies of certain *'āti* are missing, either lost or never recorded, as seems to be the case for the powerful and recent *'āti* Tetua. (2) Without any doubt, the genealogies do not retain all the names, but only those of outstanding senior or famed ancestors (*ta'ata tuiro'o*), that is, priests, warriors. The spouses of these outstanding individuals are also recorded in the genealogies but may not be recorded in their own *'āti* and thus cannot be traced. (3) Many *'āti* split into several branches and some of these branches have not been reported and "genealogized." This is particularly true for some of the *'ōpū* of the *'āti* Hoara and Fariua of Tiputa.

THE PARAU NO RA'IROA

By analyzing a very old document it is possible to gain a better idea of the ancient *'āti.* The document is the *Parau no Ra'iroa,* which is one of the oldest traditions connected with the very remote past of the atoll. This *parau,* identified with the accepted tradition of the *'āti* Hoara, provides an example of a complete genealogy which, in addition to the list of ancestors' names, gives invaluable information about the origin of the spouses, as well as about their *marae* and *'āti.*

PARAU TUPUNA NO RA'IROA—
    Tiputa. (Tera te mau tupuna i
    raro nei o Punaiteahita'a)

Taoto Punaiteahita'a ia Tutehoua no Ra'iroa, Ra'ipū te marae, *'āti* Ōio te mata'eina'a, fanau Puhenua tane, fanau Marere tane, fanau Turere'ura vahine.

TRADITION OF RANGIROA. (Here
    are the ancestors descending
    from Punaiteahita'a)

Punaiteahita'a slept with TUTEHOUA from Rangiroa. Ra'ipū was the *marae,* the *mata'eina'a* the one of *'āti* Ōio, they begot PUHENUA a male, MARERE a male, Turere'ura a female.

Taoto Puhenua ia Ouetumu vahine Aria te Ōio te fenua, Maraetapu te marae, 'āti Roa te mata'eina'a, fanau Hoara tane, fanau Ta'aroa tane (opani).

PUHENUA slept with Ouetumu a woman from the land Aria te 'Ōio (Aria from the bird 'ōio), Maraetapu was the *marae,* the *mata'eina'a* the one of 'āti Roa. They begot HOARA a male, TA'AROA a male (the end).

Taoto Hoara ia Teua, Ahe te fenua, Papatitahe te marae, 'āti Rao te mata'eina'a, fanau Ouetumu vahine (opani).

HOARA slept with Teua from the land of Ahe. Papatitahe was the *marae,* the *mata'eina'a,* the one of *'āti* Rao. They begot Ouetumu a female (the end).

Taoto Ouetumu ia Teruma, Maufano te fenua, Ta'atariri te marae, 'āti Mapu te mata'eina'a, fanau Maire tane, fanau o Tepaipaiahua vahine, fanau o Tane tane (opani).

Ouetumu slept with TERUMA from the land Maufano, Ta'atariri was the *marae,* the *mata'eina'a* the one of *'āti* Mapu. They begot MAIRE a male, Tepaipaiahua a female, TANE a male (the end).

Taoto Tepaipaiahua ia Punua, Tiputa te fenua, Ra'ipū te marae 'āti Hoara te mata'eina'a, fanau Hoara tane, fanau Temataputahi vahine, fanau u Hio vahine, fanau Hautepapa vahine, fanau o Maurea vahine (opani).

Tepaipaiahua slept with PUNUA from the land Tiputa, Ra'ipū was the *marae,* the *mata'eina'a* the one of *'āti* Hoara. They begot HOARA a male, Temataputahi a female, Hio a female, Hautepapa a female, Maurea a female (the end).

Taoto Hautepapa ia Teatua no Ra'iroa, Ra'ipū te marae, 'āti 'Ōio te mata'eina'a, fanau Matapoa vahine, fanau Piao vahine.

Hautepapa slept with TEATUA from Rangiroa, Ra'ipū was the *marae,* the *mata'eina'a* the one of *'āti* 'Ōio. They begot Matapoa a female, Piao a female.

Taoto Matapoa vahine ia Tumuteahere, Tapua'a te fenua, Naupata te marae, 'āti Tupa'ae te mata'eina'a, fanau Maire tane, fanau Teiva tane, fanau Tehau tane, fanau Tuheiroroari'i vahine (opani).

Matapoa slept with TUMUTEAHERE from the land Tapua'a, Naupata was the *marae,* the *mata'eina'a* the one of *'āti* Tupa'ae. They begot MAIRE a male, TEIVA a male, TEHAU a male, Tuheiroroari'i a female (the end).

Taoto Tehau ia Poanoano, Tapua'a te fenua, Naupata te marae, 'āti Tuapa'ae te mata'eina'a, fanau o Putahi (opani).

TEHAU slept with Poanoano from the land Tapua'a, Naupata was the *marae,* the *mata'eina'a* the one of *'āti* Tupua'ae. They begot Putahi (the end).

Taoto Putahi ia Ari'i'o'opu no Hiti'a, Fareari'i te mata'eina'a, fanau Hoara (opani).

Putahi slept with ARI'I'O'OPU from Hiti'a, the mata'eina'a was the one of 'āti Fareari'i. They begot HOARA (the end).

Taoto Hoara ia Tehuihui, Ohotu te fenua, Pari'i te marae, 'āti Moeroa te mata'eina'a, fanau Toru tane, fanau Tehipo vahine, fanau Hio vahine, fanau Ha'ahotu vahine, fanau Teiva tane, fanau Tehau tane (opani).

HOARA slept with Tehuihui from the land Ohotu, Pari'i was the marae, the mata'eina'a the one of 'āti Moeroa. They begot TORU a male, Tehipo a female, Hio a female, Ha'ahotu a female, TEIVA a male, TEHAU a male (the end).

Taoto Toru ia Ta'aroa, Teu te fenua, Toine te marae, Pahorau te mata'eina'a, fanau Teiva tane, fanau Hei vahine, fanau Ha'ura vahine, fanau Hopa tane (opani).

Toru slept with TA'AROA [or TA PUTA'AROA], Teu was the land, Toine was the marae, the mata'eina'a was the one of 'āti Pahorau. They begot TEIVA a male, Hei a female, Ha'ura a female, HOPA a male (the end).

Taoto Hopa ia Aroari'i, Tu'iare te fenua, Arehurehu te marae, 'āti Mare te mata'eina'a fanau Ha'auta tane, fanau Tehipo vahine, fanau Pahoaha tane, Teruma tane, fanau Teumahi tane, fanau Aitahu (opani).

HOPA slept with Aroari'i, Tu'iare was the land, Arehurehu was the marae, the mata'eina'a was the one of 'āti Mare. They begot HA'AUTA a male, Tehipo a female, PAHOAHA a male, TERUMA a male, TEUMAHI a male, AITAHU (the end).

Taoto Teumahi ia Tumaria, Tuherepari te fenua, O Putera'i te marae, 'āti Heiari'i te mata'eina'a, fanau Tapu tane, fanau Aroro vahine, fanau Teupoto tane (opani).

TEUMAHI slept with Tumaria, Tuherepari was the land, Putera'i was the marae, the mata'eina'a was the one of 'āti Heiari'i. They begot TAPU a male, Aroro a female, TEUPOTO a male (the end).

Taoto Teupotoa ia Tahi'ura, Avatoru te fenua, Fare'ura te marae, 'āti Niahe te mata'eina'a, fanau Hara tane (opani).

TEUPOTOA slept with Tahi'ura, Avatoru was the land, Fare'ura was the marae, the mata'eina'a was the one of 'āti Niahe. They begot HARA a male (the end).

Taoto Hoara ia Ti'ura, Harava te fenua, Maraetapu te marae, 'āti Mahinui te mata'eina'a, fanau Tuao tane, fanau Tahua (opani).

HOARA slept with Ti'ura, Harava was the land, Maraetapu was the marae, the mata'eina'a was the one of 'āti Mahinui. They begot TUAO a male, TAHUA (the end).

The genealogy established from the preceding text concerns in fact three descent lines and two 'āti, the 'āti Hoara and Ta'aroa, initiated by two sibling ancestors. For the sake of simplicity, the only names entered in Diagram A are those by whom the line is continued. The numbers beside the names indicate the order of birth within the sibling group. As for the generation levels, TUTEHOUA was TANETU'IHENUA's son and ŌIO's grandson. Thus Punaiteahita'a, TUTEHOUA's wife, well known as the "real" ancestor of the 'āti Hoara, stands at Generation Level 3.

The text and diagram reveal some of the characteristics of the ancient 'āti, including their structure, rules of affiliation, and geographical localities. Each of these aspects will be checked against other data.

'ĀTI HOARA'S GEOGRAPHICAL LOCATION

The text points out that Punaiteahita'a is "from Rangiroa." Fortunately, notes in the margins of two other copies of the same text indicate that this very remote ancestor lived at Te ava nui, literally, the large pass, the name of a part of the present site of the village of Tiputa. These marginal notes, however, confirm oral tradition. The text of the *parau* which gives the spouse's residence adds nothing for the descendants of Punaiteahita'a, who are said to "have lived where Punaiteahita'a lived." This assertion is verified by two other *parau tupuna,* those of the 'āti Mapu from Maufano and 'āti Tupa'ae from Tapua'a, which state that Ouetumu, spouse of TERUMA (Level 7), and Matapoa and TEHAU, spouses of TUMUTEAHERE and Poanoano, respectively, were from Tiputa.

According to the oral tradition, the 'āti Hoara's *marae* was erected by HOARA. Although the tradition does not give the name of this *marae,* it must have been one of the two most ancient *marae* of Tiputa, Tara'i/Opoa or Te/'iri/puhi, most probably the latter. The name means literally, moray eel's skin. This *marae* disappeared at Level 13, being replaced by Te/rua/ta'ata (literally, man's sepulcher), located nearer to the lagoon. In fact, the *fa'atara* of Tiputa relates the incident of Tehuihui's extreme grief on the tomb of TEHAU, of the 'āti Hoara, in the vicinity of *marae* Te/rua/ta'ata.

This fragment of genealogy shows that residence was one of the characteristics of the 'āti. In this case the residence has remained the same down to the present day. After more than twenty generations, Punaiteahita'a and HOARA's descendants are still living in Tiputa. From

Diagram A

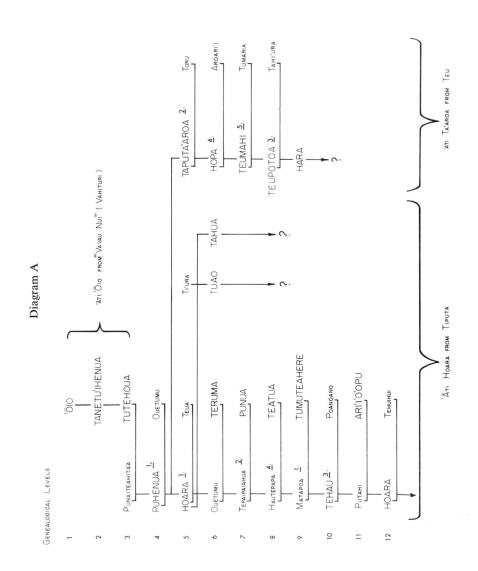

this point of view, the *'āti* Hoara provides an excellent example of continuity of occupation of a site through time by a descent group. With the exception of the *'āti* Fariua, also from Tiputa and closely related to the *'āti* Hoara, all other *'āti* have moved their residences, for historical reasons, and above all because of the fierce warfare at the end of the pre-European period. In the 19th century, with the arrival of the Europeans, the missionaries grouped the population into the three villages on Rangiroa, one of which, Tivaru, was abandoned after the hurricane of 1906.

LAND, 'ĀTI, AND MARAE

Two points are of importance here: (1) The *Parau no Ra'iroa* is concerned with the early period of the atoll's history just at the time the *'āti* began to emerge from the stem-*'āti;* (2) the indications in the text following the names of spouses of the members of the *'āti* Hoara and Ta'aroa show that they associate three terms; the name of the land, the name of the *marae,* and the name of the *'āti.*

The first period of Rangiroa history, which began with the discovery and settling of the atoll, was characterized by great mobility. Following the time of Generation Level 4, the descendants of 'ŌIO split into several branches. Each was concerned with becoming recognized and with the establishment of its territory, as outlined in the *Fa'atara no Ra'iroa.* It is noteworthy that the earlier texts and genealogies, the *Parau no Ra'iroa,* as well as the chant of Rangiroa, *Fa'atara no Ra'iroa,* refer to Rangiroa as a whole and not to the different "lands," *fenua,* and "islets," *motu,* with which the later chants and genealogies are concerned. Among the numerous branches originating from 'ŌIO, some which were located in different parts of the atoll merged into *'āti,* whereas others disappeared quickly, either by dying out or being absorbed into other *'āti.* Complete recognition of an *'āti* as a corporate unit was generally not fully achieved before Generation Level 7 or 8. This explains why the status of certain ancestors is not clearly defined, and why they are sometimes recognized as members of one *'āti,* and sometimes of another.

The case of TEATUA, studied elsewhere (Ottino, ms. in preparation) in relation to a practice of "exchange of women," is very clear in this respect. TEATUA, son of TU FARIUA, the originating ancestor of the *'āti* Fariua, and of O'ō'o, member of the *'āti* 'Ōio from Vahituri, who is listed in the *Parau no Ra'iroa* as a member of the *'āti* 'Ōio, is considered in all the genealogies of the *'āti* Fariua as a member of that *'āti.* TEATUA had simultaneously, or successively, two wives; 'Ōio from Vahituri, belonging to the same *'āti* as himself, and Hautepapa from the *'āti* Hoara of Tiputa. These two women gave rise to the lines of the *'āti* Fariua and Hoara, respectively.

Moreover, TEATUA's case gives some idea of the relations existing between *'āti* and *marae*. PUNUA, who stands at Level 7 and is supposed to have been a very close relative—perhaps a brother—of TU FARIUA, the father of TEATUA, and TEATUA himself are associated with the *marae* Ra'ipū in Vahituri. PUNUA is from Tiputa and despite the lack of any mention of Rangiroa, TEATUA himself must have been from Tiputa. This can possibly be explained by the fact that at this time the *'āti* Fariua did not yet have its own *marae;* that is to say that Tara'i/Opoa was not yet erected. Hence TEATUA, not able to or not allowed to attend the *marae* Te/'iri/puhi of Hautepapa, erected for members of the *'āti* Hoara, is always considered to have been attached to his mother's *marae,* Ra'ipū, in Vahituri. This fact may account for the assumption of greater antiquity by the members of the *'āti* Hoara as against those of the *'āti* Fariua. This example also indicates that, even though *marae* are indeed frequently associated with *'āti,* they are by no means invariably contemporaneous with the founders of the *'āti.* Ra'ipū the stem-*marae,* is supposed to have been erected, or at least completed, by TUTE-HOUA, 'ŌIO's grandson. These facts again confirm what has been said about retrospective recognition of the existence of the *'āti.* Frequently, however, the erection of the *marae* takes place when a new *'āti* is created, or a new residence is settled, as was the case for HOARA and TAPU-TA'AROA. Both built their *marae* while initiating their own *'āti.* These were *marae* Te/'iri/puhi in Tiputa, and Toine in Teu.

CONTINUATION OF THE 'ĀTI

It can be noted at first glance that all spouses' names found in the genealogies and chants are followed by the mention of but one *'āti.* As in the case of TEATUA, a comparison of different sets of documents reveals some inconsistencies, but—and this is the chief point—a single document never indicates two *'āti* for any one person. Hence, any person in any one document is always considered as a member of only one *'āti.*

A second point is that neither seniority nor sex (at least for the *'āti* Hoara), was taken into account in carrying on the descent line. In-deed, with the exception of only children, such as Ouetumu, Putahi, and HOARA, of Level 12, it is difficult to believe that the other siblings of a family were all without descendants. Moreover, the case of Matapoa carries contrary evidence, because her sister, Piao (Level 9) originated an important branch, *'ōpū,* of *'āti* Hoara, which continued for some ten generations before melting into and amalgamating with the '*āti* Fariua. From these examples, it appears that the choice of the person through whom the '*āti* continues was not made according to any formal rule.

If all persons appearing in the *Parau no Ra'iroa* had had descendants, the genealogy would appear as in Diagram B. This diagram clears up in part the problem of an identification between '*āti* and genealogies, and at the same time illustrates some examples of fission or splitting which may or may not correspond to the emergence of new '*āti* from a common stem.

At Level 4, with the siblings PUHENUA, MARERE, and Ture-re'ura, there begins a broad division into what I shall call "blocks," in order to avoid becoming involved in sociological terminology. Each block encompasses several genealogies, corresponding either to different '*āti* originating from a common stem, or to different branches, '*ōpū*, of a single '*āti*. Such alternatives are illustrated by the contrasting cases of Level 5, in which two '*āti* emerged, originating from the siblings HOARA and TAPUTA'AROA, and Level 9, in which Matapoa and Piao were responsible for the emergence of another '*ōpū*. It must be stressed that in the first case the division coincided with a shift of residence, whereas in the second case the newly begun '*ōpū* remained in the same locality. Other examples of these processes will be provided by the genealogies of Blocks II and III (Diagrams D and E).

On a more general level, another striking fact is the absence of distinction between senior and junior within the sibling groups, which is also true as far as the continuance of the line is concerned. This also makes any distinction between '*ōpū matahiapo,* senior branch, and '*ōpū teina,* junior branch, very difficult, which is a rather unusual situation in a Polynesian context.

RULES OF MARRIAGE IN RELATION TO LOCALITY

In the preceding examples, the spouses usually have been affiliated with different geographical areas, *marae,* and '*āti*. The exceptions are worth noting. Tepaipaiahua and PUNUA, of Level 7, are both said to be "from Tiputa," but affiliated with two different *marae;* Te/'iri/puhi and Ra'ipū. A related case involves PUHENUA and Ouetumu, of Level 4, and HOARA and Ti'ura of Level 5 provide a symmetrical example, coming from the same area (Ari'a/te/'ōio, literally "bird '*ōio* channel," is the ancient name for Hararu), and *marae,* but from different '*āti*. On the other hand, examples found at Levels 4 and 5 initiate a series of sequences of matrimonial unions between close relatives, born in the same

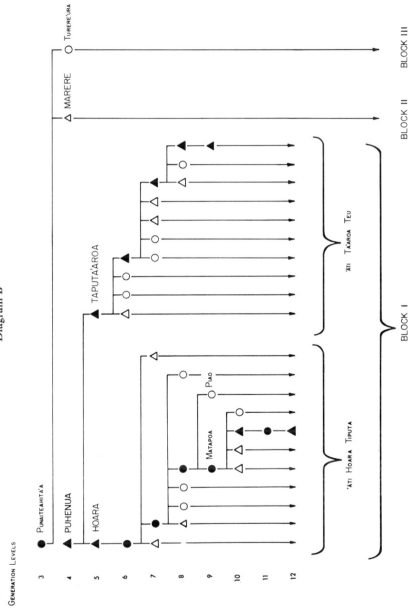

Diagram B

Diagram C

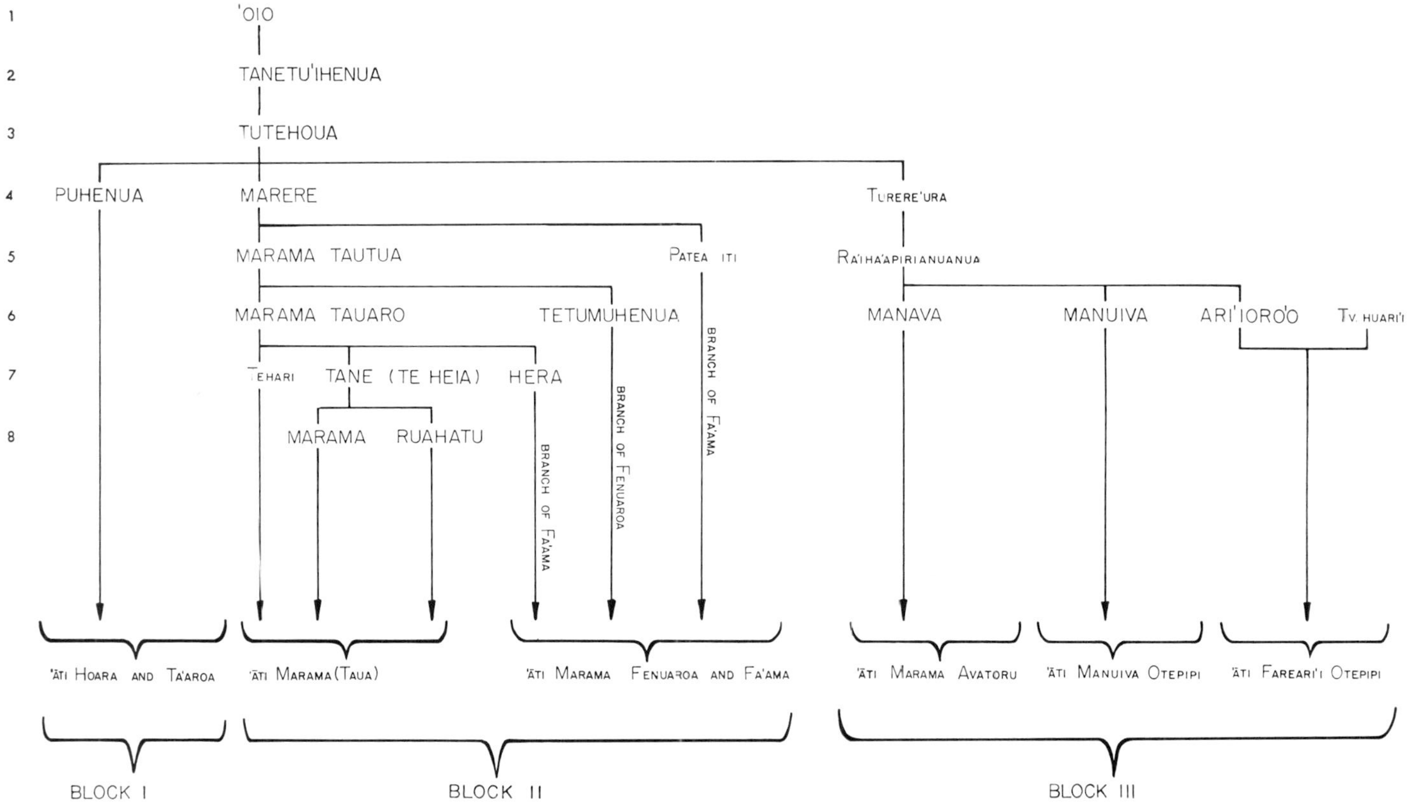

1 'OIO

2 TANETU'IHENUA

3 TUTEHOUA

4 MARERE · PUHENUA

5 MARAMA TAUTUA

6 MARAMA TAUARO · TETUMUHENUA · PATEA ITI · TU RERE'URA

7 'EHARI · TANE (TE HEIA) HERA · RA'IHAĀPIRIANUANUA

8 MARAMA · RUAHATU · MANAVA · MANUIVA · ARI'IOROO · TU HUARI'I

BRANCH OF FA'AMA
BRANCH OF FENUAROA
BRANCH OF FA'AMA

'ĀTI HOARA AND TAAROA

'ĀTI MARAMA (TAUA)

'ĀTI MARAMA FENUAROA AND FA'AMA

'ĀTI MARAMA AVATORU · 'ĀTI MANUIVA OTEPIPI · 'ĀTI FAREARI'I OTEPIPI

BLOCK I

BLOCK II

BLOCK III

Diagram D

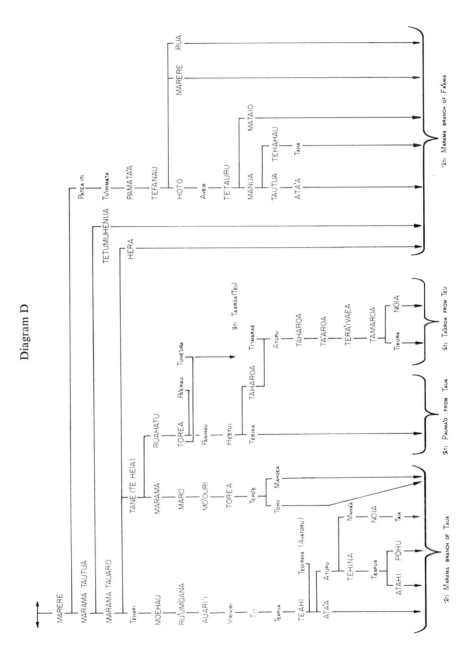

Diagram E

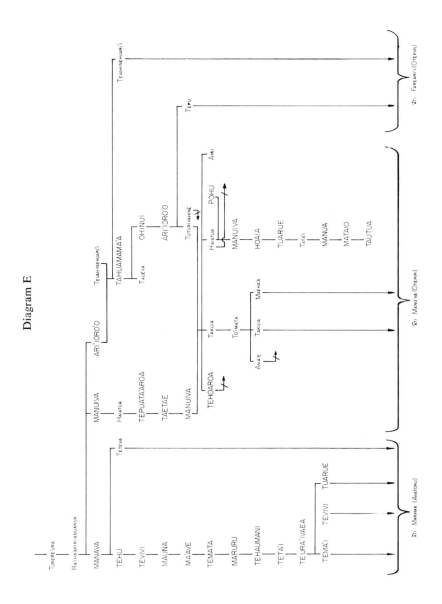

place. These are found in the Levels 7, 8, 9, and 10 of the *'āti* Hoara. There were successive unions of a mother and her daughter (Tepaipaiahua and Hautepapa) with a paternal uncle and his nephew (PUNUA and TEATUA), and also of a mother and her son (Matapoa and TEHAU) with a paternal uncle and his niece (TUMUTEAHERE and Poanoano). These practices suggest the possible existence of a regular pattern of exchanges and alliances, if not between *'āti,* at least between exogamous, localized descent groups.

Evidently these matrimonial practices were symmetrical, and if the residing members of the *'āti* Hoara and Ta'aroa received mates from other *'āti,* reciprocally, some members of the two *'āti* must go elsewhere and live viri- or uxori-locally. This explains, in part, the fluctuations of Diagram B. Some siblings may have had no descendants, while others may have "transferred away their descendants" to another *'āti.*

The *Parau no Ra'iroa* also brings to light the amazing geographical mobility of the former inhabitants. Teua, who stands at Level 5, came from the atoll of Ahe, in the old division known as Vahitu, which corresponds to the northwestern part of the Tuamotuan archipelago, now comprising Ahe, Manihi, Takaroa, Takapoto, and Tikei atolls. Similarly, for the *'āti* Ta'aroa, the women Aroari'i and Tumaria, of Levels 6 and 7, are stated as being from other atolls, unidentified for Aroari'i, probably Kaukura for Tumaria. The origin of ARI'I'O'OPU, mentioned together with the word Hiti'a, east, is difficult to ascertain, for the *'āti* Feareari'i is widely represented in several atolls of the Western Tuamotus. In Rangiroa this *'āti* has been quite restless and has been successively located in the northeastern section known as Matahoa (at Temiromiro, the current Kauraufara), and then in Otepipi, from whence it moved again toward Tae'o'o, and finally to Avatoru.[7]

To sum up the information so far provided by the *Parau no Ra'iroa,* it is possible to list some points which will serve as hypotheses: An *'āti* is associated with a geographical location, and there is also usually an

---

[7] Hiti'a as it appears together with the name of AR'I'O'OPU may be either the name of a land or of a *marae*. Both suppositions are plausible. Henry (1928, p. 106) provides the following information: "The island of Rangi-roa . . . (Long Sky). . . . The High Chief is Tute-houa (Heated-foot-run) [checked by Rangiroa traditions, TUTEHOUA was 'ŌIO's grandson] and the *marae* Hiti'a (East)." On the other hand, traditions originating from Takaroa and Takapoto atolls and collected by Kenneth P. Emory give Hitinga as the name of the *marae* of Rangiroa. I myself never heard of a *marae* of this name in Rangiroa. It may refer to a very ancient *marae* of the *'āti* Feareari'i, erected in its former residence, Te/miro/miro, land corresponding to Tupapa'urua and Tevaro, presently designated under the term of Kauraufara, and located in the eastern part of Rangiroa. It may also be another name of Ra'ipu, also known as the *marae* of the east (Hitinga or Hiti'a). I am inclined toward the second theory.

association of land with *marae* and *'āti;* affiliation of the individual can be with but one *'āti,* which results from the person's parents' choice of residence; tracing of the line of descent of the *'āti* is without regard to seniority or—at least for the *'āti* Hoara—sex; matrimonial bonds between co-resident close relatives suggest the existence of a regular pattern; and there was amazing geographical mobility, both interatoll and inside Rangiroa, especially for the members of the stem-*'āti,* who seem to have wandered extensively and to have initiated descent groups scattered in various parts of the low island.

SOUTHERN GENEALOGIES: 'ĀTI MARAMA

The genealogies of the southern part of the atoll tend largely to verify the points previously raised. In general, the relationships are consonant with Diagram C. This diagram concerns the *'āti* Marama, which has, it has been said, split since Level 4 into three blocks. Both *'āti* Hoara and Ta'aroa, with which I have been concerned, are included in Block I. Prior to examining in detail these new materials, it is necessary to clear up the apparent confusion between affiliation with the *'āti* Marama and 'Ōio during the early levels. This problem of affiliation has already been examined by means of evidence from the *Parau no Ra'iroa,* but here the issue is somewhat different.

After the general assertion that one person can only be affiliated with one *'āti,* the double affiliation of the earliest ancestors is confusing. More confusing still is the fact that MARERE and Turere'ura are considered, depending on circumstances, as members of *'āti* Marama or *'āti* 'Ōio, whereas PUHENUA is always associated with *'āti* 'Ōio. It is possible that his seniority accounts for this difference of treatment, for it was through him that 'ŌIO's line continued. This reasoning is based only on conjecture, however, and cannot be taken as fact.

It is possible that the inconsistencies are only apparent, and that they originate from the meanings given to the term *'āti,* together with the more interesting sociological notion of the continuation of the line of descent. The term *'āti* is used in two ways; it may mean "descendant," in which case the word is semantically equal to the modern word *hua'ai.* Thus *'āti* X means "X's descendants," considered together as a group. In a second interpretation, *'āti* has the precise meaning of "biologically related group originating from a sole ancestor." The term is associated with ideas of ritual, cult, and continuity of time—in a word, with a corporate group. In this meaning, *'āti* 'Ōio designated the localized descent group established in Vavau Nui, the present Vahituri, which was symbolized by the bird-guardian *'ōio* (the noddy tern, *Anous stolidus*), and associated with the *marae* Ra'ipū. The complete identification of PUHENUA with *'āti* 'Ōio can be explained by historical events. As shown by the evidence contained in the *Parau no Ra'iroa,* members of *āti* 'Ōio from Vahituri have regularly been allied with those of *'āti* Hoara, and with those of *'āti* Fariua, and thus the three *'āti* have been closely interrelated by recurrent and regular exchanges of a sort which will be presently examined. The rate of these exchanges is so high that it is sometimes difficult to distinguish between the different *'āti* involved. It is notable that the *Parau no Vahituri/mata'eina'a no te 'āti 'Ōio,* after some generations, steadily becomes a genealogy of the *'āti* Hoara from Tiputa, and also of the *'āti* Fariua, owing to the intricate and complex exchange of women between the *'āti* Hoara and Fariua.

The *'āti* 'Ōio remains distinct until Level 8. Following that time, it disappears completely, and its disappearance coincides somewhat with the emergence of the powerful *'āti* Tupa'ae from Tapua'a, which is immediately included in the net of regular matrimonial exchanges uniting the *'āti* Hoara and Fariua. For unknown reasons, perhaps of defense,[8] at about Level 8 the various *'ōpū* of the *'āti* 'Ōio abandoned their residences and joined the *'āti* Hoara, Fariua, and possibly Tupa'ae. These details explain also the statements of numerous informants, according to which the *'āti* Hoara and Fariua, stemming from the *'āti* 'Ōio, are both considered to be the "genuine" (*mau*) stem-*'āti* of Rangiroa. This is partially true, if one considers that one of the most powerful branches originating from 'ŌIO is formed by the close association of the stem-*'āti* 'Ōio with the *'āti* Hoara and Fariua.

In contrast, the position of the *'āti* as found in Blocks II and III is quite different, and the *'āti* of these times do not exhibit a similar continuity with *'āti* 'Ōio. The direction of colonization goes south, stretching along the south coast, as is suggested in two of the most ancient chants of Rangiroa, the *Fa'atara no Ra'iroa,* and one praising the land of Vaimanu, nowadays known as Fa'ama, *Fa'atara no Vaimanu/ te fa'atara ia no MARAMA TAUTUA,* meaning "Chant of Vaimanu (which is) the personal chant of MARAMA TAUTUA."

---

[8] Oral tradition retains accounts of savage fighting which took place "very long ago" in the easternmost part of the atoll, especially at Maufano and Vahituri. Vahituri was said to have been covered with human bones. However, close examination of the traditions shows that the present-day recollections confuse two distinct wars. The first one took place in the remote history of the island between the former descendants of 'ŌIO and warriors from Kaukura. The second, more recent battles, which involved not only Vahituri but the whole of the eastern part of Rangiroa, included people of Rangiroa and warriors from 'Ana'a. This is verified by precise traditions from 'Ana'a (Emory and Ottino, in press).

The various branches that sprang from MARAMA TAUTUA (Block II) are located in the southern part of the atoll from Taua to Fa'ama and Fenuaroa. For the extensive land of Fenuaroa the genealogies specify that the descendants of MARAMA TAUTUA were located in the section called *Te/pae/roa/hōā*, literally, the side of the large channel between Fenuaroa and Teha'are. As for Block III, with the exception of MANAVA, who settled on the site of the present-day village of Avatoru near the pass, Ra'iha'apirianuanua's descendants occupied the land of Otepipi. As has been said, those settling the land spread gradually from east to west, in what appears to have been a scheme of colonization of the whole of Rangiroa, by gaining control of the two broad passes of the north coast. In the earliest stages, all the *'āti* shared the emblem of the bird *'ōio*, symbol of the common ancestor. In a second stage, probably about Level 7, 8, or 9, the *'āti* located in the contiguous lands of Taua and Otepipi elected as an emblem the bird *torea* (golden plover, *Pluvialis dominica*), and still later, after Level 13, the people of Fa'ama-Fenuaroa abandoned the bird *'ōio* for the fish, *i'a,* which was to become the symbol of the new *'āti* Marere.

DESCENDANTS OF MARERE

The descendants of MARERE, Block II, are found in Diagram D.

It is sufficient to draw attention to the fact that the continuation of the branches of the *'āti* are carried through either males or females. It does not seem useful here to draw up a statistical table, which might possibly show a slight preference for males. Such a table would only have value if it were drawn on the basis of all of the *'āti* of Rangiroa.

The *'āti* Pau/ma'o (sharks/exterminated?) originated from the union of TOREA and Pa'erau, of *'āti* Ta'aroa, whereas the line which issued from Tuhe'ura, another wife of TOREA, who was a member of *'āti* Fariua from Tiputa, remained in this locality. The *'āti* Pau/ma'o seems to be named after an event, and not, as is more often the case, from its ancestor.

DESCENDANTS OF TURERE'URA

The descendants of Turere'ura, Block III, are found in Diagram E.

Block III is divided into three main branches, begun by the siblings MANAVA, MANUIVA, and ARI'IORO'O. The sign under the name of ARI'IORO'O indicates that his descent has been transferred (*'afa'ihia*) to that of his spouse's *'āti, 'āti* Fareari'i, literally royal, or chief's house.

The first line, which originated from MANAVA and was established in Avatoru, is patrilineal. This is very rare in Rangiroa, and this is perhaps the only example. However, with the exception of Te'eva, who was MANAVA's daughter and TEHU's sister, one notices the absence of female siblings, which indicates that patrilinearity in this particular case was merely the result of statistical chance. The genealogy was interrupted at the level of the siblings TEMA'I, TEVIVI, and TUARUE.

The second line was to become the important 'āti Manu/iva, literally, nine birds, named after the eponym ancestor. The example is worth noting, for immediately after MANUIVA and Tuturivahine, this line presents a good example of fragmentation into lines stemming from TEHŌ-ĀROA, Takuia, and Haiatua. The line originating from TEHŌĀROA and Amu was transferred elsewhere. The frequent recurrence of the name Amu in the genealogies prevents her exact identification. TEHŌĀROA's case is puzzling, for this name (both of person and of land) pertains without doubt to the 'āti Marama and appears at the same level in the genealogies of the branch of this 'āti which settled in Fa'ama.

Following MANUIVA and Tuturivahine, the 'āti Manuiva was carried on by Takuia and Haiatua. Two generations below, Takuia's branch split again and Amae's offspring's descent passes to her husband's 'āti, the 'āti Ta'aroa from Teu. The 'āti Manuiva continues with the second Takuia, granddaughter of the first, and possibly with Maeha'a, although I found no genealogy for this name. To return to the second Haiatua and her two mates, POHU and TUTEHARO, it appears that Haiatua's offspring by POHU became formally attached to Haiatua's 'āti, while the offspring of her union with TUTEHARO passed on to the local branch of 'āti Marama which was established in Fa'ama (See Diagram F).

MARRIAGE AND ALLIANCES BETWEEN 'ĀTI

According to the *Parau no Ra'iroa,* marital unions seem to have been contracted chiefly between mates living in distant localities. Sequences of alliances encompassing two generations might suggest, as has been noted, the existence of formalized matrimonial rules. I have also noted cases of transfer of descent resulting from the parents' choice of residence. Examples of each situation having been cited, it is now necessary to bring them together. In doing so, I wish to stress two points: first, the importance for kinship theory of the locality principle, which allows marital bonds between very close relatives provided the mates have been born and raised in separate places; and, second, the recurrent matrimonial alliances occurring between the same descent groups, whether 'āti or 'ōpū, provide evidence of close links of alliance between those groups. It is clear that matrimonial unions in Rangiroa are in fact deter-

Diagram F

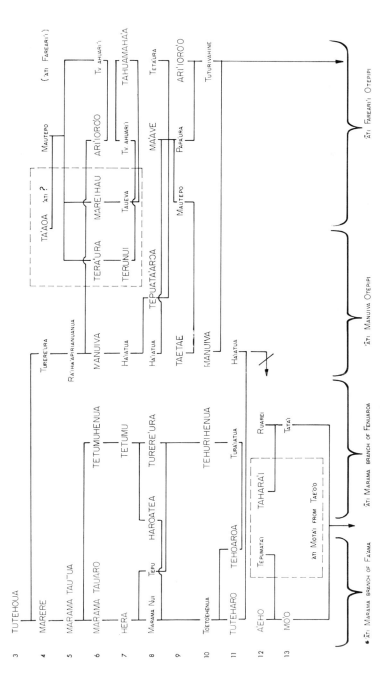

Generation Levels

mined by sociological and political necessities quite outside the self-contained realm of kinship and marriage.

From the evidence gathered, it should be possible to study the phenomenon of matrimonial union within various sets of 'āti. For the more ancient period, the best examples are offered by the northeastern 'āti Hoara, Fariua, and Tupa'ae; those of the east, chiefly located in the so-called Kauraufara section of the atoll and including the lands of Tevaro and Maufano; and in Vahituri by the 'āti Fareari'i, Pahorau, and Hiva. Later, when the 'āti Fareari'i shifted its residence to Otepipi, they formed a new set of bonds with the 'āti Manuiva. A third group is formed by the 'āti established along the southeastern part of Rangiroa from Teu to Taua and Otepipi, including one local branch of the 'āti Pahorau, and the 'āti Ta'aroa and Pauma'o. Still later, some branches of the 'āti Marere and Mota'i formed close relations and finally mingled on the extensive land of Tae'o'o. I wish to examine again here some examples which have been studied elsewhere from a quite different point of view (Ottino, 1965).

Diagram F clarifies the interrelationships in the genealogies as an examination of the genealogies separately, being merely linear lists of ancestors' names, cannot do. The examples show evidence of exogamy within the localized branches, but in the case of the 'āti Marama, there is 'āti endogamy. Yet this situation may be a mere result of chance. A similar examination of the more recent branches of the 'āti Hoara from Tiputa establishes that the criterion of geographical separation is not relevant, and that unions do occur between members of the various co-resident branches of a single 'āti. Indeed, unions between very close relatives seem to be confined to the more ancient period of atoll history, and do not extend beyond the twelfth or thirteenth generation level. After MO'O and Tata'i (Level 13) the two particular branches of 'āti Marama melt into a new 'āti Marere, then located at Porahu. The 'āti Manuiva and Fareari'i examples from Otepipi provide a quite similar pattern, rendered more intricate in the early Levels 5 through 8 by the addition of the group issuing from TA'AOA.

To sum up, the 'āti is not an exogamous entity, as was often asserted by informants. For the more ancient period, the exogamy of the various branches is always linked with the notion of separate residence, either distinct home "lands" or, as is the case for 'āti Hoara, distinct clusters of compounds within the same locality.[9]

---

[9] A consideration of the possible existence in the remote past of "long dwellings," *fare roa,* should at this point be particularly relevant. However, evidence on this point is not sufficient. Concerning Tahitian long houses, *fare pote'e,* see Handy (1932, pp. 6-10, 12; Pl. III-VIII).

'ĀTI GROUPING AND INTERDEPENDENCE

I have thus far been concerned with the *'āti* in the sense of descent groups, composed of biological relatives stemming from a common ancestor. This is a convenient fiction, because the *'āti* of ancient times were in reality communities, perhaps villages, composed both of the resident biological members of the *'āti* and their spouses. In this sense, *'āti* could appropriately be translated as community or clan.

The assertion of many informants about the demographic bases of the ancient *'āti,* that they comprised on the average thirty to fifty persons, is interesting. These low figures are in accordance with the very limited resources provided by the low coral island ecology. The ancient places of residence were always located on the major lands of Rangiroa. There were only a few sections of the northern part of the atoll, such as the contiguous lands of Otepipi-Taua, Teha'are-Fenuaroa (literally, the long island), or Tae'o'o which could support larger numbers of people, perhaps twice or three times more. The smallness of the communities makes self-evident the necessity of alliances intended to broaden their demographic bases and to facilitate the defense of the entire allied group. The patterns of marriage and transfer of descent, understood in this light, were primarily economic and safety measures.

Tuamotuan history is replete with traditions which relate the attacks on and complete destruction of isolated bands of people, or of whole *āti*. In the records of the first European explorers who, after the Spaniard Quiros, in 1616 made their way through the so-called dangerous archipelago, nothing is more convincing than the allusions to the light film of smoke rising from between the groves of the atolls (Quiros, 1876, Vol. 1, p. 249). Boenechea, another Spaniard, 130 years after Quiros, reported without any ambiguity the role of those smoke signals. Sighting of them was immediately followed by the appearance on various parts of the reef of groups of warriors armed with spears and clubs (Corney, 1913, Vol. 1, p. 228; 1914, Vol. 2, pp. 233-239).

These sociological manipulations occur within what I have called elsewhere in French, *"isolats matrimoniaux,"* thus stressing the closeness of the mates' kinship bonds. Within this broader entity, each *'āti* or *'ōpū* retains its identity. The core of its resident members insures its continuity through time. A network of cognatic bonds unites the allied *'āti* or localized branches, and every member has almost the whole of his (or her) personal kindred (Leach, 1950, pp. 61-62; Eggan, 1960, p. 30, note 7, p. 159) evenly distributed in the largest unit formed by the associated residential *'āti*. Within each *'āti* or *'ōpū,* the resident members who set up their procreative families in the place where their own parental families were established brought in their spouses and adopted children from similar neighboring groups. Considered at any one particular moment, the set of people who form the residential core of the 'āti or 'ōpū strikingly resembles a stem-kindred (Davenport, 1959, p. 565).

The choice, or, more accurately, the allocation of a parental place of residence to any young couple depended chiefly on the particular wants of the allied descent group. This had definite consequences for the future of the couple and for their children. The parent who happened to reside viri- or uxori-locally did retain personal membership in and allegiance toward the 'āti or 'ōpū in which he or she was born or raised. This fact is ascertained by many explicit annotations in the genealogies, which name the spouse's 'āti. However, the place of parental residence determines the forthcoming affiliation of the children. Thus from the very moment a member of a particular descent group leaves his or her residence to follow his or her spouse, his or her potential children are lost to his or her localized descent group. It can be said that the expatriated man or woman suffers a kind of sociological diminution, and, in spite of his biological part in parenthood, will have no influence on his child's kinship status.[10]

Such were probably the most important characteristics of the ancient 'āti which permitted them to cope with adaptation to a quite peculiar ecological milieu, as well as with difficult and unsettled historical conditions. The necessity to maintain the demographical strength of the 'āti at a satisfactory level, together with an appropriate sex ratio, explains the unusual development of what I would call their institutions of mobility. These included transfer of descent, exchange of wives— which has been studied elsewhere (Ottino, in preparation)—and a frequent resort to adoption to work out a reallocation of children which would be more in accord with specific social needs. In such a familial and social system, one can hardly expect to find any ideology of descent similar to those which are to be found in societies with linear or bilinear organization. In Rangiroa, with the exception of two or three theories obviously derived from the Bible, I have never found any trace of such ideology.

Therefore concentration upon the 'āti must not conceal the existence of broader groupings which resulted from their close alliances. Com-

---

[10] At this point, Titiev's (1943, pp. 516-519) notion of "unilocal groups," in which a bridal couple moves into and merges with the wife's or husband's household, is of particular interest.

pared with a so-called tribal organization, the individual localized descent groups are much less autonomous than are small kin-territorial segments of a tribe, and they are neither self-sustaining nor functionally independent (Sahlins, 1961, pp. 325-326). The evidence of the genealogies, together with an examination of the map, shows that these groupings usually were divided into two, three, or four residential units, either *'āti* or *'ōpū,* and exercised control on segments of the atoll about seven to fifteen miles in length. The total number of people within these groupings is, of course, difficult to estimate, but one may assume that the major ones varied between one and two hundred. Such territorial groupings, sharing usually the same guardian symbol and often the same *marae,* might have foretold the emergence of the *mata'eina'a,* the new political entities of the last period of Tuamotuan pre-European history. In contrast to the ancient *'āti,* the *mata'eina'a* were based more on the principle of locality than on the old principle of blood kinship. However, this is quite another problem, which involves the passage from a tribal stage to something which is very close to state organization (Mühlmann, 1934; Ottino, 1965).

ANCIENT 'ĀTI AND LINEAGES

As it has been defined, the *'āti* is a nonunilinear descent group in the sense of Goodenough (1955) and Davenport (1959), and is related to the concept of the cognatic system as described by Murdock (1960). Crocombe (1964, p. 25, Diagram 27), in his description of the social organization of the Cook Islands, identifies the *ngati* (*'āti*) with the lineage, and contrasts this term with *matakeinga* (*mata'eina'a*), a broader residential group which comprises the members of the *'āti*-community or clan-*'āti.* In the Western Tuamotus, at least during the early period with which I have been concerned in this paper, I think that the *mata'eina'a* is not similar to the *matakeinga* of the Cook Islands, but that this term refers only to the idea of residence, without any allusion to any social group. The term *'āti* in its ancient usage designated both all born members of the *'āti,* and, in a broader sense, the community which the resident members formed, including their spouses and adopted children; that is, in Murdock's sense, the clan. Without stressing this point, I wish only to discuss the use of the word lineage to connote the born members of the *'āti,* and to compare the rules of recruitment of the ancient *'āti* with those of the patri- or matrilineages. In so doing, I wish to discover whether the differences are great enough to justify the rejection of the term lineage, and the use of a quite different terminology.

The basic scheme governing patri- and matrilineages is quite clear. The application of the rules of exogamy and locality result in the adult members of one sex continuing to reside in their place of birth, whereas the adult members of the opposite sex are married out and go to live elsewhere. The residing adult men or women, according to the type of lineage, constitute the core of the community which includes also the spouses of opposite sex and possibly other affines or spouse's relatives. In contrast, in the case of the *'āti,* where neither sex has a specific "legal destination," the core of the residing born members is formed by both men and women. Thus the children's affiliation, which is not automatically determined by the rule of filiation and locality—here nonexistent—depends on the more complex sociological factors which decide the postmarital domicile of the parents. Whereas the predetermined place of residence of the unilinear lineages is a legal notion, the domicile of the families of orientation within the ancient *'āti* is more sociological, and was possibly established by special rites conducted at some time in the child's life.

Despite this difference, however, similarities between the nonunilinear *'āti* (in which the members trace their relationship lineally through either or both sexes to a common known ancestor) and unilinear lineages are equally striking. As Davenport (1959, p. 562) stresses, any comparison between the structural characteristics "demonstrates the need for classifying such kin groups (nonunilinear) in a manner that makes them coordinate in most structural respects with the unilinear descent groups."

A first glance at the diagrams, with their evidence of splitting processes, reminds one of the structure of a patri- or matrilineage. As in unilinear lineages, *'āti* or their branches are located in definite geographical areas, the name of which, together with the possession of a guardian symbol and frequently also of a *marae,* characterizes the *'āti.*

A guardian spirit or symbol and a *marae* implied rites, rituals, and priests—in short, a complete religious organization. An *'āti,* therefore, is a corporate group which owns rights, if not exactly in the land itself at least in its resources and in the structures which have been erected on it. It possesses a ritual, the special lore associated with it, and a collection of names of persons, lands, and properties. Thus far, there is nothing to differentiate the *'āti* from a lineage.

The most striking difference is obviously the lack of a unilineal descent principle, associated with appropriate and complementary rules of residence and exogamy. Exogamy by itself does not appear to be essential and its absence is not sufficient to separate the *'āti* from the usual lineage. It is useless to cite again the known cases of endogamic lineages such as the Tikopian *kainanga,* the Arabic lineage reported by Davenport (1959, p. 559), or the *"foko"* Merina on the Malagasy plateaus. The actual difference lies in the fact that unilinear lineages have judicial rules which regulate marriage, postmarital residence, and the affiliation of the children, whereas the *'āti* had nothing of the sort. The difference may be accounted for by a striking contrast in attitudes toward the ecological and social environment. In some societies, let us say in East Africa, the external conditions are thought of as sufficiently stable to be relied upon to remain unchanged at least for a period of time encompassing one or two generations. In the tiny Tuamotuan atolls, scattered through the Pacific, the external conditions are considered as parameters liable at any moment to sudden and drastic change, to which social groups must be prepared to adjust themselves. It would seem that, whereas in East Africa agricultural and pastoral societies can regulate marriage, postmarital residence, and affiliation of the children by formalized, judicial rules, independent of local and demographical conditions, in the Polynesian low islands the same processes, in the early days of settlement, are subject to exterior imperatives. These imperatives do not leave room for institutionalized rules which would in effect hamper any sudden necessary adaptation. In the first case, the determinant rules are those of kinship and marriage; in the second, they are merely the necessities of group survival.

From the point of view of continuity of descent, the differences, which are related to quite dissimilar environments and social and demographic conditions, are not sufficient to contrast the nonunilinear lineage known as the *'āti* with the unilinear lineage. Structurally nonunilinear and unilinear lineages are quite close. In spite of the contrasts, it is perhaps not necessary to resort to new terms or to have recourse to such dichotomies as sept versus sib, or ramage versus lineage. Following Crocombe, the use of the term lineage with the addition of a determinant qualifier seems to be quite sufficient. An appropriate qualifier might be the French term *indifférencié.*

This term, in contrast to patri- or matrilineage, seems to be more appropriate because it is neuter. Other terms such as ramage, or ambilateral, by their root meanings or by the image they evoke convey the idea of recurrent branchings, or, still more serious, of a kind of parallelism which is by no means to be found in the *'āti.* Ramage as a corresponding term for lineage is also misleading, and perhaps its usage has resulted from a mistake in historical perspective which led an observer to judge and discuss certain concepts of the ancient Polynesian social organization from or in reference to modern conditions which differ markedly from earlier ones. Confusion becomes greater in that the same terms are ordinarily used to designate institutions which in the course of time have changed completely. The label of nonunilinear descent group as used by Davenport (1959) and Goodenough (1955), has the slight disadvantage of being negative rather than positive in its connotations (Murdock, 1960, p. 2), and also is not entirely satisfactory on the grounds that this negation of linearity is apt to cause one to think of alternatives which would be contrary to the ethnographical reality of the ancient Tuamotus. It must be remembered that any child born or adopted into an 'āti of orientation was definitely affiliated with that 'āti, and no other choice was open to him.

For the Western Tuamotuan 'āti, without doubt the best term would be "utrolateral," as presented by Freeman (1960, note 7, p. 160). The term is derived from the Latin, uter, meaning "either one or the other of two." However, nothing in the structure of the ancient Tuamotuan lineage necessitates the use of complicated or quite alien terminology to describe it. Such terminology could only have the effect of separating this type of social organization farther than necessary from homologous unilinear ones.

LITERATURE CITED

CORNEY, B. G.
1913, 1914, 1918. *The Quest and Occupation of Tahiti by Emissaries of Spain during the years 1772-1776.* 3 vols. The Hakluyt Society. London: Cambridge Univ. Press.

CROCOMBE, RONALD G.
1964. *Land Tenure in the Cook Islands.* London: Oxford Univ. Press.

DAVENPORT, WILLIAM
1959. "Nonunilinear Descent and Descent Groups." *American Anthropologist* 61:557-572.

EGGAN, FRED
1960. "The Sagada Igorots of Northern Luzon." In G. P. MURDOCK (editor), *Social Structure in Southeast Asia,* pp. 24-50. Chicago: Viking Fund Pub. in Anthropology.

EMORY, KENNETH P., and PAUL OTTINO
In press. " 'Ana'a: Histoire Traditionnelle d'un Atoll Polynesien (Archipel de Tuamotu)." *J. Soc. Océanistes.*

FREEMAN, J. D.
  1960. "The Iban of Western Borneo." In G. P. MURDOCK (editor), *Social Structure in Southeast Asia*, pp. 65-87, 160-162. Chicago: Viking Fund Pub. in Anthropology.

GOODENOUGH, WARD H.
  1955. "A Problem in Malayo-Polynesian Social Organization." *American Anthropologist* 57:71-83.

HANDY, E. S. CRAIGHILL
  1932. *Houses, Boats, and Fishing in the Society Islands*. B. P. Bishop Mus. Bull. 90. Honolulu.

HENRY, TEUIRA
  1928. *Ancient Tahiti*. B. P. Bishop Mus. Bull. 48. Honolulu.

LAVONDÈS, A., and J. GARANGER
  1966. "Recherches Archeologiques à Rangiroa (Archipel des Tuamotu)." *J. Soc. Océanistes* 22:25-66.

LEACH, EDMUND R.
  1950. *Social Science Research in Sarawak*. Colonial Research Studies 1. London Colonial Office.

MÜHLMANN, W. E.
  1934. "Die Begriffe 'Ati' und 'Mata'eina'a': Ein Beitrag zur Politischen Entwicklung und Besiedlungsgeschichte Polynesiens." *Anthropos* 19:739-756.

MURDOCK, GEORGE PETER
  1960. "Cognatic Forms of Social Organization." In G. P. MURDOCK (editor), *Social Structure in Southeast Asia*, pp. 1-14. Chicago: Viking Fund Pub. in Anthropology.

OTTINO, PAUL
  1965. Ethno-histoire de Rangiroa. ORSTOM Papeete. (Provisional report.)
  1967. "Un Procédé Littéraire Malayo-Polynésien: de l'Ambiguïté à la Pluri-Signification." *L'Homme, Revue Française d'Anthropologie* 6(4):5-34.

QUIROS, PEDRO FERNANDEZ DE
  1876. *Viajes de Quiros: Historia del Descubrimiento de las Regiones Australes*. 3 vols. Madrid. English trans. by SIR CLEMENTS MARKHAM. 2 vols. London: Hakluyt Soc., 1904.

SAHLINS, MARSHALL D.
  1961. "The Segmentary Lineage: An Organization of Predatory Expansion." *American Anthropologist* 63:322-345.

TITIEV, MISCHA
  1943. "The Influence of Common Residence on the Unilateral Classification of Kindred." *American Anthropologist* 45:511-530.

OBSERVATIONS ON METHODS USED IN ASSEMBLING ORAL TRADITIONS IN THE MARQUESAS

H. LAVONDÈS*

Office de la Recherche Scientifique et Technique Outre-Mer

IN THE COURSE of his entire scientific career, Kenneth Emory has been extremely careful at all times to embellish his work with compilation of texts, always obtained in the native language and accompanied by a well-balanced and accurate translation, making no concessions to "literary" effects, which frequently are a misrepresentation. This is by no means the least of his contributions to the study of Polynesian civilization, to which he has devoted and is still devoting his life of scholarly research. This is also a sign of being up to date, since modern anthropology keeps searching with increasing persistence for objective documents free of the distortions that may be inevitably introduced through the temperament, cultural bias, and theoretical concepts of the ethnographer. A compilation formulated personally by an informant in his own tongue is one of the means of approaching this ideal of objectivity. More than anywhere else, perhaps, there is a most urgent need to accomplish this in the Pacific islands, where the few surviving cultures are in the process of change and are rapidly losing their original character, and where a certain number are irrevocably doomed. With this in mind, therefore, it is particularly important to gather as great a variety of texts as possible, because most probably these will be the only sources available for future research workers.

In the Marquesas, work of considerable importance has already been accomplished in this direction. Besides some scattered publications in

* Translated from the French by Mrs. Ella Wiswell, University of Hawaii, Honolulu.

various journals, we have important contributions by E. S. C. Handy (Handy, 1930) and S. H. Elbert's manuscript, located in the Bernice P. Bishop Museum library. This constitutes an important source of documentary material. A variety of reasons leads me to think that new texts could still be obtained in the Marquesas. Whereas the preceding scholars had carried on their research in the islands of the Southern group, there were practically no texts composed in the dialect of the Northern group. Furthermore, acquiring all the oral literature of one group is virtually impossible, so that one could hope that new narratives could be obtained, or at any rate new versions of those already known. In the meantime, the assembling of oral traditions, which was not designated as a part of my initial work program, became only gradually my principal task.

Therefore, the remarks on methodology which follow are not so much a result of a systematic planning or bibliographical research, as they are a balance sheet of my experiences and experimenting in the course of my stay in the field. This lasted a total of ten months, divided into six different visits between September, 1963, and June, 1966. On general principles, I decided to work exclusively in the Island of Ua Pou, although I was also able to profit from several trips to Taiohae (Nuku Hiva) to obtain a few texts. After specifying the type of texts which I consider worth obtaining by an ethnographer, I will outline, on the basis of my own field experience, the methods which should be adopted and precautions to be followed in selecting the texts to be assembled, the recruiting of informants, the choice among different methods of obtaining the texts, and the basic facts necessary to their proper interpretation.

Generally speaking, anthropologists in Polynesia have been gathering exclusively a corpus of texts established by tradition and transmitted orally, usually termed folklore (legends, folk tales, historical narratives, prayer texts, chants, and so forth), and yet it would seem a good idea not to limit one's efforts to compiling texts only of this type. The "folklore" texts actually all possess in various degrees a literary character and reflect ancient tradition, which accounts for the fact that the language in which they are composed is sometimes distinctly archaic and differs from current usage. It is, therefore, important in the interest of the linguists to record along with the traditional texts some modern ones of which the language reflects general present-day usage.

Therefore, on the advice of André Haudricourt, I had requested a certain number of informants to compose autobiographical narratives, texts on such subjects as fishing techniques, or the use of plants and remedies. Also, several informants composed spontaneously some texts in which they reported what they had heard from their grandparents on the subject of customs of the past (*te hana kakiu*). These latter texts, with few exceptions, are not of great interest because the customs which they describe have been presented in a much more satisfactory manner in earlier works (Handy, 1923). On the other hand, texts composed at my request on the subjects enumerated above, incomplete and confused though they may be, offer the advantage of presenting the subject matter with which they deal according to the informant's own ideas without the interfering screen present in the standard anthropological investigation procedures, no matter how careful one is. In this manner one can hope to attain a much greater objectivity and discover relations between facts which no question, no matter how cleverly formulated, would ever bring to light.

In assembling this type of text, the choice of informants is a particularly delicate matter. A difficult compromise must be established between various requirements which one single individual may not be able to satisfy: facility of expression, ability to reason so as to make his expressions coherent and clear, ability to maintain a sustained effort, and familiarity with the subject matter. In my work in the Marquesas, the nontraditional texts on various subjects which I assembled are, as a rule, compositions of storytellers. This presents one disadvantage: the more gifted the storyteller, the more likely he is to have the tendency to use a literary style. This is exactly what happened in Ua Pou and is precisely what one would hope to avoid. On the other hand, in a specific work about fishing composed by an informant without any knowledge of traditional literature, the text, though full of information, is difficult to follow because it is confused and is very clumsily put together. However, this experience presents a certain interest because it does point out to what extent knowledge of folklore contributes to the intellectual development and better means of expression of those who are familiar with it. Nevertheless, in spite of the risks involved, it is preferable to use informants who are not folklore specialists to compose the nontraditional texts. The need to obtain texts sufficiently clear for use would lead one to choose informants from among the better-known people whose means of expressing themselves are as a rule above average.

This method of "ethnography through texts," which I attempted in the Marquesas, was only tentative. For one thing, the interest which it presented and its real value occurred to me only toward the end. On the other hand, the disruption of traditional culture and the cultural vacuum which characterize the Marquesas today leaves a very limited field of action for the application of this purely ethnographic method. Nevertheless, without being a totally new idea, an attempt at requesting the informants to compose narratives different from those which are generally grouped as folklore, so long as it is done systematically and carefully, might prove to be very valuable to anthropology.

Compilation of texts established by tradition, then, constituted the major part of documentary data that I had acquired in the Marquesas. It soon became apparent to me that to be of any use such a work must be methodical, and that it is essential for the ethnographer to abide by certain self-imposed rules. An invaluable suggestion with regard to methodology, in fact, is made by Emory himself in one of his recent publications:

> I have had a particular interest in the variability of folk tales as recounted by the same story teller, as told by others in a community, and as transmitted from one generation to another. (Emory, 1965, p. 347.)

The significance of this suggestion is illustrated immediately by the author when he cites two different versions of the same narrative obtained three years apart from the same informant, one recorded on tape, the other written down by the informant. A third text of the same narrative, this time the product of a different informant, is presented with the other two versions. Emory also states later that he believes that he had recorded all the folk tales extant at the time of his visit (Emory, 1965, p. 347). All this illustrates what, in my opinion, should be the first concern of any folklorist in the field: the need to investigate to the utmost all possible sources. This latter is twofold: the ethnographer absolutely must assemble all the different narratives or fragments of distinct narratives still remembered by the members of the group; he must also try to assemble as many different formulations of these narratives and as many different versions as possible.

Different formulations in this context mean recitation on different occasions by the same storyteller. Comparison of these formulations may bring out variations which it is important to study further. It might be the presence or omission of some details or episodes, changes in the successive chronology of events, or just simple variations in the choice of expressions or vocabulary. Differences may also appear in the account of the same episode depending on whether the narrator feels more or less inspired on a particular day, or on the amount of interest demonstrated by his audience. Variations between different formulations are of interest from many points of view. They furnish valuable material to a linguist, allowing him to spot the same words in different, but comparable contexts. They are indispensable in stylistic analysis dealing with oral literature. Finally, they demonstrate the margin of freedom at the disposal of a narrator in his interpretation of tradition, which is an important element in defining the position of a narrator as an artist in the society under study and in establishing the limitations of his personal role in the field of literary creativity.

It is quite evident that a compilation of many different formulations of the same narrative by one narrator can never exhaust all the possibilities, since obviously the number of such variations is endless. What seems feasible is to obtain from the same narrator two or three formulations of two or three different narratives, selected on the basis of their special interest and because they represent different levels of the narrator's repertory, that is, tales that are less or more familiar to the narrator and to the audience. It is a good idea to obtain these formulations under different conditions or utilizing different methods; recitations in public or in private, spontaneous or upon request, tape recorded, written, or dictated.

As a general rule, one can assume he has different versions only after the same narrative has been obtained from two or more different narrators. It must be accepted from the start that there is absolutely no reason to consider any one version better than all the others. Particularly, according to Mauss' concise formula (1947, p. 98), "one never looks for the original text *because* there is no such thing" (the italics are the author's). Since I have already stressed elsewhere (Lavondès, 1964, 1966, introduction) the advantage of obtaining as great a number of different versions of one narrative as possible, I will mention this point only in passing. Let us simply keep in mind that only after acquiring several versions is it possible to formulate an opinion on the value and the authenticity of each one, that this is the best method of clarifying the meaning of a narrative, and that this approach leads to building up sources of ethnographic, linguistic, and stylistic material based on compilation of texts in native languages. Comparison of variants found in different versions of the same narrative may lead to tracing a certain number of succession links. It is only fair to assume that several versions presenting a certain number of common variants are genetically related to the same origin or to several origins which are themselves closely related, and that other versions, which systematically give variants different from the preceding ones, must go back to a different source. Following the procedure analogous to historic linguistics, it becomes possible to formulate plausible hypotheses concerning the main characteristics of a legend in the past. Finally, these comparative methods allow us to estimate, up to a point, the degree of changes in this or that narrative. In fact it becomes apparent that the more changes a narrative has undergone, the greater becomes the divergence between the different versions in meaning and the greater its incoherence.

To be sure, when one sets a goal of recording in writing all the versions of all the narratives and traditions extant in the memory of individual members of a group, at a given time, on a given area, the task soon appears out of proportion and impossible. I am certain that, even within the framework of self-imposed narrow limits, that is, the Island of Ua Pou, during the field work period, despite a simple culture of disintegrating traditions and only a small number of individuals who had any knowledge worthy of interest, with all the voluminous accumulation of records, I still did not fulfill this ambitious program and I know of certain individuals whose potential stock I did not exhaust. At a given point, therefore, one must become resigned to making a choice. But even so, one should not yield to the temptation to make an arbitrary selection, but, on the contrary, make a special effort to select on the basis of a rational criterion. This should be done at an early stage of compilation, so as to take full advantage of the limited amount of time to be spent in the field.

In this respect, I learned from my experience in the Marquesas that it is most profitable to divide the field work into two distinct stages, separated, if possible, by a summary analysis of the data assembled during the first step. This first stage should be considered as an exploratory one, to be spent in obtaining a limited number of various narratives from as many informants as possible. This part of field work, in my estimation, is similar to separating actual research work from acquiring statistical data through questionnaires and it should be spent in obtaining the first group of texts and, above all, in establishing as great a choice as possible of potential informants.

Following this phase, a summary analysis of the material obtained will aim first of all at selecting a certain number of narratives on the basis of their potential mythological, historic, or literary merit, which one will try to obtain in all possible variants during the second stage. At the same time it will also be possible to select among the available informants those who stand out because of their knowledge, their talent, the wealth of their repertory, and whose entire repertory one will attempt to record in full during the second stage. At this stage of the field work it should also be possible to determine a certain number of succession links, which will be explored fully during the following stage. This might force the investigator to record systematically the repertory of some mediocre storytellers only because their narratives are related to a specific line of succession. Finally, during the second stage one will obviously continue working at obtaining from the available narrators all the different narratives they still remember. The only point of the above selection is to avoid wasting too much time in accumulating an excess of useless versions of some of the narratives. Of course, exhausting the entire stock would appear to be safer than the above selective method, which is akin to a rational sampling in a statistical survey. But it is better to limit oneself to a rational selection than to find oneself in a situation similar to mine at the end of my field work in Ua Pou, of having gathered the entire repertory of certain mediocre informants, without even tapping the resources of better storytellers.

One can easily see that the goal of exhausting all the available material demands that special attention be paid to detecting potential informants. One should resist the temptation to use just one informant or a chance one. Much too often, in fact, former collectors of texts were content to note the repertory of just one or of a small number of storytellers, chosen because of their high repute among the natives and frequently for reasons which had no real bearing on the research project, such as ability to dictate, ability to speak the language of the field worker, and lack of timidity. This approach does not guarantee the obtaining of all the different narratives known to the people and results in leaving out numerous interesting variants. One should also bear in mind that, paradoxically, talent may diminish the ethnographic value of a myth or a legend. Gifted storytellers, in fact, tend to omit archaic or obscure sections of narratives or texts and clarify them by inventions of their own.

Finding and persuading two categories of potential informants should be done with special care. These are the timid and cautious informants, frequently quite old, who have had little opportunity to come in contact with Europeans and who prefer to remain in the background. When they are interrogated, they immediately declare that they do not know anything of interest, and the field worker will have to make use of all his anthropological acumen to establish rapport in order to persuade them to reveal their knowledge. We might mention some of the arguments which could be used to overcome this type of resistance: the promise of keeping the information secret (the recording will be done in private), citing other cases (such and such has already agreed to participate, list some of the narratives already obtained), appeal to their professional pride (repeat a few mediocre narratives; the reticent informant will not be able to resist the temptation to correct the errors).

Another group of informants not to be neglected is the one which comprises the not very gifted storytellers who deliver confused, awkward, and incomplete narratives. Some interesting variants, nevertheless, can be obtained through these channels. It is also necessary to explore regularly people who are not considered as storytellers, if only to find out to what extent the knowledge of oral literature is spread in general. Within the framework of the research done in the Marquesas, some twenty storytellers whose narratives it was possible to obtain had been found through a third person: "*I* do not know any traditional tales, but go see so and so, he knows some." One can never say enough about the need for determination and perseverance on the part of a field worker in recruiting informants. Be it in Ua Pou or in Nuku Hiva, my attempts at recruiting storytellers encountered a stone wall of proclaimed ignorance. It took me a long time to overcome this passivity and I got to know some of my best informants only toward the end of my stay.

Having settled on the informants, one has to deal with the problem of transferring into a written text the knowledge inscribed in their memories. Several methods are possible. We will first discuss the most classic method, that of dictation, then two other methods: tape recording, and texts written down by the informants themselves. The greatest majority of native language texts gathered among nonliterate peoples in our possession today have been obtained through dictation. This method therefore has been well tested and will always occupy an important place in compilation of texts. This does not mean that it is not without its well-known and evident drawbacks, which we will mention briefly. Quite obviously, in order to be able to write down a text from dictation, the anthropologist must have sufficiently mastered the language. At the beginning he will stumble over each word, trying the patience of his informant. Frequently also the informant, becoming aware of the ethnographer's language problems, tries to put himself down to his level by avoiding rare and archaic words, difficult expressions, or by simplifying syntactic structure; in a word, he tries to express himself in a sort of "basic dialect" which, in his estimation, will be more accessible to the field worker than the true language. But even without going this far, there is always the danger that dictated texts are simplified versions. The only true remedy is for the field worker to wait until his progress in mastery of the language reduces these drawbacks to a minimum; that is to say, just about the time his field trip is approaching the end. Hence a deplorable waste of time.

Furthermore, even if the field worker has mastered the language and has learned to take notes in a rapid phonetic transcription, the dictation method still retains some drawbacks. Certain informants can never adjust themselves to the restraint for which nothing in their own culture prepares them. Georges Condominas, an anthropologist who is certainly completely at home in the use of the language of the people he is working with, describes very concretely and vividly the difficulties encountered in assembling texts through dictation.

> Actually this first-rate narrator speaks much too fast to make it possible for anyone to take dictation; but when asked to repeat the legend which he had just recited more slowly, he is so completely involved in his narrative that he launches forth again at full speed, so that one cannot follow him, frequently complicating matters further by varying the narrative or adding some episode omitted the first time. Toông Oông is not the only one to act this way; it happens even among the most intelligent informants, such as Kröng-Joông, who understands very well the reason for being asked to repeat slowly what he has just said. The constraint of self-imposed discipline in slowing down his narrative interferes with his presentation and has an especially bad effect on the art of reciting, so important to a bard in his restoration of an oral tradition. (Condominas, 1965, pp. 463-464, translated.)

The difficulty experienced by the storytellers in submitting themselves to the discipline of dictation varies from individual to individual, and is stronger with those who have remained closer to a traditional background. This may force the field worker using the dictation method to begin by noting the stories of the more acculturated narrators. The texts run the further risk of being altered by the recitation in that the part left to improvisation is greater. The drawbacks of this method are at their minimum when dealing with memorized texts (certain prayers, chants, and so forth). But they become much more significant when dealing with folk tales or historical narratives. In many cases, therefore, it is worth while to have some other method at one's disposal.

Technical progress in tape recording provides the anthropologist with an easy solution of these problems. But it should be realized that the use of a tape recorder presents just as many problems as it solves, and it is necessary to know exactly what one is trying to achieve before using it and to take certain elementary precautionary measures. First of all, it should be determined in advance whether the recorder will be used to make a live recording conveying as accurate an impression as possible of the atmosphere surrounding a spontaneous recitation of oral literature, or simply as an intermediary measure before obtaining a written text. In the first instance, all the features of the background in which the storytelling is taking place can be accepted: gusts of wind and a pounding surf, roosters crowing, grunting of a hungry pig, crying children, noises of songs and games outside, outspoken reaction of the audience who laugh during the good parts, prompt the narrator, make comments, chatter, and come and go constantly. Under the circumstances, if one can succeed in placing the microphone judiciously at a well-balanced spot between the voice of the narrator and the outside noises, the recording will provide an excellent impression of the surroundings and a lifelike reconstruction of the actual atmosphere during the storytelling, all of which may be valuable ethnographic information. Furthermore, this method may occasionally provide an opportunity to record quite by chance a brilliant improvisation, a performance of a good narrator supported and inspired by the reaction of his audience, thus obtaining an interesting literary document. But we should not delude ourselves about the difficulties connected with the tape-recorder work and must keep in mind that the outside noises, whenever they become pronounced, make the work even more difficult. It happens only seldom that a tape recorded under "natural" conditions can be transcribed entirely. There are always a few passages which even a native speaker frequently is unable to transcribe. This is a major inconvenience for a collector of oral traditions whose principal aim is to assemble texts. Extraneous noises may be eliminated to a great extent by careful selection of locale (a household away from the village—if possible, not too close to the beach; an enclosure made of thatch, to avoid reverberations, and with a mud floor to avoid the creaking of the wooden planks), as well as the hour of recording (in the evening when the roosters and the babies are asleep—although one still has the dogs!). The audience interference is harder to eliminate. If the presence of the public is completely forbidden, the storyteller, not getting sufficient support from an audience limited to a lone anthropologist, will recite in a dry and uninspired manner. If one tries to control the audience by imposing absolute silence (which in any case is pretty difficult to achieve) everyone sits as if frozen, everyone is bored, and the result is the same as above. In my own case, after several unfortunate experiences, I tried to gather together around the narrator a small audience of five to ten people carefully selected from among close members of the family or old men interested in traditions, an audience which could act as a catalyst for the natural talent of the storyteller, while limiting the amount of extraneous noise interference to a minimum.

It has been demonstrated by others that a tape recording becomes a usable document from a scientific point of view only if a parallel written transcription has also been acquired. The latter has to be done by the anthropologist working with a native-speaking informant (who might easily and profitably be the storyteller himself). Thanks to the tape recording, the cadence and the contents of the narrative are fixed once and for all, and during the transcription the anthropologist may have as many repetitions as necessary to clarify the difficult passages, without the danger of changing the nature of the narrative. The greatest advantage of the tape recorder is that the job of transcribing can be delayed at will. Therefore, the ethnographer can start his work of assembling oral traditions immediately upon his arrival in the field, at a time when his command of the language is still weak, and can put off until later the task of transcribing and interpreting. However, it is necessary to point out the weaknesses of texts obtained only by means of a tape recording. The tape registers all the hesitations present in speech; the search for the right word, unfinished sentences, and wrong constructions. In certain cases, therefore, the texts obtained in a live recording may prove to be not very usable because of errors and confusion. We must also point out that transcription from a tape is a long, elaborate and, in final analysis, a very costly job, because it requires the permanent assistance of a native speaker.

Thus, the tape recorder is not a panacea, but minor inconveniences connected with its use should not outweigh the irreplaceable service which it may render. Available at all times, prepared to follow the narrator's rhythm completely, it allows the compiler of oral literature to get to work immediately upon arrival. Later on, it remains irreplaceable in capturing some points which writing cannot record; the atmosphere surrounding a spontaneous recitation, the virtuosity of expression of an orator or a storyteller, and a thousand and one nuances in pronunciation, so valuable to a linguist. In Ua Pou I used the tape recorder a great deal, recording at all possible times the important sections of the repertory of each storyteller. Nevertheless, the texts for which I have only a single tape recording represent only a small section of all the material gathered there.

Actually, it was indeed neither through dictation nor by means of a tape recorder that the corpus of Marquesas texts now being prepared for publication was assembled. Benefiting from the work of alphabetizing done in French Polynesia by the official school system, by the missionaries or, in an improvised fashion, by the Polynesians themselves, I took advantage of the fact that a great number of informants and storytellers could write, and asked them to write down their repertories. Here I should mention an unforeseen problem arising from this method. In many instances, I followed up the written rendition by asking the informants to record the text on tape. This appeared to be a mistake. In effect, the prestige of a written text is so great, that as soon as they have put it down in writing, the storytellers are paralyzed by fear of deviating from it in an oral recitation, or to forget something; they intone their narratives like a lesson, constantly asking to stop in order to check the written text. All the freshness, vigor, and spontaneity which characterize oral literature disappear. It is far better to make the tape recording before asking for a written text.

Of the eighteen storytellers whose complete or partial repertory has been obtained through written manuscripts supplied by the narrators themselves, eleven wrote the text in their own hand, and seven others dictated it to some member of the family. In the latter case, the narrator used his "poor eyesight" as the reason for not being able to write (the true reason frequently being the informant's difficulties with the alphabet). These secondhand written records apparently did not present any special difficulty when the "writer" was an older person well acquainted with traditions. The results were less satisfactory in two other cases when the texts had been dictated to a youngster trained in the official school: archaic words were not recognized, and there was general confusion because of the influence of French spelling.

Generally speaking, the drawbacks in connection with the method of texts written by the native informants concern technical matters rather than content. First of all, there is the problem of deciphering these thick notebooks covered with childish handwriting, where words are separated according to fancy. The rudimentary character of Polynesian phonology usually makes the transcription by and large correct, but the glottal stops are regularly left out or indicated irregularly by the more literate informants. Quantity oppositions, which are very slight in Marquesan, were, needless to say, always omitted. This made it necessary to spend a great deal of time on the editing of the text with the constant help of the local assistant, Mr. Samuel Teikiehuupoki, a teacher who, after a short indoctrination, was quite capable of restoring the glottals and re-establishing the word separation. Nevertheless, in certain cases, where the presence or absence of a glottal could modify the interpretation of the text, this method leads to a possible source of errors. In principle, doubtful cases were submitted to the informant. Still, some errors did remain, especially with regard to names. The delicate problem of vowel lengths had to be put aside until later. Also, it happens frequently that certain syllables, especially when doubled, are regularly omitted, as well as the unaccented grammatical words. Since these simplifications seem to be prevalent in the actual spoken language, we have, as a rule, left intact the notations in the written documents with the exception of obvious errors. This does not preclude the possibility, nevertheless, that certain astounding constructions appearing in the final text may still be simply due to *lapsus calami*.

With regard to the contents, the advantages of this method seem to compensate to a great extent for its disadvantages. Just as with the tape recorder, the work of assembling can be started well before the language has been mastered. The problems connected with the dictation method are avoided: the informant is no longer likely to substitute some currently used word for one which is rare in order to avoid the necessity of providing an explication to the recording anthropologist. Better yet, comparison between certain texts obtained through tape recording and texts written by the informant shows that the latter are usually just as good or better. Even though a certain amount of verve typical of an oral recitation does disappear, most of the unevenness of expression as well as certain unnecessary repetitions are eliminated. Above all, the informant writing down his narrative at leisure, usually for short periods at a time, has the time to think, so that the stories obtained in this manner are in general more coherent, richer in detail. The danger of some episode being completely left out is diminished.

While the recording of a narrative has always been considered as a popular distraction, and would be occasionally rewarded by some small gift, it seemed absolutely necessary to remunerate the informant for the work done in writing. To be sure, this concerns some of the private matters in anthropology, usually not mentioned, but in my opinion it is a mistake, because these details do play a part in influencing the quality of the assembled data. I have always abided by the principle stated by André Leroi-Gourhan to his students: "The best information is that which the natives give on their own." But I feel that in certain cases one has to break this rule, and that obtaining written records of oral traditions is one of these exceptional cases. This involves a long and careful task resulting in several hundred pages of closely written notebooks and, once the novelty of the job wears off, it is indeed a rare informant who will persevere in a sustained effort without some extra stimulus. Of course, handling remuneration is a delicate matter, and it is not without hesitation that I decided to take this definitely risky step.

The greatest danger of all is that the informant may produce pure inventions in the hope of increasing his gain; the least serious one is that he may elaborate the details and add unnecessary digressions. I tried to reduce these risks to a minimum by presenting the matter to the writer-storyteller in such a way that these compensations would pass for a kind of gift or special reward, rather than wages. I avoided giving them any information which would let them calculate in advance the amount which they would be getting. All I said when "placing the order" was that I would make a gift in cash, depending on the work and the quality of the manuscript. I had never had any complaints. Nevertheless, in one or two cases certain digressions did seem to appear to indicate the informant's desire to increase his profits.

These drawbacks appear very small to me as opposed to the possibility of salvaging numerous fragments of legends and less-known narratives from the repertory of certain storytellers who had started out by declaring that they "had completely exhausted the original legends which they had in their stomach" (*'u pao onaona te tekao a'akakai mei 'oto to'u kopu*). I learned indirectly that some of the informants had done actual research, consulting older men who did not know any narratives themselves, but who, having heard them, could help clarify certain details. As for gross falsification, I believe I have been spared, thanks to the self-respect of the informants who on their own had no desire to be caught in the act of "untruth" (*tivava*), and because of the cooperation of Samuel Teikiehuupoki, a man of pitilessly severe judgment of the narrators' talents, and also because of my own relative fluency in the language, long association with the same locale, and a rapidly acquired familiarity with the material concerning oral literature. All this, I hope, saved me from falling victim to these enormous jokes which the Marquesan sense of humor can invent to have a good laugh at the expense of the uninitiated.

Finally, I would like to draw attention to one rigorous rule which can never be stressed enough with regard to assembling oral traditions: the absolute necessity to obtain on the spot all the basic data related to proper interpretation of the acquired material. A text increases in scientific value with the increased wealth of accompanying annotations, and with all the essential information concerning the narrator and his background. First of all, of course, comes the precise description of the locale where the text was acquired. Emory, in my opinion, is entirely justified in regard to Stimson's *Songs and Tales of the Sea Kings,* in expressing his regret that "it is left to the reader to guess in which group of islands originated a certain chant or a particular story" (Emory,

1958, p. 791). It is true that further down he expresses even more serious criticism, but this does not detract from the extreme importance of the above remark. Nevertheless, D. S. Marshall, the editor of this work, makes a valid statement when he says: "The fact that an episode or a chant had been recorded at a recent period on some specific island cannot contribute any foolproof information as to their origin in time and space. Polynesians have always been great voyageurs and enthusiastic collectors of literature of other countries."

This receptiveness of the Polynesians to things from outside sources, this desire to enrich their own folklore with "exotic" tales, is a fact, and I saw it confirmed in the Marquesas. In fact, I have acquired quite a collection of acculturated literature, made up of narratives which are without any doubt borrowings and which are, in any case, taken as being such by the informants: a Marquesan version of "Cinderella," and "Aripapai," and some tales of still undetermined origin, which must have come in through Tahiti and which perhaps are stories of mariners. But, if it is indeed true that "determining the origin in time and space" of a given narrative does raise extremely thorny, if not insurmountable, problems, it appears to be that much more important to obtain right on the spot all possible details which may in some way start unraveling the thread and prevent making the worst errors. Two recent publications on the folklore of Oceania, that of Lessa (1961), and Elbert and Monberg (1965), are excellent illustrations of this point (we can only regret that the native versions of the texts had been omitted from the first of these two works). All the circumstances and data relative to assembling each text and to its author are noted with abundance of detail beyond comparison. In addition to indispensable information concerning the exact locale where the text had been obtained, we also learn the narrator's name and age, and have a biographical sketch describing his travels, his genealogy, and the name of the person who taught him the narrative. There is not one of these details which could be considered useless.

It is not a matter of indifference to an anthropologist that such and such a storyteller had already given a certain formulation of a certain narrative to someone else previously: hence the need to mention the names of one's informants. Knowing the biography and travels of the informant may be a decisive factor in determining whether a certain narrative had been borrowed from a neighboring island at a recent date. Discovering the last link in the chain of succession is an important element in establishing the succession. The four narrators who gave their versions of "Taheta" (Lavondès, 1966) all claim to have learned it from a certain Pupe, a famous storyteller of Ua Pou, who died August 6, 1932. Vari'i, the author of "Akahe'e-'i-Vevau," the narrative which heads the above-mentioned collection, claims to have heard this story from his adoptive grandmother, Tahiamei-ha'etiki, along with all the other narratives of his repertory. Since his version of this narrative differs considerably from the other versions (not yet published), of which some are traced back to Pupe, and since, on the other hand, his entire repertory differs significantly from those of other storytellers, critical analysis of the texts and knowledge of the last step in transmission make one assume that Vari'i and the disciples of Pupe represent two different lines of succession.

Texts compiled through assembling oral literature and traditions are frequently difficult to interpret. On the one hand, this is because it is implicitly assumed that many elements are familiar to the audience for whom the narrative is intended, and on the other hand, to the fact that they reflect the entire culture of the group. It is indispensable for the interpretation of the gathered material that all factors which may facilitate its clarification be carefully noted. Salvaging oral literature, therefore, does not simply mean compilation of texts, but also a thorough study in relation to these texts. The first step, naturally, is to seek explications of all obscure words and passages. Special attention should be paid to place names. One should know whether real places or mythical ones are mentioned, and whether a special meaning is not being attached to them because of some tradition. Certain topographic details of places mentioned may be of importance in understanding the text, and in this connection it might be useful to visit the locale in order to have the significant traits explained. It is equally important to have an exact identification of the botanical and zoological species mentioned. Recent research on American folklore by Lévi-Strauss (1964, 1966) shows to what extent native thought depends on the minutest particularities of the living world. For regions or field stations of which there are no basic studies, the anthropologist will have to collect specimens.

During the second stage, one should try to obtain from the storyteller a connected commentary on his narrative in the nature of the *explication de textes,* a technique very popular in literature classes in French high schools, aimed at developing implicitly a kind of voluntary involvement in culture on the part of the students. It is difficult to explain this system without using numerous examples. Let us just say that one has to go through the text sentence by sentence, asking the narrator to explain not only the obscure terms and passages, but also those of which the meaning appears to be clear. For instance, nothing could seem more natural than the description in a narrative of a woman with children in her lap. Yet, for the Marquesans of old, her posture had a very special meaning. The children in her lap cannot belong to her brother, or else she would have put them on her shoulders. Starting with this detail, one discovers, as far as I know, an entirely new aspect concerning the family system of the ancient Marquesans and of a joking relationship between certain categories of relatives, thus clarifying a series of obscure passages in the texts. One may similarly ask the narrator to explain the hero's behavior, which in some cases will lead to interesting anthropological findings. Thus, using these methods borrowed from modern pedagogical technique, one may find the thread which will lead to becoming aware of the real significance which these traditional narratives, reflecting the group culture, had in influencing successive generations.

This work with text commentaries requires a great deal of time and I have not carried it as far as it could have gone. Nevertheless, the results of the partial research suffice to demonstrate the importance of this approach. On the other hand, I have become aware of how vague and summary are previous explications with regard to text commentary. There is no doubt whatsoever that this is the direction in which research methods must be developed. One direction is opened by the work of Elbert and Monberg (1965), who took great care to acquire texts under conditions very close to spontaneous recitation and who noted down systematically the reactions and the commentaries of the narrator's audience. That is most certainly an important element in the interpretation of the texts themselves. Let us finally point out that all the remarks presented above are applicable only in a special context: that of the well-defined region of Oceania. Changes would have to be introduced in applying these rules elsewhere. It is quite clear, for instance, that the method of having texts written down by the informant cannot be used everywhere.

A systematic and exhaustive assembling of literature and oral traditions is an urgent task which must be carried out by present-day anthropology, especially in Oceania. The preceding comments are only a summing up of an individual experience. There is no doubt that joint research projects would be most welcome in establishing and popularizing some methods which would lead to both improving the quality of the acquired material and to increasing the output of the compilation, so great is the task which needs to be done. In this way it would be possible to make substantial progress along the way to the initiation of which Kenneth Emory has contributed so much.

LITERATURE CITED

CONDOMINAS, GEORGES
   1965. *L'Exotique est Quotidien*. Paris: Plon.

ELBERT, SAMUEL H.
   [n.d.] Marquesan Legends. Manuscript in Bernice P. Bishop Mus. Library.

ELBERT, SAMUEL H., and TORBEN MONBERG
   1965. *From the Two Canoes: Oral Traditions of Rennell and Bellona Islands*. Honolulu and Copenhagen: Univ. Hawaii Press and Danish National Mus.

EMORY, KENNETH P.
   1958. Review of J. Frank Stimson, *Songs and Tales of the Sea Kings*. *American Anthropologist* **60**(4):791-794.
   1965. *Kapingamarangi: Social and Religious Life of a Polynesian Atoll*. B. P. Bishop Mus. Bull. 228. Honolulu.

HANDY, EDWARD S. C.
   1923. *The Native Culture in the Marquesas*. B. P. Bishop Mus. Bull. 9. Honolulu.
   1930. *Marquesan Legends*. B. P. Bishop Mus. Bull. 69. Honolulu.

LAVONDÈS, HENRI
   1964. Récits Marquisiens. [1st series.] Papeete: Centre ORSTOM Mimeographed.
   1966. Récits Marquisiens. [2nd series.] Papeete: Centre ORSTOM Mimeographed.

LESSA, WILLIAM A.
   1961. *Tales from Ulithi Atoll*. Folklore Studies 13. Univ. California Press.

LÉVI-STRAUSS, CLAUDE
   1964. *Le Cru et le Cuit*. Paris: Plon.
   1966. *Du Miel aux Cendres*. Paris: Plon.

MAUSS, MARCEL
   1947. *Manuel d'Ethnographie*. Paris: Payot.

WEST POLYNESIA

PRESERVATION AND EVOLUTION OF FORM AND FUNCTION IN TWO TYPES OF TONGAN DANCE

ADRIENNE L. KAEPPLER[1]

Bernice P. Bishop Museum, Honolulu

IN MANY PARTS of Polynesia, dance has lost much of its indigenous function and become merely a form of entertainment. Performances are given as historical and intellectual exercises, or as educational activities to acquaint the new, acculturated generation with the traditions of their forefathers. Contemporary native dance combines elements from other Polynesian traditions and from Western sources with those of indigenous origin. These hybrids, with their Westernized music and their graceful and sometimes risqué movements, are enjoyed by Polynesians, and by European observers as well. At the same time, old dances have been preserved and new native forms have evolved from indigenous dance types. These dances are potentially valuable in a study of diffusion, as well as for their reflection of internal historical and social changes.

In Tonga today we find a living dance tradition that is functionally interwoven with other aspects of the culture. Tongan dance has lost some of its indigenous functions and has acquired the above-mentioned ones. In addition, it has sociopolitical implications which have developed from indigenous ones. These have risen from Tonga's own cultural environment and account for the present-day creation and performance of many of the dances.

[1] Research in the Tongan Islands was supported by a Public Health Service fellowship No. 5-F1-MH-25, 984-02 from the National Institute of Mental Health and the Wenner-Gren Foundation for Anthropological Research. The author also wishes to acknowledge Carl Wolz for checking the Labanotation scores; Barbara Smith and Penieli Fisi'ihoi for reviewing the manuscript; Alan Howard who directed the author's graduate program; and William K. Kikuchi for drawing the notations.

Much of Tonga's traditional social and cultural integrity has been retained. This is in part because of its freedom from foreign political domination, for while all other Polynesian groups were taken over by one or another of the world powers, Tonga alone managed to maintain its independence. Tonga, a constitutional monarchy under King Tāufa'āhau Tupou IV, is a Protected State of Great Britain. This status is quite different from that of a colony or a member of the British Commonwealth. The internal affairs of Tonga are Tongan matters, free to develop along strictly Tongan lines. Except for a few advisors, all government officials are Tongans. The indigenous stratified social system of chiefs and commoners still exists and is the basis of the sociopolitical system. This is not to imply that the culture is the same as, or even highly similar to what it was in pre-European times. Innumerable changes have taken place, but these changes were not induced by any outside superior political power.

The dance, too, has changed. However, these changes—along with the changes in the sociopolitical system that dance reflects—cannot be explained entirely in terms of Western acculturation. This paper will explore a number of elements which have been preserved and which have evolved in two types of Tongan group dances. It will offer some explanations as to why one of these types has come down to us virtually unchanged while the other has undergone a series of changes and, from the Tongan point of view, has died out. We are interested here in what changes have taken place in Tongan dance itself and in its context as an aid in the interpretation of cultural history.

CHANGE AND THE DANCE

Dance is subject to the same processes of change which affect all aspects of culture, both social and material. It can be considered in ways similar to any other artifact and can thus be analyzed with regard to its form and function. Because of the transitory nature of dance, existing as it does only for a certain length of time, changes in dance, and especially changes in movements, are difficult to demonstrate. Unlike the archaeologist or ethnologist who works with material culture, the dance ethnologist has no concrete objects to examine and measure in order to demonstrate changes as they occurred through examining stratified sites or a series of artifacts collected at various times. The dance ethnologist does have, however, verbal descriptions and drawings of early explorers and missionaries, as well as of later visitors and anthropologists. In themselves these descriptions are not very illuminating. However, when viewed in the light of familiarity with the present-day dance culture, the historical documents can provide an added dimension to interpretation.

Change in dance must be considered from two points of view. Change can take place in the dance itself and this change may involve both the movements and the over-all structure of the dance—or, the form of the dance. Also, change can take place in the ways in which dance is used in society and in the reasons for dance performances—or, the function of the dance. We will examine first the form of the dance, but before we do so an explanation is necessary as to how a series of quickly executed movements, which exist in the oral tradition, can be examined.

The "artifact" of dance can be represented concretely so that it can be examined and measured. Labanotation, a graphic method of recording dance, is a system in which positions and movements, no matter how subtle, can be represented (Hutchinson, 1954). Recording in Labanotation is comparable with a written phonetic record of speech, or with the notation of music on a staff, and can be analyzed in similar ways. By recording Tongan dance in Labanotation, the transitory action becomes an "object" that can be handled and compared, providing something with which to work. In a previous work I have delineated the basic movements of Tongan dance and analyzed how these movements are combined to form dances (Kaeppler, 1967). Here I will attempt to project backward in time and document the changes that seem to have taken place from the time of European contact to today. Thus, it is an ethnohistorical study using my own ethnological data plus historical documents. The verbal descriptions of previous writers will be interpreted in the light of my knowledge of Tongan dance. I will provide Labanotation of the dance positions shown in the drawings of Webber. These will be compared with the types that are considered by contemporary Tongans to be "ancient" and modern. I will concentrate on the two types of group dances that appear in the literature from the time of European contact to the present. Based on this, I will give my interpretation of preservation and evolution in these dances and their social context.

The earliest and best descriptions of Tongan dance in the immediate post-European period come from the journals of the voyages of Captain Cook. These give us the best available idea of Tongan dance before it was influenced by Western culture. The artist, John Webber, who accompanied Cook's third voyage, did some remarkable drawings and we are fortunate that two of them (Figs. 1 and 2) are of Tongan dance.

Cook visited Tonga on his second and third voyages. During the third voyage he remained in Tonga more than three months and recorded much about Tongan culture. His relations with the Tongans were for the most part very good, which prompted the name, Friendly Islands.[2] Beneath the veneer of friendliness, however, there were ulterior motives. The Tongans had planned to kill Captain Cook and take his ships, and it was only a disagreement among the chiefs about the time of attack which kept the plan from being executed. During their stay in Tonga, Cook and his men were entertained with performances of wrestling, boxing, and dancing. This seems to have been the indigenous form of entertainment for Tongan chiefs as well as for important visitors. The journals describe two types of dances, one in which men dance holding paddles, and a hand-action dance in which either men or women take part.

ME‘ETU‘UPAKI

Let us look at the descriptions from Cook's voyage of the men's paddle dance and then consider later descriptions. The journals of Cook's second voyage have no descriptions of Tongan dance. The first description of the paddle dance is from Cook's third voyage, when he observed it at a reception in Ha‘apai on May 20, 1777 (Cook, 1784, Vol. 1, pp. 247-248).

It was a kind of dance, so entirely different from any thing I had ever seen, that, I fear, I can give no description that will convey any tolerable idea of it to my readers. It was performed by men; and one hundred and five persons bore their parts in it. Each of them had in his hand an instrument neatly made, shaped somewhat like a paddle, of two feet and a half in length, with a small handle, and a thin blade; so that they were very light. With these instruments they made many and various flourishes, each of which was accompanied with a different attitude of the body, or a different movement. At first, the performers ranged themselves in three lines; and, by various evolutions, each man changed his station in such a manner, that those who had been in the rear, came into the front. Nor did they remain long in the same position; but these changes were made by pretty quick transitions. At one time they extended themselves in one line; they, then, formed into a semicircle; and, lastly, into two square columns. While this last movement was executing, one of them advanced, and performed an antic dance before me, with which the whole ended.

---

[2] The name was originally given to the Island of Lifuka in the Ha‘apai or central group of Tongan Islands, but has come to be extended to the whole Tongan group.

FIGURE 1 (opposite).

The musical instruments consisted of two drums, or rather two hollow logs of wood, from which some varied notes were produced, by beating on them with two sticks. It did not, however, appear to me, that the dancers were much assisted or directed by these sounds, but by a chorus of vocal music, in which all the performers joined at the same time. Their song was not destitute of pleasing melody; and all their corresponding motions were executed with so much skill, that the numerous body of dancers seemed to act, as if they were one great machine.

The paddle dance was again performed for Cook on Tongatapu on June 17, 1777, on the occasion of a grand entertainment. This performance lasted for four hours and included four dances, three or perhaps all four of which were done while carrying the *paki,* or paddle. Some movements are well described; for example, "They make a great many different motions; such as pointing them [*paki*] toward the ground on one side, at the same time inclining their bodies that way, from which they are shifted to the opposite side in the same manner, then passing them quickly from one hand to the other, and twirling them about very dexterously" (Cook, 1784, Vol. 1, p. 293).

The journals say that the dances were called *mai* (*me'e* in present Tongan orthography) and were accompanied by a chorus of 70 men and this time by three hollowed-out tree trunks, called *nafa,* that were struck with two wooden sticks. "Their motions were at first slow, but quickened as the drums beat faster; and they recited sentences in a musical tone the whole time, which were answered by the chorus; but at the end of a short space they all joined, and finished with a shout" (Cook, 1784, Vol. 1, p. 293). With short intervals, the dance continued for more than a quarter of an hour. During this time there were several skillful transpositions of floor plans.

In 1786 La Perouse visited Tonga, but left no description of the dances. However, Labillardière visited Tongatapu in 1793, on D'Entrecasteaux's voyage in search of La Perouse, and gave the following description of the paddle dance (Labillardière, 1802, pp. 158-159).

As soon as the women had done dancing, several men stood up, each holding in his hand a little club, nearly in the form of a paddle, which they moved about, keeping time with great correctness, and making a variety of motions with their feet. The musicians, after having sung some airs in very slow time, sang others in very quick time, which gave to this sort of pyrrhic dance, a degree of vivacity and spirit that excited our warmest admiration.

The subject of this dance greatly awakened our curiosity; but we soon learnt that its object was to celebrate the noble feats of some of their warriors. The women, from time to time, mingled their voices with those of the men, accompanying their song with the most graceful motions.

Malaspina anchored in Vava'u harbor in 1793 and has given descriptions of several dances, but it seems that he did not see a dance in which men held paddles and performed the dexterous transpositions of floor plans. He did see a dance in which he conjectured that clubs had been replaced by short sticks. This appeared to be a representation of a battle. It must have been a performance of a dance called *kailao,* which according to present-day Tongans came from Uvea. Malaspina's journal description might lead one to believe that this was a similar dance to those witnessed by Captain Cook, but my reading of the evidence leaves little doubt that it was not (Malaspina, 1885, p. 271).

The next mention of the men's paddle dance comes from Mariner's remembrances. Mariner was spared during the Tongan massacre of the ship *Port au Prince,* and lived in Ha'apai with the chief, Fīnau, from 1806 to 1810. He quotes Cook's description of the dance, but he tells us that the name of the dance is *mëë too buggi* (*me'etu'upaki*). *Me'etu'upaki* translates as dance (*me'e*) standing (*tu'u*) with paddles (*paki*). He says further that the singing was in the Samoan language (Martin, 1818, Vol. 2, p. 318).

Basil Thomson's *Diversions of a Prime Minister* (1894) takes little note of the dance, but his *Savage Island* (1902) includes an Appendix on Tongan music (pp. 218-228). His description of the *me'etu'upaki* is certainly wrong and it is probable that he never saw it performed. He says that a good drawing of this dance is to be found in Cook's journals; however, the only drawing of a men's dance in Cook (Fig. 2) is clearly not a *me'etu'upaki* because the participants are not holding paddles, and in addition Cook has a perfectly good description of what the illustrated dance is. Thomson (1902, p. 220) says further "that it is performed by men, drawn up in one line or two who perform certain slow and stately evolutions," which seems to be an attempt to describe the drawing rather than either Cook's description or what he observed in Tonga.

A Catholic priest known as P. Soane Malia, writing in 1910, noted that the *me'etu'upaki* was the most beautiful of all Tongan dances. He called it a war dance and asserted that it was practiced in the same manner at that time as it was in the time of Cook (Malia, 1910, p. 77). Collocott (1928, p. 115), a Wesleyan minister, again referred to Cook's and Mariner's accounts. Although he says the dance was still being performed, he probably did not witness a performance, because he says that the dance was performed "with spears, axes, and like manly implements and weapons." Gifford only mentions the name of the

me'etu'upaki and does not give a description (1929, p. 230). From Koch's (1955) description of the dance it does not seem that he saw it performed, although he implies that it is still practiced (p. 266).

Whether the writers about Tongan dance had actually seen the *me'etu'upaki,* had had it described to them by the Tongans, or had merely read other descriptions, they all describe it in essentially the terms used by Captain Cook. This tells us not only that Cook gave an excellent description, but also that through the years the dance has remained unchanged, or at least sufficiently unchanged so that it could still be described in the same way. This remains true today. During my first field trip to Tonga in 1964 the *me'etu'upaki* was described to me and the descriptions fit Cook's perfectly. During my second trip in 1965-1966 I saw it performed and also learned to perform it, and the descriptions above remain accurate.

As performed today, the *me'etu'upaki* is divided temporally into several sections or stanzas. Each stanza is repeated at least once, but usually twice or more, and with each repetition the movements are also repeated. Each stanza ends with a shout, *"tu!,"* and there is a short interval before the next stanza begins. One man, who might be called the director, stands to one side and indicates when the next stanza should begin by saying *"tu ki hoki."* Modern Tongans say they do not understand the meaning of that phrase or the words of the song. They say the words are Uvean, Futunan, and Samoan, but those who speak any of these languages do not understand them either. They also say that they do not know the meaning of the movements. This dance, according to the Tongans, has come down from ancient times and was performed for the Tu'i Tonga (sacred king) on ceremonial occasions such as the *'inasi,* first-fruits ceremony, at which time the people brought quantities of food to the sacred king to insure abundant harvests in the future.

In performing the *me'etu'upaki,* the dancers sometimes move as one group, or they may divide into two or three groups. While performing a number of expert turns and twirls of the *paki,* they rearrange themselves so skillfully that one must see several performances to understand what movements each person makes to take him to his new position. The performers accompany their movements with singing. A chorus of men, with one or more musicians keeping time on hollow log gongs, usually sings with the dancers. In at least one stanza the dancers divide

---

FIGURE 2 (opposite).

into three groups and each group sings a different set of words and melody, all of which have different lengths and different sets of movements. During this polyphony the chorus does not sing. Most of the movements are very graceful, and Tongans consider this a characteristic of the dance. The principal foot movements are steps in place, small steps around in a circle, side steps, small jumps, and the crossing of one foot in front of the other, pointing the toe, and passively touching it to the ground.

I would argue that this dance, the *me'etu'upaki,* has come down to us virtually unchanged from the time of European contact until today.

ME'ELAUFOLA

The other dance recorded in Cook's journals is a type in which a group of either men or women take part. Webber has done two drawings of dancers and musicians performing this type of dance (Figs. 1, 2). The musical accompaniment, as described by Mr. Anderson in the journals, is as follows (Cook, 1784, Vol. 1, pp. 249-250):

> As a prelude to them [the dances], a band of music, or chorus of eighteen men, seated themselves before us, in the centre of the circle composed by the numerous spectators, the area of which was to be the scene of the exhibitions. Four or five of this band had pieces of large bamboo, from three to five or six feet long, each managed by one man, who held it nearly in a vertical position, the upper end open, but the other end closed by one of the joints. With this closed end, the performers kept constantly striking the ground, though slowly, thus producing different notes, according to the different lengths of the instruments, but all of them of the hollow or base sort; to counteract which, a person kept striking quickly, and with two sticks, a piece of the same substance, a tone as acute as those produced by the others were grave. The rest of the band, as well as those who performed upon the bamboos, sung a low and soft air, which so tempered the harder notes of the above instruments, that no bystander, however accustomed to hear the most perfect and varied modulation of sweet sounds, could avoid confessing the vast power, and pleasing effect, of this simple harmony.

Neither of these percussion instruments—bamboo stamping tubes or a bamboo struck with sticks—is used today in Tonga. The spectators are usually arranged around an open space and before the performance begins there may be a prelude of music and singing. Stringed instruments, including ukulele and guitar, furnish the accompaniment. The rest of the group, as well as the instrumentalists, sing what are known as *hiva kakala,* or sweet songs. The voices of both men and women are often soft and sweet and the words tell of flowers, birds, and places, which obscure a deeper meaning of the song.

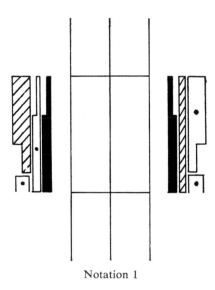

Notation 1

Webber's drawing designated "A Night Dance by Women, in Hapaee" shows two groups, one on each side of the musicians (Fig. 1). The leaders of the two groups are not in the same position. The leader on the right has her right arm raised from the elbow and the left arm bent. Her palms face backward, toward the body. Her position is written in Labanotation in Notation 1.[3] The leader of the group on the left has both of her slightly bent arms forward and both palms facing away from her. Her position is written in Notation 2.

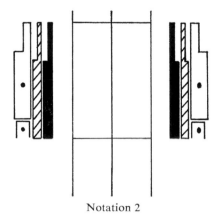

Notation 2

[3] The rotation of the torso is not notated because it is difficult to tell whether this was an artistic convention of Webber in order to show front and side views at the same time or if the torso was actually turned.

In present Tongan dance, these two positions are two stages in a single movement. The movement would start in the position of the woman on the right. From this position the lower arms are rotated outward and at the same time the fingers are bent or curled. This curling of the fingers starts with the little finger and the index finger is last to bend and does not bend as far. In Figure 1 this curling is shown in several different stages and often the index finger is curled less than the other fingers. The lower arm rotation turns the palms outward and the fingers unbend, ending in the position of the leader of the group on the left. The arms may either remain in one position or they can be moved to a different position. This whole movement is written in Notation 3. Note that the position of arms and palms are the same as the positions for Notations 1 and 2. Webber's drawing, showing the women in various positions, is similar to my photographs for at any one moment the several dancers are in slightly different stages of the movement. Reconstructing the movement from the positions in the drawing indicates that the movement is the same as that used today.

The explanation that seems to go with this plate is as follows (Cook, 1784, Vol. 1, pp. 250-251):

The concert having continued about a quarter of an hour, twenty women entered the circle. Most of them had, upon their heads, garlands of crimson flowers of the China rose, or others; and many of them had ornamented their persons with leaves of trees, cut with a great deal of nicety about the edges. They made a circle round the chorus, turning their faces toward it, and began singing a soft air, to which responses were made by the chorus in the same tone; and these were repeated alternately. All this while, the women accompanied their song with several very graceful motions of their hands toward their faces, and in other directions at the same time, making constantly a step forward, and then back again, with one foot, while the other was fixed. They then turned their faces to the assembly, sung some time, and retreated slowly in a body, to that part of the circle which was opposite the hut where the principal spectators sat. After this, one of them advanced from each side, meeting and passing each other in the front, and continuing their progress round, till they came to the rest. On which two advanced from each side, two of whom also passed each other, and returned as the former; but the other two remained, and to these came one from each side, by intervals, till the whole number had again formed a circle about the chorus.

Their manner of dancing was now changed to a quicker measure, in which they made a kind of half turn by leaping, and clapping their hands, and snapping their fingers, repeating some words in conjunction with the chorus. Toward the end, as the quickness of the music increased, their gestures and attitudes were varied with wonderful vigour and dexterity; and some of their motions, perhaps, would, with us, be reckoned rather indecent; though this part of the performance, most probably, was not meant to convey any wanton ideas, but merely to display the astonishing variety of their movements.

The description of the hand movements, "All this while, the women accompanied their song with several very graceful motions of their hands toward their faces and in other directions,"[4] is a description of what I have notated above in the progression from the position of the woman on the left in Figure 1 to the position of the woman on the right. That is, with the palm facing toward the body they bend or curl their

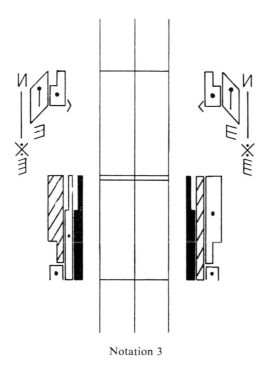

Notation 3

fingers or hands toward their faces; they then rotate the lower arm so that the hand goes to the opposite direction, and when the fingers are opened the palm is facing away from the body. This movement is the most characteristic one in Tongan dance today and we can postulate that this was also the case during Cook's time; it seems to be the move-

---

[4] Note that I have broken this sentence in two parts where it is not broken in the original. It seems to me that the comma is misplaced and should be *before* "at the same time" rather than after. I say this because one cannot move a hand toward the face and in other directions at the same time. One can, however, move the hands toward the face and in other directions, while at the same time step with the foot. This interpretation is further borne out in that in the similar description of the men's dance the comma that separates the hand movement description from the foot movement description comes before "at the same time." This makes the description meaningful instead of impossible to understand.

ment that is both described and illustrated. I emphasize this because I want to show that these basic movements are essentially the same today as they were at the time of European contact.

The explanation of the foot movements says; ". . . making constantly a step forward, and then back again, with one foot, while the other was fixed." This is not the same movement that is used today. Now the steps are taken almost in place. They are usually from side to side, but sometimes forward and back. The description sounds similar to the leg movements in the dances of the Maori of New Zealand. The Tongan women's foot movements of today seem to have become more like those of the men's, described below.

The journal description goes on to say that the dance "changed to a quicker measure, in which they made a kind of half turn by leaping,

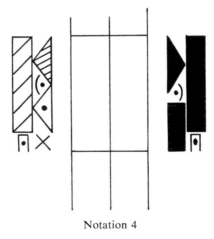

Notation 4

and clapping their hands, and snapping their fingers, repeating some words in conjunction with the chorus." This is a very good description of a group of dance movements called *fakataupasi*, which can be translated as "in the manner of hitting or clapping." The *fakataupasi* today is performed by both men and women in a dance type called *tau'olunga*, which is an individualized dance. The movement consists of snapping the fingers, clapping the hands, hitting the palms to other parts of the arms and legs, a half turn usually on one leg while the other leg is quickly raised after hitting the hand to the ankle, and sometimes by leaping. Today this group of movements usually comes at the end of the dance when the music is considerably speeded up. Occasionally

some of these movements are done during parts of a group dance called
lakalaka, but in a more controlled version, because all must perform
simultaneously.

Figure 2 reproduces Webber's drawing designated "A Night Dance
by Men, in Hapaee." The men's arm position is given in Notation 4.
This pose is very frequently used in present-day dances, especially in
the type of dance called *lakalaka.* The movements that would be done
today in this position are given in Notation 5. This involves a rotation
of the lower arm in which the palm alternates between facing up and
down. At the same time the fingers are bent or curled and then stretched
out. This is the same movement mentioned above as the most characteristic in Tongan dance, but taking a different arm position. It is easy to

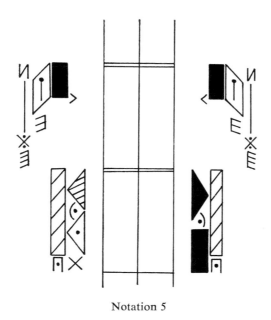

Notation 5

see the similarity of the two Labanotations. In Notation 5 the starting
position is shown below the double line. The only difference between
this starting position and the position in Notation 4 is that the latter
shows one palm facing up and one palm facing down. When the movement is made in this position the palms may face either up or down,
but they both face in the same direction at the same time. It is logical
that it would be depicted this way, however, for there are two things
that would strike the observer about this movement: the arm that is

down often has its wrist bent back and palm facing down; the arm that is held high often has the palm facing upward. These are rather unusual positions to a European. In the text there is an explanation which seems to go with this drawing (Cook, 1784, Vol. 1, pp. 251-252).

> To this grand female ballet, succeeded one performed by fifteen men. Some of them were old; but their age seemed to have abated little of their agility or ardour for the dance. They were disposed in a sort of circle, divided at the front, with their faces not turned out toward the assembly, nor inward to the chorus; but one half of their circle faced forward as they had advanced, and the other half in a contrary direction. They, sometimes, sung slowly, in concert with the chorus; and while thus employed, they also made several very fine motions with their hands, but different from those made by the women, at the same time inclining the body to either side alternately, by raising one leg, which was stretched outward and resting on the other; the arm of the same side being also stretched fully upward. At other times, they recited sentences in a musical tone, which were answered by the chorus; and, at intervals, increased the motions of the feet, which, however, were never varied. At the end, the rapidity of the music, and of the dancing, increased so much, that it was scarcely possible to distinguish the different movements; though one might suppose the actors were now almost tired, as their performance had lasted near half an hour.

The statement that "they also made several very fine motions with their hands, but different from those made by the women," probably refers to the pose in this drawing, because women do not use this pose as often as men. The explanation of the foot movements, although rather cryptic, makes sense to one who has observed Tongan dance. The journal says "at the same time inclining the body to either side alternately, by raising one leg, which was stretched outward and resting on the other." Perhaps a clearer explanation of this movement would be as follows: The foot movements consisted of resting on one foot which held the weight while the other foot was raised and stretched outward to the side where it passively touched the ground. Then the second foot stepped and took the weight and the first foot passively touched the ground to the side of it. This is written in Notation 6.

This is similar to foot movements used throughout the dance today in the *lakalaka* type of dance, except for a very infrequent moving forward and back and an occasional extra side step. The journal says the same of the dance at Cook's time, that there was a quickening of the motions of the feet, "which, however, were never varied." There is one difficulty in reconciling Figure 2 with the description in the journal. The description says that there were fifteen men, but the drawing shows at least thirty. My only explanation is that the description should refer to two groups of fifteen men each.

In the journal descriptions of the dances that follow, the reader is usually referred back for a description of the manner of the dance. There are descriptions of the transpositions of the floor plans in which the dancers retreat to the back of the dance circle, form rows, semi-circles, double circles, and triple semicircles. The main functions of the feet seem to have been to keep time and to move from place to place. The more important movements were those of the hands and head. In one dance that was particularly applauded the head is said to have been shaken vigorously from shoulder to shoulder. Movement from place to place and transpositions of the floor plan are occasionally used

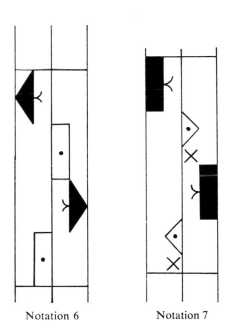

Notation 6   Notation 7

in the present-day dance form *lakalaka,* and the foot movements are not important in themselves.

The movements of importance are still those of the hands and the head. The hands allude to the most apparent level of meaning of the poetry and the interest of the spectators is often focused on how cleverly the movements interpret the words of the poetry. This cleverness is not evaluated in terms of realism, but rather in the expressing of the meaning while at the same time obscuring it. The head movements do not play an important part in interpreting the words, but they have a great deal to do with the dancer's personal interpretation of the dance. The head is moved by a quick tilt to the side and serves to give style to the dancer. This is occasionally done at prescribed places in the dance, but is usually added when the individual dancer wishes. The ambition of the dancer is to have all observers' eyes on him, and one of the ways to achieve this is to move the head in such a way and at such unexpected times as to compel attention.

Cook and his journal writers were of the opinion that the motions corresponded to the words of the song, and that "some of the gestures were so expressive, that it might be said they spoke the language that accompanied them, if we allow that there is any connection between motion and sound" (Cook, 1784, Vol. 1, pp. 254-255). They also felt that dance was one of the Tongans' favorite amusements, and that constant practice had achieved perfect discipline, which was particularly remarkable "in the sudden transitions they so dexterously made, from the ruder exertions and harsh sounds, to the softest airs and gentlest movements" (Cook, 1784, Vol. 1, p. 255).

Dance is still a favorite amusement, and for months before a large celebration the village people practice every night so that all movements are perfected and made in exactly the same timing. Quick transitions from rough movements and harsh sounds to graceful movements and soft sounds continue to characterize performances. In *lakalaka* dances, many of the stanzas of poetry have changes of melody and feeling, and movements reflect these changes. This is more apparent for the men because there are different hand movements during the soft or harsh sections. In addition, the men may strike the ground with their hands, or even roll on the ground. The women's movements also reflect change of melody, but in a more subtle way of performing the same movements either more harshly or more gracefully. Such transitions are most easily seen in a sitting dance called *ma'ulu'ulu*. One section is accompanied by drumming only, and the movements have a deliberate beat that reflects the rhythm of the drum. The other sections of the dance are accompanied by singing and more subdued drum beating, and although the same movements are used, they are softer and more graceful.

In Labillardière's account (1802), the entertainment offered by Toobou (Tupou) did not include any large-scale dances. Musicians, seated in the shade of a breadfruit tree rather than in a dance circle, struck the ground with bamboo stamping tubes and struck a longitudinally split bamboo with two sticks. "Three musicians, placed before the others, strove to explain the subject of their song by gestures, which they had no doubt perfectly studied, for they repeated them together, and in the same manner" (pp. 137-138). From reading Cook's journal one would expect that at this time there would have been large-scale dances. Perhaps the explanation lies a few pages earlier in Labillardière's journal (p. 135) where he mentions that the remains of a recently dead chief lay in a nearby hut. This may also be the reason that only "several men" performed it instead of the usual large group. Today in Tonga after a death there is a *tapu* on dancing for ten days, and after the death of a chief the *tapu* may last from thirty days to a year. It seems that in ancient times there were special dances for the funeral ceremonies of some of the chiefs, but I suspect that ordinary dancing was *tapu* then, as it is now. Whatever the explanation, Labillardière does not describe large-scale dances.

Malaspina's Vava'u account (1885) recounts dances performed by thirty men, accompanied by singing and bamboos. Although individual movements are not described, we are told that every fiber of their bodies was involved and that the movements were all uniform. The tempo gradually accelerated, figures changed twice, the music changed, and there were short intervals, at which time there was a maximum of praise and applause (p. 265). This appears to be the same dance witnessed by Cook.

Mariner describes this type of dance and tells us the name is *mëë low folla* (*me'elaufola*). He says it is danced at night, the dancers have their arms outspread, and that it "is perhaps the only one which can be considered of Tonga invention, and is the only one accompanied throughout with Tonga songs" (Martin, 1818, Vol. 2, p. 317).

The last reference to this type of dance resulted from Waldegrave's visit to Tonga in 1830. He tells of a night of dancing in which the musical accompaniment consisted of bamboo stamping tubes and the striking of bamboos. Dances of all men or all women were performed for five hours in which the "hands and head were in perpetual motion" (Waldegrave, 1833, p. 188).

The *me'elaufola* then disappears from first-hand accounts of Tongan dance, and in the Tongan view it no longer exists. Most of the present-day Tongans have never heard of it.

My view is that the *me'elaufola,* after falling into disuse for some years owing to the influence of the missionaries, reappeared in essentially the same form but with a new name, *lakalaka.* I have implied above that the transpositions of the floor plans, the foot movements, and the hand movements, can all be matched in the *lakalaka*. Let us examine the similarities and differences between the *lakalaka* and the *me'elaufola* and consider how such changes could have taken place. It is interesting to note that Mariner thought that the *me'elaufola* was the only dance that could be considered a Tongan invention. Similarly Tongans today say that the only real Tongan dance is the *lakalaka*, having been invented by Tuku'aho, a high chief of the village of Tatakamotonga.

ME'ELAUFOLA AND LAKALAKA

From journals and other early descriptions and drawings we can characterize the *me'elaufola* as being performed by either men or women. Used for accompaniment were bamboo stamping tubes and bamboos struck with sticks. Singing was in the Tongan language and motions corresponded to the words of the song. The women's hands made graceful motions toward their faces and in other directions. The men's fine motions of the hands were different from those of the women. The women took a step forward and then back with one foot while the other was fixed. The men rested on one foot while the other foot was raised and stretched outward to the side. The concluding movements were considerably speeded up, and at this time the performers leaped, clapped, and snapped their fingers. There were sudden transitions from harsh and rude sounds and motions to those that were soft and gentle.

The *lakalaka* of today is performed by men and women together who stand in two or more rows facing the audience, the men on one side, the women on the other. The two groups make different sets of movements, so that in effect they perform two dances simultaneously. The accompaniment is vocal only, sung by both the dancers and a chorus (*langi tu'a*) which stands behind the dancers. There is sometimes a section of the dance called *fakalaulausiva,* which is singing only with no movement. Words are in the Tongan language, with an occasional word borrowed from Fijian, Samoan, or English, often for the sake of rhyme. The words are often poetic allusions which many Tongans do not understand. All, however, have some idea of the surface level of meaning, or at least know which words are Tongan, and which are borrowed. Movements interpret the words of the song at the most apparent level, but not realistically. Most Tongans understand the stylistic conventions involved. The characteristic and distinctive arm movements involve curling or bending the fingers toward the face, then rotating the lower arm and opening the fingers in the opposite direction. Women's movements are soft and graceful, while the men's are more virile and vigorous. Men have more varied arm movements than women. The men's movements are larger, more loose and free, and quite often the arms are more extended, while the women's movements are smaller and more restrained. Thus, though men and women are doing "different" dances, the basic movements are very much the same. The differences lie in the order and the manner of performance and are more apparent than real.

The foot movements are basically the same for men and women. The left foot steps to the left. The right foot then moves to the left and just touches the floor next to the left foot without shifting weight. The right foot then moves right and takes the weight. Finally, the left foot moves right and just touches the floor next to the right foot. Notation 7 gives the movement in Labanotation. The whole is then repeated. Occasionally an extra step is added so that the formula is: left foot steps to the left, right foot steps to the left, left foot steps to the left, right foot touches next to left foot; right foot steps to the right, left foot steps to the right, right foot steps to the right, left foot touches next to right foot; or in Labanotation, see Notation 8. The tempo accelerates and at the end the movements are often considerably speeded up and become more emphatic. This is also true of one or more stanzas of the dance called the *tau,* where the dancers get *māfana,* "inwardly warm or exhilarated." During the *tau* and the ending stanzas the movements are freer and even the graceful stylized movements of the women tend to loosen up and become an emotional outlet.

The dancers sometimes transform their positions. For example, in the *tau* stanza of *Tapu moe Kalauni,* a *lakalaka* of Lapaha, Tongatapu, the men and women walk toward each other and the two lines become four:

0000 0000	0000 men
0000 0000	0000 women
women men	0000 men
	0000 women

The men then move to the front of the women and then all go back to their original two lines.

Another example of floor plan transpositions is the *sipa* ending of a *lakalaka* of Tatakamotonga, Tongatapu. Here the dancers turn around and move to the back of the dance space, then turn and move forward again.

Many stanzas introduce changes in melody and tempo and the movements shift to suit the character of the music. The changes are particularly noticeable in the men's movements.

The differences between *me'elaufola* and *lakalaka* are presented in Table 1.

From Table 1 we can readily perceive the elements which have changed through time. The musical accompaniment has changed, in that the bamboo stamping tubes and the struck bamboos are no longer used. It is impossible to say whether the melody has changed or not; however, the Tongans say that the melodies are taken from earlier *lakalaka* and

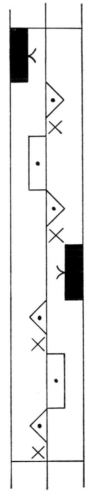

Notation 8

TABLE 1

SIMILARITIES AND DIFFERENCES IN ME'ELAUFOLA AND LAKALAKA

	ME'ELAUFOLA*	LAKALAKA**
Performers	Men or women	Men and women but different parts
Accompaniment	Bamboo stamping tubes, bamboos struck with sticks. Singing of dancers and chorus	Singing of dancers and chorus
Language	Tongan	Tongan
Movements and poetry	Movements correspond to words	Movements interpret words of song
Characteristic movements		
Hands—Women	Graceful motions toward face and in other directions	Curl fingers toward face, rotate lower arm, uncurl fingers in another direction
Hands—Men	Fine motions of the hands, different from women, arms stretched outward	Similar movements to women but with more vigorous character, more open than the women's
Feet—Women	Step forward and back again with one foot while the other foot is fixed	Men and women do same movement; step on one foot and rest there while other foot passively touches ground near it, then step to opposite side and remain there while other foot passively touches the ground
Feet—Men	Alternately step on one foot, while other foot is raised and stretched outward to side	
Tempo	Speeded up at end and movements changed to leaping and clapping	Often accelerates toward the end and during the *tau*
Floor plan	Face toward chorus which they encircle, divided circle, double rows facing each other on opposite sides of the dance circle, double and triple circles, semicircles	Two or more rows facing the audience. Men on right, women on left (from observer's point of view)
	Occasional transpositions from one figure to another	Occasional transpositions of floor plan, for example, forming four lines where there were two; all walking back, turning and walking forward again

* From journal descriptions.
** From my field observations.

old Tongan songs. Although Thomson says that the music is "composed by natives under the influence of European music" (1902, p. 226), I do not agree. To me the music seems quite similar to the Tongan-recognized ancient song forms and some of the melodies are similar to the *me'etu'upaki*. Those Tongans, who are very good at writing music in their own form of the tonic sol-fa, say that they cannot write *lakalaka* music that way, and recognize it as being Tongan and different from music that can be written down. Thus, I would say that the melody of the *lakalaka* is at least similar to the *me'elaufola*.

Besides the lack of musical instruments, the only other real difference seems to be that the same foot movements are now done by both men and women and that they have less variety.

My conclusion is that the *lakalaka* is an evolved form of the *me'elaufola*. The main differences are the absence of musical instruments, and the internal changes that became necessary when men and women were to take part in the same performance. If men and women were to dance together, at least their foot movements should be in concert, which would also be necessary for any intermixing in the floor plan transitions. The men's and women's parts retain their distinctiveness, in that each group interprets the poetry in a manner consistent with the Tongan view of movements suitable and appropriate for each sex.

Similarity can also be seen in the names of the dances. *Me'elaufola* means dance (*me'e*), reciting (*lau*), with movements of a type called *fola*, that is, movements that unfold to an outstretched position. *Me'e* seems to be the old generic name for standing dances. *Lakalaka* has now replaced this word. *Laka* means to walk and the reduplicated form *lakalaka* means to continue walking, or step out. Any Tongan will say that the word for standing dance is *lakalaka*. All Tongans know the Fijian dance form *meke*. When asked to describe a *meke* one explanation is that it is a *lakalaka faka-Fisi*, that is, a *lakalaka* done in the Fijian manner. In a *lakalaka* of Lapaha called "Sangone," one of the opening stanzas that introduce the dance says, *"Keu lau fola haka he 'aho ni,"* or "I will recite with movements this day." *Laufola* is a poetic way to describe the performance of *lakalaka*.

It would seem then, that of the two types of group dance that existed at the time of European contact, one has been preserved and come down to us today virtually unchanged (*me'etu'upaki*), and the other has evolved with only minor innovations into a new form (*me'elaufola* to *lakalaka*). We come now to the problem of why one has been preserved and the other has evolved.

THE DANCE AND CHANGES IN THE SOCIETAL STRUCTURE

It seems that from the earliest descriptions to present-day descriptions there were two types of dance performances, which can be broadly classified as formal and informal. At the time of European contact the *me'etu'upaki* was performed on formal occasions, and accompanied with large-scale food giving. Tongans today say that the main performances of the *me'etu'upaki* were at the *'inasi* ceremony when food was presented to the sacred king, the Tu'i Tonga, to assure abundant harvests in the future. This dance was seen by Cook at a formal entertainment that began at 11:00 A.M. and was accompanied by a large-scale giving of food. Cook called these dances *mai* (*me'e*). The *me'elaufola*, however, were usually performed in the evening or at night, at a gathering called *pōme'e*. Cook calls these dances *bomai,* or night dances (Cook, 1784, Vol. 1, p. 298). On one occasion, lasting for three hours, twelve of them were performed. Mariner, who continues this differentiation between night and day dances, says that the *me'etu'upaki* was a day dance and the *me'elaufola* a night dance (Martin, 1818, Vol. 2, p. 317). This distinction has been used by all succeeding writers on Tongan dance. In my view, there is a basic confusion here, not only in language but in utilizing the wrong cues to distinguish dance types from each other. The language confusion arises from the fact that Tongans speak of having a *pōula* or *pōme'e*. *Pō* means night and *ula* and *me'e* are dance types. Thus *pōme'e* could be interpreted "a night dance." However, Tongans also have *pō talanoa,* or "night of talking," but this does not mean that they talk only at night, any more than that a *me'e* is performed only at night. *Pō talanoa* or *pōme'e* can occur at any time of day. Adding *pō* before a word means only that a meeting will be held for the purpose of the word that follows *pō*. This usually implies that the participants are going to relax and enjoy themselves doing it. Their favorite time for dancing, talking, or meeting is in the evening or at night. A distinction of the highest level of contrast in Tongan dancing is between formal and informal dancing. Formal dancing usually takes place during the day and is accompanied by ceremony. Informal dancing usually takes place at night, and is for enjoyment. The time of day is not the criterion for having a *pōula* or *pōme'e*. The criterion is, rather, whether it is to be a formal or an informal occasion.

During Cook's time the *me'elaufola* was the *pōme'e* or informal dance type and the formal dance type was the *me'etu'upaki*. Today the formal dance type is *lakalaka.* Thus the *me'elaufola* has not only evolved in form but has also a new place in the society. There seem to be two reasons why the *me'etu'upaki* has ceased to be the formal dance type. The *me'etu'upaki,* although relatively intact today, is not a living dance type, in that, even though it is still performed, there are no new creations of it and it is recognized as a relic from the past. In fact, it seems to have been an old form by the time of European contact. The words even then were not understood by the Tongans and Mariner tells us that the words were Samoan. Tongans today say that the words are Uvean, Futunan, or Samoan. It seems to me, however, that the words are archaic Tongan which are no longer understood. Perhaps the words were not really understood even in Mariner's time. Mariner spoke Tongan and did not understand the words. Perhaps he just accepted the statement that the words were Samoan. If the words were archaic, or of the kind used only in poetry, he probably would not have understood them. Even if one asks, explanation of them is so difficult that most Tongans simply plead ignorance. Labillardière was told that the object of the *me'etu'upaki* was to celebrate the noble feats of some of their warriors. This seems to be a plausible explanation, because some of the poetry refers to going to Futuna and Uvea, which were at one time under the control of Tonga. These people, too, had to bring first fruits to the Tu'i Tonga at the *'inasi* ceremony, when this dance was traditionally performed. It is not unlikely that there were a few words of other languages in the poetry. In short, this dance appears to be an old form, already a classic by the time of European contact, that was rigidly passed on in the prescribed style and performed only on formal occasions. The exact meaning was not known nor was the relationship between the movements and the words. Thus it did not evolve, but was passed on just as it was learned from generation to generation.

The second reason that it is no longer the formal dance type is that the *me'etu'upaki* is associated with the Tu'i Tonga. The Tu'i Tonga was a sacred king who had spiritual power over all his subjects, including two subsidiary lines of kings, the Tu'i Ha'a Takalaua and the Tu'i Kanokupolu. Under the social system the Tu'i Tonga was not only the spiritual leader of Tonga, but also of the superior blood line from which the other two lines ramified. By the time of European contact the Tu'i Ha'a Takalaua line had lost much of its importance, but the Tu'i Kanokupolu line was ambitious and waged a number of civil wars to obtain more and more power. Christianity helped to undermine the power of the Tu'i Tonga, and finally, by force of arms, the Tu'i Kanokupolu, Tupou I, progenitor of the present dynasty, who had become a Weslcyan, became king of all Tonga. The last Tuʻi Tonga died in 1865 and the title ceased to be appointed, and for all legal purposes the Tuʻi Tonga no longer exists. However, the descendants of the Tuʻi Tonga do exist and their blood lines are as high or higher than the line of the present king. The chiefly title Kalaniuvalu has replaced the title Tuʻi Tonga and is held by the most direct descendant of the last Tuʻi Tonga. The last Tuʻi Tonga, shorn of his temporal and spiritual power, became a Catholic. His capital, the village of Lapaha, followed him and it is the most predominantly Catholic village in Tonga. The Tuʻi Tonga, Lapaha, the Catholic Church, and the meʻetuʻupaki are today inextricably interwoven.[5] The meʻetuʻupaki is performed only by the men of Lapaha. It has been passed down and taught by the ceremonial attendants of the Tuʻi Tonga known as the falefā matāpule. In Cook's description, chiefs took part in the dance and drums were beaten by persons of "first consequence," including the Tuʻi Tonga himself. At one of the last performances, it was the present Kalaniuvalu who occupied the vāhenga, or highest position in the dance.

The association of the meʻetuʻupaki with the Catholic Church and with the Tuʻi Tonga possibly accounts for the uneven descriptions of the dance throughout the literature. Cook saw the meʻetuʻupaki at an entertainment given for him in Tongatapu by the Tuʻi Tonga. He also saw it in Haʻapai. A Tongan source, Koe Taʻu ʻe Teau, also describes an occasion at which the meʻetuʻupaki was performed in Haʻapai (Collocott et al., n.d., p. 76). The Tuʻi Tonga had several estates in Haʻapai and it seems only logical that there would be men there who were skilled in its performance, including the lesser chiefs. Fīnau, who had given the entertainment in Haʻapai where Cook saw it the first time, took part in the dance in Tongatapu when it was performed for the Tuʻi Tonga. Fīnau had tried to impress Cook that he was the king of the whole Tongan group. What better way was there to show his power than to use the dance that was traditionally associated with the highest king?

Malaspina in Vavaʻu did not see the meʻetuʻupaki. This may be because the Tuʻi Tonga was not in residence, or Malaspina's visit was not considered a state occasion, or men skilled in its performance were not present in Vavaʻu. The dance that he saw I believe was the kailao. The kailao is used today when a men's group dance is required. The lakalaka is performed by both men and women, and when there are only

---

[5] It may be that the meʻetuʻupaki was not always exclusively associated with the Tuʻi Tonga. It does seem, however, to have been associated with state occasions, and state occasions were associated with the Tuʻi Tonga.

men to perform, such as an entertainment of the Wesleyan Missionary School, the dance performed would be the *kailao*.

Mariner did not live with a Tu'i Tonga chief, but he was acquainted with the *me'etu'upaki*. One of the performances he witnessed was at the end of the mourning ceremony for Fīnau. Fīnau was chief of Ha'apai and Vava'u and this was a state occasion performed in conjunction with a ceremony of food giving. Mariner could not have been overly familiar with the dance however, because he quotes Cook's description instead of giving one of his own.

In the light of all this, it is not strange that Thomson did not see the dance. He was in Tonga after the Tu'i Tonga fell from power and he was an official of the government of the Tu'i Kanokupolu. On the other hand the Catholic priest, P. Soane Malia, gives a description which shows that he did see it, and this is logical, because it is now associated with the Catholic Church. It is equally logical that the Wesleyan minister, Collocott, did not see it, and this would account for his erroneous remarks on the dance as well as his use of Cook's description.

The *me'etu'upaki* is now performed on occasions that are associated with the Tu'i Tonga line or the Catholic Church, such as the visit of a high-ranking Catholic dignitary, at graduation ceremonies of the Catholic secondary school, or at celebrations where the Tu'i Tonga Lapaha people want to show their distinctiveness, because no other village can perform this dance. It serves as a reminder of the still-exalted blood line of the Tu'i Tonga and his descendants, to the performers as well as to the spectators. It serves to separate the people of the Tu'i Tonga (*Kauhala'uta*) and the Catholic Church from the originally subordinate line, but now ruling dynasty, of the Tu'i Kanokupolu and his people (*Kauhalalalo*), and the dominant religion of the Free Wesleyan Church. The separation of the Tu'i Tonga's descendants by place and religion is intensified by exhibiting the most ancient dance form as their special symbol and property. It points out that there is something special about this group—that is, that they hold higher rank by blood because of direct descent from the first Tu'i Tonga, who descended from the sky god, Tangaloa. The dance was formerly used to pay obeisance to the Tu'i Tonga. It is now used by the descendants of the Tu'i Tonga to show that their traditionally derived exalted position is still a functioning part of the social system.

As a dance form the *me'etu'upaki* has come down to us virtually unchanged. Its function, however, has evolved because of the historical circumstances that associated the dance with the Tu'i Tonga and the

Tuʻi Tonga with the Catholic Church.[6] It serves today a different function in the society, that is, the performance of it separates the Tuʻi Tonga's descendants symbolically from the rest of the society.

The meʻelaufola has had a different history of change. Dance was suppressed by the missionaries of the Wesleyan Church as being sinful and inconsistant with the precepts of the Christian Church. The first attempt to Christianize the Tongans was by representatives of the London Missionary Society, who came on the ship Duff. This attempt was a failure. The missionaries were killed during the civil wars, except for one who had previously ceased to be a missionary, had married a Tongan, and lived as the Tongans did (Vason, 1810). However, after the conversion of Tupou I, then king of all Tonga, the populace was quickly converted and the dominant religion was Wesleyan. The Reverend Mr. Shirley Baker, originally a missionary, became Prime Minister to Tupou I, and Wesleyanism became equal to a state religion. Dancing fell into disuse, laws were passed forbidding the performance of "heathen" dances, hymn singing was instituted, and children spent their time in school. From this, a new dance form, lakalaka, was born. The official view of the government in regard to lakalaka is that it originated after the first missionaries started schools in Tonga. "The teachers would rise and repeat some of their nursery rhymes and at the same time demonstrate with their hands the various actions depicted by the rhymes. The children would follow suit and gradually this action song evolved" (Premier's Office, 1962, p. 17). The Tongans say that the first lakalaka, as dances, were originated by Tukuʻaho, chief of Tatakamotonga. Tukuʻaho was a descendant of the Tuʻi Haʻa Takalaua, the first line of kings to ramify from the Tuʻi Tonga line. This line gave rise to the Tuʻi Kanokupolu line and both lines belong to Kauhalalalo in contrast to the Tuʻi Tonga's people, who are known as the Kauhalaʻuta.[7] Tukuʻaho and his people were Wesleyan. It is said that Tukuʻaho, when he heard of the children's performances, decided that a dance built on the same principles would be appropriate. It would also be approved by the Wesleyan Church, because their missionaries had stimulated it. The dance was to consist mainly of actions of the hands that depicted poetry, and some foot movements to

---

[6] It is our good fortune that the Catholic missionaries did not suppress dancing. It is partly owing to their tolerance that the meʻetuʻupaki and other ancient Tongan dance forms, the ula and ʻotu haka, exist today. In fact the Catholic Church used the dance forms in their religion by changing the old words to Christian stories and adding appropriate movements to express them.

[7] One might consider Kauhalaʻuta and Kauhalalalo as a moiety division of the society.

keep time. Tuku'aho called upon a well-known *punake* (composer and instructor of dances and their poetry) to assist him. This *punake* was a *matāpule* ceremonial attendant who was known as Malukava. He was not of the group of *falefā matāpule* of the Tu'i Tonga who passed on and instructed the *me'etu'upaki*. Although Tuku'aho was from Tatakamotonga, it should be noted that Lapaha and Tatakamotonga are contiguous villages and that the present Malukava lives in Lapaha. Through the work of Tuku'aho and Malukava a new dance was originated and it was associated with Tuku'aho's village, Tatakamotonga. The new dance was called *lakalaka* which describes the stepping of the feet. It made use of melodies from old Tongan songs and hand actions that had not yet been forgotten, and were in fact preserved in the old dance types now associated with the Catholic Church right in the next village. Everyone liked the new dance and poets from other villages began setting their compositions to actions. A new dance, approved by the missionaries, was now available for ceremonial occasions and it became the new formal dance type.

Innovation in Tonga takes place downward from the top of the stratified society. Tuku'aho was one of the highest chiefs in the land, so there was no question of acceptance of what he had initiated, either by the common people or by the other chiefs.

It is no accident that the *lakalaka* resembles the *me'elaufola,* which had not been long suppressed. The older *punakes* no doubt remembered the old arm movements and the transpositions of the floor plan. If their memory needed help, the old dances were still preserved in Lapaha. The hand movements could be borrowed from the *ula* and *'otu haka* dance types and the floor plan transitions from the *me'etu'upaki.* Indeed these transpositions in the *lakalaka* seem more similar to those of the *me'etu'u-paki* than to the early descriptions of the *me'elaufola.* The singing or reciting of nursery rhymes by the missionaries was probably chantlike rather than hymnlike, thus there is no need to postulate European influence in the music. The Tongans simply used melodies from their old songs.

The *me'elaufola* was a living dance type during Cook's and Mariner's time. The words used with it were in the Tongan language, and had corresponding hand actions. It was performed during the *pōme'e,* or informal dancing, and was probably the type of dancing that all performed and had known from childhood. It was performed on all islands on any happy occasion, for their own and guests' entertainment, and would easily be remembered, even if officially suppressed. Thus it seems to be essentially the *me'elaufola* that evolved into the new dance type, *lakalaka*. *Lakalaka* became the official dance for formal occasions and became associated with the Tu'i Kanokupolu. Today this has become intensified and all official government *kātoanga* (celebrations) include performances of *lakalaka*. In 1962 a celebration of a hundred years of freedom under the rule of the Tu'i Kanokupolu included two whole days of *lakalaka* in Tongatapu and additional days in Ha'apai and Vava'u.

The *lakalaka* is basically an old dance with a new name. It changed from informal to formal, and in the process became more controlled and conservative. A new dance type, allegedly from Samoa, called *tau'olunga,* became the new informal dance, although this too can be shown to be an evolved form of an old Tongan dance. Everyone was pleased. The Tongans could dance again. The missionaries were content, because their converts no longer performed their old "heathen" dances, but instead used new dances stimulated by their own teachings. I would postulate that the Tongans knew they were really performing a slightly different version of their old dances, even though the missionaries believed that the *lakalaka* was a new dance stimulated by themselves.

The late Queen Salote Tupou III was one of the most prolific poets of *lakalaka,* and Malukava, who became her official *punake,* added the melodies and the movements. It was Salote who wrote the first *lakalaka* for Lapaha. Previously Lapaha had performed only their traditional *me'etu'upaki* on formal government occasions. The Queen, whose mother was from the Lapaha Tu'i Tonga line, had enough prestige to introduce the official dance type into the traditional stronghold of the Tu'i Tonga.

Thus, now even the people of Lapaha perform *lakalaka,* while at the same time they preserve their old dances as a status symbol, but perform them only for special occasions.

The *lakalaka* today is inseparable from the social structure and the official government under the Tu'i Kanokupolu, the throne now being held by Tupou IV. The order in which the performers stand in the floor plan is determined by social status and there is often a great deal of discussion and argument about who is to take the highest positions. In some cases decision is clear-cut, but in others where it is not, such as Lapaha, the Queen appointed the persons to take the highest positions.

Lakalaka poetry is a series of concepts and references which usually have several levels of meaning. Essentially an expression of allegiance to the established social and political order, the poetry honors the chiefs and reflects the Tongan preoccupation with genealogy which determines societal and interpersonal relations (see Kaeppler, in press). *Lakalaka* is basically poetry with dance accompaniment, for it is the poetry which is of prime importance, giving meaning to the dance and, indeed, the reason for its very existence. The essence of the *lakalaka* is the poetry and the cleverness with which the *punake* has expressed and yet obscured the meaning with the movements.

Dance in Tonga has a pre-eminent social function; to pay allegiance to the sociopolitical system and to reflect and validate the system of social distinctions and interpersonal relationships. The processes of preservation and evolution discussed in this paper can add a deeper understanding of these processes in the larger sphere of Tongan society. The impact of Western society, and especially Christianity, made profound changes in Tonga. Perhaps the most far-reaching change was the consolidation of power where it did not traditionally belong, that is, in the hands of the Tuʻi Kanokupolu and his nobles, and the elevation of their legal power over traditional authority.

The kingdomwide kinship system, with all highest honor and choicest goods going to the Tuʻi Tonga, was reduced to a more intimate dependence on the village noble. The noble now owed his power to the new king and the honors and goods now went to the Tuʻi Kanokupolu. The *lakalaka,* dance of the new regime, became the visual symbol of this new power. In former times the formal dance, *meʻetuʻupaki,* was given for the Tuʻi Tonga as a sacred duty and the dancers were instructed by his ceremonial attendants. Today, with a noble acting as an intermediary, the formal dance, *lakalaka,* is given to the Tuʻi Kanokupolu as a village gesture. The history of the dance provides a conspicuous demonstration of the transfer of power and honor from the Tuʻi Tonga line to that of the Tuʻi Kanokupolu. Through the dance, traditional ways were used to substantiate changes, while the poetry sung by the performers gave glory and honor to these changes, and to those who induced them.

It has been shown that change and stability in the form of dance in Tonga is at least partially dependent upon whether the dance is a living tradition or is the preservation of an earlier form. This illustrates that there is an inherent potential for change in a living "folk" tradition such as *meʻelaufola* that does not equally exist in an "art" or "court" tradition, such as *meʻetuʻupaki.* Changes in the function of the dance were shown to be related to changes in the societal structure of Tonga. Prototypes of this change were endemic to Tongan society. Additional stimulus for change was furnished by the introduction of Western society and Christianity. Extensive civil wars resulted in profound changes in power and in rivalry between Christian religions. Dance paralleled these changes and was used to validate transfers of power to a new line of kings and his legal nobles. Thus, dance is not only important and worthy of study for its own sake, but is equally valuable for what it can tell us about social change and cultural history.

LITERATURE CITED

CHURCHWARD, C. MAXWELL
 1959. *Tongan Dictionary*. London: Oxford Univ. Press.

COLLOCOTT, E. E. V.
 1928. *Tales and Poems of Tonga*. B. P. Bishop Mus. Bull. 46. Honolulu.

COLLOCOTT, E. E. V., JIONE HAVEA, JIOKATAME HAVILI, UILIAME TUPOU,
  LEJIELI TOGA, and SIONE TAUFA
 [n.d.] (c. 1926) *Koe Ta'u 'e Teau*. London: William Clowes and Sons.

COOK, JAMES
 1784. *A Voyage to the Pacific Ocean . . . in the years 1776, 1777, 1778, 1779, and 1780. . . .* 3 vols. (Vols. 1 and 2 by Cook, Vol. 3 by King.) London: Strahan.

GIFFORD, EDWARD WINSLOW
 1929. *Tongan Society*. B. P. Bishop Mus. Bull. 61. Honolulu.

HUTCHINSON, ANN
 1954. *Labanotation: The System for Recording Movement*. New York: New Directions Paperback.

KAEPPLER, ADRIENNE L.
 1967. The Structure of Tongan Dance. Ph.D. Dissertation, Univ. Hawaii.
 In press. "Folklore as Expressed in the Dance in Tonga." *J. American Folklore*.

KOCH, GERD
 1955. *Südsee—gestern und heute: Der Kulturwandel bei den Tonganern und der Versuch einer Deutung dieser Entwicklung*. Braunschweig: Limbach.

LABILLARDIÈRE, J. J.
 1802. *An Account of a Voyage in Search of La Perouse . . . in the years 1791, 1792, and 1793. . . .* London: Uphill.

MALASPINA, D. ALEJANDRO
 1885. *La Vuelta al Mundo . . . desde 1789 á 1794*. (2nd ed.) Madrid.

MALIA, P. SOANE (BISHOP JEAN MARIE BLANC)
 1910. *Chez des Meridionaux du Pacifique*. Lyon and Paris: Librairie Catholique Emmanuel Vitte.

MARTIN, JOHN
 1818. *An Account of the Natives of the Tonga Islands. . . .* 2 vols. (2nd ed.) London: John Murray.

PREMIER'S OFFICE
    1962. *Tonga*. Nuku'alofa, Tonga: Government Printing Office.

THOMSON, BASIL
    1894. *The Diversions of a Prime Minister*. Edinburgh and London: Black-
    wood Sons.
    1902. Appendix, "Tongan Music." In *Savage Island,* pp. 218-228. London:
    John Murray.

VASON, GEORGE
    1810. *An Authentic Narrative of Four Years' Residence at Tongataboo. . . .*
    London: L. B. Seeley and Hatchard.

WALDEGRAVE, W.
    1833. "Extracts from a Private Journal Kept on Board H. M. S. *Seringapatam*
    in the Pacific, 1830." *J. Royal Geographical Soc. London,* pp. 168-196.

OUTLIERS

SEA CREATURES AND SPIRITS IN TIKOPIA BELIEF

RAYMOND FIRTH

The London School of Economics and Political Science

A GREAT DEAL of scholarly attention has been devoted to the dramatic problems of Polynesian sea-voyaging and navigation, in circumstances which seem to have taken place relatively infrequently, and are not open to direct anthropological observation. Much less consideration has been given to the more mundane question of Polynesian attitudes to the sea creatures they may still encounter round their coasts, some rarely, but others almost every day. This essay is an exploration, on admittedly rather imperfect evidence, of some Tikopia attitudes in this marine sphere.

In an essay on Tikopia "totemism" (Firth, 1930-31, pp. 291-321; 377-398) I described long ago some aspects of Tikopia attitudes to sea creatures. In particular I examined the concept of "embodiment," whereby spirits were believed to use animal or fish forms as their material representations. In the present paper some new material is brought forward and I look at the matter from a more general point of view. My object is to show how, within a common framework, a considerable diversity of practices and ideas obtained, and with this in mind I attempt to indicate some of the basic principles of classification of the behavior involved.

It will be seen that the more theoretical part of my analysis follows some of the lines suggested by the very perceptive general propositions of Claude Lévi-Strauss and Edmund Leach. Although my conclusions lack their boldness and breadth, they may compensate for this by the degree in which Tikopia statement and behavior have been brought directly into the field of explanation. What I hope to demonstrate is how a set of intellectual principles of classification appears in complex pragmatic situations of emotional as well as intellectual import, and is conditioned thereby.

The analysis proceeds from consideration of attitudes toward large fish, including bonito and shark, to that of the special position of eels in the Tikopia system, and then to attitudes toward octopus, turtle, and cetaceans. From comparison of these attitudes I try to isolate the criteria which are most relevant in understanding them.

CATEGORIES OF NATURAL OBJECTS

Natural objects are divided by the Tikopia into a number of broad categories, such as *fatu* (stone, shell, and allied hard substances), *rakau* (trees and shrubs, but including also wood), *manu* (animals, including birds, insects, and reptiles), *tangata* (persons), *ika* (fish), and *paka* (crustaceans, especially crabs).

These categories do not embrace all natural objects, a few of which have specific separate designations. Again they do not correspond exactly with our English classification. Thus it is impossible to find a single-word equivalent for *manu.* The whale and other sea mammals are spoken of as *ika,* fish; while the turtle is not classed with reptiles (*manu*) but with crabs (*paka*) because it has a shell, or again as *ika* because it swims in the sea. "The turtle is *ika* indeed; its name only is ascribed as *paka.*" Within these general categories the Tikopia make many distinctions based upon size, color, habits, and so on. On my first expedition I obtained, for instance, different names for over a score of types and nearly fifty subtypes of fish, a dozen of shellfish and of land crab, and fifteen of sea crab, and I am sure that I did not nearly exhaust the lists. The Tikopia have much knowledge of the quality and habits of each type they differentiate. Thus shellfish are distinguished by their hardness or their softness, by the fact that one bleeds like a man, that another is poisonous, while others are edible, that one may be called alternatively *neve* or *vene,* and so on.

About thirty types of birds are distinguished, the classification of land birds being more precise from our point of view than that of sea birds, which are mainly petrels, some of which are not distinguished at all clearly. (It is interesting to note that after I had been given the names of various sea birds I was told of others that "it is not known whether they have names or not.")

LARGE FISH

Fish form such an important part of the Tikopia diet that it is only to be expected that they are the subject of much differentiation. Treatment of large fish, known as *para maori, para vao, para fara* or *ravenga,* and *varu,* was relatively matter-of-fact as a prized food resource. I did not identify these fish closely, but as far as I could see they included barracuda, Spanish mackerel, jewfish, and groupers. Collectively they were known as *kata,* a term for all large sea-fish irrespective of kind, and were taken by baited hook at depths down to about ten *kumi* (100 fathoms). Formulae (*tarotaro*) were recited, of a hortatory or mandatory order (Firth, 1967a, pp. 195-212), to facilitate the biting of the fish, but the fish themselves were assumed to be "natural" objects, with no specific spiritual associations. The formulae assumed only a rather vague interest of sea gods and ancestors in directing the fish to the hook for the benefit of the fisherman. The fish were not regarded as being the bodily representation of *atua,* and were not the subject of any particular myths or secular stories. They were regarded as status objects; a fisherman who caught one was very proud. But he was not expected to keep it for himself; he should present it to his chief or another man of rank in his vicinity.[1] If he caught one while fishing in someone else's canoe he was expected by custom to leave it with his host.

Such fish were measured in "cuts" and a very large fish might be divided among the chiefs. In the monsoon fishing one year the eldest son of the Ariki Kafika caught a *ravenga* described as *tuangafuru té—* ten cuts and some over. Five cuts were sent to the Ariki Taumako, the same to the Ariki Fangarere, and six to the Ariki Tafua, while the Kafika family kept only four for themselves. This fish of "twenty cuts" must have been more than six feet long. Yet such fish were not ritualized in any personal way; they were simply treated as food offerings in ritual in the same style as small fish or vegetable food.

BONITO

The treatment of bonito (*atu*) had certain similarities to this, but differed in some important particulars. A sizable fish, the bonito, too, was a prized food resource, and to catch bonito was a matter of pride. But the status aspect had a different form. Anyone who caught a bonito

---

[1] The *varu* in particular was commonly described as "the fish of chiefs."

was not expected to present it to his chief, and to catch a single bonito was not regarded as any particular achievement—in the circumstances of bonito fishing, rather a disappointment. The significant factor in this differentiation would seem to be the contrast in the fishing conditions. *Para* and similar large fish were taken with long line and baited hook; bonito with bamboo rod and barbed lure. *Para* were taken unseen in the depths of the sea, bonito on or just under the surface. *Para* fishing was an individual matter, of quiet concentration; bonito fishing was a competitive affair, with much speed, turmoil, and excitement. To catch one *para* was meritorious, to become an "expert of bonito" a sequence of fish had to be taken. If a man succeeded in hauling in twenty or thirty fish he was entitled to "stand up his rod" at the stern of the canoe when he returned; ten fish would be enough if they were very large. But very few men have had such an achievement to their credit. *Para* and its congeners were welcome food fish; bonito were invested with glamour as well, and their pursuit was a sport as well as a search for food.

During the period of my observation bonito appeared in shoals off the Tikopia coast but rarely. The season was about when the turmeric was in flower. They were pursued with keenness but with indifferent success. Paddling to intercept and keep up with a shoal was very heavy work, and even in the midst of a shoal a slight error of skill or judgment on the part of the rodsman, or what appeared to be fickleness on the part of the bonito, could mean a complete failure. Hence great attention was paid to the technical details of the lure, tension in the bonito fisherman was obvious, formulae to secure a catch were long and urgent, taboos on conduct were stringent, and the status rewards for success were marked.

A fisherman going out for bonito got up early in the morning, not having slept with a woman the night before. He put on a brand new bark waist-cloth, and removed all ornaments from his neck and arms. Then he took leaves of a fragrant shrub which he had plucked the day before, rubbed them in his hands to bruise them and smeared them over his shoulders, breast, arms, body, and legs. As he did so he murmured, "I shall go among bonito, light be the eyes of bonito to my canoe stern."

While the canoe was being carried down the beach to the reef it was taboo for any woman to be present; all kept away. The fisherman took two branches of the aromatic shrub known as *kava pi toto* and stuck them at the stern of the canoe to give added fragrance to it. All this was done for the benefit of the *tupua taufau,* the "deity of the lashing," who acted as tutelary spirit for the bonito fisherman. It was to this spirit, cited only by title and without personal name, that the main formula for success was addressed. The common means of identification of a shoal of bonito was the *fakariri,* the circling of birds over it; on sighting this in the bonito season, canoes would put to sea. While still at a distance from the shoal the fisherman called out to the bonito, "Rise up above; your sky and your ocean are fine." When by dint of skill and hard work a canoe was among the shoal of bonito, the fisherman urged on the crew; "Dig in your paddles, the canoe is speeding in the midst of bonito." He set up his rod and cast out the lure, reciting:

> Tupua taufau!
> Tou tino ka to i tafatafa o atu
> Tangata taurekareka
> Nai tauvia ou arangā vaka
> E! E! Ku roa ana tere
> Ko ai fakapoupou seua ki tua
> Kae tafuri ki tou fau tuka
> Ma tou fau tiare tonga
> Ku tere i katea
> Kai se atu i taumuri!

> Tupua taufau!
> Te fua ka feurufaki
> Fai taumafa mou i roto o atu
> Na atu piko ma na atu tonu
> Fakatonusia te matira
> Te vaka ka peia e atu
> Te fua ka fakafeurufaki
> Foaki se taumafa mou i roto o atu
> Fai ki mua ke tangi fakaue
> Tino uri, kai se atu
> Manongi, manongi
> Kai se atu i taumuri Tereiteata
> Fakaofo! Icfu!

Before translating this formula some explanation is needed of the concepts involved. One of the most critical elements in the whole complex of bonito fishing was the hook, a lure of clam-shell or pearl-shell shank with barb of turtle shell. The ordinary name for it was *pa atu.* A figurative name was *malili,* which was also the name for the *karoama,* a small white fish which was the food of the bonito; the clam-shell shank was also white and vaguely fish-shaped and the analogy was a direct one.[2] Complete, a bonito hook was a much prized object, the "property of chiefs" (Firth, 1939, p. 338),[3] that is, appropriate to chiefs, and its separate components were also valued ornaments. From the fishing point of view, a matter of prime interest was the lashing which bound barb to shank. Done by an expert, this lashing was carefully crossed at the back of the shank, and if correctly done could hold a fish. But if the lashing was not correct, when the strain came it would give way and both fish and barb be lost. Moreover, if the formula was recited without result, then the lashing of the hook might have been wrongly done. Hence it is intelligible that in the Tikopia view the correct lashing was not the invention of men but came from the gods. So the central figure in the invocation was the "deity of the lashing."

But who was this deity? According to Pa Rangifuri, himself a "man of bonito," the bonito were the product of the Female Deity and the Atua i Raropuka; it was the latter who, as deity of the lashing, went in the midst of the bonito shoal and directed fish to the hook. "He watches what the bonito do; he watches and feeds the hook." One embodiment of the Atua i Raropuka in ordinary life was the black skink, a small active lizard with a shiny body—hence the reference to this in the formula. But in this fishing context another embodiment of the deity was the bonito hook itself, which was made to "fall at the side of the bonito." The scent of the bruised leaves on the body of the fisherman was thought to be agreeable to the deity, and he was asked to turn to his headdress of frangipani and other fragrant things so symbolized. Moreover, when the bonito were taken ashore offerings of them were made to the gods in ritual, so that the deity was reminded to provide the canoe with his food portion before it left.

The whole formula, then, was a series of images of an active principle behind the fishing technology responding to stimuli of a kind recognized by Tikopia—a personification of human skill and human desires. The formula may be rendered as follows:

---

[2] In 1928 I saw a few old hooks with shank of whalebone, and one said to have come from Panapa (Ocean Island) had a shank of what appeared to be limestone stalagmite. A new hook in 1952 had a shank of conch shell.

[3] By 1966 hardly any bonito hooks were to be seen in Tikopia; their place as valuables had been taken by the turtle-shell barbs alone, which were worn as neck or wrist ornaments, and were presented to visitors or offered in exchange.

Deity of the lashing!
Your body will fall beside the bonito
Splendid fellow
He'll exchange your canoe implements
E! E! Long has been its trailing
Who opposes let him be spurned to the rear
And turn to your brow ornament
And your ornament of frangipani
It has trailed to starboard
Bite a bonito at the stern!

Deity of the lashing
The fleet will return
Make a food portion for yourself from the midst of bonito
From curved bonito and straight bonito
Confirm your rod
Let the canoe be overwhelmed by bonito
The fleet is about to return
Spread out a food portion for yourself from the midst of bonito
Perform that we cry out in thankfulness
Black body, bite a bonito
Fragrance, fragrance
Bite a bonito at the stern of Tereiteata
Rush on! Iefu!

The reference to the "splendid fellow" is to the bonito, represented as offering itself as a sacrifice ("in exchange") for the "canoe implements," that is, the hook of the deity, presented to it. The reference to Tereiteata is to the name of the canoe in which this particular reciter, Pa Rangifuri, used to go bonito fishing; the name of another canoe would be substituted where necessary. The final words are not strictly part of the formula; they are the shout of pleasure of the fisherman as he hooked a fish. Even then great care had to be exercised; his arm had to be braced strongly lest the rod be allowed to sag and the fish to come off the hook. The fish had to be pulled gently, not jerked, till it was close enough to the net to be taken in.

The formulae of all bonito fishermen followed the same general style, but different families and even individuals had some variations in phraseology. I received several versions. Pa Teva, son of Pae Ava-kofe of Taumako, gave me a formula which asked the deity of the lashing to "bathe with power" his rod, and spurred him on by alleging that his canoe gear had got all cobwebby from disuse—with the impli-

cation that he had better bestir himself and catch a fish! Pa Teva said
that he had learned this formula from his father. He also said that the
formulae of Kafika and Tafua were different, but the phrases he gave
as theirs were within the ordinary range of variation. Once the fisherman had hauled in a bonito he did not recite the formula again; he
merely called out "Your canoe gear" as he made each fresh cast with
the lure.

Correctness of the formula was thought to be important. Said Pa
Rangifuri "The diety of the lashing goes and listens to the formula
which is being recited. If the formula is correct, the bonito will bite,
but if not, then the bonito rush on, simply rush wildly. The man sits
and searches the formula, speaking thus 'My formula is wrong.' Then
he goes and asks a man who knows the formula."

At the empirical level, bonito fishing had various elements which
were very difficult if not impossible to calculate, and the margin between
success and failure was very slight. The tendency was for the Tikopia
to seek explanation of the difference in personal characteristics and
behavior of the fisherman; to place the responsibility where it belonged,
on an individual basis, but in social and ritual terms, not in technical
terms. So, success in bonito fishing was not thought to rest on the formula alone; other factors concerned with the personality of the fisherman could influence the result. A bonito rodsman operated from the
stern of the canoe. (The net for taking in the bonito after they were
hooked was used from the bow.) A man who did not get a bite while
the fleet was fishing all around was known as a "dark stern," while
one who was successful was known as a "light stern." He was light
to the eyes of the bonito, that is, the way to him was clear; fish were
attracted by him. This sign of great success was a token of pride. But
if his catch was only half a dozen or so then the rod was laid down.
Scornfully Pa Vangatau of Taumako said in 1929 that he was the only
"man of bonito" still living who had "stood up his rod."

If a man who ordinarily was a reasonably good fisherman was
"dark" to the eyes of the bonito on a certain day, then the implication
was that he had committed some breach of rules. Pa Rangifuri put this
vividly: "Great is the shame of bonito [that is, in bonito fishing]. Nothing is hidden from them. You have formed your mind [that is, have
your own ideas about your prospects], but hide it, you go to sea, and
then you are ashamed in the middle of bonito. The yelling is going on
all around, the whole fleet is catching fish, and your canoe is catching
nothing. Great is the shame." Although no word had been spoken, the

sight of bonito rushing away from a canoe was enough to tell the crew
that the man in the stern had committed some offense against taboo—
probably had had intercourse with his wife or another woman the night
before. They would all think it, and the whole fleet would see it; they
might well chaff him when they all got back ashore.

Hence when a fisherman in the stern saw that the fish were not
biting for him he would scratch gently with his fingernail the man on
the thwart in front of him, and beckon to him or whisper to him to take
his place. This man, termed the *fakasirimara,* girt also with a new
bark cloth against such eventuality, would do so, when in all likelihood the bonito, who had been waiting for him to succeed, would start
at once to bite. Even if the fish were biting, but were rushing open-
mouthed not at the hook but at the trace above, the stern fisherman
would beckon to the other man to take his place, the transfer being
accomplished as smoothly as possible lest the flow of bonito bites be
broken. Such a man succeeding would not recite the whole bonito
formula but only a brief section such as:

> Deity of the lashing
> Do your business
> That we may cry in appreciation.

Or he may simply call out "Fragrance! Fragrance!" as a pleasing suggestion to the spirit. The substitution of the second fisherman for the
first was made "to put a good face on it," and allow the canoe to get fish.

The taboo on association of women with bonito fishing also included
a bar on the presence of a woman on the fishing ground. According to a
traditional story which I heard in 1929, a chief of Tafua five generations before had said of this taboo "It's just false," and had taken his
daughter out in his canoe. Not a bonito was then to be seen; they had
deserted the fishing ground. Then, in anger, the chief jumped overboard
and excreted in the sea, calling out "There's your food"—a great insult.
He climbed back into his canoe and returned to shore. Behind him returned the bonito, trailing after.[4]

There might be other reasons for failure. The base of the bamboo
rod was held in a wooden sleeve or grip (*futia*), which was shaped to
end in a kind of ornamental curved beak. It was taboo for the bonito
fisherman to let this curved butt show in his hand above his waist.
Seeing it, the bonito would immediately dash off. The reason was that

---

[4] According to Pa Teva, the husband of a pregnant woman should not wield
the bonito rod. He may go in the bow of the canoe but should he fish and get a
catch the bonito on being cut open will be found to have maggots inside!

the butt of the *futia* was thought to have the semblance of a male organ and to represent the penis of their father the Atua i Raropuka; the bonito were greatly ashamed and offended at the sight. Seeing them rushing away, the fisherman would cast about for the cause, observe the butt of the grip projecting from his hand, ejaculate the Tikopia equivalent of "My goodness," and hastily conceal it. At the same time he shouted hopefully to the bonito "Hey! stand firm until evening." For the same reason of delicacy of the bonito, a fisherman did not tuck up the front flap of his bark-cloth girdle into his belt, as is customary in other forms of fishing, but kept it down between his legs, wrapping the immodest end of the *futia* in it. Said Pa Rangifuri "If bonito look on you, on *you* (that is, the penis) which has appeared, then bonito are ashamed; or if they feel that you have been with women, bonito will bolt off."

The interpretation of this taboo seems fairly clear. The chancy business of fishing for bonito, when skilled fishermen could fail utterly for no identifiable technical reason, demanded some explanation in terms of human fallibility. A slip in manipulation of the butt of the rod, easy to make in the rush and excitement of the moment, provided one type of reason; untimely relations with women, a foible to which most men were prone, provided another. To sensitivity to sex associations could thus be attributed the apparent whimsicality of bonito, since this was an area where, on human analogy, fastidiousness might be expected. Moreover, as explanation, offense in this field could hardly be challenged, because checking was almost impossible. This point will be taken up later, in more general terms.

In view of the value of the *pa atu* and its associations, to break one or lose it was a great disaster, and resulted in lamentation. If the lure was broken when it was taken out of the mouth of a bonito the fisherman hid it in his hand; as it was the "body" of their father the Atua i Raropuka, if they saw it they would disappear. The crew of the vessel concerned would come back weeping to their chief, to whom all bonito hooks in theory belonged. Traditionally the crew members gashed their foreheads so that blood flowed and they and the chief wailed together. An oven of food was prepared as an offering to the offended deity.

The personalization of bonito and the ritualization of their pursuit were linked with a set of fantasy elaborations in which undersea activities of bonito were described. So Pa Rangifuri told me that if a bonito hook were broken, or taken by a fish and lost, when the bonito returned to their home to sleep, their mother, the Female Deity, would scold the particular fish responsible. "Why not go and stroll properly? The canoe gear of chiefs is *tapu*." He said this was confirmed by the tale of a man who had visited the home of bonito beneath the sea.

He was a man of the lineage of Fasi. His bonito hook had been taken by a fish, which made off with it. He bewailed its loss but was not satisfied; he determined to dive down and recover it. His canoe crew waited for him while he dived down. He had first announced his intention to Feke, the Octopus God and tutelary of his lineage, asking him to divide the sea so that he might go safely in search of his hook. When he dived down he came at length to the house of the bonito. It was carpeted with mats, on which the bonito had lain to sleep, side by side. He saw the Female Deity engaged in plaiting a mat, her traditional occupation in myth. She smelt him as being a man, not a spirit. She said "Smell of living man!" and asked him whence he came. He answered that he came to recover his hook. "I have just scolded him," she replied, pointing to the culprit bonito. "Why didn't he go about things properly, and bite the hook properly; the canoe gear of chiefs is *tapu*." Then she told him that his lost hook with many others was stuck up in the thatch at the end of the house, and to go and get it— but on no account to take others too. Then she went on with her plaiting, while her husband, the Atua i Raropuka, was plaiting sinnet— also traditional in myth (Firth, 1961, p. 26).

The man went to the end of the house, and saw many hooks of all kinds stuck there. He identified his own, took it down, and with it took others. He stuck a couple in his mouth, one in each cheek, and others he put in his waist-belt, carefully folded in. His own hook he stuck in his ear lobe, which was pierced in Tikopia style, and tied its cord round his throat. When he returned the Female Deity asked him if he had identified his property. He replied in the affirmative, speaking with difficulty because of the hooks in his cheeks. She asked him if he had tampered with others, but he replied, "No." She knew he was lying but made no comment. She told him to go, but on no account to mention what he had seen. "You have seen me, and this house, and the hooks, but when you return to men, do not talk of it." He promised and went. When he had gone she went to the end of the house and saw that hooks had gone. She called out "Come back!" whereupon the hooks in the man's cheeks and waist-belt jumped out and returned to her of their own accord. The man came up to the surface, to find the canoe drifted a long way off, and his relatives almost fighting about what to do. He waved his arm, and they came and picked him up. He lay on the deck and allowed the water to run from his mouth and ears. His belly was of enormous size, full of water. When he recovered he felt for the hooks in his cheeks and belt, but they had gone. Then he knew that the Female Deity had recalled them. He felt for his own hook in his ear, and found it still there. After his return he stayed for five days and nights without saying anything, but on the sixth his desire to make a reputation overcame him—he had been to another land, so could not keep silent. He narrated all he had seen and heard. But that night, after his tale was done the man died; the Female Deity had heard him and was revenged.

From this the Tikopia obtained some idea of the state of things in bonito society. "What? A hearsay tale only? The narrative of what the man actually saw with his eyes!" said my informant.

Lack of success in bonito fishing could be because of the nonappearance of bonito off the Tikopia coast. They certainly seem to have been very variable. As far back as 1928 there was complaint of their scarcity, and in 1952 it was said by some men that they had abandoned bonito fishing because shoals were lacking. But one man who had no success attributed this possibly to his ignorance of the formula, since his grandfather, a renowned expert, had not made it known to him fully. In 1966 I was told of a crew of Taumako that had recently been after bonito using traditional gear. They knew the formula but I am not sure that they used it. Two fishermen got a couple apiece, although a third man got none.

During the period of my first stay in Tikopia, a combination of human status interest and spiritual power was held to be responsible for lack of bonito. I was told by Pa Vangatau that when his elder brother the chief of Taumako was dying, he said "When I am dead you look at the bonito fishing; if bonito do not come for the fishing of the chiefs then you will know it is true—they have come only to my *manu* [power] because I called them!" According to another account, that of Pa Rangifuri, while all bonito were under the general control of the Atua i Raropuka, he personally regulated only the main body of a shoal. Three important dead chiefs, Pu Ariki the prime ancestor of Taumako, Pu Kafika Lasi, and Pu Tafua Lasi, noted seamen, each had a wing of the shoal (*matāmafua*) assigned to him by the deity. So each clan when fishing for bonito addressed formulae to its own chiefly representative. Of old the bonito came every year. But their scarcity by 1928 was owing to Pa Veterei, eldest son of Pae Avakofe, who had died some years before. After he had "set up his rod" with a catch of twenty or so fish, he had made an offering in the sacred canoe yard to his ancester Pu Ariki, and requested that the bonito might be kept away from Tikopia, so that he might rest unchallenged in his achievement. Then after his death he crawled in homage to Pu Ariki and the other spirits, reinforcing his request that the bonito should cease to rise, that is, to shoal. Hence their disappearance in modern times. Such attribution of jealous attempts to block any rivalry, even after death, reveals another facet of Tikopia interpretation of variations in natural phenomena in terms of human intention.

It has long been a Tikopia custom to compose dance songs about objects and activities of interest, and bonito fishing has been included in these. An ancient dance song about bonito, made known to me by Pa Rangifuri, apparently describes the observations of an unlucky fisherman.

Tafito	Basic Stanza
Ko te fokoriri E!	It's the wheeling round of birds Oh!
Ka vakai i rakeiama, i katea,	(Bonito) will circle round the outrigger, and to starboard
Ku fakaino, uru moi	They have dived down, and have entered
Ki rarovaka.	Below the canoe.

Kupu	Stanza
Totoro mai ra koe taina	Crawl over here, brother
O fokosirimara	To replace me
Ki te toumuri vaka.	At the stern of the canoe.

SHARK

Sharks shared certain characteristics with bonito and other large fish already discussed. They were sought for food, their capture was a matter of some skill, elaborate formulae were recited to promote success, and the fish were regarded as being controlled in general by spirit powers. Traditionally, wooden hooks (*kau*) were used, upward of a foot long, formed from a curved branch or root of *sasa* wood, with a wooden barb strongly lashed to the point at an acute angle. But by the time I arrived in Tikopia in 1928 such hooks had been abandoned (although a few were still to be seen stowed away as relics) and replaced by iron hooks, called by the same term. Mackerel or flying fish were used as bait. When a shark of some size, say eight feet or so, was caught, great interest was taken in it, a crowd of people assembled to discuss it and the man who caught it was pleased and proud.

As an aid in shark fishing a formula of the *penu toki* was sometimes recited. Two clam shells were grated together under water, while the fisherman spoke to the following effect:

Ariki tautai, ou aranga vaka	Sea expert chief, your canoe gear
Ka ngoro i tou fonga vaka e tapu	Will snore from the deck of your sacred vessel
Taki se kau fanonga roa	Bring a great company
Mou i tou katea	With you to your starboard side
Matangore mai i ama, i katea	With dancing faces hither to port, to starboard
Taki mua na kau tamaroa	Bring on the crowd of young men
Na kau fafine taka	The crowd of maidens
Tu tokotoko atu i muri	Stand leaning on their staves in rear
Na kau matua na kau nofine valivali	The company of old men and of flabby old women
Maofa ratou nifo	With their teeth fallen
Ouia, ouia, oupa!	Ouia, ouia, oupa!
E ariki tautai, ou aranga vaka	Oh! Sea expert chief, your canoe gear
Ka fi atu ki te tai	Will be dipped in the sea
Soro manu	Grate with power
Ouia oupa.	Ouia oupa!
Sirisiria i a taufare o raro	It is asked in the abodes below
Ko ai te tupua	Whoever may be the deity
Ka maofa ki te tai ona aranga vaka	Whose canoe gear will disintegrate in the sea
Ouia oui oui oū ūpa	Ouia oui oui ou upa!

This is a sample section of a long formula, the essential purport of which is an address in figurative terms to the guardian spirit of the canoe, requesting him to bring a shark to the hook. The spirit is spoken to as "sea expert chief," the conventional form of address, and the canoe and its equipment, including the fishing gear, are treated as his property. Sharks are not mentioned by name, but referred to as persons, the spirit being exhorted to bring them along in numbers, young and old, from their home in the depths of the ocean. Such flattering speech, with pleasing images, continues throughout the rest of the formula: in other sections the shark is represented as adorned with fragrant leaf fillet in his hair (a metaphor for the noose to go over his head), and a shell plaque ornament on his breast (the hook in his gullet). The grating ("snoring") of the clam shells may have had the technical effect of attracting sharks by the noise; for the Tikopia it was the medium whereby the formula was conveyed to the guardian spirit—a kind of invisible telephone wire to the ocean depths. What was sought was efficacy for the fisherman's work; hence the ejaculation "Grate with power" (*soro manu*). Such a formula might be recited by the fisherman himself on the spot, as was the case with one example I recorded in 1929, or as with the present sample recorded from the expert fisherman Pa Teva, it might be recited by the chief ashore while the fisherman was at sea. By 1952 the formula of grating clam shells had been abandoned. The fisherman merely called out "Bite, a fish!" or, as he felt the tug of the shark on the hook "Shark! Put on your breast pendant."

Although shark fishing lacked the urgent thrill of bonito fishing in the midst of a running shoal, it had plenty of excitement when a struggling big-mawed fish was being hauled in. Moreover, when a large shark was hauled in, and the crew were paddling back, the steersman in the stern made the light dipping stroke known as *seu,* throwing up a fountain of spray as an advertisement to the people on shore. (For *para* or *varu* a less flamboyant paddling style known as *tope* was used.) In several respects, then, fishing for bonito and for shark can be seen to have presented considerable similarities. But there were also marked differences.

In the general behavior of fishermen, shark fishing was treated very much like any other kind of fishing. It was not a special exercise, but usually followed fishing for flying fish or other small catches. It required a special gear, but this gear, though valuable, was not invested with the aura of respect, even *tapu,* surrounding the bonito hook. There were no particular taboos on sex intercourse before a man went shark fishing, as there were before bonito fishing.

On the other hand, sharks were individualized in a way that bonito were not. This is intelligible, considering their greater size and diversity of shape and coloring, but the individualization was carried from the physical over to the spiritual sphere. For all ordinary practical purposes of catching, a shark was treated as a simple fish. But any abnormality in its characteristics or behavior was interpreted as evidence of spirit involvement. If a shark when caught turned out to have wounds on its body, these were interpreted as cuts inflicted by the spear or adz of the guardian spirit of the canoe in driving the fish to the canoe or in preparing it to be caught. On a sea voyage, should a shark follow a canoe closely or appear in the vicinity in a time of crisis—as not infrequently seemed to occur—this was taken to be a sign from the guardian spirit of the canoe or from a god of the lineage or clan of some member of the crew. The spirit was believed either to be actually inhabiting the fish or directing it to behave in a significant manner to indicate his interest or intent. The "appearing fish" (*ika sa*) was a portent, often of ill omen,[5] it embodied an evil spirit, coming to harm the fishermen. If there were coconuts in the canoe, one was pierced and a libation poured, with a formula to the spirit to disappear. If no coconut was available, then a libation was poured from a water bottle, and if this was lacking, from a bailer of sea water. This was the rite known as "sprinkling" (*fakaranu*), in token of respect to the spirit.

Again, if the canoe involved was one of the sacred craft, when the shark was brought ashore it was taken to the canoe yard, and a basket of food was placed beside it as an offering. The chief of the clan came to the head of the fish with his water bottle and poured water over its head. This was to render the fish agreeable to the belly of man as food.

Some of the contrast between bonito and shark may be pointed up in such terms as these: bonito were looked at in the mass, not separately, sharks were individualized; catching bonito was ritualized, shark catching—apart from the recital of a formula as with many other fish—was not; bonito were thought to be very sensitive to human frailty, sharks not at all; bonito were the children of gods, sharks their agents and tools; catching bonito was sport, catching sharks was work. To use an idiom not used by the Tikopia, though not completely alien to them since they have a class system, bonito were aristocrats, sharks were low-class. Yet outside the fishing context it was sharks who were treated with respect and credited with spirit powers, the more so as they came closer to men. Whereas once bonito were caught they were food, sharks when caught might have to be ritually asperged to render them fit for food.

There was a further contrast, to which, one may think, much of the foregoing was related. Bonito were food for man, but man was not food for bonito. With sharks the position was more complicated. Many sharks, particularly those that frequented the reef, were fish-eating; they might bite a man—when, for instance, as sometimes happened, he seized it by the tail in a flurry of a reef chase—but they did not normally attack man. Some had quite small mouths and relatively few teeth. Other sharks, the scavengers of the sea, the great white shark with large head, wide gaping mouth, and rows of razor-sharp teeth, were known to the Tikopia as *mango kai tangata,* man eaters. This posed a problem; if the shark eats man, should man eat the shark? I got no complete resolution of opinion on this point. One view was that only fish-eating sharks were used as human food; that the *atua kai tangata,* the man-eating

---

[5] This descriptive substantive can be given a verbal form: "*Ku ika saina ko tatou,*" "We have been 'appearing fished,' " a member of the crew might say.

shark, termed *atua* from its ferocity to man, did not take the hook and consequently did not become food. But another view was that while some people ate shark of all kinds, to others it was *tapu;* because they were afraid of the shark, which ate man, they refused it (Firth, 1967a, p. 255).[6] As far as I could gather, sharks of man-eating type were rarely caught, so that the practical issue did not often arise. But in general sharks were eaten freely.

EEL

With eels the Tikopia position was different again. Several kinds were recognized, the most common being the eel of the lake and the gray reef eel. By the Maori and some other Polynesians eels were eaten, even regarded as a delicacy. By Tikopia, in contrast, they were regarded as utterly unfit for food. It was said that anyone who ate eel would die. But the whole notion was repulsive; eels were treated as disgusting. There were several correlates to this Tikopia attitude. Eels, especially the reef eel, were regarded as savage and dangerous, with some justification; but this alone would not have rendered them inedible, since sharks would fall in the same category. Eels, like sharks, were associated with spirits. But what distinguished eels from sharks was the much higher degree of personification attached to them. Sharks in general were fish, and only certain individuals were directed by or vehicles for spirits, and termed *atua*. By contrast, while eels were classified as fish (*ika*) all were labeled *atua*. Moreover, while neither sharks in general nor any particular kind of shark were regarded as representative of any particular *atua*, each kind of eel was identified with a specific named *atua* of anthropomorphic quality. The eel of the lake was identified as the Atua i te Vai, the eel of the reef as the Atua i te Tai, and the eel of the channel (so-called, a brownish sea eel) as the Atua i te Ava, these being major deities of Tafua, Taumako, and Fangarere, respectively. The eel gods were thought to provide food for man by bringing sharks and other large fish to the hook. But the tendency on seeing any eel was to regard it as an embodiment of the particular deity concerned, and to treat any item of its behavior which deviated from the normal as having some special significance, probably portentous or dangerous (see also Firth, 1967a, pp. 253-255).

---

[6] Refusal to eat shark because of distaste was quite different from refusal to eat it because of respect to a dead father who had been an expert shark fisherman. This was a *tapu* of another kind; in such case, as I observed, the shark was handed over to another household not so bound by mourning restriction. See Firth, 1966, pp. 96-115.

Mythic background to these ideas was provided by various tales, including an origin myth in which the various types of eels were created by successive truncations of the elongated phallus of a generative deity. Linked with this was the notion that eels in their spirit form were essentially concupiscent; conceived as always male, they were therefore very dangerous to women. More generally, the eel gods were conceived as suspicious and jealous, personifications of the principle of punishment for offenders through their prime role as gods of the sacred adzes of their associated clans. Whereas most Tikopia gods and ancestral spirits were regarded as primarily distributing benefits and capable of harm only when offended, the eel gods were regarded as inclined to do harm to anyone causing them unauthorized disturbance. Even to be in their vicinity could be dangerous; they and a pair of female deities with no particular fish associations were the nearest equivalent to a principle of evil recognized by the Tikopia.

OCTOPUS

We now turn to other large sea creatures. The octopus, encountered sometimes on the reef, was regarded in a manner parallel to the eel. It was not taken for food and was looked upon with aversion. Instead of being referred to by a general term, *te feke,* every individual tended to be treated as an embodiment of a male deity, popularly known as the Atua i Faea, and to be referred to by his proper name, Feke. Like the eel, the octopus in his personified form was regarded as concupiscent toward women, and various tales explained how lost girl children had been carried off to be "married" by Feke. The symbolism of the octopus concentrated upon its tentacles, analogues to which were found in the rays of the sun, and in a set of springs of water originating from the hill crest of Korofau and emerging on various sides of the slope. Both sun with its rays and hill with its springs were treated as further embodiments or transformations of Feke; the rays indeed were invoked as a set of separate entities in ritual. But though dangerous, the octopus god was not regarded with the same fear as was the eel god; he seemed to be thought to lack the malignancy of the latter.

TURTLE

Another sea creature of interest in this field was the turtle; classified, as already mentioned, as *ika* because it swims in the sea, or *paka* because of its carapace. Two kinds were recognized, the green turtle, *fonu tea* (light-colored), and the hawksbill, *fonu koroa* (valuable turtle) from which was obtained "tortoise-shell." Turtles were regarded as the incarnation of a female deity, Pufine i Ravenga, and as such "belonged" to the chiefly lineage of Fangarere. But attitudes toward them were of the pattern of shark rather than of octopus (Firth, 1967a, pp. 256, 362). Individual turtles were believed to embody the deity, and to adopt protective measures toward men of Fangarere clan in peril at sea. But in general turtles were treated as animals of economic and social interest. To begin with they were regarded as edible by some Tikopia. The situation here was much as with shark; some people ate turtle while others thought it disgusting and said to eat it would make them vomit. It seemed that people of Fangarere in general abstained, from association of the turtle with their particular deity. I was told in 1928 by people of Tafua that in former times people of Matafanga, that is, Taumako, always ate turtle, but that the chiefs and their families still did not. Pa Rangifuri, eldest son of the Ariki Tafua, for instance, had never eaten turtle. It was alleged that it was John Maresere, the Uvean,[7] who had helped to introduce turtle as food to the majority of Tikopia. On the whole, even in 1928 probably fewer people ate turtle than ate shark. But when in September, 1928, a turtle was caught in a net, it was given to the Ariki Tafua, and lay on its back in his woodshed till an oven was ready for it to be cooked, after which it was eaten by a number of people.

Considerable interest was displayed in turtles that were taken in nets or which came ashore. Through dissection, no doubt, Tikopia had observed the difference of sex in turtles, and commented on the fact that the male turtle had a very long penis. Some of them told of a story brought from the Banks Islands by the Melanesian Mission teacher, to the effect that when the young turtles were hatched in the sand, some made their way to the sea in the normal manner while others stayed behind on land and grew into lizards and other reptiles. The Tikopia observed cautiously "It's a traditional tale in their country. We haven't heard it of old; we don't know if it be true or false." Occasionally turtles seem to have been kept in captivity and described as pets *(manu)*, a practice for which there was precedent in traditional tales. In 1929 a turtle with a valuable carapace was caught, and it was intended to keep it tethered by a rope on the reef. But then a wound was observed on its neck, and interpreted as an adz cut of a sea deity, who had

---

[7] See Rivers, 1914, Vol. I, pp. 299-300, for some account of Maresere. See also Firth, 1936, p. xxiv.

evidently intended it to be used as food. So it was carried off and cooked
in the oven.

CETACEANS

Toward cetaceans a different set of attitudes obtained. They were
all classed among *ika,* the term applying generally to fish, and collectively were called *tafora.* Whales, described as ten fathoms or so in
length, of a size that made a 30-foot canoe seem small, were *tafora atu*
or *tafora maori. Tafora taume* were characterized as being smaller and
addicted to curving out of the water; this term, from the pointed coconut spathe *(taume),* probably applied to beaked dolphins. The term
maranga seems to have applied to dolphins and porpoises generally. An
unidentified cetacean, said to be like a shark, and black, was termed
tafora samono by elderly informants; they also mentioned *karapesi,*
saying it was an English word—presumably *porpoise.*

I have no record of Tikopia ever having taken cetaceans in nets or
by other means; they referred to these animals always as having been
cast ashore. This was a rare phenomenon and no such animal was cast
up during my visits to Tikopia. It might be thought that the Tikopia, as
did the people of Kapingamarangi described by Emory (1965, pp. 200,
275-302), would have welcomed such cetaceans as a grand source of
fresh meat. But their views were much more sober. It seemed that while
the flesh of cetaceans might be eaten by some Tikopia, most usually
abstained, especially from the larger animals. I was told in 1928 of a
porpoise or small whale, as long as the post supporting the ridgepole of
a temple—about 15 feet—and of a girth greater than a man could span,
which stranded at Tufena some years before. Its flesh had been chewed
by sharks and had gone bad, and it was buried. But even when a carcass
was fresh it seems to have been the custom to bury it, although occasionally bones might be utilized for bonito hook shanks or betel pestles.
A *tafora* which came ashore at Te Akauroa on the east side of the island
some years before 1928 was buried, and while the flesh of another was
eaten, this was by some Anutans, the Tikopia not reckoning it as food.

So far from the emphasis being on the food value of such an
animal, it was on its ritual significance (see also Firth, 1967a, p. 251).
When a large *tafora,* that is, a whale, was cast ashore people assembled
to look at it. But as each man went to join the crowd he seized spear
or club, and with his companions brandished his weapon and shook it
violently over the dead animal. Such threatening gestures were merely
a demonstration, not a prelude to a fight. This performance was known
as *fakaveve.* At the same time green food, such as raw taro, was as-

sembled and laid before the whale; this was the *putu*. The significance of these performances lay in the belief that the whale or related animal was an embodiment of a deity. The idea of the *fakaveve* was that an *atua* had come to land in the body of the animal; it might bring disease, hence spears and clubs were brandished as a symbolic gesture of repulsion, to frighten off any evil influences that might portend. (This practice was in line with the *fakaforauatua*, the "causing of the spirits to voyage," which was another ritual of expulsion of disease-bearing spirits.) On the other hand, to appease the deity represented by the whale, the conventional offering of green food was presented to him. He was thus shown both sides of the coin, as it were—first warning, then respect. Even if the cetacean was a small one and its flesh were eaten, although the threatening *fakaveve* might be omitted, the offering of the *putu* was not. I was told by Pa Korokoro in 1929 of a type of *maranga* (dolphin) associated particularly with his lineage as being an embodiment of his sea god Semoana. If such an animal were stranded, the *putu* was first made to it. Then it was cooked, and portions were sent to the chiefs, as allocations to their respective major gods. Korokoro lineage, though responsible for the offering, the cooking, and division, did not eat at all of the flesh. It was *tapu* to them (see Firth, 1967a, p. 250).

In 1966, as the result of inquiry about a song I was recording, I was given still further details about the treatment of *tafora*. The Ariki Taumako explained that when a *tafora* came ashore it was buried in sections, with a variety of taro from the woods known as *kape* put alongside it. The burial place was known as *te umanga*, a word he said to be unknown to the modern generation of Tikopia.[8] The chief said that the reason for burying the *kape* with the whale was unknown. But I was told by the Ariki Kafika in 1928 that a distinguishing feature of the *kape* was that it was *tapu* to the Kafika clan, an *atua* to them; other clans might eat of it but they not. Hence it seems probable that the association of it with a dead whale was based upon the idea of offering to the deity of which the animal was an embodiment a vegetable already in ritual relation with a spirit.

The *tafora* referred to in the song had a proper name, Punga, and came ashore long ago, in the time of the great-great-grandfather of the Ariki Taumako. It landed in Tai, at the area known as Fasi, with its head on shore and its tail in the sea. The *fakaveve* reception over, the

---

[8] See for example, Bellona, where as Dr. Monberg informs me, *umanga* is the equivalent of the Tikopia *tofi*, orchard.

problem arose of moving it for disposal. The intention was to take it to
Uta, the ritual center of the island, for cooking in the oven. First came
sa Kafika to try to move the carcass, but they were unsuccessful; it was
too heavy. Then came sa Tafua, and failed likewise. Lastly came sa
Taumako, led by their chief. They applied their tree branch as lever,
and moved the fish over, so that it could be cut up and dealt with. It
was then taken to Uta and cooked; some people ate of it, others not.
The song was composed by the Ariki Fangarere to his brother chief,
in praise of his powers. It was chanted in the sacred dances of Uta, with
appropriate gestures, and became very popular; being dedicated to a
man, not to gods, it has been transferred to the secular dance field and
is still used nowadays, after the conversion of all the people from
paganism. Naturally, it is a favorite especially of the Taumako chiefly
family.

Tafito
Fakamama tou tino
Ke oko ki o paepae o ngoriki

Safe
Oko moi toku taina
Ma tou kainanga
Turoki moi
Ngoruru te uru o te ika.

Like many of these songs, this is a simple description with a great deal
of underlying meaning. The first stanza addresses the whale; "Let your
body be light, to arrive at the stone slabs of chiefs," that is, so that it
can be carried to Uta, figuratively designated by Pae Marae, the symbol
of the Atua i Kafika (see Firth, 1967b, p. 286). The second stanza
commemorates the achievement. The chief came, with his clan; they
stood there and applied their strength, and the head of the "fish" moved.
This celebration of the power of the Taumako chief and the discom-
fiture of Kafika and Tafua illustrates how the latent rivalry of the
Tikopia chiefs became manifest whenever an opportunity presented itself. The point here is that such an achievement was believed to be
owing to spiritual as well as to physical powers: the body of the whale
was made light for the purpose.

Behind all these dealings with cetaceans lay the idea that they represented spirit manifestations. As the Ariki Taumako said, as recently
as 1966, "People say that they are all bodies of the spirits." From this
point of view the ambiguous attitude toward them is explicable: they
were a sign of the imminence of spirits, and therefore to be regarded
with grave caution; but their appearance on shore could also be looked

upon as proof of human control over or liaison with spirits. So whenever a cetacean appeared out of its natural element there was a tendency for some chief or elder to claim that his particular spirit was responsible. In 1928 I was told by the ritual elder of Fusi that Tarikotu, his major deity, was responsible for noosing *tafora* and bringing them to shore. This deity was admitted by all Tikopia to have as his embodiment the sago palm trunk, which in its bulk was the equivalent on land of the *tafora* at sea. (It is noteworthy that when a sago trunk was grated by Fusi lineage to make flour, the *putu* offering was made by them to their god, in a fashion similar to that to a whale.) In 1966 the Ariki Taumako said there was a story about the whale that was moved by his ancestor. Pa Rarovi, a premier elder of Kafika, had composed a sacred dance song in praise of Tuaneve, Pufine i Fasi, a goddess of the traditional Nga Faea folk. It was held that the whale was her response, that she brought it to shore as the *ufi,* the reciprocity, for the song made in her honor, in general compatibility with Tikopia custom. The arrival of a cetacean ashore could therefore be made to bear a considerable load of ancillary interpretation, in terms of social relations, and could serve as focus for a complex set of beliefs.

DIFFERENCES IN ATTITUDES

We may now try to isolate those elements which seem to be most significant in the differentiation of attitude between the various types of sea creature. Can we see any clearer pattern emerging from the range of behavior? I think so, if the main features of the material be set out in systematic form, as in Table 1.

TABLE 1

CREATURE	CATEGORY IKA	FREQUENT APPEARANCE	SPIRIT EMBODIMENT ALL	SOME	AID/ HARM MAN	SOUGHT TO CAPTURE	MAGIC TO CATCH	EDIBLE	SEX SENSITIVE
Para/Varu	X	X	O	O	O	X	X	XX	O
Bonito	X	O	O	O	O	X	XX	XX	X
Shark	X	X	O	X	X/X	X	XX	XX	O
Eel	X	X	X	.	X/XX	O	O	OO	XX
Octopus	O	X	X	.	X/XX	O	O	OO	XX
Turtle	O	O	O	X	X/O	X	O	X/O	O
Whale	X	O	X	.	X/X	O	O	X/O	O

The first point to make is that the various elements overlap; no type of creature is completely distinguished in every particular from every other type. The three prime food fish types, *para,* bonito, and shark, separate fairly definitely from the rest, but one of them, shark, is sometimes a spirit embodiment whereas the others are not, and bonito are highly sex sensitive whereas the others are not. Eel and octopus share most characteristics, but one is a fish and the other an animal, and so on.

The categorization of a creature as *ika* ("fish") or not does not seem important as a regulator of or index to behavior. Categorization as an embodiment of spirit seems more significant, although sharks, which sometimes represent spirits or are conceived of as spirits, have magic to catch them, and are prized as food, while cetaceans, seemingly always conceived of as spirit embodiments, are theoretically edible in some circumstances.

The criteria which appear to me to be most useful to focus upon to begin with are whether a creature is regarded as edible or not, and whether it is regarded as aiding or harming man. Here there seems to be a clear negative correlation: those creatures which are regarded as most dangerous to man are also those which are regarded as totally inedible, while those which are regarded as neither aiding nor harming man are highly edible (compare Firth, 1967a, pp. 228, 233). A simple matrix gives two contrasted pairs of creatures:

Food	does NOT HARM man	*Para,* etc.
		Bonito
Nonfood	HARMS man	Eel
		Octopus

This seems to leave shark, turtle, and whale unaccounted for. Shark may be split between fish-eating sharks, which do not harm man and are used for food, and man-eating sharks, which do harm man and are rejected as food. But about the latter discrimination there seems to have been some difference of view among Tikopia; some people did not refuse any shark irrespective of its type. In other words, there is some uncertainty or ambiguity about the position of sharks in this categorization. This draws attention to an important feature in the criterion of "harming," that it is spiritual rather than physical damage that is implied. Eels bite and octopus can be dangerous, but the physical damage they could do to Tikopia was very small compared with the damage done by sharks. Yet it was eel and octopus that were greatly feared and shunned, and shark that was eaten. It is conceptual, not material harm that is the criterion involved in this classification.

This helps to explain to some extent the position of whale and other cetaceans in this frame of reference. An animal of this kind, emerging from its natural element, the ocean, on to land, the sphere of man, was regarded as a threat to human welfare, vague but imminent. The criterion of "out of element" seems especially relevant here. *Para,* bonito, and shark have been deliberately brought out of their element by man, for food, and therefore have been de-fused, as it were, of any dangerous potentialities they might be thought to possess. Turtles were not specifically sought at sea, but were taken in nets, and so were in somewhat the same category, although they did appear spontaneously at times on shore. Eels and octopus while never sought, had the habit of manifesting themselves on the reef, and it was even alleged that octopus might be seen wandering on the beach. Whales, above all, presented themselves unsought, and with their huge size suggested an invasion of sea representatives on to the land.

Yet there is one further criterion which needs bringing into the frame—the theme of sex sensitivity. Here again correlation seems clear: sex sensitivity of a positive kind, as the association of eel and octopus with maleness and danger to women, connotes nonfood; while sex sensitivity of a negative kind such as the prudery of the bonito, or neutral, as with fish, including shark, connotes suitability for food. Here again the criterion is a conceptual one. There is no evidence that eels and octopus are differently endowed from other creatures. But to the Tikopia they represent sex incarnate. The reason seems plain; the phallic analogy suggested by their bodily characteristics, in particular their sinuous form. In the case of the eel this analogy is supported strongly by an origin myth.

To conclude: I regard the behavioral classification of the major sea creatures coming within the cognizance of the Tikopia as explicable in terms of a combination of three primary principles: their edibility, their capacity to harm man, and their sexual suggestiveness. The first two are distinctly utilitarian criteria, and I would argue that such criteria are of distinct importance in the classification of objects in the Tikopia environment. But the criteria of utility, and of capacity to harm are not simple material characteristics; they are socially created and socially elaborated with an appartus of belief which in the case of the Tikopia brings in a range of spirit concepts which serve as reference points for much behavior. I might put this argument in another, oversimplified, way by saying that the definition of marine flesh food in Tikopia is achieved not in terms of material criteria such as consistency, taste, and flavor, but by defining marine faunal areas which can represent basic fears of physical and moral danger, and then treating as edible the major items in the rest.

LITERATURE CITED

EMORY, KENNETH P.
>
> 1965. *Kapingamarangi: Social and Religious Life of a Polynesian Atoll.* B. P. Bishop Mus. Bull. 228. Honolulu.

FIRTH, RAYMOND

> 1930-1931. "Totemism in Polynesia." *Oceania* 1 (3,4): 291-321; 377-398. (Reprinted in R. Firth, *Tikopia Ritual and Belief,* 1967.)
> 1936. *We, The Tikopia.* London: Allen and Unwin.
> 1939. *Primitive Polynesian Economy.* London: Routledge.
> 1961. *History and Traditions of Tikopia.* Wellington: Polynesian Soc.
> 1966. "The Meaning of Pali in Tikopia." In *In Memory of J. R. Firth,* C. E. BAZELL *et al.* (editors). London.
> 1967a. *Tikopia Ritual and Belief.* London: Allen and Unwin.
> 1967b. *The Work of the Gods in Tikopia.* London School of Economics Monographs on Social Anthropology Nos. 1 and 2. (2nd ed.) London: Athlone Press; New York: Humanities Press; Melbourne Univ. Press.

RIVERS, W. H. R.

> 1914. *The History of Melanesian Society.* Vol. 1. Cambridge: Univ. Press.

AN ISLAND CHANGES ITS RELIGION

SOME SOCIAL IMPLICATIONS OF THE CONVERSION TO CHRISTIANITY ON BELLONA ISLAND[1]

TORBEN MONBERG

University of Copenhagen

O NLY A FEW POLYNESIAN societies provide us with an opportunity to study religious innovation in detail. Rarely are we given a chance to gain a deeper insight in, for example, the processes of conversion from one religion to another. The majority of the islands were converted to Christianity a century or more ago, and in most cases we have only the accounts of the successful missionaries to study if we want to know what has actually taken place during the transition from one faith to another.

However, if we view a non-Christian society's conversion to Christianity as a set of complex external innovations, it may be of particular interest to consider the process involved from the point of view of the recipient society and to analyze the social and cultural elements[2] and

[1] The data for this study were collected during field work on Rennell and Bellona and among Rennellese and Bellonese in other parts of the Solomon Islands in 1958-1959, 1962, 1963, and 1966. The expeditions were sponsored by Statens Almindelige Videnskabsfond and Styrelsen for Teknisk Samarbejde med Udviklingslandene, to which institutions I convey my warmest thanks.

I also wish to thank Samuel H. Elbert, of the University of Hawaii, and Leif Christensen and Sofus Christiansen, of the University of Copenhagen, not only for their companionship in the field, but also for many helpful suggestions in connection with problems of method and analysis of the data. Samuel H. Elbert, Vernet Goldschmidt, and Leif Christensen have also read this paper and offered valuable suggestions.

The field method used and the problems of collecting retrospective data in a nonliterate society have been discussed in Monberg, 1966. This discussion also applies to the present study.

[2] In the use of the words "social" and "cultural" I follow the suggestions for a distinction between these two analytical aspects made by Geertz (1957, p. 33) and by Parsons and Shils (1951): culture is an ordered system of meanings and symbols in terms of which social interaction takes place, whereas a social system is the pattern of social interaction itself.

the set of choices and decisions which have made the innovations possible and which have determined their status within the society.

Rennell and Bellona, two Polynesian Outliers in the Solomon Islands, provide us with some material for an analysis of this kind. They were among the last of the Polynesian islands to accept Christianity. The conversion took place in 1938. Fairly detailed accounts by some Rennellese and Bellonese of the dramatic events on Rennell which led to the abandonment of the old beliefs and rituals have been published elsewhere (Elbert and Monberg, 1965), and some aspects of these events have been analyzed briefly (Monberg, 1962).

This paper is only indirectly concerned with the actual process of conversion; it is rather an attempt to present and analyze some of the social configurations which took place on the smaller of the two islands, Bellona, after the new faith had been accepted.

It has been shown previously (Monberg, 1966) that religious change itself is nothing new in Bellonese society. The pre-Christian religion seems to have undergone a number of rather important transformations even before contact with Europeans or other outsiders. These were the introduction of new ritual formulas or new rites, the institution of new deities and also the abandonment of certain old rites and ritual formulas (Monberg, 1966, pp. 72-74). Compared to the religious change which took place in 1938 with the introduction of Christianity, these changes were, however, slight. In the old religion the worship of new gods was introduced occasionally but the old gods were not discarded. Christianity, however, brought entirely new gods, the god-in-the-sky (*te 'atua i te ngangi*) and his son (*te 'aitu*), and the old deities were dismissed from the island. New rites and new sets of values were introduced and some major social changes took place.

The actual chain of events from 1938 onward can be analytically divided into three periods or phases, which I have chosen to label the phases of acceptance, of adjustment, and of readjustment. In these three phases different processes were at work.

PHASE I: ACCEPTANCE (1938)

Rennell and Bellona have a common language and culture; of the two, Rennell, the larger island, had had most contact with the outside world before the advent of Christianity. Accounts of these contacts are given elsewhere (Birket-Smith, 1956; Broek d'Obrenan, 1939; Deck, 1945; Elbert and Monberg, 1965; Hogbin, 1931; Lambert, 1941; Macgregor, 1943; Monberg, 1962; Stanley, 1929; Young, no date).

An attempt by the South Seas Evangelical Mission (SSEM) to establish Chistianity on Rennell resulted in 1910 in the killing of a missionary and his two helpers on the island in the same year. During the 1930's several Rennellese were taken to mission stations on other islands in the Solomons where they received from six weeks to twelve months training before they were returned to Rennell. This paved the way for the island's conversion to Christianity in 1938. During a harvest ritual in the Lake District the Rennellese attempted to establish a joint worship of the old deities and the Christian God. The first rite of this kind, however, developed into mass hysteria and complete ritual anarchy. The dramatic events have been related in Elbert and Monberg (1965). The Rennellese interpreted this chaos and violence as a struggle between the Christian God and the old gods in which the latter were expelled from the island by the new power, and as a result, mass conversion to Christianity took place.

In comparison with Rennell, the smaller island of Bellona led a very isolated life until 1938. Bellona had been visited by a few anthropologists and government officers in the 1930's, and a Seventh Day Adventist mission ship had called there in 1934 or 1935 on its way to Batuna, the mission station in the Western Solomons, with a shipload of Rennellese. No Bellonese wanted to go, however, allegedly because they were afraid at that time of contact with the white man. The Bellonese assert that the reason they wanted to be left alone on their island was that they had heard that contact with Europeans resulted in the introduction of new and hitherto unknown infectious diseases. Earlier, sporadic contact had, they believed, brought yaws and other diseases to the island.

In spite of their comparative isolation, the Christian religion was not totally unknown to them. Rennellese visitors to Bellona and Bellonese going to see their kinsmen on Rennell had naturally exchanged news, and the Bellonese had learned about the two gods in the sky, God and "Sisas," but, according to the Bellonese themselves, they saw no reason why they should give up the worship of the old deities and turn to the new god, especially because they knew very little about his powers and also because they feared that the old gods might be angered. The deities of Bellona had already expressed their points of view through their human mediums: it was taboo to mention the name of the Christian deities because they were bad gods.

In November, 1938, Christianity was introduced on Bellona through the back door, so to speak. When the madness on Rennell was over and Christianity had been generally accepted, Moa, a powerful lineage elder of the Lake District, decided to go to Bellona to tell about the new faith (Elbert and Monberg, 1965, pp. 394-419). When he arrived there, Bellona was engaged in an extensive interlineage fight, particularly involving the lineages of the eastern district, Matangi, and the middle district, Ghongau. For fear of surprise attacks people had moved from their homesteads in the interior of the island to small places of refuge in the bush which covers the entire outer rim of the island.

A detailed account of the events of Moa's arrival has been given elsewhere. The following little incident may, however, give an impression of the atmosphere in which the conversion took place. One of the first men whom Moa met when he arrived on Bellona was the influential lineage elder, Takiika, of Nuku'angoha lineage (Monberg, 1966, p. 18). Takiika recently told me of their first conversation when they met in his homestead, Hanakaba. The two men greeted each other with elaborate and stylized formulas, indicating mutual respect, but in concluding his speech Moa deviated from the traditional pattern by saying: "I am only worthy of saluting your entrails and those of your older classificatory brother in the sky." The usual formula is: "I am only worthy of saluting your entrails and those of your older classificatory brother (or your father)." Takiika tells how astonished he was and that he wondered who his older classificatory brother in the sky could be. It was Jesus. God being everyone's Father, it was obvious to a Rennellese that His Son must be everyone's Older Brother.

Moa now told why he had arrived. According to Takiika he said approximately the following: "I have come to enlighten you and your house because we (the people of the Lake District on Rennell) have been punished. We had received knowledge of Father (God) and of our Older Brother (Jesus) and we mixed (the rites). We worshiped our Father in Heaven, and we worshiped the gods of this world. And time went on and Father sent a punishment; we were punished in Niupani; we fought, killed people, set fire to one another's hair and pulled down the temple house in Mangama'ubea; I set fire to the hair of my older classificatory brother, Taupongi; women made dances to the sounding board; we ended the brother-sister avoidance and brother and sister spoke to one another. Then everything became well and we made churches, and I thought of coming to your land which still worships the gods whom we have abandoned. . . ."

Moa held many meetings on Bellona in which he prayed to the Christian God and cursed the old gods. On at least one occasion, during a large feast in one of the homesteads, the gods answered back through their mediums. The result was a verbal fight between Moa and the old gods, and it was so fierce that the audience was said to have fled in horror (Elbert and Monberg, 1965, p. 417). But the outcome was that the mediums were silenced. The gods left them and mediumship was then given up.

The arriving missionary had other victories. He broke the two stones, the "bodies" of the two most powerful and sacred gods of the Rennellese and Bellonese, and he was not killed by them because of this. Only a splinter of one of the stones hit Moa when he crushed it with his ax. This was interpreted as a sign of the gods' comparative weakness. Moa also mediated between the fighting parties on the island, and peace was restored on Bellona. His prayers were even claimed to have had healing powers. A number of sick Bellonese were restored to health when he prayed for them. He describes these achievements, very modestly, in Elbert and Monberg (1965, p. 405).

Moa's message had obviously been very simple. He had had very little training in the teachings of Christianity. During his meetings in 1938 he told the Bellonese the outlines of Genesis, the story of Noah, and about the birth, life, and death of Christ. We have no detailed data on what went on in the minds of the Bellonese when they heard these strange stories. Such things are difficult to remember after twenty-five years. Several informants have told how surprised they were to hear about a god who was powerful enough to flood the whole world but save only one family in a canoe. The story about the Deluge must have appealed to the Bellonese who knew that a man in danger at sea who appealed to the gods would be saved from disaster (Elbert and Monberg, 1965, pp. 298-299). They knew of the sinking of all but two of the canoes of the immigrants from 'Ubea going to Rennell and Bellona, and the drowning of a hundred people. This resemblance has never been expressed by the Rennellese or Bellonese themselves, but it is obvious that the story of Noah has elements which they could conceive.

The teachings of Moa were almost devoid of specific dogma. He stressed the power of God and of His Son; that His wrath would fall upon those who did not worship Him; that it was taboo to kill each other; that one should like one's neighbor; that one should give up rigid brother-sister avoidance; that one should keep the Sabbath, and build churches and pray and sing to God there.

A few months after Moa's arrival another party of missionaries came. This was a group of Rennellese, led by two men, Puka and Tangokona, who represented another Christian sect, the South Seas Evangelical Mission (SSEM). Their teachings were on the same elementary level as those of Moa and his group, who represented the Seventh Day Adventists (SDA).

From the beginning the two groups of missionaries stressed that they represented different schools. One of the differences was that for the SDA the day of worship was Saturday, whereas the members of the SSEM held their services on Sundays. Obviously this difference cannot have meant much to the Bellonese, who at that time had no names for the days of the week, but it was at least an indication that the missions were different.

Within a few weeks after Moa's arrival in the island the old temples had been torn down, the ritual paraphernalia and the sacred stones destroyed, and the rituals abandoned.

An overwhelming majority of the Bellonese now accepted the new religion. I have records of only five men who, with their wives and children, still objected to the introduction of the new god and who went on performing the minor household rituals (*hainga 'atua*) to the old deities. These five families gave up their resistance after one or two months and joined one of the two missions. Their reason for initially objecting to the introduction of Christianity was in all cases said to be that they thought the old gods were stronger and that they would take revenge on all those who deserted them.

We may now pose the one question which seems of most interest in connection with this first phase of the process of religious innovation on Bellona: Why did the 430 inhabitants on the island so readily accept a new religion about which they had received such scant information?

If new culture traits or inventions "are on the one hand suggested by a device already in operation (using the same principle) and on the other hand are intended to be a substitute (an 'improvement') for another one also already in operation but using a different principle" (Barnett, 1942, p. 16), we may be close to an answer. In the Bellona case the device already in operation was, naturally, the old religion whose practitioners, like Christians, believed in supernatural beings and had temples and performed rites in these temples. We shall return to this later.

As for the question of the innovation intended to be an improvement, it poses certain theoretical problems. It is unlikely that an innovation will survive and spread within a society, whether introduced from the outside or not, unless the members of the society believe that they will profit from accepting the new, or, as a minimum, that the innovation is considered of equal value to the trait for which it is to substitute. It may be argued that new traits (taxation, legal or political institutions) are sometimes forced upon a society from the outside under threats of sanctions if these traits are not accepted. Such forcefully introduced traits, however, only offer an extreme example of what has been said above. They are accepted because the receiving society realizes that it will gain from accepting them, the gain being that the sanctions are not put into force.

From available data it is obvious that the Bellonese accepted Christianity because they believed that they would profit from it in various ways. It would be misinterpretation to state that the Bellonese began to worship the new god because they suddenly realized that what Moa told them was the universal and final truth and that the Christian God was the only existing god. The Bellonese have never been inclined to discussion of, or belief in, ultimate truths. They seem to share a general Polynesian concept that there are many kinds of worlds with many kinds of gods, and that people worship different gods who are all true and existing, for otherwise it would be sheer foolishness to worship them. An example of this attitude may be that the Bellonese until this day believe that their old deities exist. To them the Christian God is merely powerful enough to keep them away.

There are probably at least two reasons why the Bellonese so readily accepted Christianity without knowing much about it. The Christian God had proved that he was more powerful than the old gods of Bellona. The people had seen Moa destroy the sacred objects without being punished, and exercise extraordinary powers in curing sickness and restoring peace; they had also heard his words that the Christian God would punish those who did not follow Him, and they had heard about the madness in the Lake District on Rennell, a result of God's punishment.

This is not just the anthropologist's speculation. The Bellonese themselves assert that these were the reasons they accepted the new faith. They considered it an improvement, and they thought that they had, so far, made a good trade.

To this we may add another reason. Although Moa's message was revolutionary, it was simple. Moa spoke the language. He had had little training in Christianity and in European thought. He translated the teachings of Christianity into Rennellese and Bellonese concepts, because

he basically shared these concepts. His message was coded to the Bellonese set of concepts, his words were understood, and his acts showed
that what he said was true.

The Christian God was now accepted as the supernatural power on
the island. The worship of Him was to be a substitute for the old religion, not an addition to it. How could people adjust themselves to the
new God and how could He be integrated into Bellonese life?

PHASE II: ADJUSTMENT (1938-1949)

It need not be emphasized that the abandonment of an entire religion with its beliefs and rituals which are interdependent with a number
of the society's institutions, and with the behavior of the individual
in his daily life, is a complex affair. Numerous examples in the literature have shown this. We are here concerned with how the people
of Bellona attempted to solve the problems which arose from their
religious revolution in 1938.

During his first stay on Bellona, Moa held his meetings when people
were gathered in a homestead to perform the ceremonial distribution of
a harvest or a fish catch. Before the actual acceptance of Christianity,
Moa and his followers prayed and sang during the rites performed to the
old deities. When Christianity had been generally accepted and the old
temple sites destroyed, Moa helped to build churches. Bellonese churches
had at that time close resemblance to ordinary dwelling houses, which
were wooden frameworks thatched with pandanus leaves. Their size
varied from three to eight fathoms (*ngoha*) in length. "Chapels" might
have been a more appropriate term for these rather unimpressive edi-
fices. I have, however, chosen to use the word "church" because the
Bellonese refer to them as *tiosi,* church.

The first church was built in 1939 at Ngongona, which was the
homestead of the important lineage elder, Takiika, mentioned above.
When Moa left Bellona, he appointed Takiika "teacher," although the
latter had never attended a school and at that time knew just as little
about Christianity as the rest of the Bellonese. Even the adherents of
the SSEM mission built churches. By approximately the end of 1940
there were nine churches on the island, six belonging to SDA, and three
to SSEM.

We shall later discuss the question of church building from a political
point of view. Let us first consider some examples of how the Bellonese
reacted to the abandonment of the rites. It was from the beginning
obvious to them that it was impossible merely to carry on with the old

rituals and substitute the names God and Jesus for those of the old gods. For one thing, the Christian God spoke a different language. When Moa prayed and sang hymns it was mostly in Pidgin English. His teachings were in Rennellese, but only a few hymns had been translated into this language. Also the temples and all ritual paraphernalia had been destroyed, and the worship of the Christian God required churches.

None of the Rennellese missionaries were apparently of much help in telling the Bellonese what kind of rites they were to perform. When they returned to Rennell, the Bellonese were left with very little knowledge of Christian rituals. One informant expressed it by saying that, "When Moa and the others left us the only thing we really knew about the new faith was that Christ would come soon, and that the worship of God was different from our rituals to the old gods."

Garden work, fishing, and other economic activities went on, however, in spite of the fact that the Bellonese were ignorant of how to worship the new God. In their attempt to create a pattern for their religious behavior they tried to imitate the little they had learned from the Rennellese about the ways of the European and Melanesian followers of the new God.

Before Christianity came to Bellona, offerings and ceremonial distributions of food were a part of any major garden activity. If a man was to plant a large garden he summoned his kinsmen to help him. Some time during the work day a ceremonial distribution, 'oso hekau, of food would take place. The food was dedicated to the deities and then given to the people working in the garden. The dedication of the food to the gods was accompanied by the recitation of certain ritual formulas, and customarily the person of highest social status received the first share. Obviously the 'oso hekau could not be given up entirely because a new god had arrived. It was part of the system of economic compensation. The Bellonese told how they, in an attempt to do everything in a new way, adopted a new procedure for the reward to workers. When the food was to be distributed by the owner of the garden, he lined up those who had helped him, and he and his wife then went down along the line of people and shook hands repeatedly with every man, woman, and child. Thereupon the food was distributed in the reverse order: the first share was given to the youngest child present, and the last to the most important man. Unfortunately, it is impossible to tell exactly how common this procedure was, but a number of informants have told that this was the way in which they did it. The custom of shaking hands had been taught the Bellonese by the Rennellese missionaries who had learned it during their brief sojourns at the SDA and SSEM mission stations in Malaita and the Western Solomons. It seemed to them an important part of the missionaries' ways.

Other white men's customs had been taught the Bellonese. One was quickly adopted, namely that of taking European or Melanesian names. A number of Bellonese began to call themselves such names as Alon (Aron), Polo (Paul), Luku (Luke), Nomoa (no more), Basiana (Bastian), and Kanighae.

During the reign of the old gods, the harvest with its produce distribution was the most important occasion for the performance of elaborate rituals. These rites took place in a homestead. Food was distributed among the various deities and then redistributed among the participants in the feast, the amount given to each guest being dependent on his social status and on his specific kin ties to the person giving the feast. Immediately after the acceptance of Christianity there was said to have been a brief period in which this distribution was abandoned, allegedly because Moa had told people that Christ would come soon and take his faithful worshipers, those who had already been converted, to Heaven (Elbert and Monberg, 1965, p. 418). People pulled up the seed tubers in their gardens in the belief that Jesus would come "tomorrow," in order to have provisions to take with them to Heaven. When Jesus failed to come, the gardens were replanted. At harvest time the following year the garden produce had to be distributed, and people went on with it in the traditional way. The tubers were gathered in the homestead of the garden and handed out according to the traditional pattern.

The Bellonese state that at that time they were completely bewildered as to how to proceed with the rituals. One of the arriving Rennellese had, however, taught them how to invoke the Christian God. The prayer tells something, not only of how little the Bellonese knew at that time but also about the amount of knowledge of Christianity possessed by the Rennellese missionaries. It ran as follows: *O Lord, tasi kiu, tasi kiu. Father Lord hapemu power. Jesus seee. Amen.* The prayer was as unintelligible to the Bellonese as it is to us. *Tasi kiu* in this context is meaningless to the Bellonese, as well as to the English speaker; *hapemu* is the Bellonese version of the Pidgin word "havim," to have; *seee* is the Bellonese pronunciation of say. These were the words which the Bellonese assert were used during the rites of distribution of food. A similar and equally unintelligible formula was used at church services and at birth and death.

The above are obviously only a few, scattered examples of the state of ritual confusion which existed on Bellona in the earliest phase of the life under a new faith. Based as they are on Bellonese accounts twenty-odd years after the events took place, we have no means of knowing in detail what took place or what actually went on in the minds of the people who took part. From informants' accounts we get an impression, but only a glimpse, of the bewilderment which must have reigned. It is worth noting that the Bellonese are far more precise and distinct in their accounts of events which happened before the arrival of Christianity. I venture a psychological explanation of this: The pre-Christian events took place within a structure of relatively fixed values. The rituals had their patterns and so had the behavior of the individual. It may be easier to recall events which have such a pattern than it is to remember what has taken place in a period of frustration. And the Bellonese themselves see this period as a time of confusion and trauma. They say that they were bewildered (*tootoobasi'a*), stupid (*hu'u*), and afraid (*mataku*).

In the year 1939 about 65 percent of the total population belonged to the SDA mission and the remainder had joined the SSEM. An exact figure cannot be given, primarily because there was a certain fluctuation in the mission affiliations also at that time. We shall deal with these fluctuations below.

There were from the beginning strong feelings of antagonism between the members of the two missions. When Puka and Tangokona brought the teachings of the SSEM mission to Bellona, both Moa and those Bellonese who had joined the SDA objected to the establishment of a new mission on the island. This antagonism resulted in open fights between members of the two groups, verbally as well as physically, and these fights were to last throughout the next decade.

With the establishment of the two missions, new social groups were formed. The Bellonese assert that each person chose to join the mission which he or she liked best, and that it was purely a matter of personal choice (*noko manga hano i te pengea*). This is in a way true, but it is nevertheless possible to point to some social determinants for the individual's choice of mission affiliation.

Wives, for instance, joined the same mission as their husbands. Only three exceptions to this rule have been recorded from Phase I. The patrilineal descent groups being exogamous and patrilocal, a married woman commonly belonged to the same mission as her husband's kinfolk, thus often being a member of a mission other than that to which her own agnatic group belonged.

Also, the rest of a male landholder's (*matu'a*) household, his sons, and unmarried daughters commonly joined the same mission.

A survey of some deviations from these general rules may provide us with further insight as to how the mission groups became organized. In all three recorded cases of wives joining a mission other than that of their husbands, the husbands belonged to the SDA and the wives left them to live, in two cases with kinsmen of their own patrilineal descent groups, and in one case with a *tu'aatina,* a mother's classificatory brother, who was a man of considerable social prestige and who had established an important SSEM church. In one case the husband later joined his wife's mission and lived for a time with her agnatic kinsmen. In the other two cases the wives later rejoined their husbands and became members of the SDA mission. In two cases the reason for the split between the spouses seems to have been temporary personal disagreement over purely secular matters. In the third case the reason was said to be that the wife "preferred SSEM to SDA." More data on this case have not been available; both persons are dead.

Of the eighteen major patrilineal descent groups on the island (Monberg, 1966, Fig. 3) all individuals inhabiting the land owned by members of five of the lineages belonged to the SDA mission, and the individuals inhabiting the land of two lineages were all members of the SSEM mission. The remaining eleven patrilineal descent groups were split up. We shall consider the reason for some of these rifts.

In one lineage, all belonged to the SDA with the exception of one young and unmarried landholder (*matu'a*) who was on bad terms with his kinsmen and therefore chose to join the SSEM. In three lineages, groups of young people whose fathers had died lived with kinsmen of other lineages and joined their missions rather than those chosen by the majority of their own lineages. In six lineages, long-standing disagreements over land or other matters had split the members into two groups, and each chose to join a different mission. The reasons for the furcation of one lineage have not been recorded.

Space does not permit a detailed exposition of these data, but from the above, it is obvious that social and political determinants for the choice of mission affiliation were very strong indeed. In fact I have found no cases (with the possible exception of the one mentioned above) of Bellonese claiming that they chose to become members of a certain mission because they thought that its teachings were more true than those of the other. The Bellonese knew that members of SDA and SSEM worshiped the same deity, but that they worshiped in different ways, a concept well known to them from their old religion in which rituals of the two clans of the island showed minor differences. A similar attitude toward the differences of two missions on a Polynesian island has been shown by Emory (1965, p. 103) for Kapingamarangi.

It is, however, evident that factors other than lineage affiliation have acted as determinants of membership in a certain mission. Common residence before the arrival of Moa was important. People chose to join the same mission as those with whom they had most social interaction in daily life. These were usually people of their own lineage, but where individuals resided with others than their agnatic kinsmen, this affected their choice.

As time went on and new cleavages arose between groups and individuals, this principle acted in reverse: co-residence of people of different missions became impossible. If one changed from one mission to the other, one had to move.

Even though the Bellonese seem to have had difficulties with the conceptual adjustment to Christianity because of their ignorance of the teachings of the two missions, it seems clear that the new religion quickly became an important social and political instrument on the island.[3] The history of church building on Bellona offers examples of this. As mentioned previously, the first SDA church was built in Ngongona, a homestead belonging to one of the important lineage elders, Takiika. Each lineage had a number of male landholders—women as a rule did not own land—and some had higher prestige and authority than others. This was to a great extent due to their outstanding abilities as gardeners, fishermen, warriors, or performers of rituals (Monberg, 1966, pp. 29-30). Bellona had no chiefs in the Tikopia sense of the word. The first churches were built by those lineage elders (hakahua) who at that time had the highest prestige on the island, Takiika of Nuku'angoha lineage (SDA), Taungenga of Ghongau lineage (SSEM), Pongi of Ngikobaka lineage (SDA), Sa'engeika of Ngikobaka lineage (SSEM), Ngibauika of Pangangiu lineage (SDA), Sa'omoana Taupongi of Sauhakapoi lineage (SSEM), and Taaika of Matabaingei lineage (SDA). This was in 1939-1940. The Bellonese say that during these first years, on each Saturday or Sunday, depending on the mission, they prayed in the churches which had been made by the important lineage elders. The traditional homesteads of the Bellonese lay scattered along the main trail which runs through Bellona and as it was often a long walk during which one had to pass homesteads of the people of the opposite mis-

---

[3] The fact that persons of high status accepted the new religion in the earliest phase probably also paved the way for its general acceptance among the Bellonese, and it may also be one of the reasons why the pre-Christian distribution of power was carried over into the new phase.

sion with whom one's relations were strained, a gradual change in the
residence pattern began to emerge. Some individuals set up their residences in the near vicinity of the church to which they went to pray
most often and which belonged to the lineage elder to whom they were
most closely related. This tendency was, however, slow in the beginning
and it was counteracted by another development. In the years 1941 to
1949 more and more new churches were built. By approximately 1943
there were twenty-three SDA churches and ten SSEM churches, one for
about every thirteen of the island's people.

The three major factors which supported this development were the
prestige involved in having one's own church, the traditional pre-
Christian system of frequently founding new temples, and the fights between members of the original churches which made them split up.

When considering the specific cases in which new churches were
founded it is often analytically impossible to determine which of these
three reasons has weighed most heavily when a landholder established
himself as church owner. There are, however, at least three clear cases
of people worshiping at the same church who came to disagreement
and separated accordingly. The majority of churches were, however,
said to have been made because the founder "wished to have a church
of his own." This is not a surprising statement when seen in the light of
the pre-Christian social and religious organization on the island. The
majority of landholders on the island then had their own little temples
(*nganguenga*) in which minor rituals to certain gods were carried out.
According to the Bellonese traditions they were offshoots of a number
of larger temples on the island in which the more important rituals took
place. Before 1939 Bellonese lineage elders established new temples
when they considered themselves powerful enough to make larger ritual
distributions. Sometimes they would, however, merely take over the
temple of a deceased kinsman. A Bellonese in danger at sea or elsewhere might promise the deities to found a new temple if he were
saved from disaster. The foundation of new temples was thus on the
one hand a means of acquiring or confirming one's social prestige, and
on the other, the individual's means of establishing good relations with
the deities.

During the first phase of Christianity, the Bellonese contented themselves with having only a few churches, but gradually they reverted to
the traditional system of each lineage having at least one place of worship of its own. In 1947 the members of one of the major lineages had
six churches, mainly because this lineage was split into a number of

groups which were opposed to each other, chiefly because of long-standing disagreements over land rights.

The Bellonese themselves saw the gradual emerging of more and more churches as a reversion to the pre-Christian system of founding new temples. One informant made this particularly explicit: "The land-holders wanted to have their own churches because they were like temples. We did not know how to make churches then, so we just did as before"—that is, before Christianity.

Another example of this tendency to organize the new religion according to the forms and principles of the old was the invention of certain official positions at the many churches built in the years 1939 through 1949.

The Bellonese created three ritual roles at each SDA or SSEM church, that of *hetimane,* headman, that of *bosi,* boss, and that of *tisa,* teacher. These English words had been taught them by the Rennellese missionaries. At the minor churches whose congregations consisted of only a few people, sometimes only the members of one household, the church owner held all three posts; but at a few major churches owned by lineage elders of higher social status, and with larger congregations consisting of several households, the posts were each filled by a different person. It was, however, more common that the same man would be *tisa* and *hetimane,* whereas another kinsman would act as *bosi.* This system of positions corresponds rather closely to the pre-Christian religious system. The role of *hetimane* resembles that of the *tunihenua,* priest-chief, in the old religion. The role of *bosi* corresponds to that of the *haihenua,* second priest-chief. The *tisa,* who was supposed to be the actual religious authority, reflects the old *ta'otu'a* institution in which a man might ritually assume the role of a deity or an ancestor, thus securing closeness to the sacred sphere. To the Bellonese, the *tisa* was the person in closest contact with the new God. During the old religion the role as *ta'otu'a* was most commonly assumed by the priest-chief, just as it was common under the new religion that the owner of the church was both *hetimane* and *tisa* at the same time.

Between 1939 and 1949 the Bellonese distinguished between two types of worship: the distribution of food in the ritual grounds of the homestead with accompanying prayers, and the actual church services held on Saturdays (SDA) or Sundays (SSEM). This duality also resembles the old religious practices in which important distributions of food took place on the ritual grounds (*ngoto manga'e*) in front of the living houses, and other rituals were performed in the temples.

Bellonese churches were built in close proximity to the living houses of the homestead, often next to the old ritual grounds. Services on Saturdays and Sundays were held in the churches with no distribution of food, whereas the feasts involving the distribution of the harvest or of fish took place in the ritual grounds. On these latter occasions the *hetimane,* who was usually also the *tisa,* conducted the short prayer (see above), and the food was then distributed by the *bosi.* The first shares of food were given to any other *hetimane* of Bellona present. The next shares were given to the affinal kinsmen of the *hetimane* who conducted the feast. The following shares were given to other *tisa* and *bosi* who were present as guests. Finally other persons present received their share. This procedure is similar to that followed during pre-Christian rites: important lineage elders and the affinal kinsmen of the host received the first shares, and younger persons or those of lower social status received their food baskets later. The similarity even went further in that it was the important lineage elders who filled the roles as headmen and teachers under the new religion, the same persons who would have held posts as priest-chiefs at the old temples. Younger people or those of lesser social status who would have held posts as minor religious officials had similar posts under the new faith.

One feature of the old religion was carried over into the new era without much alteration. When the food had been distributed in the pre-Christian times, dancing and singing took place in the ritual grounds. This also happened after Christianity had been introduced. Even some songs mentioning the names of the old deities were sung, but the more sacred songs were abandoned. In the pre-Christian rites it was customary that a group of men from the same district as that of the host began the dancing to the accompaniment of the sounding board. Then members of one of the other two of the island's three districts took over. The dancing had an element of competition in that which district had produced the best dancing and the best songs was a subject of discussion. The rivalry of the districts on Bellona has been attested in many of the oral traditions (Elbert and Monberg, 1965).

With the arrival of Christianity new groups were formed across the borders of the districts, namely the SDA and the SSEM. Post-Christian dancing came to be a competition between members of the two missions rather than between districts. During a feast in a homestead of a member of the SDA mission, people of this mission danced first, and members of the SSEM followed.

The decade following conversion was, as mentioned, full of tension between members of the two groups. Open violence broke out frequently. Several groups of teachers (who had little or no training as such) who came from Rennell made matters worse by inciting fights between the two sects. They were supposed to help the Bellonese in their struggles to adjust themselves to the new life, but they had apparently little to offer. The relations between the adherents of SDA and SSEM worsened. Traditionally the Bellonese were of a rather bellicose disposition. One reason for this was that the various lineage elders constantly strived to gain higher social prestige than others. This often resulted in feuds, but also found other manifestations.

The years after the introduction of Christianity saw another development. The Bellonese tell how the traditional competitions among landholders to make the largest gardens and the most elaborate feasts with distribution of their garden produce reached a climax at that time. Landholders planted enormous prestige gardens, some of which were said to have yielded more than 10,000 yams. Rival landholders then attempted to plant gardens which were even larger. The garden produce was distributed at enormous feasts which included Christian prayers and dancing. The prestige in making a large garden lay chiefly in enabling the maker not only to display his wealth and generosity, but also his ability to make many people assist him in cultivation.

There may be several explanations for this curious outbreak of planting activities on Bellona after the old religion had been abandoned: as actual fights, with elaborate displays of physical skill and intelligence in planning attacks, had been abandoned entirely, the Bellonese lineage elders may have sought other ways of manifesting their abilities and superiority. The old religion, which was so closely linked with social prestige, had been given up, and the individual lineage elder may have felt the need for a reconfirmation of his status within the new system and on a new basis. An obvious way was to stress another value highly praised, namely one's skill as a gardener and one's generosity as a host, both qualities which might give a man status as a *hakahua,* important lineage elder.

Another reason may be that, whereas the pre-Christian rituals took up considerable time, the worship of the Christian God was a far less time-consuming affair. When Christianity was introduced, people simply had a surplus of time for garden work and fishing. To this may be added that, whereas many Bellonese landholders had to spend considerable time hiding in their bush homesteads for fear of being attacked by

enemies, the restoration of peace after 1939 also gave them more time
to devote to food production.

The introduction of Christianity is, under most circumstances, a
highly complex cluster of innovations in a non-Christian society. On
Bellona, however, Christianity was introduced in a fairly simple form,
and it was not to any considerable degree accompanied by the introduction of material innovations. What the Bellonese received was a
brief message about the existence of a new supernatural power, and a
few hints on how the distant European and Melanesian adherents of
this new god behaved. Lack of knowledge of the rituals to some extent
left them bewildered and frustrated, but the general ignorance of the
dogmas and ethics of this new religion enabled them to integrate it within their own political and economic system, and, especially as the new
religion arrived in two different versions, to utilize it as a political
weapon. During the first decade of Christianity, to a large extent, the
new religion became adjusted to Bellonese culture and society rather
than the opposite. The island was relatively isolated during this period.
Once Christianity had been accepted, there was very little pressure
from the outside forcing new changes and people were comparatively
free to manipulate the new religion as suited them best. It is obvious
that such a situation is likely to result in an attempt to adjust the new
faith to the already existing concepts and social structure. When the
new religion is utilized to enforce changes in the social organization it
is likely to be in those institutions which members of the society consider it advantageous to reorganize or eliminate, but whose previous
structure has been strongly sanctioned by certain values in the old
religion.

From what has been said above it will, however, be obvious, that
this process of adjustment was full of social and political tension. This
seems only natural, not only because the introduction of the new religion
involved conflicting interests of various members of the society, but
also because tension was inherent in the old religious system, in which
beliefs and rites often acted as religious sanctions for strife and configurations within the society.

In the period which followed, the situation on Bellona was the
reverse of that in the first decade. With the arrival of trained teachers
and missionaries, the previous religious organization broke up. Pressure
from the outside forced the Bellonese to begin a complete reorganization
of many of its social institutions.

PHASE III: READJUSTMENT (1949-   )

Until 1949 contact with the outer world was very slight, but the island was not completely isolated. In 1941 four Bellonese were taken to the mission stations in the Solomons. One man went to Onepusu, the SSEM school, and three went to Batuna, the school of the SDA. They returned to Bellona after six months, but, according to the Bellonese, without having learned much. Their presence on the island in their new roles as scholars did not do much to enlighten the Bellonese on the intricacies of Christian beliefs and rituals.

In 1942 the first larger influx of Euro-American goods took place on the island. An American warship anchored at the north coast and its crew traded tobacco, trousers, calico, soap, pencils, and paper for local goods. It has been impossible to determine the exact amount of goods; the Bellonese just remember that the crew gave them "very many things."

During World War II no Bellonese went abroad. Their only contact was with the crews of the few ships and seaplanes which called at the island. No missionary vessels arrived at Bellona before 1946, and then only to hold a few meetings and services before the visiting missionaries left for Rennell. The Bellonese tell how after accepting Christianity they waited anxiously for proper missionaries to arrive to instruct them in the new faith: "We waited, waited in vain; no one came. Our worship was bad and we fought. Fought all the time because there was no one who could teach us about God and Jesus." In 1946 the Bellonese felt that they had been isolated long enough and three groups of men set out in canoes. They had decided to undertake the hazardous 100-mile voyage to Guadalcanal to ask the government and the missions to send them proper teachers. All the men stayed at the mission stations in the Solomons to receive training, and some of them returned after six months; others stayed longer. Those who returned tried to establish actual schools on the island but had to give up because their knowledge was inadequate.

In 1949 a radical change took place. The SDA mission ship brought two Melanesian teachers to the island to stay over a longer period. They were immediately accepted by the Bellonese as authorities on religious matters and their advice was followed to a considerable degree.

A few samples will give a picture of the forces which were at work during this period of cultural and social change on the island.

The two missionaries taught the Bellonese the proper forms of Seventh Day Adventist services which they had wished to know for so very long, and also induced other changes which, at least socially, may have had an even greater influence. They made the Bellonese give up their many churches and centralize their worship in certain key places. Churches in Matahenua in Ngango district, in Angaiho and Ngongona in Ghongau district, and in Pangangiu in Matangi district (maps in Elbert and Monberg, 1965, and in Monberg, 1966) became the centers of the religious activities of the SDA mission. The missionaries' reason for taking this step was allegedly that they considered it impossible to set up a proper church organization when deacons, teachers, and church elders were scattered throughout the island in more than twenty churches.

This organizational pressure from the outside not only resulted in a centralization of the churches, but also in a change in the island's residential pattern. Until 1949 people had still to a great extent lived in the old homesteads along the main trail. Now larger villages grew up around the churches. The majority of the members of the SDA mission built houses in close proximity to the church at which they worshiped. The members of the SSEM mission also had a tendency to move together in larger villages, and the fact that such a development took place among the adherents of the SDA, seems to have accelerated the centralization also of the members of the SSEM.

In the years after 1949 a number of other important innovations took place: a proper school was started in Ngongona; the Melanesian missionaries banned all dancing on the island, deeming it sinful. They also tabooed polygyny. (Nine of the eleven existing polygynous marriages were dissolved as a result of the new taboo.) Smoking of tobacco was forbidden and so were those types of food which are traditionally taboo for members of the Seventh Day Adventist sect. As a result, the adherents of the SDA could not eat such important and highly prized foods as sharks, flying foxes, coconut crabs, lobsters, or shellfish. The two missionaries also tried to discourage the members of the two missions from fighting each other, and they stressed the white man's ways as the best of ways.

The Bellonese responded eagerly to these teachings and followed the missionaries obediently. They assert that they knew so very little about the outside world then that they had no reason to doubt that what the missionaries said was true, or that the white man was actually better and more intelligent than themselves—in fact they still to a great extent believe this. Their aim was to live as the white man did, to abandon their old way of life and imitate their missionary teachers as much as possible.

The Bellonese had hoped that contact with the external world and the teachings of Christianity would restore peace completely on the island. This was not the case; tension was there as it had been before. The two missions still constituted opponent groups and people still used them as political instruments. If two individuals of the same mission and village came to disagreement, one of them would leave the village, either to join other members of his mission in another village or to join another mission. Changes in mission affiliation induced in this way seem to have been more common in the earlier stages of the process of acculturation than later when the individual became better acquainted with the teachings of his mission and thus might be more reluctant to convert to a new school, preferring instead to move to another village belonging to his mission. It should perhaps be noted that we have no records of cases in which persons changed from one mission to the other because of preference for its ideas. We cannot claim that no such conversions took place, but it seems obvious that the majority of people who left one to join the other did so for political reasons. The situation on Bellona is very similar to the one observed in Pangai village in Tonga by Beaglehole and Beaglehole (1941, pp. 129-130): ". . . changing church affiliation provides a means of solving on the social plane interpersonal conflicts that might otherwise become strong enough to result in social disorganization and disintegration."

The new church order introduced with the arrival of the Melanesian missionaries in 1949 also affected the social status system on Bellona. Between 1939 and 1949 the lineage elders could retain some of their earlier status by making elaborate feasts of distribution in the homesteads. When the residential pattern changed, the old homesteads lost their importance as centers of social activities. A number of lineage elders moved to the villages and this influenced the system of economic distribution. Large feasts became increasingly rare. The lineage elders still had their wealth in land, and it was vested in their sons according to the traditional pattern. But along with the wealthy young men, a new class of people grew up: the bright young men who received more extensive training as mission teachers abroad and who returned to the island with a wealth of equal value to that of land, knowledge of reading and writing and of the world of the white man. In the villages it was their activities as conducters of the rituals and as school teachers which counted. Naturally some sons of wealthy landholders went to the mission schools and a number of them are mission teachers and pastors today with high prestige. But there were others who came from poorer families but who showed particular abilities during their training at the mission schools and who returned to acquire high prestige in the present-day society. One of them, the head teacher of the SDA mission on the island, is even a man born out of wedlock, which would have meant low status in pre-Christian Bellona.

In this way the external selection as to who should receive further training has been a strong factor in the remodeling of the status system of the island. In a more authoritarian society with a strong centralized political power, the island chief or chiefs might have reacted against this tendency. Such powerful men could have allowed only persons of high status to go abroad for mission training. On Bellona this was impossible; everybody was free to go to the mission stations, for who could forbid them to do so?

SUMMARY AND SOME CONCLUSIONS

The new culture trait, the belief in the Christian god as the great supernatural power, had certain elements which could easily be identified by the Bellonese as operating on the same principle as their old religion. Both religions involved supernatural beings with power to bring welfare and to punish humans. They also both involved rituals with songs and sacred formulas and temples in which the supernaturals were invoked. These similarities, and also the fact that the Bellonese did not realize that acceptance of the Christian God also involved acceptance of a number of dogmas which were entirely alien to Bellonese culture and society (for example, monogamy and certain food or dancing taboos) made it possible for the Bellonese to accept the new trait.

With this possibility at hand, it became a question of advantages and disadvantages whether the new trait should be accepted or not. The advantages seemed overwhelming and the incentives for acceptance were strong. The new God had shown His power by punishing people on Rennell and also by giving Moa strength to annihilate the sacred objects belonging to the old deities. Also the fact that the island was engaged in a long and exhausting interlineage fight at the time when Moa arrived may have made the Bellonese more susceptible to change. Several informants have said that before 1938 people were fed up (*hiu*) with the incessant fights on the island, but could see no way out of them. Moa's new religion provided the Bellonese with a supernatural sanction which prevented further fights.

Once the new God had been accepted, the problem of integration became pertinent. The Bellonese knew that the new religion operated on the same basic principles as their old religion. It seems obvious that there must have been a need for knowledge of how to perform the new rites, for how else could the new religion become an adequate substitute for the old?

They did not get this knowledge at first, and as it was the Bellonese substituted those few culture traits of Melanesian and European Christians known to them for some of their old, and otherwise adapted what they knew of Christianity to the existing pattern of behavior. The social organization of the island remained chiefly as it was before 1939. Certain configurations took place, new alliances were created, and others split up, but this had also happened in the years prior to Moa's arrival.

In the next phase of the development the external influences became stronger. The Melanesian missionaries and other visiting strangers introduced a considerable number of entirely new traits. Among these the introduction of the principles of European church organization induced some of the most important changes. The innovation process took a new turn. Whereas in the first phase of adjustment only relatively few and insignificant traits were brought to Bellona together with the simple message about the Christian God, and whereas the majority of the island's basic institutions changed little, the situation was the opposite in the second phase: the political and religious organization became more and more susceptible to change, and where this created conflicts with the existing Bellonese organization, the latter became more and more suppressed.

This may sound somewhat simpler than it is. In actual fact a number of conflicts were not solved in this way, but the general tendency for the Bellonese was to let themselves be led by their foreign political and religious supervisors.

This is perhaps the most surprising part of the whole story. Why have the Bellonese until recently been so willing to accept what the Europeans have taught them to do? (Mark that I do not say that they have always succeeded in letting themselves become acculturated. Below the level of political and religious organizations there is a stratum of social interaction, ripe with conflicts, which, interesting though it is, cannot be dealt with here.)

On the basis of available data it is not possible to give an exhaustive answer to this question, but only to suggest some possible explanations.

As in all other cases which concern decision making, the conversion to Christianity seems to have been a process involving an appraisal of social values. Does one, by making a specific decision, gain more than one loses?

By accepting Christianity in the first place, the Bellonese obviously believed that they gained more than they lost. We have discussed this above. In the second phase the Bellonese realized that they had to face certain losses—the old rites in their original form and the social prestige involved in being religious officials—but that these were small in comparison with what was gained—protection from a powerful deity and peace on the island. Moreover some of the losses could be compensated for by carrying on with the feasts involving distributions, thus not breaking up the economic system, and also by holding overly large feasts, thus compensating for the loss of such prestige-stimulating acts as fights and rites. In the third phase of closer contact with people of other parts of the Solomons, particularly with missionaries, the Bellonese have to a great extent gone along with the suggestions for innovations made by strangers because these innovations have so far mostly been evaluated as a gain. These included medical assistance, teachers, a local council, and a native court. The value lost has been considered much smaller than the profit obtained. In a few cases where the Bellonese considered that they had made a bad bargain with the Europeans, the introduction of the culture trait in question was rejected. A case of this kind was the attempt to introduce a cooperative society on Bellona. It failed because it conflicted with the economic and political system and brought the Bellonese what they believe was a considerable financial loss.

This analysis of the situation is very similar to the one which the Bellonese make themselves. When asked whether they preferred life in the "heathen days" to life as it is today, they unanimously say no. They regret that the old rites and the dancing had to be abandoned, but they prefer life as it is today because "we can learn from the white man and the white man helps us with medicine and councils and courts."

So far the extremely high evaluation of contact with the white man and his ideas has made the Bellonese willing to pay what to us may seem a rather high price for its continuation. This is of course an ethnocentric point of view. The Bellonese do not consider the costs too high. It seems, however, likely that the increasing interaction with the outside world will result in a drop in the market price on Bellona of the white man's ideas. How this will affect Bellonese religion is difficult to say; but it would not be surprising if the Bellonese will in the future become increasingly reluctant to sacrifice their own ideas and institutions in order to please the Christian God and His white followers.

LITERATURE CITED

BARNETT, H. G.
1942. "Invention and Cultural Change." *American Anthropologist* **44**:14-30.

BEAGLEHOLE, ERNEST, and PEARL BEAGLEHOLE
1941. *Pangai: A Village in Tonga.* Polynesian Soc. Mem. 18. Wellington.

BIRKET-SMITH, KAJ
1956. *An Ethnological Sketch of Rennell Island. A Polynesian Outlier in Melanesia.* Det Kongelige Danske Videnskabernes Selskab, Historisk-filologiske Meddelelser Bind 35 Nr. 3.

BROEK D'OBRENAN, CHARLES VAN DEN
1939. *Le Voyage de la Korrigane.* Paris.

DECK, NORTHCOTE
1945. *South from Guadalcanal. The Romance of Rennell Island.* Toronto.

ELBERT, SAMUEL H., and TORBEN MONBERG
1965. *From the Two Canoes. Oral Traditions of Rennell and Bellona.* Honolulu and Copenhagen: Univ. of Hawaii and Danish Nat. Mus.

EMORY, KENNETH P.
1965. *Kapingamarangi. Social and Religious Life of a Polynesian Atoll.* B. P. Bishop Mus. Bull. 228. Honolulu.

GEERTZ, CLIFFORD
1957. "Ritual and Social Change: A Javanese Example." *American Anthropologist* **59**:32-54.

HOGBIN, H. IAN
1931. "A Note on Rennell Island." *Oceania* **2**:174-178.

LAMBERT, S. M.
1941. *A Yankee Doctor in Paradise.* Boston: Little, Brown.

MACGREGOR, GORDON
1943. "The Gods of Rennell Island." *Peabody Mus. American Archaeology and Ethnology Pap.* **20**:32-37.

MONBERG, TORBEN
1962. "Crisis and Mass Conversion on Rennell Island in 1938." *J. Polynesian Soc.* **71**:145-150.
1966. *The Religion of Bellona Island. A Study of the Place of Beliefs and Rites in the Social Life of Pre-Christian Bellona. Part 1: The Concepts of Supernaturals.* Language and Culture of Rennell and Bellona Islands Vol. 2(1). Copenhagen: Danish Nat. Mus.

PARSONS, TALCOTT, and EDWARD A. SHILS
1951. *Toward a General Theory of Action.* Cambridge.

STANLEY, G. A. V.
1929. "Report on the Geological Reconnaissance of Rennell Island, British Solomon Islands Protectorate." *British Solomon Islands. Report for 1927, Appendix A. Annual Colonial Report No. 1421.* London.

YOUNG, FLORENCE S. H.
[n.d.] *Pearls from the Pacific.* London.

INDEX